The Multilingual Internet

The Multilingual Internet

Language, Culture,
and Communication Online

Edited by
Brenda Danet
and Susan C. Herring

2007

OXFORD
UNIVERSITY PRESS

Oxford University Press, Inc., publishes works that further
Oxford University's objective of excellence
in research, scholarship, and education.

Oxford   New York
Auckland   Cape Town   Dar es Salaam   Hong Kong   Karachi
Kuala Lumpur   Madrid   Melbourne   Mexico City   Nairobi
New Delhi   Shanghai   Taipei   Toronto

With offices in
Argentina   Austria   Brazil   Chile   Czech Republic   France   Greece
Guatemala   Hungary   Italy   Japan   Poland   Portugal   Singapore
South Korea   Switzerland   Thailand   Turkey   Ukraine   Vietnam

Published by Oxford University Press, Inc.
198 Madison Avenue, New York, New York 10016

www.oup.com

Oxford is a registered trademark of Oxford University Press

Library of Congress Cataloging-in-Publication Data
The multilingual internet : language, culture, and communication
online / edited by Brenda Danet and Susan C. Herring.
    p. cm.
Includes bibliographical references and index.
ISBN 978-0-19-530479-4; 978-0-19-530480-0 (pbk.)
1. Communication—Data processing.   2. Internet.
3. Multilingualism—Data processing.
4. Written communication—Data processing.
5. Sociolinguistics—Data processing.
6. Language and culture—Data processing.
I. Danet, Brenda, 1937–   II. Herring, Susan C.
P96.D36M85 2007
302.20285—dc22   2006043764

9 8 7 6 5 4 3 2 1

Printed in the United States of America
on acid-free paper

We dedicate this collection to Jacques Anis (January 8, 1953–December 16, 2005), whose research on computer-mediated communication in French was perhaps the first large, coherent body of work to apply linguistic methods of analysis to online communication in a language other than English.

Preface

This book marks the culmination of the second stage of a two-stage project initiated in 2002. In that year, we co-edited a special issue of the *Journal of Computer-Mediated Communication* about multilingualism on the Internet (published in 2003). Our call for papers, distributed online, yielded far more proposals than we had expected, and many of high caliber. Because of this evident interest in online multilingualism, and knowing that we could include only a limited number of articles in the special journal issue, we conceived the idea of an extended volume.

This book reproduces the eight articles originally published online, some in slightly abridged or modified form. These studies were authored by David Palfreyman and Muhamed Al Khalil, Yukiko Nishimura, Hsi-Yao Su, Dimitris Koutsougiannis and Bessie Mitsikopoulou, Salvador Climent and colleagues, Mercedes Durham, Sandi de Oliveira, and Siriporn Panyametheekul and Susan Herring.

Most of the other chapters were commissioned by us in response to proposals submitted by authors, with a few exceptions. Two pioneering attempts to investigate aspects of multilingualism online that had previously been published elsewhere are reprinted here, with minor modifications—these are the chapters by Mark Warschauer and colleagues about online communication in Egypt and by Ann-Sofie Axelsson and her collaborators on attempts to switch languages in a graphical chat environment. We invited several other scholars to submit articles based on their expertise in relevant areas. Ruth Wodak agreed to prepare a chapter about her work on multilingualism in Europe and in the European Union; she was joined by Scott Wright, whose doctoral dissertation at Lancaster University proved relevant. Jannis Androutsopoulos contributed a study of language choice and code switching online in a German-speaking context. The chapter by the late Jacques Anis on deviant spelling in French SMS (short message service) messages makes accessible to English-speaking readers the work of an established researcher in the French-speaking world. We also commissioned a chapter from cultural anthropologists Hirofumi Katsuno and Christine Yano on *kaomoji*—"face marks" (the Japanese equivalent of "smiley" icons)—in Japanese online communication. Finally, while gathering material for a review of the literature on multilingual computer-mediated communication (CMC), we encountered a paper by Carmen Lee, now a doctoral student at Lancaster University, on CMC in Hong Kong based on her master's thesis and invited her to rework her analysis for this book.

In our introductory chapter, we aimed to survey linguistic studies of Internet communication in languages other than English and in non-English-dominant contexts. In the past few years, the amount of available research on the topic has expanded considerably, and we discovered more work than we previously thought existed. As a result, the introduction provides only an overview, rather than exhaustive coverage of the body of research currently available.

This book was made possible by the medium that is fundamental to its subject matter—the Internet, especially email. While we had met at several conferences in the past, we had worked together only once before (to co-organize a panel at the 1993 International Pragmatics Conference in Kobe, Japan), and that collaboration took place entirely via email. The present book was also produced almost exclusively via email, because we live nearly 1,000 miles apart, including all correspondence between us as co-editors and correspondence with prospective and actual authors around the globe and with outside reviewers. The story of how email facilitates academic collaboration is a fascinating topic in its own right, one that deserves another book.

We thank our authors for their patience and cooperation as we asked for yet further revision of their drafts. We also thank the external reviewers of chapter drafts and of the book proposal, who provided important feedback and suggestions. Deborah Anderson, head of the Script Encoding Initiative in the Department of Linguistics at the University of California–Berkeley, made useful comments on a draft of the section in our introduction on writing systems and the Internet. John Paolillo read and commented on a draft of the entire introduction. Finally, we extend our thanks to Peter Ohlin, our editor at Oxford University Press, for his enthusiastic support of this project.

Contents

PART V   BROADER PERSPECTIVES:
LANGUAGE DIVERSITY

Contributors

Åsa Abelin is a lecturer in linguistics at Göteborg University. In addition to her work on language encounters in virtual reality, she has conducted research on emotional prosody in cross-cultural perspective, attitudes to foreign accent, and sound symbolism. abelin@ling.gu.se.

Muhamed Al Khalil teaches in the Arabic Studies Department at Zayed University, Dubai. His research interests include Arabic dialectology, socio-linguistic influences on Arabic rhetoric, and the interplay of the literary and the political in the Middle East. oryxius@gmail.com.

Jannis Androutsopoulos is Junior Professor of Mediated Communication at the Universität Hannover. His current research areas are media discourse and the sociolinguistics of CMC. androutsopoulos@fbls.uni-hannover.de.

Jacques Anis was Professor of Linguistics at the University of Paris X Nanterre until his death in 2005. He had researched CMC since 1985, with special attention to unconventional spelling (*neography*).

Ann-Sofie Axelsson is a researcher at Chalmers University of Technology, Sweden. She studies social interaction in virtual environments. annaxe@mot.chalmers.se.

Salvador Climent is Professor of Humanities and Catalan Language and Linguistics at the Universitat Oberta de Catalunya. His research areas are computational linguistics and language and cognitive science. scliment@uoc.edu.

Brenda Danet is Professor Emerita, Sociology and Communication, Hebrew University of Jerusalem, and Research Affiliate in Anthropology, Yale

University. She has been researching language, play, and performance online since 1991 and has a special interest in online adaptations of writing systems. brenda.danet@yale.edu.

Sandi Michele de Oliveira is Associate Professor of Portuguese linguistics at the Institute of Romance Studies of the University of Copenhagen and has served as President of the Research Committee on Sociolinguistics, International Sociological Association. Her research focuses on the linguistic construction and negotiation of identity in Portuguese and Japanese. smo@hum.ku.dk.

Mercedes Durham is completing her Ph.D. at the University of Fribourg (Switzerland) and is a research assistant and tutor at the University of York (U.K.). She studies the acquisition of variation by nonnative speakers and by children. md503@york.ac.uk.

Ghada R. El Said is a doctoral candidate in the Department of Information Systems and Computing, Brunel University (U.K.), and information systems senior technical advisor on an international development project in Egypt. Her research focuses on human–computer interaction. ghada.elsaid@brunel. ac.uk.

Susan C. Herring is Professor of Information Science and Linguistics at Indiana University, Bloomington, and editor of the *Journal of Computer-Mediated Communication*. She has been researching online communication, with special attention to gender and discourse, since 1991. Her current research focuses on multimodal CMC and weblogs. herring@indiana.edu.

Hirofumi Katsuno is a doctoral candidate in anthropology at the University of Hawaii, Manoa. His dissertation research focuses on the relationship between gender and technology in the consumption of robots in contemporary Japan. hirofumi@hawaii.edu.

Dimitris Koutsogiannis is Assistant Professor of Linguistics, Faculty of Philology at Aristotle University of Thessaloniki, and director of the Portal for the Greek language, Centre for the Greek Language. His interests include literacy and technology, educational linguistics, literacy education, e-learning, and Critical Discourse Analysis. dkoutsog@lit.auth.gr.

Carmen K. M. Lee is a Ph.D. student in linguistics and English language at Lancaster University (U.K.). She is interested in the relationship among language, literacy, and new technologies. Her M.Phil. thesis examined CMC in Hong Kong within the theoretical framework of new literacy studies. kmcarmen@graduate.hku.hk.

Bessie Mitsikopoulou is Assistant Professor of Language and Linguistics, Faculty of English Studies, National and Kapodistrian University of Athens. She specializes in educational linguistics, Critical Discourse Analysis, social and political implications of new technologies, information and communication technologies and language pedagogy, and critical and academic literacy. mbessie@enl.uoa.gr.

Joaquim Moré is a computational linguistics technician in the Linguistic Service and a researcher at the Internet Interdisciplinary Institute of the Universitat Oberta de Catalunya. jmore@uoc.edu.

Yukiko Nishimura is Professor of Linguistics, Toyo Gakuen University, Japan. She has also taught Japanese at Yale University and was a Visiting Researcher at the University of California–Santa Barbara. Her interests are in contrastive English/Japanese discourse studies. yukiko.nishimura@tyg.jp.

Antoni Oliver is a computational linguistics technician in the Linguistic Service and a researcher at the Internet Interdisciplinary Institute of the Universitat Oberta de Catalunya. aoliverg@uoc.edu.

David Palfreyman works at Zayed University, Dubai, contributing to ESL-related programs in the English Language Centre and educational development in the Centre for Teaching and Learning. His research interests include the role of sociocultural context in education and the use of information and communication technology. David.Palfreyman@zu.ac.ae.

Siriporn Panyametheekul is a lecturer in linguistics at Srinakharinwirot University, Thailand, specializing in discourse analysis, semantics, and pragmatics. Her Chulalongkorn University dissertation was titled *Coherence of Interactions in a Thai Chatroom: Interplay of Cohesion, Turn-Allocation, and Relevance.* panyametheekul@hotmail.com.

John C. Paolillo is Associate Professor of Informatics and Information Science at Indiana University, Bloomington. He has been researching CMC with an emphasis on social networks and language issues since 1995. His current research includes amateur multimedia and semantic web technologies. paolillo@indiana.edu.

Míriam Salvatierra is a language technician in the Linguistic Service of the Universitat Oberta de Catalunya. msalvatierra@uoc.edu.

Imma Sànchez is director of the Linguistic Service of the Universitat Oberta de Catalunya. isanchez@uoc.edu.

Ralph Schroeder is a research fellow at the Oxford Internet Institute at Oxford University; previously he was Professor of Technology and Society, Chalmers University, Sweden. He has been researching virtual environments since 1993, including issues of intercultural communication. Ralph.Schroeder@oii.ox.ac.uk.

Hsi-Yao Su is Assistant Professor of Linguistics in the Department of English, National Taiwan Normal University. She received her Ph.D. in linguistics from the University of Texas–Austin in 2005, specializing in sociolinguistics, with a regional interest in Taiwan and transnational Chinese communities. hsysu@ntnu.edu.tw.

Mariona Taulé is Professor of Linguistics at the Universitat de Barcelona and at the Universitat Oberta de Catalunya. mtaule@uoc.edu.

Theodora Tseliga is a teaching associate in ELT and ESP at the Technological Educational Institute of Epirus (Ioannina, Greece) and a lecturer in the Foreign Language Centre, University of Ioannina (Greece). Her main research interests focus on literacy and technology. thtselig@cc.uoi.gr.

Mark Warschauer is Associate Professor of Education and Informatics at the University of California–Irvine, and associate director of the Ada Byron Research Center for Diversity in Computing and Information Technology. He researches the integration of information and communication technologies in schools, their impact on language and literacy practices, and their relationship to institutional reform, democracy, and social development. markw@uci. edu.

Ruth Wodak is Professor of Discourse Studies at Lancaster University (U.K.) and head of the Wittgenstein Research Center, "Discourse, Politics, Identity," at the University of Vienna. Her research interests include discourse analysis, gender studies, language and/in politics, prejudice and discrimination, and ethnographic methods of fieldwork. r.wodak@lancaster.ac.uk.

Scott Wright is a research fellow at the Local Governance Research Unit at De Montfort University (U.K.). His University of East Anglia Ph.D. thesis was an analysis of government-run online forums at the local, national, and European levels. SWright01@dmu.ac.uk.

Christine Yano is Associate Professor of Anthropology at the University of Hawaii, where she researches gender and Japanese popular culture. Her current research subjects include Hello Kitty, Pan American flight attendants, and a Japanese postwar diva. cryano@hawaii.edu.

Ayman Zohry is a research associate in the Forced Migration and Refugee Studies Program, the American University in Cairo. He is the founding editor of "Demographers Without Borders," the first e-group for demographers. azohry@aucegypt.edu.

The Multilingual Internet

BRENDA DANET AND SUSAN C. HERRING

Introduction

Welcome to the Multilingual Internet

A GLOBAL NETWORK

In recent years, the Internet has become a truly global communication network. According to a late 2004 compilation (Computer Industry Almanac, 2004), approximately one billion people—one-sixth of the world's population—are now online. Internet services have become so common that the city of Budapest has installed an "@" sign on a central street to inform locals and visitors of the presence of a cybercafé (figure 1.1).[1]

Table 1.1 lists the top 15 nations using the Internet as of 2004. The United States has the largest proportion of users, 20% of the total. This reflects not only its large population size and advanced technological infrastructure, but also the fact that the technology that makes the Internet possible was created in the 1960s in the United States (Hafner & Lyon, 1996; O'Neill, 1995). Notably absent from the list are regions with a high concentration of small languages, such as Africa and Oceania.

Many scholars have expressed concern about the dominance of world English, and the Internet as a new arena for its spread (Dor, 2004; Mair, 2002; Nunberg, 2000; see chapter 18). A 2002 survey found that more than 56% of all webpages were in English.[2] Also, in July 2000 more than 94% of links to pages on secure servers were in English (OECD, 2001). Some view the spread of English as a "natural" or benign extension of globalization (Crystal, 2001, 2003; Fishman, 1998; Fishman, Conrad, & Rubal-Lopez, 1996). Others take a dimmer view, writing of "linguistic imperialism" and its threat to the status

FIGURE 1.1. "@" sign in central Budapest, informing pedestrians of the cybercafé ahead. Photograph by Brenda Danet, April 2005.

of smaller languages (Pakir, in press; Phillipson, 1992; Phillipson & Skutnabb-Kangas, 2001).

Regardless of one's position in this debate, when taken out of context statistics highlighting the prevalence of English on webpages or secure servers can be misleading. Already by 2003, roughly two-thirds of users were not native speakers of English (CyberAtlas, 2003). In only 4 of the 15 top countries online in 2004 (the United States, United Kingdom, Canada, Australia) was English the official or dominant language (table 1.1). China and Japan together accounted for nearly another fifth of the total. Moreover, growth in the next few years is predicted to accelerate, especially in China and India.[3] Thus, hundreds of millions of people are already participating online today in languages other than English, in some form of nonnative English,[4] or in a mixture of languages, and this trend is projected to continue in the years to come.

Academic research published in English on language use in computer-mediated communication (CMC) has only recently begun to take account of

TABLE 1.1. Top 15 countries on the Internet, year-end, 2004.

Country	In thousands	Percent
United States	185,550	19.86
China	99,800	10.68
Japan	78,050	8.35
Germany	41,880	4.48
India	36,970	3.96
United Kingdom	33,110	3.54
South Korea	31,670	3.39
Italy	25,530	2.73
France	25,470	2.73
Brazil	22,320	2.39
Russia	21,230	2.27
Canada	20,450	2.19
Mexico	13,880	1.49
Spain	13,440	1.44
Australia	13,010	1.39
Top 15 countries	662,360	70.88
Worldwide total	934,480	100.00%

Source: Computer Industry Almanac, September 2004, http://www.c-i-a.com/pr0904.htm; retrieved December 15, 2005. Reproduced with permission.

this complex empirical reality. Most researchers publishing in English venues have generalized about the language of computer-mediated *communication*, whereas in fact they were describing computer-mediated *English,* sometimes in a single CMC mode (see, e.g., Ferrara, Brunner, & Whittemore, 1991). Exceptions are publications by Naomi Baron (2000) and David Crystal (2001, 2004), which contextualize English-based CMC within the history of the English language.

In recent years, researchers have turned their attention to other languages on the Internet, often their native languages. This book is devoted to that research, presented in English in order to be accessible to a wide audience. As native speakers of English, we have both enjoyed the benefits of reading and writing about CMC in our first language, which, conveniently, is the lingua franca of scientific and academic publishing (Ammon, 2001). In the long run, however, this state of affairs can breed insularity. In a review of David Crystal's *Language and the Internet* (2001), the German scholar Dieter Stein (2003) observed that "a large body of research is simply not represented: research that is not in English. . . . There is a danger . . . of misrepresenting the state of the art. There is by now a large body of linguistic and communicational studies of Internet language in German" (pp. 162–163).[5] In recognition of this bias, in this chapter we survey some of the work on CMC that has been reported in languages other than English. However, a full review of that body of work for English-language readers must await a future time.

Our perspective on multilingualism is both microsociolinguistic and macrosociolinguistic. The chapters in this book focus mainly on microlevel patterns of use in a variety of languages and language combinations and in a variety of digital media. At the same time, a number of chapters are concerned with issues of language choice, linguistic diversity, and developments regarding specific languages online, including the use of English as a lingua franca in non-English-dominant contexts.

The media analyzed include instant messaging (IM), bulletin board systems (BBSs), email, and chat.[6] A chapter about French mobile phone communication is also included, since cell phone and Internet-based communication have converged and since asynchronous SMS (short message service) and synchronous IM share many constraints and features (Baron & Ling, 2003). All of these media are interactive and text based, text being the most popular form of CMC in use today, even in graphical chat environments (see chapter 16). Communication in all these media can be characterized as "interactive written discourse" (Ferrara et al., 1991).

This book is a considerably expanded version of a special issue of the online *Journal of Computer-Mediated Communication* that we published in 2003 (Danet & Herring, 2003). That was, to our knowledge, the first major publication in English about multilingualism online. Soon after, a UNESCO-sponsored team published another special issue about multilingualism online (Sue Wright, 2004). Their emphasis was macrosociological, and the authors were members of the same team: All papers were based on the same survey of students of English in 10 countries (Tanzania, Indonesia, the United Arab Emirates, Oman, France, Italy, Poland, Macedonia, Japan, and Ukraine). In contrast, the authors in this book and in our earlier special issue responded to an online solicitation for proposals or were invited to contribute based on their previous work, with the goal of representing a diversity of languages, methods, and CMC types.

In this introductory chapter, we first describe our theoretical approach. Thereafter, we review literature on multiple language use and the use of languages other than English online, as a backdrop for the 17 research studies in this book and as our own contribution to the emerging area of Internet language study. In this introduction, as in the remainder of the book, we group this research into five thematic sections: writing systems, linguistic and discourse features of CMC, gender and culture, language choice, and linguistic diversity. Finally, we summarize the book's contents and contributions and outline what research remains to be done.

LANGUAGE, CULTURE, AND COMMUNICATION: THEORETICAL APPROACH

The concept of culture has long proved elusive in many academic disciplines (see Duranti, 2003). Globalization, increased interconnectedness across international boundaries via electronic media, and hybridization of cultural content and identity further problematize the notion of culture (Hannerz, 1996; Holton, 2000). Our approach is consistent with Clifford Geertz's (1973) view of culture as shared ways of life and webs of meaning, with a focus on language as a repository and transmitter of culture. Just as it has traditionally been in offline interactions, in today's dynamic, mediatized world language is "a cultural resource and . . . a social practice" (Duranti, 2003, p. 323). Indeed, language choice and language use are the primary means of signaling cultural identity in text-based CMC, which transcends geographical boundaries and in which physical and social cues are reduced (Herring, 2004a). At the same time, online interlocutors live in the physical world and are grounded in offline cultures, defined by national, ethnic, religious, and other boundaries.

CMC and Speech Communities

Drawing on conceptualizations from the ethnography of communication (Bauman & Sherzer, 1989; Gumperz, 2001; Saville-Troike, 1989), sociolinguistics (Hymes, 1974; Labov, 1989; Romaine, 1982), and linguistic anthropology (Duranti, 1997, 2004), we view Internet users as members of one or more *speech communities* who bring to their online encounters shared knowledge, values, and expectations for linguistic interaction (for extensions of these notions to online contexts, see Baym, 1995; Cherny, 1999).

Geographical boundaries do not coincide neatly with linguistic ones. Whether residing within a country or living abroad, participants online share sociolinguistic norms acquired originally in a face-to-face context, which are not static but themselves change over time. Individuals may belong to more than one speech community. Thus, for example, a native of Greece who came to the United Kingdom at age 21, and has a good command of U.K. English, is a member both of the global Greek-speaking speech community and of a subgroup of immigrant, nonnative speakers of English in Britain. The email of this person to other Greek immigrants in the United Kingdom may reflect her membership in both speech communities (Georgakopoulou, 1997).

Context

Two further concepts that are pertinent are *context* (Duranti & Goodwin, 1992; Giglioli, 1982) and *performance* (Bauman, 1992). In the physical world, context includes demographic characteristics of speakers, their communicative competence and repertoire, the physical and social setting, relationships among speakers, and general cultural norms and expectations, as well as norms pertaining to language use itself (Hymes, 1974).

In CMC, identifying context can be problematic: In chat rooms where participants are geographically dispersed and whose identities are heavily masked,[7] context is largely emergent from online interaction. However, when participants belong to groups clearly located within specific real-world cultural and institutional settings—as in Sandi de Oliveira's study of online communication at a Portuguese university (chapter 11)—offline culture can often be shown to play an important role. Cultural context, however, is not always relevant. In Jacques Anis's study of French SMS (chapter 4), it is not French culture but rather the transcultural properties of the medium that condition linguistic strategies.

Performance

Digital writing often takes on characteristics of artful, playful, stylized performance, thereby partially resembling traditional oral genres (Bauman, 1992; Edwards & Sienkewicz, 1990; Finnegan, 1992). Performance aspects are salient in synchronous and even asynchronous modes (Baym, 1995, 2000; Danet, 1995, 2001), In this book, performance figures prominently in Taiwanese BBS language (chapter 3 by Hsi-Yao Su) and in emoticon use by Japanese housewives (chapter 12 by Hirofumi Katsuno and Christine Yano). Before discussing these and other behaviors in textual CMC, however, we start with the basics: the writing systems and fonts through which online communication is represented.

WRITING SYSTEMS AND ONLINE COMMUNICATION

ASCII Encoding and Its Unintended Consequences

Because early planners of the Internet were North American and sought only to facilitate communication in English, they did not anticipate problems encountered by speakers of other languages trying to communicate online. The text-transmission protocol on the Internet is based on the ASCII (pronounced AS-kee) character set (figure 1.2). ASCII is an acronym for "Ameri-

	!	"	#	$	%	&	'	(	)	*	+	,	−	.	/
0	1	2	3	4	5	6	7	8	9	:	;	<	=	>	?
@	A	B	C	D	E	F	G	H	I	J	K	L	M	N	O
P	Q	R	S	T	U	V	W	X	Y	Z	[	\	]	^	_
`	a	b	c	d	e	f	g	h	i	j	k	l	m	n	o
p	q	r	s	t	u	v	w	x	y	z	{			}	~	

FIGURE 1.2. The ASCII character set. *Source*: http://www.cs.tut.fi/~jkorpela/chars. html, retrieved December 15, 2005.

can Standard Code for Information Interchange"; established in the 1960s, it contains 128 seven-bit codes (unique combinations of 1's and 0's), 95 of which are available for use as graphical characters. This character set is based on the Roman alphabet and the sounds of the English language. "Plain text," as in email and chat, is often understood to mean text that contains only basic ASCII characters, whether written in English or in some other language.

The ASCII character set has privileged English online. Whether it concerns HTML (the markup language for webpages), domain names on the Web (URLs), email addresses, or the content of instant messages, email, discussion list postings, and chat, speakers of many languages have faced varying degrees of difficulty. Speakers of languages using the Roman alphabet but with only a few characters missing, such as the Scandinavian languages, suffer least, although the consequences may be embarrassing. ASCII does not include the last three letters of the Swedish alphabet, å, ä, and ö. The URL of a Swedish town called Hörby is http://www.horby.se. Swedes must live with the fact that without the two dots over the "o," the name of this town means "fornication village"[8] (Pargman, 1998). Another example is Hawaiian, which is written in Roman characters with additional use of macrons.[9] Warschauer and Donaghy (1997) note that "incorporation of diacritical marks is crucial, since they define meaning in Hawaiian; for example, *pau* means finished, *payu* means soot, *payü* means moist, and *päyü* means skirt" (p. 353).

Speakers of languages with non-Roman writing systems, such as Greek, Russian, Arabic, Hebrew, Chinese, Korean, and Japanese, have been especially disadvantaged, being dependent on special character sets for word processing and online communication.[10] In 1998, the editors of *Foreign Policy* claimed that "English remains the only language that can be used without distortion on virtually every computer in the world" (cited in Fishman, 1998, p. 34). Since then, the situation has improved. Nevertheless, many people today still cannot assume that their interlocutors will be able to read messages containing characters other than basic ASCII, even if their own computers accommodate their non-English language needs.

Problems engendered by the dominance of the ASCII character set online might lead some to speak of "typographic imperialism" as a subcategory of linguistic imperialism (Pargman & Palme, 2004). More neutrally, we ask: How have people communicating online in languages with different sounds and different writing systems adapted to the constraints of ASCII environments? What problems have they encountered, what progress has been made in solving these problems, and what remains to be done?

Ad Hoc Improvisation by Users

Elke Hentschel (1998, n.p.) describes how speakers of Serbian, German, and other languages have compensated for the limitations of ASCII (and the ISO Latin eight-bit character set[11]) in Internet Relay Chat (IRC):

German IRC users write ae, oe, ue and ss for ä, ö, ü and ß; Serbian IRC'ers just write the basic letter without the diacritic sign; Russian users . . . make use of the English transcription of the Russian letters, and the Japanese use special ANSI escape control sequences to represent the Kanji signs.[12]

For speakers of many languages, the solution has been to write in their language but using the Roman alphabet, rather than its conventional script. One of the first to document romanization was John Paolillo (1996), who in the mid-1990s studied the Usenet newsgroup *soc.culture.punjab* in which Punjabi (normally written in either an Indic or Arabic script) was written in Roman characters. Similarly, in emails of Chinese students in the United States, writers represent Chinese characters in the Roman alphabet, inserting numbers next to syllables to indicate tone (Gao, 2001).[13] Romanization has also been documented for both email and chat in Greek (Androutsopoulos, 1999; Androutsopoulos & Hinnenkamp, 2001; Georgakopoulou, 1997, 2004) and Assyrian (McClure, 2001a).[14]

Other research problematizes romanization. Spelling has been inconsistent in languages for which transliteration norms have not yet emerged, including Punjabi, Greek, and Assyrian. Theodora Tseliga (chapter 5) finds substitutions based both on similar graphic shape and on sound. The use of "Greeklish" (romanized Greek) is hotly contested in Greece. Dimitris Koutsogiannis and Bessie Mitsikopoulou (chapter 6) identify three trends in the Greek press: a retrospective trend that views Greeklish as a serious threat to the Greek language, a prospective trend that argues that Greeklish is a transitory phenomenon that will disappear as technology advances, and a resistive trend that points to the negative effects of globalization.

Arab countries are characterized by *diglossia* (Ferguson, 1972): high-prestige, written, literary, classical Arabic coexists with a low-prestige, local spoken variety, that is ordinarily not written. When people type local colloquial Arabic online, they resort to romanization (Berjaoui, 2001; Palfreyman & Al Khalil, chapter 2; Warschauer, El Said, & Zohry, 2002; chapter 13). Some users in Dubai "script switch," alternating between conventional, right-to-left Arabic script and Arabic rendered left to right in the Roman alphabet. As in Greek, Arabic Internet users also use numerals to represent sounds of Arabic that cannot otherwise be represented in the Roman alphabet.

In chapter 3, Hsi-Yao Su identifies four creative uses of writing systems on Taiwanese BBSs: rendering the sounds of English in Chinese characters, rendering Taiwanese (normally not written) in Chinese characters, writing Taiwanese-accented Mandarin in Chinese characters, and recycling a transliteration alphabet ordinarily used in elementary education. There is a strong component of playfulness in the use of these systems. Patterns of adaptation are quite different in Hong Kong (chapter 8 by Carmen Lee). Whereas Taiwanese users play with Chinese characters, Hong Kong users prefer using the Roman alphabet to represent Cantonese elements.

Beyond Ad Hoc Improvisation:
The Search for Solutions

Over time, developers expanded character sets to eight-bit profiles that facilitated use of specific languages and/or groups of languages online. Thus, the
extended ASCII character set (ISO Latin 1, alias ISO 8859–1) added enough
characters, including letters with diacritics, to accommodate many European
languages (figure 1.3).[15]

Globally, however, ISO 8859–1 was still unsatisfactory. Eventually, the
Unicode Standard was established (Anderson, 2004; Consortium, 2003;
Everson, 2002; Paolillo, chapter 18). Unicode is "the universal character
encoding, maintained by the Unicode Consortium (http://www.unicode.org/).
This encoding standard provides the basis for processing, storage and interchange of text data in any language in all modern software and information
technology protocols."[16]

Whereas the original ASCII character set employs only seven bits per
character, in Unicode each character has a unique 16-bit profile. The vision
behind Unicode is that ultimately there will be one encoding for all the scripts
in the world. Developments in Unicode are now greatly expanding the possibilities for multilingual word processing and communication online, reducing
the need for improvisation.[17]

In its latest version (4.1.0), Unicode can accommodate more than a
million characters; at this writing, 97,000 different characters have been
defined.[18] As of August 2004, Unicode included 50 scripts, seven of which
accommodated hundreds of the world's languages. The Roman alphabet
serves more languages than any other script. As of early 2005, more than 80
scripts awaited encoding (Anderson, 2005).

¡	¢	£	¤	¥	¦	§	¨	©	ª	«	¬		®	¯
°	±	2	3	´	µ	¶	•	,	1	°	»	¼	½	¾	¿
À	Á	Â	Ã	Ä	Å	Æ	Ç	È	É	Ê	Ë	Ì	Í	Î	Ï
Ð	Ñ	Ò	Ó	Ô	Õ	Ö	×	Ø	Ù	Ú	Û	Ü	Ý	Þ	ß
à	á	â	ã	ä	å	æ	ç	è	é	ê	ë	ì	í	î	ï
õ	ñ	ò	ó	ô	õ	ö	÷	ø	ù	ú	û	ü	ý	þ	ÿ

FIGURE 1.3. The ISO (International Standards Organization) Latin 1 character set
(alias ISO 8859-1). *Source*: http://www.cs.tut.fi/~jkorpela/chars.html#latin1,
retrieved December 15, 2005.

LINGUISTIC AND DISCOURSE FEATURES OF CMC
IN LANGUAGES OTHER THAN ENGLISH

English-based research over the last decade shows that CMC tends to display both speechlike and written language features, as well as distinctively digital ones (Baron, 2000; Crystal, 2001; Danet, 2001; Herring, 1996b, 2001; Yates, 1996a). These features, and their frequency of use, vary considerably according to CMC mode. Synchronous modes tend to be more speechlike than asynchronous ones (Baron, 2000; Cherny, 1999; Herring, 2001, 2004c; Ko, 1996; Werry, 1996; Yates, 1996a). However, many features are shared across modes: the emoticon or "smiley face"; abbreviations (*LOL*, "laughing out loud"), rebus writing (*c u* for "see you"), and a tendency toward speechlike informality.

Research on other languages has observed similar phenomena. Summarizing features of chat, Androutsopoulos and Ziegler (2004) write:

> In German, as well as in other languages, typical vernacular features include:
> * the graphic representation of colloquial standard pronunciation or non-standard accents
> * typical syntactic patterns of spoken language, e.g., for German, the deletion of clause-initial subject pronouns
> * discourse markers, colloquial and slang vocabulary. (p. 101)[19]

In a local IRC channel called #*mannheim*, they also found evidence of the representation of regional dialect features.

These features of CMC are generally thought to result from two constraining forces: a tendency toward reduction in the number of keystrokes typed, to increase speed and efficiency of communication, and a tendency toward expressivity and creativity, to convey social and affective meanings (Anis, chapter 4 this volume; Cho, in press; Herring, 2001). This latter tendency often manifests itself in language play.

Orthography, Typography, and Playful Performance

In the 1990s, a tendency toward playful performance was documented for many genres of CMC in English (Baron, 2005; Cherny, 1999; Danet, 1995, 2001; Danet, Ruedenberg, & Rosenbaum-Tamari, 1998; Meyer & Thomas, 1990; Reid, 1991; Werry, 1996). There was widespread play with identity (Bechar-Israeli, 1995; Bruckman, 1992, 1993; Danet, 1998; Donath, 1999; Kendall, 1998; Turkle, 1995) and with language and typography.

The flouting of orthographic and typographic norms, and linguistic and typographic playfulness, is evident in many other languages: in Greeklish email (Georgakopoulou, 1997), Swedish chat (Hård af Segerstad, 2000, 2005; Sveningsson, 2001), and German CMC (Durscheid, 2000). Beißwenger and Pütz (2001) analyzed elements of theatricality in German chat. Online play with spelling and typography is also very common in French (Anis, 1999a, chapter 4 this volume; Dejond, 2002; Marcoccia, 2004a).

Second-language learners are playful online (Belz & Reinhardt, 2004; Warner, 2004). Zhao (2002) found linguistic and typographic playfulness in English IRC by native speakers of Chinese. Unintentional misspellings can also produce humorous effects in chat.

In her study of Swedish chat, Hård af Segerstad (2000, 2005) found emoticons (smiley faces), words bracketed in asterisks, play with fonts and colors, extreme use of punctuation, abbreviations and acronyms, ellipsis, and tolerance for deviant spelling. Citing Werry's (1996) study of English and French IRC, Hård af Segerstad (2000, n.p.) concludes, "There is nothing to indicate that the adaptations found [in Swedish] are significantly different [from] online adaptations [in] English or French."

In IM and cell phone text messaging (short messaging service, SMS), two modes that are especially popular with younger users, play with spelling and typography is an apparent mixture of playful expressivity and problem-solving in many languages.[20] Anis (chapter 4) suggests that structural reduction in French SMS language reflects natural linguistic and semiotic processes common to all human languages, triggered by technical, economic, and communicative constraints on text messaging.

It may be helpful to situate the typographic and orthographic features of CMC alongside other characteristics of computer-mediated discourse by considering the case of two very different languages: Japanese and Greek.

CMC in Japanese

The use of Japanese online is interesting because of the language's unusually complex writing system (Griolet, 2002; Nishimura, 2003a, 2003b). Four scripts are used: (1) *kanji*, ideograms of Chinese origin; (2) *hiragana* and (3) *katakana*, systems for representing syllables; and (4) *romaji*, use of the Roman alphabet to transliterate Japanese words and to represent originally foreign terms, such as "CD," in otherwise Japanese contexts. *Hiragana* is used for grammatical endings and to represent Japanese concepts and objects for which *kanji* do not exist, whereas *katakana* is used for foreign names and the representation of natural sounds.

In an analysis of private Japanese email, Fais and Ogura (2001) found nonstandard punctuation, fillers paralleling English "um" or "ah," sentence-final particles, use of *katakana* to highlight expressions normally written in *hiragana* or *kanji*, vertical Asian-style emoticon *kaomoji* ("face marks"), and considerable variation in openings and closings. In the Japanese newsgroup *fj.soc.men-women* (Yamakazi, 2002), Western-style "smileys" also occurred, alongside *kaomoji* (e.g., ^-^), and use of sentence-final particles made the discourse conversation-like. However, in TESOL link, an asynchronous forum for teachers of English in Japan, communication was characterized by "the consistent and reciprocal use of formal verb endings, honorifics, and a formal address term" (Matsuda, 2002, p. 48). In *lig.soc.men-women,* in contrast to many English-language newsgroups (Kim & Raja, 1990), mature adults discussing serious matters mostly maintained standards of politeness, addressing one another by name with the honorific *san* appended (Yamakazi, 2002).[21]

Yukiko Nishimura (2003b, chapter 7 this volume) finds many similarities between English-language CMC and Japanese BBS communication, but also distinctive differences. Similarities include multiple punctuation, eccentric spelling, all caps, written-out laughter, verbal descriptions of actions, and emoticons. Differences include use of final particles, and insertion of icons such as musical notes for expressive purposes. Analysis of other Japanese BBSs (Nishimura, 2003a) identified further differences: *kanji* punning, in which a *kanji* symbol is used to represent a homonym, and play with script shape similarity to create neologisms. In an investigation of Japanese weblogs, Michaela Oberwinkler (2005) found unconventional spelling resembling speech, frequent use of intensifiers, multiple abbreviations, and heavy use of *kaomoji.*

In chapter 12, Hirofumi Katsuno and Christine Yano focus on playful performance via *kaomoji* among Japanese housewives.[22] Whereas earlier *kaomoji* are typographically compact, Japanese women have developed feminized, wider, "cuter" ones. The authors argue that expressive use of *kaomoji* online helps Japanese housewives defuse their real-world frustrations and that their use has connections with Japanese popular culture, including *manga* (comics), a cult of cuteness, and a tradition of feminized handwriting. Centuries-old veneration of calligraphy as an art form (Boudonnat & Kushizaki, 2003) probably also fostered the elaboration of *kaomoji.*[23]

CMC in Greek

The Greek language is interesting not only for its non-Roman writing system that has led to the creation of "Greeklish" online (see chapters 5 and 6), but as a language that until recently was diglossic, with a High (Katharevousa) and a Low (Demotic) style. Katharevousa was used in writing and official functions associated with government, education, and religion, and Demotic was used in informal speech and ordinary affairs. Demotic was made the official language in 1976, but many Katharevousa words and grammatical structures remain in the linguistic repertoire of contemporary Greek speakers (Joseph, 2001; see also chapters 5 and 6).

Oral features and play with register are often found in Greek CMC. Personal email by Greeks writing in Greeklish and English is a hybrid communicative genre, having continuities both with letter writing and with oral aspects of Greek culture and communication. In a study of private email by Greeks living in England (Georgakopoulou, 1997), openings and closings were absent or highly routinized. The discourse style was one of informal, playful pastiche; for example, some emails contained an incongruous, humorous mixture of Demotic Greek and Katharevousa. Style shifts and code switches between Greek and English served as contextualization cues (Gumperz, 1982). Emailers preferred positive politeness strategies, to cultivate solidarity with fellow Greeks abroad.

Tereza Spilioti (2005) identified continuities in Greek SMS with patterns of communication in Greek face-to-face and mediated communication, including telephone conversations and answering machine messages. Because messages were embedded in close social relationships, openings and even closings were mostly absent; participants again expressed solidarity via affective elements including emoticons. Recounting events in personal email by Greeks also shows culture-specific features. While email stories tend to exhibit features of letter writing, they also reflect narrative norms governing Greek face-to-face interaction (Georgakopoulou, 2004).

GENDER, LANGUAGE, AND CULTURE ONLINE

Gender differentiation is an important aspect of culture that is often reflected in language use. In English-language CMC, men and women use different discourse styles online much as they do offline (Herring, 1996a, 2003, 2004b; compare Bucholtz, 2004; Lakoff, 1975; Tannen, 1990). We know of no studies yet to identify systematic "women's language" and "men's language" features in CMC in other languages. However, a growing number of case studies have examined gender and Internet use in non-English contexts.

Politeness

In a study of gender and politeness in email in India, Asha Kaul and Vaibhavi Kulkarni (2005) analyzed 494 work- and task-related emails. Although all messages were in English, reflecting its use as a lingua franca and language of white-collar professionals, all were written by employees in Indian workplaces and reflect the Indian cultural context. Women were more polite than men, as in studies of gender and politeness in English CMC. However, men used flattery more than women, communicating praise and approval of the recipient's actions—a behavior more commonly associated with women in English CMC (Herring, 1996a). Kaul and Kulkarni (2005, n.p.) suggest that "this could be attributed to the cultural backdrop in which the emails were written where men take on the patronizing role and compliment frequently to motivate the team players/members."

In chapter 11, Sandi de Oliveira analyzes politeness violations on the users' discussion list of a university in Portugal. While grammar and spelling were standard, messages sometimes failed to observe the requirement—of utmost importance in Portuguese culture—to use the appropriate term of address. Thus, a participant entitled by rank to be addressed as *Professor Doutor* [+ first name + last name] should not be addressed as *Senhor* (Mr.) [+ first name + last name]. Although women participated less often, messages posted by women were more often treated as transgressions. Men were quick to chastise transgressions, in contrast to English-based claims that men are less concerned than women with maintaining politeness norms (see Herring, 1996a). At the same time, the behavior of the Portuguese men asserted their traditional gender roles as interactionally dominant and representative of "authority."

Turn Taking

Focusing on the mechanics and power dynamics of interaction, Siriporn Pan-yametheekul and Susan Herring (chapter 10) analyzed gender in relation to turn-allocation patterns in a Web-based Thai chat room. They found that females made greater use of strategies like those found in face-to-face conversation and enjoyed greater power in the chat room, chatting with whom they chose and receiving more responses to their messages, than did males. Flirtatious initiations were infrequent and generally lacking in sexually explicit content. The authors interpreted their findings in relation to the gender demographics of the chat room, the norms of the website, and Thai cultural values of politeness and respect—all of which favor female participation.

Internet Communication and Social Change

The three studies above demonstrate that gender interacts with culture online in ways that shape language and communication. It has also been sug-gested that the Internet has the potential to empower women and members of other traditionally subordinate groups (see Herring, 2003). This poten-tial takes on special significance for women in traditional patriarchal cultures. For example, Katsuno and Yano (chapter 12) argue that ex-pressive use of *kaomoji* online helps Japanese housewives defuse their real-world frustrations associated with meal preparation, child care, and boring husbands.

The Middle East is another region in which gender roles are traditionally segregated. Deborah Wheeler (2001) studied women's use of the Internet in Kuwait, where access is mainly through cybercafés in which men and women sit in separate sections. Wheeler's evidence suggests that the greater freedom available online to chat with young people of the opposite sex could potentially break down traditional Islamic barriers to mixed-sex interaction. In an Internet kiosk in Essaouira, Morocco (figure 1.4), a young woman wearing the traditional Muslim *hijab* (head covering) and young man are not separated by a barrier, but they are seated maximally far apart.

FIGURE 1.4. Users in an Internet kiosk, Essaouira, Morocco. Photograph by Brenda Danet, March 2002.

LANGUAGE CHOICE AND CODE SWITCHING

Wherever multilingualism exists, language choice becomes an issue. Language choice online depends on the technological, sociocultural, and political context. One commonality across contexts, however, is the use of English as a lingua franca. English-educated bilinguals often use both English and their national language online (Kelly Holmes, 2004; Sue Wright, 2004).

The Less Developed World

Tanzania is fairly representative of the less developed world in that large areas are not connected to the electricity grid (Mafu, 2004). During British rule, Africans were educated in Swahili while Europeans and Asians were educated in English. After independence, Swahili became the language of instruction, but only at the elementary level.[24] Swahili and English are both official languages today. While Internet use has grown in the last five years, only elites usually have access. Students and professionals interviewed by Mafu (2004) reported some use of Swahili in email, but English predominated, reflecting and perpetuating the elite status of users and the functions of English as a language of wider communication. More than a hundred minority languages spoken in Tanzania are unrepresented online and are likely to remain so.[25]

The situation is similar in the Arab world. English is the main language of email among young Egyptian professionals (Warschauer et al., 2002; also chapter 13). There is no single standard for communication in Arabic online; many computers lack operating systems that can handle Arabic. As discussed above, many people romanize colloquial Arabic. English is more common in formal email communication, again reflecting its function as a language of wider communication.

Uzbekistan is a newly independent country in Central Asia, formerly part of the Soviet Union. Uzbek is the official language. Between 1989 and 1995, Russian was the officially sanctioned main language of wider communication. In 1993, a law was passed changing the Uzbek script from Cyrillic to the Roman alphabet. As of 2003, not many Uzbekis reported having used the Internet. Among those who did, nearly all reported using Russian, and more than 70% said they used English, while only 13% claimed to use Uzbek online (Wei, 2004). The absence of material on the World Wide Web in Uzbek may explain its underuse.

Language Choice in Europe

The nations of Europe speak different languages and are technologically developed. Europeans online should thus use multiple languages, both in national contexts and in the European community as a whole. The available research suggests that this is true but that local languages often cede to English and regional lingua francas when speakers of different language backgrounds seek to communicate.

Switzerland is an example of a multilingual nation, with four national languages, German, French, Italian, and Romansh, of which the first three are official languages used in government and federal administration. English has slowly gained ground as a lingua franca since World War II (Demont-Heinrich, 2005; Dürmüller, 2002). Mercedes Durham (chapter 14 this volume) studied the languages used on a Swiss medical students' list. In less than four years, English went from being used a little more than 10% of the time to more than 80% of the time. The main reason for this development, Durham speculates, is that in Switzerland, English is no one's native language and hence privileges no group of speakers over another.

At the regional level, the European Union currently has 25 member states and 21 official languages. Romania, Croatia, and Bulgaria are due to join in 2007, and Turkey is knocking at the door. With so many languages represented among its membership, the European Union "is committed to the principle of multilingualism and to the fundamental rights of non-discrimination and equality of its citizens. This implies, in particular, equal rights of all citizens for information and access to legal documents in their national language" (Ginsburgh & Weber, 2005, p. 2). Accordingly, the European Union maintains a veritable army of translators for all written documents and interpreters who perform direct and relay oral interpretation.[26]

Between July 2001 and October 2004, citizens could also participate in a Web-based discussion forum called Futurum about the E.U. constitution, in languages of their choosing. Ruth Wodak and Scott Wright (chapter 17; Scott Wright, 2004) investigated the languages actually used in the Futurum forum.[27] English was by far the main language; more than 90% of all threads or topics introduced in English were conducted only in English. Threads introduced in other languages—mostly French and German—used a greater diversity of languages, but this trend was minor.

Negotiating Language Choice in Global Forums

How do participants negotiate language choice in global forums where participants hail from many countries, speak many different languages, and there is no overt link to a specific national or regional context, no official commitment to a given language, and no moderator to police language choice? This situation is common; most discussion forums do not specify what language should be used, and many are in principle open to participants from any country. Yet research on language choice in global forums is rare, perhaps because context usually sets a default expectation for language choice even when no explicit language policy is articulated.

An exception is Active Worlds,[28] a Web-based environment that supports text chat in three-dimensional graphical "worlds." Allwood and Schroeder (2000, p. 1) describe the environment as "a potentially multilingual and multicultural setting"; it is popular with users from many countries, and it has worlds devoted to particular language groups and general worlds that are cosmopolitan. However, in a study of AlphaWorld chat involving speakers from mixed language backgrounds, Allwood and Schroeder found that 68% used English only, while only 2% participated exclusively in a language other than English; the remainder alternated between English and another language. Axelsson, Abelin, and Schroeder (2003, chapter 16 this volume) studied efforts to switch languages in Active Worlds and the response to these efforts. English dominated, generally in a nonconflictual manner. Non-English speakers, being generally bilingual, were willing to switch to English even in settings where the majority of the users were non-English speaking.

Language Use in Diasporic Online Communities

Among immigrants to a new country, use of the home language with compatriots may be associated with alienation from the local culture and a desire for cultural maintenance and solidarity. Fialkova (2005) studied online discussion forums for Russian Jews living in Israel. Russian dominated in the forums, even in ethnic community sites for Ukrainians and Byelorussians; Ukrainian and Byeloruss were found only in familiar cultural artifacts such as poems and songs. In contrast to situations in which non-Roman scripts were rendered in ASCII characters, the Russian script, Cyrillic, is used in the Israel-based forums; transliteration into Roman script is actively discouraged on some sites (Fialkova, 2005).

John Paolillo (1996) investigated *soc.culture.punjab*, a Usenet newsgroup populated mainly by Punjabi expatriates living in Canada, the United Kingdom, and the United States. In contrast to the situation described by Fialkova (2005), Paolillo found very little use of the home language; English was the unmarked language. Punjabi was the functionally marginalized, marked choice, used primarily for conventional and expressive purposes (e.g., greetings and jokes). Paolillo attributed the dominance of English to the presence of nonfluent second- and third-generation Punjabis in the newsgroup, widespread use of English in India by the educated classes, and the status of English as the language of Usenet. Having to type Punjabi in Roman characters may also have discouraged its use.[29]

In a third type of diasporic situation, Jannis Androutsopoulos (chapter 15) reports that German is the online lingua franca among migrants in Germany. In Web-based discussion forums for Persians, Indians, and Greeks living in Germany, German predominates, although there is much use of migrant languages, too. In this case, the language of the host country serves as the primary lingua franca, rather than English. Androutsopoulos attributes the prominence of German to language shift among second- and third-generation immigrants, its utility as a regional lingua franca, and the language policy of webmasters.

In contrast to the limited Ukrainian and Byeloruss usage on Russian emigrant sites in Israel, or the use of Punjabi on *soc.culture.punjab*, the migrants' home languages on the sites studied by Androutsopoulos alternate with German in locally meaningful ways, in a pattern of code switching. Androutsopoulos noted that written code switching online resembles conversational code switching, an observation also made by Jayantilal (1998), McClure (2001a), and Hinrichs (2006).

THE INTERNET AND GLOBAL LINGUISTIC DIVERSITY

The discussion of language choice shows that languages used online form global and regional hierarchies, with English at the top, followed by important regional languages, and finally (if at all) users' local languages (see Graddol, 1997/2000). This raises the broader issue of the effects of the Internet on linguistic diversity worldwide, including the fate of small and endangered languages online, and the status of English in the Internet age.

Small and Endangered Languages

The number of languages spoken in the world has been in decline since well before the invention of computer networking (Graddol, 1997/2000; Krauss, 1992). Some people claim that the Internet has the potential to support and even revitalize endangered languages (Cunliffe & Herring, 2005; Danet & Herring, in press). Here we are interested in the extent to which speakers of minority and endangered languages use their indigenous languages online.

Several studies have examined CMC involving minority language speakers. Luis Fernandez (2001) reports several discouraging situations involving language choice. The manager of a list discussing the future of Ireland warned those posting in Gaelic (rather than English) that their posts would be removed (Ostler, 1999; cited in Fernandez, 2001, p. 24). On Leonenet, a current events list in Sierra Leone, when some people posted in Krio, the country's lingua franca, others thought this impolite vis-à-vis non-Sierra Leonean subscribers, or that the practice discriminated against speakers of other ethnic languages (Wright, 1996, p. 24; cited in Fernandez, 2001, p. 25). Fernandez found almost no use of Basque in ostensibly Basque fora, although many users were bilingual in Basque and Spanish or French. Most messages were in Spanish.[30]

In another Spanish-dominated context, Salvador Climent and his colleagues (chapter 9) found that three-quarters of all postings on a Usenet newsgroup based in a Catalan-language university were in Catalan. However, among postings spontaneously responding to previous ones, Catalan speakers were more likely to switch to Spanish than vice versa, a trend that bodes ill for the future of Catalan, according to the authors. Issues of wider intelligibility again arise: Spanish is the preferred language for interacting with foreigners, for example, who are more likely to know Spanish than Catalan. Climent and colleagues propose machine translation as a potential solution to enable minority language speakers to use their local languages online, yet still communicate with larger audiences.

Cunliffe and Harries (2005) analyzed the language and functions of posts to a bilingual Welsh–English Web community, Pen i Ben, created to encourage communication in both languages. However, over time Welsh use decreased, as did the range of functions expressed by Welsh posts, while English use increased. The authors suggest that minority languages may have a difficult time maintaining an online presence without supporting strategies, social as well as technological.

A more successful case is that of Assyrian, a Semitic language spoken by a mainly diasporic community of Assyrians, an ancient people whose homeland is in the Middle East. McClure (2001a, 2001b) collected samples from Usenet newsgroups including *soc.culture.Assyrian*, chat rooms, and online publications, with special attention to the forms and functions of code switching in these media genres (McClure, 2001a). In the 1990s Assyrian was mostly transliterated into the Roman alphabet for online purposes, because of font difficulties. McClure (2001a) reports a good deal of code switching to

Assyrian in mainly English-based chat rooms and newsgroup postings. Greetings and closings were frequently written in romanized Assyrian to express solidarity with others. McClure (2001b) concludes, "Assyrians have found in the Internet a strong tool in the fight for the maintenance of their language" (p. 74).

The Status of English

English has a historical advantage in relation to the Internet and continues to dominate many online contexts (Paolillo, chapter 18; Yates, 1996b). Offline, as well, interest in English as a second language is growing: Globally, more young people are learning English now than at any other time (Graddol, 1997/2000). The Internet alone is not responsible for this growth: Other political, economic, and cultural forces had already made English a global lingua franca (Crystal, 2003). The Internet has, however, facilitated interaction among participants in multilingual nations, regions, and around the world, a number of whom employ English as a language of wider communication. This, in turn, further strengthens the global position of English, online and offline. Thus, it seems likely that the Internet is accelerating the global spread of English, as have previous mass communication technologies such as film and popular music recording.

The question arises: Does the spread of English pose a threat to other languages and, more generally, to language diversity on a global scale? The possibility of a single language prevailing to the exclusion of all others seems remote. Graddol (1997/2000) foresees, instead, an oligarchy of the world's largest languages—Chinese, Spanish, English, Arabic, Malay, Hindi, Russian—each of them dominating in its geographical region, where it also enjoys economic and cultural influence. Graddol estimates that by the year 2050, about 90 national languages will remain, and the number of local and minority languages will continue to decline, consistent with the ongoing trend toward language loss (Krauss, 1992).

Paolillo (chapter 18) also finds that ongoing trends favor large languages, especially English. He addresses the question of linguistic diversity online quantitatively, by developing a diversity index that allows for comparison of the relative diversity of polities with different population sizes. The linguistic diversity of Internet users is considerably lower than that of global linguistic diversity; moreover, the regions with the lowest linguistic diversity, especially North America and Europe, have the largest share of Internet resources. Projected trends suggest that linguistic diversity online is on the rise but that it is leveling off after a period of rapid increase since 1996. Paolillo concludes that the concentration of resources in North America, and the economics of Internet technology development and use, will necessarily mean continued greater use of English than any other language on the Internet in the foreseeable future.

It is often claimed that Chinese, as the language with the largest number of speakers in the world, will eventually become the dominant language online. Chinese Internet use has been growing rapidly: As of November 2005, an estimated 124 million Chinese speakers used the Internet, second only to English with 310 million speakers.[31] However, Paolillo notes that current estimates tend to be based on the usage of urban, educated Chinese, who represent a relatively small proportion of Chinese speakers. Moreover, for socioeconomic reasons, Internet penetration levels for China will probably be lower than in English-speaking countries, resulting in a leveling off below projected levels (Lin, 2002). In any case, Bruthiaux (2002) argues, the writing system and other features of the Chinese language will prevent it from displacing English globally.

THE CONTENTS OF THIS BOOK

This book contains 18 chapters, including this introduction. The heart of the book is 15 empirical case studies of online communication in a variety of languages and CMC modes. An additional chapter (chapter 6) is a critical analysis of discourse about CMC, and the last chapter is a quantitative survey of language diversity on the Internet (chapter 18).

A range of languages and language varieties is represented, including three varieties of Chinese: Hong Kong Cantonese, Taiwanese, and Mandarin Chinese (chapters 3 and 8, by Su and Lee). Two chapters analyze Japanese, the third most popular Internet language (after English and Chinese): Nishimura (chapter 7) examines Japanese BBS communication, and Katsuno and Yano (chapter 12) focus on *kaomoji* in Japanese chat. Panyametheekul and Herring (chapter 10) report on turn taking in Thai chat. Androutsopoulos (chapter 15) discusses Persian online, as well as Indian languages and Greeklish. The Middle East is represented by studies of Arabic in Egypt and Dubai (chapters 2 and 13, by Palfreyman & Al Khalil, and Warschauer et al.).

European languages discussed include French, German, Italian, Catalan, Spanish, and Portuguese (chapters by Anis, Androutsopoulos, Durham, Climent et al., and Oliveira). Two chapters focus on "Greeklish": chapter 5 by Tseliga and chapter 6 by Koutsogiannis and Mitsikopoulou. The latter chapter is about *attitudes* toward the use of Greeklish; it complements Tseliga's empirical analysis of Greeklish online. Greek is also one of the diasporic languages on German-based websites considered in chapter 15 by Androutsopoulos. Finally, varieties and aspects of nonnative English are investigated by Su, Lee, Warschauer et al., Durham, Axelsson et al., and Wodak and Wright.

Eleven studies analyze various forms of asynchronous CMC, as used by different populations of users. Two discuss personal email, among Hong Kong students (chapter 8 by Lee) and Egyptian professionals (chapter 13 by Warschauer et al.). Three chapters deal with asynchronous CMC among students, in a recreational context in Taiwan (chapter 3 by Su), and in academic or professional contexts, among computer science students in Catalonia (chapter 9 by Climent et al.), and Swiss medical students (chapter 14 by Durham). Other varieties of asynchronous CMC studied include a faculty/ staff forum at a Portuguese university (chapter 11 by Oliveira), a European Union citizens' discussion list (chapter 17, Wodak & Wright), discussion lists and a newsgroup in Greek (chapter 5, Tseliga), electronic BBSs in Japan (chapter 7, Nishimura), and Web-based discussion forums for migrants in Germany (chapter 15, Androutsopoulos). In chapter 4, Jacques Anis discusses SMS messages circulated among French students and other young people.

Six chapters discuss synchronous CMC, one-to-one modes such as IM and ICQ ("I Seek You"), as well as public group chat. Palfreyman and Al Khalil (chapter 2) and Warschauer et al. (chapter 13) investigated IM use by students and young Arabic professionals. Lee (chapter 8) analyzes ICQ chat by young people in Hong Kong. Panyametheekul and Herring (chapter 10) and Katsuno and Yano (chapter 12) investigated Web chat among Thai young people and Japanese housewives, respectively. Finally, Axelsson et al. (chapter 16) examine text chat in the three-dimensional graphical environment Active Worlds.

Table 1.2 summarizes the case studies in this book by CMC mode, the populations studied, the language(s) investigated, and the linguistic phenomena that are the research focus.

CONCLUSIONS

Despite its broad scope, the coverage of this book is limited in several respects. Most chapters are case studies of a single language in a single online context. Of the approximately 190 countries in the world, fewer than 20 are represented here. In geographical terms, no indigenous languages from Central America, South America, or outlying areas such as New Guinea are included; also missing are major languages such as Russian and Malay.

The book includes more asynchronous than synchronous studies, and no chapter that addresses the currently most rapidly growing mode of asynchronous CMC, weblogs.[32] Finally, the language use analyzed in this collection is textual, rather than audio or graphical (with the exception of Active Worlds as studied by Axelsson et al.), or mixed modality.

Summary of Findings

The above limitations notwithstanding, certain generalizations can be made from the studies in this collection, considered together with the research summarized in this introductory chapter. Many of these point to commonalities associated with CMC in different languages.

TABLE 1.2. Classification of case studies by CMC mode, population and languages investigated, and research focus.

Synchronicity/CMC mode	Population	Language(s)	Focus	Chapter author(s)
Asynchronous				
Personal email	High school, university students	Cantonese, English	Code mixing, representations of Cantonese, romanization	Lee
Personal email	Young professionals, 24–36 years old	Classical, colloquial Egyptian Arabic, English	Language choice	Warschauer et al.
BBSs	University students, young people	Taiwanese, Taiwanese-accented Mandarin, English	Writing systems, dialects, language play	Su
Discussion list	Medical students	English, French, German, Italian	Language choice over time	Durham
Discussion list	University faculty, staff	Portuguese	Politeness, gender	Oliveira
Discussion list	E.U. citizens, all ages	Multiple, English	Language choice, dominance	Wodak & Wright
BBSs on fan websites	Young people	Japanese	Orthography and typography	Nishimura
Local Usenet newsgroups	Computer science students	Catalan, Spanish	Netspeak and Spanish interference in Catalan; issues for machine translation	Climent et al.
Discussion lists, newsgroup	Unspecified, presumably adults all ages	Greek, "Greeklish"	Romanization; uses and features of Greeklish; relation between Greeklish and English borrowing	Tseliga

continued

25

TABLE 1.2. (continued)

Synchronicity/CMC mode	Population	Language(s)	Focus	Chapter author(s)
Web-based, diasporic discussion forums	Adolescents, young adults, migrants, children of migrants to Germany	German, Persian, Hindi, Punjabi, other Indian languages, Greek(lish)	Language choice, code switching	Androutsopoulos
SMS (mobile phone text messages)	University students, young people	French	Orthography and typography	Anis
Synchronous				
Instant messaging	Female students	Arabic, ASCII-ized Gulf Arabic	Orthography and typography	Palfreyman & Al Khalil
ICQ chat	High school, university students	Cantonese, English	Code mixing, representations of Cantonese, romanization	Lee
Webchat	Young people 11–25 years old	Thai	Turn taking, gender	Panyametheekul & Herring
Chatroom	Housewives	Japanese	*Kaomoji* (Japanese emoticons), gender	Katsuno & Yano
Chat	Young professionals 24–36 years old	Classical, colloquial Egyptian Arabic, English	Language choice	Warschauer et al.
Graphical chat (Active Worlds)	Unspecified	English, miscellaneous European languages	Language choice	Axelsson et al.

First, writing systems influence the linguistic features of CMC. The ASCII bias in textual CMC is not just a limitation for languages that use non-Roman fonts, but also, in many cases, an impetus for orthographic and typographic innovation. This trend goes hand in hand with the tendency for language play in CMC, which has been observed for every language used online, including those written in Roman script.

Considerable evidence has accumulated that distinctive CMC features recur in languages besides English, for example, abbreviations, emoticons, and conversational usage. Shared features may have originated from a single source (e.g., North American English users) and spread through contact, although some may be local responses to technical constraints of the medium, as Anis proposes for French SMS. More generally, online communication tends to be less formal and more oriented toward interpersonal interaction than other registers of writing, especially in synchronous modes.

Gender is reflected in online discourse in every language context studied, typically reproducing offline gender patterns (see Herring, 2004b). This finding runs counter to popular claims that gender is invisible in textual CMC, due to its paucity of social cues (Herring, 2003). The studies in this book show that gender can be indexed through online behaviors including politeness, emoticon use, and turn taking.

In several online multilingual contexts (e.g., chapter 15), language alternation has been observed to resemble face-to-face, conversational code switching. This CMC evidence presents an empirical counterpoint to theoretical claims that code switching is an exclusively conversational phenomenon (see Gumperz, 1982).

Finally, English is often used as a lingua franca in public online contexts, even when no native English speakers are present. Longitudinal studies such as Durham's (chapter 14) lend particularly compelling support to the notion that the Internet is accelerating the global use of English.

Alongside these shared tendencies, variation can be observed across different language contexts. The characteristics of non-Roman scripts will evidently shape how they are adapted in ASCII, for example, whether numerals can be used to stand in for sounds. Acronyms are not universally common (chapter 4); conversely, writing words together in an unbroken string may be more characteristic of CMC in French than in English, which may reflect language-internal preferences, for example, for synthetic as opposed to analytic morphology.

Some apparently culture-based differences are found in the chapters on gender. Thai women (chapter 10) come off better than Portuguese women (chapter 11) in terms of control of, and obtaining positive outcomes from, online mixed-sex discourse. Another intriguing comparison is that between CMC in Hong Kong and Taiwan: Despite similar Chinese/English bilingualism, different patterns of use are evidenced by young people that cannot be explained as differences between one-to-one (chapter 8) and many-to-many (chapter 3) modes of CMC.

Even emoticons reflect cultural practices. Two radically different sets of emoticons correspond roughly to Western versus Asian usage, the latter category reflecting, in the case of *kaomoji*, Japanese comic book representation and a popular cult of "cuteness" (chapter 12).

Finally, English does not dominate in every multilingual situation: Russian dominates Internet use in Uzbekistan (Wei, 2004), Spanish dominates in Catalunya (chapter 9), and German is the matrix language among immigrants to Germany (chapter 15). There is also some evidence that the online presence of speakers of (relatively) smaller languages is increasing (chapter 18). Case studies such as those presented here can begin to shed light on what circumstances—linguistic, communicative, cultural, demographic, and technological—condition such variation.

Directions for Future Research

There is a pressing need for systematic cross-linguistic studies that make use of similar methods in similar contexts involving different languages. Studies that assess the actual extent and nature of CMC use in different parts of the world, rather than relying on estimates of number of Internet hosts or numbers of computers, would also be valuable. Given that technology choices determine with whom one can converse (e.g., currently, IM users cannot necessarily chat with people using a different IM client) and that features of CMC technology can shape language use, mapping out who is communicating via what modes of CMC, where, and to what extent is a vital prerequisite to an eventual understanding of CMC on a global scale.

In the meantime, Internet use continues to rise, and Internet technologies continue to evolve. Unicode and new fonts have partially obviated the need for romanization of non-Roman scripts; does this mean that the use of Greeklish, for example, will ultimately disappear? What fonts will be used by speakers of languages that were previously unwritten before being expressed in CMC, such as Sardinian, Romani, and vernacular Gulf Arabic?

Consider, too, the recent rise of weblogs (blogs), a technology that allows individuals to self-publish their thoughts on the Web. How does the public broadcast nature of blogs, and their global audience, affect language choice? Blog publishing is also having a popularizing effect, as seen in its use to challenge the authoritarian character of the current regime in Iran. This challenge is partly linguistic; the deliberately informal, ostensibly illiterate style of some Persian bloggers conflicts with conventional expectations for writing in Persian and has given rise to a "vulgarity debate" (Doostdar, 2004). Such uses, in addition to raising sociolinguistic issues of language prescriptivism and standardization, are culturally embedded and critical in nature, calling for a diverse set of analytical methods.

It is our hope that these observations and those in the following chapters will serve as a starting point for further research on Internet language use that adopts as its premise that the Internet is a multilingual domain.[33]

Acknowledgment

This chapter incorporates material from Danet and Herring (2007).

Notes

1. This example shows how the meaning of the character "@"—the separator between username and server name in an email address—has come to symbolize Internet-mediated communication in general (see Danet, 2001, pp. 2–3).

2. Internet Statistics: Distribution of languages on the Internet, http://www.netz-tipp.de/languages.html, retrieved December 16, 2005.

3. Internet World Stats, Internet usage in Asia, http://www.Internetworldstats.com/stats3.htm; retrieved December 16, 2005.

4. See Block (2004) and papers in Sue Wright (2004).

5. See English abstracts for Beißwenger (2001) at http://www.chat-kommunikation.de/chat2001/index.html and Beißwenger's multilingual bibliography at http://www.chat-bibliography.de/, both retrieved December 16, 2005; see also references in note 19.

6. On CMC modes, see Herring (2002).

7. See Danet (1998), Donath (1999), and Turkle (1995).

8. *Hor* means "fornication" and *by* means "village." See Pargman (1998) and Pargman and Palme (2004).

9. See http://www.omniglot.com/writing/hawaiian.htm; retrieved December 5, 2005.

10. On word processing in Chinese and Japanese, see Su (chapter 3) and Nishimura (2003b).

11. See the discussion of the extended ASCII character set below.

12. See also Durscheid (2000).

13. This is apparently not spontaneous improvisation. In one method of inputting Chinese characters, typists type romanized syllables and then further key sequences to produce Chinese characters. Evidently, in the United States they stop at the first stage. See Su (chapter 3) and http://www.pinyin.info/, retrieved December 5, 2005.

14. Today Syriac fonts are freely available (McClure, 2001b).

15. ISO stands for the International Organization for Standardization; see http://www.iso.org/iso/en/ISOOnline.frontpage, retrieved December 5, 2005. On pre-Unicode solutions, see http://www.cs.tut.fi/~jkorpela/chars.html, retrieved December 5, 2005.

16. Unicode Home Pages, http://www.unicode.org/glossary/, retrieved December 6, 2005.

17. See http://www.linguistics.berkeley.edu/sei/ and http://www.evertype.com/, both retrieved December 6, 2005.

18. See http://www.unicode.org/versions/Unicode4.1.0/, retrieved December 5, 2005; page last updated March 31, 2005.

19. On German CMC, see also Beißwenger (2001), Beißwenger and Storrer (2005), Durscheid (1999, 2000), Hentschel (1998), Stein (2003), Warner (2004), and Zitzen and Stein (2004). On French CMC, see Anis (1999b; chapter 4 this volume) and Marcoccia (2004a, 2004b).

20. Studies of these practices include Thurlow and Brown (2003) on SMS, Baron (in press) on IM in English, Ling (2005) on Norwegian SMS, Baron and Ling (2003) on English IM and Norwegian SMS; Hård af Segerstad (2005) on Swedish SMS, Kasesniemi and Rautiainen (2002) on Finnish SMS, Pietrini (2001) on SMS in Italian, Almela Perez (2001) and Galan Rodriguez (2001) on Spanish SMS, Spilioti (2005) on Greek and Greeklish SMS, Androutsopoulos and Schmidt (2002) and Döring (2002) on German SMS; Anis (2001; chapter 4) on French SMS, and Miyake (2005) on Japanese SMS.

21. "*San* is used between equals regardless of gender.... [It] is the least marked of all address terms for gender or social status" (Matsuda, 2002, p. 45).

22. See also Katsuno and Yano (2002) and Miyake (2005).

23. *Kaomoji* are common in Japanese CMC in general (Fouser, Narahiko, & Chungmin, 2000; Sugimoto & Levin, 2000). Even Japanese professionals and seniors use them (Kanayama, 2003; Matsuda, 2002).

24. Tanganyika and Zanzibar gained independence in 1962 and 1963, respectively. In 1964, they became the nation of Tanzania (http://www.african.gu.se/tanzania/weblinks.html, retrieved December 6, 2005).

25. See the discussion of linguistic diversity online in chapter 18.

26. See http://europa.eu.int/comm/education/policies/lang/languages/index_en.html, retrieved December 4, 2005. Only a "handful" of languages were actually used (Fishman, 1998, p. 29).

27. The forum was closed in October 2004. Futurum debates are archived at http://europa.eu.int/constitution/futurum/index_en.htm, retrieved December 5, 2005.

28. See http://www.activeworlds.com/, retrieved December 5, 2005.

29. On the Punjabi script, see http://www.omniglot.com/writing/gurmuki.htm, retrieved December 16, 2005.

30. See also Arbelaiz (2001) and Uberuaga (2001).

31. Internet World Stats, Internet users by language, http://www.Internetworldstats.com/stats7.htm, retrieved December 5, 2005.

32. On weblogs in English, see Herring, Scheidt, Bonus, and Wright (2004). Japanese and Israeli weblogs are the subject of Ph.D. theses by Oberwinkler (2005) and Vaisman (in preparation), respectively.

33. For more recent sociolinguistic work on computer-mediated communication using a multilingual perspective that appeared after this book went to press, see Androutsopoulos (2006).

References

Allwood, J., & Schroeder, R. (2000). Intercultural communication in virtual environments. *Intercultural Communication, 3.* Retrieved December 5, 2005, from http://www.immi.se/intercultural/nr3/allwood.htm.

Almela Perez, R. (2001). SMS: Short messages via the mobile telephone. *Español Actual, 75,* 91–99.

Ammon, U. (Ed.). (2001). *The dominance of English as a language of science.* New York: Mouton de Gruyter.

Anderson, D. (2004). The Script Encoding Initiative. *SIGNA, 6,* 1–12. Retrieved December 5, 2005, from www.linguistics.berkeley.edu/~dwanders/SIGNAEnglish.pdf.

Anderson, D. (2005). Global linguistic diversity for the Internet. *Communications of the ACM, 48*(1), 27–28.

Androutsopoulos, J. (1999, April). Spelling variation in Latin alphabeted Greek email messages (English abstract). Paper presented at the 20th Working Meeting, Linguistics Department, Aristoteles University of Thessaloniki, Thessaloniki, Greece. Retrieved December 5, 2005, from http://greekweb.archetype.de/greekmail/abstracts.htm.

Androutsopoulos, J. (Ed.) (2006). Sociolinguistics and computer-mediated communication (Special issue). *Journal of Sociolinguistics, 10*(4).

Androutsopoulos, J., & Hinnenkamp, V. (2001). Code-Switching in der bilingualen Chat-Kommunikation: Ein explorativer Blick auf #hellas und #turks. In M. Beißwenger (Ed.),

Chat-Kommunikation. Sprache, Interaktion und Sozialität in synchroner computerver-mittelter Kommunikation (pp. 367–401). Stuttgart: Ibidem.

Androutsopoulos, J., & Schmidt, G. (2002). SMS-Kommunikation: Ethnografische Gattungs-analyse am Beispiel einer Kleingruppe. *Zeitschrift für Angewandte Linguistik, 36,* 49–80.

Androutsopoulos, J., & Ziegler, E. (2004). Exploring language variation on the Internet: Regional speech in a chat community. In B.-L. Gunnarsson, L. Bergström, G. Eklund, S. Fridell, L. H. Hansen, A. Karstadt, et al. (Eds.), *Language variation in Europe* (pp. 99–111). Uppsala: Uppsala University.

Anis, J. (1999a). Chat et usages graphiques. In J. Anis (Ed.), *Internet, communication et langue française* (pp. 71–90). Paris: Hermes.

Anis, J. (Ed.). (1999b). *Internet, communication et langue française.* Paris: Hermes.

Anis, J. (2001). *Parlez vous texto? Guide des nouveaux langages du réseau.* Paris: Le Cherche Midi.

Arbelaiz, A. M. (2001). Basque, the Internet, and new language policies. In C. Moseley, N. Ostler, & H. Ouzzate (Eds.), *Endangered languages and the media: Proceedings of the fifth FEL conference, Agadir, Morocco, September 20–23, 2001* (pp. 98–103). Bath, UK: Foundation for Endangered Languages.

Axelsson, A.-S., Abelin, Å., & Schroeder, R. (2003). Anyone speak Spanish? Language encounters in multi-user virtual environments and the influence of technology. *New Media & Society, 5*(4), 475–498.

Baron, N. S. (2000). *Alphabet to email: How written English evolved and where it's heading.* London: Routledge.

Baron, N. S. (with L. Squires, S. Tench, & M. Thompson). (2005). Tethered or mobile? Use of away messages in instant messaging by American college students. In R. Ling & P. Ped-ersen (Eds.), *Mobile communications: Renegotiation of the social sphere* (pp. 293–311). London: Springer.

Baron, N. S. (in press). Discourse structures in instant messaging: The case of utterance breaks. In S. C. Herring (Ed.), *Computer-mediated conversation.* Cresskill, NJ: Hampton Press.

Baron, N. S., & Ling, R. S. (2003). *IM and SMS: A linguistic comparison.* Paper presented at the fourth international conference of the Association of Internet Researchers, Toronto, October 16–19.

Bauman, R. (1992). Performance. In R. Bauman (Ed.), *Folklore, cultural performances, and popular entertainments* (pp. 41–49). New York: Oxford University Press.

Bauman, R., & Sherzer, J. (Eds.). (1989). *Explorations in the ethnography of speaking* (2nd ed.). Cambridge: Cambridge University Press.

Baym, N. (1995). The emergence of community in computer-mediated communication. In S. G. Jones (Ed.), *Cybersociety: Computer-mediated communication and community* (pp. 138–163). Thousand Oaks, CA: Sage.

Baym, N. (2000). *Tune in, log on: Soaps, fandom, and online community.* Thousand Oaks, CA: Sage.

Bechar-Israeli, H. (1995). From <bonehead> to <clonehead>: Nicknames, play and identity on Internet Relay Chat. *Journal of Computer-Mediated Communication, 1*(2). Retrieved December 5, 2005, from http://jcmc.indiana.edu/vol1/issue2/bechar.html.

Beißwenger, M. (Ed.). (2001). *Chat-Kommunikation. Sprache, Interaktion und Sozialität in synchroner computervermittelter Kommunikation [Chat communication. Language, interaction, and sociality in computer-mediated communication].* Stuttgart: Ibidem.

Beißwenger, M., & Pütz, U. (2001). Das interaktive Lesespiel: Chat-Kommunikation als mediale Inszenierung. In M. Beißwenger (Ed.), *Chat-kommunikation. Sprache, Interaktion und*

Sozialität in synchroner computervermittelter Kommunikation (pp. 403–465). Stuttgart: Ibidem.

Beißwenger, M., & Storrer, A. S. (Eds.). (2005). *Chat-kommunikation in Beruf, Bildung und Medien: Konzepte–Werkzeuge–Anwendungsfelder.* Stuttgart: Ibidem.

Belz, J. A., & Reinhardt, J. (2004). Aspects of advanced foreign language proficiency: Internet-mediated German language play. *International Journal of Applied Linguistics, 14*(3), 324–362.

Berjaoui, N. (2001). Aspects of the Moroccan Arabic orthography with preliminary insights from the Moroccan computer-mediated communication. In M. Beißwenger (Ed.), *Chat-Kommunikation: Sprache, Interaktion, Sozialität & Identität in synchroner computerver-mittelter Kommunikation* (pp. 431–465). Stuttgart: Ibidem.

Block, D. (2004). Globalization, transnational communication and the Internet. *International Journal on Multicultural Societies, 6,* 13–28.

Boudonnat, L., & Kushizaki, H. (2003). *Traces of the brush: The art of Japanese calligraphy.* San Francisco: Seuil & Chronicle Books.

Bruckman, A. (1992). *Identity workshop: Emergent social and psychological phenomena in text-based virtual reality.* Retrieved December 6, 2005, from http://www.cc.gatech.edu/~asb/papers/old-papers.html#IW.

Bruckman, A. (1993). *Gender swapping on the Internet.* Retrieved December 5, 2005, from http://www.cc.gatech.edu/~asb/papers/old=papers.html#INET.

Bruthiaux, P. (2002). Predicting challenges to English as a global language in the 21st century. *Language Problems and Language Planning, 26*(2), 129–157.

Bucholtz, M. (Ed.). (2004). *Language and woman's place: Text and commentaries.* New York: Oxford University Press.

Cherny, L. (1999). *Conversation and community: Chat in a virtual world.* Stanford, CA: CSLI Publications.

Cho, T. (in press). Linguistic features of electronic mail in the workplace: A comparison with memoranda. In S. C. Herring (Ed.), *Computer-mediated conversation.* Cresskill, NJ: Hampton Press.

Computer Industry Almanac. (2004). Press release, *Worldwide Internet users will top 1 billion in 2005.* Retrieved December 5, 2005, from http://www.c-i-a.com/pr0904.htm.

Consortium, The Unicode. (2003). *The Unicode Standard, version 4.0.* Boston: Addison-Wesley.

Crystal, D. (2001). *Language and the Internet.* Cambridge: Cambridge University Press.

Crystal, D. (2003). *English as a global language* (2nd ed.). Cambridge: Cambridge University Press.

Crystal, D. (2004). *The stories of English.* New York: Overlook Press.

Cunliffe, D., & Harries, R. (2005). Promoting minority language use in a bilingual online community. *The New Review of Hypermedia and Multimedia, 11*(2). Retrieved December 5, 2005, from http://www.aber.ac.uk/~merwww/english/events/mercSym_03-04-08.htm.

Cunliffe, D., & Herring, S. C. (Eds.). (2005). Minority languages, multimedia and the Web (Special issue). *The New Review of Hypermedia and Multimedia 11*(2).

CyberAtlas. (2003, June 6). *Population explosion!* Retrieved December 5, 2005, from http://www.clickz.com/stats/sectors/geographics/article.php/5911_151151.

Danet, B. (Ed.). (1995). Play and performance in computer-mediated communication (Special issue). *Journal of Computer-Mediated Communication, 1*(2). Retrieved December 5, 2005, from http://jcmc.indiana.edu/vol1/issue2/.

Danet, B. (1998). Text as mask: Gender, play and performance on the Internet. In S. G. Jones (Ed.), *Cybersociety 2.0: Revisiting computer-mediated communication and community* (pp. 129–158). Thousand Oaks, CA: Sage.

Danet, B. (2001). *Cyberpl@y: Communicating online.* Oxford: Berg. Companion website: http://pluto.mscc.huji.ac.il/~msdanet/cyberpl@y/.

Danet, B., & Herring, S. C. (Eds.). (2003). The multilingual Internet: Language, culture and communication in instant messaging, email and chat (Special issue). *Journal of Computer-Mediated Communication, 9*(1). Retrieved December 5, 2005, from http://jcmc.indiana.edu/vol9/issue1/.

Danet, B., & Herring, S. C. (2007). Multilingualism on the Internet. In M. Hellinger & A. Pauwels (Eds.), *Handbook of applied linguistics:* Vol. 9. *Language and communication: Diversity and change.* Berlin: Mouton de Gruyter.

Danet, B., Ruedenberg, L., & Rosenbaum-Tamari, Y. (1998). "Hmmm . . . Where's that smoke coming from?" Writing, play and performance on Internet Relay Chat. In F. Sudweeks, M. McLaughlin, & S. Rafaeli (Eds.), *Network and netplay: Virtual groups on the Internet* (pp. 47–85). Cambridge, MA: AAAI/MIT Press.

Dejond, A. (2002). *La cyberl@ngue française.* Tournai, Belgium: La Renaissance du Livre.

Demont-Heinrich, C. (2005). Language and national identity in the era of globalization: The case of English in Switzerland. *Communication Inquiry, 29*(1), 66–84.

Donath, J. (1999). Identity and deception in the virtual community. In P. Kollock & M. Smith (Eds.), *Communities in cyberspace* (pp. 29–59). London: Routledge.

Doostdar, A. (2004). "The vulgar spirit of blogging": On language, culture, and power in Persian weblogestan. *American Anthropologist, 106*(4), 651–662.

Dor, D. (2004). From Englishization to imposed multilingualism: Globalization, the Internet, and the political economy of the linguistic code. *Public Culture, 16*(1), 97–118.

Döring, N. (2002). "Kurzm. wird gesendet"—Abkürzungen und Akronyme in der SMS-Kommunikation [Short message will be sent—abbreviations and acronyms in SMS communication]. *Muttersprache, 112*(2), 97–114.

Duranti, A. (1997). *Linguistic anthropology.* New York: Cambridge University Press.

Duranti, A. (2003). Language as culture in U.S. anthropology. *Current Anthropology, 44*(3), 323–347.

Duranti, A. (2004). *A companion to linguistic anthropology.* Malden, MA: Blackwell.

Duranti, A., & Goodwin, C. (Eds.). (1992). *Rethinking context: Language as an interactive phenomenon.* Cambridge: Cambridge University Press.

Dürmüller, U. (2002). English in Switzerland: From foreign language to lingua franca. In D. J. Allerton, P. Skandera, & C. Tschichold (Eds.), *Perspectives on English as a world language* (pp. 115–123). Basel: Schwabe.

Durscheid, C. (1999). Zwischen Mundlichkeit und Schriftlichkeit: Die Kommunikation im Internet. [Between the spoken and the written: Communication on the Internet.] *Papiere zur Linguistik, 1*(60), 17–30.

Durscheid, C. (2000). Spelling of electronic texts. *Muttersprache, 110*(1), 52–62.

Edwards, V., & Sienkewicz, T. J. (1990). *Oral cultures past and present: Rappin' and Homer.* Oxford: Basil Blackwell.

Everson, M. (2002, May). *Leaks in the Unicode pipeline: Script, script, script. . . .* Paper presented at the 21st International Unicode Conference, Dublin, Ireland. Retrieved December 5, 2005, from http://www.unicode.org/notes/tn4/.

Fais, L., & Ogura, K. (2001). Discourse issues in the translation of Japanese email. *Proceedings of PACLING2001.* Retrieved December 5, 2005, from http://afnlp.org/pacling2001/pdf/fais.pdf.

Ferguson, C. (1972). Diglossia. In P. P. Giglioli (Ed.), *Language and social context* (pp. 232–252). Harmondsworth, UK: Penguin.

Fernandez, L. (2001). Patterns of linguistic discrimination in Internet discussion forums. *Mercator Media Forum, 5*, 22–41.

Ferrara, K., Brunner, H., & Whittemore, G. (1991). Interactive written discourse as an emergent register. *Written Communication, 8*(1), 8–33.

Fialkova, L. (2005). Emigrants from the FSU and the Russian-language Internet. *Toronto Slavic Quarterly, 12*. Retrieved December 6, 2005, from http://www.utoronto.ca/tsq/12/fialkova12.shtml.

Finnegan, R. (1992). *Oral traditions and the verbal arts.* London: Routledge Chapman Hall.

Fishman, J. (1998). The new linguistic order. *Foreign Policy,* Winter, 26–40.

Fishman, J. A., Conrad, A. W., & Rubal-Lopez, A. (Eds.). (1996). *Post-imperial English: Status change in former British and American colonies, 1940–1990.* New York: Mouton de Gruyter.

Fouser, R., Narahiko, I., & Chungmin, L. (2000). The pragmatics of orality in English, Japanese and Korean computer-mediated communication. In L. Pemberton & S. Shurville (Eds.), *Words on the web: Computer-mediated communication* (pp. 52–62). Bristol, U.K.: Intellect Books.

Galan Rodriguez, C. (2001). SMS? A new language model? *Español Actual, 76,* 93–103.

Gao, L. (2001). Digital age, digital English. *English Today, 17*(3), 17–23.

Geertz, C. (1973). *Interpretation of cultures.* New York: Basic Books.

Georgakopoulou, A. (1997). Self-presentation and interactional alliances in e-mail discourse: The style- and code-switches of Greek messages. *International Journal of Applied Linguistics, 7,* 141–164.

Georgakopoulou, A. (2004). To tell or not to tell? Email stories between on- and off-line interactions. *language@Internet, 1.* Retrieved December 5, 2005, from http://www.digijournals.de/languageatinternet/articles/36.

Giglioli, P. P. (Ed.). (1982). *Language and social context: Selected readings* (rev. ed.). London: Penguin.

Ginsburgh, V., & Weber, S. (2005). Language disenfranchisement in the European Union. *Journal of Common Market Studies, 43,* 273–286.

Graddol, D. (1997/2000). *The future of English.* London: The British Council. Retrieved December 5, 2005, from http://www.gre.ac.uk/~ds42/pages/future%20of%20English.pdf.

Griolet, P. (2002). Writing in Japan. In A.-M. Christin (Ed.), *A history of writing: From hieroglyph to multimedia* (pp. 123–141). Paris: Flammarion.

Gumperz, J. (1982). *Discourse strategies.* Cambridge: Cambridge University Press.

Gumperz, J. (2001). The speech community. In A. Duranti (Ed.), *Linguistic anthropology: A reader* (pp. 43–52). Malden, MA: Blackwell.

Hafner, K., & Lyon, M. (1996). *Where wizards stay up late: The origins of the Internet.* New York: Simon & Schuster.

Hannerz, U. (1996). *Transnational connections: Culture, people, places.* London: Routledge.

Hård af Segerstad, Y. (2000). Swedish chat rooms. *M/C: A Journal of Media and Culture, 3*(4). Retrieved December 5, 2005, from http://journal.media-culture.org.au/0008/swedish.php.

Hård af Segerstad, Y. (2005). Language use in Swedish mobile text messaging. In R. Ling & P. Pedersen (Eds.), *Mobile communications: Renegotiation of the social sphere* (pp. 313–334). London: Springer.

Hentschel, E. (1998). Communication on IRC. *Linguistik online, 1*(1). Retrieved December 5, 2005, from http://www.linguistik-online.de/irc.htm.

Herring, S. C. (1996a). Posting in a different voice: Gender and ethics in computer-mediated communication. In C. Ess (Ed.), *Philosophical perspectives on computer-mediated communication* (pp. 115–145). Albany, NY: State University of New York Press.

Herring, S. C. (Ed.). (1996b). *Computer-mediated communication: Linguistic, social and cross-cultural perspectives.* Amsterdam: John Benjamins.

Herring, S. C. (2001). Computer-mediated discourse. In D. Tannen, D. Schiffrin, & H. Hamilton (Eds.), *Handbook of discourse analysis* (pp. 612–634). Oxford: Blackwell.

Herring, S. C. (2002). Computer-mediated communication on the Internet. *Annual Review of Information Science and Technology, 36,* 109–168.

Herring, S. C. (2003). Gender and power in online communication. In J. Holmes & M. Meyerhoff (Eds.), *The handbook of language and gender* (pp. 202–228). Oxford: Blackwell.

Herring, S. C. (2004a). Computer-mediated discourse analysis: An approach to researching online behavior. In S. A. Barab, R. Kling, & J. H. Gray (Eds.), *Designing for virtual communities in the service of learning* (pp. 338–376). New York: Cambridge University Press.

Herring, S. C. (2004b). Computer-mediated communication and woman's place. In M. Bucholtz (Ed.), *Robin Tolmach Lakoff, Language and woman's place: Text and commentaries* (pp. 216–222). New York: Oxford University Press.

Herring, S. C. (2004c). Slouching toward the ordinary: Current trends in computer-mediated communication. *New Media & Society, 6*(1), 26–36.

Herring, S. C., Scheidt, L. A., Bonus, S., & Wright, E. L. (2004). Bridging the gap: A genre analysis of weblogs. In *Proceedings of the 37th Hawai'i International Conference on System Sciences.* Los Alamitos, CA: IEEE Computer Society Press. Retrieved December 5, 2005, from http://www.blogninja.com/DDGDD04.doc.

Hinrichs, L. (2006). *Codeswitching on the Web: English and Jamaican Creole in e-mail communication.* Amsterdam: John Benjamins.

Holton, R. (2000). Globalization's cultural consequences. *Annals of the American Academy of Political and Social Science, 570*(1), 140–152.

Hymes, D. H. (1974). *Foundations of sociolinguistics.* Philadelphia: University of Pennsylvania Press.

Jayantilal, R. (1998). Code-switching and transfer in email correspondence exchanged between four Malaysian women. *Jurnal Pendidikan Tigaenf, 2*(2), 63–78.

Joseph, B. (2001). Modern Greek. In J. Garry & C. Rubino (Eds.), *The encyclopedia of the world's major languages: Past and present* (pp. 263–270). Dublin: H. W. Wilson.

Kanayama, T. (2003). Ethnographic research on the experience of Japanese elderly people online. *New Media & Society, 5*(2), 267–288.

Kasesniemi, E.-L., & Rautiainen, P. (2002). Mobile culture of children and teenagers in Finland. In J. E. Katz & M. Aakhus (Eds.), *Perpetual contact: Mobile communication, private talk, public performance* (pp. 170–192). Cambridge: Cambridge University Press.

Katsuno, H., & Yano, C. R. (2002). Face to face: On-line subjectivity in contemporary Japan. *Asian Studies Review, 26*(2), 205–231.

Kaul, A., & Kulkarni, V. (2005). *Coffee, tea, or . . . ? Gender and politeness in computer-mediated communication (CMC).* Indian Institute of Management Ahmedabad Working Papers. Retrieved December 5, 2005, from http://ideas.repec.org/p/iim/iimawp/2005-04-02.html.

Kelly Holmes, H. (2004). An analysis of the language repertoires of students in higher education and their language choices on the Internet (Ukraine, Poland, Macedonia, Italy, France, Tanzania, Oman and Indonesia). *International Journal on Multicultural Societies, 6*(1), 29–52.

Kendall, L. (1998). Are you male or female? The performance of gender on MUDs. In J. Howard & J. O'Brien (Eds.), *Everyday inequalities: Critical inquiries* (pp. 131–153). London: Basil Blackwell.

Kim, M.-S., & Raja, N. S. (1991). *Verbal aggression and self-disclosure on computer bulletin boards.* (ERIC document ED334620.) Lanham, MD: ERIC (Education Resources Information Center). Retrieved July 17, 2006, from http://www.eric.ed.gov/.

Ko, K.-K. (1996). Structural characteristics of computer-mediated language: A comparative analysis of interchange discourse. *Electronic Journal of Communication, 6*(3). Retrieved December 5, 2005, from http://www.cios.org/www/ejc/v6n396.htm.

Krauss, M. (1992). The world's languages in crisis. *Language, 68,* 4–10.

Labov, W. (1989). The exact description of the speech community. Short-a in Philadelphia. In R. W. Fasold & D. Schiffrin (Eds.), *Language change and variation* (pp. 1–57). Amsterdam: John Benjamins.

Lakoff, R. T. (1975). *Language and woman's place.* New York: Harper & Row.

Lin, J. (2002, August). *A comparison of Internet diffusion patterns in China and the U.S.—a preliminary study of longitudinal demographics of Internet population.* Paper presented at IAMCR 2002 Conference, Barcelona, Spain. Retrieved December 5, 2005, from http://www.portalcomunicacion.com/bcn2002/n_eng/programme/prog_ind/papers/l/pdf/l003se03_linpaper.pdf.

Ling, R. S. (2005). The sociolinguistics of SMS: An analysis of SMS use by a random sample of Norwegians. In R. S. Ling & P. Pedersen (Eds.), *Mobile communications: Renegotiation of the social sphere* (pp. 335–349). London: Springer.

Mafu, S. (2004). From the oral tradition to the information era: The case of Tanzania. *International Journal on Multicultural Societies, 6,* 53–78.

Mair, C. (2002). The continuing spread of English: Anglo-American conspiracy or global grassroots movement? In D. J. Allerton, P. Skandera, & C. Tschichold (Eds.), *Perspectives on English as a world language* (pp. 159–169). Basel: Schwabe.

Marcoccia, M. (2004a). *La communication écrite médiatisée par ordinateur: Faire du face à face avec de l'écrit.* Retrieved December 5, 2005, from http://www.up.univ-mrs.fr/~veronis/je-nfce/Marcoccia.pdf.

Marcoccia, M. (2004b). On-line polylogues: Conversation structure and participation framework in Internet newsgroups. *Journal of Pragmatics, 36,* 115–145.

Matsuda, P. K. (2002). Negotiation of identity and power in a Japanese online discourse community. *Computers and Composition, 19,* 39–55.

McClure, E. (2001a). Oral and written Assyrian codeswitching. In R. Jacobson (Ed.), *Codeswitching worldwide II* (pp. 157–191). Berlin: Mouton de Gruyter.

McClure, E. (2001b). The role of language in the construction of ethnic identity on the Internet: The case of Assyrian activists in diaspora. In C. Moseley, N. Ostler, & H. Ouzzate (Eds.), *Endangered languages and the media: Proceedings of the fifth FEL conference, Agadir, Morocco, September 20–23, 2001* (pp. 68–75). Bath, UK: Foundation for Endangered Languages.

Meyer, G., & Thomas, J. (1990). The baudy world of the byte bandit: A postmodernist interpretation of the computer underground. In F. Schmalleger (Ed.), *Computers in criminal justice* (pp. 31–67). Bristol, IN: Wyndham Hall.

Miyake, K. (2005, August). *Young Japanese people's construction of relationships in mobile communication: An analysis based on empathy, emotion and context.* Paper presented at the Eleventh Annual Meeting of the European Association for Japanese Studies, University of Vienna, Vienna. Abstract retrieved December 5, 2005, from http://www.univie.ac.it/eajs/sections/abstracts/Section_2/2_5b.htm.

Nishimura, Y. (2003a). Establishing a community of practice on the Internet: Linguistic behavior in online Japanese communication. In P. M. Nowak, C. Yoquelet, & D. Mortensen (Eds.), *Proceedings of the 29th annual meeting of the Berkeley Linguistics Society* (pp. 337–348). Berkeley, CA: Berkeley Linguistics Society.

Nishimura, Y. (2003b). Linguistic innovations and interactional features of casual online communication in Japanese. *Journal of Computer-Mediated Communication, 9*(1). Retrieved December 5, 2005, from http://jcmc.indiana.edu/vol9/issue1/nishimura.html.

Nunberg, G. (2000). Will the Internet always speak English? *The American Prospect Online, 11*(10). Retrieved December 6, 2005, from http://www.prospect.org/print/V11/10/nunberg-g.html.

Oberwinkler, M. (2005, August). *New tendencies in the Japanese language on the Internet: Analyzing Japanese Internet diaries.* Paper presented at the annual meeting of the European Association for Japanese Studies/JAWS (Japan Anthropology Workshop), University of Vienna, Vienna. Abstract retrieved December 5, 2005, from http://www.univie.ac.at/eajs/sections/abstracts/Section_2/2_6b.htm.

OECD (Organization for Economic Co-operation and Development). (2001). *Understanding the digital divide.* Retrieved December 5, 2005, from http://www.oecd.org/dataoecd/38/57/1888451.pdf.

O'Neill, J. (1995). The role of ARPA in the development of the ARPAnet, 1961–1972. *Annals of the History of Computing, 17*(4), 76–81.

Ostler, N. (1999). Fighting words: As the world gets smaller, minority languages struggle to stake their claim. *Language International, 11*(2), 38–45.

Pakir, A. (in press). Linguistic imperialism? English as a global language. In M. Hellinger & A. Pauwels (Eds.), *Handbook of applied linguistics:* Vol. 9. *Language and communication: Diversity and change.* Berlin: Mouton de Gruyter.

Paolillo, J. C. (1996). Language choice on soc.culture.punjab. *Electronic Journal of Communication, 6*(3). Retrieved December 5, 2005, from http://ella.slis.indiana.edu/~paolillo/research/paolillo.publish.txt.

Pargman, D. (1998). Reflections on cultural bias and adaptation. In C. Ess & F. Sudweeks (Eds.), *Proceedings, cultural attitudes towards communication and technology '98* (pp. 81–99). Sydney, Australia: University of Sydney. Retrieved December 5, 2005, from http://www.it.murdoch.edu.au/~sudweeks/catac98/pdf/06_pargman.pdf.

Pargman, D., & Palme, J. (2004). Linguistic standardization on the Internet. In F. Sudweeks & C. Ess (Eds.), *Proceedings of CaTaC'04: Cultural attitudes towards technology and communication 2004* (pp. 385–388). Murdoch, Australia: Murdoch University Press.

Philllipson, R. (1992). *Linguistic imperialism.* Oxford: Oxford University Press.

Phillipson, R., & Skutnabb-Kangas, T. (2001). Linguistic imperialism. In R. Mesthrie (Ed.), *Concise encyclopedia of sociolinguistics* (pp. 570–574). New York: Elsevier.

Pietrini, D. (2001). "x'6:-(?": The SMS and the triumph of informality and ludic writing. *Italienisch, 46*, 92–101.

Reid, E. (1991). *Electropolis: Communication and community on Internet Relay Chat.* Unpublished senior honors thesis, University of Melbourne, Australia. Retrieved December 5, 2005, from http://www.crosswinds.net/~aluluei/electropolis.htm.

Romaine, S. (1982). *Sociolinguistic variation in speech communities.* London: Arnold.

Saville-Troike, M. (1989). *The ethnography of communication: An introduction* (2nd ed.). New York: Basil Blackwell.

Spilioti, T. (2005, July). *Managing closings and intimacy in text-messaging.* Paper presented at the 9th International Pragmatics Conference, Riva del Garda, Italy.

Stein, D. (2003). Book review, David Crystal, *Language and the Internet. Linguistics, 41*(1), 158–163.

Sugimoto, T., & Levin, J. A. (2000). Multiple literacies and multimedia: A comparison of Japanese and American uses of the Internet. In G. E. Hawisher & C. L. Selfe (Eds.), *Global literacies and the World-Wide Web* (pp. 133–153). London: Routledge.

Sveningsson, M. (2001). *Creating a sense of community: Experiences from a Swedish web chat.* Linköping, Sweden: Linköping Universitet.

Tannen, D. (1990). *You just don't understand: Women and men in conversation.* New York: Morrow.

Thurlow, C. W., & Brown, A. (2003). Generation txt? The discourses of young people's text-messaging. *Discourse Analysis Online, 1*(1). Retrieved December 5, 2005, from http://www.shu.ac.uk/daol/articles/v1/n1/a3/thurlow2002003-t.html.

Turkle, S. (1995). *Life on the screen: Identity in the age of the Internet.* New York: Simon & Schuster.

Uberuaga, B. P. (2001). The Basque presence on the Internet: Yesterday, today and tomorrow. *Journal of the Society for Basque Studies in America, 20.* Retrieved December 6, 2005, from http://www.buber.net/Basque/Web/basque_rev4.html.

Vaisman, C. (in preparation). *Writing, play and performance in an Israeli teenage girls' blog.* Unpublished Ph.D. thesis, Department of Communication and Journalism, Hebrew University of Jerusalem.

Warner, C. N. (2004). It's just a game, right? Types of play in foreign language CMC. *Language Learning & Technology, 8*(2), 69–87.

Warschauer, M., & Donaghy, K. (1997). *Leoki*: A powerful voice of Hawaiian language revitalization. *Computer-Assisted Language Learning, 10*(4), 349–361.

Warschauer, M., El Said, G. R., & Zohry, A. (2002). Language choice online: Globalization and identity in Egypt. *Journal of Computer-Mediated Communication, 7*(4). Retrieved December 5, 2005, from http://jcmc/indiana.edu/vol7/issue4/warschauer.html.

Wei, C. (2004). Language and the Internet in Uzbekistan. In F. Sudweeks & C. Ess (Eds.), *Proceedings of CaTaC'04: Cultural attitudes towards technology and communication, 2004* (pp. 393–396). Murdoch, Australia: Murdoch University Press.

Werry, C. C. (1996). Linguistic and interactional features of Internet Relay Chat. In S. C. Herring (Ed.), *Computer-mediated communication: Linguistic, social and cross-cultural perspectives* (pp. 47–64). Amsterdam: John Benjamins.

Wheeler, D. (2001). New technologies, old culture: A look at women, gender, and the Internet in Kuwait. In C. Ess & F. Sudweeks (Eds.), *Culture, technology, communication: Towards an intercultural global village* (pp. 187–211). Albany: State University of New York Press.

Wright, H. K. (1996). Email in African studies. *Convergence: The Journal of Research into New Media Technologies, 2*(1), 20–30.

Wright, Scott. (2004). *A comparative analysis of government-run discussion boards at the local, national and European Union levels.* Unpublished Ph.D. thesis, University of East Anglia, Norwich.

Wright, Sue. (Ed.). (2004). Multilingualism on the Internet (Special issue). *International Journal on Multicultural Societies, 6*(1). Retrieved December 5, 2005, from http://portal.unesco.org/shs/en/ev.php-URL_ID=3996&URL_DO=DO_TOPIC&URL_SECTION=-465.html.

Yamakazi, J. (2002). Global and local in computer-mediated communication: A Japanese newsgroup. In R. T. Donahue (Ed.), *Exploring Japaneseness: On Japanese enactments of culture and consciousness* (pp. 425–442). Westport, CT: Ablex.

Yates, S. J. (1996a). Oral and written linguistic aspects of computer-conferencing. In S. C. Herring (Ed.), *Computer-mediated communication: Linguistic, social and cross-cultural perspectives* (pp. 29–46). Amsterdam: John Benjamins.

Yates, S. J. (1996b). English in cyberspace. In S. Goodman & D. Graddol (Eds.), *Redesigning English: New texts, new identities* (pp. 106–140). London: Routledge.

Zhao, Y. (2002). Linguistic features of the English of Chinese Internet Relay Chat. *Haerbin Gongye Daxue Xuebao (Shehui Kexue Ban)/Journal of the Harbin Institute of Technology (Social Sciences Edition)*, *4*(2), 99–102.

Zitzen, M., & Stein, D. (2004). Chat and conversation: A case of transmedial stability? *Linguistics*, *42*(5), 983–1021.

PART I

WRITING SYSTEMS
AND THE INTERNET

2

DAVID PALFREYMAN AND MUHAMED AL KHALIL

"A Funky Language for Teenzz to Use"

Representing Gulf Arabic in Instant Messaging

The global growth of computer-mediated communication (CMC) has led to changes in how language is used, including faster composition and reading of texts (Baron, 2002) and diffusion of oral discourse features into written language (Werry, 1996; Yates, 1996). Research into these phenomena has focused mainly on the English language; expanding the focus to other languages highlights new research issues. This chapter presents a small-scale, exploratory study of how female Arab university students in the United Arab Emirates use the Roman alphabet to write vernacular Arabic online, in instant messaging (IM; using MSN Messenger, Yahoo Messenger, or ICQ, "I seek you").

The short extract in table 2.1 shows a sample of the type of discourse studied. The left-hand column is the opening of an online conversation in the corpus used for this study; the right-hand column shows an approximate English translation.

Although some features of this extract are familiar from other types of CMC in other contexts (turns are short, and emoticons such as ^_^ represent emotive content),[1] even a reader with no knowledge of Arabic will notice some linguistic complexity. The first two turns are in Arabic script, and then both participants start to use the Roman alphabet instead. The latter part of this extract, although using the Roman alphabet, still represents Arabic, but letters are interspersed with numerals, and Arabic with English words. In this chapter, we discuss characteristics of this ASCII-ized Arabic (AA), in which ASCII (American Standard Code for Information Interchange) symbols are used to represent Arabic in IM and other electronic written communication.

TABLE 2.1. Opening of a typical messenger conversation.

Conversation opening	Approximate English translation
D: السلام عليكم ورحمة الله وبركاته	D: Hello there.
D: مرحبا حمده،، شحالچ؟	D: Hi Hamda, how are you doing?
F: w 3laikom essalaaam asoomah ^_^	F: Hi there Asooma ^_^
F: b'7air allah eysallemch .. sh7aalech enty??	F: Fine, God bless you. How about you?
D: el7emdellah b'7eer w ne3meh	D: Fine, great thanks.
D: sorry kent adawwer scripts 7ag project eljava script w rasi dayer fee elcodes	D: Sorry, I was looking for scripts for the java script project and my head is swarming with code.
F: lol	F: lol

The IM users studied are university students in the United Arab Emirates (UAE), mainly on the Dubai campus of Zayed University (ZU), a university for female UAE nationals. All ZU students are required to have a laptop, and the campus offers almost unrestricted intra- and Internet access. ZU aims to produce students who are bilingual in English and Arabic, and the majority of courses are conducted in English. Students' familiarity with technology and with English contrasts greatly with UAE women (and many men) of their mothers' generation, who often did not receive even primary schooling. AA is one product of such dramatic changes in the UAE. An analysis of the form and use of AA illustrates some of the interrelations among language, literacy, technology, and globalization.

This study involves two writing systems (the Arabic and Roman alphabets) that are closely linked to two world languages (Arabic and English). The interaction among these four language systems takes place within a particular social context (a traditional community in the midst of rapid modernization), which shapes the linguistic and technical resources used by our informants. In the following sections, we first discuss writing systems—the mapping of sounds and symbols—and how orthography relates to macro and micro aspects of social context, as well as psycholinguistic and social psychological processes. We then provide some explanation about Arabic in particular: the Arabic language and its script, romanization, and the different varieties of Arabic and their social significance. To complete the background, we discuss the phenomenon of ASCII-ization. Then we describe an exploratory study of Arabic IM discourse and discuss its implications for the global study of CMC.

BACKGROUND

Linguistic Aspects of Writing Systems

The majority of the world's writing systems employ conventions that link the sounds of spoken language with written symbols. In this chapter, phonemes (sounds used to distinguish meaning in a particular language) are shown as International Phonetic Alphabet (IPA) symbols between slashes (e.g., /s/), while written symbols (e.g., letters) are shown as follows: <s>. The conventions that link sounds and symbols vary widely among languages and can be complex. The symbol <c> can be pronounced in various ways in English (e.g., as /k/ in <cat> and as /s/ in <cent>) and in yet other ways in other languages (e.g., as /θ/ in Castilian Spanish and as /dʒ/ in Turkish). Conversely, the sound /k/ can be written with <c> or <k> in English (as in <cat>, <keep>) or with the completely different symbol <ك> in Arabic. In English, single sounds may also be represented by digraphs—sequences of two symbols such as <sh> or <oo> in <shoot>, which uses five letters to represent the three sounds /ʃu:t/.

The standard English alphabet contains 26 letters, which generally correspond, individually or in combination, to phonemes in the spoken language; each letter comprises a lowercase and an uppercase form. Other languages use basically the same set of characters as English but with some letters omitted and/or added—thus, the Spanish and Turkish versions of the Roman alphabet comprise 27 and 29 letters respectively. Non-Roman alphabets such as Arabic use entirely different characters to represent sounds, but Arabic script is still based on correspondences between letters and sounds, and the set of symbols used in Arabic is comparable in size to the English alphabet.

Sociolinguistic Perspectives

Beesley (1998, n.p.) states that "many language communities adopt their standard orthography more or less by historical accident." He cites the distribution of the Roman and Cyrillic alphabets in Europe, which largely reflects whether these areas were, in the early centuries A.D., occupied and/or proselytized under Roman or Greek influence. Similarly, the use of Arabic script has in the past been closely associated with the spread of Islam, being used to represent languages unrelated to Arabic (e.g., Turkish and Persian) in Muslim societies.

Grivelet (2001) uses the term "digraphia" to describe societies where two different writing systems with different social functions are used to represent essentially the same language (e.g., the Cyrillic and Roman scripts for Serbo-Croatian in pre-1990s Yugoslavia). Often the relative statuses of the writing systems are contested to some extent: In general, any decision about orthography constitutes a social/political statement (Unger, 2001), and in the modern world such decisions are linked with access to various types of literacy and to technology and power (Bruthiaux, 2002; Street, 1995). These connections are apparent in choices between different orthographic systems such as Roman and Arabic: The new Turkish Republic of the 1920s, for example, pursued a very effective alphabet revolution, converting from Arabic to Roman script with the aim of facilitating access to Western discourse. Conversely, the Syrian Ba'ath party in the 1980s orchestrated the smashing of shop signs written in Roman script, in the name of Arab purism.

The importance of social norms in orthography is also visible at a more micro level. One pervasive feature of CMC discourse that has attracted the attention of researchers is phonological simulation—representation of spoken features in online text, for example, the written use of English contractions such as "gonna" and "wanna." Documenting such features, Werry (1996) states that "the conventions that are emerging are a direct reflection of the physical constraints on the medium combined with a desire to create a language that is as 'speech-like' as possible" (p. 48). However, this downplays the social significance of this way of writing. Research shows that accents and other aspects of language act as markers of in-group and out-group identity (Abrams & Hogg, 1987; Cargile & Giles, 1997). Stevenson (2000, n.p.) suggests that phonological simulation in Internet Relay Chat (IRC), rather than being motivated simply by individual desire to mirror spoken features, "is a result of social pressure to break conventional spelling rules and comply with IRC's nonconformist, hacker image." It is therefore important to bear in mind the sociolinguistic norms that users embrace or distance themselves from as they make decisions about writing online.

Psycholinguistic Perspectives and Language Change

Orthographic representation of language also has implications for the study of the mental processing of language. On the one hand, literacy may affect processes of perception as well as production of spoken language: Read et al. (1987) found that familiarity with the Roman alphabet (compared with the logographic Chinese script) correlated with Chinese speakers' awareness of individual sounds, while Mann (1986) and Leong (1991) found that the Japanese syllable-based writing system helped Japanese children to segment heard utterances into syllables but not phonemes. On the other hand, psychological representations may also influence orthographic ones, making orthography a valuable source of evidence in historical linguistics. For example, nonstandard spellings in graffiti and other nonformal inscriptions in ancient Roman sites provide evidence as to the actual pronunciation of Vulgar Roman, which illuminates the evolution of Proto-Romance in a way that the standardized texts of Classical Roman do not (Sampson, 2002).

One modern equivalent of this is online phonological simulation, which Li (2001) uses as evidence for local changes in the use of tones in Chinese. As well as reflecting pronunciation, such nonstandard texts also point to the ways in which speakers understand the structure of their own language. For example, Hentschel (1998) notes that in Serbian chat, people write the negative particle *ne* joined to the verb rather than, as in standard orthography, writing it as a free morpheme.

Arabic

Arabic belongs to the Semitic family of languages, which also includes Hebrew. The study of Arabic e-discourse and Gulf Arabic in particular is of interest for several reasons. First, Arabic, like English, may be described as a world language—it ranks fifth among the world's languages on an index based on number of speakers, geographical spread, and socioliterary prestige (Weber, 1997). Another reason for interest in Arabic is that the grammar, vocabulary, sounds, and writing system of Arabic are strikingly different from those of English and other Indo-European languages and have in the past challenged and expanded assumptions of European-based linguistics.

The sound system of modern standard Arabic (MSA) includes more consonant sounds and fewer vowel sounds than does that of English. In addition to /t/, /d/, /s/, and /ð/ (the first sound in "this"), pronounced more or less as in English, Arabic distinguishes the "emphatic" consonants /s'/, /d'/, /t'/, and /ð'/ (written <ص>, <ض>, <ط>, and <ظ> respectively), which are pronounced with a tense and somewhat retracted tongue, moving any vowels adjacent to them backward in the mouth. Another set of distinctive Arabic consonants are known as the gutturals: sounds produced by constricting the throat. These include the sounds /x/ (written <خ>), /ɣ/ (<غ>), /ʕ/ (<ع>), /ʔ/ (<ء>), /q/ (<ق>), and /ħ/ (<ح>). Conversely, there are six consonant sounds in English that are not seen as distinct sounds in MSA: /g/, /v/, /ŋ/ (as in "sing"), /p/, /ʒ/ (the <s> in "pleasure"), and /tʃ/ (the first sound in "chip"). The MSA vowel system is generally taken to include the short vowels /i/, /a/, and /u/ and their long counterparts /i:/, /a:/, and /u:/—although the actual pronunciation of these phonemes may vary widely.

The sounds of Arabic are normally represented with a 28-letter alphabet (with no uppercase forms). Broadly speaking, Arabic orthography is phonemic: One letter represents one sound, and "silent" letters (e.g., <gh> in English <night>) and digraphs (e.g., English <sh> or <th>) do not occur. However, there are significant exceptions. For example, vowel sounds may be represented using a set of diacritics, but these are restricted mainly to religious or literary texts and are used only selectively in books. In Arabic newspapers, magazines, and handwriting (as in Hebrew), only consonants and long vowels are written. In this respect, the Arabic writing system depends on the background knowledge of the reader to accurately pronounce the written word— much as a reader in English needs to decide on the basis of context whether <read> is to be pronounced /ri:d/ (present tense) or /red/ (past tense). Another case in which Arabic orthography does not reflect the surface pronunciation is the definite article. This is pronounced /əl/ before words beginning with vowels or some consonants but assimilates before words beginning with certain consonants, such that it is pronounced as /əs/, /ər/, /əθ/, or other pronunciations depending on the initial sound of the word that follows. However, Arabic orthography represents the article consistently as <ال>, as if it were always pronounced /al/.

Only one language of the Semitic family (Maltese) uses the Roman alphabet as its standard orthography, but Arabic (like Hebrew) does have some more or less established conventions for writing Arabic words in Roman script for particular purposes. The most authoritative of these are the conventions used by the Library of Congress and by the *Encyclopedia of Islam*. The latter uses, for example, <kh> for the sound /x/ (retained in the spelling but normally not the pronunciation of English "sheikh" and "Khartoum"), <q> for the guttural sound /q/ (hence the spelling <Iraq>), and capitals for the emphatic sounds described above (e.g., <S> for "emphatic" /s'/ and <s> for "normal" /s/). It also represents the definite article always as <al>, regardless of its pronunciation.

People in the UAE are accustomed to seeing romanized representations of Arabic names on road signs or in English-medium institutions such as the university where this research took place. In these contexts, a de facto romanization system resembling the academic standard is used, although with less effort to represent all sounds consistently. Since this is the kind of romanized Arabic most likely to be familiar to the informants in this study, we refer to it as "common romanized Arabic" (CRA). In CRA, the guttural sounds and vowels tend to be represented less consistently than in the academic standard. For example, /ħ/ (<ح>) and the English-type /h/ are both represented with <h>; /ʕ/ (<ع>) is represented with an apostrophe (e.g., <Mazra'a>) or not shown at all (e.g., <Al Ain> for /il ʕain/). In representing vowels, <mina> and <meena>, for example, appear variably to represent the same word, as do <sheikh> and <shaikh>.

Beesley (1998, n.p.) distinguishes orthographic *transcription* of sounds ("orthography devised and used by linguists to characterize the phonology or morphophonology of a language") from *transliteration* of an existing orthography, which uses "the exact same orthographical conventions [as the language's customary orthography], but using carefully substituted orthographical symbols"; for example, one transliteration of the Arabic word <كتب> (= "books", pronounced /kutob/) would be <ktb>, with each of the three Arabic letters converted into a Roman character; whereas one transcription of the same word would be <kutob>. In Beesley's terms, the romanization conventions for Arabic described above are more transcriptions than transliterations, since they aim to represent pronunciation. However, the rendition of the definite article as <al> regardless of pronunciation represents a transliteration of Arabic <ال>, which reflects the underlying grammatical identity of the word, rather than its varying surface pronunciation. Both transcriptions and transliterations provide ways of relating Arabic to Roman script, but ambiguities often result. For example, the character sequence <kh> has two readings: either as a digraph representing /x/, as in the name <Shaikha> (/ʃeixa/), or as a sequence of two consonants /k/ and /h/, as for example in <samakha> (/səməkha/, "her fish"), formed from "samak" ("fish") and the possessive particle "-ha" ("her").

Arabic has been cited as a textbook case of diglossia (Ferguson, 1959): the systematic use of distinct High and Low forms of the same language for different purposes. Today Arabic exists in two forms: formal MSA and the several vernaculars derived from it. While all Arabs necessarily speak at least one of these vernaculars in their daily communication, an educated Arab by definition must add to that a fair mastery of MSA. MSA is today's version of Classical Arabic, the language of the Quran and Classical Arabic literature. MSA is mainly a written language, spoken only in very formal settings (e.g., judicial proceedings, parliamentary deliberations, religious sermons), often from a prepared script (e.g., news broadcasts, dedications). MSA, as the official language of some 20 Arab countries, is also the written language that students learn in primary education, although verbal communication in the classroom is usually conducted in the local vernacular.

The UAE vernacular Arabic spoken in Dubai is part of the group of dialects known as Gulf Arabic. Despite rapid urbanization, most of these dialects still reflect strong Bedouin characteristics that they share with other Bedouin-rooted dialects across the Arab world. Consonants in particular exhibit considerable variation from MSA. The sounds /g/ or /dʒ/ are typically used instead of MSA /q/ (e.g., /ħari:ga/ or /ħari:dʒa/ for MSA's /ħari:qa/, "fire"); the /k/ sound is replaced with a /tʃ/ sound in certain positions (compare MSA /samak/ [fish] with UAE /sɨmatʃ/. Other characteristics include the pronunciation of /dʹ/ as /ðʹ/ and occasional use of /y/ instead of /dʒ/ (e.g., /yɨlas/ for MSA /dʒalas/ ["he sat"] (Hoffiz, 1995).

Until approximately 40 years ago, the UAE vernacular was used by often nomadic communities that were almost entirely illiterate. UAE Arabic, like other Arabic vernaculars, is not normally written, since doing so is often thought to undermine the stature of MSA and corrupt its image. Yet Arabic script may be used to write the vernacular in certain circumstances. In the UAE, popular poetry composed in the vernacular is written using Arabic script. Other uses include cartoons in newspapers and magazines, and to a lesser extent TV advertisements and street billboards, to capture a local flavor, and the spontaneous creativity of wall graffiti. Online communication is another area where the script is sometimes used, as computer support for Arabic script becomes more accessible and more efficient.

The ASCII-ized Arabic (AA) used in the computer-mediated conversations studied here differs from traditional ways of writing Arabic in several ways. Most obviously, it uses ASCII characters rather than Arabic letters; this in turn means that AA is read from left to right (the opposite direction from normal Arabic script) and that the letters are always separate from each other, rather than joined together (in slightly varying forms) as letters in the cursive Arabic script often are. Warschauer et al. (chapter 13 this volume) studied the use of English and Egyptian vernacular AA in CMC and provide some initial observations about the prevalence of these two varieties in contrast to the use of MSA in nonelectronic written communication. They also note in passing some orthographic features of the ASCII-ized variety, including the use of numerals to represent certain sounds. Their main focus is on the balance between English and Arabic, rather than features of AA itself, but they point out the great volume of use of AA, compared with regular Arabic script. A previous email survey of 83 students at ZU Dubai (Palfreyman, 2001b) supports the view of AA as a significant medium for online communication: Approximately 25% of respondents said they used mainly Arabic script in IM, 25% AA, and 50% English.

ASCII-ization

In CMC situations where people use informal ASCII-ized representations, several factors seem to influence the choice of symbols. Androutsopoulos (2000) and Tseliga (2002, chapter 5 this volume) note that ASCII-ized "orthographies" do not typically have the consistency characteristic of other orthographic systems: They may vary among writers or within an individual writer's usage. However, they highlight some clear patterns in usage that relate indirectly to the distinction between transcription and transliteration made by Beesley (1998).

The primary principle is that of phonological similarity to a sound in the language in question. In many cases, a sound in this language resembles a sound in English and/or another familiar language using the Roman alphabet, and there is a widely accepted and fairly consistent Roman alphabet spelling for this sound. Note that this varies with the spelling conventions of particular foreign languages. For example, the sound /u/ in Arabic tends to be represented as <ou> in Moroccan romanized Arabic, on the basis of French spelling, and as <oo> in the UAE, where English is the main foreign language. Another key principle is that of visual similarity to a character in the normal alphabet of the language in question. Androutsopoulos (2000) and Tseliga (chapter 5) note the use in ASCII-ized Greek CMC of representations such as <h> for the Greek letter <η>, based on visual similarity, rather than on the sound (/i/) associated with the Greek letter.

In general, ASCII-ization (like traditional orthographic systems) seems to produce competing alternate representations (Palfreyman, 2001a); however, the factors that affect such variation remain to be investigated. Attitudes to this lack of consistency are often ambivalent: ASCII-ized varieties (in common with other new varieties of e-language) appear to be perceived as modern, but also as somewhat sloppy and perhaps as a threat to the language (Koutsougiannis & Mitsikopoulou, 2003, chapter 6; Tseliga, chapter 5).

RESEARCH QUESTIONS

The aim of the present study was to analyze ASCII-ized representations used in IM conversations and the social factors that impinge on these representations. The discussion above highlights some factors that are potentially relevant to the analysis of AA. These include technical factors (notably computer character support), linguistic factors (phonological patterns and orthographic conventions linked to English and Arabic), and social-psychological factors (ways in which users orient to social values through choices of linguistic resources). The main research questions were as follows:

- How do IM users represent (or not represent) Arabic sounds in AA?
- How consistent are these representations across interactions and across users?

- What linguistic resources do users draw on in representing Arabic?
- What purposes does AA serve for those who use it?

METHODOLOGY

This study involved three sources of data: a corpus of messenger conversations (supplemented by short interviews with core informants), responses to a short email survey, and informal observation. We collected the corpus by asking three student volunteers to provide sample conversations. These core informants were female UAE nationals 18–19 years old, in their first or second year in ZU. They all had some experience of IM before entering the university but began using it more extensively once they began their university studies; all three were comfortably literate in both Arabic and English. Their interlocutors were of a similar background (all female UAE nationals in higher education), except for B, a male cousin of one of the core informants. Since the focus of this study was AA, we asked the core informants to provide conversations including examples of this variety. The IM programs used by students all include a feature for archiving or saving conversations, and students were asked to obtain consent, where feasible, from their interlocutor to save the conversation and use it anonymously for research. The students collected these conversations between November 2002 and January 2003. After this we conducted a short interview with each core informant to gather background information and clarify a few points in the conversations.

Each conversation included two interlocutors, a core informant and another acquaintance, and the conversations used added up to approximately the same size sample for each core informant. The resulting corpus included a total of approximately 2,400 words of AA (in 543 conversational turns), approximately 2,000 words of English (in 571 turns; many turns included both AA and English items), and a small amount of material in Arabic script. This is not a large corpus, but it includes contributions from 10 different interlocutors and seemed sufficient for an initial exploration in this variety of Arabic. We refer to users throughout by the pseudonyms A, B, C, and so forth (* = core informants):

*A: interacts with B (a male cousin) and C (a female friend).
*D: interacts with E and F (female friends).
*G: interacts with H, I, and J (female friends).

The corpus was analyzed initially by counting instances of particular key symbols known to be used for particular Arabic sounds (e.g., <q>, <ai>, and numerals), checking that each instance did indeed represent that sound. An Arabic speaker then read through the conversations to locate instances where sounds or words were represented in unexpected ways; a few segments of the corpus were shown anonymously to UAE vernacular speakers to check their pronunciation. A few obvious typos were discounted from the analysis.

FIGURE 2.1. Student cartoon. The fifth, sixth, and eighth names from the right incorporate numbers—6, 5, and 3, respectively—to represent Arabic sounds. For a large color version of this image, see http://jcmc.indiana.edu/vol9/issue1/palfreyman .html, Figure 1. Photograph by David Palfreyman.

Following this quantitative analysis of the conversations, the following four open questions were emailed to all of the approximately 1,000 students at ZU Dubai, in order to elicit their perceptions of the wider social context of AA:

1. Why do people sometimes write Arabic with English letters instead of using Arabic letters?
2. Do you remember when and how you learned to write Arabic like this?
3. Where do you think this way of writing came from—who *first* used these symbols?
4. Do you ever see or write Arabic like this in other situations (*not* in Messenger)?

Seventy-nine individuals responded to this survey by email. Responses were coded, and where necessary the respondents were asked (by email) to clarify parts of their responses. Throughout the period of this research, we also collected examples of AA that we observed in other settings, for example, on a Student Council "friendship wall" on campus (see figure 2.1).

FINDINGS

The conversations in this corpus share some features with English CMC. The register used is generally informal, turns typically short (often four words or less), and the language stripped down and abbreviated. Letters are almost exclusively lowercase, with capitalization used mainly for emphasis (this may be reinforced by the lack of uppercase letters in Arabic script). In addition, typographical conventions are used to represent stylized verbal or attitudinal effects: Vowels are reduplicated for emphasis or expressiveness (e.g., when greeting someone by name), as are punctuation marks such as <!> and <?>. Emoticons such as <^_^> occur, although those that are standard in English CMC were often converted automatically by the messaging program to icons, which were subsequently lost in the text-only saved versions of the conversations. Abbreviations based on English are also used, such as <lol> (= "laugh out loud"—normally a turn on its own). There were also various typos, as one might find in English chat or messaging.

Concerning the use of Arabic vis-à-vis English, the corpus included a fair amount of code switching (changing mid-utterance or mid-sentence from one language to another) and code mixing (using words or phrases from one language within sentences in the other language—see Warschauer et al., chapter 13). This mixing of varieties often correlated with different functions or topics, with Arabic being used for more formulaic phrases, and English for topics such as university courses. In the extract shown in table 2.1, the formulaic greetings are entirely in Arabic, whereas D's final utterance includes a number of English words related to the student's (English-medium) university course, for example, <project eljava script>, which consists of English words concatenated with Arabic word order and the definite article <el>. It should be remembered, however, that this corpus cannot be used to make valid quantitative generalizations about the proportions of the different varieties, since students were specifically asked to provide conversations including some AA.

The AA used by these students broadly follows romanization conventions used in Dubai signage. AA is in many respects a transcription of what writers would say, rather than a transliteration of Arabic script: Although the initial motivation for using AA may be the difficulty of using Arabic characters themselves, the students do not simply turn each Arabic letter into a corresponding Roman one. For example, short vowels, which are not normally written in Arabic orthography, are often included in AA.

ASCII-izing Consonants

Some Arabic sounds are represented in AA by single ASCII letters, based on the usual pronunciation of these letters in English. For example, the sound /t/ is represented by <t>, and /s/ by <s>. Other sounds are represented by digraphs clearly drawn from English; for example, <th> is used for the sounds /θ/ and /ð/, and <sh> for the sound /ʃ/. These may seem natural and inevitable to native speakers of English, but they are based in a particular representation system used in English. In contrast to CRA, several sounds that do not exist in English are represented with numerals that are seen by the informants as having some visual resemblance to the corresponding Arabic letters. The Arabic sounds and the symbols used to represent them in normal and ASCII-ized orthography are shown in table 2.2. The visual resemblance is clearer in some cases than in others, and in some cases involves mirror-image reversal of all or part of the symbol.

TABLE 2.2. Numerals used to represent Arabic sounds.

Sound	Arabic letter	ASCII representation	Example (English translation)
/ħ/ (a heavy /h/-type sound)	<ح>	<7>	<wa7ed> (one)
/ʕ/ (a tightening of the throat resembling a light gargle)	<ع>	<3>	<ba3ad> (after)
/t'/ (the emphatic version of /t/)	<ط>	<6>	<6arrash> (he sent)
/s'/ (the emphatic version of /s/)	<ص>	<9>	<a9lan> (actually)
/ʔ/ (glottal stop)	<ء>	<2>	<so2al> (question)

TABLE 2.3. Numerals used with apostrophe.

Sound	Arabic letter	ASCII representation	Example (English translation)
/x/ (final sound in Scots "loch")	<خ>	'7	<'7ebar> (news)
/ɣ/ (voiced version of above)	<غ>	'3	<'3ada> (lunch)
/ð'/ (the emphatic version of /ð/, the first sound in English "that")	<ظ>	'6	<'6ahry> (my back)
/d'/ (the emphatic version of /d/)	<ض>	'9	<man3ara'9> (not shown)

Several letters in Arabic are distinguished only by the presence or absence of a dot above them. Some of the dotted letters correspond to sounds existing in English and are replaced with the English letters for these sounds (e.g., <ز> is replaced by /z/ on the basis of pronunciation, rather than by <j>, which looks similar). However, where the sounds do not occur in English, they are represented in AA by visual analogy with Arabic characters, using digraphs consisting of a numeral preceded by an apostrophe. Note that in the AA segments of this corpus, the apostrophe is not used alone (e.g., to represent a glottal stop). The conventions used are shown in table 2.3.

The numeral <5> is also used as an alternate to <'7> to represent the sound /x/. This appears to derive from the fact that the Arabic word for "five," /xamsa/, begins with this sound. Looking at the corpus as a whole, it appears that individuals use consistently either <'7> or <5>. A, B, I, and J use only <5>, while D, F, G, and H regularly use <'7>. This sound happened not to occur in any of the words used by C and E.

Notice the logic of the symbols above: Arabic sounds with clear equivalents in English are represented according to English conventions, but those that have no clear English equivalent are represented by symbols based on familiar Arabic letters and sounds. This reflects the background of the writers as native speakers of Arabic who are familiar with the writing systems of both languages (as opposed to being linguists or native speakers of English).

It is interesting to consider possible conventions that have not been adopted by these writers. For example, if native English speakers who do not speak Arabic were asked to represent /s'/, they would probably use <s> (the closest correspondence in English), but none of the conversations in the corpus used <s> to represent this sound. For an Arabic speaker, /s/ and /s'/ are quite distinct phonemes, as distinct as the sounds at the beginning of "sing" and "thing" are for English speakers. Likewise, the writers here do not necessarily use ready-made forms from CRA. For example, they never represent the sound /x/ by using the digraph <kh> (which suggests some relation with the sound /k/), nor <gh> for /ɣ/, but instead use distinct symbols derived mainly from the corresponding Arabic letters (<'7>) but in at least one case from a familiar spoken Arabic word (<5>). In the process, the transcription becomes in some ways less ambiguous and less dependent on contextual cues and background knowledge than in CRA; for example, in contrast with the ambiguity of <kh> in CRA mentioned above, in AA <kh> unambiguously represents the sequence of two sounds /k h/ (rather than the sound /x/, which would be written <'7> or <5>).

The variety of Arabic used in the corpus is the UAE vernacular, and this affects the written symbols that are used in the conversations. As noted above, the sound /tʃ/ (usually represented in English as <ch>, as in <chair>) is specific to Gulf vernaculars; it does not occur in MSA, and there is no standard Arabic letter to represent it. When Arabic writers wish to represent words with this sound, they try to use an Arabic letter that is in some sense close to this sound. In this case, English spelling provides a ready-made solution where MSA does not: In the corpus, the writers regularly use <ch> to represent this sound. The extract in table 2.1 provides interesting examples. Both D and F write the vernacular expression /ʃha:litʃ/ (= "how are you-FEMININE"), corresponding to MSA /kaifa ħa:luki/. D, using Arabic script at this stage, writes the final /tʃ/ sound as <چ>, which normally represents the similar, but voiced, sound /dʒ/. By doing so, she makes an effort to represent the vernacular pronunciation, deviating from the standard spelling with <ك> (/k/), which reflects the MSA pronunciation of this expression. F, on the other hand, makes use of English conventions to represent the vernacular and writes the same expression as <sh7aalech>.

Another difference between UAE vernacular and MSA is in the pronunciation of the sound /q/, written <ق> in Arabic and <q> in CRA. For the most part, the MSA sound /q/ is represented in this corpus using <g>, reflecting (in terms of the conventions of English) its local vernacular pronunciation, for example, <gooli> (tell me). If the conversations were pure vernacular, then the letter <q> would presumably not be used at all; however, there are a few occurrences of this letter in the corpus. For example, when informant A writes <fe i qanah?> ("on which [TV] channel?"), she uses the CRA character <q> to reflect a pronunciation with the MSA /q/ sound. Checks with other UAE Arabic speakers confirmed that they would be likely to give this word the MSA pronunciation, reflecting recent borrowing of this word from MSA.

Another sign of influence from "outside" is one example of the use of <t> for the emphatic /t'/, in the word <fattoom> (a diminutive of the name "Fatima"). This is the only example in the corpus of <t> (as opposed to <6>) being used for this sound and is an exception to the overall tendency described above for Arabic consonant phonemes to be kept distinct from each other in the ASCII-ized version. It seems plausible that this is influenced by the writer having often seen personal names such as "Fatima" written in this way at the university and elsewhere.

Influence from "official" CRA spellings might also help explain the spellings used in the student-drawn cartoon shown in figure 2.1, which was observed on a "friendship wall" set up in the university cafeteria by the Student Council for graduating students to write messages to each other. As discussed further below, AA has come to be used for stylistic effect in some offline contexts as well as in CMC. Besides many inscriptions in Arabic and some in English, the friendship wall included several examples of AA, including this cartoon, drawn by one student to represent members of her class. Note that the name "Sheikha" (the "official" name of the seventh student from the right, apparently nicknamed "Blossom") is written <sheikha>, using the CRA form that would be familiar from university contexts. However, the diminutive of "Sheikha," which would not normally be seen in official contexts, is written beneath the caricature of another student (fifth from the right) as <shwee5>, using the numeral <5> to represent the /x/ sound, as in AA. Numbers indicating sounds are also visible in the nicknames below the sixth and eighth figures from the right.

More idiosyncratic examples of CRA also occur in the IM corpus. For example, on one occasion, D writes <9ah> for the more common <9a7> (= "true"); although this is not typical of AA, it is presumably not a random typo, since it reflects the English spelling for the English sound that is perceptually closest to Arabic /ħ/, as well as being the CRA representation for this sound.

ASCII-izing Vowels

Whereas Arabic has more consonants than English provides ready symbols for, in the case of vowels English offers a wider range of letters and digraphs than does Arabic script. Furthermore, UAE vernacular distinguishes more vowel sounds than does MSA. Probably for both reasons, the representation of vowels in the corpus is considerably less consistent than that of consonants. As in Arabic script, short vowels are often left out entirely. In some cases, this reflects reduction of syllables in UAE vernacular; in others, a vowel that would be pronounced is left out (e.g., <97> for /s'aħ/). However, short vowels are also represented in many cases, following the convention for English and in contrast to Arabic script, where they would not normally be marked at all. When vowels are marked, each may be represented by a variety of written symbols. Table 2.4 summarizes the most noticeable patterns in representing vowels.

Although there is considerable variation, as in the case of <'7> and <'5> mentioned above, individual informants show some consistency in their use of symbols. For example, although the vernacular sound /i/ is variably written (/yimkin/ (= "could be") appears in the corpus as <yumkin>, <yemken>, and <yemkin>), each writer tends to use either <i> or <e> fairly consistently to represent this sound. Similarly, <ai> and <ei> alternate as in the word "laish" in the following exchange:

> C: laish (= why?)
> A: sho leish?? (= why what?)
> C: laish ma 3ndch friends (= why don't you have any friends?)

The influence of English and CRA orthography is detectable not only in correspondences such as <oo> for /u:/, but also in the choice of variant. For example, <y> is used for /i/ only at the end of words of more than one syllable, reflecting a similar convention in English. Furthermore, as in the examples of <fattoom> and <sheikha> mentioned above, there are indications that personal names are more likely to be influenced by CRA conventions, since the only case of <i> being used for the vowel /i:/ is in the personal name <iman> (see table 2.4).

TABLE 2.4. Representation of vowels.

Sound	Most frequently represented as:	Less frequently represented as:
/a/	<a>—e.g. hala (= hello)	—
/a:/ (long /a/)	<a>—e.g. <kaif al7al?>(= How is it going?)	<aa>—e.g. <7elwah hay el aflaam?> (= are these films good?)
/i/	<e>—e.g. <kent malaaaaanaaaah> (= I was boooooored)	<i>—e.g. <ana kint achoof Angel> (= I was watching *Angel*)
/ei/	<ai>—e.g. <enzain> (= all right)	<ei>—e.g. <nseit> (= I forgot)
/i/	<i>—e.g. <almohim> (= the important thing)	<y>—e.g. enty (= you)
/i:/	<ee>—e.g. tadreeb (= drill, exercise)	<i>, <e>—e.g. <iman> (= girl's name), <el moderah> (= headmistress)
/u/	<u>—e.g. <shukran> (= thanks)	<o>—e.g. <sho ishtraiti?> (= What did you buy?)
/u:/	<oo>—e.g. <kent ashoof> (= I was watching)	<ou>—e.g. <you9al> (= delivered, done)
/o/	<o>—e.g. <w 3laikom essalam> (= and peace upon you)	<u>—e.g. <wa 3alaikum essalam> (= and peace upon you)
/o:/	<o>—e.g. <a'7ar yom> (= last day)	<oo>—e.g. <el yoom> (= today)

ASCII-izing Arabic Morphophonology

We consider here two examples where AA in this corpus represents not only the phonology (pronunciation) of Arabic but also its morphophonology (grammatical units that underlie these sounds). The first example is the definite article, consistently written <al> in CLA and <الـ> in standard Arabic orthography, and typically pronounced as /il/ in UAE vernacular. As mentioned above, the pronunciation of the consonant in the definite article often assimilates to the sound that follows it, for example, being pronounced as /s'/ before /s'/ and /t/ before /t/. In the corpus, the definite article is most frequently represented as <el>; the vowel reflects its vernacular pronunciation. As noted earlier, the definite article "el-" is pronounced as /əs/, /ər/, /əθ/ or other pronunciations, depending on the initial sound of the word which follows. However, Arabic orthography represents the article consistently as if it were always pronounced with an /l/. The consistent use of <el> in these IM conversations (e.g., <el 9eb7> rather than <e9 9eb7>) therefore reflects Arabic spelling, rather than pronunciation. Nevertheless, there were a few examples of phonological spelling, in common phrases and vernacular words involving assimilation to /s/, for example, <essalam 3aleikom> ("peace upon you, hello") and <essa3ah 3> ("3 o'clock"—note that the second <3> here represents the number three). In these phrases, the definite article is also orthographically attached to the word that follows it, whereas in other cases a space is usually inserted between the article and the following word.

Another case where AA reflects an underlying grammatical distinction is the representation of the feminine "-a" ending. This ending is generally pronounced /a/ but is realized in certain contexts as /at/, for example, in /dʒa: mʕat zayed/ ("Zayed University"). In CRA, words with this ending tend to be written with final <ah>, distinguishing them from nonfeminine words such as /ana/ ("I"), which always end in /a/. In AA this ending is transcribed as /et/ when the /t/ would be pronounced, but even when it is pronounced simply /a/, the underlying distinction is largely maintained, with <ah> and <eh> used for the feminine ending. Some informants (e.g., B) use <ah> throughout; others (e.g., D) mainly use <eh> but still used <ah> for words that tend to be pronounced according to MSA. One example of this is the word <qanah> referred to above.

A particularly striking example is <elmoderah mb 3arfeh shai 3n essalfeh> (= "the headmistress does not know anything about the story"). Here D uses <ah> in <moderah>, an item of institutional vocabulary normally pronounced as in MSA, but uses <eh> in the more vernacular words <3arfeh> and <salfeh>. Both <ah> and <eh>, however, are much more common than <a>, which represents the pronunciation rather than the underlying form. We can thus see influence from three sources: CRA spelling (associated with MSA pronunciation), vernacular pronunciation, and an underlying awareness of the morphophonemic patterns that both varieties share.

The Social Context of AA

In interviews, core informants did not use a particular term to refer to AA. "Arabic English," "writing Arabic with English letters," and "Arabenglish" were all used to refer to it; note the equation in all these cases of the ASCII symbols with the English language. Ease of typing was mentioned by most informants as a motivation for using AA, and they pointed out that they had had little experience of using a keyboard before coming to the largely English-medium university. Privacy (particularly from parents) and the intrinsic interest of writing in an unusual script were also cited. In addition to IM, chat rooms, emails, URLs, and mobile phone text messaging (SMS) were mentioned as contexts where AA is used extensively. In general, the core informants had perhaps seen AA before coming to university but had started to use it themselves only after starting their studies. One student said that she had first encountered it in communicating with her brother who was living in Sweden and who had no Arabic script functionality on his computer there.

In order to expand the database on these topics, all students on the Dubai campus were sent an email survey, to which 79 students responded. Their responses are summarized below.

1. *Why do people sometimes write Arabic [on a computer] with English letters instead of using Arabic letters?* Fifty-five percent of respondents said that they use AA because they find it easier to type in English than in Arabic. In most cases, it was implied or stated that this was a matter of greater familiarity with English keyboard layout, for example, "because we type most of our projects, homework etc in English." Thirty percent mentioned technical factors, specifically, lack of support for Arabic script, but several noted that this lack of support was true in the past rather than now. Fifteen percent mentioned using English letters for vernacular sounds not represented in Arabic script, citing <ch> and <g> as examples.

Ten percent commented explicitly on positive social connotations of AA. One, for example, felt that "people who are higher educated use this way of writing and others use original Arabic writing letters . . . in another word the one who is used to English right in this way and the one who is not used to English use the original writing way"; another described AA as "kind of a code, we feel that only ppl of our age could understand such symbols and such way of typing . . . i guess its kind of a funky language for teenzz to use." Both comments in different ways link AA to positive, in-group local values of education, competence in English, and peer group prestige.

Interestingly, one informant contrasted AA with CRA: "[AA makes] the word sound more like 'Arabic' pronunciation rather than English. For example, we would type the name ('7awla) instead of (Khawla). It sounds more Arabic this way:)." Here the CRA form of a personal name seems to be associated with "out-group" discourse, possibly through its association with formal university contexts; this is contrasted with AA, which is paradoxically seen as more "locally authentic"—paradoxically because AA is in orthographic terms no more "Arabic" than CRA. Compare this with the contrast in figure 2.1, between the spelling of /x/ in the full name <sheikha> and in its diminutive <shwee5>.

2. *Do you remember when and how you learned to write Arabic like this?* Seventy percent of those who mentioned when they learned to use AA said that they had encountered this variety before entering the university. All of those who mentioned how they learned AA said that they had learned it from other people with whom they interacted online, including relatives and online acquaintances. None of them mentioned learning it from sources such as websites or print materials.

3. *Where do you think this way of writing came from—who first used these symbols?* The most common answer to this question was "I don't know," but guesses tended to focus on Arabs abroad (citing lack of Arabic script support) and/or on positively evaluated groups, including "chatters," "young people," and "creative people."

4. *Do you ever see or write Arabic like this in other situations (not in Messenger)?* No one mentioned seeing AA in more official public settings (although it appears in URLs such as the music site www.6arab.com, and has been used in a fast food advertisement in Dubai), focusing instead on personal communications. Most mentioned using AA in emails, and 40% mentioned using it in mobile phone text messaging. Note that mobile phones, like computers, are often Arabic script enabled; however, default settings can make Arabic script more complicated to set up and/or use than Roman script. The second most frequently cited genre of offline communication (25%) was notes and cards to friends. One student said that "my 15 years old sister uses it to write her friends short messages that her teachers won't understand during class in case they get caught"—this contrasts the in-group aspect of AA with privacy and exclusion of "outsiders." This was mentioned by several respondents, especially in relation to secret communication in class; one stated that "I have seen some girls back in high school use this sort of language to cheat in arabic tests. An arabic supervisor when reading it won't understand anything written there. And the same goes for English supervisor!" After reading this response, we showed samples of AA to a few non-UAE Arab teachers older than 40 and found that they found it almost impossible to read.

CONCLUSION

Warschauer et al. (chapter 13) note that the private, relatively unregulated world of CMC may foster the development of linguistic varieties that will reflect and contribute to changes in the linguistic balance of the Arab world. The phenomenon of ASCII-ization, as noted above, is apparently a response to a technical constraint (lack of script support), but the ways users get around this constraint, and the ways they use AA in contexts where this constraint does not apply, reveal much about their use of linguistic and other resources. These resources include the spoken languages with which they are familiar, the orthographic symbols and conventions of these languages, and, beyond this, the social meanings surrounding various kinds of literacy.

The interaction between English and Arabic in AA involves a combination of transcription of spoken language and mediation from the properties of the Arabic and Roman writing systems. While in many cases AA follows patterns drawn from CRA romanizations used on road signs and in other public contexts, there is also idiosyncratic influence from English (e.g., the use of <y> for /i/ in final position, which is not common in CRA in Dubai). On the other hand, where English does not provide a phonologically comparable and fairly consistent orthographic convention, ASCII symbols outside the English alphabet (notably, numerals) are used. In these cases numerals based on a purely visual resemblance to Arabic characters are used to maintain the distinctness of sounds. AA in fact represents these sounds more faithfully and consistently than do the CRA forms found in public domains.

There is also the issue of vernacular versus MSA. In effect, in the ASCII-ized Arabic of these students, we can observe the first extended written use of the UAE vernacular. This variety has previously been written down only in very brief texts, in specialized genres such as poetry, cartoons, and linguistic studies. Now, however, under the combined pressure of technical and social change, it is being used routinely in written form, for everyday interactions. Standardization of this form of Arabic is almost entirely informal, but it draws on other linguistic resources as outlined above.

The use of AA also highlights the use of symbolic resources current among young Gulf Arabs. Shigemoto (n.d.) notes in relation to formal language planning that "a writing system legitimates literacy efforts, which, in turn, contribute to the cultural production and vitality of a community." In the UAE context, the informal use of AA appears to be enabling a vernacular with local prestige. Users apparently choose to bypass the Arabic writing system—to which UAE vernacular has the closest historical relation, and from which it has historically been excluded because of the low social status of vernaculars in the Arab world in general—and instead draw on the orthographic system of another language (English) that has a different prestige base, in the broader context of globalization.

All but one of the informants are female—a consequence of our sampling methodology, which capitalized on online social networks that are typically female. The single male informant did not appear to use AA in a way different from the others, but it would be interesting to examine the characteristics of AA in mixed or male-predominant samples. Other research possibilities related to AA include analyzing a larger corpus, perhaps drawn from emails and chatrooms as well as from IM. Various aspects of such a corpus could be studied, including the representation of sounds (particularly vowels) and the representation of underlying and surface forms, as well as of vernacular versus MSA. Although this study has looked at AA as a set of orthographic items, a similar corpus offers the possibility of studying from a discourse analysis perspective how AA use develops through an interaction: In table 2.1, for example, what factors influence D's change from Arabic script to AA? It would be interesting to examine the speed and accuracy of people's comprehension of AA, compared with Arabic script, and their attitudinal responses to these varieties (Dahlbäck et al., 2001).

Acknowledgment

A previous version of this chapter was published in the *Journal of Computer-Mediated Communication* (volume 9, issue 1, 2003).

Note

1. On Asian-style, vertical emoticons, see chapters 7 and 12 on Japanese; they are also frequent in Hong Kong online communication; see chapter 8.

References

Abrams, D., & Hogg, M. A. (1987). Language attitudes, frames of reference, and social identity: A Scottish dimension. *Journal of Language and Social Psychology*, 5, 202–213.

Androutsopoulos, J. (2000). Latin-greek spelling in e-mail messages: Usage and attitudes (Greek). *Studies in Greek Linguistics*, *20*, 75–86.

Baron, N. (2002, October). *Text in the fast lane*. Paper presented at AoIR 3.0: 3rd International Conference of the Association of Internet Researchers, Maastricht, Holland.

Beesley, K. R. (1998). *Romanization, transcription and transliteration*. Retrieved June 25, 2005, from http://www.xrce.xerox.com/competencies/content-analysis/arabic/info/romanization.html.

Bruthiaux, P. (2002). Hold your courses: Language education, language choice, and economic development. *TESOL Quarterly, 36*(3), 275–296.

Cargile, A. C., & Giles, H. (1997). Understanding language attitudes: Exploring listener affect and identity. *Language and Communication, 17*, 195–217.

Dahlbäck, N., Swamy, S., Nass, C., Arvidsson, F., & Skågeby, J. (2001). Spoken interaction with computers in a native or non-native language: Same or different? In *Human Computer Interact '01* (pp. 294–301). Retrieved June 25, 2005, from http://www.stanford.edu/~nass/comm369/pdf/InGroupVs.OutGroupPrompts.pdf.

Ferguson, C. (1959). Diglossia. *Word, 15*, 325–340.

Grivelet, S. (2001). Introduction. *International Journal of the Sociology of Language, 150*, 1–10.

Hentschel, E. (1998). Communication on IRC. *Linguistik Online, 1*(1). Retrieved June 25, 2005, from http://viadrina.euv-frankfurt-o.de/~wjournal/irc.htm.

Hoffiz, B. T. (1995). *Morphology of UAE Arabic, Dubai dialect*. Ph.D. dissertation, University of Michigan (microform).

Koutsogiannis, D., & Mitsikopoulou, B. (2003). Greeklish and Greekness: Trends and discourses of "glocalness." *Journal of Computer-Mediated Communication, 9*(1). Retrieved December 3, 2005, from http://jcmc.indiana.edu/vol9/issue1/kouts_mits.html.

Leong, C. K. (1991). From phonemic awareness to phonological processing to language access in children developing reading proficiency. In D. J. Sawyer & B. J. Fox (Eds.), *Phonological awareness in reading: The evolution of current perspectives* (pp. 217–254). New York: Springer-Verlag.

Li, W. -C. (2001, March). *Where have all the neutral tones gone? Charting neutral tone decline in Taipei Mandarin, with evidence from online phonological simulation.* Paper presented at the American Oriental Society 211th meeting, Toronto.

Mann, V. A. (1986). Phonological awareness: The role of reading experience. *Cognition, 24,* 65–92.

Palfreyman, D. (2001a). *LINGUIST List 12.2760: Informal Romanized Orthographies.* Retrieved June 25, 2005, from http://www.ling.ed.ac.uk/linguist/issues/12/12-2760.html.

Palfreyman, D. (2001b). *Keeping in touch: Online communication and tradition in a Gulf Arab context.* Unpublished manuscript.

Sampson, G. (2002). *Pronunciation of Greek and Roman two thousand years ago.* Retrieved July 4, 2003, from: http://www.linguistlist.org/~ask-ling/archive-most-recent/msg06865 .html (no longer active).

Shigemoto, J. (n.d.) *Language change and language planning and policy.* Pacific Resources for Education and Learning (PREL). Retrieved June 25, 2005, from http://www.prel.org/ products/Products/language-change.pdf.

Stevenson, J. (2000). The language of Internet Relay Chat. Retrieved June 25, 2005, from http://www.demo.inty.net/Units/Internet%20Relay%20Chat.htm.

Street, B. V. (1995). *Social literacies.* London: Longman.

Tseliga, T. (2002). Some cultural and linguistic implications of computer-mediated Greeklish. Paper presented at the annual meeting, Association of Internet Researchers, Maastricht, The Netherlands, October 13–16, 2002.

Unger, J. M. (2001). Functional digraphia in Japan as revealed in consumer product preferences. *International Journal of the Sociology of Language, 150,* 141–152.

Weber, G. (1997). Top languages. *Language Today, 3,* 12–18. Retrieved June 25, 2005, from http://www.andaman.org/book/reprints/weber/rep-weber.htm.

Werry, C. (1996). Linguistic and interactional features of Internet Relay Chat. In S. C. Herring (Ed.), *Computer-mediated communication: Linguistic, social and cross-cultural perspectives* (pp. 47–63). Amsterdam: John Benjamins.

Yates, S. J. (1996). Oral and written linguistic aspects of computer conferencing. In S. C. Herring (Ed.), *Computer-mediated communication: Linguistic, social and cross-cultural perspectives* (pp. 9–46). Amsterdam: John Benjamins.

3

HSI-YAO SU

The Multilingual and Multiorthographic Taiwan-Based Internet

Creative Uses of Writing Systems on College-Affiliated BBSs

Hundreds of millions of people around the globe communicate daily through the Internet, for both instrumental and recreational purposes. Along with the growing influence of English as the international language of choice in both online and face-to-face interactions, the seemingly ubiquitous nature of the Internet has created a myth in some parts of the Western world that this online environment is a culturally and linguistically transparent global village (Hawisher & Selfe, 2000). Contributing to the rise of this myth are the prominent role of English globally and the fact that the Internet was first created in the United States in the late 1960s and early 1970s (Hafner & Lyon, 1996) and popularized in Western countries where English is prominent. The myth of linguistic transparency is reflected in the relative lack of research on computer-mediated communication (CMC) in non-English-based Internet environments.

Although the Internet may be accelerating the globalization process, each society or culture tends to have a set of localized linguistic practices online that distinguishes its members from other significant groups (Appadurai, 1996; Hongladarom, 2000). This study investigates the linguistic features of CMC in the Taiwan-based Internet, sites that are frequented by Taiwanese users and for which servers are housed in Taiwan. Specifically, this chapter examines creative uses of writing systems in college-affiliated Electronic Bulletin Board Systems (BBSs), including the rendering in Chinese characters of the sounds of English, Taiwanese, and Taiwanese-accented Mandarin, and the recycling of a transliteration alphabet used in elementary education.

The investigation aims to contribute to research on non-Western Internet practices in several ways. First, the primary writing system used on the Taiwan-based Internet is the Chinese writing system. The morphosyllabic, logographic characteristics of this system contrast markedly with the more familiar alphabetic systems examined in the majority of research on CMC and allow us to investigate how the nature of writing systems affects Internet users' linguistic practices. Second, Taiwan is a multilingual society composed of speakers of various languages and dialects. Examining how Taiwan's multilingual environment and the language attitudes associated with each linguistic variety interact with online language use can provide insights into how Internet users employ the various linguistic and cultural resources at hand, in response to changes in their mode of communication. The written nature of the Internet medium, the orthographic systems available in Taiwanese society, and the multilingual situation in Taiwan all contribute to the emergence of linguistic practices unique to the Taiwan-based Internet.

This chapter is organized as follows: Research questions and methodology are presented first, followed by a brief review of the theoretical frameworks drawn upon in the study, an introduction to the sociolinguistic situation in Taiwan, and a brief overview of writing systems and word processing there. Four creative uses of writing systems are then introduced and analyzed with respect to their linguistic characteristics and social meanings.

RESEARCH QUESTIONS AND METHODOLOGY

This study is part of a research project investigating language identities and ideologies as manifested in both online and face-to-face interactions in Taiwan (Su, 2005). I examine creative uses of writing systems on two recreational BBSs and a Web-based BBS belonging to two college student organizations at National Taiwan University (NTU) in Taipei, Taiwan. The BBSs and Web-based BBS differ in their interfaces but function similarly with regard to message posting. Except for the Web BBS, the BBSs in question do not set restrictions on access, but those who post are usually members of the student organizations, and posters usually know each other, at least by their online identities.

This study takes a qualitative and ethnographic approach (Hymes, 1974). A primary set of interactional data was collected between summer 2002 and spring 2003. Participant observation and logging of messages were the primary methods for data collection. I gained access to the BBSs of the two student organizations by personally participating in the two online communities. During this period, a total of 235 messages containing the four creative uses of writing systems were collected out of approximately 3,500 messages posted. Linguistic practices informally observed in portal websites and chat rooms, along with a set of data collected in 1998 from two Taiwanese campus-based BBSs, are used as supplementary data. A final set of data comes from semi-structured interviews in an informal context, students' lunch gatherings, in which 11 students from the two student organizations were asked to comment on the four forms of play with writing systems and on Internet language use generally. All interviewees were active on the BBSs in question, and some of their postings were among those analyzed in this study. The interviewees' ages ranged from 18 to 22 years.

The focus of this chapter is an analysis of four forms of play with writing systems. The research questions I posed were the following:

> In what ways do the distinctive features of the Chinese writing system affect user interactions on the Taiwan-based Internet?
>
> In what ways does Taiwan's multilingual society contribute to the various online linguistic practices exhibited by Taiwanese college students?
>
> What are the functions of the various linguistic practices and the implicit language ideologies underlying such practices?

KEY THEORETICAL CONCEPTS

In this section, I briefly review two theoretical concepts explicitly drawn upon in the analysis: indexicality and playfulness.

Indexicality

Elinor Ochs (1992) investigated how "gender ideologies are socialized, sustained, and transformed through talk, particularly through verbal practices that recur innumerable times in the lives of members of social groups" (p. 336). The present study does not touch upon gender issues. However, the theory of indexicality Ochs developed is helpful in understanding how certain languages, dialects, or forms of language use come to convey various social meanings. Ochs identifies two kinds of indexicality: direct and indirect. An example provided by her illustrates their differences and how ideological connections are made through them. In Japanese, the use of the sentence-final particle *wa* is often associated with feminine speech, while the use of the sentence-final particle *ze* is linked with masculine speech. This connection is made through two layers of indexicality: *Wa* directly indexes delicateness, and since delicateness is a preferred social quality for women, the particle comes to indirectly index female voice. Similarly, *ze* is directly linked to coarseness and indirectly indexes male voice. Through indexicality, ideological connections between linguistic forms and gender are made. Through similar processes, the various languages and dialects spoken in Taiwan come to convey certain social meanings, as discussed below.

Playfulness

The term "playful" connotes "a mood of frolicsomeness, lightheartedness, and wit" (Sutton-Smith, 1997, p. 147). Of three components of playfulness—

spontaneity, manifest joy, and a sense of humor (Lieberman, 1977)—it is humor that is most in evidence in this study, although fun and joy may also be involved. Generally, the humor derives from the incongruous discrepancy between literal and intended meanings (Palmer, 1994). Regarding language play, Crystal (1998) notes:

> We play with language when we manipulate it as a source of enjoyment, either for ourselves or for the benefit of others. . . . We take some linguistic feature— such as a word, a phrase, a sentence, . . . a group of sounds, a series of letters—and make it do things it does not normally do. . . . We do it . . . for fun. (p. 1)

Researchers have noted a tendency toward playfulness in online communication. Werry (1996) suggests that CMC places physical constraints on the display of contextualization cues (Gumperz, 1982), such as prosody, gesture, and addressivity. As the link between speakers and listeners is weakened, speakers must add variety in written discourse to compete for attention. Herring (1999) proposes that loose coherence and disrupted adjacency in both synchronous and asynchronous CMC invite humorous play.

Danet (2001) identifies four factors fostering online playfulness in the mid- to late 1990s: (1) objective features of the medium itself, particularly its interactive, dynamic, immersive nature; (2) hacker culture with its valorization of wit and play with symbols and typography, and a predilection for various forms of subversiveness; (3) the "Wild West" quality of cyberspace as a new and relatively unsettled social and cultural frontier governed by few norms; and (4) the masking of identity—the lack of cues to physical appearance, ethnic identity, gender, and so on (pp. 362–363).

The present study examines four forms of play with writing systems and factors that foster playfulness on the Taiwanese BBSs.

TAIWAN'S SOCIOLINGUISTIC BACKGROUND

An introduction to the historical development and sociolinguistic situation in Taiwan is necessary to facilitate understanding of linguistic practices on the Taiwan-based Internet. The better known part of Taiwanese history begins with the Chinese settlement established by immigrants from the coastal areas of mainland China in the seventeenth and eighteenth centuries. The majority of immigrants came from Fujian province and spoke various dialects of Southern Min, a southern Chinese language from mainland China, which eventually became the predominant language in Taiwan. The dialect of Southern Min spoken in Taiwan today is referred to as *Taiwanese*. In 1949, the mainland China–derived Nationalist government lost the civil war against the Chinese Communist Party and subsequently retreated to Taiwan, which created another wave of immigration to the island. Mandarin Chinese was later promoted by the Nationalist government as the only legitimate language in Taiwan and literally became known as the "national language" or *guoyu*.

Since the mid-twentieth century, the influence of Taiwanese has gradually declined, despite being the native language of up to 70% of Taiwanese people (Huang, 1993). However, a dramatic political change took place in the mid-1980s, which contributed to the emergence of Taiwanization in political, cultural, and social arenas and a Taiwanese language movement in the 1990s (Hsiau, 1997). The sociolinguistic status of Taiwanese has improved since then, yet the general attitude toward Taiwanese tends to be disparate and sometimes contradictory. On the one hand, its use may directly index age and rurality and may further be indirectly linked to undesired qualities such as backwardness or, inversely, to positive qualities such as congeniality (Ochs, 1992). On the other hand, Taiwanese is promoted by native activists as a valuable, sophisticated, and somewhat "purer" language than Mandarin, since its sound structure is closer to that of Middle Chinese, the Chinese language spoken during the sixth to tenth centuries. It is also valued as a symbol of Taiwanese independence in certain contexts (Hsiau, 1997). However, although gaining in prestige, the Taiwanese language is still more of a spoken than a written language, and it lacks a standardized writing system. Various writing systems have been proposed, ranging from character based to alphabetic (Chiung, 1999; Hsiau, 1997; Huang, 1993). Agreement has not been reached among either the public or scholars, and the ability to read and write Taiwanese texts is generally restricted to a small circle of scholars and political activists.

The coexistence of Mandarin and Taiwanese in Taiwan inevitably leads to mutual influences resulting from contact between the two languages. Among the many examples is Taiwanese-accented Mandarin (*Taiwan guoyu*), which refers to Mandarin as spoken by speakers having a strong Taiwanese accent and is stereotypically associated with members of older generations and less educated rural residents. Note that the Taiwanese-accented Mandarin discussed here is a cultural stereotype of the nonstandard Mandarin spoken by native speakers of Taiwanese. It does not refer to the national dialect of Mandarin spoken in Taiwan, called "Taiwan Mandarin" in linguistic research such as that by Cheng (1997), as contrasted with the Mandarin spoken in mainland China or Singapore and elsewhere.[1]

Taiwanese-accented Mandarin shares with Taiwanese the sociolinguistic meanings of backwardness and congeniality but lacks the purist value Taiwanese holds and thus is a highly stigmatized variety among Taiwanese speakers. In sum, these three linguistic varieties—Mandarin, Taiwanese, and Taiwanese-accented Mandarin—enjoy different overt prestige: In formal contexts, Mandarin holds the highest prestige, while Taiwanese-accented Mandarin is generally the most stigmatized. Taiwanese seems to be located in between.

In addition to Mandarin and Taiwanese, English plays an increasingly important role in Taiwan. Although not spoken natively, with its global importance English is emphasized in Taiwanese education and, moreover, is considered highly prestigious. Nonetheless, it is not used in everyday speech. Only a very small portion of the population (usually people who have lived in English-speaking countries) speaks English fluently. In daily interactions, educated Taiwanese speakers may use English words or insert common phrases (e.g., "Oh, my god") into their Chinese language conversations, but the opposite does not tend to occur.

WRITING IN TAIWAN

A brief explanation of the relationship between the Taiwanese language and Chinese characters is necessary to facilitate understanding of the examples analyzed below. As mentioned above, Taiwanese derives from a dialect of Southern Min, a Chinese language from southern China. Taiwanese and Mandarin, a Chinese language from northern China, belong to the same language family, Sino-Tibetan, but are mutually unintelligible. In many introductory linguistics books, this unique relationship between Chinese languages is often cited. Despite differences as vast as those between Dutch and English (Chao, 1976), Chinese languages are often reported as sharing a common writing system that renders texts mutually intelligible (e.g., Wardhaugh, 1992).

While this simplified explanation of the relationship between Chinese languages is informative, it creates an imprecise impression that the Chinese languages spoken today—such as Southern Min, Cantonese, and Mandarin—can be written with a shared set of Chinese characters. Instead of claiming that Chinese languages share a common writing system, it is probably more appropriate to say that many Chinese languages make use of Chinese characters as part of their writing system. Historically, Chinese characters were developed to write Classical Chinese (also called literary Chinese), a written language functionally different from the vernacular languages spoken in different areas in China. Until as recently as the beginning of the twentieth century, Chinese characters were still used mostly for Classical Chinese.

In the 1920s, a movement advocating a colloquial writing style emerged in China. This movement managed to reform Classical Chinese writing practices and to develop a new form of writing based on colloquial Mandarin, then China's national language. Since then, a misconception that equates Chinese characters with Mandarin has become increasingly prevalent among the Taiwanese. The Taiwanese government's promotion of Mandarin and the lack of standardized writing systems for other Chinese languages further reinforce this impression. Today, an educated Taiwanese speaker may find it relatively easy to read a Classical Chinese text aloud in Taiwanese, but to write colloquial Taiwanese poses a major problem. Associations between some Taiwanese words and Chinese characters can be found, and according to Hsiau (1997), approximately 70% of Taiwanese can be codified through Chinese characters, but the other 30% of Taiwanese words cannot be written with the characters in current use. Moreover, Taiwan's populace is not adequately educated about the relationship between the Taiwanese language and

Chinese characters (Cheng, 1989; Chiung, 1999; DeFrancis, 1984; Hsu, 1992; Huang, 1993; Norman, 1988).

The Chinese writing system is morphosyllabic (DeFrancis, 1984): Each character has an inherent meaning and is associated with a single-syllable pronunciation. The inherent meaning usually stays constant across Chinese languages, while the phonological realizations of each character may vary among these languages. However, for social and historical reasons, the Mandarin pronunciation is the most salient both in print texts and in the online environment in Taiwan. In this chapter, all indications of the pronunciations of Chinese characters refer to Mandarin pronunciations, in which case the above description that each character is associated with a single-syllable pronunciation mostly holds true.

WORD PROCESSING IN TAIWAN

Since Chinese characters are totally different from the Roman alphabet and are far greater in number, keyboard entry of Chinese requires special software programs that map each character onto two to five keys, typically based on either the shape or the pronunciation of the character. Various input methods have been proposed, among which the most popular in Taiwan are the *Zhuyin* input method, the *Cangjie* method, and the *Wuxiami* method. *Zhuyin* inputs by sound, while *Cangjie* and *Wuxiami* input by shape and the composition of characters.[2]

Zhuyin, or Mandarin phonetic symbols, is an alphabetic writing system used exclusively in Taiwan to aid in the acquisition of Chinese characters during elementary education. The *Zhuyin* alphabet is composed of 37 symbols, each of which is part of a Chinese character. Thus, *Zhuyin* symbols resemble characters to a certain degree but are easily differentiated by literate Chinese readers. Each symbol represents either a vowel or a consonant in Mandarin. On a typical Taiwanese keyboard (figure 3.1), the *Zhuyin* symbols appear in the lower right corner of the keys. Thus, the "A" key also represents "ㄇ", the third symbol of the *Zhuyin* alphabet, which is pronounced approximately as "mo" or "m" in English. To enter a character such as 米("rice," pronounced as "mi"), a user of the *Zhuyin* method switches from the default Roman alphabet to the *Zhuyin* alphabet and then carries out four steps: (1) first, he or she keys in "ㄇ"; (2) next, he or she inserts "—" (which reads as "yi," looks something like a dash, and shares a key with the Roman letter "U"); then (3) a tone marker that shares a key with the numeral "3" is entered: "ˇ." This produces a list of homonyms from which a user must choose (step 4).

Figure 3.2 shows the windows appearing on the computer screen immediately after the *Zhuyin* symbols are entered. The left window indicates the *Zhuyin* symbols that have been keyed in, while the right window displays a list of characters that are pronounced as "mi" with the intended tone. The last step is to select the intended character from the list, which is number 1 in this case.

FIGURE 3.1. A Taiwanese computer keyboard.

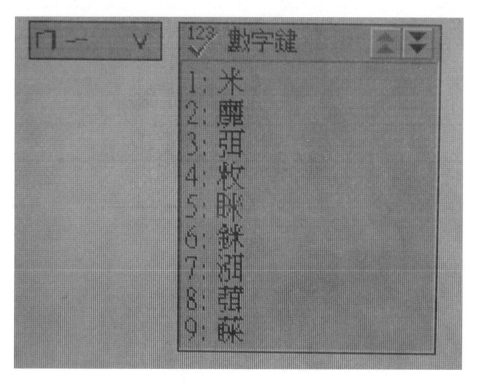

FIGURE 3.2. The last step in the *Zhuyin* input method: a list of homonyms.

The *Cangjie* input method, on the other hand, is shape based. It assigns keys to 24 radicals, or character roots. The radicals appear in the lower left corner of the keys (see figure 3.1). The first step when inputting is to divide each character in one's mind into one to five parts, depending on how complex the character is. Each part is mapped onto a radical. Inputting the correct sequence of radicals produces the intended character. For example, the character 明 ("bright") can be divided into two parts, left and right. The left part is mapped onto the "A" key, which also represents the radical 日 ("sun"), while the right part is mapped onto the "B" key, representing the radical 月 ("moon"). Striking the sequence A, B outputs the intended character (Juni'chiro, 1999–2001; Friends of *Cangjie*, n.d.). *Wuxiami*, an input method gaining popularity among professional typists, is similar to *Cangjie* in its shaped-based principle but differs significantly in details.

Among the three, the *Zhuyin* input method is probably the most accessible to the public, since the *Zhuyin* alphabet is acquired in elementary education in Taiwan. Mastery of *Cangjie* or *Wuxiami*, on the other hand, requires memorization of the mapping principles for character parts, radicals, and keys at the initial stage. Once the principles are memorized, these methods input much more speedily and accurately than the *Zhuyin* method, mainly because the number of keys involved in inputting a character is usually smaller in *Cangjie* and *Wuxiami*. *Cangjie* and *Wuxiami* are therefore preferred among professional typists or those whose life involves a large amount of Chinese word processing. They also require a slightly higher level of literacy in Chinese. That is, one has to know the shape of the character, not simply the pronunciation of a word, to be able to make use of such an input method.

LANGUAGE USE ON THE TAIWAN-BASED INTERNET

I now analyze patterns of language use on Taiwan-based BBSs, focusing on three creative uses of writing systems, which I call Stylized English, Stylized Taiwanese-accented Mandarin, and Stylized Taiwanese, notions based upon Rampton's (1995) and Coupland's (2001) concepts of stylization. A comparison of the three stylized uses is followed by a discussion of *Zhuyin Wen*, writing involving the alphabetic transliteration system used in elementary education. Among the 235 messages collected for this study, 34 contain switching between Chinese characters and English (example 1 below), 17 contain Stylized English (example 2 below), 44 contain Stylized Taiwanese-accented Mandarin (example 3 below), 39 contain Stylized Taiwanese (example 4 below), 87 contain *Zhuyin Wen* (example 5 below), and 14 contain more than one of the aforementioned patterns of writing.

Stylized Representations (Use of Chinese Characters to Represent Linguistic Varieties Other Than Mandarin)

In addition to being used in everyday interactions, the languages spoken in Taiwan also serve as linguistic resources for a variety of discursive practices on the Taiwan-based Internet. The main language on Taiwanese BBSs is Mandarin, which users write in standardized, traditional Chinese characters.[3] Occasionally, English words or expressions written in the Roman alphabet appear in this otherwise Chinese-dominant environment. An example of an English word embedded in a Chinese sentence is given in example 1.

Example 1: English word embedded in a Chinese sentence

印象中上回麗麗學姊的 suggestion 好像沒什麼回應ㄚ～～～[4]
"From what I can recall, no one seemed to respond to Lily's last suggestion. . . ."

This pattern of language use is reminiscent of spoken Mandarin–English code switching that occasionally occurs between educated speakers in Taiwan. In contrast to the linguistic practices discussed further below, this pattern does not seem to involve playfulness, though it does represent the construction of complex multilingual identities (Myers-Scotton, 1993).

In addition to Mandarin and occasional English code switching, other languages and dialects—such as Taiwanese, Taiwanese-accented Mandarin, English, Hakka-accented Mandarin, or even Japanese—are also playfully written with Chinese characters in BBS postings. The most popular creative uses of writing systems involve the stylized use of Chinese characters to mimic Taiwanese, Taiwanese-accented Mandarin, and English. Use of the term "stylized" to describe the representation of other languages in Chinese characters is based on Rampton's (1995) and Coupland's (2001) concepts of stylization. In his study of cross-ethnic interaction among adolescents in a multiethnic neighborhood in England, Rampton (1995) reported a phenomenon in which young people put on an "Asian" accent to project a comic persona, which he termed "stylized Asian English." Coupland (2001) later explicitly defined stylization as "the knowing deployment of culturally familiar styles and identities that are marked as deviating from those predictably associated with the current speaking context" (p. 345). He emphasized that "stylization operates in a specific mode of social action, PERFORMANCE in the strong, theatrical, and quasi-theatrical sense of that term" (p. 346, emphasis original).

The terms "Stylized English," "Stylized Taiwanese-accented Mandarin," and "Stylized Taiwanese" are so named because, first, such practices are marked choices on the Taiwan-based Internet, and their use connotes playfulness and performs an online persona. Second, the online practices they denote carry the social meanings of English, Taiwanese-accented Mandarin, and Taiwanese from more familiar daily contexts. The everyday meanings of these languages and dialects are appropriated and reproduced through these practices, resulting in a unique mode of communication.

In these playful linguistic practices, characters are adopted that represent sounds similar to the phonology of the target languages or accents, regardless of their original meanings. While the string of characters may not be readily transparent, to the initiated the characters are easily recognized as representing sounds that humorously mimic their English, Taiwanese, or Taiwanese-accented Mandarin counterparts.

Two examples of Stylized English are given in example 2. Each example presents a case of this form of language play and its intended meaning. The actual production of Stylized English is indicated by an arrow. *Hanyu Pinyin* (hereafter *Pinyin*), a Mandarin romanization system, is also provided to indicate the sound structure of the two phrases.[5] In example 2a, for instance, the phrase in Chinese characters reads as "ou-mai-ga," which is close to the pronunciation of the common English phrase "Oh, my god." Yet the literal meaning of each character tells a different story.

Example 2: Stylized English

Example 2a

→	Character	噢	買	尬
	Pinyin	ou	mai	ga
	Gloss	interjection	to-buy	to-embarrass
	Tone contour	high-level	low-dipping	high-falling

Intended meaning: "Oh, my god"

Example 2b

→	Character	古	耐
	Pinyin	gu	nai
	Gloss	ancient	endure
	Tone contour	low-dipping	high-falling

Intended meaning: "Good night"

In addition to creative exploitation of the morphosyllabic nature of Chinese orthography, the tonal characteristics of Mandarin Chinese are often employed in stylized English. In example 2a, the high-low-high-falling tone contour of the three characters mimics the intonation often associated with the familiar English expression "Oh, my god." The missing "d" in the final position of "god" is also reminiscent of the preference in Taiwanese-style English for open syllables, making the phrase sound as though it were uttered by a Taiwanese rather than a native English speaker.

In example 2b, the low-high-falling tone contour resembles the intonation associated with the phrase "good night," as well. Stylized English plays down the stiffness and arrogance often linked in Taiwan with the use of English, a language with international status and overt prestige, lending this alternative linguistic practice a sense of locality and congeniality while simultaneously maintaining a level of sophistication associated with English.

Taiwanese-accented Mandarin is often playfully written using Chinese characters, as well. Two examples of Stylized Taiwanese-accented Mandarin are given in example 3.

Example 3: Stylized Taiwanese-Accented Mandarin

Example 3a

Intended meaning:

Character	**很**	多	人	**去**	考
Pinyin	**hen**	duo	ren	**qu**	kao
Gloss	**very**	many	people	**go**	take-exam

"Many people took the exam."

Stylized Taiwanese-accented Mandarin → actual production

→	Character	**混**	多	人	**企**	考
	Pinyin	**hun**	duo	ren	**qi**	kao
	Gloss	**mix**	many	people	**business**	take-exam

Example 3b

Intended meaning:

Character	是	個	帥	**哥**
Pinyin	shi	ge	shuai	**ge**
Gloss	is	CL[6]	handsome	**brother**

"(He) is a good-looking guy."

Stylized Taiwanese-accented Mandarin → actual production

Character	是	個	帥	**鍋**
Pinyin	shi	ge	shuai	**guo**
Gloss	is	CL	handsome	**pot**

The boldface font in examples 3a and 3b draws attention to the exact loci of language play. (BBS users don't replace every word, otherwise the result would be totally indecipherable.) Comparing the marked characters in the upper section (the intended meaning) and the lower section (Stylized Taiwanese-accented Mandarin), we see that the lower section replaces the intended character with another character that has a twist in pronunciation. The words in regular font remain the same.

This pattern of writing has been used on the Taiwan-based BBSs for at least half a decade. The chat room data collected in 1998 already contained a large amount of Taiwanese-accented Mandarin. However, with the passage of time, the novelty and creativity involved in this linguistic practice seem to be declining, and the characters involved are more conventionalized in the 2002 data.

In addition to Taiwanese-accented Mandarin and English, Taiwanese expressions also appear on the Taiwan-based Internet. When users attempt to write Taiwanese, two strategies are often employed. One involves finding the Chinese character that corresponds exactly with a Taiwanese word. The other is to pick characters whose Mandarin pronunciations resemble those of the intended Taiwanese expressions. Since many Taiwanese words do not have corresponding Chinese characters that remain in use—and even if there were, the general public is usually not aware of their existence—the second strategy is much more frequently used. The result of this second strategy is a creative use of writing similar to the Stylized English and Taiwanese-accented Mandarin presented above. Two examples of Stylized Taiwanese are given in example 4. The characters in bold refer to the exact place where Stylized Taiwanese occurs. The *Pinyin* provides the Mandarin pronunciation for each character.

Example 4: Stylized Taiwanese

Example 4a

→	Character	開始	天天	**趴**	**趴**	**造**
	Pinyin	kaishi	tiantian	**pa**	**pa**	**zao**
	Gloss	begin	everyday	**prostrate**	**prostrate**	**build**

Intended meaning: "(I) begin to **run around energetically** everyday."

Example 4b

→	Character	我	**熊**	**熊**	想	起來
	Pinyin	wo	**xiong**	**xiong**	xiang	qilai
	Gloss	I	**bear**	**bear**	recall	ASP[7]

Intended meaning: "I **suddenly** recalled (something)."

The Mandarin pronunciation of *pa pa zao* and *xiong xiong* in example 4a and 4b represent approximate pronunciations of the intended Taiwanese expressions "running around energetically" and "suddenly," respectively. Although such a strategy seems to be a simple expedient, it has become increasingly popular due to its novelty and the playful incongruity it engenders between literal and intended meanings. In both examples, the repetition of sounds connotes childlike speech and enhances the playfulness associated with such practices.

The novelty of this linguistic practice arises from two sources. First, it is uncommon to find Taiwanese in written form, and second, even in cases where written Taiwanese is attempted (e.g., in articles by advocates of Taiwanese standardization), Taiwanese expressions are rarely represented in this way. Although viewed negatively from a purist's perspective, such unorthodox representations of Taiwanese expressions provide Internet users an opportunity to play creatively with available linguistic resources.

Zhuyin Wen (Recycling of a Transliteration Alphabet Used in Elementary Education)

In addition to the three patterns of writing discussed above, a new linguistic practice is emerging on the Taiwan-based Internet that is being criticized, even as it gains in popularity. Unlike the above three forms, this newer practice has a widely recognized name: *Zhuyin Wen*. Specifically, *Wen* refers to "written language." *Zhuyin* is the alphabetic writing system used exclusively in Taiwan and discussed above.

Zhuyin Wen refers to an online writing style in which some or all Chinese characters are replaced by *Zhuyin*, as example 5.

Example 5: Zhuyin Wen

		ㄧ	ㄍ	ㄏ	ㄗ
→	*Zhuyin Wen*				
	Pinyin of *Zhuyin Wen*	i	g	h	z
	Intended character	一	個	盒	子
	Pinyin of intended character	yi	ge	he	zi

Phrasal meaning: "a box"

In *Zhuyin Wen*, the complete phonetic representation of a character is reduced to a consonant (or, less commonly, a vowel). Recovery of the referential meaning in *Zhuyin Wen* is not always easy: A reader has to figure out the missing vowels. In addition, tonal information, an important aspect of Chinese languages, is not provided in *Zhuyin Wen*. Thus, a reader has to infer the intended meaning based on context and partial linguistic clues. Unlike Stylized English, Stylized Taiwanese-accented Mandarin, and Stylized Taiwanese, all of which highlight incompatibility between sound and meaning, the playfulness of (as well as resentment toward) *Zhuyin Wen* derives from its underspecified quality and the juxtaposition of Chinese characters, the norm of writing, and an alphabet associated with imperfectly acquired literacy. The use of *Zhuyin Wen* also conveys a sense of cuteness or naïveté because it is reminiscent of compositions written by elementary school students, which mix Chinese characters and *Zhuyin* symbols.

One may wonder whether the emergence of *Zhuyin Wen* is related to the prevalence of the *Zhuyin* method of word processing in Taiwan. Since it is easier to type *Zhuyin* symbols than to use the shape-based *Cangjie* or *Wuxiami* methods, their use might encourage the practices of *Zhuyin Wen*. While the *Zhuyin* input method has been used since the early 1990s, the prevalence of *Zhuyin Wen* online is a relatively recent development. There are two possible reasons for its increasing popularity. First, as one interviewee suggests, as the Internet becomes more accessible to the public, the average age of initial contact with the Internet has been lowered. Many young students, who have not yet mastered the Chinese writing system or have not acquired an alternative input method by shape such as *Cangjie* or *Wuxiami*, are already frequent Internet users. They may well display a greater tendency than older people to use the *Zhuyin* input system and to write in *Zhuyin Wen*. In turn, their language use may influence language practices on the Taiwan-based Internet to a certain degree. A second possibility is that the use of *Zhuyin Wen*, along with other creative writing practices, engenders group solidarity among Taiwanese Internet users, and that this in turn reinforces its use (cf. Baym, 1995).

ATTITUDES TOWARD THE FOUR CREATIVE WRITING PRACTICES

As noted above, the three stylized representations create humor through incongruity between the visual and the auditory at the linguistic level. Sociolinguistically, the humorous effects evoked by the representations can also be traced to the sociocultural situation in Taiwan and the ideologies and stereotypes associated with the use of each linguistic variety. The three linguistic varieties involved—English, Taiwanese, and Taiwanese-accented Mandarin—enjoy different forms of prestige in various speech contexts: English is the most overtly prestigious, Taiwanese in the middle, and Taiwanese-accented Mandarin the most stigmatized. At the same time, this ranking concerns only overt prestige; the social meanings attached to each linguistic variety are usually multiple and sometimes contradictory. A highly respected linguistic variety may not be used in familiar contexts for its lack of warmth or humanity, while a stigmatized linguistic variety may remain popular because of the solidarity and friendliness it conveys (Labov, 1972; Trudgill, 1972).

On the Taiwanese BBSs, this explicit ranking of overt prestige in speech contexts interacts with multiple social meanings associated with the Chinese writing system. The result is an "averaging" effect; Stylized English, Stylized Taiwanese, and Stylized Taiwanese-accented Mandarin can no longer be distinguished clearly with regard to their functions on the Internet. All three patterns of writing are taken as a way to show congeniality, humor, and an online persona. In other words, the explicit ranking and the functional differentiation among the three in speech contexts become much more obscure in online contexts.

Why the averaging effect? One may wish to argue that, in online contexts, the social meanings each linguistic variety carries are no longer important and that, since the production of all three forms of language play involves similar processes, the sources of humor are the same. However, I propose that the averaging effect is related to the interaction between the social meanings attached to each linguistic variety and the multiple connotations associated with the Chinese writing system. Indeed, as demonstrated above, all three forms of language play involve exploitation of the morphosyllabic nature of the Chinese writing system. Yet their similarity is only superficial: Stylized English, Stylized Taiwanese, and Stylized Taiwanese-accented Mandarin are linked with different language ideologies and stereotypes prevalent in Taiwanese society.

Stylized Representations

A detailed analysis of each pattern of stylized writing is necessary to facilitate an understanding of this point. I first provide an analysis of Stylized Taiwanese-accented Mandarin, followed by a discussion of Stylized English and Stylized Taiwanese. As mentioned above, in speech contexts, Taiwanese-accented Mandarin is more common among older generations and among younger generations from rural areas. Hence, in the spirit of Och's (1992) theory of indexicality, the heaviness of a speaker's Taiwanese accent when speaking Mandarin directly indexes age and region. Furthermore, since rurality and older age often indicate a lack of adequate educational access or facilities, Taiwanese-accented Mandarin is indirectly linked with undesirable qualities such as ignorance or backwardness. At the same time, like many regional varieties reported in other societies, the accent has local prestige and is associated with friendliness, congeniality, and a local (Taiwanese) persona.

In online contexts, Stylized Taiwanese-accented Mandarin still carries the social connotations of the spoken variety. Yet the transformation from an accent to a playful pattern of language use in a written medium complicates the interpretation of this practice. Competing and conflicting voices coexist in Stylized Taiwanese-accented Mandarin. On the one hand, the writer's voice is present each time it is used; the sentential meaning expresses the referential content the writer attempts to convey. On the other hand, Stylized Taiwanese-accented Mandarin evokes the voice of a speaker with a Taiwanese accent, albeit in a twisted way. The familiar, congenial persona associated with a Taiwanese accent is integrated into the writing of Stylized Taiwanese-accented Mandarin. On this level, the author aligns him/herself with the indexical values associated with the accent and its local prestige. However, the transformation from a spoken accent to written word play, which implies the ability to manipulate language, filters out the negative connotation of backwardness often linked with a Taiwanese accent. Users' access to computers and modern technology also distinguishes them from speakers of the stigmatized linguistic variety. On this level, the writer positions him/herself away from negative representations of speakers with such an accent. Hence, by using Stylized Taiwanese-accented Mandarin, Internet users simultaneously associate themselves with and dissociate themselves from connotative meanings associated with a Taiwanese accent.

As with Stylized Taiwanese-accented Mandarin, each instance of Stylized English conveys multiple and conflicting voices. However, in the case of Stylized English, the Chinese writing system plays a quite different role, particularly in terms of its formation and associated social meanings. As mentioned above, English, with its international prestige, has received great emphasis in Taiwanese education. In addition to the presence of an English curriculum in Taiwan's formal educational institutions, learning English has emerged as a national movement on its own. Parents send their children to expensive bilingual kindergartens, many English radio or TV language programs are broadcast every day, and English classes are offered in many places for learners of different ages and competences. Moreover, English fluency is a highly valuable skill in Taiwan's competitive job market.

However, despite its high prestige, English is still a foreign language and is not welcome in all contexts in Taiwan. The sense of sophistication attached to English use by Taiwanese speakers has a negative side: It is also interpreted as a sign of arrogance and a lack of appreciation for local Taiwanese culture. In daily conversation, the "overuse" of English vocabulary and phrases is often criticized as showing off. In online contexts, the reaction toward the use of English is less harsh, as English appears to be the default language in the world of computer technology. In addition, although very few Taiwanese Internet users are unable to read and input Chinese characters, some consider keyboarding in English more convenient. However, it is important to note that this acceptability is often conditional. Chinese is still the predominant language on BBSs and online discussion groups, and postings in English are frequently accompanied by a paragraph justifying its use.

Stylized English is much more widely accepted than English itself. Like Stylized Taiwanese-accented Mandarin, in addition to conveying the writer's voice and the referential meaning of the sentence, it conveys social meanings associated with both English and the Chinese writing system. However, whereas the sophistication linked with English is evoked in Stylized English, too, its negative connotations, such as arrogance and lack of local identification, are mitigated by the use of the Chinese writing system. Through the use of Chinese characters, Stylized English becomes nativized: It no longer represents a foreign product, but rather a combination of the imported and the local. Although this study does not focus upon language ideologies associated with the Chinese orthographic system, it seems that many educated Taiwanese feel pride in the traditional Chinese writing system, and several interviewees implicitly or explicitly expressed positive attitudes toward Chinese orthography.[8] To them, Chinese orthography distinguishes Taiwanese/Chinese speakers from the rest of the world. These positive attitudes carry over into the use of Stylized English, making it seem cute and friendly rather than arrogant.

In short, the Chinese writing system plays different roles in Stylized Taiwanese-accented Mandarin and Stylized English. While the use of Chinese characters transforms a stigmatized variety into a form of language play, it also renders Stylized English local. Superficially similar forms of language play carry dramatically different social meanings. At the same time, functional differentiation between Stylized Taiwanese-accented Mandarin and Stylized English in online interaction is not as sharp as that between English and Taiwanese-accented Mandarin in speech contexts.

The above analyses are supported by interviewees' comments. When asked about the functional differences between the three patterns of writing, several interviewees stated that the three are similar in terms of language play and the jocular and friendly effects they produce. This claim jibes with the view that functional differentiation between the three forms of language play is less salient than between their spoken counterparts. Still other interviewees pointed out subtle differences between Stylized Taiwanese-accented Mandarin and Stylized English. Consider the following example:

Example 6

DJJ: *Ziji jiang taiyu ranhou zheyang xie wo juede hai hao, keshi Taiwan guoyu wo jiu juede youdian song.*
"If you speak Taiwanese and then write this way, it's ok. But (Stylized) Taiwanese-accented Mandarin sounds a little outdated."

HY: *Youdian song dui bu dui?*
"A little outdated, right?"

DJJ: *Dui a.*
"Right."

HY: *Na xie yingwen de hua ne?*
"How about (Stylized) English?"

DJJ: *Da yingwen de hua hui bijiao shengying.*
"If you type English, it seems stiff."

HY: *Hmhmm.*

DJJ: *Da guowen de hua hui bijiao you qinqie gan.*
"If you type Chinese, it sounds friendlier."

HY: *Da shenme?*
"Type what?"

DJJ: *Da guowen de hua hui [bijiao you qinqie gan.*[9]
"If you type Chinese, it sounds friendlier."

HY: *[Oh, jiuxiang xiamian xie o-mai-ga ganjue bijiao haowan.*
"I see, just like the example below, *o-mai-ga* ("oh my god")[10] seems funnier."

DJJ: *Dui a. Da yingwen de hua you bijiao gaoji yidian de ganjue (laugh).*
        "Right. English sounds a bit more sophisticated."

HY: *Hmhmm.*

DJJ: *Na da zheyang de hua hui bijiao keai yidian de ganjue.*
        "Typing like this (referring to Stylized English) gives a cuter impression."

In this excerpt, DJJ offers his impressions of Stylized Taiwanese-accented Mandarin and the localizing effect of Stylized English. He first describes Stylized Taiwanese-accented Mandarin as conveying a sense of outdatedness and then points out the functional differences between English and Stylized English, thus supporting the above analysis that the two superficially similar forms of writing, Stylized Taiwanese-accented Mandarin and Stylized English, convey different social meanings.

Among the three types of stylized language, Stylized Taiwanese is considered to contain the least language play. Four of the interviewees commented that it represents an expedient: Given that Taiwanese lacks a standardized writing system, Stylized Taiwanese is simply the most intuitive way to represent Taiwanese expressions. Indeed, some of the sociolinguistic characteristics of Stylized Taiwanese are different from those of Stylized English and Stylized Taiwanese-accented Mandarin. While English is based on the Roman alphabet, Taiwanese-accented Mandarin is a verbal accent not normally associated with an autonomous orthographic system. Neither English nor Taiwanese-accented Mandarin necessarily requires using the Chinese writing system. Taiwanese, however, is regarded as a language independent from Mandarin, at least by educated speakers, although it lacks a standardized orthography. In comparison, Stylized Taiwanese seems more natural or less playful, perhaps an inevitable consequence of the fact that it is fairly natural to use the Chinese writing system for it, after all.

However, the belief that it feels natural for a language, but not an accent or a dialect, to have a system of literary representation is itself an ideology about language and literacy. Linguistically, the element of language play inherent in Stylized Taiwanese is not fundamentally different from that of Stylized English or Stylized Taiwanese-accented Mandarin: All involve incongruity between the intended and literal meanings of characters. However, due to Taiwanese speakers' attitudes toward Stylized Taiwanese and their ideologies about languages, dialects, and literacy, it is considered to be less a form of language play than a "natural" form of writing.

Zhuyin Wen

Although *Zhuyin Wen* is the most popular of the four types of creative use of writing systems, it is most heavily criticized by interviewees. Blunt, negative comments such as *Zhuyin Wen hen taoyan* ("*Zhuyin Wen* is annoying"), *zhuyin wen shi meiyou shou guo jiaoyu de biaoxian* ("*Zhuyin Wen* is a sign of a lack of education on the part of the writer"), and *xiedu wenzi* ("it degrades our written language") were made during the interviews (there may be some inconsistency between actual practice and professed attitudes of students interviewed). From a purely linguistic point of view, the production and interpretation of all four strategies require metalinguistic skill on the part of users. The level of linguistic competence involved in producing and interpreting *Zhuyin Wen* does not seem to be particularly lower than that required to produce the three other forms of language play. If this is the case, why are attitudes toward *Zhuyin Wen* so negative?

I propose that the different attitudes are related to the social meanings attached to Chinese orthography and the *Zhuyin* system. Well-educated Taiwanese take pride in the morphosyllabic Chinese writing system; interviewees' negative reactions toward *Zhuyin Wen* seem to be another illustration of this attitude. The role of the *Zhuyin* system as a subsidiary and transitional stage in the acquisition of Chinese characters links *Zhuyin* indirectly with a lack of education or formality. Furthermore, the alphabetic nature of *Zhuyin* also differs from the widely cherished morphosyllabic Chinese writing, which partially defines the uniqueness of the Chinese languages.

It is understandable that *Zhuyin Wen* evokes such criticism among my interviewees, who are students at one of the most prestigious universities in Taiwan. The elite in any society usually comprise those individuals who invest the most social capital in the orthography of their language. These attitudes toward *Zhuyin Wen* are reinforced as more and more college BBSs proscribe the use of *Zhuyin Wen*, an interesting trend in its own right. During my interviews, criticism of *Zhuyin* was also linked to the diminishing future of the Chinese language. For many interviewees, *Zhuyin Wen* was regarded not simply as a creative use of a writing system but as a sign that users' knowledge of traditional Chinese characters was declining. Consequently, *Zhuyin Wen* and the other three stylized patterns of writing are assigned different social meanings. While Stylized English, Stylized Taiwanese, and Stylized Taiwanese-accented Mandarin exploit the characteristics of Chinese characters, and thus are compatible with the indexical values associated with the Chinese writing system, *Zhuyin Wen* represents a lack of either the ability or the willingness to master the use of Chinese characters. Whatever the reason, its use offends my interviewees' positive attitudes toward Chinese orthography.

CONCLUSION

In this chapter, I have explored four creative uses of writing on the Taiwan-based Internet. This analysis demonstrates how Taiwanese college students use the linguistic resources at their disposal to create innovative linguistic styles in response to a new medium. At the same time, this study illustrates how linguistic practices in different media are situated within the larger social context.

A number of technological, linguistic, and social factors collectively contribute to the emergence of these linguistic practices. The written basis and the interactivity of the Internet encourage written forms of language play (Danet, 2001; Herring, 1999; Werry, 1996). Linguistically, the morphosyllabic nature of the Chinese writing system makes it possible to direct one's attention to the incompatibility between the sound structure and the meaning of a word/phrase in these creative uses of writing systems. Stylized Taiwanese, Stylized Taiwanese-accented Mandarin, and Stylized English all convey multiple and sometimes conflicting social meanings associated with their spoken counterparts. The processes of transforming spoken English, Taiwanese, and Taiwanese-accented Mandarin into forms of online language play involve mitigation of some of the connotations associated with spoken varieties, on the one hand, and the addition of some of the social meanings linked to the Chinese writing system, on the other. Similarly, *Zhuyin Wen* conveys negative stereotypes associated with the use of this alphabetic system.

In addition to the social meanings they inherit from their spoken linguistic varieties and associated orthographic systems, all four forms accrue various connotations as they become more and more widely used on the Internet and as BBS users interactively negotiate the meaning of their experiences and online practices. Further research is needed to investigate to what extent methods of word processing in Taiwan affect posters' choices, and how this may be changing over time, as young participants on the Internet gain increased literacy and improve their word-processing skills.

Acknowledgments

I thank Brenda Danet, Susan Herring, Keith Walters, Alice Chu, and two anonymous reviewers for feedback on earlier versions of this chapter, and the National Science Foundation (project no. 0236473) and the University of Texas–Austin for funding the research project of which the present study is a part.

A previous version of this chapter was published in the *Journal of Computer-Mediated Communication* (volume 9, issue 1, 2003).

Notes

1. A description of the linguistic features of Taiwanese-accented Mandarin is not provided in this study, since I focus on Taiwanese-accented Mandarin as a local stereotype rather than as an autonomous linguistic system. For further discussion of the linguistic contrasts between Taiwan Mandarin, Taiwanese-accented Mandarin, and Peking Mandarin spoken in China, see Cheng (1997), Kubler (1979), and Li (1992).

2. See http://www.honco.net/japanese/05/page4.html, retrieved December 15, 2005.

3. There are two systems of Chinese characters in current use in Chinese-speaking communities. Traditional Chinese characters are used mainly in Taiwan and Hong Kong. Simplified Chinese characters are used mainly in China and Singapore.

4. The last symbol is not a Chinese character but a *Zhuyin* symbol, discussed later in this chapter.

5. *Pinyin* is a Mandarin romanization system created in the 1950s in China (DeFrancis, 1984; Norman, 1988). Until very recently, the *Pinyin* system remained unknown to the majority of Taiwanese. The *Pinyin* system, employed frequently by linguists presenting Mandarin Chinese data, is used here as a means of transliteration to aid readers' understanding of the sound structure of Chinese characters. In practice, *Pinyin* is hardly ever seen on the Taiwan-based Internet.

6. CL refers to a classifier.

7. ASP refers to an aspectual marker.

8. The general attitude toward the logographic Chinese writing system can be observed in debates surrounding the standardization of Taiwanese. The proposal to write Taiwanese with the Roman alphabet seems to be the most feasible, since there has been a tradition of such a writing system among Christian missionaries in Taiwan. Yet this proposal is not well accepted in Taiwanese society. Chiung (1999) surveyed language attitudes toward a Taiwanese text written in seven different orthographies and found that the Chinese character-only orthography received the highest rating.

9. The transcript of my interview data partially follows the conventions of Conversational Analysis (CA; Sacks, Schegloff, & Jefferson, 1974). According to the conventions of CA, the sign "[" refers to overlapping conversational turns between two or more speakers.

10. See example 2a of Stylized English.

References

Appadurai, A. (1996). *Modernity at large: Cultural dimension of globalization.* Minneapolis: University of Minnesota Press.

Baym, N. (1995). The performance of humor in computer-mediated communication. *Journal of Computer-Mediated Communication. 1*(2). Retrieved December 5, 2005, from http://jcmc.indiana.edu/vol1//issue2/baym.html.

Chao, Y. R. (1976). *Aspects of Chinese sociolinguistics.* Stanford, CA: Stanford University Press.

Cheng, R. L. (1989). *Zou xiang biaozhunhua de Taiwan yuwen* [Walking toward a standardized Taiwanese]. Taipei: Zili News.

Cheng, R. L. (1997). A comparison of Taiwanese, Taiwan Mandarin, and Peking Mandarin. In R. L. Cheng (Ed.), *Taiwanese and Mandarin structures and their developmental trends in Taiwan: Vol. 2. Contacts between Taiwanese and Mandarin and restructuring of their synonyms* (pp. 27–62). Taipei: Yuan-Liou.

Chiung, W. T. (1999). *Language attitudes toward Taibun, the written Taiwanese.* Unpublished master's thesis, University of Texas at Arlington.

Coupland, N. (2001). Dialect stylization in radio talk. *Language in Society, 30*(3), 345–375.

Crystal, D. (1998). *Language play.* Chicago: University of Chicago Press.

Danet, B. (2001). *Cyberpl@y: Communicating online.* Oxford: Berg. Companion website: http://pluto.mscc.huji.ac.il/~msdanet/cyberpl@y/.

DeFrancis, J. (1984). *The Chinese language: Fact and fantasy.* Honolulu: University of Hawaii Press.

Friends of *Cangjie*. (n.d.). Self-learning *Cangjie* Input Method. Retrieved December 5, 2005, from http://www.chinesecj.com/.

Gumperz, J. J. (1982). *Discourse strategies.* Cambridge: Cambridge University Press.

Hafner, K., & Lyon, M. (1996). *Where wizards stay up late: The origins of the Internet.* New York: Simon & Schuster.

Hawisher, G. E., & Selfe, C. L. (2000). Introduction: Testing the claims. In G. E. Hawisher & C. L. Selfe (Eds.), *Global literacies and the World-Wide Web* (pp. 1–18). London: Routledge.

Herring, S. C. (1999). Interactional coherence in CMC. *Journal of Computer-Mediated Communication, 4*(4). Retrieved December 5, 2005, from http://jcmc.indiana.edu/vol4/issue4/herring.html.

Hongladarom, S. (2000). Negotiating the global and the local: How Thai culture co-opts the Internet. *First Monday 5*(8). Retrieved December 5, 2005, from http://www.firstmonday.dk/issues/issue5_8/hongladarom/index.html.

Hsiau, A. (1997). Language ideology in Taiwan: The KMT's language policy, the tai-yu language movement, and ethnic politics. *Journal of Multilingual and Multicultural Development, 18*(4), 302–315.

Hsu, J. (1992). *Taiyu wenzihua de fangxiang* [The direction of Taiwanese standardization]. Taipei: Zili News.

Huang, S. (1993). *Yuyan, shehui, yu zuqun yishi: Taiwan yuyan shehuixue de yanjiu* [Language, society, and ethnic identity: A sociolinguistic study on Taiwan]. Taipei: Crane.

Hymes, D. (1974). *Foundations in sociolinguistics: An ethnographic approach.* Philadelphia: University of Pennsylvania Press.

Jun'ichiro, K. (1999–2001). *Word-processing in the world of kanji.* Retrieved December 5, 2005, from http://www.honco.net/japanese/05/page3.html.

Kubler, C. (1979). Some differences between Taiwan Mandarin and textbook Mandarin. *Journal of the Chinese Language Teachers Association, 14*(3), 27–39.

Labov, W. (1972). *Sociolinguistic patterns.* Philadelphia: University of Pennsylvania Press.

Li, W. (1992). *Four mergers in the Mandarin finals of the speech of Taipei.* Unpublished doctoral dissertation, Oxford University, Oxford, UK.

Lieberman, J. N. (1977). *Playfulness: Its relation to imagination and creativity.* New York: Academic Press.

Myers-Scotton, C. (1993). *Social motivations for codeswitching: Evidence from Africa.* Oxford: Oxford University Press.

Norman, J. (1988). *Chinese.* Cambridge: Cambridge University Press.

Ochs, E. (1992). Indexing gender. In A. Duranti & C. Goodwin (Eds.), *Rethinking context* (pp. 335–358). Cambridge: Cambridge University Press.

Palmer, J. (1994). *Taking humor seriously.* London: Routledge.

Rampton, B. (1995). *Crossing: Language and ethnicity among adolescents.* London: Longman.

Sacks, H., Schegloff, E., & Jefferson, G. (1974). A simplest systematics for the organization of turn-taking for conversation. *Language, 50*(4), 696–735.

Su, H. (2005). *Language styling and switching in speech and online contexts: Identity and language ideologies in Taiwan.* Unpublished Ph.D. thesis, University of Texas at Austin.

Sutton-Smith, B. (1997). *The ambiguity of play.* Cambridge, MA: Harvard University Press.

Trudgill, P. (1972). Sex, covert prestige, and linguistic change in the urban British English of Norwich. *Language in Society, 1*, 179–195.

Wardhaugh, R. (1992). *An introduction to sociolinguistics* (2nd ed.). Cambridge, MA: Blackwell.

Werry, C. (1996). Linguistic and interactional features of Internet Relay Chat. In S. C. Herring (Ed.), *Computer-mediated communication: Linguistic, social, and cross-cultural perspectives* (pp. 47–63). Amsterdam: John Benjamins.

4

JACQUES ANIS

Neography

Unconventional Spelling in French
SMS Text Messages

WHAT IS SMS?

In today's Global System for Mobile Communications (GSM) telephony, short message service (SMS)[1] allows mobile phone users to exchange text messages of up to 160 characters.[2] In the United Kingdom, this phenomenon is known as text messaging or texting. In France, the company Cégétel (SFR) invented the term "texto," while France Télécom (Orange) coined the term "mini-message." Both terms are used in France, although "texto" is more popular (Anis, 2001), as is the acronym SMS.

According to Cor Stuttentheim, the Dutch inventor of SMS,

> [SMS] started as a message service, allowing operators to inform all their own customers about things such as problems with the network. . . . [I]t was not really meant to communicate from consumer to consumer and certainly not meant to become the main channel which the younger generation would use to communicate with each other.[3]

Only when operators in the United Kingdom and in France interconnected their networks at the end of the twentieth century did ordinary users make SMS an interpersonal communication medium. The years around the beginning of the millennium saw an explosion of mobile telephony[4] in which SMS played a significant role. In 2003, 9.8 billion SMS messages were sent in France, including 88 million on New Year's Day alone.[5]

SMS and Linguistic Prescriptivism

France has long been known for its language academy, founded in 1635 (Judge, 1993), and for preoccupations with linguistic prescriptivism and language purism (Dewaele, 1999; Judge, 1993, 1999; Walter, 1994, 1999, 2001). "The mission of [the] forty hand-picked members [of the Academy] was to observe the language, supervise it, channel its development and contain its excesses" (Walter, 1994, p. 67).

Although in many respects there is tolerance today for the view of French as a "living language," which cannot be kept in a strait jacket, spelling is still considered important:

> All those children who today struggle to learn the spelling of French can curse Monday 8 May 1673, that dreaded day on which the members of the Academy decided to adopt a single, standardized spelling . . . and which they they tried to force on the public. This spelling, which was both abhorred and venerated, continues even today to have its martyrs . . . and its admirers. (Walter, 1994, p. 70)

Many SMS users are young people, whose messages tend to be social in purpose and informal in style. It is not surprising that the abbreviated and often nonstandard orthography and grammar used in SMS messages have provoked the ire of language purists, both online and offline. SMS spellings are controversial[6] or prohibited[7] in some French newsgroups. There is even a *comité de lutte contre le langage SMS et les fautes volontaires* (committee fighting against SMS language and deliberate errors), which claims to have more than 2,000 members. Its website displays the banner shown in figure 4.1.

A Typology of Neographical Transformations

This chapter presents a linguistic analysis of neography—unconventional spelling—in electronic messages conveyed by a French GSM mobile phone network. Central to the study is the development of a typology of neographical transformations: phonetic reductions, syllabograms (rebus writing), and logograms (symbols, uniliteral abbreviations, acronyms), based on a corpus of attested examples. The analysis illuminates the heterogeneity, polyvalence, and high degree of variation in spellings. I propose that neography is a dynamic phenomenon based on local combinations of general mechanisms, which are also in evidence in other languages and in other modes of computer-mediated communication (CMC). At the same time, neography is not a standard, but a set of procedures writers use in particular communication situations, while writing a specific message, and under pressures from various constraints.

This chapter is organized as follows: First I provide background on the phenomenon of neography in CMC, with a focus on French. I then introduce

**C'EST UN FORUM
PAS UN PORTABLE**
Ici on parle un langage que les humains
peuvent comprendre...
Si tu veux une réponse à ta question,
essaye toi aussi de te faire comprendre

**Comité contre le langage SMS
et les fautes volontaires**

FIGURE 4.1. The fight against SMS language in France: Banner displayed on a French-language purist website. The text can be translated: "IT'S A FORUM/NOT A MOBILE: Here we speak a language human beings can understand. . . . If you want your question to be answered, try to make yourself understandable too." *Source*: http://sms.informatiquefrance.com/, retrieved December 6, 2005.

a model of the economic, technological, communicative, psychosocial, and linguistic constraints on SMS production, with an especially detailed account of the latter. The typology of neographical transformations in French SMS is then presented and illustrated with examples. In the conclusion I compare SMS features with those of other communication media and suggest future directions for research to expand investigation to other alphabetical and non-alphabetical CMC phenomena and to refine the study of orthographic variation more generally.

BACKGROUND

Neography

The term "neography" is used here as shorthand to designate unconventional spelling. More strictly than for other European languages, the rules of French orthography are considered to be absolute law. Spoken language forms are typically not acceptable in writing. For example, when a French person says the equivalent of "I do not know" in a medium register style, s/he would say: *Je sais pas*, whose written transcription would be *Je ne sais pas*. In English, the contracted forms "I don't know," "it's fine," and so on, are accepted spellings. Moreover, if English writers wish to emphasize familiar or popular ways of speaking, they can use unconventional spellings such as "I ain't" and "I wanna." In French novels and songs such transcriptions exist, but their stylistic effects are much stronger.

The situation is different in CMC, where permissiveness seems to triumph, for several reasons. In France, people educated in the humanities have been late to enter the computer world. Even when prescriptively oriented adults started using the Internet, they usually had little awareness of what was going on in synchronous chat environments, which are typically frequented by young people. Cyberspace thus initially developed as a space with no orthographic law—or so it seemed. In fact, the use of unconventional spelling in messages designed to be sent and received in a short time, which are informal, or intended for young people and their peers, is acceptable in many online environments. Moreover, as I suggest here, SMS spellings (and chat spellings in general) are not random transcriptions but, rather, follow systematic processes.

Neography is a commonly observed feature of CMC in English, including rebus writing (*b4* for "before"), Internet-specific acronyms (*lol*, "laughing out loud"), reduplication of letters ("soooon"), exuberant repetitive punctuation ("wow!!!!!!"), and comics-like marking of words within asterisks ("*grins*"). According to previous research, motivations for use of neography include to save time and typing effort through abbreviation, to make the message more expressive, to exhibit the user's ego, to play with language and communication, to contest standards, to express solidarity with the group, or to manifest adhesion to a counterculture (Crystal, 2001a; Danet, 2001; Herring, 2001; Raymond, 1996).

Previous research on electronic communication in French found rather restricted use of neography on the Minitel system, which predated the Internet in France (Anis, 1998, chapter 3).[8] However, neography is one of the most striking features of Internet Relay Chat and other chat interfaces in French (Anis, 1999a, 1999b, 2003); and includes the following:

- Omission of accents (*peut-etre* instead of *peut-être*—"perhaps")
- Substitution of *k* for *qu* (*je croyais ke tu sortais!* instead of *je croyais que tu sortais!*—"I thought you were going out")
- Phonetic realizations (*moua* instead of *moi*—"me")
- Truncations (*comme d'hab* instead of *comme d'habitude*—"as usual")
- Suppression of vowels (*tjrs* instead of *toujours*—"always")
- Syllabograms (*c* instead of *c'est*—"it is, this is")
- Numerals substituting for syllables (*qq1* instead of *quelqu'un*—"someone"/ "anyone")

The case of SMS in French is similar (Anis, 2001, 2003). In comparing neographic spellings in chat and SMS corpora, I did not find phenomena specific to either kind of communication (Anis, 2003). This observation applies to instant messaging as well (Anis, 2004a).[9] In contrast, in email, newsgroup postings (Anis, 1998), and discussion list postings (Anis, 2004b), neography is marginal. The difference seems to be in large part a function of a temporal

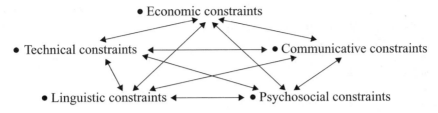

FIGURE 4.2. A model of mediated communication.

dimension: instantaneity or very short term versus medium or long term; a relational dimension: intimacy or group dynamics versus a generic audience; and differences of genre: ludic versus serious communication. As a preliminary to further discussion, in the next section I outline a rough model of mobile-mediated written communication with specific application to SMS.

A Constraint-Based Model of Mobile-Mediated Written Communication

In general terms, any goal, functionality, or limit of a communication system can be seen as a constraint. In natural vocal communication, the vocal apparatus, sounds, and so forth, are part of the constraints that shape output; in written communication, technical and economic constraints become relevant. In CMC, the technologies involved are very sophisticated; for this reason, their role has often been overestimated and conceived in a deterministic way. A multiple-constraint-based model can help to show that technical constraints do not mechanically influence linguistic content and expression. Instead, they interact with other economic, communicative, and psychological constraints. Figure 4.2 illustrates my model,[10] which is intended to characterize mediated human communication in general and can be applied to SMS to shed light on the factors that shape its use. The following characterizations focus on personal, nonprofessional, and informal text messaging.

Technical Constraints

The Network   Text messaging is an asynchronous communication mode. Therefore, no interaction is possible while the sender is writing the message. Once sent, however, the message can be read almost immediately, given that the mobile phone of the recipient is receiving. The sender must know the mobile number of the recipient, which requires a preexisting social link. Messages are limited to 160 characters; longer messages are possible by concatenating several individual messages but entail a proportionally higher cost. As discussed in the next paragraph, there is also pressure for brevity generated by the nature of the terminal.[11]

The Terminal   The screen of a standard device displays only a few lines of text at a time. Therefore, the following 158-character message must be displayed over three screens. For this example I insert a sequence of pictures simulating mobile screen shots, then a transcription into conventional French spelling (without normalization of punctuation), followed by translation into colloquial English conventionally spelled. In this example only do I use a slash (/) to mark line ends.

coucou mon pti goré!G penC a toi mé G du jeT lé cour daber pdt	mon Dménajment je lé retrouv + kan es tu dispo pr kon se	voi?we du 13 on fête l'aniv nico surpriz

1st screen
coucou mon petit/ goret [?])! J'ai pensé à/ toi mais j'ai dû jeter les/ cours d'Habert [proper noun] *pendant*
2nd screen
mon déménagement/ je les retrouve plus/ quand es-tu disponible/ pour qu'on se
3rd screen
voit? week-end du 13 on/ fête l'anniversaire Nico/ surprise

1st screen
"Hey my little/ piggy! I thought of/ you but I must have thrown away/ Habert's lessons as/ I was"
2nd screen
"moving/ can't find them/ when are you free/ for us"
3rd screen
"to meet? the weekend of the 13th we/ 're celebrating Nico's birthday/ surprise"

Figure 4.3 shows a standard mobile phone keyboard. The keyboard is rudimentary; most characters are accessed through multiple button presses, as shown in table 4.1. In contrast, the set of available characters is very wide. It includes many letters written with diacritics (not all of which are used in French),[12] all punctuation marks,[13] and a number of symbols, for example, +, @, ¥.

Economic Constraints

In France, from the inception of SMS services in 1999 to spring 2004, the cost of an SMS message hardly varied and then only because of the adoption

FIGURE 4.3. Keyboard of the Alcatel One Touch 756. *Source*: Alcatel.

TABLE 4.1. Characters available on a mobile phone.

1	. , ? ! ' "
2	a b c 2 à â æ ç ä á ã
3	d e f 3 é è ê ë
4	g h i 4 ï î
5	j k l 5
6	m n o 6 ô ö œ ñ ò ó
7	p q r s 7 $ ß
8	t u v 8 ù û ü
9	w x y z 9 ý
*+	[triggers the opening of a window with the table shown in next column] . , ? ! " – ( ) @ / : _ ; + & % * = < > £ ¥ ¤ [ ] { } \ ~ ^ ¡ ¿ $ # ¦ ↵

of the euro: FF 1, then €0.15 (about US$0.18)—a 2% reduction. In 2004, some SMS plans offered by several companies reduced the price to €0.10. Prices were lowered further after an active consumer movement, which exposed the huge profits of the telecom operators. Even at the higher price, however, an SMS was cheaper than a voice call, thanks to the expressive power of written language and the drastic reduction of salutations and various forms of *captatio benevolentiæ* tolerated in SMS messages.[14] In addition, mobile phone subscriptions that parents took out for their children—teenagers are the main SMS consumers—allow only a limited time for voice communication.

Communicative Constraints

Text messaging is typically dedicated to satisfying immediate or short-term communicative aims—maintaining a link with friends and loved ones and coordinating physical interaction, such as making an appointment or planning a meeting or a shared activity. In contrast with vocal mobile communication, the discretion and noninvasiveness of an asynchronous written medium allows for quite intimate content (see Rivière, 2002, on SMS messages as a new form of love correspondence).

Psychosocial Contraints

Most nonprofessional SMS messages are sent within a narrow circle of friends and relatives. The partners are peers, most often intimate. A certain complicity originates in their affective and social links. They share some knowledge, references, and values, as in the following example in which a shared memory (associated with an American popular song) is recalled:

> coucou je ss en tr1 d ecou t no woman no cry ca te rap l ri1 kiss maëlle
> (coucou je suis en train d'écouter no woman no cry ça ne te rappelle rien kiss maëlle)
> "hey I'm listening to no woman no cry doesn't it remind you of something kiss maëlle"

Linguistic Constraints

The theoretical model shown in figure 4.2 postulates that linguistic features are not the final link in a causal chain but, rather, can occupy a higher position. Linguistic constraints themselves interact in complex ways, as represented in figure 4.4. The features of this model can be explained and exemplified with respect to SMS as follows.

Writtenness   That SMS is a *written* medium is self-evident, but it is nevertheless important to emphasize this point, insofar as the adoption of oral features in CMC is often overestimated (Anis, 1999a; Debyser, 1989; Jeay, 1991).[15] Further below I discuss how conventional some of these features are. Moreover, the feeling of spokenness can be the simple result of the use of written language for linguistic interactions that are typically conveyed by spoken language (see "Dialogism," below).

Conciseness   Conciseness is another obvious feature of SMS messages, one that in some respects recalls traditional telegraphy. The motivation for being concise seems to lie mainly in the limited length of messages and the urgency of the communicative aims. Short spellings are the core of this

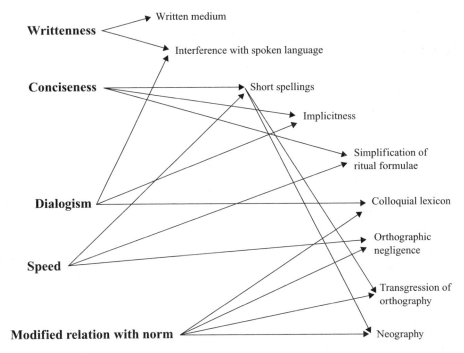

FIGURE 4.4. Linguistic constraints.

variety of written language, which is often characterized as a set of abbreviations (Anis, 2004a). Short spellings can include standard abbreviations, such as "US" or "PhD," but also unconventional abbreviations and thus participate in the trend toward transgressive orthography.

Dialogism   The phrase "dialogal dynamics" implies that most messages are components of regular exchanges. The example above regarding the shared memory of a popular song reflects this interactive dimension, which can be expressed implicitly. Dialogism partially explains interferences with spoken language, since the SMS communication situation recalls face-to-face conversation; it is also linked to the use of colloquial lexicon.

Speed   Speed fosters short spellings (which save time), simplification of ritual formulas, and orthographic negligence.

Modified Norms   The loosening of norms can be related to three causal factors: (1) Orthographic negligence reflects the reduction of cognitive resources allocated to spelling; (2) transgression of orthography implies deliberate discrepancies; and (3) neography is an alternative orthography based on a few general processes whose nondeterministic combination generates numerous spelling variants. One could say that transgression of orthography leads naturally to neography, whereas orthographic negligence can be considered negative interference, for both users and observers. In the SMS corpora analyzed here, actual spellings can rarely be attributed with absolute certainty to neography.

THE CORPUS

SMS messages are private correspondence. For the purpose of this study, messages were collected by young volunteers, since regular users are typically members of younger generations. The writers gave permission for their messages to be studied for research purposes. A total of 750 messages were collected by four volunteers, all of whom are very productive texters. RM is a 24-year-old worker; he collected messages he received himself. The others are students in linguistics. JDV collected messages from students and high school pupils for his maîtrise (fourth year of university, sanctioned by a diploma) in linguistics. OR collected three corpora (ORA, ORV, ORD), also for her maîtrise in linguistics. DA compiled a large corpus for her dissertation in Diplôme d'Études Approfondies (fifth year); she included messages she wrote herself, practicing participant observation in her research. The others did not include messages they themselves had written, although they were often the receivers of the messages they collected from their intimates. The data sources that comprise the SMS corpus for this study are summarized in table 4.2.

At present, no devices are available that allow the direct capture of SMS messages. The volunteers who collected the messages were instructed to copy them literally, although of course some mistakes may have occurred. All of the examples cited in this chapter are drawn from this combined corpus.

TABLE 4.2. SMS message sources.

Collector	Number of messages	Producers	Dates
RM	10	Young people around 20 years old	November 2003
JDV	57	High school and college students	Spring 2002
ORA	74	Teenagers	June–October 2003
ORV	61	Older than 25 years (mostly 25–30)	Winter 2003
ORD	160	Teenagers; 20–25 years old; older than 25 years	October 2003–March 2004
DA	388	20–25 years old	October 2003–February 2004

A TYPOLOGY OF NEOGRAPHIC TRANSFORMATIONS

This section presents a typology of neographic transformations observed in the French SMS corpus. These are categorized into three broad types: phonetic spelling, syllabograms (rebus writing), and logograms (symbols, uniliteral abbreviations, acronyms), each of which comprises subtypes.

Any typology of neographic transformation depends upon the levels of the linguistic units represented by the graphic units. A user can encode a phoneme or a sequence of phonemes; an alternative alphabetic system simplifies relations between graphemes and phonemes and thus can be qualified as phonetics oriented. The systematic elision of graphic vowels evokes the Middle Eastern alphabets; here, the traditional term "consonantal skeleton" is used. If a character corresponds to a syllable (as in Japanese *katakana*), I call it a syllabogram. For larger units corresponding to a morpheme, a word, or a phrase, I employ the term "logogram"[16] somewhat broadly.

Neographic Processes

Phonetic Spelling

Phonetic spelling involves transcription of standard pronunciations (e.g., English almost-standard "nite" for "night," or unconventional "guyz" for "guys") or socially marked variants ("luv" for "love," "wanna" for "want to").

Reduction of qu *to* k   This phenomenon has been mostly documented in the grammatical words qui ("who"), que ("what" or the conjunction "that"), and quoi ("what"), which occur with high frequency. However, it occurs in other contexts as well (e.g., example 18).[17]

   1. ORA

   *j'esper **ke** tu va bien.*
   *(J'espere **que** tu vas bien.)*
   "I hope you're doing well"

Substitution of k *for* c, *a Nonabbreviated Spelling (compare English* "kool" *for* "cool").

   2. ORA

   *Slt **komen** va tu?*
   *(Salut **comment** vas-tu?)*
   "Hi how are you doing?"

Substitution of z for s (compare English "pleaze" for "please")

3. DA

tu vil kan tu ve.bizou
(*tu viens quand tu veux. bisou*)
"come when you want to. Kiss"

Simplification of Digrams and Trigrams   In the consonantal domain, the digram *ss*, which is the transcription of /s/ in intervocalic position (a simple *s* would be pronounced [z]),[18] is reduced to *c* following the vowels *e* or *i*.

4. ORA

Moi G repri lé cour oci
(*Moi j'ai repris les cours aussi*)
"Me too I'm back at school"

In the vocalic domain, *au* and *eau* are reduced to *o* (compare English "coz" for "(be)cause"), as is shown in example 5; *ai* is reduced to *é* (example 6) or—less often—to *è* (example 7). *Eu* [ø] is reduced to *e* (example 8).

5. ORV

jmeclate avec mon nouvo forfai!
(*je m'éclate avec mon nouveau forfait!*)
"I'm having so much fun with my new plan!"

6. JDV

Si t na vréman rien a faire
(*Si tu n'as vraiment rien à faire*)
"If you really have nothing to do"

7. ORD

Je te lèss gro bisou.chachou ki t'adore trè fort.
(*Je te laisse gros bisous. chachou qui t'adore très fort.*)
"I must leave you big kisses. chachou who adores you so much."

8. ORD

bah alor si tu pe pa 1 otr foi kan tu ve
(*bah alors si tu peux pas une autre fois quand tu veux*)
"well then if you can't another time whenever you want"

Substitutions of Certain Digrams for Others   *Oi* results from the evolution of the old diphthong /oi/, which survives in English words borrowed in
the eleventh century, such as "poison," whose French homograph is pronounced [pwazɔ]. A phonetic reduction gives *wa*.

9. ORA

rappel mwa a 6h
rappelle-moi à six heures
"call me back at 6 pm"

To type *oi* one needs to make six key presses (three for each letter), and only
two for *wa*. We also find the variant *oa* (requiring four key presses), which
could correspond to an expressive phonetic variation.

10. JDV

BIZ A TOA ET A TON BOY
(*Bises à toi et à ton boy*)
"Kisses to you and your boyfriend"

Substitution of oo *for* ou   In a society highly influenced by American
culture—much as it was by British culture through the nineteenth and the
beginning of the twentieth centuries—high-frequency words borrowed from
English (e.g., football, look, cool) are familiar, and so is the correspondence
/u/—*oo*. This spelling often connotes youth and modernism.

11. ORA

bon ben c tout bizooxxx frérot
(*bon (eh) bien c'est tout bisous frérot*)
"well then that's all, kisses little brother"

Substitution of o *for* a   This variation only affects the *a* of the negative
word *pas*. In standard dialects of modern French, /a/ and /ɑ/—a front
vowel and a back vowel—have merged in a rather front sound. In some
nonstandard dialects, the inverse phenomenon has occurred, that is, a dis-
similation, producing /æ/ and /ɔ/. Thus, *pas* could be pronounced [pɔ], as
a regional or colloquial variant, although in most cases it is used in a humorous way. In written French, *po* has become a conventionalized marker of
spokenness.[19]

12. JDV

tu peux po etre + fatigué que moi
(*tu peux pas être plus fatigué que moi*)
"you can't be more tired than I am"

Deletion of Silent Letters—or Mutograms   For consonants:

13. DA

je ne sai pa pkoi tu ne répon[20] *jamai*
(*je ne sais pas pourquoi tu ne réponds jamais*)
"I don't know why you never answer"

The mute consonants[21] often have a morphological function (e.g., first-person singular present tense in *sais*, and second-person singular present tense in *réponds*), a fact that has been emphasized by a number of specialists of French orthography (Catach, 1980, 1986; Gak, 1986; Jaffré, 2003).

For vowels, deletion of silent vowels almost exclusively affects the famous *e muet* (silent e) of French, that is, a letter corresponding to a weak vowel pronounced in the same way as *eu* in *peur* {in International Phonetic Alphabet [ə], but often deleted in speech: The deletion is mandatory at the end of a rhythmical group or when *e* is followed by another vowel (e.g., in *je n'ai pas d'autre élève*: [ʒənepadotʁelɛv]—"I have no other student"), optional within a rhythmical group (e.g., *je n'ai pas* . . . : [ʒnepa]), which is the colloquial (medium style) pronunciation}. However, standard spelling always conserves the graphical vowel.[22] The mere transcription of the deletion of [ə] produces a suggestion of spokenness; if the deletion is optional, the transcription gives an even stronger feeling of spokenness. Example 14 belongs to the first category. It is noteworthy that this example shows a spelling that breaks a rule of French orthography: Only before an *e* or an *i* can the letter *g* correspond to [ʒ]. In the final position, *g* is either mute (as in "rang") or, in exotic or onomatopoeic words, pronounced [g] (as in "hot dog", borrowed from English, and in the onomatopoeia *dring*—English "ding-a-ling").

14. ORA

vil on boug.
(*viens on bouge.*)
"come on we're moving."

We also find optional deletions that affect clitic forms such as pronouns, prepositions, and determiners. In example 15, *profit bien d ton chéri* and *on s tien* show natural deletions generalized in most regions of France. The other deletions are more interesting, insofar as they would hardly correspond to a possible pronunciation. Actually, [puʁsvwarynotʁfwa] includes two heavy consonantal sequences that are unpronounceable (the transcription corresponds to *pr c voir 1 otr foi*). This shows that phonetic spellings in SMS are not simply the transcription of spoken pronunciations, but that they provide shortened variants for writing.

15. *DA*

*profit bien **d** ton chéri on **s** tien o couran pr **c** voir 1 otr foi, bone soiré,bisou*
(*profite bien **de** ton chéri on se tient au courant pour **se** voir une autre fois, bonne soirée, bisou*)
"just enjoy being with your darling we'll keep in touch to meet another time, have a good evening, kiss"

Amalgamated Spellings   Some sequences of words are written without the commas or spaces that normally separate them. The words involved are syntactically linked. A sequence generally contains a lexical unit preceded (example 5 above) or followed (example 16) by a clitic element, but other sequences can be found, such as two clitic elements, for example, *j'y vais* ("I'm going there") written *jy vai*.

16. *JDV*

*JVS **VÉRÉPA?***
(*je vous **verrai pas?***)
"I won't see you?"

Amalgamated spellings can also contain features that signal phonostylistic variation. In example 17, *chui* for *je suis* shows the transcription of an informal pronunciation, which goes beyond a regular assimilation: The deletion of [ə] allows the assimilation of the voiced spirant [ʒ] to the unvoiced spirant [s], which should produce [ʃs], difficult to articulate; the result is a lengthened [ʃ], represented simply by "ch."

17. *ORA*

***chui** pas né en 89 ms en 87!*
(***je (ne) suis** pas né en 89 mais en 87!*)
"I wasn't born in 89 but in 87!"

Consonantal Skeletons

Information theory has long claimed that consonants have a higher information value than do vowels (Knowles, 1986; Pierce, 1981; Shannon, 1948). The Phoenician alphabet, which is the common origin of all alphabets, was exclusively consonantal, as are the Hebrew and Arabic alphabets. It has been demonstrated that a short text written in a French or English deprived of all vowels can be read rather easily (see Masson, 1999, for French). Omission of vowels has long been used to abbreviate words in lecture notes.

The French written word—like the English written word—has a heavy consonantal framework. In English CMC corpora, one finds "pls" for "please" and "ppl" for "people." But a specific feature of the French written word is that some of its consonants do not have any phonetic counterpart, as in the final *s* of *vous*. Many of the consonantal skeletons we find in our corpora do not include all consonants. Nonetheless, the first and last consonants of the written word are almost always preserved, for example, for the transcription of *toujours* ("always"), *tjs* and *tjrs* are more typical than *tj* and *tjr*, although all appear in the corpus. Sometimes, all the other letters are eliminated (example 18, *vs* for *vous*; example 19, *ac* for *avec*). In particular, the nasals *n* and *m* followed by another consonant, which we characterize as weak consonants,[23] are generally omitted (e.g., *lgtps* for *longtemps*, "a long time"). In most cases, geminate consonants are simplified (e.g., *msg* for *message*).

18. *JDV*

VS ME MANKÉ MÉ GRAV.
(***Vous** me manquez mais grave.*)
"I seriously miss you."

19. *ORA*

*fo tro ke ti aille **ac** monica oci*
*faut trop que tu y ailles **avec** Monica aussi*
"you should really go there with Monica too"

Syllabograms or Rebuslike Spellings

The second category of neography in our typology is the use of a letter or a number to represent the phonetic sequence that constitutes its realization in spoken language, known as a syllabogram or rebus writing. Thus, "be4" or "**B4**"[24] stands for "before" in English, and *Kdo* for *cadeau* [kado] in French. The homophony is often approximate, as when *2*—pronounced [tu:] in English—is used for [tə] in "2nite" ("tonight"). In French, *2* [dø] can be used for the sound [də] or even for the spelling *de* in a context where the final *e* would be silent in spoken language (example 20).

20. *DA*

G** pa eu le temps **2** voir ca avec tou le mon**2
(***J**'ai pas eu le temps **de** voir ça avec tout le mon**de***)
"I didn't get the time to look at that with everybody"

The term "syllabogram" itself is approximate, insofar as when an originally syllabic element has been inserted into a longer graphic sequence, sometimes this element does not correspond to a syllable. It can be integrated into a more complex syllable: In English, 8 in *sk8* for *skate*, or in French *1* [ɛ] in *2m1* for *demain* [dəmɛ̃], "tomorrow."[25] It can also be split by a syllable boundary: In English, ICQ for "I seek you" is made up of three elements, the last one standing for *k#you*; in French *N* [ɛn] in *NRV* stands for [e#n] to spell énervé [ɛ̃nɛʁve] (example 21).

21. JDV

*MANIF AGAINST JEAN MARIE CE SOIR A REPUBLIK, VER 19H, FAITES PASSER ET VENEZ NOMBREUX, MOTIVÉ, PA **NRV**, A CE SOIR!*

(*Manifestation contre Jean-Marie ce soir à République, à 19h, faites passer et venez nombreux, motivés, pas **énervés**, à ce soir!*)

"Demonstration against Jean-Marie,[26] forward it and come in large numbers, motivated, not upset, see you tonight!"

Among the most striking features in our French corpus are the following: Syllabograms often allow a drastic reduction of the number of characters, for example, *CT* [sete] (two characters) for *c'était* (seven characters) (example 22). They are also often polyvalent: *c* stands for *c'est, c'é* . . . (example 22), and *s'est* (example 23), and other values are theoretically possible, such as *sais* from *savoir* ("to know"), *ces* ("these"), and *ses* ("his/her/its").

22. ORD

***c** maelle **ct** pr savoir si ya match samedi biz maelle*
(***c'est** maelle **c'était** pour savoir s'il y a match samedi bises maelle*)
"it's maelle it was to ask if there's a game on Saturday kisses maelle"

23. ORA

*Coucou moi sa va la rentré **c** bien passé a par ke ya tro **2** devoir*
(*Coucou moi ça va la rentrée **s'est** bien passée a part qu'il y a trop **de** devoirs*)
"Hi I'm fine the term began well except there is too much homework"

Syllabograms remodel the graphic string, which is made up of a sequence of words, separated by spaces in the general case, commas in some specific cases.[27] As for the phonic string, it is based on syllables, which in French often cross word boundaries. In fact, there is a strong trend toward open syllabification, that is, sequences of syllables ending in vowels. *Elle appliquait très exactement les indications* ("She very strictly applied the instructions") is oralized as [ɛ-la-pli-kɛ-tʁɛ-zɛg-zak-tə-mã-le–zɛ̃-di-ka-sjɔ̃]. When one uses syllabograms, sometimes oral syllabification is violated, and sometimes written word structure is violated.

In standard French, monosyllabic grammatical words such as *ce, de, je, le, la,* and so forth, lose their vowels when the next word begins with a vowel, but the elision is marked by an apostrophe that preserves the identity of each word. In example 24 from the SMS corpus, *G* for *j'ai* [ʒe] merges the two words, *U* for *eu* [y] corresponds to one word and one phonic syllable, and *L* for "elle" corresponds to one word but can be split into two phonic syllables.

24. ORA

G U *ma moman o tel é el été super content car* **L** *a reçu ta cart avec baloo.*
(**J'ai eu** *ma maman au téléphone et elle était super contente car* **elle** *a reçu ta carte avec baloo.*)
"I spoke with my mom on the phone and she was really happy because she received your postcard with baloo [a pet?]"

Not only commas but also word spaces can be eliminated (examples 25 and 26). In the first case, merging the preposition *de* and the clitic pronoun is irrelevant; in the second case, *de rien* is a phrase.

25. DA

Ca sera donc tjs 1 plaisir **2te** *revoir! :-)*
(*Ça sera donc toujours un plaisir* **de te** *revoir! :-)*)
"So it will always be a pleasure to meet you again! :-)"

26. ORA

2rien mai **c** la veri **t**
(**De** rien mais **c'est** la vérité)
"You're welcome but it's the truth"

Words are sometimes broken up by syllabograms. In example 26, *vérité* becomes *veri t*, while in example 27, *t* represents the pronoun *t(e)* and the first syllable of the verb *écouter*.

27. DA

Je **t koute** *mai tu me fai peur . . .*
(*Je* **t'écoute** *mais tu me fais peur . . .*)
"I'm listening to you but you are making me afraid"

To conclude this section, it is noteworthy that to prevent misreadings, many writers use a graphic marker, a capital letter, to indicate that a letter should be read as a syllabogram (examples 24 and 28). In example 28, *rest* could correspond to *reste*; *resT* here denotes *restait* (in context, i.e., after the pronoun *il* (he) it cannot refer to the infinitive *rester* or to the past participle *resté*).

28. DA

> *tu madi kil te res**T** du forfé alor apel ta cousine pr prendre **D** nouv**L***
> (*tu m'as dit qu'il te res**tait** du forfait alors appelle ta cousine pour prendre **des** nouv**elles**)
> "you told me you had time left on your plan so call your cousin to get some news"

Logograms

The third common category of neography is logograms. I use the term here somewhat broadly, applying it not only to word signs such as "@" for "at" or "$" for "dollar" or "2" for "two," but also to single-letter abbreviations such as "f" for "female" or acronyms made up of initials such as "CNN" (Cable News Network) or "IMHO" (In my humble opinion).

In our SMS corpus, *1* is used for the numeral *un* (one), but also for the indefinite article *un* (a), thanks to the homonymy of these two words.

29. ORD

> *on se voi ou pa a 13h pr prendre **1** café?*
> (*on se voit ou pas à 13h pour prendre **un** café?*)
> "are we or aren't we going to meet at 1 pm to have coffee?"

The plus sign (+) is often used as the equivalent of the very common adverb *"plus"* ("more," "most"; example 30). The colloquial expression *à plus*, derived from *à plus tard* ("see you later"), written as *a+* or *@+*, is a frequent message closure (example 30).

30. DA

> *C bizar mé n **+** t voir me mank. C ptetr pa l msg k tu attendai Ptetr a+*
> (*C'est bizarre mais ne **plus** te voir me manque. C'est peut-être pas un message que tu attendais Peut-être à **plus***)
> "It's strange but I miss not seeing you any more. You maybe weren't expecting such a message Maybe see you later"

Single-letter abbreviations (e.g., *k* for *que*, *t* for *tu*) are not frequent, possibly to avoid confusion with syllabograms. I return to this topic in the section on "spelling variation."

Phrasal acronyms are not as popular in French as in English. In common language, we write *s.v.p.* (*s'il vous plait* = "please"), *r.a.s* (*rien à signaler*, old-fashioned military formula meaning "nothing to report"), and a few others; these also appear in SMS messages. Often in chat, and from time to time in SMS messages, *lol* is used; however, it is directly borrowed from the English acronym "laughing out loud";[28] thus, it is not an acronym in the French context. The French acronym to express loud laughter is *mdr* (*mort de rire*), literally "dead from laughing" (example 31), used only in electronic communication. It is very frequent in chat but is used less in SMS messages.

31. ORA

tro je croyé ke ta cop ct toi! **mdr**
(*trop je croyais que ta copine c'était toi!* **mort de rire**)
"it's too much I thought your friend was you! lol"

Truncations and Other Morpholexical Alterations

In concluding this taxonomy, I address two phenomena that are not part of the core of neography: truncations and the morpholexical alternations known as *verlan*.

Truncations exist both in spoken and written language. The deletion of the beginning of a word is called *apheresis*; the deletion of the end of a word is *apocope*. It seems that only truncations of the second type can be lexicalized. For example, we find *intello* for *intellectuel* ("intellectual" with pejorative connotations) and *ciné* for *cinema* ("movie," old shortening of *cinématographe*). The present corpus contains nicknames such as *seb* for *Sébastien* and *delph* or *del* for *Delphine*, *cop* for *copine* (example 31), *vac* for *vacances* ("holiday"), and *dèf* for (*La*) *Défense* (example 32).

32. ORA

RDV a la **dèf** *dvnt mcdo*
(*rendez-vous à la* **Défense** *devant McDonald's*)
"let's meet at the Défense in front of McDonald's"

Apheresis belongs to a quite colloquial register of language and is thus more marked in written language.

33. DA

Lu! *Alors tu vien 2 main ou bien?*
(**Salut**! *Alors tu viens demain ou bien?*)
"Hi! so you're coming tomorrow, right?"

The second phenomenon is *verlan*, a form of spoken wordplay practiced by many teenagers in France. *Verlan* is intended to communicate without being understood by adults, to establish complicity with peers, and to have fun (Andreini, 1985; George, 1993). The name *verlan* is meaningful: The coding is based on the inversion of syllables or syllabic elements, and *verlan* represents the inversion of the syllables of *l'envers* [lãvɛʁ] (the reverse). The basic procedure is complicated by the fact that an audible final consonant is transformed into a syllable followed by [ə] and by deletions of some elements: For instance, *flic* (cop) gives [flikə], and [kəfli] gives [kœf] written *keuf*. Through the progressive integration of *verlan* words into the colloquial lexicon, new spellings have appeared, some of which can be found in dictionaries. In example 34, the initial syllable of *énervé* has been cut, and the others reversed [venɛʁ]. Note that the spelling of the syllables does not deviate from traditional spelling. In contrast, when the monosyllabic personal pronoun *moi* [mwa] is written *oim*, the spelling is far from standard (example 35).

34. ORA

T **vénère**?? tu sai tré bien ke jrigolé?!? xcus si ca ta vexé
(*Tu es **énervé**?? tu sais très bien que je rigolais?!? excuse si ça t'a vexé*)
"You're annoyed?? You know perfectly well I was kidding?!? sorry if it upset you"

35. ORA

jvoulé te demandé si tu pouvé vnir ché **oim** 7apré
(*je voulais te demander si tu pouvais venir chez **moi** cet après-midi*)
"I wanted to ask if you could come to my place this afternoon"

In this section, I have presented a taxonomy of neographic processes in French SMS. However, this approach does not account for the way SMS messages are written, which is dynamic, complex, and variable. The following section considers variation in SMS orthography.

Spelling Variation

French orthography is an institutionalized norm, upon which all written documents are supposed to be modeled. However, the frequency of deviations is highly variable; the demand for conformity with the norm is strong in documents destined to be published and weak in private correspondence. In French SMS, unconventional spelling occurs as an intentional strategy in short texts produced in informal and short-term communication with peers. This section considers three aspects of variation in SMS: heterogeneity, polyvalence, and variants.

Heterogeneity

Heterogeneity is defined here as the co-occurrence of multiple strategies within the same textual unit. A few messages in this SMS corpus are written, except for punctuation, according to the orthographic norm (example 36). In most messages, however, standard orthography and neography are mixed, producing heterogeneous spelling. Example 37 is an extreme case, in which neographic or misspelled words make up 90% of the words. However, neography rarely affects the whole expression; even in example 37 there are segments in standard French (shown in boldface). This is not surprising, insofar as neography operates by modifying the orthographic system, which constitutes its substrate.

36. *DA*

petite précision importante c'est le samedi 24 janvier la soirée!
"a small but important detail the date of the party is saturday january 24!"

37. *ORA*

C **bon** *ya pa 2 prob, yora 2 la plac pr remné tt l mde:* **mélaine** *vil ns ch ver*
20h *é apré on pd* **Clémence**. *ya vrémen ok1 pb é pui ça tévitra 2 payé l tr1.*
tr1[29] *moi o couran biz*
(*C'est bon il n'y a pas de problème, il y aura de la place pour remmener*
tout le monde: mélaine vient nous chercher vers 20h et après on prend
Clémence. il y a vraiment aucun problème et puis ça t'évitera de payer
un train. tiens-moi au courant bises)
"It's fine no problem, there will be enough room to drive everybody back:
mélaine is going to pick us up at about 8 pm and afterward we'll pick up
Clémence. There's really no problem and besides it will save you the cost of
the train. keep me updated kisses"

A second source of heterogeneity is the combination of different processes to transcribe one word, such as *ok1* for *aucun* in example 37, which involves phonetic reduction for *auc-* and syllabography for *un*. Similarly, *k* for *que* could be interpreted as the result of a phonetic reduction to *ke* followed by a logographic reduction selecting the initial letter. However, the form also could be the result of two phonetic reductions. The same analysis could be applied to *je* transcribed *g* in example 38. Here we enter the field of polyvalence.

38. *DA*

G *SÉ PLU SI* **G** *TÉ ENVOYÉ MON NOUVO NUMERO*
(*je (ne) sais plus si je t'ai envoyé mon nouveau numéro*)
"I've forgotten if I sent you my new phone number"

Polyvalence

Except for some cases of logography, spellings are based on a selection among the different values attributable to alphabetic characters and certain character deletions and substitutions applied to conventional spellings. Readers must make an effort and use their linguistic and contextual knowledge to arrive at the intended meanings, similar to the skills necessary to decipher a text written in ancient Egyptian hieroglyphs. Spellings that can be assigned multiple values are described as polyvalent.

Consider a borderline but instructive case in which a single letter can be read as a syllabogram, a logogram, or a phonetic reduction. Examples 39 and 40, which correspond to two successive sentences, illustrate contextual disambiguation. *t* first represents *te* in the logographic or phonetic—deletion of silent e—mode, then *tu* in the logographic mode. A syllabographic interpretation is excluded by the syntactic and semantic structure. The pattern *ça . . . dit de . . .* (literally = "does it say . . . to [verb]") needs to fill its gap with a dative clitic pronoun. In the sequence *si . . . n'a(s)*, a subject pronoun must be put before the verb. The numerous syllabographic readings such as the sequences *tais* (verb), *tes* (plural of second person possessive determinant), or *t'es* (*tu es* = "you are"), and so on, are contextually impossible.

39. *JDV*

sa *t* dit 2 mapelé?
(*ça* ***te*** *dit de m'appeler?*)
"do you feel like calling me?"

40.

Si *t* na vréman rien a faire
(*Si* ***tu*** *n'as vraiment rien à faire*)
"If you really have nothing to do"

For frequent words we find many spelling variants in the corpus, insofar as conventional spelling and neographic processes can combine in various ways. For example, *salut* ("hi") is written *salut, salu,* and *slt.* The word *nouvelles* ("news") appears as *nouvelles, nouvel,* and *nouvL.* More varied yet are the spellings of *demain* ("tomorrow"): *demain, demin, dem1, 2main,* and *2m1.* Moreover, a single writer can use variant spellings:

41. *DA*

tout ("every")
tou
tt

It appears that neography is not a standard but a set of procedures each writer uses in a particular communication situation while writing a specific message, and under the pressure of various constraints, as noted in the section above on modeling mediated communication.

CONCLUSION

The language used in SMS messages deviates in many ways from the prescriptive norms of standard French. This study has presented a systematic characterization of neography in French text messaging. Starting from a model of mediated communication that views language output as the interaction of technical, economic, communicative, and psychosocial constraints, I first described the context for text message production in France. Then followed the presentation of a taxonomy of linguistic phenomena, motivated by natural linguistic and semiotic processes, observed in a corpus of messages produced by young people. The realization of these processes is highly variable, reflecting the personalized and often playful nature of the private exchanges studied, and the freedom from prescriptive norms enjoyed by participants in this emergent form of mobile electronic communication. Some uses result in cryptic messages that must be deciphered as though in a secret code. However, such messages are intentional and creative, not intended to be incomprehensible to their recipients, and certainly not "inhuman," as some language purists have implied. Rather, they demonstrate common human characteristics, documented for a variety of languages, including tendencies toward economy of expression (Andrieux-Reix et al., 2004) and language play, seen earlier in many varieties of speech and paper-based writing, among children, young people, and adults,[30] as well as in various modes of CMC and other new media.[31]

This study raises several questions to which we cannot yet give definitive answers, although the available data suggest promising directions for future research. To what extent are the neographic formations identified here specific to French? To mobile text messaging? In which languages and modes of electronic communication are they preferentially found? How does electronic neography differ from that in nonelectronic environments, in speech and on paper?

Neography in SMS is a dynamic phenomenon based on local combinations of general mechanisms. Those mechanisms seem to be cross-linguistic, at least for Indo-European languages written in Latin characters. For example, Spanish text messages also contain phonetic spellings (*eyos* for *ellos*, "them"), deletion of mute consonants (*aces* for *haces*, "you make"), consonantal skeletons (*dnd* for *donde*, "where"), and logograms (*X favor* for *por favor*, "please").[32] Many of these same processes are evident in chat in English (Anis, 2004a) and may be characteristic of synchronous CMC in general, while not excluding the possibility of their occurrence in asynchronous CMC, especially in playful communication between friends or intimates.

As regards the relation between text messaging and nonelectronic writing, there is evidence that neographic spellings influence or at least coexist with conventional orthography. Advertisers use neography to seduce teenagers. The syllabogram *C* for *c'est* also appears in titles of TV programs, such as *C du sport* ("That's sports"). The similarity between SMS writing and informal daily correspondence seems to be another promising topic, in view of some examples and testimonies, for example, short messages produced within the family or messages written by teenagers during a boring class.

The exportation of SMS-like neographies to formal written documents raises educational concerns. Teachers are naturally worried about the acquisition of orthography, yet teaching spelling has always been difficult. Veith (2005) maintains that SMS spelling is too recent to be responsible for the problem and that SMS spellings are not typically found in school papers. Marty (2001) notes the positive linguistic skills stimulated by SMS neography but worries about its negative influence on primary-level pupils. She suggests writing class activities inspired by SMS processes that could make mastering orthography easier.

There is clearly a need for further empirical research into SMS language and its effects. To study variation seriously, we need a number of delimited studies focusing on criteria such as age, school level, adaptation of the sender to the receiver, communication objective, and so forth. The scope of the research should be enlarged to include languages represented in nonalphabetic scripts. Above all, much research remains to be done regarding orthographic variation in different languages, in order to confirm or disconfirm the naturalness of the processes posited here.

Acknowledgment

I'm very grateful to Hillary Bays, of the University of Cergy-Pontoise, who patiently helped make an earlier version of this text readable. Thanks to my young friends Delphine, Océane, Jean-David, and Rachid, who compiled the corpora, and to the anonymous reviewer. I express my deepest gratitude to Brenda Danet and Susan Herring, who gave me the opportunity to contribute to the development of a global approach to CMC and who helped improve my text.

Notes

1. SMS appeared with GSM standard in 1992.
2. Messages have become longer in the past two or three years but more expensive through the concatenation of two messages. A 163-character message costs the price of two messages.
3. Interview by Richard Wray, *The Guardian*, March 16, 2002.
4. There have been more mobile phones than land lines in France since September 2001: 34.6 compared to 34 million. By the end of March 2005, France had 44.9 million mobile phone subscribers (http://www.art-telecom.fr, retrieved June 25, 2005).
5. Paper by Estelle Dumout. Retrieved April 1, 2005 from http://www.zdnet.fr (no longer available).

6. See http://www.cultureco.com/forum/ (students in marketing), http://cera-astronomie .forumactif.com/ (astronomy), http://forum.pcastuces.com/ (PC hints), http://sortons.net/ forum/ (leisure plans in Normandy), all retrieved April 5, 2005.

7. See http://forum.aceboard.net/21288-3288-7792-0-.htm (ancalimëa, witchcraft), http:// www.expreg.com (PHP language), http://www.indierockforum.com/ (indie-rock), all retrieved June 29, 2005. The indie-rock site warns, *L'écriture texto ou sms est strictement interdite sur le forum* ("texto or SMS writing is strictly forbidden in the forum").

8. For discussion of the speechlike nature of Minitel messages, see Luzzati (1991).

9. In Anis (2004a), I analyze abbreviations in both French and English modes of CMC, using some of the same analytic categories as in this chapter, and conclude that similar mechanisms appear in both languages.

10. This model is an adaptation of Langacker's (1987) approach to language production, which draws on the connectionist framework.

11. I use the word "terminal" here to draw a comparison with other forms of CMC.

12. For example, *ý* never occurs in French. However, a typographer would note the omission of *ÿ*, which occurs in proper names such as Pierre Louÿs (a writer) and L'Haÿ-les-roses (a city).

13. The inverted interrogative and exclamation marks used only in Spanish are included.

14. In Latin rhetoric, *captatio benvolentiæ* ("search for benevolence") designates elements inserted to win the hearer's sympathy.

15. The "spokenness" of CMC is a topic favored by French researchers. A number of scholars interested in telematic messages, beginning with Minitel, have evoked hybridization between spoken language and written language. Debyser (1989, p. 18) suggested *un oral transcrit à la va-vite* ("spoken discourse transcribed in a rush"), and Jeay (1991, pp. 31–32) invented the *portemanteau* word *parlécrit* (*parlé* = spoken, *écrit* = written), which, according to French syntax, prioritizes spokenness. Following Vachek and his model of spoken norm and written norm (see Vachek, 1973), I proposed (Anis, 1999a) a third norm: "scripto-conversational": written language characterized by interactive features. See also Luzzati (1991).

16. Logograms are used in old Egyptian hieroglyphic script, e.g., ☉ for sun, ⊏⊐ for house. Many linguists (see Bloomfield, 1933) use the term "logogram" instead of "ideogram."

17. The closest parallel in English is the digrams ("th", "ch") when they correspond to the occlusive consonants /t, k/, as in such words as "Thomas" and "chaos," which could in theory be spelled "Tomas" and "caos."

18. Phonetic pronunciations are given in square brackets [ ] using the International Phonetic Alphabet. Phonemes are given between /slashes/.

19. A very popular cartoon for children, *Titeuf*, by Jep, rejuvenated this form.

20. In these examples, the letter printed in bold characters in the original is the letter that precedes the missing one; in the orthographic form, it is the missing letter.

21. We adopt here the terminology of Lucci and Millet (1994).

22. English inherited from French an "e" that is always silent, not only in words with a French origin such as *"page"* and *"savage"* but also in Saxon words such as "love" and "sleeve."

23. This qualification was proposed in the theoretical framework of autonomic graphematics, which studies written language independent of graphophonic correspondence (see Anis 1988a, 1988b, inspired by J. Vachek, most of whose papers have been collected in Vachek, 1989).

24. See B4 U GO at www.ezzetravel.com/B4UGO/. In French, *K7* was coined upon the arrival of the audio cassette: cassette audio ([kasɛtodjo]).

25. The symbol # denotes a syllable boundary.

26. This is a reference to Jean-Marie Le Pen, the far right rival of Jacques Chirac in the second round of the French presidential elections in May 2002.

27. We discard hyphens that are internal separators in compound words.

28. lol ("laughing out loud") is used as a signal of happiness and conviviality. In Anis 1999a, I compare it with a smiley.

29. This is an obvious mistyping, resulting from a confusion with the previous word. The expected form would be *til* for *tiens*.

30. See Huizinga (1955), Kirshenblatt-Gimblett (1976), George (1993), Crystal (2001b), and Sebba (2003a).

31. See Danet (1995, 2001), Werry (1996), Durscheid (2000), Sebba (2003b), and Androutsopoulos (2000, 2004).

32. The Spanish examples were extracted from a corpus of text messages produced by teenagers in interaction with a TV program, collected by Alcalá-Santaella Oria De Rueda (2004).

References

Alcalá-Santaella Oria De Rueda, M. (2004). Los SMS en los programas de televisión: De la economía lingüística a la ley del mínimo esfuerzo. *Información Pública*, 2(1), 143–163.

Andreini, L. (1985). *Le verlan. Petit dictionnaire illustré.* Paris: Henri Veyrier.

Andrieux-Reix, N., Branca-Rosoff, S., & Puech, C. (Eds.). (2004). *Ecritures abrégées (notes, notules, messages, codes . . .): L'abréviation entre pratiques spontanées, codifications, modernité et histoire.* Paris: Ophrys.

Androutsopoulos, J. (2000). Non-standard spellings in media texts: The case of German fanzines. *Journal of Sociolinguistics*, 4(4), 514–533.

Androutsopoulos, J. (2004). Typography as a resource of media style: Cases from music youth culture. In K. Mastoridis (Ed.), *Proceedings of the 1st International Conference on Typography and Visual Communication* (pp. 381–392). Thessaloniki: University of Macedonia Press.

Anis, J. (1988a). Une graphématique autonome? In N. Catach (Ed.), *Pour une théorie de la langue écrit* (pp. 213–223). Paris: Éditions du CNRS.

Anis, J. (with J-L. Chiss & C. Puech). (1988b). *L'écriture: Théories et descriptions.* Bruxelles: De Boeck-Wesmael.

Anis, J. (1998). *Texte et ordinateur: L'écriture réinventée?* Paris: Broché.

Anis, J. (1999a). Chats et usages graphiques. In J. Anis (Ed.), *Internet, communication et langue française* (pp. 71–90). Paris: Hermes.

Anis, J. (Ed.) (1999b). *Internet, communication et langue française.* Paris: Hermes.

Anis, J. (Ed.) (2001). *Parlez-vous texto? Guide des nouveaux langages du réseau.* Paris: le Cherche Midi.

Anis, J. (2003). Communication électronique scripturale et formes langagières: Chats et SMS. *Actes des quatrièmes rencontres réseaux humains/Réseaux technologiques.* Poitiers: Université de Poitiers. Retrieved July 5, 2005, from http://oav.univ-poitiers.fr/rhrt/2002/actes%202002/jacques%20anis.htm.

Anis, J. (2004a). Les abréviations dans la communication électronique (en français et en anglais). In N. Andrieux-Reix, S. Branca, & C. Puech (Eds.), *Écritures abrégées (notes, notules, messages, codes . . .)* (pp. 97–112). Paris: Ophrys.

Anis, J. (2004b). La dynamique discursive d'une liste de diffusion: Analyse d'une interaction sur typographie@irisa.fr. In S. Reboul-Touré, F. Mourlhon-Dallies, & F. Rakotonoelina (Eds.), *Les discours de l'internet: Nouveaux corpus, nouveaux modèles? [Les Carnets du Cediscor, 8]* (pp. 39–56). Paris: Presses Sorbonne nouvelle.

Bloomfield, L. (1933). *Language.* New York: Holt.

Catach, N. (1980). *L'orthographe française.* Paris: Nathan.

Catach, N. (1986). The grapheme: Its position and its degree of autonomy with respect to the system of the language. In G. Augst (Ed.), *New trends in graphemics and orthography* (pp. 1–10). Berlin: de Gruyter.

Crystal, D. (2001a). *Language and the Internet.* Cambridge: Cambridge University Press.

Crystal, D. (2001b). *Language play.* Chicago: University of Chicago Press.

Danet, B. (Ed.) (1995). Play and performance in computer-mediated communication. *Journal of Computer-Mediated Communication, 1*(2). Retrieved July 2, 2005, from http://jcmc .indiana.edu/vol1/issue2/.

Danet, B. (2001). *Cyberpl@y: Communicating online.* Oxford: Berg. Companion website: http//:pluto.mscc.huji.ac.il/~msdanet/cyberpl@y.

Debyser, F. (1989). Télématique et enseignement du français. In A. Dugas (Ed.), *Langue fran-çaise 83, Langue française et nouvelles technologies* (pp. 14–31). Paris: Larousse.

Dewaele, J.-M. (1999). Is it the corruption of French thought processes that purists fear? A response to Henriette Walter. *Current Issues in Language and Society, 6,* 231–234.

Durscheid, C. (2000). Spelling in electronic texts. *Muttersprache, 110*(1), 52–62.

Gak, V. G. (1976). *L'orthographe française.* Paris: Selaf.

George, K. (1993). Alternative French. In C. Sanders (Ed.), *French today: Language in its social context* (pp. 155–170). Cambridge: Cambridge University Press.

Herring, S. C. (2001). Computer-mediated discourse. In D. Schiffrin, D. Tannen, & H. Hamil-ton (Eds.), *The handbook of discourse analysis* (pp. 612–634). Oxford: Blackwell.

Huizinga, J. (1955). *Homo ludens: A study of the play element in culture.* Boston: Beacon.

Jaffré, J.-P. (2003). Orthography. In W. J. Frawley (Ed.), *The international encyclopedia of linguistics* (2nd ed., Vol. 4, pp. 386–390). Oxford: Oxford University Press.

Jeay, A.-M. (1991) *Les messageries télématiques.* Paris: Eyrolles.

Judge, A. (1993). French: A planned language? In C. Sanders (Ed.), *French today: Language in its social context* (pp. 7–26). Cambridge: Cambridge University Press.

Judge, A. (1999). Is French really open to outside influences? A response to Henriette Walter. *Current Issues in Language and Society, 6*(3–4), 250–255.

Kirshenblatt-Gimblett, B. (Ed.). (1976). *Speech play: Research and resources for the study of linguistic creativity.* Philadelphia: University of Pennsylvania Press.

Knowles, F. (1986). Information theory and its implications for spelling reform. *Simplified Spelling Society Newsletter,* Spring, 5–13.

Langacker, R. (1987). *Foundations of cognitive grammar: Vol. 1. Theoretical prerequisites.* Stanford, CA: Stanford University Press.

Lucci, V., & Millet, A. (Eds.) (1994). *L'orthographe de tous les jours, enquête sur les pratiques orthographiques du français.* Paris: Champion.

Luzzati, D. (1991). Oralité et interactivité dans un écrit Minitel. *Langue Française, 89,* 99–109.

Marty, N. (2001) Les textos, un danger pour l'orthographe? Retrieved July 1, 2005, from http:// www.enseignants.com/mag/article.asp?num_rbq=3&num_art=571.

Masson, M. (1999). Lire sans voyelles. *Panoramiques, 42,* 100.

Pierce, J. R. (1981). *An introduction to information theory: Symbols, signals and noise* (2nd ed.). New York: Dover.

Raymond, E. S. (1996). *The new hackers' dictionary* (3rd ed.). Cambridge, MA: MIT Press.

Rivière, C. (2002). La pratique du mini-message, une double stratégie d'extériorisation et de retrait de l'intimité dans les interactions quotidiennes. *Réseaux, 112–113,* 139–168.

Sebba, M. (2003a). Spelling rebellion. In J. K. Androutsopoulos & A. Georgakopoulou (Eds.), *Discourse constructions of youth identities* (pp. 151–172). Amsterdam: John Benjamins.

Sebba, M. (2003b). Will the real impersonator please stand up? Language and identity in the Ali G websites. *Arbeiten aus Anglistik und Amerikanistik, 28*(2), 279–304.

Shannon, C. E. (1948). A mathematical theory of communication. *Bell System Technical Journal, 27,* 379–423, 623–656.

Vachek, J. (1989). *Written language revisited* (edited, selected, and introduced by P. A. Luelsdorff). Amsterdam: John Benjamins.

Veith, M. (2005). Nuls, les élèves d'aujourd'hui? Retrieved July 1, 2005, from http://www3.clicanoo.com/impression.php3?id_article=98763 (no longer available).

Walter, H. (1994). *French inside out: The worldwide development of the French language in the past, present and the future.* London: Routledge.

Walter, H. (1999). French—an accommodating language: The chronology, typology and dynamics of borrowing. *Current Issues in Language and Society, 6*(3–4), 227–230.

Walter, H. (2001). *Honni soit qui mal y pense: L'incroyable histoire d'amour entre le français et l'anglais.* Paris: R. Laffont.

Werry, C. C. (1996). Linguistic and interactional features of Internet Relay Chat. In S. C. Herring (Ed.), *Computer-mediated communication: Linguistic, social and cross-cultural perspectives* (pp. 47–64). Amsterdam: John Benjamins.

5

THEODORA TSELIGA

"It's All Greeklish to Me!"

*Linguistic and Sociocultural Perspectives on
Roman-Alphabeted Greek in Asynchronous
Computer-Mediated Communication*

The advent of Internet technologies and computer-mediated communication (CMC) has given rise to novel linguistic phenomena. Early technical constraints privileged English on the Internet (Yates, 1996), and most earlier published scholarship focused on English-based interaction (Herring, 1996a). Subsequent technological developments, however, have facilitated the use of local and minority languages that are not written with the Roman alphabet (Nunberg, 1998; Paolillo, 1996; Warschauer, El Said, & Zohry, 2002, chapter 13 this volume).

This chapter investigates "Greeklish," the use of Roman-alphabeted Greek online. The first section presents a corpus-based analysis of Greek versus Greeklish postings to public discussion lists. The second section presents findings from a qualitative investigation, conducted via face-to-face interviews, of users' perceptions and value judgments of Greeklish. The overall aim is to contribute new perspectives to the study of electronic discourse in general and to the Greek sociocultural context in particular, where "in all controversies about every issue and at all levels, ranging from the scientific to the practical and from the ideological to the educational, language has always been at the forefront of discussion" (Babiniotis, 1995, p. 238).

HISTORICAL BACKGROUND
AND PREVIOUS RESEARCH

Greeklish is not the first instance of romanized Greek in the history of the Greek language. The idea of writing Greek with the Roman alphabet dates back to Byzantine times (Giofyllis, 1980). Zachos-Papazachariou (1999) refers to communities of Greeks who lived in nineteenth century Smyrni (in Asia Minor, at that time Greek); having experienced difficulties learning Greek spelling due to the great memory load imposed by its historical orthography, they resorted to use of the Roman alphabet. This practice was similarly adopted by Chiotes[1] and other Greek traders, who would send telegrams to their fellow Greeks in Roman-alphabeted Greek; it eventually became known as "Langue Francochiotica." However, none of these practices led to an expanded use or establishment of Roman-alphabeted Greek in any official practice in Greece or abroad.

The disposition of some scholars toward the adoption of romanized Greek surfaced in the 1930s, when Giofyllis and other linguists undertook a structured effort to reform the orthography of the Greek language. One of the main arguments of these scholars against the use of historic orthography was the confusion and the burden on memory it caused Greek writers, who were obliged to memorize a number of different letters or combinations of letters representing the same phoneme (Filindas, 1980a; Giofyllis, 1980; Karthaios, 1980). The adoption of the Roman alphabet would not confuse people with two alternative spellings of the same words in the same alphabet, the old, orthographic one, and the proposed phonetic spelling (Filindas, 1980a).

The supporters of romanized Greek, aware of the deep sentimental, traditional, and patriotic value that the Greek language and writing system held for the Greek people, contended that establishing Roman-alphabeted Greek would not negatively influence the formation of the Greek national identity. In particular, Filindas (1980b) argued:

> Every nation differs from each [sic] other, not of course in terms of the type of digits or letters of the alphabet it uses, but on the basis of its national character and its language, etc. . . . Thus, if we accept the symbols of the Latin alphabet, we have nothing to lose from our nationalism, nor will we stop speaking our language or be[ing] descendants of the ancient Greeks. (p. 34)

In this way, supporters of the Roman script dissociated the alphabet from sentimental or ideological beliefs, asserting that it was simply a tool for representing phonemes (Sideris, 1980). Nevertheless, official establishment of the Roman alphabet for the transcription of the Greek language was never realized.

The use of Roman-alphabeted Greek has recently become ubiquitous again with the spread of CMC, giving rise to a form of "digraphia" (DeFrancis, 1984), where users employ two different scripts in the composition of their emails: the Roman (in so-called Greeklish emails) and the Greek (in standard Greek emails). The functional motivation for the emergence of Greeklish can be traced to technical limitations that originally constrained language interaction in CMC in non-Roman-alphabeted languages such as Greek (Alevantis, 2001), Arabic (Palfreyman, 2002; Palfreyman & Al Khalil, chapter 2 this volume), Russian, and Bulgarian (Palfreyman, 2001).

In early computer systems, the most common coding system for the transmission of data was the ASCII code (American Standard Code for Information Interchange), which supported only the basic Roman characters, digits from 0 to 9, and a restricted number of punctuation marks and symbols. Greek CMC users were obliged to employ the Roman alphabet for their electronic communication. However, technological advances, particularly the development of the Unicode Worldwide Character Standard (Unicode Standard, 2002), have recently enabled CMC in a variety of scripts and languages. As of summer 2005, the Unicode system encodes more than 50 different scripts for European, Middle East, and Asian languages, including Greek.[2]

Despite this, Greeklish is still widely used in both synchronous and asynchronous CMC, including private email, mailing lists, chat rooms, electronic magazines, and webpages. Its main feature is spelling variation, whereby some Greek characters are transliterated with more than one Roman character (Androutsopoulos, 1999, 2000). These transliterations can be classified as "phonetic" (e.g., the Greek graph [η] is represented with the Roman [i]) or "orthographic/visual" (e.g., [η] is represented as [h]; note the visual similarity). In the former case, users employ Roman characters in order to represent the sounds/phonemes of the corresponding Greek characters, while in the visual/orthographic pattern, users conform to the orthographic conventions of the Greek language by visually representing the Greek letters with Roman characters, or even numbers.

Once again, then, it seems that Greek writers are faced with a dilemma as to whether the phonetic or the orthographic transliteration of their spelling system is the most appropriate. This is illustrated in figure 5.1. If a Greek user wants to type the word *Aθήνα* in the Roman alphabet, the two main options are "Athina" and "A8hva." The phonetic alternative, "Athina," should be familiar to most Greeks and foreign visitors to Greece since it is identical to the official transliteration according to ELOT standards[3] and is found on road signs, maps, and passports. Conversely, "A8hva" would be intelligible only to a competent—if not native—Greek user who could identify the visual similarity between "8" and [θ].[4]

The persistent use of Greeklish lends itself to a number of interpretations. First, technological limitations are still present in CMC due to the Greek Internet infrastructure, which lags behind that of other European countries, having not yet reached full compatibility. Furthermore, an incipient tendency has been documented by CMC researchers for sociolinguistic and social-psychological nuances to become interwoven with the practice of Greeklish,

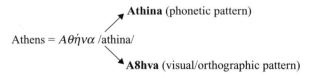

Athens = *Aθήνα* /athina/
→ **Athina** (phonetic pattern)
↘ **A8hva** (visual/orthographic pattern)

FIGURE 5.1. Phonetic versus orthographic transliteration.

for example, ease of writing and acquired habit, a communication strategy loaded with cultural semiosis (Androutsopoulos, 1999; Giannakoulopoulos, 1999; Koutsogiannis, 2004).

Greeklish has provoked extensive discussion in Greek society. The Academy of Athens released a declaration on June 1, 2001, expressing growing concern about threats posed to the Greek writing system and language as a result of the extensive use of the Roman alphabet in Greek contexts. Numerous publications followed in the Greek press by renowned scholars and linguists, and the issue was extensively covered in news portals on the Internet. Although some writers attributed negligible significance to the phenomenon, Greeklish was still perceived by many as a grave threat to the Greek language (Koutsogiannis & Mitsikopoulou, chapter 6 this volume).

Similar concerns are shared by Greek Internet users. In a study by Androutsopoulos (1999), nearly one-quarter (23.6%) of subjects identified the use of Greeklish as a problem for the Greek language. Similarly, respondents to an exploratory electronic survey (Tseliga, 2002) maintained that Greeklish is an unorthodox way of writing that restricts and undermines the quality of communication. They also attributed specific language practices to the influence of Roman-alphabeted Greek, such as increased use of English loan words, little editing resulting in more syntactic and grammatical errors, and an overall informal message structure in Greeklish emails. However, these perceptions and reports have not been verified with reference to authentic material.

This study seeks to examine the extent to which such observations are evidenced in actual emails, and whether and how Greeklish emails differ in their linguistic makeup from Greek emails. One motivation underpinning this empirical focus is the observation that "in many cases, humans tend to notice unusual occurrences more than typical occurrences, and therefore conclusions based on intuition can be unreliable" (Biber, Conrad, & Reppen, 1998, p. 3). Also, until now, no study has been conducted of Greek-to-Greek CMC tailored to the theoretical principles and practical requirements of the corpus-based approach. To the best of my knowledge, the only large collection of Greek emails (around 500) previously analyzed was that reported in Georgakopoulou (1997), who based her analysis mainly on methods of interactional sociolinguistics and the ethnography of communication. Georgakopoulou's study does not take Greeklish into account as a situational parameter.

This study investigates contrasting patterns of regularities and distributions of use of specific features in two small corpora of Greek and Greeklish emails. The main aim is to analyze the corpora with respect to the use of romanized Greek and perceptions associated with its use, as these interact dynamically with the context of communication, and especially with the Greek cultural context.

The study endorses Lee's (2002) view that "cultural and linguistic backgrounds of CMC users should . . . be taken into consideration because it is these properties which generate unique practices of CMC texts in different cultural settings (p. 22)." In Lee's research (2002, chapter 8 this volume), she showed that, although Cantonese electronic communication shares a number of textual features with CMC in other languages, many of these features (e.g., shortenings, verb form errors, creative orthographic representations, and code mixing) are employed in unique ways that reflect the specific linguistic and cultural setting. Similarly, Georgakopoulou (1997) concluded that the code alternations found in her study (e.g., word-internal or turn-internal alternations between standard modern Greek and *katharevousa*[5]) were contingent on the linguistic and sociocultural characteristics of the particular discourse community.

From a cultural perspective, Dragona and Handa (2000) have claimed to observe a process of "hellenization" of the Web, according to which Greeks

> are beginning to employ the Web as an economic tool and a mask offering the world the "Greek face" it expects, while manipulating the Web in a way that preserves Greek privacy from being overrun by yet another in a long series of conquerors, albeit a technological rather than an armed one. (p. 63)

Similarly, romanized varieties of colloquial Arabic (Palfreyman, 2002; Warschauer et al., 2002, chapter 13 this volume) are used extensively in informal online communication and seem to be challenging established norms since their use "in a new realm in which informality is considered acceptable and in which no authority has stepped forward to discourage its use . . . represents the appropriation of technology toward people's own communicative needs" (Warschauer et al., 2002, n.p.).

In contrast, Paolillo (1996), studying the use of Punjabi (a South Asian language) in an online newsgroup, reported that although "the strategic and selective use of Punjabi serves to signal Punjabi identity . . . Punjabi words are embedded in a kind of codeswitching that heavily favors English, because of its prestige and inter-ethnic value, and because of its associations with the modern technological environment of Usenet," (n.p.). Hence, Paollilo predicted that Punjabi language use will become even more marginalized in the future in online communities. Ess and Sudweeks (2003, n.p.) similarly warn that

> despite initial promises of democratization and liberation, CMC technologies can be easily appropriated by the powerful and only with difficulty by the powerless, so that the implementation and use of these technologies, in the end, only mirrors and reinforces prevailing patterns of power and advantage.

This debate points to the importance of embedding a study of Greeklish within the context of Greek language and culture and the larger global linguistic context, as it is unavoidably influenced by existing sociocultural dynamics.

METHODOLOGY

In an attempt to capture both the empirical facts about Greeklish and the sociocultural context in which it is embedded, this study combines quantitative and qualitative methods. An analysis of linguistic features in two corpora of Greek messages is followed by discussion of interviews with Greek CMC users about Greeklish.

Linguistic Features

The linguistic features analyzed in the two corpora were drawn from responses to an earlier electronic survey (Tseliga, 2002) and from previous literature on the email register in English (Baron, 1998; Cho, in press; Collot & Belmore, 1996). The features analyzed are grouped into three broad categories, as follows.

Use of Foreign Language Material

Employing a nonnative alphabet (i.e., the Roman alphabet) to compose an email was expected to accentuate users' motivation to integrate foreign words and expressions into their writing.

Informal Register

Analysis was conducted of specific lexical items and markers, classified according to their shared functions as hedging expressions, interactional discourse particles, and fillers. Greeklish emails were expected to display a higher concentration of informal linguistic features in comparison to Greek emails.

Register Markers as Paralinguistic or Extralinguistic Cues

Register markers are the distinctive features that distinguish particular registers or genres of discourse (Biber, 1995). The use of emoticons constitutes a unique feature of the electronic language register and has been interpreted as an indicator of emotional expressiveness and a means of conveying nonverbal communication in the absence of paralinguistic or extralinguistic cues (Crystal, 2001). The use of multiple punctuation, capitalization for emphasis, and lack of sentence-initial capitalization were also analyzed. These have been reported as means for compensating for the absence of oral and verbal cues and have been associated with playfulness and informality in the CMC context (Cherny, 1999; Cho, in press; Danet, 2001; Davis & Brewer, 1997; Tella, 1992).

Data

The data for the first part of the study are Greek and Greeklish postings to four Greek discussion lists and one newsgroup on the Internet in March and April 2001. The main criterion for selection of the lists was a high frequency of message posting, as this could indicate contributions from a great number and variety of users. Furthermore, all postings were drawn from open-access discussion lists and newsgroups (Ess and the AoIR Ethics Working Committee, 2002; Herring, 1996b). The lists covered a wide variety of topics. In all the selected forums, posters were free to use either Greek or Greeklish. Table 5.1 presents details of the two corpora.

The goal was to include the same number of authors and approximately the same number of words in each corpus, to make them comparable. Email authors were selected randomly, the only restriction being that they had to be consistent and not alternate between Greeklish and Greek writing. A sample of around 80 words was selected per author in order to ensure equal representation of each author and facilitate comparison among them. Because no average email length per message has been proposed for Greek or Greeklish postings in any previous study, the selection of 80 words per author was based on a calculation of the average posting length per day for each of the selected forums. In cases where postings had more or fewer than 80 words, the researcher used either excerpts or more than one posting per author, in order to reach the word limit.

The concordance package MonoConc Pro 2.0[6] was employed for automated quantitative analysis of the data, supplemented by manual analysis.

Interviews

A qualitative and contextualized approach was adopted for the second part of the study, comprising a series of semistructured interviews with a group of Greek Internet users. The main aim was to investigate users' preferences and stances toward Greeklish, the underlying motives behind the use of different discourse patterns and contrasting transliteration patterns, and the relationship of Greeklish to broader sociocultural phenomena.

A general interview protocol with three main parts was developed:

(a) "Knowledge questions" about users' experience with email generally (e.g., When did you start using email? What are the main reasons you use it? How many emails do you send per week?) and with Greeklish more specifically (How many of your emails are in Greeklish?) were asked as a means of creating a profile about the interviewee. Interviewees were also asked about the reasons behind their use of Greeklish.

(b) The theme of transliteration in Greeklish was approached from different perspectives (e.g., Do you write in Greeklish in a specific way? Do you

TABLE 5.1. Profile of the Greek and Greeklish corpora.

	Source					Total
	www .flash.gr	www .otenet.gr	www .pathfinder.gr	www .in.gr	grk.forthnet .users	
Greek corpus						
No. of authors	10	15	43	25	34	127
No. of words	811	1,215	3,495	1,998	2,752	10,271
Greeklish corpus						
No. of authors	10	15	43	25	34	127
No. of words	788	1,213	3,478	2,046	2,726	10,251

write in a way that sounds like or looks like Greek? Which of the two ways do you prefer?). Several more indirect questions were incorporated to elicit honest assessments of the prestige and status of Greeklish (e.g., Would you like to have a specified/standard way of writing in Greeklish? Do you communicate in Greeklish only with friends or with your boss/teacher/ organizations, too?). Questions about interviewees' aesthetic evaluation of Greeklish were also included (e.g., Do you like writing in Greeklish and why? Do you find Greeklish ugly, funny, difficult, etc?). Interviewees were also asked to reflect on the linguistic makeup of Greeklish by invoking examples from their own email communication (e.g., Does the fact that you use the Roman alphabet affect the way you compose an email? Can you give some examples?).

(c) I also investigated the perceived position of Greeklish in relation to the Greek language (e.g., What do you think of the state of Greeklish in relation to the Greek language? Does it pose a threat/is it just a tool for communication? How do you see the future of Greeklish?). These open-ended questions were to induce interviewees to think more deeply about the common perception of the Greek language as "weak," "threatened," and undermined by linguistic, social, political, and economic inequalities.

All interviews were carried out during December 2001 and January 2002 in three different cities in Greece: Athens, Thessaloniki, and Ioannina. Twenty-nine participants were recruited based on the following criteria: Participants had to be computer-literate Internet and email users with at least two years' experience using Greeklish. They also had to send a minimum of 10 emails per week. Effort was made to select a sample that would represent a diversity of participant characteristics, such as age, gender, and occupation. Although this lack of homogeneity could hinder the identification of shared patterns, it could equally be viewed as a strength of the study, since common patterns would cut across a heterogeneous sample (Patton, 1990).

Twenty-five out of the 29 interviews met the selection criteria and were included in the analysis. There were 12 males and 13 females, most between 25 and 34 years old. They represented various occupations (e.g., mass media, business, computing, languages, engineering). Most (16 interviewees) had between three and five years' experience with email use; seven interviewees had more than six years' email experience.

RESULTS

Analysis of Linguistic Features

Owing to the small size of the two email corpora, the present study does not purport to produce results generalizable to all Greek CMC. Nevertheless, the quantitative results shed light on many linguistic features used in authentic Greeklish, as compared to popular beliefs about the nature of Greeklish.

Use of Foreign Language Material

Because there was no extensive previous study of the use of foreign language material in Greek or Greeklish emails, analysis could not be based on a pre-defined list of foreign words or phrases. After perusal of the postings, cases of foreign language instances were noted and their frequency was subsequently tested in the corpus using the KWIC (Key Word In Context) format. This method was chosen because it displays occurrences of the search term with surrounding context, so that the researcher can evaluate which findings match the original query, eliminating irrelevant hits.

A "foreign language instance" is any word or phrase identifiable as a borrowing from or as a code switch to a language other than Greek. Foreign names of people, places, brands, companies, and so forth, were excluded. The results of this analysis are summarized in table 5.2.

TABLE 5.2. Frequency of foreign language material.

Corpus	Instances	Users	Frequency per user
Greek	74	39.4% (127)	1.48
Greeklish	124	53.5% (127)	1.82

Some of the most popular foreign words in the Greeklish corpus were "email," "forum," "CD," "sorry," "video," "internet," "sex," "message," and "pc" (= personal computer). Similarly, in the Greek corpus, words such as "forum," "humor," "post," "group," "sorry," "email," and "CD" were among the most frequent occurrences.

The tendency of Greeklish authors to incorporate more foreign-language material into their emails concurs with the hypothesis stated above that use of the Roman alphabet could motivate the incorporation of words and phrases from Roman-alphabeted languages. This prediction is further supported by the observation that 54% of the foreign language instances observed in the Greek corpus were written in the Roman alphabet. Users might find it more appropriate to write a foreign word in its original alphabet rather than adapt it to Greek spelling and morphological rules. It should also be noted that incorporating Roman-alphabeted units while typing a Greek email is time-consuming, since authors have to switch from one alphabet to the other (either by clicking on a particular icon on their desktop or by pressing Alt+Shift). Conversely, when composing a Greeklish email, users are already typing in Roman-alphabeted Greek; thus, to incorporate an English word requires no extra effort.

The possible contribution of other factors should also not be underestimated. It is likely that a greater number of the Greeklish postings were generated abroad, where there are often more technical problems with the use of the Greek alphabet. Furthermore, Treffers-Daller's (1994) distinction between "attested" and "nonattested" loans, borrowings that are or are not recurrent, widespread, and fully accepted in the speech community, is relevant here. In the Greek corpus, the nonattested loans were written in the Roman alphabet, probably because their use has not yet been widely established in the Greek speech community. Thus, "humor," classified as an attested loan, was never found in the Roman alphabet in the Greek corpus, but the nonattested loan "post" was written in the Roman alphabet in three out of four of its occurrences.

Informal Register

Informality was analyzed in the two corpora according to the use of the linguistic features listed earlier. The KWIC format was employed to analyze the linguistic patterns; the overall results are summarized in table 5.3. The two corpora are very similar along the dimension of informality.

Table 5.4 shows the results of analyzing each grouping of features individually. No major differences emerged from the analysis of the above categories by frequency per user for each feature. This can be attributed partly to the small sample of words that was collected per author (80 words), within which instances of the linguistic features did not always appear.

TABLE 5.3. Frequency of all informal features.

Corpus	Instances	Users	Frequency per user among those using at least one feature
Greek	148	70% (127)	1.7
Greeklish	144	64% (127)	1.8

TABLE 5.4. Frequencies of individual informal features.

	Instances per user	
Category	Greek corpus	Greeklish corpus
Mitigating/aggravating expressions		
Diminutives	1.30	1.40
Lexical items denoting diminution	1.25	1.23
Augmentatives	1.00	0.00
Intensifiers	1.20	1.10
Interactional discourse particles		
Amplifiers, emphatics	1.10	1.60
Discourse particles	1.10	1.20
Contractions	1.40	1.10
Fillers	1.00	1.25

Register Markers

Emoticons

A search for emoticons was conducted using KWIC, where the "word" was one of the emoticons presented in table 5.5. Although there was no great difference in the variety of icons used in the two corpora, Greeklish users were somewhat more likely to use emoticons. Given that emoticons are an exclusively digital phenomenon, their higher frequency in Greeklish may be associated with users' greater familiarity with or preference for a digital, innovative style of writing.

Multiple Punctuation

Multiple punctuation was examined with respect to exclamation marks and question marks, which are commonly repeated in CMC contexts. Greek users

TABLE 5.5. Frequency of emoticons.

Greek corpus		Greeklish corpus	
Emoticon	Instances	Emoticon	Instances
:)	2	:)	12
:))	1	:))	5
:)))	2	:)))	4
:-)	2	:-)	4
:-)))))))	1	:(	1
;-)	1	:-((	1
;-))	1	;)	1
;pppp	1	:>	3
;pppppppppppp	1	;p	3
Total	13	Total	34
Mean = 1.3 instances per user		*Mean = 1.9 instances per user*	

TABLE 5.6. Frequency of multiple punctuation.

Category	Greek corpus		Greeklish corpus	
	Instances	Frequency per user	Instances	Frequency per user
Exclamation point	28	2	32	2
English question mark	9	1.8	14	1.4
Greek question mark (;)	3	1	0	0

employ either the Greek question mark, which resembles the English semi-colon (;), or the English question mark (?); these two types were examined separately (table 5.6). No combinations of question marks and exclamation marks were noted in the corpora.

Use of multiple exclamation and question marks was almost identical in the two corpora. The main difference was that there were a few cases where Greek users employed the Greek question mark, while no Greeklish user did so.

Sentence-Initial Capitalization

The use of capitalization to mark a new sentence was analyzed by examining the first letter of all words after periods, question marks, and exclamation marks. This fell into three categories:

TABLE 5.7. Frequency of sentence-initial capitalization.

	Greek corpus users	Greeklish corpus users
Always capitals	91%	67%
Always lowercase	3%	18%
Mixed	6%	15%
N	127	127

- Consistent sentence-initial capitalization
- No use of capitals sentence-initially
- Alternation between capitals and small letters sentence-initially

The frequency of each category is summarized in table 5.7. Significant differences were found between the two corpora, with the Greek users showing a clearly higher tendency to conform to prescriptive grammatical rules about sentence-initial capitalization. This is despite the fact that capitalizing the first letter of each sentence slows down typing in that it requires an additional keystroke.

Capitalization for Emphasis

This category was also analyzed with the KWIC method in order to evaluate which cases could be classified as instances of "capitalization for emphasis." Two examples are presented below (with translations provided by the researcher).

> 1. . . . *aylia tous stis 27/10 kai htan panw apo [[TELEIA]]!!!!!!!Dystyxws den phga kai stis 28 all* . . .
> ". . . their concert on 27/10 and it was more than [[PERFECT]]!!!!!!! Unfortunately I didn't go on the 28th too but . . .)

> 2. . . . *a den katalaveno Na ton kleisoume sto [[PSIHIATRIO]], giati eine epikindinos. Kathe vradi* . . .
> ". . . I don't understand We should put him in a [[PSYCHIATRIC CLINIC]], because he is dangerous. Every night . . .)

Overall, emphatic capitalization appeared in both corpora with almost identical frequency: 27 Greek and 25 Greeklish email writers capitalized for emphasis.

Interview Results

Out of a number of interesting issues to emerge from the interviews, only those most relevant to the topics discussed in the preceding sections are pre-

TABLE 5.8. Emails sent per week by 25 interviewees.

Number of emails per week	Number of interviewees
≤10	8
10–30	7
30–50	3
>50	7

TABLE 5.9. Frequency of Greeklish emails among 25 interviewees.

How many of your emails are in Greeklish?	Number of interviewees
Almost all	15
Only a few	4
It varies	6

sented here. All responses were translated from Greek into English by the researcher.

Email Use

The interviewees' self-reported weekly production of emails in general and in Greeklish in particular is presented in tables 5.8 and 5.9.

Reasons for Using Greeklish

When asked to explain their reasons for using Greeklish, interviewees revealed multiple motivations. Although all referred to technical difficulties that had originally obstructed their email communication in Greek, the majority (16 out of 25) attributed their current use of Greeklish mainly to acquired habit. The following response is typical:

> There was a time when most programs wouldn't read Greek. Then, I learned the "language" of Greeklish, and since then, even from my company's account . . . from which I can send and receive [emails] in Greek, I write in Greeklish . . . it's a matter of habit now. (female, age 25, advertiser)

Interviewees' comments such as the following suggest that this habitual use is maintained because writing in Greeklish is more convenient, faster, and easier than writing in Greek, due to the lack of stress marks, lack of rigid grammatical rules, and the overall greater tolerance associated with Greeklish: "I would try to write Greek correctly, with stress marks and everything . . . but I got bored with it . . . the Latin [alphabet] helps me as a lot of abbreviations are used, half of the words are shortened . . . it is easier this way." (male, age 27, civil engineer).

Transliteration Patterns

Nearly half of the interviewees (11 out of 25) favored orthographic over phonetic transliteration. The main reason put forward was the visual similarity it affords with the original Greek text, thus preserving visually the original and "correct" spelling of words.

> I use all these [symbols], e.g., "8", "3" . . . I want the word to look exactly the same [as the Greek one] in terms of orthography . . . It's ok to use Greeklish but we should at least write orthographically. (female, age 25, law student)

> I was already annoyed that I had to use Latin characters and I said. . . . I don't want to stop using the alphabet . . . the Greek orthography . . . so, I will do it simply for this reason . . . as if I'm doing something in Greek . . . an illusion. (female, age 30, business manager)

At the same time, strong opinions were expressed by 12 participants that transliteration should not be standardized in Greeklish since Greeklish does not constitute a separate, codified language with grammatical or orthographic rules.

> Greeklish is a very special innovation . . . which should not be restricted by any grammatical or orthographic limitations in order to have one day a grammar of Greeklish let's say . . . (male, age 21, student of mass media)

> Everyone writes as they like . . . of course . . . this doesn't happen in Greek, but Greeklish is not a language in the sense of Greek or English . . . it is a hybrid, a combination and since each one has the opportunity to write it as they like, why not? (female, age 30, journalist)

These value judgments indicate that Greeklish is not accorded the same status and prestige as Greek, which is associated with standard, established norms. However, this lack of overt social valuation does not necessarily mean that Greeklish rates low in all users' value systems. A few users indicated that romanized Greek and its spelling variation enjoy a localized covert prestige relating to a within-users social significance or, in Labov's (1972) terms, group solidarity:

People who use Grenglish don't find it difficult to read ... Grenglish has become an issue by people who don't use it. The ones who use it, don't make an issue of it ... it's like asking an engineer if he would like his tools to have a different shape! (male, age 40, journalist)

This is not a language which has rules like all the other languages and no one can specify that this is wrong and this is right ... everything is comprehensible by both the sender and the receiver. (female, age 27, lawyer)

Use of Foreign Language Material

Contrary to the findings of the corpus-based study, more than half the interviewees (15 out of 25) claimed that writing in Greeklish does not increase their use of foreign expressions, and only nine people indicated that they use more foreign words when writing in Greeklish.

According to five interviewees, foreign abbreviations and short foreign words, mainly from English, are used in place of longer Greek words or expressions in order to compose messages faster and more easily:

There might be also a greater number of abbreviations in Greeklish ... you shorten words ... In chat ... "lol" which means "laugh out loud" ... and you adopt these generally ... [but] you can't write these [in Greek]. (male, age 28, computer engineer)

Yes ... There are many English words which in Greek are very long ... e.g., "λεωφορείο" [= bus] ... while you can write "bus" and that's it ... I think it's part of the whole game. (female, age 20, student of architecture)

Opposite views were expressed by other interviewees, who found mixing the two languages more confusing than facilitating:

If you write Greek with Latin characters, you get confused with the foreign words, because where /d/ is read as /δ/ [in Greeklish], all of a sudden it has to be read /d/ [in a foreign word]. (male, age 41, telecommunications manager)

This comment suggests that confusion caused by the use of foreign words is due to the use of the phonetic pattern of transliteration in Greeklish. Testing this claim with the whole group of participants generally confirmed it. As shown in figure 5.2, users of the orthographic rather than the phonetic transliteration pattern displayed a greater tendency to use foreign-language material in their emails.

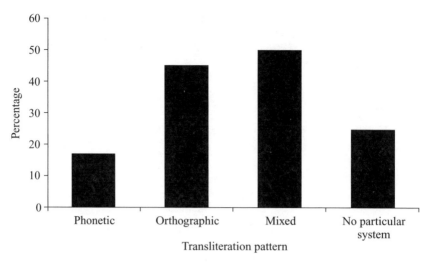

FIGURE 5.2. Users of each transliteration pattern who use foreign words in their emails.

Less Careful Editing

The interviewees appeared divided about the perceived association of Greeklish with a less carefully edited writing style. On the one hand, 12 interviewees admitted to careless use of punctuation marks, capitalization, slips, and typos when composing Greeklish messages. Typical are the following observations:

> Most Greeklish emails don't have punctuation marks . . . the question mark is always strange, because when you write Greeklish . . . others use the question mark and others the semicolon . . . There are no commas. (male, age 37, business manager)

> Generally you write a bit more messy . . . at least personally, because I write very fast . . . strange writings appear some times . . . and some letters will appear in the wrong place. (female, age 25, advertiser)

The main reason put forward for this practice was that Greeklish is a fast, modern, and easy means of communication characterized by a lack of explicit rules and a tolerance for deviance, as long as communication is effective and convenient:

> I won't pay attention . . . I will almost never use capitals . . . because when you write in Greek or English, you draw on the relevant rules; now that you don't

have any rules, or you use a combination, you don't really care to use all the necessary conventions. (female, age 27, language teacher)

As stated by the following interviewee, Greeklish is associated with a trend, a novel writing culture on the Internet that serves practical communicative functions and does not conform to traditional norms:

Here's an interpretation: what's the basic reason to communicate? To say something, to be understood, I'm in a hurry, I'm a busy person, I'm modern, why should I have to correct a small error when the other will understand what I want to say anyway? It's a kind of trend . . . not to correct the mistake . . . we don't have time for such things . . . Some try to invent rules . . . theoretically from what we have been taught . . . being faithful to a model of correctness . . . Older users, in order to show their authority, [have said to me]: "No, this is not written like this in Greeklish", but . . . who says that? (male, age 38, magazine editor)

Different views were expressed by 13 participants who argued that loose structure and inconsistency are not exclusive to Greeklish emails but relate to the overall informal, rapid, and spontaneous nature of electronic communication. This comment is representative:

The fact is that electronic messages are not composed carefully . . . they are written in haste, mistakes are made and . . . he [the sender] won't correct it, he won't read it again . . . he clicks on [a button] and it's gone! It has this element of rapidness, which of course is against quality . . . It's not only in Greeklish . . . it's generally [because] email is closer to spoken language, rather than written. (male, age 41, telecommunications manager)

Use of Greeklish in Formal/Informal Contexts

At first sight, interviewees' answers to this question appeared divided again: 11 interviewees said that they would use Greeklish in a formal context, while 12 answered that they use Greeklish only in informal situations. Overall, however, Greeklish was perceived as more appropriate for friendly and informal electronic communication, and Greek was reserved for more formal and official communication. Thus, three of the 11 interviewees reported that they would resort to Greeklish only if Greek were not available. Four participants noted that they would send a Greeklish email in the context of an official interaction, after ensuring that standard orthography, grammar, and overall structure were adhered to:

In my communication with people I didn't know from organising committees, conferences, universities, etc., at a more serious level . . . I have written Greeklish emails, adhering, however, to all the other forms of a formal type of communication, e.g., "Dear Sir, I thank you in advance . . ." (female, age 40, lecturer in linguistics)

Yes, I would write it, but I would maybe be more careful with my structure than when I am with a friend of mine . . . I'd be more careful to use the same letters for the same phonemes, so as not to confuse them. (male, age 36, information technology teacher)

Interestingly, two participants observed that use of Greeklish is mainly associated with digital literacy rather than with contexts of formality or informality:

If you are technologically literate and you address people who know about computers, you have to write Greeklish . . . so, I will use Greeklish only with [online] communities that have to do with computers . . . irrespective of their formality. (male, age 38, magazine editor)

Conversely, the others clearly differentiated functions and contexts of use for Greek and Greeklish. This distinction was attributed mainly to the playful, casual nature and the lower official prestige associated with Greeklish:

For me, Greeklish is a practical language but not a formal one . . . it seems funny to use Latin characters to give a formal tone to my text. (male, age 21, student of mass media)

Even if the organization was Greek, I would still prefer to write to them in English . . . it's more formal, it's not that the one who owns the organization is my best friend so that I can send it [email] in Greeklish . . . it might be misjudged, they might think it's carelessness . . . I don't think it has become acceptable to that extent so as to risk it on that level. (female, age 30, journalist)

Four interviewees stressed misunderstandings that could result from loose grammatical structure and carelessness in punctuation:

I sent an email to a publishing company one . . . and I wrote it in Greek . . . because I wanted there to be no doubt about the text I had written . . . I assume if I had written it in Greeklish some meanings might not have been conveyed correctly. (male, age 21, student of mass media)

Aesthetic Perceptions of Greeklish

Interviewees expressed varied aesthetic evaluations of Greeklish. Seven interviewees described it as a challenging, funny, and interesting linguistic innovation, owing to its peculiar spelling variations and creative writing practices:

Greeklish has a certain kind of charm . . . chat, for example . . . it's been there since the beginning of the Internet . . . it has charm as a way of writing. (male, age 28, computer engineer)

I like Greeklish . . . it's a challenge . . . sometimes, I try to write something, and the words don't look right to me . . . some diphthongs . . . some spellings . . . don't look nice and might confuse the other. So, I have to try to find something else. (male, age 27, information technology manager)

It is not surprising that most participants who made such comments preferred the orthographic way of transliterating their messages, which is also the most innovative. Use of Greeklish evoked negative feelings in seven interviewees:

I don't find it cute . . . because I have been used to considering that the orthographic picture of the words also has a practical value, the fact that I lose this when I'm obliged to use the Latin alphabet . . . is annoying to me. (female, age 40, lecturer in linguistics)

The majority of those who expressed such views preferred the phonetic/mixed transliteration pattern, that is, the more "traditional" one.

However, quite a few interviewees (10 out of 25) ascribed neither positive nor negative value to Greeklish, describing it rather as a neutral tool for facilitating communication:

[I find it] useful I would say . . . I do my job . . . it doesn't annoy me aesthetically, nor do I particularly like it . . . it's just that I can communicate this way. (female, age 27, language teacher)

It looks exactly the same as Greek to me . . . with just a little bit different way of writing, neither ugly nor charming . . . neutral . . . same thing, it doesn't look strange to me. (female, age 31, English as a foreign language teacher)

Use of Greeklish in the Future

The majority of the interviewees (14 out of 25) were confident that Greeklish would continue to be used in Greek-to-Greek CMC in the foreseeable future. Four participants based their view on the status of Greeklish as an established, convenient and unique tool of communication among Greek Internet users that allows for creativity and playfulness to emerge:

I think we will be writing in this alphabet for quite a long time . . . it's not necessarily bad; I think a lot of times it is used by the writers themselves, so as to lend a mysterious nature to what they write . . . as a secret code with the person they are communicating, precisely because it's not something conventional . . . they create a type of game with the system of writing, or otherwise, are ironic towards it. (female, age 40, lecturer in linguistics)

Two interviewees suggested that the inventiveness afforded by this novel practice will contribute to its future existence as it relates to a cultural characteristic of Greek users:

I think it [Greeklish] will exist as long as there are Greeks all over the world . . . A lot of times you have to experiment, and I think that for Greeks, the fact that they invent these tricks is . . . is part of their character, their nature . . . we Greeks have millions of things like that . . . and Greeklish is one of them. (male, age 37, business manager)

Conversely, quite a few interviewees associated future use of Greeklish with the overall domination of English on the Internet and global financial interests, which do not promote the use of less commonly used languages such as Greek:

In mobiles, there's a reason why I don't use Greeklish: it's because their technology is set up in a way that when you write a message, the first letter which appears is the Greek, not the English one . . . In PCs now, because . . . the whole environment on the Internet is English . . . and also the keyboards are made for Latin characters, I believe we'll continue using Greeklish. (male, age 21, student of mass media)

As for computers, basically everything happens as Microsoft wants . . . So, this is a very big hassle for a very minor issue . . . out of the 20 million people on earth [sic], there are around 500,000 Greek users for whom the issue should be resolved. Thus, neither Microsoft nor anyone else will bother to deal with it for such a small number of people. (male, age 40, journalist)

I remember one of my lecturers had created this computer program [for Greek] . . . which counted, searched for words, etc. . . . He rang an American company and told them that he wanted to co-operate with them . . . They told him: "Nobody cares. Dead language."[7] . . . Now, with the great rhythms of globalization, I don't know . . . I'm Greek, I want us to survive . . . but I see it as very difficult. (male, age 38, magazine editor)

Although future use of Greeklish was not viewed as a problem, concerns were expressed about the perceived endangered position of the Greek alphabet and Greek language in general on the Internet.

I think that as long as there is email, Greeklish won't die . . . but I hope that it won't prevail as the first alternative. I only hope that it won't be exaggerated . . . If there's a sensible use, I don't think there's a problem. (female, age 30, journalist)

CONCLUSION

The findings of this study indicate that Greeklish messages are generally more conducive than those typed in Greek to the activation of discourse strategies such as simplification, informality, and deviance. This conclusion is based on quantitative analyses of a set of linguistic features. Differences in the frequency and distribution of these features can be associated with different functional bases underlying the two corpora. The greater frequency of emoticons and less consistent sentence-initial capitalization in the Greeklish emails as compared to the Greek ones can be interpreted as evidence of the more informal character associated with Greeklish.

While both multiple punctuation and use of capitalization for emphasis are discouraged in formal writing, their use is familiar in comics and street graffiti, where they are regarded as standard conventions and not as mistakes (Danet, 2001). At the same time, "writing in this manner [in all lower case] probably also came to signal membership in the new culture" (Danet, 2001, p. 18), a culture that challenges traditional nor-mative expectations. The tendency to disregard sentence-initial capitalization is not surprising either, since tolerance of deviance is in the nature of Greeklish.

Viewed within the wider context of interaction between language and technology, Greeklish constitutes an example of the ability of modern *Homo flexibilis* (Hård af Segerstad, 2002) to display linguistic creativity so as to adjust to the exigencies of global and local networks of communication. As Warschauer (2002) explains, "while the Internet has strengthened the need for an international *lingua franca*—and that *lingua franca* is most frequently English—there are present other online dynamics that contribute to new forms of language pluralism" (p. 62). In response to such needs, Greek Internet users started using romanized Greek as a means of facilitating their online communication. Further evidence from interviews, however, suggests that—in addition to being a technological compromise—Greeklish has come to constitute for quite a few users a hybrid form of writing with a distinctive function (appropriate for use in informal contexts) and a culture-specific code that resists standardization and rigid rules and allows greater structural and spelling creativity and innovation.

No claim is made here that Greeklish constitutes a register in itself—not yet, at least—since its linguistic profile remains controversial and variable. However, Greeklish could be conceded as a case of marginal digraphia (DeFrancis, 1984; Grivelet, 2001) in the context of Internet communication, where it coexists with the use of the Greek alphabet. There also seems to be some indication that its overtly unofficial status and lower prestige are counterbalanced by a covertly positive evaluation by some users, for the freedom and novelty it affords. These findings show that analysis of users' expectations, evaluative stances, and attitudes toward linguistic phenomena can bring to the fore interesting aspects of their underlying motivations for the use of specific linguistic features.

Although these findings are of most interest within the Greek context, the perspectives emerging from this study could undoubtedly help to illuminate similar situations. The fusion of linguistic, cultural, and technological forces in the generation of novel literacy practices described here has also been aptly described by Kress (2000):

> Partly because of electronic technologies we live in an age in which the boundaries around cultures are becoming increasingly permeable . . . in this context, the rules about "proper behaviour", of which spelling is one instance, are now no longer controlled in one place, but are controlled in several places. (p. 25)

Rather than lamenting the "Anglification of the planet" (Nunberg, 1998), it is more fruitful to investigate current linguistic diversity in online cultural settings so as to gain a deeper understanding of the dynamics that will shape future developments in both online and offline linguistic contexts.

Notes

1. Chiotes were Greeks who lived on the island of Chios, famous for its sea trading.
2. Anderson (2005). Editors' note: This figure was given by Deborah Anderson, director of the Script Encoding Initiative (http://www.linguistics.berkeley.edu/sei/), in a lecture, Sterling Memorial Library, Yale University, June 30, 2005.
3. ELOT is the Hellenic Organization for Standardization responsible for creating national and international standards for the classification of Greek characters and words, the codification of Greek characters in 7-, 8-, and 16-bit representations, and the transliteration and transcription of Greek characters into Roman script.
4. The use of numerals such as 3, 9, or 7 to represent visually similar letters is also observed in Arabic online communication (Palfreyman, 2002; Palfreyman & Al Khalil, chapter 2 this volume; Warschauer et al., 2002, chapter 13 this volume).
5. *Katharevousa* is "a form of Greek using a mixture of words and forms from Ancient and Modern Greek, formerly used as the official language of Greece" (Holton, Mackridge, & Philippaki-Warburton, 1997, p. 510).
6. MonoConc Pro 2.0. is text analysis software written by Michael Barlow for corpus analysis. Its functions include searching for words, parts of words, whole phrases, and collocations and producing concordances, word lists, and frequencies of the search words.
7. This sentence was uttered by the interviewee as transcribed here, in English.

References

Alevantis, P. (2001). *I eisagogi ton ellinikon sta sustimata pliroforikis tis Europaikis Epitropis. Technika provlimata kai thetikes epiptoseis* [The introduction of Greek in the information systems of the European Commission. Technical problems and positive consequences]. Retrieved October 18, 2002, from http://users.skynet.be/p.alevantis/gr/index_gr.htm; no longer available.

Anderson, D. (2005). *Unicode and the university: How script encoding can change future research.* Guest lecture, Sterling Memorial Library, Yale University, June 30, 2005.

Androutsopoulos, J. (1999, April). *Latino-elliniki orthographia sto ilektroniko tachidromeio: chriseis kai staseis.* [Latin-Greek orthography in electronic mails: Use and stances]. Paper presented at the 20th annual meeting of the Linguistics Department, Aristotle University of Thessaloniki.

Androutsopoulos, J. (2001). From "dieuthinsi" to "diey8ynsh." Orthographic variation in Latin-alphabeted Greek (Greek). In: Y. Agouraki, A. Arvaniti, J. Davy, D. Goutsos, M. Karyolemou, A. Panayotou-Triantaphylopoulou, A. Papapavlou, P. Pavlou, & A. Roussou (Eds.), *Greek Linguistics '99: Proceedings of the 4th International Conference on Greek Linguistics, Nicosia, September 1999* (pp. 383–390). Thessaloniki: University Studio Press. English abstract retrieved December 15, 2005, from http://greekweb.archetype.de/greekmail/icgl99.html.

Babiniotis, G. (1995). The blending of tradition and innovation in modern Greek culture. In D. Constas & T. Stavrou (Eds.), *Greece prepares for the twenty-first century* (pp. 223–252). Baltimore: John Hopkins University Press.

Baron, N. S. (1998). Letters by phone or speech by other means: The linguistics of email. *Language and Communication, 18,* 133–170.

Biber, D. (1995). *Dimensions of register variation: A cross-linguistic comparison.* Cambridge: Cambridge University Press.

Biber, D., Conrad, S., & Reppen, R. (1998). *Corpus linguistics. Investigating language structure and use.* Cambridge: Cambridge University Press.

Cherny, L. (1999). *Conversation and community: Chat in a virtual world.* Stanford, CA: CSLI Publications.

Cho, T. (in press). Linguistic features of electronic mail in the workplace: A comparison with memoranda. In S. C. Herring (Ed.), *Computer-mediated conversation.* Cresskill, NJ: Hampton Press.

Collot, M., & Belmore, N. (1996). Electronic language: A new variety of English. In S. C. Herring (ed.), *Computer-mediated communication: Linguistic, social and cross-cultural perspectives.* Amsterdam: John Benjamins.

Crystal, D. (2001). *Language and the Internet.* Cambridge: Cambridge University Press.

Danet, B. (2001). *Cyberpl@y. Communicating online.* Oxford: Berg. Companion website: http://pluto.mscc.huji.ac.il/~msdanet/cyberpl@y/, retrieved September 13, 2005.

Davis, B. H., & Brewer, J. P. (1997). *Electronic discourse: Linguistic individuals in virtual space.* Albany: State University of New York Press.

DeFrancis, J. (1984). Digraphia. *Word, 35*(1), 59–66.

Dragona, A., & Handa, C. (2000). *Xenes glosses*: Literacy and cultural implications of the Web for Greece. In G. E. Hawisher & C. L. Selfe (Eds.), *Global literacies and the World-Wide Web* (pp. 52–73). London: Routledge.

Ess, C., & the AoIR Ethics Working Committee. (2002). *Ethical decision-making and Internet research. Recommendations from the ethics working committee of the Association of Internet Researchers.* Retrieved September 13, 2005, from http://aoir.org/reports/ethics.pdf.

Ess, C., & Sudweeks, F. (2003). Technologies of despair and hope: Liberatory potentials and practices of CMC in the Middle East. *Journal of Computer-Mediated Communication, 8*(2). Retrieved September 13, 2005, from http://jcmc.indiana.edu/vol8/issue2/essandsudweeks.html.

Filindas, M. (1980a). *Prepei na grafoume me to Latiniko alfavito* [We must write with the Latin alphabet]. In *Phonitiki grafi* [Phonetic spelling]. Athens: Kalvos. (Original work published 1929)

Filindas, M. (1980b). *To Latiniko alfavito apo oikonomiki apopsi* [The Latin alphabet from a financial point of view]. In *Phonitiki grafi* [Phonetic spelling]. Athens: Kalvos. (Original work published 1930)

Georgakopoulou, A. (1997). Self-presentation and interactional alliances in email discourse: The style- and code-switches of Greek messages. *International Journal of Applied Linguistics, 7*(2), 141–164.

Giannakoulopoulos, A. (1999). *I chrisi tis Ellinikis Glossas sto Diktyo I.R.C.* [Use of the Greek language in IRC channel]. Retrieved September 13, 2005, from http://www.utopia.gr/archive/irc.doc.

Giofyllis, F. (1980). *I aplopoiisi tis grafis me to Latiniko alfavito* [The simplification of spelling with the Latin alphabet]. In *Phonitiki grafi* [Phonetic spelling]. Athens: Kalvos. (Original work published 1930)

Grivelet, S. (Ed.). (2001). Digraphia: Writing systems and society (Special issue). *International Journal of the Sociology of Language, 150.*

Hård af Segerstad, Y. (2002, October). *Mobile text messaging and Homo flexibilis.* Paper presented at AoIR 3.0: 3rd International Conference of the Association of Internet Researchers. Maastricht, Holland.

Herring, S. C. (Ed.). (1996a). *Computer-mediated communication. Linguistic, social and cross-cultural perspectives.* Amsterdam: John Benjamins.

Herring, S. C. (1996b). Linguistic and critical analysis of computer-mediated communication: Some ethical and scholarly considerations. *The Information Society, 12*(2), 153–168.

Holton, D., Mackridge, P., & Philippaki-Warburton, I. (1997). *Greek. A comprehensive grammar of the modern language.* London: Routledge.

Karthaios, K. (1980). *I chrisi ton latinikon charaktiron gia ti grafi tis neas ellinikis* [The use of Latin characters for the writing of modern Greek]. In *Phonitiki grafi* [Phonetic spelling]. Athens: Kalvos. (Original work published 1934)

Koutsogiannis, D. (2004). Critical techno-literacy and "weak" languages. In C. Beavis & I. Snyder (Eds.), *Doing literacy online: Teaching, learning and playing in an electronic world* (pp. 163–184). Cresskill, NJ: Hampton Press.

Kress, G. (2000). *Early spelling: Between convention and creativity.* London: Routledge.

Labov, W. (1972). *Sociolinguistic patterns.* Philadelphia: University of Pensylvania Press.

Lee, C. (2002). Literacy practices in computer-mediated communication in Hong Kong. *Reading Matrix, 2*(2). Retrieved July 15, 2002, from http://www.readingmatrix.com/articles/lee/article.pdf.

Nunberg, G. (1998, October). Languages in the wired world. Paper presented at the Politics of Language and the Building of Modern Nations conference, Institut d'Etudes Politiques de Paris. Retrieved September 13, 2005, from http://www-csli.stanford.edu/~nunberg/WebPaper.html.

Palfreyman, D (2001). LINGUIST List 12.2760: Informal romanized orthographies. Retrieved September 13, 2005, from http://www.ling.ed.ac.uk/linguist/issues/12/12-2760.html.

Palfreyman, D. (2002, November). *Informal romanized orthographies in online communication.* Paper presented at 2. Tage der Schweizer Linguistik, Bern University.

Paolillo, J. C. (1996). Language choice on soc.culture.punjab. *Electronic Journal of Communication, 6*(4). Retrieved September 13, 2005, from http://ella.slis.indiana.edu/~paolillo/research/paolillo.publish.txt.

Patton, M. Q. (1990). *Qualitative evaluation and research methods* (2nd ed.). London: Sage.

Sideris, G. (1980). *I simasia tou agona gia to Latiniko alfavito* [The significance of the fight for the Latin alphabet]. In *Phonitiki grafi* [Phonetic spelling]. Athens: Kalvos. (Original work published 1930)

Tella, S. (1992). *Talking shop via email: A thematic and linguistic analysis of electronic mail communication.* Research Report No. 99. Helsinki: University of Helsinki, Department of Teacher Education.

Treffers-Daller, J. (1994). *Mixing two languages. French-Dutch contact in a comparative per-spective.* New York: Mouton de Gruyter.

Tseliga, T. (2002, October). *Some cultural and linguistic implications of computer-mediated Greeklish.* Paper presented at AoIR 3.0: 3rd International Conference of the Association of Internet Researchers, Maastricht, Holland.

Unicode Standard (2002). Retrieved September 13, 2005, from http://www.unicode.org/unicode/standard/principles.html.

Warschauer, M. (2002). Languages.com: The Internet and linguistic pluralism. In I. Snyder (Ed.), *Silicon literacies: Communication, innovation and education in the electronic age* (pp. 62–74). London: Routledge.

Warschauer, M., El Said, G. R., & Zohry, A. (2002). Language choice online: Globalization and identity in Egypt. *Journal of Computer-Mediated Communication, 7*(4). Retrieved December 5, 2005, from http://jcmc/indiana.edu/vol7/issue4/warschauer.html.

Yates, S. J. (1996). Oral and written linguistic aspects of computer conferencing. In S. C. Herring (Ed.), *Computer-mediated communication: Linguistic social and cross-cultural perspective* (pp. 29–46). Amsterdam: John Benjamins.

Zachos-Papazachariou, E. A. (1999). *Valkaniki Vavel. Politiki istoria ton alfaviton pou chrisi-mopoiithikan sta Valkania* [Balkan Babel: Political history of the alphabets that were used in the Balkans]. In K. Tsitselikis (Ed.), *Glosses, alfavita kai ethniki ideologia stin Ellada kai ta Valkania* [Languages, alphabets and ethnic ideology in Greece and the Balkans] (pp. 17–95). Athens: Kritiki.

6

DIMITRIS KOUTSOGIANNIS AND BESSIE MITSIKOPOULOU

Greeklish and Greekness

Trends and Discourses of "Glocalness"

The turn from page to screen has positioned the computer and the Internet at the center of the new postmodern communication ecosystem and has brought changes to the communication landscape and to language- and communication-related fields of study. Several studies have already attempted to outline the new communicative order and to analyze its consequences (Crystal, 2001; Herring, 2001). However, although much discussion has focused on computer-mediated discourse (CMD) and globalization, most theoretical analyses and empirical investigation have exclusively focused on the English language. Except for a "phobic" approach that views the Internet as a threat to less widely spoken languages (Crystal, 2001, pp. 1–2), there has been little research on social attitudes towards CMD, on specific discursive practices of CMD, or on the effects of the Internet on other languages.

Paolillo (1996) found that the use of South Asian languages online is rather restricted among native speakers. He notes, however, that the situation may change due to technological advances and the change from colonial heritage within the home culture. Yoon (2001) suggests that the symbolic power of technology in combination with the commercialization of the mass media leads to an uncritical acceptance of the dominance of English online. Hawisher and Selfe (2000) challenge the view of the Web as a culturally neutral literacy environment, in which, liberated from geographical, linguistic, cultural, and technical constraints, people enjoy the advantages of unimpeded contact and communication. They propose an alternative version of the global village narrative and note the emergence of a postmodern identity whose literacy practices are characterized by dynamic hybridity.

Acknowledging that there has been little attention to culture and communication in relation to computer-mediated communication (CMC), Ess and Sudweeks (2003) show that cultural values and communication preferences have played a significant role in the design and implementation of CMC. Using the example of Arab-speaking countries, they argue:

> CMC technologies operate less as the vehicles for intractable homogenization and more as catalysts for significant processes for hybridization, as individuals are able to consciously choose for themselves what elements of "the west" and their own local cultural identities and traditions they wish to hold to. . . . The powers of globalization and new technologies are not absolute; rather, they can be refracted and diffused through the specific values and preferences of diverse individuals and local cultures. (p. 3)

Warschauer, Said, and Zohry (2002) examined the interaction of the English and Arabic languages in online practices and found that, parallel to the English language, a romanized version of colloquial Egyptian Arabic is used extensively in informal email messages and online chats. They analyzed this tendency as an attempt by users to participate in the global, taking into account their local identity. A similar explanation is offered for the extensive use of Singlish (the colloquial dialect of English spoken in Singapore) in literacy practices on the Internet, despite systematic efforts by education policy makers and government officials to promote use of a standard variety of English (Warschauer, 2002).

The phenomenal growth of the Internet has also raised concerns regarding the future of local identities in some Asian countries. Arguing that the globalizing trend of the Internet is tempered by local sensitivities and concerns, Hongladarom (2000) suggests that local cultures are finding ways to cope with the impact of the Internet and are absorbing it without losing their identity. Hongladarom analyzed a Thai cybercommunity, showing that its participants do not wish to shut themselves off completely from the world, yet they do not want to become "mere blank faces in the globalized world."

Explanations for cross-cultural and cross-linguistic literacy practices on the Internet and social attitudes toward CMD practices often reference a contradiction noted in postindustrial societies between global networks and local identities, leading to the construction of hybrid postmodern identities. The concept of "glocal" has recently been employed as a refinement of the concept of "global" and a more descriptive term for what is happening today. It assumes a view of global culture not as a "unified" or a "socializing" institution into which local cultures integrate, but as a contradictory phenomenon, entailing a dialectical relationship between the global and the local. To describe this process, Robertson (1995) coined the term "glocalization," "the universalization of the particular and the particularization of the universal." We view glocalization as a dynamic negotiation between the global and the local, with the local appropriating elements of the global that it finds useful, at the same time employing strategies to retain its identity.

Recent research has also paid little attention to electronic literacy environments as "cultural maps" that represent the culture and the ideology of their origins (Selfe & Selfe, 1994). It is well known, for example, that the choice of ASCII (American Standard Code for Information Interchange) as the character set for the first personal computers and online communication created less serious problems for languages whose writing system is based on the Roman alphabet, such as German, French, and English, but greater problems for non-Roman-based languages, such as Greek and Chinese (Yates, 1996).[1] This long-standing difficulty goes beyond technical constraints and is related to ideological factors having to do with the use of English on the Internet (Koutsogiannis, 2004).

An example of a discursive phenomenon that developed in a non-Latin-based language is the use of "Greeklish" among Greeks in CMC contexts. Despite advances to overcome the technical constraints of the ASCII code, and despite the fact that Unicode has been designed to support the Greek writing system, problems persist with the use of the Greek alphabet in online communication. To avoid this problem, Greek Internet users began to make extensive use of the Roman alphabet in their writing of Greek, transliterating Greek with Roman characters, producing what is commonly known as "Greeklish" (Greek + English). Greeklish is characterized by spelling variation in which Greek alphabet characters may be transliterated with one or more Roman equivalents. It is used quite extensively in emails and chat groups and tends to become a script register among young people. Although it is used more in social than professional communication, Greeklish is also found in formal electronic communication (e.g., in government departments and universities), where both writing systems—Greek and Greeklish—are often employed to avoid communication problems due to technical constraints (e.g., varied technological platforms, or international communication in Greek).

Greeklish has become the focus of linguistic and sociolinguistic research (Georgakopoulou, 1997; Androutsopoulos, 2000; Tseliga, chapter 5 this volume). However, Greeklish is not merely a new variety of writing but a wider sociocultural and ideological phenomenon that causes heated debates in the media and divides intellectuals, academics, and the public. This is understandable considering that writing is not simply a means of recording the spoken word but is also a cultural symbol, one that, in the case of Greece, has been in use since ancient times.

The issue of language has long been a minefield of confrontations and conflict in Greek social and political life. As we argue further below, the duration and intensity of this conflict are not due to issues of language as such, but to ideological, social, and political questions at stake in critical periods of Greek history. Moreover, although in the past the debate was primarily at the level of language planning, in recent years discussions concerning the Greek language have focused on the effects of Greece joining the European Union and on the effects of extensive use of English. Since the end of the last century, like a number of other countries on the (European) periphery, Greece has been in a critical transitional stage regarding full membership in the European Union and the more general economic and sociopolitical changes that globalization entails. This new reality means new challenges and an overall reexamination of what has hitherto been regarded as given. We argue that, just as issues of the country's increasingly global orientation have found expression in language debates in critical historical periods in the past, the same process can also be traced in today's debate about Greeklish.

THE GREEK LANGUAGE AND ALPHABET AS IDEOLOGICAL SIGNS

The Language Issue

Positioning Greeklish within its wider sociocultural context entails an understanding of age-old confrontations about the Greek language, known as the "language issue"—confrontations with broader ideological, social, and political content (Christidis, 1999). The history of these confrontations provides the context for our discussion of Greeklish. It is our contention that attitudes and positions concerning Greeklish today have the same origin as positions in past debates concerning the Greek language.

Already in the first century B.C., a linguistic "schism" was evident between spoken and written Greek. The written language, used by the intellectuals of the age, ignored the spoken language, regarding it as the result of a process of corruption and thus inferior to its ancestor, and sought to imitate classic Attic language. This continued in the following centuries and during the Byzantine period.

In modern times, conflict over language made its appearance for the first time in the early nineteenth century, within the context of efforts of intellectuals to discover an appropriate vehicle for the dissemination of ideas of the Enlightenment (Delveroudi, 2000) and to establish a national language for the modern Greek state. It was then that *Katharevousa* was adopted as the official language.[2] The choice was not random but expressed specific ideological and political tendencies (Fragoudaki, 2001) that aimed to prune out foreign influences and to link modern to ancient Greek. This option was also a declaration of Greece's European orientation, given the high regard for the ancient Greek heritage in Europe. This resulted in diglossia (Ferguson, 1972), a linguistic split between *Katharevousa*, which was closer to ancient Greek and was used in administration and education, and the everyday language spoken by the majority of the population, *Demotic* Greek.

After 1870, when an attempt at broader modernization of the Greek state began (Terzis, 1998), diglossia began to fuel acute confrontations between the supporters of the two differing approaches to the country's official language: supporters of *Katharevousa* versus those of *Demotic* Greek. With the passage of time, these two poles came to be the expression not simply of two different approaches, but of two different worlds upholding entirely different views on education and the general orientation of the country (Stavridi-Patrikiou, 1999). Although the debate officially ended in 1976 in favor of the spoken language, fierce confrontations over issues of language—conflicts that are in essence about the broader orientation of education and of the country—continue today, to such an extent that some people talk about the creation of a "new language issue" (Fragoudaki, 2001).

The Greek Alphabet

It is estimated that the alphabet as a system of writing was first used by the Greeks in the eighth century B.C.[3] and was an adaptation of the Phoenician system of writing (Woodard, 1997). In spite of the changes that took place in the meantime in the pronunciation of Greek, the alphabet had already acquired its own authority, since it was in this that ancient Greek thought had been set down and remained to a significant degree unchanged down to the ninth century A.D. (Byzantium). Then, together with the introduction of lowercase script, diacritics,[4] which had already been used since the second century B.C. by the grammarians of Alexandria, came to be employed more extensively.

The accent system of Greek was simplified in 1982, retaining only one accent and abolishing the two breathings (see note 4). This reform also provoked resistance and has not been adopted universally even today (Hatzisavvidis, 1986). Generally, the introduction of the single-accent system was seen as a transitional stage that could lead to abandonment of the Greek alphabet, and for this reason was regarded by many as an "antinational" act.

A symbolically and ideologically charged attitude toward the alphabet is not exclusive to Greeks. It is well known that the choice of writing systems by various communities is often an ideological sign of national orientation and identity[5] and that attempts at spelling reforms in various languages have encountered major opposition, deriving from a view that the historicity of the languages is being lost (Karantzola, 1999). Consequently the emergence of Greeklish could not have remained merely that of a new writing variety for electronic environments, but sooner or later would turn into a new ideological and political issue. This is precisely the stance of the Academy of Athens, which deplores the phenomenon and warns of the wide-ranging dangers with which it is fraught.

Moreover, from the brief review presented above, it becomes clear that the question of the language and its alphabet is not an exclusively linguistic issue. It has provided a fertile field in which serious confrontations of ideas and behaviors have been cultivated in crucial phases of the development of Greek society. These confrontations expressed the ideological conflicts of society as a whole and have crystallized into two clearly distinguishable trends: one devoted to the greatness of the past, and the other open to new explorations.

The words and symbols with which we grow up and that we inherit shape us as specific historical and sociocultural subjects (Bakhtin, 1986). In this reasoning, the views that have been argued on the "language issue" during its long history have played and continue to play a determining role in the shaping of modern Greek identity. Thus, discussions about the authenticity of the language have been, at a deeper level, discussions about the authenticity of Greek identity (Fragoudaki, 2001), on the basis of which the "linguistic mythology of the nation" (Christidis, 1999, p. 156) has been created.

The "language issue" bequeathed to Greek society ready-made patterns of interpretation of linguistic phenomena, a repertoire or "tool kit" of habits and beliefs from which people construct "strategies of action" (Swidler, 1986). These ready-made patterns of interpretation are the key to understanding any new attitude to questions of language from that point on (e.g., simplification of the Greek accent system, threats from the dominance of English, romanization of the Greek alphabet).

DESCRIPTION OF THE STUDY

In January 2001, the Academy of Athens, a prestigious Greek social body known for its conservative orientation, issued a statement concerning the rise of Greeklish and the possible substitution of the Greek by the Roman alphabet, as a result of increased use of Greeklish on the Internet. This statement, which was signed by 40 distinguished members of the Academy of Athens, was released to the press and gave rise to a heated debate in the media.

The corpus used in this study consists of 58 newspaper texts that appeared between January and March 2001 in the Greek press, all written as a reaction to the Academy's text on Greeklish. It makes available a condensed expression of a variety of views, put forward in the heat of the moment in a very short period. In order to ensure that the corpus is representative of the different types of texts that appeared in the Greek press, we used the archive of the Greek Language Center (GLC), a research institute of the National Ministry of Education and Religious Affairs, which is located in Thessaloniki. The GLC uses a press clipping service that searches in the Greek daily and Sunday press nationwide on a daily basis and locates all publications concerning the Greek language.

The texts in the corpus are drawn from 23 different newspapers. Twelve texts come from morning newspapers (*Avgi, Vima, Kathimerini, Makedonia, Ellinikos Vorras*), 25 from evening papers (*Vradini, Elefteri Ora, Eleftheros, Eleftherotipia, Estia, Thessaloniki, Nea*), 2 from the daily financial press (*Express, Naftemporiki*), 14 from Sunday papers (*Apogevmatini tis Kiriakis, Avgi tis Kiriakis, Ethnos tis Kiriakis, Prin, To Paron, Tipos tis Kiriakis*), 1 from a weekly newspaper (*Nei Anthropi*), and 2 from provincial papers (*Eleftheria Larissas, Tipos Chalkidikis*). These texts cover a variety of newspaper genres—articles, editorials, interviews, readers' letters, statements by professional organizations—and vary in length. They were written by linguists, philologists, journalists, professors from various fields, computer experts, and a few laypeople.

This study is a Critical Discourse Analysis of views of Greeklish in the texts. Adopting a critical discourse-analytic perspective from Fairclough (1992, 2003), the study views discourse both as action, a form of social practice, and as a social construction of reality, a way of representing social practice. Viewing discourse as interaction relates discourse to other social practices, thus establishing a relationship between the discursive event and the social practice. It promotes an understanding of discourse as always social and cultural, thus excluding a view of language as a purely individual activity. Viewing discourse also as constructing social reality allows an understanding of discourse as representing forms of knowledge and aspects of social reality. Our analysis of the corpus subsumes both uses of the term, attempting to bring them together. It starts with the analysis of "discourses," defined as the language used in representing social practice from a particular point of view. This analysis reveals the various heterogeneous and conflicting representations of Greeklish online.

The next section presents the three main trends identified, with the purpose of examining the various elements of their stances and attitudes. At the same time, we investigate the degree to which these views reflect deeper upheavals and aspirations that are the result of new situations and quests worldwide. We are also concerned with the following questions: To what extent do attitudes toward Greeklish highlight the phenomenon of "glocalness," which recent literature has pinpointed as predominant in the age of globalization? To what extent is this phenomenon truly recent? What are its main features in the case of Greeklish?

ANALYSIS

First Trend: A Retrospective View

This seems a rather strong and solid view that is developed in 38 of the total of 58 texts in the corpus. It is "retrospective" in the sense that it is shaped by national, religious, and cultural narratives (Bernstein, 1996) that are recontextualized to ensure the stability of the past into the future. What primarily characterizes this trend is the use of the glorious past as a reference point to provide answers for the future.

The texts following this trend come from 15 different, mainly conservative, newspapers, support the Academy's view and provide further argumentation in its favor. They praise the Academy for the specific initiative that they often view as an act of resistance to the threat of globalization. The Academy is represented as the "guardian of our language" (*Vradini* 18.1[6]). Two metaphorical discourses hold a prominent position in this trend. The first is a metaphorical discourse of resistance whose traces are frequently found in formulations such as "we should extol the vigorous resistance of the Supreme Intellectual Institution of our country" (*Vradini* 18.1), "forty

Academics express their intention to resist" (*Kathimerini* 7.1), "angry reaction" (*Tipos Chalkidikis* 7.1), and "to fend off the threat and ward off the dangers" (*Vradini* 15.1).

This discourse of resistance is embedded within a metaphorical discourse of military attack. Greeklish is construed as a threat against the Greek language that needs to be protected from "foreign" invasion: "standing guard over the Greek language," "we are called upon to defend it with vigor" (*Ellinikos Vorras* 21.1), "they [academics] draw attention to the major danger of a very heavy blow" (*Estia* 31.1), "others too will wake up to this national danger" (*Vradini* 18.1), "in the battle for Greek" (*Tipos tis Kiriakis* 6.1). The Academy's statement was primarily about the danger of substituting the Roman for the Greek alphabet. However, in texts of this trend, discussion about the Greek alphabet soon moves on to discussion about defending the Greek language and consequently Greek culture and the country. As stated in one of the articles, "throwing off the national system of writing is a betrayal of the national ethos" (*Tipos tis Kiriakis* 6.1):

> The Academy of Athens . . . sounds the warning bell and calls upon the people in a reveille sounded against this unholy and senseless movement . . . [The language] is the breakwater for every foreign influence and propaganda. "If you want a people to lose its national consciousness, make it lose its language," Lenin used to say.
>
> The nation is living through critical times. What is needed is watchfulness, alertness, planning, A REPLY.
>
> **We have nothing "save Liberty and Language." Solomos.**
>
> **Let us do it !!!** (*Nea* 16.1g) (emphasis and bold in original)

Formulations such as "[the language] is the breakwater for every foreign influence and propaganda," "[the Academy] sounds the warning bell and calls upon the people in a reveille," "The nation is living through critical times," "What is needed is watchfulness, alertness, planning," together with the reference to Lenin and to the national poet Dionysios Solomos strongly evoke a national discourse. The language needs to be defended in the same way that a country needs to be defended from an external threat. According to this view, Greeklish constitutes a threat to the language and to the country. We must protect the Greek language, the argument goes, from any "external" invasion that threatens it. This metaphorical discourse of national threat is also found in the titles of articles, as lexical items such as "danger signal," "attack," "guard," and "protection" indicate: "Warning signal from 40 Academics" (*Kathimerini* 7.1), "The attack upon our language" (*Estia* 7.3), "For the protection of the Greek Language" (*Eleftheri Ora* 23.3).

Other prominent discourses in this trend are historical. In many newspaper texts, the theme of ancient Greek history is prominent: "Our language . . . has for 3,000 years enlightened the whole world" (*Apogevmatini tis Kiriakis* 14.1g), "Our language, the most ancient, but always contemporary and alive, this language may not suffer degradation by the abolition [of the alphabet] at our own hands" (*Ellinikos Vorras* 21.1). The ethnocentric view developed here is based upon the importance of Ancient Greek culture:

> The Greek language has deep historical roots which it has maintained throughout its age-old history and development, and it is neither conceivable nor permissible for us to adulterate our pronunciation by the introduction of Latin characters. . . . This language of ours has preserved our culture and history in the multifarious vicissitudes of the nation, and, moreover, under harsh Ottoman tyranny. (*Vradini* 18.1)

Within the ethnocentric historical discourse, a number of comparisons are made that are important for their ideological underpinnings. For instance, the Greek language is praised for its aesthetics: "The Greek alphabet takes precedence over the Latin because it comes from the Phoenician and the Phoenicians were among the first civilized peoples upon earth. Consequently, there is also chronological precedence" *(Eleftheros* 15.1). Moreover, the Latin (or Roman) alphabet was not only the second to appear but is also a "subproduct" of the Greek alphabet: "Now, in the very nature of things we are obliged also to use the Latin alphabet, which is, of course—as everybody knows—a subproduct of the Greek alphabet; and this too is Greek, it is the Chalcidian alphabet of Aeolian Cyme" (*Apogevmatini tis Kiriakis* 14.1g).

Embedded in the historical discourses is a religious discourse that connects the Greek Orthodox tradition with Greek history: "The Greek communities with a holy zeal maintained Greek schools to preserve our language, with the Church as protagonist, under the aegis of the Ecumenical Patriarchate" (*Elefterotipia* 22.1). The Church is construed as the "protagonist," the main institution that at difficult times in Greek history served as a connecting link of Hellenism. The diachronic element is often stressed, and the connection between the ancient Greek spirit and Christian tradition is represented as strong: "From the works of Plato, Aristotle, Sophocles, Socrates, Thucydides, and the other classical authors, but also from texts of the Fathers of our Christian religion, the Gospels, the Byzantine hymnographers and of all the other written texts of our Church, the Greek language took on a universal character, of diachronic importance" (*Ellinikos Vorras* 21.1). Moreover, the role of the Greek language, in which most books of the New Testament were written, in the spread of Christianity is stressed: "The Greek language was the world of the Gospel and the means of preserving Christian ideas" (*Vradini* 18.1).

New technologies are represented as threatening the extinction of the Greek alphabet and consequently of the Greek language: "Our language . . . is being displaced by the new technology," "Computers have now forced us in our everyday life to use the Latin alphabet" (*Apogevmatini tis Kiriakis* 14.1g). A distinguished member of the Academy of Letters, when asked by a journalist: "Is what you are saying above all that the main danger comes from computers?" replied: "Yes. I'm not going into these mechanical means, I'm going into the issue itself, which is precisely what is being cultivated. And what is being cultivated is not only the replacement of the alphabet, but even of our spelling" (*Apogevmatini tis Kiriakis* 14.1b).

Of particular interest are conflicting representations of globalization in this trend. In the Academy's text and in the newspaper texts that support the Academy's view, globalization is construed negatively in the case of Greeklish and the spread of new technologies. On the other hand, globalization is construed somewhat positively in the case of ancient Greek as the global language of its time: "The universality of the Greek language is demonstrated by the conception, the originality, the profundity and the wealth of ideas and by its globalization through Alexander the Great" (*Vradini* 18.1), "The Greek language has been for thousands of years the instrument of the intellectual cultivation and development of the whole of humanity" (*Ellinikos Vorras* 21.1). The role of the Greek language, the "source and mother of other languages" (*Nea* 16.1g), in the foundation of important fields of study such as philosophy and mathematics is praised, and so is its contribution to world literature: "At its very first historical steps it produced the two immortal Epics the Iliad and the Odyssey" (*Ellinikos Vorras* 21.1). It is of considerable interest that whereas the importance of the Greek language at a global level is praised, and Greek culture is construed as the main element of global culture, the current globalization phase is construed negatively as a threat to the Greek language.

Second Trend: A Prospective View

Texts in this trend position themselves against the Academy's statement and attack its arguments that Greeklish is a threat to the Greek language. They generally adopt a positive stance toward technology. They minimize the importance of arguments presented in the Academy's statement by criticizing the rhetoric of the Academy's text, the language features selected, the exaggeration embedded in the arguments, and the technophobia that seems to penetrate the text. Interestingly, there is frequent reproduction of the arguments of the first trend. This reproduction, however, serves as a starting point in the process of refuting these arguments as wrong or lacking in importance. The Academy's text is called a "panic-stricken" statement and "a monument of language-defensive frenzy" (*Vima* 21.1).

It is often suggested in texts in this trend that the Academy's text involves traditional rhetoric concerning the Greek language, which represents it as ancient, as having "enriched Latin and all main European languages" and "transmitted culture all over the world." This rhetoric, also supported by historical and religious discourses as mentioned in the preceding section, is not new. It views Greeklish as a threat and has been present in other discussions concerning the Greek language in the past (e.g., discussions concerning *Demotic* and *Katharevousa*). The language used in the Academy's text is also a target of criticism. The use of *Katharevousa* expressions and vocabulary not used today is mentioned in a number of different texts in this trend:

"Moreover, [the Academy's text] employs a spelling of other times (not the official spelling taught in schools today) and a vocabulary which arbitrarily lapses into *Katharevousa*" (*Nea* 20.1).

At this point, it is worth drawing attention to some differences concerning the language features selected in the texts of the first two trends. Whereas texts in the first trend to a great extent draw upon vocabulary that has its origins in *Katharevousa*, texts in the second trend are characterized by a tendency toward conversationalization and informalization of discourse (Fairclough, 1992), as the following formulations indicate: "I'll explain that right away" (*Thessaloniki* 15.1), "let's say this once and for all" (*Vima* 28.1b), "I hope the ladies and gentlemen of the Academy will forgive me, but I think . . ." (*Nea* 20.1).

Another point of criticism of the original text refers to the use of exaggeration. The argument that is developed in a number of texts in the second trend is that the Academy's text deals with a nonexistent problem: "Do we, perhaps, like worrying? Do we, perhaps, feel better when we are in danger?" (*Vima* 28.1a), "the concern is unjustified" (*Kathimerini* 1.2), "the Academy of Athens has invested the issue with its authority and elevated it into a serious matter which is in essence non-existent" (*Vima* 28.1b).

Moreover, it is repeatedly stressed that the Academy's text is imbued with technophobia: "some kind of phobia has afflicted these distinguished intellectuals" (*Kathimerini* 1.2), "the careful reader can detect certain misunderstandings or imperfect knowledge of the actual facts—even a veil of technophobia" (*Kathimerini* 14.1). It is suggested that this technophobia is the result of misunderstanding or inadequate knowledge of technological advances. It is also pointed out that the Academy's text came late, when the problem with Greek fonts no longer existed: "Instead of proposing solutions, they denounce . . . computers and world-wide communication, instead of helping to deal with a technical problem" (*Nea* 20.1).

Two types of discourses are mainly employed in this trend. The first is an instrumental technical discourse that identifies the source of the problem: "The reason why this form of Greek is widely used has to do with computer software, which initially did not make it possible to use the Greek alphabet" (*Makedonia* 14.1), and offers solutions: "Today, in all the software commonly in use on the Internet you can use the complete alphabet, in accordance with ISO-8889-7 standards. Also, very soon, when the international Unicode standard is in general use, the Greek alphabet (and the polytonic system) will be inherently supported" (*Kathimerini* 14.1).

Moreover, unlike the texts in the first trend, which approach the global from the point of view of the glorious (global) past that provides (or should provide) the basis for the local today, the texts in this trend develop a view of glocalization that relates primarily to the localization of technology. The issue of localization of the software interface is predominant in these texts. As is pointed out in one of the texts: "This is a purely technical problem. In order to communicate in Greek on the Internet, our interlocutor's computer must have uploaded the appropriate software, which is of Greek manufacture. . . .

Even in Greece, compatibility is lacking between the systems of the different companies" (*Elefteria Larissas* 18.1). This technical discourse employs a view of technology as value neutral and ideology free.

Second, there are traces of sociolinguistic discourses in the second trend. A descriptive sociolinguistic discourse identifies elements of what is referred to as a "technological idiolect":

> E.g., "θ" is written not with "th" but with "8". "Ξ" not with "x" but with "3", and so on. . . . Even English on the Internet has undergone similar syntactical and grammatical changes. E.g., the prepositions "to" and "for" are rendered by the arithmetical symbols "2" and "4". The purpose of these alterations is to ensure speed. (*Vima* 28.1a)

On another occasion, Greeklish is seen as a kind of "glossary" used by the young among themselves (*Nea* 16.1f) or as a "jargon" that distinguishes insiders and outsiders: "it operates as a jargon in which the initiated are differentiated from the uninitiated who enter the Internet" (*Vima* 28.1a). Elements of this new "language variety" are described: "Electronic script is halfway between written and oral conversation" (*Vima* 28.1a), "Greeklish does not have rules . . . It is a spontaneous script and everybody formulates it in his own way . . . For example, the Greek letter 'beta': Some write it as 'b' and others as 'v'" (*Makedonia* 13.1).

Third Trend: A Resistive View

Texts in this trend differentiate themselves from the Academy's text, yet they take the opportunity to raise a number of critical issues concerning the challenges the Greek language faces today within the context of global change. Although they share some views with texts in the second trend, they do not merely attempt an explanation of Greeklish. They also raise issues such as the pressure of the dominant English language on the Internet on the "small languages" and the role of English on the Internet, and they generally develop a resistive view of the effects of globalization. The catalytic changes brought about by globalization, the changing European dynamic, and advances in information and communication technologies are seen to have led to a restructuring of social identities and to concerns about the role "weaker" languages are expected to play in the future. Proposals are also put forward concerning initiatives to be taken in the new situation.

As with texts in the first trend, here, too, there is a metaphorical discourse of resistance, which is, however, differently realized. Specifically, this discourse of resistance is not based on a retrospective discourse that has its origins in the greatness of history or in ethnocentric views concerning the importance of the Greek language. Neither is it inspired by "a fear of every change, every discovery . . . and a nostalgia for the past" (*Nea* 3.3) that is always considered to be better than the present and the future. On the contrary, it originates from an interest in the "weaker" languages, an interest in preserving "small" languages such as Greek, and the need to struggle for linguistic equality. Moreover, as is stated in one of the texts, "resistance is legitimated by a principle similar to that which is supported in the natural environment. A need to preserve bio-diversity. Just as for balance in nature, the variety of biological species must be maintained, so in culture, differences need to be maintained by positive measures" (*Vima* 28.1a). According to this view, it is a matter of "linguistic ecology" to protect languages from extinction in the same way that we preserve the various living species around us.

The same text also comments on the Academy's statement, notes its contradictory arguments, and suggests that any distinction between more important and less important languages leads toward homogenization and the dominance of English, which the Academy strongly opposes:

> The Greek language, it is stated in the text "has enriched not only Latin, but the principle European languages." It fails to mention, however, that the Greek language has also been enriched by other languages . . . Anyway, what is this argument suggesting? That the small languages which have not enriched others are worth less protection? (*Vima* 28.1a)

Resistance in the texts in this trend is motivated by the need to promote linguistic diversity through a multilingual, heteroglossic, and polyphonic ethos (Dendrinos, 2001). Although the use of the Roman alphabet in CMC is not a real threat since "nobody has ever suggested the adoption of the Latin alphabet" (*Nea* 16.1e–f), it is acknowledged that "This does not mean that the absolute dominance of English and, as a consequence, of the Latin alphabet should not be faced up to. Many countries promote specific measures for the presence of their languages in cyberspace" (*Nea* 16.1d). Resistance becomes a result of pressure that the weaker languages undergo today, primarily as "a result of globalization" (*Prin* 14.1): "in recent years, the Greek language has undergone 'pressures' at a multiplicity of levels, both in the spoken and the written word" (*Avgi* 21.1). Most important, the discourse of resistance that is proclaimed here is not a retrospective but a prospective one, which looks into the future using the past as a base, and which attempts to "create appropriate attitudes concerning current change" (Bernstein, 1996, p. 77). As stated in one text:

> If, then, there is this strong trend towards English-speaking, and, even more so, towards techno-English which will steam-roller national languages, and in fact there is, there is just as much an equally strong trend on the part of cultures and languages not to submit, to resist, to preserve themselves, not as romantic nostalgia, but an active value towards their present and their future. (*Avgi tis Kiriakis* 14.1)

There is a strong urge to resist the homogeneity brought about by globalization and its promoted monolingual, monoglossic, and uniphonic ethos.

After all, it is argued, "Culture . . . is the result of relations. Communication relations, but also conflict relations in which opposing tendencies, opposed values, different ways of life, social relations and interests which do not come out of the mold of a uniformity dictated from above are expressed" (*Avgi tis Kiriakis* 14.1). We cannot, therefore, remain "passive witnesses of a world cultural re-ordering which tends to strike a blow especially at Greek, mainly because of the particularity, the rarity, but also the prestige of its alphabet" (*Nea* 16.1a). However, this resistance cannot be restricted to the Greek language since "if, then, our language is in danger, are not all the languages of the world in danger, and with them local cultures, from the whirlwind of globalization and cultural homogenization?" (*Elefteria Larissas* 18.1).

At a surface level, it might seem that texts in this trend adopt a rather negative stance toward globalization and its avant garde instrument, the Internet. Formulations such as "steam-rolling" and "setting aside history, culture" evoke a pessimistic discourse of globalization and express a negative stance toward it: "The steam-rolling brought by globalization, a levelling which sets aside history, culture, traditions, manners, and customs, the identity, that is, of each state, disturbs many Greek citizens as to the 'day after' of our country" (*Paron* 21.1). Several texts in this trend note the concern that the Greek language might become a victim of globalization. It is even suggested that "national languages, particularly those of small nations, like the Greek nation, are condemned to deterioration and final annihilation in the melting-pot of globalization" (*Avgi tis Kiriakis* 14.1). On the other hand, an optimistic discourse of globalization is evoked through formulations that recognize existing linguistic imperialism, but which also argue that

> other ages have experienced similar forms of linguistic imperialism which have wiped out linguistic particularities within the sphere of their influence. And Greek, like Latin, was once in the position now occupied by English. Printing and nation-states annihilated hundreds of dialects, and a good deal more effectively than the Internet. (*Vima* 28.1a)

Moving away from the deterministic position of the first trend, which does not offer any solutions, and from the restricted view of the second trend, which approaches English as a technical problem, the texts in the third trend place Greeklish within its sociohistorical context, attempt an analysis of its ideological underpinnings, and provide suggestions for the future by looking into possibilities offered by the electronic communications media. Most important, texts in this trend do not revert to grand narratives of the past, but turn to history to develop "a social, historical understanding of current reality" (*Nea* 16.1d). Here, languages are viewed as "open communications systems," language users as active social agents who "often borrow, appropriate, assess and re-assess, or even reject various linguistic sources" (*Avgi* 21.1), and new technologies and the Internet as "working tools" (*Nea* 16.1e).

Against the "ideology of linguistic (and more general) conservatism which has marked Greek history" (*Nea* 16.1d) and the "ahistorical, ethnocentric, conservative, and, in the end, misleading footing on which the issue is placed" (*Nea* 16.1f) in texts in the first trend, skepticism is expressed as to the "replacement of the Greek alphabet by the Latin and the production of this *sui generis* linguistic idiom" (*Avgi* 21.1) of Greeklish and its ideology. "The preservation of particularity—including national particularity" (*Nea* 16.1d) is considered important. However, the position here is not one against globalization "but against Americanization and their value of money and consumption. Against the culture of Macdonald's French fries and of Coca Cola" (*Elefteria Larissas* 18.1).

Technology is not here to destroy us (*Nea* 16.1f). On the contrary, "The use of the Latin alphabet to write Greek in communication on the Internet is not only not a bad thing, but, rather, a good one, since even when we cannot write in Greek, because of technical difficulties, we find a way of doing it. We insist by every means upon our language" (*Elefteria Larissas* 18.1). Turning the Academy's argument around, a text argues: "we know, however, from history that the only way of surviving for a culture at such critical periods is creative assimilation of the new challenges to its benefit, and not its obstinate isolation on the pretext of non-existent dangers" (*Nea* 16.1e). It is therefore important to explore how "technology can be used as a tool for the dissemination and spread of our language to the ends of the earth" (*Elefteria Larissas* 18.1).

In fact, texts in this trend are the only ones that consider this "creative assimilation of new challenges" and move a step forward to propose specific initiatives that must be taken in this direction. Suggestions include that "the whole of ancient literature should be digitized and made available in cyberspace, so that anyone can have direct access to any text," "the world-wide electronic library should be supplemented with Greek texts of all periods" (*Nea* 3.3), the Academy "should put the whole of Greek poetry, the whole of ancient Greek literature on a site on the Internet" (*Elefteria Larissas* 18.1). Other suggestions concern the financing of programs to teach Greek through the Internet, and the financial support of a program to provide software for communicating in Greek, free of charge.

CONCLUSIONS

From the above analysis it can be seen that attitudes toward the use of Greeklish are deeply embedded in the Greek sociocultural context, where, from its beginning as a nation-state in the nineteenth century, questions about the official language and the graphic system have been central to long, heated social and political debates. Responses to Greeklish are linked to a view of the Greek graphemic system as inseparable from the Greek language and national identity. Among the three main trends that have been identified (retrospective, prospective, and resistive), the *retrospective* view is numerically the strongest. Its arguments do not differ substantially from those used in the past in support of *Katharevousa* and, to a large degree, in support of other meta-linguistic views after 1980. Its roots deep in the past make it a clear-cut point of view, to which a solid shape has already been given. Analysis of the corpus suggests that this view serves as a powerful pole that attracts supporters from the full range of Greek society: intellectuals, university teachers, journalists, those engaged in politics, and lay people. It views the issue of Greeklish as one of exceptional importance, as the "thin end of the wedge" for further risk to the Greek language and the Greek identity, which are under direct threat. The elegiac tone is marked, as is the note of protest and indignation that imbues most of the texts. References to history are frequent, not only to bring out the magnitude of the "good" that is at risk but also to demonstrate the resilience of the Greek alphabet, which, in spite of the dangers, has survived. To the urgent question of the reorientation of the country's role in this critical period the answers are ready to hand—answers drawn from the well-stocked quiver of the past (Swidler, 1986).

The *prospective* view minimizes the importance and extent of the issue by approaching it either in terms of technology (a technical weakness that will be overcome) or in terms of sociolinguistic factors (a new variety of script). This stance may also be seen as a reflex reaction to the Academy of Athens itself, an institution tinged with specific conservative linguistic and political ideologies. This is the second important viewpoint in quantitative terms. There can be no doubt that it expresses part of the ideas that were expressed by Demoticism in the past, particularly that part which had to do with the rebuttal of retrospective arguments. Moreover, supporters of this view—particularly the older generations—take care to point out the close link with this tradition (democratic principles, linguistic options). This is an outward-looking trend, prospective and future oriented, which, in no circumstances, however, denies the importance of the Greek alphabet. In light of the observations in the literature reviewed above, it is perhaps the most authentic trend of glocalness.

The *resistive* view dissociates itself from the observations of the Academy but takes the opportunity to raise issues that touch on the crucial problems that Greek is facing in this critical transitional period. Views held by the prospective trend are frequently found in its argumentation. The difference is that the resistive view does not confine itself to a description of Greeklish. Subjects debated include pressure on "small languages" because of the dominance of English on the Internet, and in some cases proposals for options, plans, and the undertaking of initiatives in the new world situation are put forward. This is a combative viewpoint that does not ignore particularity but regards it as a starting point for an outward-looking stance. In place of an American-dominated globalization, texts in this trend propose a more critical, multicultural, and multilingual world. This view is related to the part of the *Demotic* movement that was associated with innovative options in educational matters.

The two differing approaches that came into intense conflict over the country's political orientation in the past, again with language issues as the point of departure, are condensed in these three viewpoints. The extent to which retrospective arguments and in part prospective arguments are a reformulation of similar arguments from the past is particularly striking. The phenomenon of Greeklish seems to serve, like similar phenomena in the past, as a stimulus for highlighting sharp differences over the country's orientation and the shaping of modern Greek identity at a critical moment.

However, despite the disagreements that are recorded, none of these texts raised any question about the introduction of the Roman alphabet to write Greek routinely. It is interesting that sporadic voices raised in the past to urge the adoption of the Roman or the phonetic alphabet in the writing of Greek have not found a single echo in this debate. In this respect, there is a closing of ranks despite disagreements as to the absolute acceptance of the use of the Greek alphabet both in conventional and in electronic environments of literacy practices. Both in this example and in the discussions as a whole, the dimension of localness is apparent. However, the content of localness is not unified; it differs significantly in the three views.

Matters seem to be equally complex in the case of globalness. In the retrospective trend, it can be observed that the "international" is passed over in total silence, while there is absolute dedication to the "local"—as this approach apprehends it. Nevertheless, more research is needed to discover to what degree this viewpoint is a form of self-absorption and denial of the international, as it would seem from many of the texts in the present analysis, or a trend that looks for the international only in terms of the local. But in the case of the resistive view also, there could be no question of speaking of a simple trend toward globalness, but rather of a trend toward a reappraisal of its content.

One conclusion to be drawn from the foregoing analysis is that the pattern of glocalness that characterizes many practices of contemporary societies—particularly in relation to CMD practices—seems a good deal more complex than it is usually represented. Another conclusion is that the tug-of-war between local and global is not just a contemporary but an ongoing phenomenon that has *always* been related to the political and ideological orientations of various countries, and that manifests itself most forcibly in critical periods of transition. At the same time, we do not underestimate the changes that are taking place today, or their effects on countries, cultures, and social groups. A historically contextualized, diachronic approach may make a significant contribution toward a more comprehensive, deeper understanding of the significance of the changes of our age and of CMC practices in the context of a multilingual Internet.

Acknowledgment

A previous version of this chapter was published in the *Journal of Computer-Mediated Communication* (volume 9, issue 1, 2003).

Notes

1. See the discussion of writing systems and the Internet in chapter 1.

2. Three proposals were suggested in that period (Christidis, 1999): the adoption of Ancient Greek as the only form of "pure" and "uncorrupted" Greek; the adoption of Demotic,

the spoken language, as first-born daughter of Ancient Greek (Skopetea, 1998); and the adoption of *Katharevousa*, which recognized the importance of the spoken language but held that it had undergone "corruption" and aimed at "purifying" and "correcting" it.

3. The oldest system of writing used for Greek, the syllabic Linear B script, had already been abandoned by the twelfth century B.C.

4. These included mainly three accents (which indicated the raising and lowering of the voice) and two breathings (which showed the presence or absence of the aspirate [h]). They were used to show changes in pronunciation and were addressed mainly to fellow grammarians rather than to the general public. Their use in the writing of Greek was widely adopted in Western Europe after the invention of printing (Petrounias, 1984).

5. The examples of Romania, Albania, Turkey, and the countries that resulted from the dissolution of the former Yugoslavia are typical.

6. The numbers that follow the name of the newspaper indicate the date of publication of each text. Since all texts were published in 2001, the year has been omitted. In cases where there is more than one text in the same newspaper and the same day, the letters a, b, c, and so on, are used to identify each text.

References

Androutsopoulos, J. (2000). Latin-Greek spelling in email messages: Usage and attitudes (in Greek). *Studies in Greek Linguistics, 20,* 75–86.

Bakhtin, M. (1986). *Speech genres and other late essays* (C. Emerson & M. Holquist, Eds.; V. W. McGee, Trans.). Austin: University of Texas Press.

Bernstein, B. (1996). *Pedagogy, symbolic control and identity: Theory, research, critique.* London: Taylor & Francis.

Christidis, A.-F. (1999). *Language, politics, culture* (in Greek). Athens: Polis.

Crystal, D. (2001). *Language and the Internet.* Cambridge: Cambridge University Press.

Delveroudi, R. (2000). *La variation linguistique et la formation de la langue nationale Grecque.* In A.-F. Christidis (Ed.), *La langue Grecque et ses dialects* (pp. 117–126). Athens: Ministère de l'Education et des Cultures.

Dendrinos, B. (2001). Language education to meet the new social challenge: Linguistic diversity in Europe. In B. Dendrinos (Ed.), *The politics of ELT* (pp. 63–84). Athens: National and Kapodistrian University of Athens.

Ess, C., & Sudweeks, F. (2003). Technologies of despair and hope: Liberatory potentials and practices of CMC in the Middle East. *Journal of Computer-Mediated Communication, 8*(2). Retrieved December 5, 2005, from http://jcmc.indiana.edu/vol8/issue2/essandsudweeks.html.

Fairclough, N. (1992). *Discourse and social change.* Cambridge: Polity Press.

Fairclough, N. (2003). *Analyzing discourse.* London: Routledge.

Ferguson, C. (1972). Diglossia. In P. P. Giglioli (Ed.), *Language and social context* (pp. 232–252). Harmondsworth, UK: Penguin.

Fragoudaki, A. (2001). *Language and the nation* (in Greek). Athens: Alexandria.

Georgakopoulou, A. (1997). Self-presentation and interactional alliances in email discourse: The style- and code-switches of Greek messages. *International Journal of Applied Linguistics, 7,* 141–164.

Hatzisavvidis, S. (1986). Ideological and political quests in the field of accentuation marks. *Anti, 322,* 47–49.

Hawisher, G., & Selfe, C. (Eds.). (2000). *Global literacies and the World-Wide Web.* London: Routledge.

Herring, S. C. (2001). Computer-mediated discourse. In D. Schiffrin, D. Tannen, & H. Hamilton (Eds.), *The handbook of discourse analysis* (pp. 612–634). Oxford: Blackwell.

Hongladarom, S. (2000). Negotiating the global and the local: How Thai culture co-opts the Internet. *First Monday, 5*(8). Retrieved December 5, 2005, from http://www.firstmonday .dk/issues/issue5_8/ hongladarom/index.html.

Karantzola, E. (1999). Spelling reform in the "strong" and "weak" languages in the EU. In A.-F. Christidis (Ed.), *"Strong" and "weak" languages in the European Union* (Vol. 2, pp. 825–833). Thessaloniki: Center of the Greek Language.

Koutsogiannis, D. (2004). Critical techno-literacy and "weak" languages. In I. Snyder & C. Beavis (Eds.), *Doing literacy online* (pp. 163–184). Cresskill, NJ: Hampton Press.

Paolillo, J. C. (1996). Language choice on soc.culture.Punjab. *Electronic Journal of Communication, 6*(3). Retrieved December 5, 2005, from http://www.cios.org/www/ejc/v6n396 .htm.

Petrounias, E. (1984). *New Greek grammar and comparative analysis.* Thessaloniki: University Studio Press.

Robertson, R. (1995). Glocalization: Time-space and homogeneity-heterogeneity. In M. Featherstone, S. Lash, & R. Robertson (Eds.), *Global modernities* (pp. 25–44). Thousand Oaks, CA: Sage.

Selfe, C., & Selfe, R. (1994). The politics of the interface: Power and its exercise in electronic contact zones. *College Composition and Communication, 45*(4), 480–504.

Skopetea, E. (1998). *The "model kingdom" and the great idea* (in Greek). Athens: Polytypo.

Stavridi-Patrikiou, R. (1999). *Language, education and politics* (in Greek). Athens: Olkos.

Swidler, A. (1986). Culture in action: Symbols and strategies. *American Sociological Review, 51,* 273–286.

Terzis, N. (1998). *The pedagogy of Alexandros Delmouzos* (in Greek). Thessaloniki: Kyriakidis.

Warschauer, M. (2002). Languages.com: The Internet and linguistic pluralism. In I. Snyder (Ed.), *Silicon literacies. Communication, innovation and education in the electronic age* (pp. 62–74). London: Routledge.

Warschauer, M., Said, G., & Zohry, A. (2002). Language choice online: Globalization and identity in Egypt. *Journal of Computer-Mediated Communication, 7*(4). Retrieved December 5, 2005, from http://jcmc.indiana.edu/vol7/issue4/warschauer.html.

Woodard, R. (1997). *Greek writing from Knossos to Homer.* New York: Oxford University Press.

Yates, S. J. (1996). English in cyberspace. In S. Goodman & D. J. Graddol (Eds.), *Redesigning English: New texts, new identities* (pp. 108–140). London: Routledge, in association with the Open University.

Yoon, S. (2001). Internet discourse and the habitus of Korea's new generation. In C. Ess (Ed.), *Culture, technology, communication* (pp. 241–260). Albany: State University of New York Press.

PART II

LINGUISTIC AND DISCOURSE
FEATURES OF COMPUTER-
MEDIATED COMMUNICATION

7

YUKIKO NISHIMURA

Linguistic Innovations
and Interactional Features
in Japanese BBS Communication

In 2003, the Japanese Internet user population was almost 77.3 million, more than 60% of the entire Japanese population (Soumushou, 2004). Japanese speakers are the third largest language group on the Internet (Global Internet Statistics, 2004). Not much is known, however, about how Japanese speakers use language online, in contrast to voluminous research on computer-mediated communication (CMC) among English speakers (Herring, 1996, 2001). This chapter describes aspects of Japanese speakers' Internet communication. Specifically, it analyzes linguistic and interactional features of informal CMC in Japanese, using as data messages posted asynchronously to message boards (bulletin board systems, or BBSs) on websites.

Previous studies in English on Internet communication have dealt mainly with CMC that utilizes Roman-based scripts, neglecting CMC in languages not utilizing Roman-based characters, such as Japanese. An exception is Matsuda (2001), who analyzed Japanese Web diaries, focusing on the construction of "voice," and discussed one of the four Japanese scripts, *katakana*, as contributing to "voice" construction. Matsuda (2002) also examined the negotiation of identity and power in email messages of Japanese teachers of English. In Nishimura (2003a), I presented analyses of innovative and playful uses of *kanji* and other scripts on a Japanese message board website called *ni channeru* ("channel 2"), where users form a community of practice and have developed highly specialized, unconventional language use. Satake (1995, 2002) gave an account of the styles used by contemporary Japanese youth in general as well as in CMC.

Such journals as *Nihongogaku* [*Japanese Linguistics*] (1996, 2001) and *Gendai no Esupuri* [*Esprit of Today*] (1998) have produced special issues on communication via computers and cell phones. Tanaka (2001) compared exchanges of email messages by computer versus cell phone. Katsuno and Yano (2002, chapter 12 this volume) investigated face marks (*kaomoji*, the Japanese equivalent of emoticons) used in email and cell phone messages. Sugimoto and Levin (2000) compared how American and Japanese users identify themselves and use emoticons in email messages sent to discussion groups.

Except for the studies by Matsuda (2001), who discusses *katakana*, and Nishimura (2003a), these studies of Japanese CMC, both in English and in Japanese, overlook one of the key elements that characterizes Japanese online communication: the wide variety of scripts that are used innovatively by Japanese speakers. Through the variety of orthographic choices available to them, Japanese Internet users create rich online discourse that suits their communicative and interactional purposes. Compared with English CMC users, Japanese users devise creative, sometimes amusing, orthography and punctuation in similar as well as distinctive ways, supported by Japanese CMC technology. A variety of features in informal spoken Japanese such as sentence-final particles reinforce this tendency. Thus, Japanese Internet users have a high degree of freedom in CMC. They exploit it to recreate or construct "informal friendly talk" online, appropriate to the cultural expectations of their communities.

In this chapter I attempt to explain how the Japanese orthographic system enriches Japanese CMC in linguistic, interactional, and sociocultural contexts. The chapter is an abridged version of Nishimura (2003b), where background information about written Japanese not included here (e.g., the four major scripts, details on word processing, and additional examples) is available.

After identifying briefly the data on which this study is based, I compare Japanese CMC with its close equivalents in English, in order to clarify what orthographic means are shared by users of both languages and what features are distinctive. I use Danet's (2001, p. 17) "common features of digital writing" as a frame of reference, supplemented by studies by several other researchers, in order to enrich the comparison of the specific means of compensating for and adapting to the limitations of CMC in the two languages.

A taxonomy based on English CMC alone is of limited use in accounting for the rich variety of Japanese CMC. Various features specific to informal spoken Japanese are found in Japanese CMC. After considering briefly how informal spoken interactions take place, I examine the way such informal features as sentence-final particles are transferred to Japanese CMC. Finally, by examining closely what users do, I suggest that online interaction is a reflection of communicative styles that occur in casual face-to-face conversation, even though BBS communication is asynchronous. Because the present study is based on a limited set of data, I do not claim that my results necessarily apply to Japanese CMC in general. Rather, they reflect the specific kinds of BBS interactions studied.

DATA: ASYNCHRONOUS BBSs

The data for this study come from messages sent asynchronously to BBSs that are part of several personal fan websites featuring popular actors, films, music, and so forth, where young people spend a great deal of time reading and posting messages. The data were collected between July and October 2000 and in January 2001. Participants appeared to be mostly women in their mid-teens to thirties, based on the content of their messages. One reason for using these asynchronous BBS messages is their accessibility. Messages stored on these sites can be visited and viewed by anyone interested. A more substantial reason to examine these messages relates to their personal nature. This point is best illustrated by comparing these BBS messages with email messages as investigated in the literature.

Herring (2001) points out that synchronicity is one of the major factors that shapes CMC discourse (p. 6). Both BBS and email messages are exchanged asynchronously. While email messages are typically exchanged between individuals and are private, BBS messages are posted on websites and are public. In BBS settings there is an audience; messages can be read by posters and others. In one-to-one email, no one other than the recipient typically reads the message. Concerns about who reads the messages, and to whom they can be addressed, may influence BBS message contributors and their discourse.

Another aspect to be considered is whether messages are of a personal nature. Both email and BBS messages can further be divided into two types: personal and nonpersonal. Email messages of a personal nature are located in the computer files of senders and recipients, and nobody "would volunteer his or her 'in' and 'out' baskets for public scrutiny" (Baron, 2000, p. 248). In contrast, postings to BBS and other publicly archived asynchronous systems are readily accessible to researchers.

This distinction is by no means clear-cut. Gimenez (2000) compared features of email messages in business communication with business letters. Cho (in press) examines work-related emails exchanged in a university setting in comparison with memoranda. Both studies can be regarded as investigating emails of a nonpersonal nature, although the communication is private. Matsuda (2002) analyzed email messages sent to a professional discussion group, TESOL Link; these emails are also of a nonpersonal nature. Other researchers, such as Danet (2001), have analyzed emails addressed to them on business-related matters. Although the distinction between personal/nonpersonal emails can be a matter of degree, it is useful to separate them for the purposes of this study.

The messages analyzed here are of a personal nature, even though they are publicly posted. Their subjects relate to personal likes and hobbies. Since

personal email messages are often difficult to obtain, there is a strong rationale for studying personal BBS messages in order to examine how personal
subject matter affects this form of discourse.

The BBS websites studied here also contrast with others examined thus
far concerning users' purpose for posting messages. Collot and Belmore
(1996) consider BBS users' goals to be requesting and giving information,
making announcements, and engaging in discussion. The BBS users in my
study, in contrast, post messages in order to share common interests in particular actors, films, music, and so on, and to interact with others who share
the same interests. This goal of entertainment and enjoyment on the part of
the users should be taken into consideration when interpreting the messages
under investigation.

Table 7.1 gives a profile of three representative BBS websites studied here.
Although these websites are no longer available, similar BBS websites can
easily be found elsewhere. Each such site is managed by a site manager, in
many cases the site creator, who sets rules and guidelines regarding conduct

TABLE 7.1. Profile of representative BBSs.

| | Name of BBS | | | | | | | | |
| | Confession room | | | Idol BBS | | | No name | | |
Participants	Manager	Others	Total	Manager	Others	Total	Manager	Others	Total
Number of participants in the logs retrieved	1	5	6	1	7	8	1	8	9
Number of messages	8	6	14	16	17	33	9	11	20
Total message length (number of lines)	43	38	81	106	196	302	84	86	170
Average length per message	5.3	6.3	6.1	6.6	11.5	9.1	9.3	7.8	8.5
Number of messages posted by each participant	8	6	14	16	17	33	9	11	20
P1		1			7			2	
P2		1			1			1	
P3		2			3			2	
P4		1			2			1	
P5		1			1			2	
P6					1			1	
P7					2			1	
P8								1	

on the website including the use of appropriate language. The attitudes of the manager might influence participants' message production, especially given that interaction takes place asynchronously, and writers have time to edit and revise their messages to meet the guidelines.

All participants use nicknames called *handoru neemu* ("handle names") when posting messages. When a new participant appears at the site, the site manager normally asks for a brief self-introduction. After this self-introduction, the newcomer is treated as a member.

The site manager usually responds every time someone posts a message. Thus, as shown in table 7.1, the site manager posts messages far more frequently than other users, while other participants usually post once or twice. On average, the messages are long and elaborated, as senders have time to compose and edit their postings in this asynchronous Web environment.

COMPARISON BETWEEN ENGLISH AND JAPANESE CMC

In order to clarify what aspects of Japanese CMC are distinctive, I compare features of messages written by Japanese CMC users with their English counterparts. Ideally, the comparison should be made with English BBS messages posted on fan sites. However, this is not practical, since, to my knowledge, no study of such sites exists. English messages in asynchronous exchanges such as email offer a second-best comparison with Japanese CMC messages with asynchronous characteristics.

Danet's (2001) general characterization of digital discourse provides a useful frame of reference. She identifies nine common features (p. 17; table 7.2). To widen the scope of my study, I supplement Danet's characterization with additional features reported by other researchers (Cho, in press; Gimenez, 2000; Lan, 2000; Lee, 1996, Werry, 1996), all of whom studied email except for Werry (1996), who provides a detailed description of spoken features characterizing Internet Relay Chat (IRC). As Danet (2001) cautions, differences between synchronous IRC and asynchronous BBS should be kept in mind. Thus, I incorporate from Werry's data only those features that are not directly related to the issue of synchronicity. In table 7.2, features of Japanese BBS discourse are juxtaposed with their English counterparts, mainly based on Danet's classification of nine common features. Each category of features is discussed below.

Multiple Punctuation

First, consider multiple punctuation, a feature shared by the two languages. Punctuation marks that come at the end of a sentence, such as periods, exclamation points, and question marks, are multiply employed by users of both Japanese and English. One difference is the Japanese use of wavy lines, which

TABLE 7.2. Common features of digital writing, based on Danet (2001).

	Examples	
	English (from several sources)	Japanese (from Nishimura, 2001)
Multiple punctuation	Type back soon!!!!!! (Danet 2001) Annny pwoblewms???? (Werry, 1996)	読みたいですぅ〜〜〜!!! Yomitai desuu〜〜〜!!! "I really, really want to read it."
Eccentric spelling	Type back soooooooon! (Danet, 2001) more work, she sez (Lee, 1996)	はっじめまして〜[はじめまして〜] Hajjimemashite〜 [Hajimemashite〜] "First time (to see you)" 終わりましたかあ〜 [終わりましたか] owari mashita kaa〜 [owari mashita ka] "Was it really over?" ありがと〜 [ありがとう] arigato〜 [arigatou] "thank you" [Unconventional notation underlined]
Capital letters	I'M REALLY ANGRY AT YOU (Danet, 2001)	HAPPYな気分です HAPPY na kibun desu "I'm feeling happy."
Asterisks for emphasis	I'm really *angry* at you. (Danet, 2001)	ヨロシクお願いしますっ! Yoroshiku [in katakana] onegai shimasu? [glottal stop]! "Please remember me!"
Written-out laughter	hehehe hahahaha (Danet, 2001)	ふふふ huhuhu "laughing"
Other vocalizations	—	え〜ん! E〜n! Weeping! きゃあ kyaa [cry for surprise] "Wow!"
Music/noise	Mmmmmmmmmm MMMMMMMM poc poc poc poc (Werry, 1996)	チャンチャン♪ chan chan ♪ [sound of bells often heard at the end of comical stage performance]
Description of actions	*grins* <grin> <g> (Danet, 2001)	（笑）, [笑いwarai "laughter" or 笑うwarau "laugh"] （殴）naguru "kicking" etc （手に汗握りつつ）(Feeling uneasy; literally, meaning "holding sweat in the palm")
Emotions	:-) (smile) ;-) (wink) :-((frown) (Danet, 2001)	(^_^) [a smiley face without rotation] ナンダ!これわ (@_@) もう びっくりです nan da! Kore wa (@_@) mou bikkuri desu. "What! Is it? (@_@) I'm very surprised." [image of eyes wide open]
Abbreviations	pls. [please]; tks [thanks] (Gimenez, 2000) LOL; BRB (Danet, 2001)	あけおめことよろ ake ome koto yoro, [akemashite omedetou kotoshimo yoroshiku] "New Year's Greeting/ Happy New Year"

168

TABLE 7.2. (continued)

	Examples	
	English (from several sources)	Japanese (from Nishimura, 2001)
Rebus writing	CU [see you] (Danet, 2001)	こからもどうか4649です!!（笑）korekara mo douka *yoroshiku* desu !! (wara) "please remember me from now on, too!! (*kanji* for laughter)"
All lower case	hi, how are you? (Danet, 2001)	n/a
Other features not included in Danet (2001):		
Multiple/ nonlinguistic symbols	I'm running out of $$$$$$$$$$$$ $$$$$$$$$$ (Cho, in press)	頑張ってくださいっ☆★☆ ganbatte kudasai ☆★☆ "Please do your best ☆★☆" 見ようと思ってます♪ miyuou to omotte masu ♪ "I'm thinking of looking at it ♪"

are not found in English, nor are they conventional symbols in Japanese writing. The standard symbol for lengthening is a straight line. The use of wavy lines invokes a long, undulating span of time. CMC users type multiple wavy lines to emphasize visually the length of time. This practice is reminiscent of the typographic simulation of smoking marijuana on IRC analyzed by Danet and her colleagues (Danet, 2001; Danet et al., 1998), in which the main participant typed decreasing numbers of the letter "s" to simulate dissipating smoke.

Eccentric Spelling

Attempts to reproduce spoken pronunciation in typed messages are the major causes for eccentric spellings. For prolonged pronunciation, letters are reduplicated, and words are spelled in what is called "pronunciation spelling" in English, such as "sez" for "says."

The Japanese examples in row 2 of table 7.2, which use unconventional orthography to indicate colloquial style, show the highly expressive nature of some *hiragana*. The smaller sized symbol つ is conventionally used to represent a long consonant. The inclusion of this symbol in はっじめまして (*hajjimemashite*, "first time to see you") is unconventional because the standard orthography for this expression is はじめまして (*hajimemashite*). The inclusion of つ gives the viewers a more vivid sound image of how this expression might be pronounced, suggesting a clear and cheerful, high-spir-ited articulation. Via this symbol the writer conveys a high degree of affect and closeness, as if sharing the same physical space and time of conversation with the viewer.

This inclusion does not cause any difference in lexical meaning. In some other words, the presence or absence of this symbol is contrastive in meaning, such as きって (切手) (*kitte*), which means "stamps," versus きて (来て) (*kite*), meaning "please come" or the gerundive form of the verb *kuru* ("come"). The difference conveyed by the inclusion of っ in the example here is in the degree of emphasis and is pragmatic in nature.

Another form of unconventional writing in row 2 of table 7.2 is the inclu-sion of smaller sized symbols, あ at the end of 終わりましたかあ (*owarimashita ka a*, "was it really over"). These might look like reduplicated letters, but the reduplication takes place on the vowel, and not on the typed symbols; か *ka* and あ *a* are not the same symbols. These smaller sized scripts signify empha-sis in spoken articulation, in which the phrase-final vowel is stressed. Such added vowels normally do not cause a difference in meaning. In conventional writing, these smaller scripts are not used; the expressions are 終わりました か *owarimashita ka* and 久しぶり *hisashiburi*.

While the conventional writing is ありがとう (*arigatou* "thank you"), あ りがとー (*arigatoo*) is used in the BBS messages. The use of a lengthening symbol, whether straight or wavy, in place of the *hiragana* う *u* is seen often not only in CMC but also in informal writing, where the long vowel [o:] is used as in speech. Such unconventional orthography conveys the user's voice more directly when the gap between pronunciation and conventional writing is noticeable, as in this case.

Capital Letters

There are English examples of all capital letters in row 3 of table 7.2, while in the Japanese example, an English word, *HAPPY*, is given in capital letters along with Japanese symbols. This is an example of a use of *eimoji*—an English word. Since the Roman alphabet is not a predominant script in the Japanese writing system, English words are seen only sporadically. Their use stands out among the Japanese scripts and has an attention-catching function. This user's choice of capital letters over lower case probably lies in the fact that capital letters are even more visually prominent. The function of capital letters in entirely alphabetic writing and in the middle of *kana* and *kanji* writing obviously differs. Thus, the use of capital letters in English CMC to signify shouting does not occur in Japanese CMC, though the function of emphasis seems to be present. The user could employ *katakana*, ハッピー (*happii*), following the convention of using *katakana* for loan words. The use of *eimoji* here gives viewers some sense of emphasis on the feeling of happi-ness, though the difference between *katakana* and *eimoji* would be slight and can be a matter of the message sender's taste.

Asterisks for Emphasis

I did not find Japanese examples of asterisks used for emphasis. Instead, the example in table 7.2 is given in *katakana*. Since *yoroshiku* is a native expression, the standard convention is to write it in *hiragana* (よろしく) or in *kanji* (宜しく). The use of *kanji* conveys a rigid or formal feeling and is not suitable in informal casual interaction. *Hiragana* would be the most unmarked expression. A marked means, *katakana*, is employed, suggesting that the user attempts to place emphasis on this expression as *katakana* can be used as a kind of italic script for words that are "unique and special" (Stanlaw, 2002, p. 549). The function of asterisks for emphasis and its distribution in English CMC may differ from that of the marked use of *katakana* in Japanese CMC. However, since they seem to work for the same purpose, it may be appropriate to regard *katakana* used in marked ways as an approximate counterpart to the asterisk in English.

Written-Out Laughter

The category of written-out laughter can be extended to include other vocalizations and nonlinguistic sound/noise such as music. Because interactions are not face to face, several kinds of extralinguistic information are missing in CMC. In order to supply as much missing information as possible, users in both languages strive to express various nonlinguistic sounds visually by keyboarding in similar ways. One difference is the use of musical notes in Japanese examples to show explicitly that the expressions belong to music or have some musical characteristics. The use of musical notes and other non-linguistic symbols also appears at the end of table 7.2, under "Multiple/non-linguistic symbols" and is discussed further below.

The Japanese examples for auditory information (sound/noise) can be classified as onomatopoetic or mimetic words, such as *kyaa, uumu, chan chan*, and *een*, which are also abundant in informal spoken conversation. Because such vocabulary encodes high affect (Baba, 2001), its inclusion in CMC evokes a high degree of involvement and a sense of participation in "conversation."

Description of Actions

Three different notations for "grin" are given in the English examples: asterisks enclosing the verb, the verb spelled out between angle brackets, and the initial letter alone of the verb in angle brackets. In the Japanese examples, parentheses differentiate expressions from the main text itself. One type of action description is to give the verb stem in *kanji* alone enclosed by parentheses. *Kanji* are not normally used in isolation as verbs; they are used with *hiragana* for inflectional endings, tense, and so on. Yet even when the characters are used without accompanying *kana*, their meaning is clearly

172 FEATURES OF COMPUTER-MEDIATED COMMUNICATION

understandable by readers with basic literacy in Japanese, because the characters are ideographs and convey meanings.

Use of isolated *kanji* in parentheses is typical of Japanese CMC; it is very frequently found not only in BBSs but also in informal email messages and chat. Senders can communicate their feelings, actions, and so on, by means of *kanji* instantaneously and easily. Recipients can get the message at a glance, as well. However, this way of expressing feelings is rather unconventional and not often used in other communication modes except for personal casual letters (Kataoka, 1997).

Not only *kanji* in parentheses but also other types of expressions indicate actions, gestures, and mental states. Parentheses are used to separate this kind of comment from the messages themselves. In row 6 of table 7.2, the writer explains the situation using a somewhat metaphorical expression, "holding sweat in the palm."

Emoticons

A major difference between emoticons in English CMC and in Japanese is that in English they are read sideways, while Japanese *kaomoji* are right-side up, as illustrated in row 7 of table 7.2 (see also Katsuno & Yano, chapter 12 this volume). Emoticons rendered in Roman typographic characters consist of colons, parentheses, and other characters. Because symbols available in Japanese are more varied, including nonlinguistic symbols, there appears to be more variety in Japanese "face marks." The following face mark represents the mouth wide open, laughing loudly and cheerfully, with asterisks used to indicate rosy cheeks.

Example 1

復活おめでと～♪良かったね (*＾▽＾*)
hukkatu omedeto～♪yokatta ne   (*＾▽＾*)
"Congratulations on your comeback [as if singing] That was good
(*＾▽＾*)"

Such examples illustrate that variety in face marks is enhanced by variety in scripts. Some *kaomoji* are used so frequently that they are "lexicalized" in dictionaries, many of which are available online. Message writers can create face marks manually, or they can copy and paste ready-made marks. When face marks are entered manually in asynchronous messages, users can take time to create more expressive messages.

Abbreviations

Abbreviations are the result of at least two different processes: acronyms such as LOL for "laughing out loud" and rebus writing. In English, acronyms are encoded by stringing together the initial letters of words in phrases; what the acronyms mean may not always be understood by users, unless they are already familiar with the language used in CMC. Although the Japanese examples for abbreviations in table 7.2 may not be the exact counterpart of the English examples, they involve a process of shortening from full phrases. The whole expression for the new year's greeting in Japanese is a long one, and the first two syllables from each of the four phrases that make up the greeting are used to form this abbreviated greeting. This expression is not limited to CMC, but is in circulation especially among young people.

Regarding rebus writing—the use of a single symbol to represent a word or syllable with a similar sound—the English example seems clear, while the process by which the sequence of numbers "4649" in the Japanese example can be rebus writing needs explanation. In Japanese the number 4 is pronounced *yon* or *shi*; 6, *roku*; and 9, *ku* or *kyuu*. The first number, 4, is read *yo* from *yon*, the second number, 6, as *ro* from *roku*, the third number, again 4, is this time read *shi*, and the final number 9 is read *ku*. When strung together, we get *yoroshiku*. This replacement of words by numbers seems motivated at least as much by word play and play with writing as by a desire to speed up typing.

In general, to be able to type messages fast is preferred in all modes in CMC, although there is a tendency for abbreviations to occur more often in synchronous than asynchronous modes. Since the Japanese data are from asynchronous CMC, it is not absolutely necessary for users to type quickly.

All Lower Case

Since the Roman alphabet is not a predominant script, I did not find examples typed in all lower case in the Japanese data. One possible phenomenon similar to this would be to write everything in *hiragana* or *katakana*, without taking the trouble of converting to *kanji*. However, there are a great many homophones in Japanese, and it would be difficult for readers to understand the intended meaning without the use of *kanji*, even with the help of context. This would thus be an unlikely counterpart to writing in all lower case in English. Another possibility would be to send misconverted *kanji* as is, before or without correcting it, because all lowercase writing has errors that need to be corrected, from a prescriptive perspective, and misconverted *kanji* are also errors that should be corrected, as well. However, misconverted *kanji* could cause misunderstanding, while all lower case would not; thus, these processes cannot be considered exactly the same.

Other Features

In the final row of table 7.2, I have included a few examples that are not specifically discussed in Danet (2001). One example is from Cho (in press), multiple uses of $, which expressively emphasizes money as visually represented by the dollar symbol. Similar Japanese examples include use of nonlinguistic symbols such as stars and musical notes. The message accompanied by the symbols conveys encouragement; the effect of the ☆★☆ symbols is to cheer up someone in a light-hearted manner. Similarly, the use of musical notes (♪), which denote music and singing, suggests that the writer feels merry, as if about to sing. Although these examples could have been discussed under multiple punctuation, the dollar symbol and ☆ are not punctuation marks, strictly speaking.

To sum up, as shown in table 7.2, CMC users in Japanese and English employ similar methods to supply information that cannot otherwise be conveyed through this medium. CMC users in both languages devise various innovative and unconventional ways of writing in order to supply prosodic, paralinguistic, phonological, and auditory information through language-specific means.

The analysis presented here has been based on Danet's (2001) common features on English CMC. However, this classification cannot account for the rich variety of Japanese CMC. In fact, various features specific to informal spoken Japanese are also found in Japanese CMC. I have already pointed to Japanese CMC users' extensive use of colloquial vocabulary. Another important feature is expressions of familiarity and politeness. In the next section, I examine the way informal spoken features showing politeness and familiarity are transferred to Japanese CMC.

ONLINE JAPANESE DISCOURSE AS "CONVERSATION"

Features of Informal Spoken Japanese

As shown in the discussion above, computer-mediated discourse shares a number of features with informal spoken language. It is useful to examine characterizations of informal face-to-face conversation in Japanese. Maynard (1989) presents a detailed description of Japanese conversational language, which is characterized by (1) fragmentation of talk, (2) final particles, (3) fillers, (4) ellipsis, (5) postposing (movement of sentential elements after the verb, which is normally in final position), (6) verb morphology (plain vs. polite), (7) sentence-final forms, (8) insertion of meta-communicational remarks, (9) propositional twisting, (10) questions as conversational elicitors, and (11) rhythmic ensemble.

Among these features, the fragmentation of talk is based on pauses within utterances; since no auditory information is communicated in BBS exchanges, this characteristic is not discussed. However, it should be pointed out that BBS users show a tendency to create fragmentary messages through innovative use of symbols such as punctuation marks between chunks of words and phrases, as well as the use of short messages that do not form full sentences syntactically. Similarly, the feature of rhythmic ensemble will not be considered, since it concerns the tempo of each syllable and nonverbal behavior such as head movement (e.g., nodding), also unavailable in online interaction.

Final Particles

Among the remaining characterizations, I mainly focus on particles and verb morphology or, more specifically, the polite and plain styles of verb endings. Particles can be categorized into two groups: grammatical particles, and particles that express the speaker's attitude. The first type encodes the grammatical structure of the sentence and is not of concern here. The second type can be further subcategorized into particles in sentence-initial position that draw interactants' attention, such as *e* and *aa*, and particles that ensure rapport, which normally appear at the end of phrases, clauses, and sentences.

According to Maynard (1989), the particles of rapport, sometimes referred to as sentence-final particles, include *ne(e)*, *sa(a)*, *no*, *ka na* and *yo na*, *yo*, *ka*, *wa*, and *ze*. A brief summary of their functions and uses (except for the combined particles, *ka na* and *yo na*) is given in table 7.3. These particles have been studied by Uyeno (1971), Cook (1990, 1992), McGloin (1990), and Barke (2001). Maynard (1989) observes that "in general frequent insertion of particles encourages rapport between the conversation partners and achieves a closer monitoring of the partners' feelings" (p. 28).

A number of particles appear in my data; the most widely used particle of rapport is *ne(e)*, and next is *yo*. All participants ($N = 23$ in the representative three BBSs) used at least one particle once in their messages, as in example 2 below. Underlining indicates politeness.

Example 2: Final particles (boldface)

1   Re: そうな**の**? 投稿者: GMTNでちゅ 2000/10/08(Sun) 13:51:30
2   あ、リンク<u>貼らせて頂きました</u>ｖｖ逃がさん**よ**?
3   最近、踊るから離れてるGMTNだけど仲良くして**ね**。
4   只今GMTNの心は富樫でいっぱいいっぱい。可愛い**よね**?
5   ホワイトアウトのサイトになっちゃおうか**なあ**? (死)

1   *Re: sou na **no** ? Sender: GMTN dechu Date and time*
2   *A, rinku <u>harasete itadaki mashita</u> vv nigasan **yo** ?*
3   *Saikin, Odoru kara hanareteru GMTN da ke do nakayoku shite **ne**.*
4   *Tada ima GMTN no kokoro wa Togashi de ippai ippai. Kawaii **yo ne** ?*
5   *Howaito auto no saito ni nattchaou ka **naa** ? (shi)*

1   "Re: Title: Is that **so**? Sender: GMTN Date and Time
2   Oh, you <u>let me put a link</u> [to your website], vv I won't let you get away, **OK**? [vv replaces the heart symbol]
3   Recently, I'm not really into Odoru [title of film], but let's stay in touch, **okay**?

TABLE 7.3. Summary of final particles.

Function	Connotation	Particle	Notes	Typical gender
Insistence	"I'm telling you"	よ *yo*	Implies that you're telling something others don't already know; not always polite to use to a superior	—
		ぜ *ze*	A strong *yo*	Male
		ぞ *zo*	The strongest particle of all; can add a commanding or threatening tone to a sentence	Male
		さ(あ) *sa(a)*	To add emphasis, surprise, etc.	—
Confirmation/rapport	"...you know?" "...right?" "...isn't that so?" "we feel the same way"	ね(え) *ne(e)*	Directly indexes affective common ground, indirectly indexes various conversational functions that require the addressee's cooperation (requesting confirmation) (Cook, 1992)	—
		な *na*	A strong *ne*	—
Rapport	Create feminine tone	の *no*	Indexes knowledge shared by the speaker and the addressee or the third party; can function as politeness	Female
		わ *wa*	Indexes softness or hesitant attitudes, the speaker's female gender	Female
Question	"Am I right to understand...?"	か *ka*	Used to form a question	—

Based on studies by Barke (2001), Cook (1990, 1992), and McGloin (1990).

4 Now my heart is full, full of Togashi [character in film]. He is cute, **isn't he?**

5 Shall I make my site a Whiteout site, **do you think**? [*kanji* for death]"

Example 2 has a particle of rapport in every line: *no* in line 1, *yo* in 2, *ne* in 3, *yo ne* in line 4, and *naa* in 5 within the five lines of the message. This indicates how widely these particles are used. The contributor "talks" to the previous message sender, using multiple rapport-providing final particles. A particle, *no*, even occurs in the title of the message. This type of particle aspires to elicit the partner's reaction on the topic discussed; in the BBS setting, these reactions will be elicited later, when the message is read. Also, since messages posted on BBSs can be read by other users who may have the same interests, the writer may also be addressing other readers as well in this affect-encoding manner.

Polite versus Plain Styles

Let us now turn to levels of politeness. I examine sentence-ending forms, specifically the polite and plain verb forms in CMC in comparison with face-to-face conversation. There are at least two levels of politeness and formality in Japanese conversational discourse: polite/formal and plain/informal, distinguished by verb endings typically known as *desu/masu* polite style and *da/(r)u* plain style. Maynard (1989) states that polite/formal uses of sentence endings in her data on Japanese conversation are limited and that, when they appear, there are reasons, such as quoting other people who might be the speaker's superior. Utterances directly addressed to the conversational partner in her data are all in nonpolite forms. In conversation among peers, the most unmarked form is the plain *da/(r)u* ending. Maynard's data are consistent with cultural expectation of conversational behavior among people of equal status.

BBS writers, however, show different behavior regarding polite and plain verb endings. In my data, about two-thirds of the verbs have polite/formal forms, and plain forms, when they are used, are rather scattered. Normally, a user is consistent regarding verb ending use in a single message. This phenomenon can be interpreted by taking the BBS setting into account. Since the users do not share physical space, they generally do not know other users, even though they share common interests and expect to interact. Interlocutors may be their senior/superior in age. Thus, it would be more appropriate to address their fellow users with polite forms. Users who are not very conscious of relative age or status differences may assume that others are their equals; they would be more likely to use plain address forms. Also, since most users are likely to be women, and women tend to use polite language more often than men, this may explain why more cases of polite endings appear. (For a discussion on politeness and women's use of Japanese, see Ide and Yoshida

[1999].) Another factor that might contribute to using polite language is the site manager's guidelines. If the site manager expects her contributors to use such language on her website, users comply with her request by using these polite forms.

There are, however, cases where a writer mixes these two styles in one message. Maynard summarizes the views of scholars who have discussed the phenomenon of mixing polite *desu/masu* and plain *da/(r)u* forms, citing Haga's (1962) remark, "in a discourse where *da*-endings dominate with occurrences of sporadic *masu/desu* endings, the latter functions to (1) mark formality, (2) express humor and sarcasm, (3) insert personal comment, and (4) mark vocatives directly addressing the partner" (pp. 77–83, cited in Maynard, 2002, p. 278). Example 2 shows this situation, in which one occurrence of a polite form, which is the underlined part in line 2, is surrounded by plain forms in the rest of the lines.

By contrast, in example 3, more polite forms (lines 4, 6, and 7) appear with one plain form in the parentheses of line 5:

Example 3: Polite forms bolded and honorific forms underlined

1 Re: ハジメマシテ。 投稿者: MSSG K ＠管理人 2000/09/30(Sat) 23:24:31
2 わっvvv(*^_^*)
3 いらっしゃい**ませ**〜♪いつもメールでは<u>お</u>世話に... (笑)
4 そっ、そんなに緊張<u>な</u>**され**<u>まし</u>たかっ!!!!(*>_<*)
5 別にとって食いはし**ません**から *(あたりまえだ...)*
6 フフフ〜♪7日やり**ます**ね〜。
7 標準で録画<u>され</u>**ます**か? (笑) じっくり! まったり! (謎) 見**ましょ**う ね〜
　　(-_-)予告は見れ**まし**たか? (*^_^*)

1 *Title Re: Hajime mashite Sender: MSSG K @Manager Date and time*
2 *Wa* [symbol to represent long consonant] *vvv(*^_^*)*
3 *Irasshyai**mase** ～♪itsu mo meeru de wa <u>o</u> sewa ni...[kanji for laughter]*
4 *So* [long consonant] *sonna ni kinchyou <u>nasare</u> **mashi**ta ka* [long consonant] *!!!! (*>_<*)*
5 *betsu ni totte kui wa shi**masen** kara (atarimae da...)*
6 *Huhuhu ～♪nanoka yari**masu** ne～*
7 *Hyoujun de rokuga <u>sare</u>**masu**ka? [kanji for laughter] jikkuri ! mattari ! [kanji for puzzlement] mi**masyou** ne～(-_-) yokoku wa mire**mashi** ta ka? (*^_^*)*

1 Title Re: First time [to post] Sender: MSSG K @Manager Date and time
2 "Oh Wow vvv(*^_^*)
3 **Welcome** ～♪Thank you (for your honorable labor in) email as always . . . [*kanji* for laughter]
4 [Stuttering] Were, **were** you that nervous [honorific]! ! ! (*>_<*)
5 [No one] **will** take you and eat you up. (Of course not . . . [plain form])
6 Huhuhu [laughter] ～♪on the 7th they **will** show it, right～

7 **Are** you going to record [honorific] in standard [playing mode] [*kanji* for laughter] **Let's** watch [it] leisurely! appreciatively [*kanji* for puzzlement] ~(-_-) **Were** you able to see the preview? (*^_^*)"

According to Haga (1962, p. 74, cited in Maynard, 2002, p. 278), such informal use surrounded by formal style "expresses an interpersonal familiarity and closeness with the partner." Formal *desu/masu* endings create distance between the speaker and the hearer, and informal *da* forms can shorten such psychological distance. Maynard (2002) presents her own analysis of mixing and concludes that in a *desu/masu* dominant discourse, *da* is selected:

> (1) when the speaker takes a perspective internal to the narrative setting and immediately responds within that framework, (2) when the speaker presents background information semantically subordinate within the discourse structure, and (3) when the speaker finds the partner close enough and the speaker uses a style similar to the style in which he or she self-addresses. (p. 280)

This analysis fits example 3. The writer feels very close to the addressee. The remark after "no one will take you and eat you up" has the plain *da* form, in *atarimae da*, and is not important semantically; it could be an afterthought, subordinate to the main discourse. The use of parentheses also supports this analysis.

Finally, there is a new element in my data, which to my knowledge has not been accounted for in the literature. It appears in line 5 in example 3. After an ordinary (yet very playful) sentence *betsu ni totte kui wa shimasen kara* ("[No one] will take you and eat you up"), this user adds the remark *atarimae da* ("of course not") in parentheses. Though this addition is extremely obvious and might sound odd, it is not strange, especially to those who are familiar with popular Japanese comic dialogues.

In Japanese comic dialogues, one actor typically poses as a man of common sense, while the other behaves like a trickster. Every time the man of common sense states something ordinary and unwitty, the trickster reacts with a witty and sometimes sarcastic reply. In the example just described, the writer apparently mimics this comic dialogue all by herself. The main part is a statement by a person of common sense, and this statement is commented on by a trickster in parentheses. What is extraordinary here is that one writer plays a double role: a person of common sense and a trickster. In a sense, the writer creates dramatic discourse or a stage performance online.

This is not so strange if one takes account of the situation. Interaction on BBS websites can be viewed by other users who visit the site. The writer is well aware of such viewers. Moreover, this BBS website is for entertainment, so that the writer, the creator of the site, expects to present a humorous dramatization that can be enjoyed by visitors. Frequent uses of the *kanji* character for laughter and various amusing emoticons and innovative punctuation marks such as a musical note also exemplify the writer's intention to make messages enjoyable.

The *da* form in *atarimae da* in the example is used for an additional reason. Since it is extremely noticeable, both because it has an abrupt sound (Maynard, 2002), and because it is surrounded by so many polite expressions, including three honorific forms, such a great gap between very polite language and a short sudden plain form creates a humorous effect.

CONCLUDING REMARKS

This study has shed light on the communicative behavior of young, mostly female Japanese BBS users. We have seen that they employ a variety of flexible options to address readers with varying degrees of familiarity and involvement. Their use of language largely resembles that of informal spoken Japanese with the addition of genuinely creative orthography. Users employ informal spoken features such as final particles, interacting with other users online as if they were in face-to-face conversation. We have also seen greater use of polite than plain forms. Some users may be very involved and assume a highly interactive stance by using more plain forms, while others who may not be as involved but are more concerned with avoiding making a rude impression may convey social distance with polite *masu* forms. If they are quite familiar with each other, they may engage in message exchange without *masu/desu* polite forms. When the participants are new or do not have sufficient familiarity to use plain forms, they may use more *masu/desu* polite forms than *da/suru* forms. Thus, the varying degrees of style mixture in CMC may be related to the extent to which the users feel involvement and closeness to other users.

The above findings come from Japanese fan sites. If we were to look at other kinds of websites, different phenomena might be observed. Users in the sites studied seem to aim at being friendly with each other because of shared interests. It might be harder to find friendly interaction on websites where conflicting opinions and interests coexist. It would be intriguing to investigate how users on other websites employ language, and how they interact. It would be of great interest, for example, to see whether culturally constrained Japanese communication patterns are maintained, or whether novel behavior is found. This type of research could make a theoretical contribution to our knowledge of Japanese online communication.

Studies of CMC owe a great deal to previous studies of spoken versus written language (e.g., Chafe, 1982; Ochs, 1979; Tannen, 1982). CMC research strengthens the claim that various genres of communication (regardless of medium) are located along a continuum and that there is no clear dichotomy between speech and writing (Baron, 1984; Collot & Belmore, 1996; Yates, 1996). CMC occupies an intermediate position between spoken and written language, sharing certain features with both, while displaying at the same time other features unique to online genres. The investigation of online discourse deepens our understanding of communicative behavior generally, in that we encounter types of communicative events that have not previously been observable for study. At the same time, this study shows the importance of attending to the characteristics of the specific language involved, and to the sociocultural context of its online use, for an understanding of emergent patterns in online communication.

Acknowledgments

I thank Brenda Danet and Susan Herring for their helpful suggestions. I am also grateful to Patricia M. Clancy and Mary Bucholtz for their valuable comments on earlier versions of this chapter. My thanks also go to my colleague Charles Muller for his assistance in preparation of the manuscript. Any errors that may remain are my responsibility.

A previous version of this chapter was published in the *Journal of Computer-Mediated Communication* (volume 9, issue 1, 2003).

References

Baba, J. (2001). *Pragmatic function of Japanese mimesis in emotive discourse*. Paper presented at the Southern Japan Seminar, Atlanta, GA. Retrieved December 5, 2005, from http://web.aall.ufl.edu/SJS/Baba.pdf.

Barke, A. J. (2001). Inconspicuous gender marking: The case of Japanese sentence-final particles, *yo* and *ne*. In K. Horie & S. Sato (Eds.), *Cognitive-functional linguistics in an East Asian context* (pp. 235–255). Tokyo: Kuroshio.

Baron, N. S. (1984). Computer mediated communication as a force in language change. *Visible Language, 18*(2), 118–141.

Baron, N. S. (2000). *Alphabet to email: How written English evolved and where it's heading*. London: Routledge.

Chafe, W. L. (1982). Integration and involvement in speaking, writing, and oral literature. In D. Tannen (Ed.), *Spoken and written language: Exploring orality and literacy*. Advances in Discourse Processes Series (Vol. 9, pp. 35–53). Norwood, NJ: Ablex.

Cho, T. (In press). Linguistic features of electronic mail in the workplace: A comparison with memoranda. In S. Herring (Ed.), *Computer-mediated conversation*. Cresskill, NJ: Hampton Press.

Collot, M., & Belmore, N. (1996). Electronic language: A new variety of English. In S. C. Herring (Ed.), *Computer-mediated communication: Linguistic, social and cross-cultural perspectives* (pp. 13–28). Amsterdam: John Benjamins.

Cook, H. M. (1990). An indexical account of the Japanese sentence-final particle *no*. *Discourse Processes, 13*, 401–439.

Cook, H. M. (1992). Meanings of non-referential indexes: A case study of the Japanese sentence-final particle *ne*. *Text, 4*, 507–539.

Danet, B. (2001). *Cyberpl@y: Communicating online*. New York: Berg. Companion website: http://pluto.mscc.huji.ac.il/~msdanet/cyberpl@y/.

Danet, B., Ruedenberg, L., & Rosenbaum-Tamari, Y. (1998). "Hmmm . . . where's that smoke coming from?" Writing, play and performance on Internet Relay Chat. In F. Sudweeks, M. McLaughlin, & S. Rafaeli (Eds.), *Network and netplay: Virtual groups on the Internet* (pp. 47–85). Cambridge, MA: AAAI/MIT Press.

Gendai no Esupuri [Esprit of today]. (1998). Intaanetto Shakai [Internet Society] (Special issue). Vol. 370. Tokyo: Shibundo.

Gimenez, J. C. (2000). Business email communication: Some emerging tendencies in register. *English for Specific Purposes, 19,* 237–251.

Global Internet Statistics (by language). (2004). Retrieved December 5, 2005, from http://global-reach.biz/globstats/index.php3.

Haga, Y. (1962). *Kokugo hyougen kyooshitsu* [Classrooms for/lessons in expressions in Japanese]. Tokyo: Toukyoudou.

Herring, S. C. (Ed.). (1996). *Computer-mediated communication: Linguistic, social and cross-cultural perspectives.* Amsterdam: John Benjamins.

Herring, S. C. (2001). Computer-mediated discourse. In D. Tannen, D. Schiffrin, & H. Hamilton (Eds.), *Handbook of discourse analysis* (pp. 612–634). Oxford: Blackwell.

Ide, S., & Yoshida, M. (1999). Sociolinguistics: Honorifics and gender differences. In N. Tsujimura (Ed.), *The handbook of Japanese linguistics* (pp. 444–480). Malden, MA: Blackwell.

Kataoka, K. (1997). Affect and letter-writing: Unconventional conventions in casual writing by young Japanese women. *Language in Society, 26,* 103–136.

Katsuno, H., & Yano, C. R. (2002). Face to face: On-line subjectivity in contemporary Japan. *Asian Studies Review, 26,* 205–232.

Lan, L. (2000). Email: A challenge to standard English? *English Today, 16,* 23–29, 55.

Lee, J. Y. (1996). Charting the codes of cyberspace: A rhetoric of electronic mail. In L. Strate, R. Jacobson, & S. B. Gibson (Eds.), *Communication and cyberspace: Social interaction in an electronic environment* (pp. 275–296). Cresskill, NJ: Hampton Press.

Matsuda, P. K. (2001). Voice in Japanese written discourse: Implications for second language writing. *Journal of Second Language Writing, 10,* 35–53.

Matsuda, P. K. (2002). Negotiation of identity and power in a Japanese online discourse community. *Computers and Composition, 19,* 39–55.

Maynard, S. K. (1989). *Japanese conversation: Self-contextualization through structure and interactional management.* Norwood, NJ: Ablex.

Maynard, S. K. (2002). *Linguistic emotivity: Centrality of place, the topic-comment dynamic, and an ideology of pathos in Japanese discourse.* Amsterdam: John Benjamins.

McGloin, N. H. (1990). Sex difference and sentence-final particles. In S. Ide & N. H. McGloin (Eds.), *Aspects of Japanese women's language* (pp. 23–41). Tokyo: Kuroshio.

Nihongogaku [Japanese Linguistics]. (1996, November). Denshi shakai no komyunikeisyon [Communication in electronic society] (Special issue). Tokyo: Meiji Shoin.

Nihongogaku [Japanese Linguistics]. (2001, September). *Keitai meeru* [Cell phone (e)mail] (Special issue). Tokyo: Meiji Shoin.

Nishimura, Y. (2001). *Kakareru hanashi kotoba—intaanetto jyou ni mirareru atarashii komyunikeeshon sutairu* [Written "spoken" discourse: Novel communication style found on the Internet]. In Toyo Gakuen University and Toyo Women's College Association for Studies on Language (Ed.), *Shiriizu kotoba no supekutoru Taiwa [Dialogue: Series in spectrum of languages]* (pp. 27–57). Tokyo: Liber Press.

Nishimura, Y. (2003a). Establishing a community of practice on the Internet: Linguistic behavior of online Japanese communication. In P. M. Nowak, C. Yoquelet, & D. Mortensen (Eds.), *Proceedings of the 29th annual meeting of the Berkeley Linguistics Society* (pp. 337–348). Berkeley, CA: Berkeley Linguistics Society.

Nishimura, Y. (2003b). Linguistic innovations and interactional features of casual online communication in Japanese. *Journal of Computer-Mediated Communication, 9*(1). Retrieved December 5, 2005, from http://jcmc.indiana.edu/vol9/issue1/nishimura.html.

Ochs, E. (1979). Planned and unplanned discourse. In T. Givón (Ed.), *Discourse and syntax* (pp. 51–80). New York: Academic Press.

Satake, H. (1995). *Aratana buntai wo mosaku suru* [Exploring new styles]. *Gengo [Language]*, *24*(1), 52–59.

Satake, H. (2002). *Hugou no mondai* [Issues on signs and symbols]. In Y. Hida & T. Sato (Eds.), *Gendai Nihongo Kouza [Contemporary Japanese linguistics series]* (Vol. 6, pp. 104–126). Tokyo: Meiji Shoin.

Soumushou [Ministry of Public Management, Home Affairs, Posts and Telecommunications, Japan]. (2004). *Information and communications in Japan white paper: Building a ubiquitous network society that spreads throughout the world.* Retrieved December 5, 2005, from http://www.johotsusintokei.soumu.go.jp/whitepaper/eng/WP2004/2004-index.html.

Stanlaw, J. (2002). "Hire" or "fire"? Taking AD-vantage of innovations in the Japanese syllabary system. *Language Sciences, 24*(5–6), 537–574.

Sugimoto, T., & Levin, J. (2000). Multiple literacies and multimedia: A comparison of Japanese and American uses of the Internet. In G. Hawisher & C. Selfe (Eds.), *Global literacies and the World-Wide Web* (pp. 133–153). London: Routledge.

Tanaka, Y. (2001). *Keitai denwa to denshi meeru no hyougen* [Expressions in messages via cell phones and email on the computer]. In Y. Hida & T. Sato (Eds.), *Gendai Nihongo Koza [Contemporary Japanese language series]*: Vol. 2. Hyougen [Expressions] (pp. 98–127). Tokyo: Meiji Shyoin.

Tannen, D. (Ed.). (1982). *Spoken and written language: Exploring orality and literacy.* Advances in Discourse Processes Series, Vol. 9. Norwood, NJ: Ablex.

Uyeno, T. (1971). *A study of Japanese modality: A performative analysis of sentence particles.* Unpublished Ph.D. thesis, University of Michigan.

Werry, C. C. (1996). Linguistic and interactional features of Internet Relay Chat. In S. C. Herring (Ed.), *Computer-mediated communication: Linguistic, social and cross-cultural perspectives* (pp. 47–63). Amsterdam: John Benjamins.

Yates, S. J. (1996). Oral and written linguistic aspects of computer-conferencing. In S. C. Herring (Ed.), *Computer-mediated communication: Linguistic, social and cross-cultural perspectives* (pp. 29–46). Amsterdam: John Benjamins.

8

CARMEN K. M. LEE

Linguistic Features of Email and ICQ
Instant Messaging in Hong Kong

While most previous research has investigated English-based computer-mediated communication (CMC; Baron, 1998, 2001; Danet, 2001; Herring, 1996, 2001), a growing number of studies are investigating the linguistic features of CMC in non-English-speaking communities (Danet & Herring, 2003; see chapter 1 this volume for an overview). Among these are several studies of Chinese (Bodomo & Lee, 2002; Cheng, 2002; James, 2001; Lee, 2002a, 2002b; Su, chapter 3 this volume).

In this chapter I examine linguistic features of CMC in Hong Kong, a special administrative region of China in Southeast Asia. The analysis is based on a 70,000-word corpus of email and ICQ messages ("I Seek You," a form of instant messaging), collected mainly from undergraduate students in Hong Kong whose first language is Cantonese, with English as their second language. A questionnaire survey was also conducted. While some of the findings are comparable to those in previous studies of CMC in Chinese-speaking communities, the present study provides a more comprehensive overview of features in Hong Kong, such as the mixture of Cantonese and English elements (i.e., code-mixed messages) and morpheme-by-morpheme literal translations. It reveals that CMC features in Hong Kong differ from those of other Chinese-speaking communities, such as Taiwan (Su, chapter 3 this volume).

ICQ

Hong Kong, with an Internet penetration rate of 69.9%,[1] has the highest number of instant messenging (IM) users (65% of its Internet population) and the highest number of ICQ users in Asia (NetValue, 2001a, 2001b). ICQ is an IM application that was launched in July 1996 by Mirabilis Ltd. (now ICQ Inc.). As of December 2005, the latest version of the software was available in eight languages, and previous versions in another 10 languages.[2] By April 2005, there were more than 180 million registered ICQ users from at least 245 countries (ICQ Inc., 1998–2005).

With ICQ, users can chat via text, send asynchronous text messages, share website addresses, and exchange files. Users can search for chat partners freely, although authorizations are required before one can actually communicate with another registered user. Every ICQ user has his or her contact list that stores information about chat partners. The contact list appears in the form of a popup menu (figure 8.1).

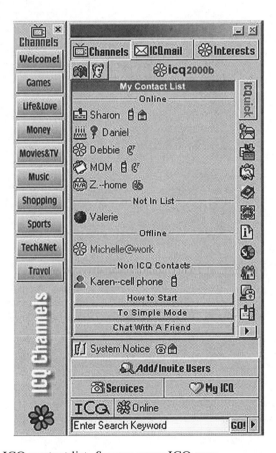

FIGURE 8.1. An ICQ contact list. *Source*: www.ICQ.com.

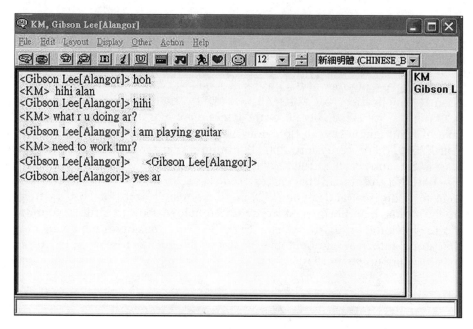

FIGURE 8.2. ICQ chat mode, IRC format.

ICQ offers two possibilities for synchronous communication: chat mode, in which the contributions of two or more participants are simultaneously visible on the screen, and IM mode, in which only one contribution at a time is displayed. Participants in full chat mode may further choose to have the exchange of messages displayed in Internet Relay Chat (IRC; line-by-line) format (figure 8.2) or in separate subwindows (character-by-character format) for each participant (figure 8.3). Most of the ICQ data in this study come from the IM mode (figure 8.4). In this mode, the sender selects a person from his or her contact list (by double-clicking on a name), and a message dialogue box then pops up for the message (of no more than 450 characters).[3]

THE SOCIOLINGUISTIC BACKGROUND
OF HONG KONG

Language(s) Spoken and Written

Cantonese, a Yue dialect of Chinese, has long been the dominant variety of Chinese spoken in Hong Kong. Although Hong Kong is essentially a Cantonese-speaking community, with more than 90% of its population being Cantonese speakers, English is also very important. The 2001 census revealed that 43% of the population had "knowledge" of English (cited in Bolton, 2002). Chinese (including both written Chinese and spoken Cantonese) and

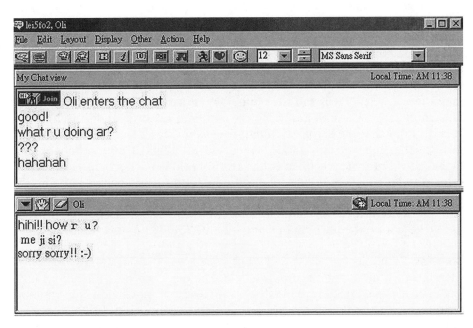

FIGURE 8.3. ICQ chat mode, split-screen format.

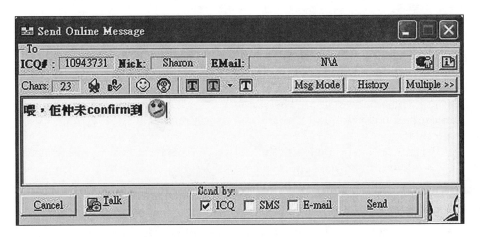

FIGURE 8.4. ICQ message window, IM mode.

English have been Hong Kong's official languages since the early 1970s when the region was still a British colony. Even though it has been argued that English should be treated as Hong Kongers' "second language," Luke and Richards (1982) claim that English is neither a second language nor a foreign language but an "auxiliary" language. It is not a second language because it is not spoken at home or in any interpersonal communication situations.

However, it is not a foreign language, either, because it has been used widely in many domains, including government, education, business communication, and the mass media (TV, magazines, and newspapers).

After the handover of its sovereignty to China in 1997, Hong Kong became a Special Administrative Region (SAR) of China. The SAR government's major language policy is to foster biliteracy in written Chinese and English, and trilingualism in Cantonese, English, and *Putonghua* (Mandarin Chinese). It is believed that the status of Mandarin has increased with the closer business partnership between Hong Kong and Mainland China, although the language is not widely spoken in the territory. Many schools in Hong Kong offer Mandarin classes along with traditional Chinese (see below) and English classes.

The written form of Cantonese has never been officially standardized, nor is there formal education in Cantonese writing. *Baihua*, a traditional and standard form of written Chinese, is used widely in official and formal domains, including in government and education. It corresponds closely to Mandarin Chinese, but it is different from spoken Cantonese phonologically, syntactically, and lexically. Although Cantonese does not have a conventional writing system, this does not mean that Cantonese cannot be written. Recently, many advertisements and youth magazines have started to incorporate informal representations of Cantonese.

Languages Used on the Internet

Many Hong Kong–based official and business websites are bilingual, with English and standard written Chinese versions. With the growing partnership between Hong Kong and Mainland China, many websites provide a simplified Chinese character version.[4] The simplified character writing system is used in most parts of Mainland China, while traditional character writing is used in Hong Kong.

Part of the questionnaire for this study asked participants what language(s) they would use in online communication. The results show that most respondents prefer a mixture of language varieties or codes. Forty-nine respondents (68%) indicated that code mixing of Chinese and English was a preferred means of communication via the Internet. Twenty-two respondents (30%) would use English as the *only* language of online communication. Surprisingly, *none* reported using only Chinese online.

Chinese Character Inputting Systems Used in Hong Kong

The Chinese inputting methods used in Hong Kong partially resemble those available to users in Taiwan (Su, chapter 3 this volume). However, as Su points out, some of these methods are not very popular, because they require a

TABLE 8.1. Familiarity with Chinese inputting methods.

Chinese inputting system	No. of respondents ($N = 72$; respondents may choose more than one)
Simplified	41
Pen-based/handwriting	35
Changjie	25
Romanized Cantonese	21
English–Chinese Conversion	14
Hanyu Pinyin	10

certain level of proficiency in decoding Chinese characters. Moreover, while *Zhuyin*, a phonetic inputting system, is the most popular in Taiwan, Hong Kong users are more skillful in simplified[5] and handwriting[6] inputting methods. *Changjie*, a well-known, widespread Chinese inputting method, was used by fewer than half the respondents. The overall responses are summarized in table 8.1.

Respondents are more familiar with ideographical, shape-based inputting methods than with sound-based, phonetic methods. This is because Hong Kong users are not familiar with the romanization of Cantonese. However, being familiar with character inputting systems does not necessarily mean that CMC users prefer inputting characters. Of the 167 email messages and 155 ICQ exchanges collected, only 17 email messages (10%) and 72 ICQ sessions (46%) contain Chinese characters.

PREVIOUS STUDIES OF CHINESE CMC

In a study of writing systems in Taiwan-based BBSs, Su (chapter 3 this volume) identified four creative uses of writing systems: stylized English, stylized Taiwanese, Taiwanese-accented English, and recycling of a transliteration alphabet used in elementary education. Situated within Taiwan's multilingual social context, these writing systems have spawned unique patterns of use among Taiwanese online. As discussed below, patterns of use online in Hong Kong are rather different.

Research into CMC in Hong Kong does not have a long history. Much of it is devoted to the educational or pedagogical implications of CMC in the English language classroom. L. Li (2000) and Y. Li (2000), for example, address linguistic issues of CMC from a Chinese perspective. L. Li identifies linguistic differences between email written by native and nonnative English speakers (native Mandarin speakers) in Hong Kong. Y. Li focuses on code mixing and code switching in a CMC corpus of English and Mandarin email messages written by native Mandarin speakers. In response to L. Li and Y. Li, Gao (2001) analyzed Chinese–English code mixing in CMC from a pedagogical perspective. Although these studies are Chinese based, little attention is accorded to Cantonese.

In one of the few CMC studies devoted to Hong Kong Cantonese, James (2001) focuses on one of its most distinctive aspects—sentence-final particles—and discusses how ICQ language may be adapted in the language classroom. Cheng (2002) investigated the ICQ chat history of two Hong Kong users and identified creative ways of representing Cantonese: informal romanization of Chinese characters, direct translations of Chinese, and sentence-final particles. In this chapter I discuss similar phenomena, via qualitative and quantitative analyses of a larger corpus including both synchronous ICQ and asynchronous email data, and also investigate code mixing.

DATA AND METHODOLOGY

The data for this study were collected from 72 Cantonese speakers in Hong Kong, who were mainly secondary school and university students. The young age of these subjects is in line with findings reported in NetValue (2001b) that the 15–24 year age group accounts for the highest percentage of Internet users in Hong Kong (41.8%), followed by those 25–34 years of age (26.7%).

Questionnaire Survey

A survey was conducted at the end of 2001, shortly before the collection of email and ICQ texts. Its purpose was to investigate general habits of CMC use in Hong Kong and participants' attitudes toward CMC. The survey was administered in face-to-face interviews, telephone interviews, and via a self-administered questionnaire in the absence of the investigator. Questions were written in both Chinese and English in order to minimize misinterpretations.

Collection of Messages

At the end of the questionnaire, respondents were asked whether they would agree to make their CMC messages available for this research. The investigator would then approach them for details and procedures regarding data collection. An instruction sheet specifying the criteria for text messages was attached to the questionnaire. The messages should be

- One-to-one exchanges, that is, only two participants involved
- Written in Chinese/Cantonese, English, or a mixture of both
- Written by native Cantonese speakers who have English as their second language

Data providers copied and pasted their messages as MS Word documents and emailed the files to the investigator. For ICQ messages, they were requested to save their personal message "history" as text or document files. There was no restriction regarding how many or what kind of messages they should provide. A total of 167 email messages and 155 ICQ exchanges[7] were collected, constituting a corpus of approximately 70,000 words.[8] The data involve mainly private communications. Of the 167 email messages, 121 are personal exchanges between friends and 46 messages involve tutor–student correspondence. The ICQ data are mostly casual exchanges between friends and classmates.

Translations and Glosses of Cantonese Data

Chinese/Cantonese examples in this chapter are glossed and translated into English using the following format:

我	試	試	啦	(Chinese/Cantonese characters)
ngo5	si3	si3	laa1	(Cantonese romanization with tones)
1.SG[9]	try	try	PART	(morpheme-by-morpheme translation)
"I'll have a try."				(free translation in English)

Cantonese romanizations are based on the Cantonese romanization scheme developed by the Linguistic Society of Hong Kong (LSHK). Tones in Cantonese are marked with numbers: 1, high level; 2, high rising; 3, mid level; 4, low falling; 5, low rising; and 6, low level.

LINGUISTIC FEATURES OF CMC TEXTS IN HONG KONG

Representations of Cantonese in Hong Kong CMC

Although there is no standard writing in Cantonese, in order to represent it in CMC, Hong Kong users have created a number of strategies involving different combinations of Chinese and English and their writing systems. This study identified five main strategies to represent Cantonese words: romanized Cantonese, literal translations, Cantonese characters, standard Chinese characters, and a combination of "o" or "0" and a standard Chinese character.

Romanized Cantonese and Literal Translations of Cantonese

Whereas Taiwanese BBS participants often play with Chinese characters to represent their target language (as in stylized Taiwanese and stylized English; Su, chapter 3 this volume), in Hong Kong CMC, many users prefer using the

TABLE 8.2. Romanized Cantonese sentence-final particles.

Particle in CMC	Target particle: character and (romanization)		Example
ar (aa/a/ah/aar)	啊/呀	(aa3/4)	yes *ar* ... just set up my computer *ar* ...
ga (gar/ka)	嘿/㗎	(gaa3/4)	hahahhahaha!! That's true *ga*!
ge (geh/gee/gei)	嘅/嘅	(ge2/3)	oh!! not waiting for me *gei*!!!!
gwa (kwa)	啩	(gwaa3)	u might argue for that *gwa*
jar (ja)	咋	(zaa3)	i don't think so just joking *jar*
la (lah/laa/lar)	啦/嚹	(laa1/3)	sleep *la* ... goodnight ...:)
lor (low/lo/law)	囉/囉	(lo1/3)	sorry again *lor*
mei (me/meah)	咩	(me1)	are u very busy now *mei*????
tim	添	(tim1)	wo, quite want u to phone me *tim*!!!!
wor (woo)	喎/喎/喎	(wo3/4/5)	she seems not so interested in him *wor*!!

Roman alphabet to represent Cantonese elements; they either create Cantonese spellings or directly translate the intended Cantonese expressions in a morpheme-by-morpheme manner.

Unlike *Hanyu Pinyin* for Mandarin, the romanization of Cantonese has never been fully standardized, although a variety of romanization schemes have been adopted by linguists and dictionary makers, such as the Yale system developed by Parker Huang and Gerald Kok at Yale University[10] and the *JyutPing* scheme developed by LSHK,[11] the system used here. Romanization of sentence-final particles is very common: In the corpus (a total of 322 messages/exchanges), 1,740 romanized sentence-final particles were found. Examples are shown in table 8.2.

Cantonese Characters and Homophony

Although Cantonese does not have a very developed set of characters for writing, it is still possible to word process these characters on the computer. In order to process such characters, the Hong Kong Supplementary Character Set (HKSCS)[12] must be installed. The following example from an ICQ message contains (bracketed) Cantonese characters:

Excerpt 1

haha.......	喂,	諗	唔	諗	到	[啲]	**Fill in**	比	**Reality**	呀?
(laughter)	*wai3*	*lam2*	*m4*	*lam2*	*dou2*	*di1*	*fill-in*	*bei2*	*Reality*	*aa3*
(laughter)	hey	think	NEG	think	able	CL	fill-in	give	Reality	PART

"Hey, have you thought of the 'fill-in' for *Reality*?" (talking about a guitar performance)

你	淨	係	彈	solo	好	[嗮]	喎
nei5	zing6	hai6	taan4	solo	hou2	saai1	wo3
2.SG	just	be	play	solo	INTENS	waste	PART

"It's a waste if you only play the solo part."

Some users may find it inconvenient to install an extra set of characters onto their computers and may resort to using homophones in the standard Chinese character set, that is, characters that are different in form but have the same pronunciation as the intended Cantonese characters. For example:

Excerpt 2

K:

做	[緊]	咩	[野]	呀?
zou6	gan2	me1	je5	aa3
do	PROG	what	thing	PART

"What are you doing?"

N:

關	你	咩	[野]	事?
gwaan1	nei5	me1	je5	si6
relate	2.SG	what	thing	matter

"It's none of your business."

K uses 緊 (*gan2*) and 野 (*je5*) to represent 嚟 (*gan2*) and 嘢 (*je5*), respectively. Both characters have the same pronunciation as their target expressions. This strategy is comparable to Su's (chapter 3 this volume) stylized Taiwanese. Since, according to her, it is not common to see Taiwanese in writing, CMC users would rather find a Chinese character that resembles the pronunciation of the intended Taiwanese expression. I prefer to call this phenomenon "homophony" because it captures an important linguistic feature of Cantonese: It is a tone language, and there are a large number of morphemes (represented as characters) that are the same in pronunciation (and tone) but differ in meaning and form. Cantonese-speaking CMC users are well aware of this and make use of this linguistic knowledge in their messages.

Combination of Letters and Standard Chinese Characters

Hong Kong CMC users may also represent a character by combining the letter "o" or the number "0" with an existing Chinese character. Many Chinese characters can be "dismantled" into different parts. In Cantonese, many characters are represented in print by attaching the radical 口 to the left-hand side of an existing Chinese homophonic character (as in 咗 = "口" + "左").

Since the shape of □ roughly resembles that of "o" or "0," some CMC users skillfully combine "o" or "0" with an existing Chinese character to form the intended Cantonese character, as shown in the bracketed characters of the following excerpt from an email:

Excerpt 3

佢成日叫我唔好[o係]佢[o地]面前提起佢,驚佢[o地]唔會接受佢[o既]建議

(NB: "o係" for 喺; "o地" for "哋"; "o既" for 嘅)

Gloss and translation:

佢	成日	叫		我		唔	好
keoi5	*seng4_jat6*	*giu3*		*ngo5*		*m4*	*hou2*
3.SG	always	ask		1.SG		NEG	good
o係	佢o地	面	前	提	起	佢	
hai2	*keoi5_dei6*	*min6*	*cin4*	*tai4*	*hei2*	*keoi5*	
at	3.PL	face	front	remind	up	3.SG	

"S/he always says I shouldn't mention him/her in his/her presence."

驚	佢o地	唔	會	接受	佢	o既	建議
geng1	*keoi5_dei6*	*m4*	*wui5*	*zip3_sau6*	*keoi5*	*ge3*	*gin3_ji5*
fear	3.PL	NEG	will	accept	3.SG	POSS	suggestion

"S/he fears that they won't accept his/her suggestions."

Forming characters this way ensures that they will display properly without installing the Cantonese character set onto one's computer. To better understand users' preferences regarding the representation of Cantonese in CMC, I asked respondents to select their preferred form of Cantonese representation from the five strategies described above (they could choose more than one; figure 8.5).

The use of Chinese/Cantonese characters was not the preferred method reported by these Hong Kong CMC users. The most popular method turned out to be literal translation; 42 of the 72 respondents reported having used this method. In addition, 35 respondents created their own romanization of Cantonese, while 22 reported combining alphabetic symbols and Chinese characters to form Cantonese characters. Only 17 indicated the use of homophones for Cantonese representation, and four said they had never composed their messages with Cantonese elements. Although character inputting is still among the most preferred methods, a large number of respondents like to represent Cantonese elements in the Roman alphabet. In fact, very few messages in the corpus are represented solely in characters. This suggests that Hong Kong CMC users are constrained by factors such as typing effort and proficiency in Chinese inputting systems.

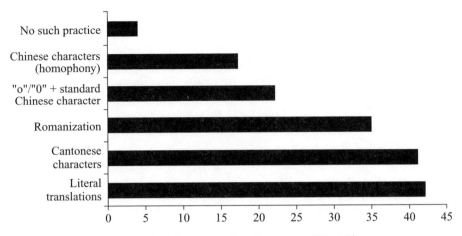

FIGURE 8.5. Reported modes of representing Cantonese ($N = 72$).

Code Mixing in Hong Kong CMC

Code mixing is a well-known linguistic phenomenon in Hong Kong and has been the focus of many sociolinguistic studies (Chan, 1998; Gibbons, 1987; D. C. S. Li, 1994, 1998, 2000; Luke, 1998). It generally refers to the existence of two or more linguistic systems within an utterance (Kamwangamalu, 1989). However, the meaning of code mixing may vary in different contexts. In D. C. S. Li's research, for instance, the term "code switching" is preferred. To avoid terminological controversy, this study adopts the traditional view of code mixing, that is, switching between two or more languages at an intra-sentential level.

In the context of CMC in Hong Kong, code mixing is not restricted to Cantonese–English mixing as it is in naturally occurring conversation. This study has identified five forms of "code" created and used in different combinations by Hong Kong CMC users: standard English, standard Chinese, Cantonese represented in characters, romanized Cantonese, and morpheme-by-morpheme literal translations.

Type 1: Standard English.   This refers to the form of English that is used in education and other formal contexts in Hong Kong; it is the variety that is intelligible to the general native English speaker.[13] In the data collected, messages written in this form are mainly formal email exchanges and are rarely found in ICQ. However, "standard" in this context does not refer to a perfect or error-free variety. The following example is an email communication between a tutor and her student:

Excerpt 4

Dear YC,
I am glad to receive your email and learn that you can join my tutorial
group on Friday morning. There are totally three tutorials for this course.
In case you couldn't come to any of these tutorials, would you please inform
me in advance so that I could make proper arrangement for you, say, to
assign you to another tutorial session which you are able to attend.
Sincerely yours,
WM

Type 2: Standard Chinese.   This refers to the variety of formal and
traditional written Chinese that is widely accepted in domains of education,
business, and other official settings. The following is an email extract primarily in standard Chinese:

Excerpt 5

有些中文文件必須通過電腦的 "編碼",然後解碼,方能閱讀

Gloss and translation:

有些	中文	文件	必	須
jau5_se1	*zung1_man4*	*man4_gin2*	*bit1*	*seoi1*
some	Chinese	document	must	need
通過	電腦	的	"編	碼"
tung1_gwo3	*din6_nou5*	*dik1*	*pin1*	*maa5*
through	computer	POSS	arrange	code

"Some Chinese documents have to be encoded by the computer"

然　後	解	碼,	方	能	閱　讀.
jin4_hau6	*gaai2*	*maa5*	*fong1*	*nang4*	*jyut6_duk6*
then	solve	code	then	able	read

"and then it [the Chinese document] has to be decoded before it is
readable."

In this variety, there are no Cantonese items. For example, 有些 (*jau5se1*,
"some") would be 有啲 (*jau5di1*, "some") in Cantonese. However, standard
Chinese writing is rarely found in the corpus. Only five email messages are
written mainly in standard written Chinese, and only one ICQ exchange
contains significant elements of this form of Chinese writing.

Type 3: Cantonese in Characters.   In contrast to standard Chinese
(type 2), this form of written language is rarely used in other media
except colloquial or youth publications, because it directly reflects spoken
Cantonese. Here is an ICQ example:

Excerpt 6

A: 聽日點玩?
B: 到時好似會有張紙比我地填上台時啲嘢點擺 . . .
A: 聽日我都唔知點算呀 . . .

Gloss and translation:

A:	聽日		點		玩?	
	ting1_jat6		*dim2*		*waan2*	
	tomorrow		how		play	

"How should we play tomorrow?" [talking about the arrangement of their music performance]

B:	到	時	好	似	會	有
	dou3	*si4*	*hou2*	*ci5*	*wui5*	*jau5*
	arrive	time	INT	similar	will	have
	張	紙	比	我地	填	上
	zoeng1	*zi2*	*bei2*	*ngo5_dei6*	*tin4*	*soeng5*
	CL	paper	give	1.PL	fill	up
	台	時	[啲	嘢]	點	擺
	toi4	*si4*	*di1*	*je5*	*dim2*	*baai2*
	stage	time	CL	thing	how	place

"We will be given a form to indicate the setting requirement when we are on stage."

A:	聽	日	我	都	唔	知	點	算	呀
	ting1_jat6		*ngo5*	*dou1*	*m4*	*zi1*	*dim2*	*syun3*	*aa3*
	tomorrow		1.SG	also	NEG	know	how	count	PART

"I really don't know what to do tomorrow."

This exchange between two secondary school students contains no English or alphabetic writing. The bracketed items indicate Cantonese characters not found in standard written Chinese. In CMC, character representation of Cantonese is not very common, even though it directly reflects the language with which users are most familiar. This is because of the extra typing effort required to input Cantonese characters. Although Cantonese characters can be found in both the email and ICQ data, the messages within this category are restricted to informal exchanges between friends.

Type 4: Romanized Cantonese.   Romanization in CMC is quite common for languages that do not conventionally use the Roman alphabet (see, e.g., Palfreyman & Al Khalil, chapter 2 this volume; Tseliga, chapter 5 this volume). In this study, the most commonly romanized items are sentence-final particles in Cantonese. Cantonese particles occur primarily at the end of a sentence and indicate speech-act types such as questions and requests, attitudinal factors, and emotional coloring. They have no direct counterpart in English, although they are comparable in function to question tags such as "right?" and "do you?" (Matthews & Yip, 1994).

In the list of romanized Cantonese particles (with examples) identified in both email and ICQ (table 8.2), the spellings of some particles are quite consistent in the data. For instance, *la* (for *laa1/3*), one of the most common final particles in spoken Cantonese, appears 579 times in the 155 ICQ exchanges and 149 times in the 167 email messages. In everyday speech, *laa1* with a high-level tone as in *gwo3 lei4 laa1* ("Come here!") is used for "requesting," and *laa3* with a mid-level tone as in *keoi5 lei4 gan2 laa3* ("S/he's coming") usually has the function of emphasizing the current relevance of a situation (Matthews & Yip, 1994).[14] The use of *la* and several other sentence-final particles in the corpus is exemplified in the following email message:

> *Excerpt 7*
>
> The ocamp is ok *la*, except that the beach programs and nite journey were cancelled because of the bad weather. And ah sun quarrelled with "ha jong" *lor*, as u know his character *ga la*. But in our ocamp gp ah sun and jessic got along very well with the cores and freshmen *geh*. Ok *la*, keep contact thru email. One yr is not very long.

Table 8.3 lists some other romanized expressions identified in the corpus. Note that some users enclosed these romanizations in quotation marks (e.g., "*che chai min*"). This suggests that users are aware of the nonstandardness of incorporating Cantonese spellings in an English sentence.

Type 5: Morpheme-by-Morpheme Literal Translations.   These are direct translations of Cantonese elements into English in a syllable-by-syllable (or morpheme-by-morpheme) manner. They would make no sense to readers not acquainted with Hong Kong culture as reflected in the Cantonese language (table 8.4). Many of these examples are culture specific and do not have equivalents in English.

> *Excerpt 8*
>
> Dear DD,
> Hee hee . . . dunno why I always like to send u mails *ar*! Part is becoz I wanna keep contact with u *la*! Another reason is I am having "*sky and land*" lessons today!

The phrase "sky and land lessons" is university jargon common among undergraduate students. The target expression in Cantonese is 天地堂 (*tin1 dei6 tong4*, "sky-land-lesson"), which metaphorically refers to a large gap in time between two lectures on the same day (e.g., one lecture at 9:30 A.M. and the other at 4 P.M.).

TABLE 8.3. Selected romanized Cantonese expressions in the data.

Romanized expression	Target Cantonese expression	Example from data
bei sum gei	俾 心 機 *bei2 sam1_gei1* give effort "Work hard!" (an encouragement)	then "*bei sum gei*" la cu next time!
che chai min	車 仔 麵 *ce1 zai2 min6* car little noodle (a kind of Hong Kong style noodle)	We've tried a newly-opened "*che chai min*" shop outside the campus, very delicious *ar*!
dim aaaaaaaa	點 呀 *dim2 aa3* how PART "What's up?"	*Dim aaaaaaaaaaaaaa?* I don't want to be so bad to you *laa*
ma fan	麻 煩 *maa4 faan4* "troublesome"	i can use e-mail to contact ja,icq is so *ma fan ar* coz i have to secretly download and use it
mo liu	無 聊 *mou4 liu4* "feeling bored"	not so early, 10 sept, but in fact, i want early cos' i gain weight and "*mo liu*" more and more~~hee

TABLE 8.4. Examples of morpheme-by-morpheme literal translation.

Example	Target expression
Add oil	加 油 *gaa1jau2* add oil "Work hard!" (an encouragement)
BIG-HEAD-SHRIMP	大 頭 蝦 *daai6 tau4 haa1* big head shrimp "careless and absent-minded"
Black eye circle	黑 眼 圈 *hak1 ngaan5 hyun1* black eye circle "darkness around one's eyes due to lack of sleep"
Hand letter	手 信 *sau2 seon3* hand letter (a souvenir/gift brought back home from somebody who just traveled overseas)
Sky and land lessons	天 地 堂 *tin1 dei6 tong4* sky land lesson (a long period of time between two lessons)

Another example requiring explanation is "hand letter." In Hong Kong, people like buying small gifts and souvenirs for their friends and relatives at home when they travel overseas. Small gifts of this kind are called *sau2 seon3* in Cantonese, literally translated as "hand-letter." The origin of this expression is unknown, but it is likely to mean a letter sent by hand/in person rather than through the post, which is now used metaphorically to mean "gift." The following is part of an ICQ exchange in which "hand letter" is used:

Excerpt 9

A: . . . u wanna come to airport? no need *la*!! Thanks!!!
B: . . . i just want to say: pls give me "*hand letter*" as u come back *jar* . . . hhahahaha
A: hahah!!! what's that? I've never heard about such a thing *worrrrr*!!!

In this exchange, A is going to France, and s/he is asking whether B will go to see her off at the airport. However, B only wants A to bring her some souvenirs ("hand letter") from France.

It is also very common for CMC users to combine romanization and morpheme-by-morpheme literal translations to form a full English sentence in a message, as in the examples shown in table 8.5. These examples contain reduplication (e.g., "*see see*" for 睇睇 *tai2 tai2*, "*try try*" for 試試 *si3 si3* . . . etc.). The reduplication of verbs serves to convey a meaning similar to "have a . . . ," as in "have a try" and "have a look" in English. The following ICQ excerpt contains the second reduplicated construction:

Excerpt 10

A: u need bass tab?
B: yes *ar*
A: try to follow guitar chord^^
B: um . . . . i try try *la~*

TABLE 8.5. Combining romanized Cantonese and morpheme-by-morpheme translation.

Example	Target and interpretation
Let me see see *sin laa*	等 我 睇 睇 先 啦 *dang2 ngo5 tai2 tai2 sin1 laa1* wait 1.SG see see first PART "Let me think about it first."
I try try *la*	我 試 試 啦 *ngo5 si3 si3 laa1* 1.SG try try PART "I will have a try."

"I try try *la*" (last reply of B) is a direct translation of the target Cantonese construction:

Cantonese expression:	ngo5	si3	si3	laa1
Gloss:	1.SG	try	try	PART
Meaning:	"Let me have a try."			

Shortenings

In CMC, shortenings may be used to indicate familiarity and intimacy between users or to facilitate fast typing, especially in synchronous CMC. Table 8.6 presents selected shortenings reported by interviewees and their frequency of actual usage in the email and ICQ corpora.

U ("you"), *ur* ("your"), *coz* ("because"), *thx* ("thanks"), and *oic* ("oh I see") are the five most commonly used CMC shortenings. Shortened expressions occur more frequently in ICQ than in email. Most are English based or are common to English speaking CMC users, as has been documented in previous studies (Crystal, 2001; Danet, 2001; Werry, 1996). However, some deserve further explanation. Consider the use of number homophones, as in *88, 886*, and *99*.

88.   The pronunciation of the number "8" in Cantonese is *baat3*. For some Cantonese CMC users, the sound resembles the pronunciation of "bye"

TABLE 8.6. Shortenings self-reported by respondents and frequency of actual usage in email and ICQ.

Shortening	Target expression	No. reported in questionnaire	No. of uses in email data	No. of uses in ICQ data
88/886	Bye bye	3	0	8
99	Nighty night	1	0	1
ar	Are	1	2	12
B4/b4	Before	6	0	19
Bb/BB	Bye bye	12	5	33
BF	Boyfriend	2	4	2
BTW	By the way	19	0	2
cos	Because	2	1	44
Coz/bcoz/ becoz	Because	4	28	37
oic	Oh I see	3	0	47
R	Are	3	0	23
sth	Something	1	4	18
Thx/thx	Thanks	1	0	87
TMR	Tomorrow	9	2	26
U/u	You	19	117	589
ur	Your	3	6	68

in English; 88 is thus used to represent "bye bye," as in the closing of the following ICQ exchange:

Excerpt 11

> *A*: haha, ok, i have to leave now for dinner.
>   see you later. ^_^[15]
> *B*: 88
> *A*: bye.
> *B*: CU
> *A*: see you.

886.   Some CMC users think that the pronunciation of "6" (*luk6*) in Cantonese resembles the pronunciation of the sentence-final particle *laa3* or *lo3* in Cantonese. *laa3* serves as a confirmation of an action or an affirmative marker in utterances. Cantonese speakers like to say "bye-bye laa3" as a farewell, meaning that one really "has to go now." In the following ICQ exchange, one of the participants uses "886" in the closing:

Excerpt 12

> *J*: oh, take care.
> *B*: thx!! I will!
> *B*:   I leave lu!! 886 Have a nice and sweet dream!
> *J*: same to you.

99.   The target expression of "99" is "night night," meaning "good night." To some Hong Kong CMC users, the pronunciation of "9" in English, "nine" /najn/, resembles that of "night" /naɪt/. Instead of writing out the full expression, users write "99." This phenomenon is not new; English CMC, for example, uses "b4" for "before" and "GR8" for "great." These uses are all sound based. Some represent English sounds ("99" for "night night"), while others are used because they resemble the pronunciation of their target Cantonese expressions ("88" for "bye-bye"). "99" is used in the following closing of an ICQ session:

Excerpt 13

> *K*: ok . . . have to go *lar* . . . BB
> *N*: 99 . . . cu tmr
> *K*: CU . . . nite

These number shortenings are not commonly used. None occurred in the emails, and only nine ICQ sessions contain one or more.

TABLE 8.7. Examples of emoticons reported by respondents.

Emoticon	Meaning	No. reported
:)	Happy/smiling	17
: (	Sad	10
^_^	Happy	8
-_-	Not in mood	8
>.<	Angry/disappointed/unhappy/embarrassed	7
=p	Joking/mischievous/happy	7
=)	Happy	6
=(	Unhappy	6
^v^	Smiling/happy/"that's okay!"	6
^.^	In good mood	5
@.@	Idle/sleepy/bored	5
>o<	Angry	5
><	Annoyed/angry/dissatisfied	4
^3^	Kiss	3
^^	Smiling	3
:米	User is "dead"	2
:-(	Sad	2

Emoticons

Inserting emoticons in computer-mediated messages is fairly universal (Crystal, 2004). However, some culture-specific features can be observed. This study confirms that Hong Kong users tend to use "Asian" or vertical emoticons such as ^v^ (Nishimura, chapter 7 this volume; Katsuno and Yano, chapter 12 this volume) more frequently than Western or horizontal emoticons. Of the 56 emoticons reported by the respondents, only 19 are horizontal; the rest are Asian style (table 8.7).

Even though emoticons are very popular, users do not always include them in messages. A significant difference is found between email and ICQ. Only 13 emoticons were found in the emails, versus 204 in the ICQ data. This again confirms that users tend to employ more CMC features in synchronous than in asynchronous systems.

COMPARING EMAIL AND CHAT

There are striking differences between the email and ICQ data. Table 8.8 compares the frequency of five features in the two modes: code mixing, shortenings, "Asian" emoticons, morpheme-by-morpheme literal translations, and creative Cantonese romanization.

Code mixing is much more common in the ICQ data. All but one of the ICQ exchanges are written in more than one code, whereas fewer than half of the email messages are written in mixed code. The most prominent linguistic feature is romanization of sentence-final particles. There are nearly

TABLE 8.8. Linguistic features of email and ICQ.

Feature	Frequency in email data		Frequency in ICQ data	
	N	%	*N*	%
Code-mixed messages/sessions	69	41.3	154	99.4
Shortenings using numbers (88, 886, 99)	0	0	9	5.8
"Asian" emoticons	7	4.2	79	51.0
Morpheme-by-morpheme literal translations	2	1.2	7	4.5
Creative Cantonese romanization —sentence-final particles	51	30.5	143	92.3

N = number of messages/exchanges containing the specified feature. % = percentage of total messages (167 email messages/155 ICQ exchanges).

two romanized particles in each email message, and up to nine in an ICQ exchange. The least adopted feature is number shortenings. This does not necessarily imply that shortenings are not common in Hong Kong; use of "u" for "you" is still one of the most common features. Hong Kong-style shortenings such as "88" and "99" are not frequent because they are used only among a small group of locals and may not be known to most CMC users in the region. The second least frequently occurring feature is literal translations. This can be accounted for by the fact that literal translation is not the most economical way of representing Cantonese elements. Translation, whether in formal writing or CMC, requires a certain level of language proficiency. Since this feature violates the principle of economy in CMC, some users may prefer not to employ it in their messages.

The linguistic differences between ICQ and email may be attributed to synchronicity. According to Herring (2001), in synchronous CMC contexts users are more bound by time constraints, resulting in a lower degree of linguistic complexity compared to asynchronous CMC such as email. Herring also suggests that the level of formality of a communication situation affects users' preference for the use of standard or nonstandard linguistic features in their messages. In the context of this study, for example, some of the social situations of the email messages collected are quite formal, including academic discussion, whereas ICQ use is overwhelmingly social. For this reason, as well, fewer nonstandard or playful features are found in email.

SUMMARY AND CONCLUSIONS

Creative Representations of Cantonese

This study identified five methods of representing Cantonese in Hong Kong CMC: Cantonese romanizations, literal translations, homophony, Cantonese characters, and combinations of "o" or "0" and Chinese characters. In the survey, interviewees claimed that translating Cantonese words into English in a morpheme-by-morpheme manner is the most popular strategy to represent Cantonese elements. However, in practice this strategy is rather rare.

Code Mixing

Most messages are creative combinations of various codes, including standard English, standard Chinese, Cantonese, Cantonese romanization, and morpheme-by-morpheme literal translations. While the dominant language in everyday conversational code mixing is typically Cantonese, many examples use English as the "matrix" code (Myers-Scotton, 2001), with elements of Cantonese mixed into the sentences. The pervasiveness of English in Hong Kong CMC suggests that the Internet has become a medium in which young people in Hong Kong use English more than they do in everyday speech or in the classroom.

Shortenings

While some of the shortened expressions in the corpus are similar to those identified in previous CMC studies, there are also Hong Kong–specific shortenings, such as "88" for "bye-bye" and "99" for "good night."

Asian Emoticons

Vertical emoticons are more common in Hong Kong CMC than are horizontal ones. They are also much more frequent in the ICQ data than in email.

Overall, this study indicates that CMC features in Hong Kong differ from those of other Chinese-speaking communities, such as Taiwan (Su, chapter 3 this volume). It follows, therefore, that research on CMC features must take account of not only the linguistic backgrounds of CMC users but also the cultural contexts in which they live.

Acknowledgments

I thank Brenda Danet and Susan Herring for helpful comments on earlier drafts of this chapter. I am also very grateful to Adams Bodomo, University of Hong Kong, for his constant support throughout this study.

Notes

1. Source: http://www.internetworldstats.com/top25.htm, retrieved December 5, 2005.
2. See http://www.icq.com/download/, retrieved December 31, 2005.

3. See Herring (2002) for a detailed discussion of the various modes of CMC.

4. See, for example, the Hong Kong SAR government website: http://www.info.gov.hk, retrieved December 5, 2005.

5. A simplified version of *Changjie* inputting method. See Tang and Clubb (1992).

6. Handwriting inputting method uses a handwriting recognition system that allows users, without using a keyboard, to "write" on a handwriting pad specially designed for the computer to recognize and display the required characters.

7. An ICQ exchange in this study refers to a sequence of messages from the initiation of talk to the end of an interaction between two participants.

8. Names of participants have been changed.

9. The following abbreviations are used throughout the chapter: 1/2/3.SG/PL = first/second/third-person singular/plural, CL = classifier, INTENS = intensifier, NEG = negative marker, PART = particle, POSS = possessive marker.

10. See http://www.chinawestexchange.com/Cantonese/Pingyam/, retrieved December 5, 2005.

11. See http://lshk.ctl.cityu.edu.hk/Jyutping.php, retrieved December 5, 2005.

12. HKSCS is available for downloading at http://www.info.gov.hk/digital21/eng/hkscs/download.html, retrieved December 5, 2005.

13. What is considered standard English has long been controversial. See Bex and Watts (1999) and Trudgill (2002).

14. Different particles serve different functions in Cantonese utterances; see Luke (1990).

15. ^_^ (a happy face) is one of the most common Asian emoticons in the data.

References

Baron, N. S. (1998). Letters by phone or speech by other means: The linguistics of email. *Language and Communication, 18*, 133–170.

Baron, N. S. (2001). *Alphabet to email: How written language evolved and where it's heading.* London: Routledge.

Bex, T., & Watts, R. J. (1999). *Standard English: The widening debate.* London: Routledge.

Bodomo, A. B., & Lee, C. K. M. (2002). Changing forms of language and literacy: Technobabble and mobile phone communication. *Literacy and Numeracy Studies, 12*(1), 23–44.

Bolton, K. (2002). The sociolinguistics of Hong Kong and the space for Hong Kong English. In K. Bolton (Ed.), *Hong Kong English: Autonomy and creativity* (pp. 29–55). Hong Kong: Hong Kong University Press.

Chan, B. H.-S. (1998). How does Cantonese-English code-mixing work? In M. Pennington (Ed.), *Language in Hong Kong at century's end* (pp. 191–216). Hong Kong: Hong Kong University Press.

Cheng, J. K. Y. (2002). *Internet chatting as an emergent register: A study of ICQ talk in Hong Kong.* Unpublished M.Phil. thesis, University of Hong Kong.

Crystal, D. (2001). *Language and the Internet.* Cambridge: Cambridge University Press.

Crystal, D. (2004). *A glossary of textspeak and netspeak.* Edinburgh: Edinburgh University Press.

Danet, B. (2001). *Cyberpl@y: Communicating online.* Oxford, UK: Berg. Companion website: http://pluto.mscc.huji.ac.il/~msdanet/cyberpl@y/.

Danet, B., & Herring, S. C. (Eds.). (2003). The multilingual Internet: Language, culture and communication in instant messaging, email and chat (Special issue). *Journal of Computer-*

Mediated Communication, 9(1). Retrieved December 5, 2005, from http://jcmc.indiana .edu/vol9/issue1/.

Gao, L. (2001). Digital age, digital English. *English Today, 17*(3), 17–23.

Gibbons, J. (1987). *Code-mixing and code choice: A Hong Kong case study.* Clevedon, UK: Multilingual Matters.

Herring, S. C. (1996). Two variants of an electronic message schema. In S. C. Herring (Ed.), *Computer-mediated communication: Linguistic, social and cross-cultural perspectives* (pp. 81–108). Amsterdam: John Benjamins.

Herring, S. C. (2001). Computer-mediated discourse. In D. Schiffrin, D. Tannen, & H. E. Hamilton (Eds.), *The handbook of discourse analysis* (pp. 612–634). Oxford: Blackwell.

Herring, S. C. (2002). Computer-mediated communication on the Internet. *Annual Review of Information Science and Technology, 36,* 109–168.

James, G. (2001). Cantonese particles in Hong Kong students' English emails. *English Today, 17,* 9–16.

Kamwangamalu, N. (1989). *Code-mixing across languages: Structure, functions, and constraints.* Unpublished Ph.D. dissertation, University of Illinois, Urbana.

Lee, C. K. M. (2002a). *Chinese and English computer-mediated communication in the context of new literacy studies.* Unpublished M.Phil. thesis, University of Hong Kong.

Lee, C. K. M. (2002b). Literacy practices in computer-mediated communication in Hong Kong. *Reading Matrix, 2*(2). Retrieved December 5, 2005, from http://www.readingmatrix.com/ articles/lee/article.pdf.

Li, D. C. S. (1994). *Why do Hongkongers code-mix? A linguistic perspective.* Research Report No. 40. Department of English, City University of Hong Kong. Hong Kong: City University of Hong Kong.

Li, D. C. S. (1998). The plight of the purist. In M. C. Pennington (Ed.), *Language in Hong Kong at century's end* (pp. 161–190). Hong Kong: Hong Kong University Press.

Li, D. C. S. (2000). Cantonese-English code-switching research in Hong Kong: A Y2K review. *World Englishes, 19*(3), 305–322.

Li, L. (2000). Email: A challenge to standard English? *English Today, 16*(4), 23–29.

Li, Y. (2000). Linguistic characteristics of ESL writing in task-based e-mail activities. *System, 28,* 229–245.

Luke, K. K. (1990). *Utterance particles in Cantonese conversation.* Amsterdam: John Benjamins.

Luke, K. K. (1998). Why two languages might be better than one: Motivations of language mixing in Hong Kong. In M. Pennington (Ed.), *Language in Hong Kong at century's end* (pp. 145–159). Hong Kong: Hong Kong University Press.

Luke, K. K., & Richards, J. C. (1982). English in Hong Kong: Functions and status. *English World-Wide, 3*(1), 47–64.

Matthews, S., & Yip, V. (1994). *Cantonese: A comprehensive grammar.* London: Routledge.

Myers-Scotton, C. (2001). The matrix language frame model: Development and responses. In R. Jacobson (Ed.), *Codeswitching worldwide II* (pp. 23–58). Berlin: Mouton de Gruyter.

NetValue. (2001a). Hong Kong leads Asia's instant message market. March 1. Retrieved December 5, 2005, from http://hk.netvalue.com/presse/cp0016.htm (link no longer active).

NetValue. (2001b). Instant Messaging war. August 9. Retrieved December 5, 2005, from http:// hk.netvalue.com/presse/cp0035.htm (link no longer active).

Nishimura, Y. (2003). Linguistic innovations and interactional features of casual online communication in Japanese. *Journal of Computer-Mediated Communication, 9*(1). Retrieved December 5, 2005, from http://jcmc.indiana.edu/vol9/issue1/nishimura.html.

Tang, C. M. W., & Clubb, O. L. (1992). *Chinese computing: History and current trends.* Hong Kong: Tamarind Books.

Trudgill, P. (2002). *Sociolinguistic variation and change.* Washington, DC: Georgetown University Press.

Werry, C. (1996). Linguistic and interactional features of Internet Relay Chat. In S. C. Herring (Ed.), *Computer-mediated communication: Linguistic, social, and cultural perspectives* (pp. 47–63). Amsterdam: John Benjamins.

9

SALVADOR CLIMENT, JOAQUIM MORÉ, ANTONI OLIVER,
MÍRIAM SALVATIERRA, IMMA SÀNCHEZ, AND MARIONA TAULÉ

Enhancing the Status of Catalan versus Spanish in Online Academic Forums

Obstacles to Machine Translation

This work presents a linguistic analysis of a corpus of messages in Catalan and Spanish, from several informal newsgroups on the Universitat Oberta de Catalunya (Open University of Catalonia, henceforth UOC) Virtual Campus. The surrounding environment is one of extensive bilingualism and contact between Spanish and Catalan. The main goal of the study was to ascertain the linguistic characteristics of the email register in the newsgroups, to assess their implications for the creation of an online machine translation environment to facilitate cross-linguistic communication on the Internet, and to prevent the subordination of Catalan.

Catalonia is an autonomous bilingual region of Spain[1] where the native language, Catalan, is being displaced to a great extent by Spanish when Catalan speakers communicate with members of different linguistic groups. Usually, Catalan speakers tend to use Spanish if they know the addressee is not a native Catalan speaker, even if the addressee is able to understand Catalan. In addition, they tend to use Spanish as the default language when they are unsure of the addressee's level of understanding of Catalan. In computer-mediated communication (CMC), the tendency of Catalan speakers to use Spanish by default is even more noticeable. Thus, we reasoned that the gradual replacement of Catalan by Spanish could be prevented if those writing in Catalan felt that, thanks to human language technologies, they did not need to shift to Spanish. The existence of a machine translation (MT) system that could automatically translate emails into the language of the addressee would make it unnecessary for users to write in Spanish. Users' confidence in translation quality would lead to their using their own language regardless of the other's language. With this idea in mind, we started the INTERLINGUA project, to promote MT to enable users to employ Catalan online.

However, MT systems are currently not capable of translating spontaneous emails accurately. Such systems work reasonably well if the input is in a standard form, but as we show below, emails often contain spelling mistakes, typing errors, and the like. Moreover, the systems are not prepared to cope with the creative and spontaneous use of language typical of emails, especially in a bilingual community. Thus, email presents new challenges for MT. On the one hand, nonstandard forms must be converted into standard forms recognizable by the MT system, a challenge that the MT community has not yet addressed (Climent, Moré, & Oliver, 2003). On the other hand, the project must also take into consideration the use of language in a bilingual society.

In this chapter, we present the results of a study of emails written on the UOC Virtual Campus, carried out as part of the INTERLINGUA project. The emails were first translated from Catalan to Spanish or vice versa using an MT system. On the basis of translation errors, we classify and quantify the linguistic features in the original messages that have a negative impact on translation quality, stressing features that involve bilingualism, and analyze their distribution in the two languages.

THE SOCIOLINGUISTIC SITUATION IN CATALONIA

Catalan is still recovering from the extreme measures imposed under the rule of Spain's former dictator Francisco Franco, who prohibited the public use of Catalan. Since the return of democracy after Franco's death, Catalan and Spanish have been co-official languages in Catalonia, and linguistic and educational policies have attempted to redress the situation of Spanish dominance over Catalan. However, according to official statistics, although these policies have improved the levels of understanding and ability to speak Catalan, they have not succeeded in improving levels of spontaneous usage. These levels are shown in table 9.1. The data on people's understanding and ability to speak are from a survey by the Centro de Investigaciones Sociológicas (Sociological Research Centre; CIS, 1998). The usage data are from an analysis by Cerdà (2001, Section 5.2.2) from the same CIS survey.

Another survey, carried out by the Catalonian Institute of Statistics (IDESCAT, 2001), shows that the percentages for reading and writing Catalan are lower than those for oral comprehension and use (table 9.2). The ability to read and write is obviously essential in CMC. Thus, the growth of Spanish at the expense of Catalan is expected to be greater in this form of communication than in spoken contexts.

These statistics support the impression of Catalans that the Catalan language is not essential for living in Catalonia. Moreover, the situation

TABLE 9.1. Percentage of the population in Catalonia
able to understand and speak Catalan and Spanish
(Cerdà, 2001; CIS, 1998).

Understand Catalan	97%
Speak Catalan	79%
Spontaneously use Catalan	41%
Spontaneously use Spanish	43%
Spontaneously use both	16%

TABLE 9.2. Percentage of the population in Catalonia
able to understand, speak, read, and write Catalan
(IDESCAT, 2001).

Understand Catalan	95%
Speak Catalan	75%
Read Catalan	74%
Write Catalan	50%

has worsened in the last decade due to massive immigration from Africa
and Latin America. According to the CIS (1998) survey, 18% of the immigrant population in Catalonia did not understand any Catalan at all in
1998.

Immigrants learn Spanish because it is the official language of Spain and
a widespread means of communication. They do not feel compelled to learn
Catalan since, on the one hand, Spanish is omnipresent in mass media, books,
shops, law, and so forth, and on the other hand, Catalans communicate with
them in Spanish. The tendency of Catalan speakers to shift to Spanish when
the addressee uses Spanish is an example of code switching. Some people also
code switch to Spanish because they feel more competent in that language
(Pujolar, 2000).[2]

The presence of code switching on the Internet is particularly apparent
as interactions between Catalans and those from outside Catalonia through
chats, email, and so forth become increasingly common. Aside from the fact
that Spanish has a far greater presence on the Internet than Catalan, the possibility of addressing a wider group of people from all over Spain and the
world encourages the use of Spanish when writing to someone for the first
time or when replying to a message in Spanish, even in cases where the
addressee understands Catalan. This trend goes against the perception of
many scholars that the Internet can promote minority languages and multilingualism (Mensching, 2000; Warschauer, 2000).

LANGUAGE CHOICE IN A PRELIMINARY
EMAIL SAMPLE

In order to assess the current status of Catalan on the Internet, we analyzed a sample of emails from the UOC-Catalonia[3] Virtual Campus. Catalan is the institutionalized language of the Virtual Campus, used in educational material as well as by teachers when addressing students online. Although there are no official restrictions on the spontaneous use of other languages, it is assumed that people who register for instruction through UOC-Catalonia will be fully competent in Catalan.

As a test bed for the research, several computer science newsgroups were chosen. In these informal newsgroups, students exchange information and opinions related to computers, software, bugs, cheats, academic subjects, and so forth. These newsgroups are not, by themselves, representative of text-based, asynchronous CMC in Catalonia as a whole. Both linguistically and sociolinguistically, the communicative situation in Catalonia is too diverse and complex to be represented by a single group. Nonetheless, we believe that these newsgroups are good examples of contemporary practice and that by analyzing them we can learn how languages are currently used in Catalonia in online communication.

Although the official language of UOC-Catalonia is Catalan, messages and replies are posted in the forums in both Catalan and Spanish, sometimes mixing the two. In an attempt to quantify the degree of code switching between messages (as opposed to within messages), we analyzed all messages mailed to the forums between July and December 2002: 533 messages sent by 254 users (an average of 2.1 messages per user). In this sample, 76% of the messages were in Catalan and 24% were in Spanish. To infer the degree of code switching in the group, we considered only the 189 emails that were spontaneous replies in one or the other language. The criteria for defining spontaneous users are described in Climent, Moré, Oliver, Salvatierra et al. (2003). Table 9.3 shows the results of applying this classification scheme to the messages in the sample.

Although these results may not be statistically significant because the sample size is small, they suggest that code switching between messages is an important phenomenon among spontaneous users of Catalan (43% of messages) but less so among spontaneous users of Spanish (15% of messages). This, and the fact that only 69% of messages were sent by spontaneous

TABLE 9.3. Classification of messages in terms of spontaneous language use.

Spontaneous Catalan users		Spontaneous Spanish users		Indifferent	Undetermined
68.9%		18.1%		1.2%	11.8%
Reply to emails written in Spanish		Reply to emails written in Catalan			
In Catalan	In Spanish	In Catalan	In Spanish		
57.1%	42.9%	15.4%	84.6%		

Catalan users, appears paradoxical when we recall that, in the environment studied, Catalan should be the only language used. This evidence suggests a trend that is endangering Catalan on the Internet.

THE ROLE OF MACHINE TRANSLATION

MT systems allow users to employ their own language, regardless of whether the addressee can read it. If the quality of the translation is sufficiently high, the sender can trust the MT system and avoid having to code switch in order to guarantee communication. In this way, the better the quality of the translation, the more likely the sender is to use his or her native language.

However, to guarantee quality in the translation of emails, certain factors need to be taken into account. The MT systems currently in operation depend on the input text being correct and standardized; that is, the systems' rules and lexical databases are able to recognize only standard words and correctly written texts. Even when working with standardized texts, MT systems make mistakes; the greater the structural differences in the languages involved, the more mistakes the systems make. Thus, it is generally assumed that MT systems are not able to produce perfectly correct translations, merely approximate translations that allow the addressee to understand the gist of the text. In the case of nonstandardized texts, such as emails, the quality may be even lower. Moreover, messages written by bilingual users may contain further deviations: Users might mix languages when quoting or linking to previous articles, employ words of the other language, make spelling and grammatical mistakes due to language interference, and so on.

Currently, MT specialists take for granted that texts submitted for automatic translation should be manually preedited to overcome errors and deviations from the standards, as well as postedited to correct the remaining mistakes. However, in email communication, human pre- and postediting are not feasible, because the system has to work in real time and automatically. For this reason, an in-depth analysis of the email register is needed to shed light on the problems an MT system might be required to overcome in order to produce a quality translation in an unsupervised environment.

THE EMAIL REGISTER

CMC researchers have studied various aspects of the email register. We focus here on the relationship between the linguistic structure of emails and non-standard features.[4] According to Herring (2001), most nonstandard features in English emails are deliberate choices made by users to

- Economize on typing effort
- Mimic spoken language features
- Express themselves creatively

Murray (2000) claims that CMC uses "simplified registers," characterized by short sentences, special lexicon, feedback devices that facilitate the reader's comprehension, and simplifications, including the use of abbreviations and omission of articles, pronouns, and copulae. According to Murray, the technology constrains time and space. CMC relies on typing, computer, and network speed and provides no visual paralinguistic or nonverbal cues. Consequently, users employ strategies that reduce the time needed to write messages or that substitute for the lack of paralinguistic and nonverbal cues.

According to Yates and Orlikowski (1993), the mimicking of spoken language features in email results in unconventional orthography, such as textual indications of emphasis (e.g., "If an implementation DOES support vectors . . ."), informal words typically used in speech (e.g., "groove," "stuff"), and syntactic informality often taking the form of incomplete sentences and conversational cadences, usually combined with word choice and punctuation in order to simulate oral communication, as in "Hmm, I see. . . ."

As for the creative use of language, Alonso, Folguerà, and Tebé (2000), focusing on the Catalan Internet lexicon ("Internet slang"), identify a category of informal, expressive lexical elements, such as *correu tortuga* ("snail mail"; literally "tortoise mail") and *emili* ("email" referred to humorously, due to its resemblance to the proper noun *Emile*). These lexical items are common and convey a recreational, creative, ironic, or informal attitude.

For Fais and Ogura (2001), there are features that are exclusive to email, causing it to differ significantly from both formal textual and spoken language. These include visual and discourse-level phenomena such as (1) the use of indentation and spacing to be interpreted as cues to a change in the topic; (2) nonstandard punctuation, which invites the reader to draw inferences, supplementing the explicit meaning in the text; (3) nonstandard spelling (e.g., elongating a sound by repeating a letter several times); and (4) the attempt to capture the flavor of speech and employ typically spoken discourse markers to do so, for example, "mmm" or "ah."

These studies tend to focus on new, intentionally expressive devices. This may be because, as Herring (2001) concludes, "Actually, although computer-mediated language often contains non-standard features, only a relatively small percentage of such features appears to be errors caused by inattention or lack of knowledge of the standard language forms" (p. 616).

However, in the email register, texts may contain many unintentional language mistakes if the user writes quickly and carelessly. Likewise, the assertion that lack of knowledge of standard language forms is relatively minor may be true in monolingual English-speaking environments; however, in a bilingual community, lack of knowledge of standard forms of one language or the other can be significant. For instance, in Catalonia, some users writing in Catalan have less command of Catalan than Spanish; they may not have studied Catalan at school or may not be used to reading Catalan. Their lack of knowledge may be displayed, unintentionally, in emails. Another factor inadequately discussed in the CMC literature is interference between two languages in the messages of bilinguals.

EVALUATING TRANSLATION QUALITY: THE IMPACT
OF NONSTANDARD FEATURES

The MT system used in the INTERLINGUA project is Comprendium Trans-
lator (www.comprendium.es), an application to translate between Catalan
and Spanish and vice versa that is based on the prestigious METAL system.
METAL is the result of decades of research starting at the University of Texas
in the 1960s and culminating at the German electronics company Siemens in
the 1990s. It is broadly assumed to be the best-performance MT system, as it
is based on deep linguistic knowledge—complex lexical entries and syntactic
rules augmented with semantic information. Versions of the system have been
developed through years of research by different projects and/or companies
for several language pairs mainly involving major European languages
(Hutchins & Sommers, 1992). The METAL system was evaluated in the first
stage of the study in order to find out how it worked and what its shortcomings
were. By analyzing the results of the evaluation, we would know to what
extent nonstandard features were responsible for poor-quality translations
and to what extent these features were attributable to specific aspects of the
email register or to users' lack of awareness of standard language forms.

Evaluation of the system followed the International Standards for
Language Engineering for MT evaluation (ISLE, 2000) and consisted of two
processes: macro- and microevaluation (Van Slype, 1979). The macroevaluation provided information about the acceptability of the translation system
from a global perspective (intelligibility, fidelity, readability of the emails
translated). The goal of the macroevaluation was to validate the translations
performed in order to assess the usability of the system, without detailing its
limitations. In contrast, the microevaluation identified the system's limitations and was required in order to establish a strategy for improvements. The
microevaluation provided information about the origin of translation errors,
whether they came from the system's shortcomings or from the user's writing.
In this chapter, we focus on the microevaluation.

Since the system translated segment by segment (roughly sentence by
sentence), the microevaluation was carried out on text segments. The corpus
prepared for the microevaluation amounted to 1,239 segments in Catalan and
1,128 segments in Spanish, taken from 129 randomly selected emails for each
language.[5] There was a total of around 25,000 words. All segments were sent
to the MT system; the corpus was constituted by juxtaposing each segment
with its automatic translation.

The evaluation of each segment was carried out in five steps. First, a
human evaluator judged whether the translation was intelligible without reference to the source segment. Second, given both the source segment and the
translation, the evaluator decided whether the translation was faithful to the
original in content, intelligibility, and style. Third, if the translation was not
fully intelligible or faithful, the evaluator graded the translation errors that
led to the problem. The fourth step was to analyze the original and the translation and to classify the translation error as either caused by the writer of

the input or by inadequate functioning of the system. If caused by the writer, the evaluator stated whether the writer had expressed him- or herself infelicitously, written a syntactically incorrect sentence, or used a nonstandard language form (a typing error, a spelling error, or an intentional or unintentional lexical deviation). The evaluator also considered "language interference," a category that affects expression, syntax, and lexicon. If the translation error was caused by the system, the evaluator had to state whether the translation error was morphologic or syntactic or whether there were words, terms, or expressions that were not translated or translated badly. Fifth, after having performed these steps, the evaluator could write comments that would be an important source of information for future improvements and research into email writing and MT.

The evaluation was carried out by six bilingual language consultants whose usual job is to proofedit documents for grammar and style. At least two evaluators examined each segment of text. The results were then collected and analyzed.

DATA ANALYSIS

In this chapter, we show only the results concerning what the evaluators regarded as translation errors caused by the input. Errors caused by malfunctioning of the MT system are not presented here.

Analysis of the data was carried out by systematizing the classification and comments of the evaluators regarding translation errors, and quantifying the results. Our aim was to determine which characteristics of the text were attributable to the writer's intention to use language that differed from formal norms, and which characteristics were attributable to other factors, focusing on language contact, a significant aspect of the area under study. Another important aim was to quantify each type and subtype of phenomenon. We believe this approach to be innovative, as the CMC literature to date has often pointed out certain phenomena without quantifying their actual relevance. We think that certain overvalued phenomena actually have little effect, while other important phenomena have been neglected.

Due to the size of the corpus studied, the background of the users, and the specific nature of their communication needs, the conclusions we have drawn from the analysis of the results cannot describe email communication in general. However, as shown below, we can infer certain interesting points.

CLASSIFICATION SCHEME

We have empirically classified the linguistic characteristics that cause translation errors into three broad areas: (1) unintentional nonstandard features, (2) intentional nonstandard features, and (3) terminology.

The full classification scheme produced for the empirical analysis of the corpus is summarized below. Following that, we describe each category and subcategory in turn.

1. Unintentional nonstandard features
   1.1 Mistyping
   1.2 Deviations from prescriptive language norms
      1.2.1 Orthographic
         1.2.1.1 Accents
         1.2.1.2 Phoneme–grapheme confusion
         1.2.1.3 Composition and separation symbols
         1.2.1.4 Capitalization
         1.2.1.5 Errors in abbreviations and acronyms
      1.2.2 Lexical
         1.2.2.1 Barbarisms
         1.2.2.2 Recurrent mixups
         1.2.2.3 Oral reproduction
         1.2.2.4 Loan-word errors
      1.2.3 Syntactic
      1.2.4 Cohesion
         1.2.4.1 Verb tense errors
         1.2.4.2 Anaphoric errors
         1.2.4.3 Punctuation errors
2. Intentional nonstandard features
   2.1 Language shift
      2.1.1 Lexical
         2.1.1.1 Expressive
         2.1.1.2 Terminological
      2.1.2 Phrasal
   2.2 New forms of textual expressivity (characteristic of the email register)
      2.2.1 Orthographic
         2.2.1.1 Orthographic innovations
         2.2.1.2 Systematic lack of accentuation
      2.2.2 Lexical
         2.2.2.1 Internet user vocabulary
         2.2.2.2 Informal (oral-like) language
         2.2.2.3 Prosodic reproduction
         2.2.2.4 Shortenings
      2.2.3 Visual
      2.2.4 Pragmatic
      2.2.5 Simplified punctuation
      2.2.6 Simplified syntax
3. Terminology
   3.1 Domain terminology
   3.2 User community terminology

Main Categories

Our first main category is unintentional nonstandard features. These differ from the second main category, intentional nonstandard features, since they are not deliberately chosen by the writer. In some cases, doubt arises as to whether a nonstandard feature is intentional. These cases are considered in relation to the context of the email as a whole. If the case appears to be embedded in a system of coherent odd features, it is classified as intentional. For instance, with regard to accents, if only one or a few words in the email lack the necessary accentuation, we classify it as unintentional. However, when the user does not use accents at all in the message, or where the lack of accentuation is consistent with a rationale, then we regard this as voluntary deviation, that is, systematic lack of accentuation.

Accordingly, our second main category, intentional nonstandard features, is characterized by deliberate choice. One main group of intentional deviations is that which, according to the literature, defines the email register itself: new forms of expressivity—oral patterns, shortenings, simplified punctuation or syntax, specific pragmatic resources, visual information, and so on. The other main group is language shift, use of words or constructions from other languages, even though well-known equivalents exist in the language in which the text is written. Both the categories and their subcategories are explained below.

In the third and final main category, we classified as terminology vocabulary that is specific to either the domain of knowledge and communication (in this case, computer science) or the particular user community under consideration (in this case, UOC students). This differs from vocabulary that can be considered part of the general register of Internet users, classified as new forms of expressivity.

Mistyping

These are mainly deviations caused by neighboring key strikes ("*Cstalonia" instead of "Catalonia"), extra strikes ("*Caatalonia"), inverted strikes ("*Catlaonia"), missing strikes in a word ("*Ctalonia"), or connecting two words "*toCatalonia"). (Asterisks indicate forms that are not acceptable in either Catalan or Spanish.) We also include here the mistyping of a symbol similar to one that the user intends to strike; a typical example is the use of accents instead of apostrophes.

Deviations from Prescriptive Language Norms

In this case, the deviation is caused by users not being aware of a rule or a norm of the language they are using. This occurs at different linguistic levels, as described below. In Catalonia, a number of these deviations can be seen to be caused by language interference, although it is difficult to say exactly how many, since it depends greatly on the social and educational backgrounds of individuals. We return to this point further below.

Orthographic Deviations

We found different types of orthographic deviations, from erroneous capitalization (i.e., asystematic noncapitalization) to errors in writing acronyms and abbreviations or in the use of certain characters (e.g., apostrophes and hyphens in Catalan to affix clitics, as in *dona'me-l* for *dona-me'l*, "give + to me + it"). However, the most common orthographic deviation comes from accentuation and phoneme-grapheme confusions (*andavant*, *adreçes*, *trovar* instead of *endavant*, *adreces*, *trobar*), typically when one phoneme can be spelled by many graphemes. For instance, both "a" and "e" can represent the schwa sound in Catalan, and writers sometimes choose the wrong letter, as in the case of *andavant* ("forward"), which should be written *endavant*. Similarly, "s," "c," and "ç" can all represent the /s/ sound, and writers sometimes choose the wrong option, for example, *adreçes* should be *adreces* (addresses).

This happens in our corpus in four cases: (1) a/e and o/u alternation to represent the schwa sound and the unstressed /u/ sound, (2) c/s/ç to spell /s/, (3) b/v for /b/, and (4) confusion in the use of digraphs: s/ss to spell /s/, and l/l·l and n/nn. The digraphs "l·l" and "nn" represent a combination of two /l/ and two /n/, respectively, which are prescribed by spelling norms but are hardly ever pronounced in the oral language. For instance, speakers pronounce a single /l/ when saying "*pel·licula*" (film).

Lexical Deviations

We found four types of lexical units that differ from standard language use. The first are what in Catalonia are called barbarisms, words or lexical constructions that the speaker believes are genuinely Catalan but that are Spanish. Examples of these are *insertar* (instead of *inserir*, "to insert") and *recent* (instead of *acabat de fer*, "fresh"). These are archetypal cases of interference between languages in contact. In Catalonia, they also occur in Spanish due to the influence of Catalan, as in *antes de nada* instead of *en primer lugar* ("first of all"). This particular example is caused by the speaker translating the lexical construction word for word from the Catalan equivalent *abans de res* (*abans* = *antes* = "before," *de* = *de* = "of," *res* = *nada* = "nothing").

The second type is lexical mixups, which are caused by similarity of form but difference of meaning, for example, *si no/sinó* ("but"/"otherwise"), *per què/perquè* ("why"/"because"), *per/per a* ("for" or "by"/"in order to") in Catalan, and *a parte/aparte* ("in part"/"apart") in Spanish. These are very common in some people's writing. Some of these mixups may also be caused by language interference due to false analogies between similar forms in Spanish and Catalan.

The third type of lexical deviation is caused by attempts to reproduce oral forms in writing. There are different subtypes, but all are distinct from phoneme–grapheme confusion, in which one phoneme can be spelled by two or three alternative letters, constraining the deviation in terms of available options. The scope is wider in the case of oral spelling, since it might affect several phonemes/graphemes, or the whole word, thus changing the overall form of the lexical unit; for this reason, it has been classified as lexical. Typical cases are *vols* or *a veure*, Catalan words that some speakers pronounce /bos/ and /abere/, so those speakers sometimes mistakenly write them as *vos and *avere. Another case is the pronunciation of *donés* /dunes/ (a subjunctive form of "to give") with an epenthetic velar consonant, /dunges/, thus leading the word to be written as *dongués. Deviations caused by oral reproduction are dialect dependent, inasmuch as pronunciation in different dialects resembles to a greater or lesser extent the standard in Catalan or Spanish.

Last, we also found cases of errors in the spelling of loan words, for example, mistakenly writing the English word "cookies" as *cookis, or "Access" (the database software) as *Acces.

Syntactic Deviations

This category covers the nonstandard use of grammatical categories (e.g., incorrect choice of verbal mood, as in the use of infinitive instead of imperative in *decirme instead of *decidme* ["tell me"] in Spanish) and other cases of syntactic ill-formedness. Relevant examples are the omission or addition of pronouns, prepositions or other function words, as in Catalan's *jo vull ("I + want") instead of *jo en vull* ("I" + direct object pronoun + "want") to mean "I want (that thing)" or, in Spanish, *pienso de ir for *pienso ir* ("I think I'll go"); as well as typical cases of lack of agreement (subject–verb, determiner–noun). Although it is difficult to generalize due to the sparseness of this type of data in the corpus, it is clear that at least some syntactic deviations are caused by language interference, as in the first two examples above, where (1) the incorrect omission of the pronoun *en* in Catalan reflects Spanish norms, and (2) the incorrect addition of the preposition *de* in Spanish reflects Catalan norms.

Cohesion Deviations

Textual cohesion is negatively affected in our corpus by inappropriate use of punctuation marks (colons, semicolons, hyphens, etc.), incorrect choices of verbal tenses to express temporal relations, and lack of concordance between pronouns and their antecedents.

Language Shift

As mentioned above, intentional deviations from language standards are classified into two main categories, the first being language shift—the voluntary use of words or phrases from other languages. In Catalonia, where there is close contact between Catalan and Spanish, language shift is very common in informal speech since all speakers have a degree of knowledge of both languages. A consequence is that sometimes, when speaking in language A, a lexical choice corresponding to language B comes naturally to the speaker's mind. Since the language shift does not usually affect communication, inasmuch as the interlocutor is also bilingual, the speaker uses the other language's word, or even sometimes a phrase, not by mistake but for the sake of fluency or other expressive reasons. For instance, it is typical to swear in Catalan using Spanish *joder* ("fuck") or to say goodbye in Spanish using Catalan *adéu*. This also happens to Catalan and Spanish speakers with third languages. Sometimes people say goodbye by using Italian *ciao*, express gratitude by using French *merci*, or ask for aid with English "help."

Not every intentional use of language shift is expressive: Many shifts involve terminology that either has been learned or is better established in another language. A typical example is the use of English "software" instead of Catalan *programari*. This case is debatable, in as much as some speakers might simply be unaware of the existence of the Catalan term. However, we have classified these cases as intentional since we assume that our users either know the terminology of their field in their language (but that they still prefer using English terms) or else are aware that there must exist a word in their language for the term (but do not wish to think about it or look it up in a dictionary when writing email). Finally, those foreign terms that lack a well-known equivalent in Spanish or Catalan have been classified as domain terminology.

Two characteristics should be highlighted about such language shifts in emails: (1) They are related to the written reproduction of informal speech, and (2) they are related to language interference.

New Forms of Textual Expressivity

These are the features that, according to the literature, best define the email register. We find here simple categories such as visual resources—typically, smileys; the pragmatic resource of dialogue simulation in quoting part of a previous message; and simplified punctuation or syntax. We classified as simplified syntax cases involving the lack of a function word in intentionally telegraphic constructions, for example, the lack of an article in *M'adreço a aquest fòrum amb l'esperança de trobar tècnic disposat a* . . . instead of . . . *l'esperança de trobar un tècnic* . . . (". . . I'm hoping to find [a] technician . . ."). To distinguish between punctuation errors and simplified punctuation, we counted as the latter any lack of (expected) punctuation marks in emails lacking any punctuation at all.

Similarly, for accentuation, we counted those emails that did not have any accents at all separately, so that any lack of an accent within them was classified as a case of systematic lack of accentuation. Otherwise, when occurring in emails that did have accents, lack of an accent was counted as an error.

Systematic lack of accentuation is one subtype of the category new orthography. The other main class includes a wide range of innovations such as capitalization or the use of a range of symbols to show emphasis (*necessito ajuda URGENT* . . . "I need help URGENTLY; *no funciona!!??!!* "it doesn't work!!??!!"), use of symbols as meaning components in words (*tod@s* covering both masculine and feminine genders instead of "*todos y todas*") or the use of ['s] to pluralize acronyms, as in CD's.

The other main class categorized as new forms of expressivity includes a variety of lexical units that are not found in formal texts. First, we have colloquial Internet user vocabulary such as "online," "hoax," "*nick*," *àlies* ("nickname"), or *xat* ("chat"). These are usually English terms or adaptations from English. We have not classified English terms as language shifts or terminology because they belong to an emerging Internet register more than to the domain of computer science.

The second subtype includes general-purpose informal vocabulary, typically used in speech but never in formal texts, for example, *mates* ("maths") for *matemáticas* ("mathematics"), *profe* for *profesor* ("teacher, lecturer"), or *yuyu* (a colloquial term in Catalan and Spanish for either feeling under the weather or unusual behavior).

Another class is that of intentional reproduction of spoken prosody used as an expressive resource. For instance, *modessssno* contains a graphical reproduction of a very long [s] sound; this "word," which represents *moderno* ("modern/fashionable"), means something or someone pretending to be fashionable but who in fact seems ridiculous. We also include here reproduction of oral sounds such as *hmmm* (expressing doubt) or *psé* (indifference).

The last category is that of SMS message-like (short message service) shortenings, such as *tb* instead of *també* ("as well") or *k* for *que* ("who, what, which . . ."). See also Anis (chapter 4 this volume) for a description of similar phenomena in French.

Terminology

As expected, we found many examples of terminology in our corpus. This finding is crucial for machine translation, since these are words that are usually missing in the lexical databases of MT systems and could therefore cause errors in translation. Most of the time, such terminology is associated with a specialized knowledge domain: in the case of our newsgroups, computer science. Thus, we find words such as "XML," *disc dur* ("hard disk"), and "script." However, we also find terms particular to the community of users, UOC students. These include *PACs* (a kind of academic assignment) and *MIC* (an acronym for an academic subject, *Multimèdia i comunicació*, "Multimedia and communication").

Such terms cannot be considered characteristic of the CMC register. In a newsgroup devoted to medicine, for example, we will find medical terms instead of terms for computer science. Furthermore, in a newsgroup devoted to computer science in another kind of community, for example, professionals instead of students, we would not expect to find student vocabulary such as *MIC* or *PAC*.

QUANTIFICATION OF FEATURES THAT CAUSE TRANSLATION PROBLEMS

Having classified the errors and deviations from standard language use found in the corpus, we present the quantitative results of the classification in table 9.4. These results are analyzed in the next section.

DISCUSSION

It appears that the emails in the sample are characterized not only by new forms of expressivity, as is often claimed in English CMC research, but also by at least as many unintentional infelicities, mistypings, and deviations from prescriptive norms. Most of these deviations seem to be due to a weak awareness of the language, especially Catalan, as the data show that the number of unintentional deviations from prescriptive norms is noticeably higher in Catalan than in Spanish. We have analyzed only a specific group of highly educated users—university students. It is likely that among less well-educated users, the incidence of unintentional infelicities would be higher.

Analogy with Spanish sheds light on a number of deviations from norms in Catalan, such as accentuation of the common ending "-ia" (e.g., *enginyería* instead of *enginyeria*, "engineering") or phoneme–grapheme confusions such as the failure to use "ss" to represent the phoneme /s/, as in *asociació* instead of *associació*, "association." The interference is clear in such cases, since the norms of Spanish demand both accentuation of "-ía" and use of "s" instead of "ss." Language interference is also evident in the lexicon (barbarisms) and explains certain recurrent confusions. In Spanish, language interferences are mainly cases of analogy in accentuation as well (Catalan *exàmens* ["exams"], Spanish *exámen* instead of *examen*). However, the impact of these spelling confusions is not as great as in Catalan. The number of barbarisms in Spanish emails is also lower, and in recurrent mixups the difference disappears.

Many types of deviations cannot be explained in terms of interference. However, language interference is the single most important influence on the deviations found in the corpus. We hypothesize that each of the following types of deviation was caused mostly or entirely by linguistic interference:

TABLE 9.4. Frequency and distribution of features that caused translation errors.

	Catalan		Spanish		
	AF	RF	AF	RF	IT
1. Unintentional nonstandard features	512	46.7	322	30.7	
1.1 Mistyping	92	8.4	55	5.2	H
1.2 Deviations from prescriptive language norms	420	38.3	267	25.4	
1.2.1 Orthographic	296	27.0	169	16.1	
1.2.1.1 Accents	233	21.2	149	14.2	H
1.2.1.2 Phoneme–grapheme confusion	49	4.5	2	0.2	H
1.2.1.3 Composition and separation symbols	3	0.3	0	0.0	H
1.2.1.4 Capitalization	9	0.8	7	0.7	L
1.2.1.5 Errors in abbreviations and acronyms	2	0.2	11	1.0	L
1.2.2 Lexical	54	4.9	19	1.8	
1.2.2.1 Barbarisms	17	1.5	8	0.7	H
1.2.2.2 Recurrent mixups	5	0.4	4	0.4	H
1.2.2.3 Oral reproduction	29	2.6	7	0.7	H
1.2.2.4 Loan-word errors	3	0.3	0	0.0	M
1.2.3 Syntactic	36	3.3	48	4.6	H
1.2.4 Cohesion	34	3.1	31	2.9	
1.2.4.1 Verb tense errors	8	0.7	3	0.3	M
1.2.4.2 Anaphoric errors	1	0.1	9	0.8	H
1.2.4.3 Punctuation errors	25	2.3	19	1.8	H
2. Intentional nonstandard features	155	14.1	346	32.9	
2.1 Language shift	24	2.2	46	4.4	
2.1.1 Lexical	24	2.2	45	4.3	
2.1.1.1 Expressive	5	0.4	4	0.4	M
2.1.1.2 Terminological	19	1.7	41	3.9	L
2.1.2 Phrasal	0	0.0	1	0.1	M
2.2 New forms of textual expressivity	131	11.9	300	28.6	
2.2.1 Orthographic	71	6.5	250	23.8	
2.2.1.1 Orthographic innovations	53	4.8	86	8.2	M
2.2.1.2 Systematic lack of accentuation	18	1.6	164	15.6	H
2.2.2 Lexical	36	3.3	39	3.7	
2.2.2.1 Internet user vocabulary	8	0.7	18	1.7	L
2.2.2.2 Informal (oral-like) language	9	0.8	8	0.8	M
2.2.2.3 Prosodic reproduction	6	0.5	5	0.5	H
2.2.2.4 Shortenings	13	1.2	8	0.7	M
2.2.3 Visual	9	0.8	3	0.3	L
2.2.4 Pragmatic	2	0.2	3	0.3	L
2.2.5 Simplified punctuation	2	0.2	0	0.0	H
2.2.6 Simplified syntax	11	1.0	5	0.5	H
3. Terminology	396	36.1	437	41.6	
3.1 Domain terminology	268	24.4	293	27.0	L
3.2 User community terminology	128	11.7	144	13.7	M
Total	1,063	96.8	1,105	105.2	

The columns labeled AF (absolute frequency) show the total occurrences of each category in the corpus. RF (relative frequency) shows the number of occurrences of each category per thousand words in the corpus. IT (impact on translation) indicates the high (H), medium (M), or low (L) expected impact of the category on the quality of translation, independent of the number of occurrences.

incorrect accentuation, grapheme–phoneme confusions, barbarisms, recurrent mixups, syntactic errors, and language-shift deviations. This hypothesis is supported by the comments of the language experts who evaluated the data, all of whom registered statements to this effect. Adding up these categories results in an estimate that 49.1% of the errors in Catalan and 31.3% of the errors in Spanish were caused by language interference. Focusing on deviations from norms (not counting language shifts), we find that as many as 59.4% of deviations from prescriptive norms in Catalan and 50.6% in Spanish were plausibly caused by interference. The high incidence of interference-induced errors and deviations is no doubt due to the fact that the users in our sample must deal with language contact on a daily basis. This situation represents a unique challenge for the application of MT to email communication in Catalonia.

On the other hand, the ratio of intentional language shifts is not very significant (only 2.2 per 1,000 words in the corpus). Therefore, it appears that the main influence of linguistic interference in spontaneous texts is that it causes deviations from prescriptive norms.

Adaptation to intentional deviations through customization of the MT system in both directions would be worthwhile, as well. Among new forms of expressivity, the feature that best characterizes the register is "new orthography," much more noticeable in Spanish (83.3% of intentional features) than in Catalan (54.1%). There seems to be greater impact in terms of intentionality and the creative use of language in Spanish than in Catalan. In Spanish, fully intentional nonaccentuation is more evident. Likewise, there are more orthographic innovations in Spanish than in Catalan.

Lexical forms of new expressivity, considered together, have some effect in characterizing the register, although their relative frequency in terms of the corpus as a whole is low (3.3 for Catalan and 3.7 for Spanish). In contrast, visual and pragmatic resources, simplified syntax and simplified punctuation, despite having been paid a great deal of attention in the CMC literature (Herring, 2001; Murray, 2000), appear to be insignificant in either direction.

Another aspect often characterized as significant is oral patterns. However, the impact of the features related to this in our study did not reach expected levels. The features selected as oral patterns were barbarisms, oral reproduction, language shift, informal oral-like language, and prosodic reproduction. It is not completely clear whether all of the barbarisms or language shifts reproduce oral behavior, but they are included here because they refer to vocabulary that is used when speaking but not usually when writing a formal text. Counting all of these features as oral patterns, they represent 12.7% in Catalan and 11.0% in Spanish, of all of the nonstandard features. If unintentional features are set aside and we concentrate on intentional aspects, oral patterns are, in Catalan, 25.1% and, in Spanish, 17.0% of all of the intentional deviations. Compared to the total number of words in the corpus, oral patterns make up 7.7 per 1,000 words in Catalan and 7.0 per 1,000 words in Spanish. Therefore, it seems that in our sample emails are to a large extent textual in nature, with little evidence of oral patterns. However, oral features deserve special attention due to their negative impact on translation quality.

The results indicate that successful application of MT to the online translation of emails in our environment would require customizing the MT system, taking into account the following information.

For Catalan, the main efforts should focus on automatic correction of unintentional deviations from language norms, mainly mistyping, orthography, and mistakes caused by language contact. The results show that unintentional deviations represent more than three times the amount of intentional nonstandard features.

The situation for Spanish is more balanced. In terms of frequency, efforts should be focused on feeding the MT system with terminology, because the incidence of nonstandard terminology is slightly higher than that of unintentional and intentional nonstandard features.

For both languages, unintentional deviations and terminology as well as intentional deviations are issues sufficiently important to require customizing the system. Regarding terminology, both domain terminology and user community terminology have to be dealt with, but the impact on translation is greater in the case of user community terminology, because most of the domain terminology is in English and does not usually need to be translated to be understood. The impact on translation of Internet vocabulary is not significant, because the terms are widespread and commonly understood (they are usually English terms). Apart from terminology, the main sources of problems for translating emails in both languages are orthography and the lexicon; errors and deviations in syntax and pragmatics are scarcely significant. In terms of orthography, the most common problem is accentuation: 37.6% in Catalan and 46.8% in Spanish of all deviations involve accentuation, regardless of the fact that in Spanish this seems, for the most part, to be intentional (systematic lack of accentuation) and in Catalan to be unintentional mistakes.

CONCLUSIONS

In this chapter, we have presented an in-depth linguistic evaluation of a corpus of approximately 260 emails and 25,000 words, written in Catalan and Spanish, from four informal computer science newsgroups at the Universitat Oberta de Catalunya Virtual Campus. Messages were produced within a situation of bilingualism and language contact, where Spanish is progressively substituting for Catalan as the language of daily use.

The main goal of the study was to identify the linguistic characteristics of the email register for our universe of study in order to assess their impact on machine translation and, based on our findings, to make recommendations on how to improve the quality of translation. The emails in our corpus were translated by an MT system, and the translations were evaluated in order to formulate an improvement strategy: We classified and analyzed the features of the original messages that caused problems. The study was part of the INTERLINGUA project, which aimed to adapt a system for online unsupervised translation of emails from Catalan to Spanish and vice versa, to avoid the marginalization of Catalan as a language for communication on the Internet. Our main conclusions are as follows.

For our sample, the email register is characterized both by unintentional mistyping and deviations from prescriptive language norms and by intentional use of features usually considered typical of emails. In Spanish, the two kinds of features are balanced, while in Catalan, unintentional nonstandard features outnumber their intentional counterparts by 3 to 1.

One of the main reasons for nonstandard input that results in translation errors in the sample is the interference of one language with the other. Language interference can account for up to half of the errors; however, some of these may be due to a lack of awareness of prescriptive norms. Interference affects Catalan more than Spanish, confirming marginalization of the former. The analysis has shown that, despite educational efforts made over recent decades, gaps still exist in many people's knowledge of Catalan.

The intentional nonstandard feature that best defines the email register is nonstandard orthography, in particular, orthographical innovations in Catalan and systematic lack of accentuation in Spanish. The use of visual information, new pragmatic resources, simplified syntax, and simplified punctuation is not significant in quantitative terms.

From an MT perspective, the extremely high ratio of spelling mistakes, barbarisms, and so forth, in emails severely threatens the feasibility of online automatic translation, since MT systems are not currently prepared to deal with noisy input. The MT community has not addressed such a challenge as yet. Therefore, we believe that this study and the project of which it forms a part represent an important innovation in the fields of both MT and CMC.

An implication of these findings is that the MT system must be fine-tuned in order to build software modules for the automatic correction of input, and of accents in particular. To the extent that the feasibility of incorporating minority languages such as Catalan into the multilingual Internet will depend on natural language processing, which usually deals with standard texts, difficulties might be expected for these languages in the future. An important question arises: Should MT systems bear the responsibility for correcting input in order to preserve users' spontaneity when writing, or should users be more careful in their use of language? While in theory the effort to write accurately might help increase the status of minority languages online, the Internet is a medium that encourages nonstandard writing and expressive innovation. In the environment studied, we cannot expect users always to write carefully, making the effort to look up words in the dictionary, use spelling and grammar checkers, and so on. We think it unrealistic to rely on users to facilitate MT and therefore believe that fine-tuning MT systems is essential for the survival of Catalan in newsgroups, chat, and elsewhere online.

The future of Catalan depends on its users. However, on the multilingual Internet, it also depends on the help of technological tools such as MT systems. We have seen that gaps in knowledge of the language are a very serious handicap in the usability of systems that aim to translate Catalan into other languages. We have also seen that these gaps are significantly present in one of the principal groups of Internet users, university students, and predict that they will also be significant in the other principal group, teenagers. It is obvious that email is a medium that encourages linguistic innovations and creativity. This trend is not likely to change in the future. Consequently, we would encourage MT developers to fine-tune their systems to make them error-proof, yet also flexible enough to deal with the nonstandard features typical of the email register. Otherwise, if MT continues to focus only on controlled, standard, well-written texts containing no deviations from linguistic norms, Catalan is likely to disappear from the Internet in a few years.

Acknowledgment

A previous version of this chapter was published in the *Journal of Computer-Mediated Communication* (volume 9, issue 1, 2003).

Notes

1. Catalonia is an autonomous region in Spain that has self-governing powers guaranteed by the Spanish Constitution and the Catalan Statute of Autonomy. Although its actual political status is highly controversial, it can be seen as a kind of a "stateless nation" or "a nation within a nation."

2. On the sociolinguistic situation in Catalonia, see Strubell and Hall (1992), Pujolar (2000), and Castells and Díaz de la Isla (2001).

3. We term it UOC-Catalonia because the institution has recently opened studies in Spanish for the rest of Spain and Latin America.

4. See Danet (2001, chapter 1) for a more comprehensive and in-depth review on this topic.

5. This corpus is a subset of the one used for the analysis of code switching in the first phase of this study.

References

Alonso, A., Folguerà, R., & Tebé, C. (2000). Del tecnolecte al sociolecte: consideracions sobre l'argot tècnic en català. In N. Alturo, Ll. Jardí, M. Torres, Ll. Payrató, & F.X. Vila (Eds.), *CMO-Cat I Jornada sobre comunicació mediatitzada per ordinador en català*. Retrieved December 5, 2005, from http://www.ub.es/lincat/cmo-cat/tebe-alonso-folguera.htm.

Castells, M., & Díaz de la Isla, M. I. (2001). *Diffusion and uses of Internet in Catalonia and Spain*. Project Internet Catalonia (PIC) Working Paper Series, PICWP 1201. Barcelona, Spain: Universitat Oberta de Catalunya / IN3. Retrieved December 5, 2005, from http://www.uoc.edu/in3/wp/picwp1201/.

Cerdà, R. (2001). *Castellano y catalán en Cataluña y las Islas Baleares. II Congreso Internacional de la Lengua Española. 2001 Valladolid, Spain: Proceedings*. Retrieved August 29, 2006, from http://cvc.cervantes.es/obref/congresos/valladolid/ponencias/unidad _diversidad_del_espanol/4_el_espanol_en_contacto/cerda_r.htm.

CIS (Centro de Investigaciones Sociológicas). (1998). Uso de lenguas en comunidades bilingües (II): Cataluña. In *Catálogo del banco de datos del Centro de Investigaciones Sociológicas, estudio 2298, Madrid, Spain*. Retrieved December 5, 2005, from http://www.cis.es/File/ ViewFile.aspx?FileId=1743.

Climent, S., Moré, J., & Oliver, A. (2003). Building an environment for unsupervised automatic email translation. In *EAMT-CLAW 2003, Joint conference combining the 7th international workshop of the European Association for Machine Translation and the 4th Controlled Language Applications Workshop, Dublin: Proceedings*. Retrieved December 5, 2005, from http://www.uoc.edu/in3/dt/20292/index.html.

Climent, S., Moré, J., Oliver, A., Salvatierra, M., Sànchez, I., Taulé, M., & Vallmanya, L. (2003). Bilingual newsgroups in Catalonia: A challenge for machine translation. *Journal of Computer-Mediated Communication, 9*(1). Retrieved December 5, 2005, from http://jcmc .indiana.edu/vol9/issue1/climent.html.

Danet, B. (2001). *Cyberpl@y: Communicating online*. Oxford: Berg. Companion website: http://pluto.mscc.huji.ac.il/~msdanet/cyberpl@y/.

Fais, L., & Ogura, K. (2001). Discourse issues in the translation of Japanese email. In *Conference of the Pacific Association for Computational Linguistics, PACLING 2001. Kitakyushu, Japan: Proceedings*. Retrieved May 9, 2005, from http://afnlp.org/pacling 2001/pdf/fais.pdf.

Herring, S. C. (2001). Computer-mediated discourse. In D. Tannen, D. Schiffin, & H. Hamilton (Eds.), *Handbook of discourse analysis* (pp. 612–634). Oxford: Blackwell.

Hutchins, W. J., & Sommers, H. L. (1992). *An introduction to machine translation*. London: Academic Press.

IDESCAT (Institut d'Estadística de Catalunya). (2001). (source data as of 2001). Retrieved May 9, 2005, from http://www.idescat.net/cat/societat/soclleng.html.

ISLE (International Standards for Language Engineering). (2000). *The ISLE classification of machine translation evaluations*. Retrieved December 5, 2005, from http://www.isi .edu/natural-language/mteval.

Mensching, G. (2000). The Internet as a rescue tool of endangered languages: Sardinian. Retrieved December 5, 2005, from http://www.gaia.es/multilinguae/pdf/Guido.PDF.

Murray, D. E. (2000). Protean communication: The language of computer-mediated communication. *TESOL Quarterly, 34*(3), 397–421.

Pujolar, J. (2000). *Gender, heteroglossia and power. A sociolinguistic study of youth culture*. Berlin: Mouton de Gruyter.

Strubell, M., & Hall, J. (1992). Problems and prospects of small linguistic societies—Catalonia. *EMI Education Media International, 29*(1), 26–37.

Van Slype, G. (1979). *Critical study of methods for evaluating the quality of machine translation*. Report BR 19142. Brussels: Bureau Marcel van Dijk/European Commission. Commission of the European Communities Directorate General Scientific and Technical Information and Information Management.

Warschauer, M. (2000). Language, identity, and the Internet. In B. Kolko, L. Nakamura, & G. Rodman (Eds.), *Race in cyberspace* (pp. 151–170). New York: Routledge.

Yates, J. A., & Orlikowski, W. J. (1993). *Knee-jerk anti-LOOPism and other e-mail phenomena: Oral, written, and electronic patterns in computer-mediated communication.* MIT Sloan School Working Paper 3578-93. Center for Coordination Science Technical Report 150. Retrieved December 5, 2005, from http://ccs.mit.edu/papers/CCSWP150.html.

PART III

GENDER AND CULTURE

10

SIRIPORN PANYAMETHEEKUL AND SUSAN C. HERRING

Gender and Turn Allocation in a Thai Chat Room

A growing body of research finds that females and males display different participation patterns online. Females tend to participate less and receive fewer responses than do males in mixed-sex asynchronous discussion forums (Herring, 1993, 1996), whereas in chat rooms, females sometimes participate more actively and get more responses than do males, for example, because they are objects of flirtatious attention (Bruckman, 1993; Rodino, 1997). At the same time, gender roles vary across cultures and, along with them, norms associated with how appropriate it is for women to speak and be heard in public, as well as attitudes toward flirtation. Thus far, however, most research on online participation patterns has focused exclusively on English-speaking contexts. We might reasonably ask whether gender roles differ across cultures with respect to participation in computer-mediated communication (CMC).

This chapter is part of a study of initiation and response patterns manifested through the exchange of messages, or turn taking, in a recreational Thai-language chat room (located at http://pantip.com/). In considering questions such as who responds to whom and how participants keep track of conversational threads in this popular multiparticipant chat environment, we were struck by the fact that participants were predominantly female, in contrast to English-language chat forums, which tend to have more male participants (Herring, 2003). This piqued our curiosity—what are the interactional dynamics in a predominantly female Thai chat room? Are patterns of dominance reproduced from offline Thai culture—in which women are socialized to be docile and pleasing to men—or do women control the conversational floor because they are more numerous (and perhaps also liberated by the online environment)?

To address these questions, we investigated the effects of gender on turn allocation in the chat room. Our analysis draws on the model of turn allocation developed by conversation analysts Sacks, Schegloff, and Jefferson (1974), who posit three strategies for change of speaker turn in face-to-face conversation. The current speaker may use names or vocatives, gaze, posture, or targeted moves such as direct questioning to select the next speaker (strategy A). Alternatively, next speakers may select themselves (strategy B). If no one self-selects, the current speaker may continue speaking (strategy C). Sacks et al. (1974) order the three strategies, noting that A is preferred over B and B over C.

In chat rooms, in contrast, gaze or gesture cannot be used to select the next speaker as in a face-to-face conversation. Moreover, everyone is in principle free to self-select (Lunsford, 1996), and turns are posted democratically in the order received by the system. These features lead to the prediction that chat rooms will have more self-selecting conversational "floors" (strategies B and C) than does face-to-face communication, with implications for gender equality (see Edelsky, 1981). Since flirtation plays an important role in English-language chat room interactions, we also analyzed flirtatious behavior in relation to turn initiations and responses, predicting that cross-sex initiations would be more frequent than same-sex initiations[1] and that males would attempt to initiate more flirtatious conversations with females than vice versa (Bruckman, 1993).

We found that females participated more often and receive a higher rate of response from both females and males. Females used strategy A more than did males, and they were more likely to select other females to take the next turn. Perhaps for this reason, males used strategy B, the next speaker self-selects, and strategy C, the current speaker continues, more than did females. Males, who were in the minority, had to work harder to take the floor, even in their attempted flirtatious interactions. These results suggest that gender interacts with culture online in complex ways: Contrary to previous findings on gender in chat rooms, and contrary to culturally based expectations about the subordinate status of Thai women, females appeared to be relatively empowered in the Thai chat room studied here, as assessed through turn allocation patterns.

The following section describes the Sacks et al. (1974) model of turn allocation, along with two approaches to analyzing turn taking in computer-mediated chat. This is followed by a review of literature on gender and computer-mediated discourse and gender roles in Thai culture. We then describe the Thai chat data and the methods used to analyze turn allocation and flirtation. The results of the analysis are then presented and interpreted in light of the effects of Web chat systems on turn taking, majority group gender effects on online participation, and Thai cultural values.

BACKGROUND

Turn Allocation in Spoken Conversation

Conversation is composed of speech between at least two people, organized by turns. The turn is the period of talk for each speaker; ideally, only one person talks at a time. In formal situations such as rituals, meetings, and public lectures, turns are often allocated by a moderator or predetermined according to participant roles. In unstructured, spontaneous conversation, however, participants must determine from moment to moment when it is appropriate to take the next turn. Sacks et al. (1974, p. 704) propose the following rules governing turn allocation in such contexts:

(1) For any turn, at the initial transition-relevance place of an initial turn-constructional unit:
   A. The current speaker selects the next speaker and transfer occurs at that place.
   B. The next speaker self-selects, the first starter acquires rights to a turn, and transfer occurs at that place.
   C. If neither (A) the current speaker selects the next speaker nor (B) another party has self-selected, then the current speaker may, but need not, continue, thereby claiming rights to another turn-constructional unit.
(2) If, at the initial transition-relevance place of an initial turn-constructional unit, neither 1A nor 1B has operated, and, following the provision of 1C, the current speaker has continued, then the rule-set A–C re-applies at the next transition-relevance place, and recursively at each next transition-relevance place, until transfer is effected.

In order to converse smoothly, conversationalists must further coordinate transfer to minimize gap and overlap between adjacent turns (Sacks et al., 1974). In face-to-face conversation, transition-relevance places (places where turn exchange is likely to occur) are indicated by a variety of prosodic and visual cues. These include utterance-final intonation, deceleration, final stress, pausing, sustained eye contact, and signaling gestures of the head or hands (Duncan, 1972). In telephone conversations, where prosodic but not visual cues are available, turn transitions can still occur smoothly (McLaughlin, 1984). Text-only CMC lacks both prosodic and visual cues, however.

Turn Allocation in CMC

Disrupted Adjacency

Participants in CMC face certain challenges compared to face-to-face conversation. In addition to lacking nonverbal cues, text-only CMC is characterized by disrupted turn adjacency; logically related turns are separated by unrelated turns, sometimes from other conversations (Herring, 1999). Disrupted adjacency is especially common in multiparticipant CMC. It is caused by technical properties of CMC systems such as delays in message transmission (e.g., system "lag") and the linear display of messages in the order received by the system, without regard for senders' intentions to respond to a particular message. This is illustrated by the following sample of Internet Relay Chat (IRC):

[4]   ashna: hello?
[5]   dave-g it was funny
[6]   how are u jatt
[7]   ssa all
[8]   kally you da woman!
[9]   ashna: do we know eachother? I'm ok how are you

Herring (1999) represents the connections between turns in this sample schematically as in figure 10.1. The perspective in figure 10.1 is anaphoric—the message lower in the diagram is considered to be responding "backward" (or in this case, upward) to a previous message in each case.

In this example, every pair of logically related turns (or adjacency pair, Schegloff & Sacks, 1973) is disrupted by a message from another exchange. Participants in synchronous chat face the problem of how to keep track of who is talking to whom. A common strategy for creating cross-turn coherence is addressivity—the vocative use of the intended addressee's name (Werry, 1996). This can be seen in every turn in the example above except for message [7], which is addressed to "all."[2] By explicitly naming the intended next "speaker" in each turn, chat participants compensate for the lack of nonverbal cues in the text-only medium.

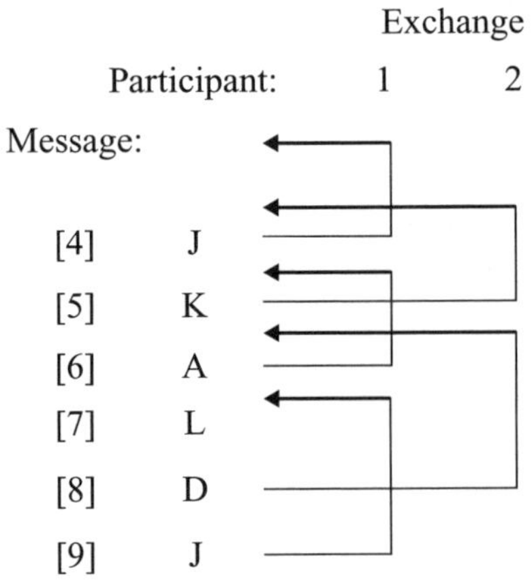

FIGURE 10.1. Schematic representation of turn taking in an IRC sample (adapted from Herring, 1999).

Turn-Allocational Techniques

Lunsford (1996) systematically compares turn-taking organization in IRC with the turn allocation model of Sacks et al. (1974) and concludes that turn allocation in IRC is fundamentally different from that in spoken discourse. According to Lunsford (1996), everyone in a chat room has an equal opportunity to transmit a message at any given time. A speaker can then allocate the next turn by means of three turn allocational techniques:

1. Speaker[3] addresses individual participants by their screen name. This is the same as the practice of addressivity described above. For example:

   WildRoseTX: Dagny, you DO live in Texas, right? I mean, you
                    used to be my neighbor in Dallas and you do

2. Speaker addresses the whole group within a given room. The implication is that all present should respond. For example:

   → NAA4EVER: age/sex check
     HOOKNLOOP: 32/f and you?
     CM622:   hello 30/f
     S Jolene: 33/f

3. Speaker elicits reactions from anyone who cares to respond, often by making a provocative statement. For example:

   → A W MN: Women are taught to manipulate men, sexual
                    harassment is just another way of doing so.
     Doc Yeah: AWMN, how is a man harassing a woman a way of a
                    woman manipulation a man?

Lunsford (1996) notes that a chat message is usually, but not always, equivalent to a turn, as in the case of a turn that is too long to be sent as a single message or a message that contains more than one functional turn.

Further evidence of turn allocation strategies can be found in Cherny (1999)'s observations of interaction patterns in a social Multi-User Dungeon or Dimension (MUD), another form of synchronous text chat. Cherny finds frequent use of an address term (name), which she claims serves the function of eye gaze in face-to-face communication. The social MUD she observed also made conventionalized use of routines that allocate the "next" turn to all who wish to respond, such as the ROLLCALL routine, which Cherny describes as follows: "A character announces a roll call in capital letters, and the characters present who feel they fit the subject or attribute in the name of the roll call answer with their names on a line alone" (p. 102).

In addition to the above strategies, Cherny (1999, p. 181) notes the use of third-person present-tense descriptive actions to simulate bids for the conversation floor, such as "X raises her hand [to request permission to speak]." However, such simulated bids were not common in her spontaneous, recreational MUD data.

From this survey, it emerges that chat participants use various means to circumvent the coherence problems caused by lack of nonverbal cues and disrupted adjacency, including addressing others by name and engaging in conversations with the group at large rather than with targeted individuals. However, it is not apparent that turn allocation in chat rooms is fundamentally different from that of face-to-face speakers in groups. Addressivity is a form of "current speaker selects next" (strategy A) in the Sacks et al. (1974) turn allocation model, and Lunsford's (1996) claim that any participant can "self-select" at any time is similar to Sacks et al.'s strategy B and can subsume strategy C ("same speaker continues"), as well. Moreover, the technical *ability* to take a turn must be distinguished from the social *appropriateness* of doing so, both face to face and in CMC. Social appropriateness is determined in part by speaker identities and roles, as discussed with respect to gender below.

Gender Differences in CMC

Despite early claims that CMC filtered out social cues and was therefore gender neutral, research has found that gender remains socially important online. Herring (1992, 1993, 1996, 1998, 2003) found systematic differences in the participation patterns and discourse styles of males and females in both asynchronous and synchronous CMC in English. These differences are summarized in tables 10.1 and 10.2.

TABLE 10.1. Gender differences in asynchronous CMC (Herring, 1992, 1993, 1996, 2003).

Males	Females
Participation	
Longer messages and greater variability in message length	Short messages
Post more messages	Post fewer messages
Receive more responses	Receive fewer responses
Discourse styles	
Strong assertions; absolute and exceptionless adverbials (e.g., certainly, definitely, obviously, never, by no means)	Attenuated assertions; hedges and qualifiers (e.g., perhaps, may, might, seems, sort of, rather, somewhat, a bit)
Impersonal, presupposed truths (e.g., It is obvious/clear/a fact that . . .)	Speaker's feelings/experiences (e.g., I feel that . . . , I am intrigued by . . .)
Exclusive first-person plural pronouns	Inclusive first-person plural pronouns
Rhetorical questions	Questions as a means to elicit a response
Self-promotion	Apologies
Disagreement with others	Support and agreement with others
Opposed orientation	Aligned orientation
Less polite	More polite

TABLE 10.2. Gender differences in synchronous CMC (Herring, 1998, 2003; Bruckman, 1993; Cherny, 1994).

Males	Females
Participation	
May get fewer responses	May get more responses
Discourse styles	
Use more violent verbs (e.g., "kills")	Use more neutral and affectionate verbs (e.g., "hugs" and "whuggles")
More profanity and more offensive swear words	More emoticons and laughter
More sexual references	Attribution of feelings to self and others
Evaluative judgments, sarcasm, insults	Appreciation and support

These findings are in many respects similar to those of language and gender research in face-to-face public contexts (see Coates, 1993). That is, males tend to dominate in amount and manner of communication, using confrontational and self-promotional talk, while females tend to be attenuated, self-deprecating, and supportive of others. These patterns reenact a familiar gender power hierarchy, with males in the dominant and females in the subordinate position.

At the same time, gender patterns in asynchronous and synchronous CMC differ. Males post longer messages and get more responses than do females in asynchronous discussion groups (Herring, 1993, 2003). For participants in chat rooms, by contrast, messages are similar in length, and females not infrequently get more responses than males (Bruckman, 1993; Herring, 2003). At first blush, this might appear to suggest that females enjoy greater equality in chat rooms than in other forms of CMC, because it is more anonymous and more egalitarian (Danet, 1998; Grossman, 1997). However, many reported cases of females receiving more responses than males in mixed-sex chat rooms involve flirtatious interactions in which one or a small number of females are the focal point of attention, often explicitly sexual in nature, from a larger number of males (e.g., Rodino, 1997). Herring (1998) calls this the "belle of the ball" phenomenon, illustrating the dynamic with the following exchange from IRC:

⟨Dobbs⟩ come on, Danielle!!
⟨Danielle⟩ No.
⟨Danielle⟩ You have to SEDUCE me . . .
*** Action: jazzman reaches out for Danielle's soft hand.
*** Danielle has left channel #netsex
*** Action: Dobbs whispers sweet nothings in Danielle's ear
*** Action: Butthead moves closer to Danielle
⟨jazzman⟩ danielle's gone dumbass

While the female in this example appears to be in control and is the center of attention, it is as an object of sexual desire, not as an intellectual equal. Thus, this interaction reproduces the traditional (Western) gender role of female as sex object, rather than eliminating or equalizing gender roles.

A further qualification concerns the majority gender in the CMC environment under consideration. In asynchronous discussion lists, Herring (1996) finds that the numerically predominant gender establishes the overall discourse norms for the group. She calls this the "list effect." Groups with more females will tend to exhibit, and value, female discourse styles for both females and males. Moreover, Herring (in press) finds that in groups with a majority of females, women are more likely to introduce new topics and have them taken up by others in the group; the converse is true for groups with a majority of males. If the same principle holds in chat rooms, we would expect the relative proportion of males and females in a chat room to influence its gender dynamics. Specifically, we would predict that a chat room with more females than males would show more active female participation and that female patterns of participation would prevail. We would further predict that sexualization of females by males would be less evident than in male-predominant environments, since female discourse norms would not favor such behavior. As yet, however, no research has systematically investigated the effect of majority gender in chat rooms.

Gender in Thai Culture

Women in Southeast Asia are generally thought to enjoy high status, in contrast to the male dominance characteristic of traditional Indian and Chinese societies (van Esterik, 1982). In Thailand, women enjoy a relatively active role and high status in society (UNESCO, 1990). Historically, Thai women controlled household financial expenditures, and Thai society was, and remains, quasi matrilineal (Suriyasarn, 1993). Modern urban Thai women are encouraged to pursue higher education and occupy important, even dominant, roles in public professions such as television broadcasting and some areas of university teaching (Suriyasarn, 1994).

At the same time, Thai males occupy most of the high-paying professions, and women are excluded from many leadership roles. From an early age, females are socialized to be care-giving, submissive, and pleasing to men. Women's language is expected to be more polite than the language of men (Simpson, 1997). Van Esterik (1982) concluded more than 20 years ago that the presumed high status of Thai women is "a delightfully refreshing cliché [. . .] and very little else" (pp. 2–3). However, as Suriyasarn (1994) notes, Thai women are making inroads into increasingly important positions in Thai society.

On the U.S.-dominated Internet (Paolillo, chapter 18 this volume), Thai women are stereotypically portrayed as beautiful, exotic, and eager to meet foreign men. Approximately 90% of the hits in the first five pages produced by an English-language Google search in April 2003 for the terms "Thai," "women," and "Internet" led to sex sites and dating services. Suriyasarn (1997) also found an active discourse sexualizing Thai women on the newsgroup *soc.culture.thai*, produced mostly by Western men posting messages seeking and debating the merits of Thai women as prospective girlfriends, wives, and sexual partners. Thai women posted very little to these discussions.[4] The reputation of Thai women as sexually available can be traced to the widely publicized prostitution services made available to American military personnel during and after the Vietnam War (Gay, 1985). Although the Thai government has in recent years taken actions to restrict prostitution, stereotypes about Thai women persist, especially in the West.

Among online Thais themselves, the situation is quite different. According to S. Hongladarom (2000), Thais preserve their cultural ("local") identity on the Internet despite Western dominance of the medium. On *soc.culture.thai*, Thai men did not participate in objectifying discourse about Thai women; some protested against it (Suriyasarn, 1997).[5] Thai women (especially urban, middle-class women) are supposed to be modest and chaste (VanLandingham et al., 1993);[6] (male) participants defended these traditional virtues.

More generally, crude discourse is considered impolite in Thai culture, and avoided online as well as offline. For example, the netiquette guidelines posted on the pantip.com website and analyzed for politeness behaviors by K. Hongladarom and S. Hongladarom (2005) prohibit messages that contain foul language and sexually explicit content, and disrespectful comments about the king of Thailand and the Buddhist religion. At the same time, gender plays a role in online interaction among Thais. S. Hongladarom (2000, n.p.) describes the Internet as "a place where [Thai] teenagers hang out and find their girlfriends or boyfriends," adding "as with other cybercommunities elsewhere, women, or those who identify themselves as such on the Net, are instantly popular and can attract a lot of traffic." Conversely, although gender is not a focus of the K. Hongladarom and S. Hongladarom (2005) study, it appears from their examples that most of the participants in the asynchronous science and philosophy discussion forum they analyzed were male.

As yet, no research has systematically investigated the discourse of men and women in Thai Internet contexts. The available evidence, however, points to the importance of distinguishing between Thais participating in English-language, Western-dominant Internet contexts and Thais communicating online among themselves. The present study analyzes participation patterns of Thai speakers communicating with other Thais in a Thai-language chat room popular with young, educated, urban users, focusing on the effects of participant gender. Significantly, the participants in this chat room are predominantly female.

DATA AND METHODOLOGY

The primary research question in this study is how gender affects turn taking in Thai chat. To answer this question, we analyzed turn allocation and response patterns in light of Sacks et al.'s (1974) claims regarding face-to-face conversation, taking into consideration the independent variable of participant gender. Sacks et al.'s model was chosen because it allows us to test whether turn allocation in the chat room is similar to face-to-face strategies (i.e., favors selecting a next speaker, strategy A) or whether it is fundamentally different, as Lunsford (1996) suggested (i.e., favors self-selection, strategies B and C). We also analyzed use of, and responses to, flirtation, in order to test whether females are selected as conversational participants with flirtatious intent, as in English-language chat.

Data

The data were collected from the Thai chat room #*jaja5* (located at http://www.pantip.com). The name of the site, "pantip," is derived from Pantip Plaza, a large shopping center in Bangkok specializing in computer hardware and software (S. Hongladarom, 2000). This site was selected because it is the most popular chat website in the Thai language.[7] In addition to 11 chat rooms, the site includes asynchronous discussion forums, news, and links to commercial and technical resources. The #*jaja5* chat room, like the other chat rooms on the site,[8] is intended for general social chat (*jaja* is a combination of two final particles in Thai that signal intimacy between speaker and hearer). Most messages posted to the chat room are in Thai script in the Thai language.[9] From the information they provide about themselves in their chat messages, it appears that most participants live in Thailand and are between the ages of 11 and 25. The chat room interface is shown in figure 10.2.

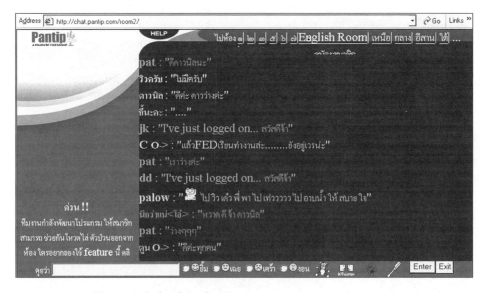

FIGURE 10.2. The #*jaja5* chat interface.

Thai chat is especially amenable to the study of gender since the Thai language has sentence-final particles that can be used to classify whether participants are female or male; that is, gender is grammatically visible. These particles, which occur frequently in the chat data, include

- Final particles for men such as /khráp/ (with variants /khráap/, /khrâap/, /khâap/, /kháap/, and /há/)
- Final particles for women such as /khà/, /khá/, and /khâa/

In addition, the Thai language has gender-specific first-person pronouns (*phom* for males and *dichan* or *chan* for females), although the male pronoun is more common in everyday use than are its female counterparts, which sound somewhat formal. Either can be omitted, or a gender-neutral pronoun or self-referential nickname can be used in its place; the latter strategy is especially common among females (Simpson, 1997).

Participants were classified as female or male on the basis of their use of sentence-final particles, first-person pronouns (when available), and nicknames. Regarding nicknames, for example, "Roy," "Jay," "dul," and "Maunjalho" were classified as male;[10] "Prim," "Pimja," "Namfon," "Maunsuey," and "Viva" as female;[11] and "O," "Nut" (possibly from English "peanut"), and "Nangmannoi" ("devil") as gender indeterminate.

The data consist of 917 messages produced over a two-hour period in July 2001. This sample was part of a 60-hour corpus collected in two-hour intervals three times a week over a 10-week period from the six #*jaja* chat rooms,[12] for a total of 10 hours per chat room. All data collection took place on weekdays from 6:00 P.M. to 8:00 P.M., the most active period in Thai chat rooms and the time when the widest range of participants are present, since it is both after school hours and working hours in Thailand (Todla, 1999). For the purposes of the present analysis, one two-hour interval was selected from the larger corpus. The interval was chosen because it contained the largest number of messages, but otherwise appeared to be typical. As in English-language chat rooms, participants joined and left the room continuously during the sample period. In total, the sample contains messages from 52 individuals: 25 females, 12 males, and 15 participants whose gender could not be identified,[13] Five hundred ninety-eight female messages, 269 male messages, and 50 messages from participants of indeterminate gender were posted during the sample period.

Methodology

Herring's (1999) schematic representation of coherence in turn taking was adapted for identifying turn initiations and responses. We coded each initiation ($N = 576$) in terms of the three basic strategies of turn allocation identified by Sacks et al. (1974). In addition, we analyzed which initiations received no response, and whether males or females received more responses in the chat room. Finally, we classified flirtatious initiations in terms of the nature and explicitness of their flirtatious content.[14]

We coded three basic strategies of turn allocation used in the Thai chat room, adapted from the classification scheme of Sacks et al. (1974). (All examples given below were translated from the original Thai by the first author.) Arrows indicate the message that illustrates each category of phenomenon in examples with more than one message.

>A. The current speaker selects the next speaker by using a name (nickname) or kinship term such as "sister," "brother," and so on.
>
>   *Prim*:   Hey *roy*, have you given me your email [address]?
>
>B. The next speaker self-selects
>
>   1. By responding to a previous conversation. That is, the speaker "interrupts" a conversation between other speakers. For example, Fon asks dul a question, and Omyinlaksi comments on his answer:
>
>   *Fon*:   What is your telephone number?
>
>   *dul*:   01-3636655
>
>   → *Omyinlaksi*:   Fon, don't believe it. It is a wrong number.
>
>   2. By changing the topic or initiating a new conversation.
>
>   *Prim*:   Hey girl, can you give me your email. I'll send you a card.
>
>   *POOH BEAR*:   xxxxxxXX@hotmail.com
>
>   → *Prim*:   POOH, are you feeling sleepy? Do you need my lap?
>
>C. The current speaker continues
>
>   1. Immediately
>
>   *Roy*:   POOH, do you have a special friend yet?
>
>   → *Roy*:   Prim and I will find one for you.
>
>   2. After a pause (stops posting for a while)
>
>   *POOH BEAR*:   What are your real names? They are Prim and Roy, right?
>
>   *Peesaew*:   IE4 or IE5 or IE6
>
>   *Pimja*:   Hi TAR
>
>   *Pimja*:   What's IE? Peesaew. I don't know.
>
>   *[[TAR]]*:   Hi too.
>
>   → *POOH BEAR*:   Hey, please answer.

Strategy A can co-occur with either B or C; that is, in self-selecting or continuing to take a turn, a speaker can simultaneously select a next speaker. Thus, a turn may be coded for multiple turn allocation strategies.

A grounded theory approach was used to identify categories of flirtation (Glaser & Strauss, 1967). Specific behaviors observed to be used flirtatiously in the data were first listed and then generalized to a smaller set of coding categories:

>*Flirtation strategies*
>
>*1. Request/give personal contact information*
>
>   1.1 Email
>
>   1.2 Phone number
>
>   1.3 Home address/office address

2. *Talk about relationships*
   2.1 Do you have a boyfriend/girlfriend?
   2.2 Can I date you?
   2.3 Sexual proposition or sexual reference
3. *Request/offer personal contact*
   3.1 Chat with me
   3.2 Email me/I will email you
   3.3 Phone me/I will phone you
   3.4 See me

The coded data were entered into Microsoft Excel 98 and analyzed statistically using GLMStat, a generalized linear model statistical analysis program for the Macintosh, set up to run log-linear models. This method was chosen because log-linear models are better suited than linear regression and analysis of variance models to analyzing count data that do not show a normal distribution, as was the case for the data in this study.

RESULTS

Turn Allocation

The results of the analysis of turn allocational strategies for all participants combined are shown in table 10.3. Current speaker selects the next speaker was used the most (66.5%), followed by next speaker self-selects (25.9%), while current speaker continues was least exploited (7.6%).

GLMStat was used to determine the relationship between turn allocational strategies and gender. The turn allocation strategies (A, B, and C) reported in table 10.3 were set as dependent variables, and the independent variables were FS (female speaker), MS (male speaker), FA (female addressee), and MA (male addressee). In addition, the software automatically generated interaction categories for the speaker and hearer combinations FS.FA (female speaker, female addressee), FS.MA (female speaker, male addressee), MS.FA (male speaker, female addressee), and MS.MA (male speaker, male addressee).[15] An iterative process of model selection and refinement was followed in the statistical analysis. We started by including all the main variables

TABLE 10.3. Percentage of use of turn allocational strategies.

Turn allocation strategy	N	Frequency (%)
A. The current speaker selects the next speaker	525	66.5
B. The next speaker self-selects	205	25.9
C. The current speaker continues	60	7.6
Total	790	100

in each analysis, weeding out those that proved to be nonsignificant, and then adding in the interaction variables and weeding out those that were non-significant, to arrive at the best model for each analysis. Only the best model in each case is presented in the tables below (i.e., no nonsignificant results are included). All results are significant at $p < 0.05$.

The numbers yielded by the statistical analysis show either positive or negative values. In table 10.4, a positive value means that the speaker, hearer, or speaker–hearer combination is associated with significantly greater use of the specified turn allocational strategy than the mean.[16] A negative value means that the speaker, hearer, or speaker-hearer combination significantly avoids use of the turn allocational strategy relative to the mean. In the tables, "variable" refers to the independent variables, and "estimate" refers to the size of the contribution of each variable to the statistical model.

In table 10.4A, the current speaker selects the next speaker. Both females and males significantly use strategy A. However, females use A more than do males, because the value of the estimate is higher. In addition, males use A in order to talk to females. None of the other interaction combinations was significant.

In table 10.4B, the next speaker self-selects. Male speakers make significant use of strategy B, but female speakers do not differ significantly from the mean, inasmuch as they do not appear in the model. Moreover, when B is used by males, the addressee is usually female.

In table 10.4C, the current speaker continues. The use of strategy C is again significant for male speakers but not for female speakers. That is, males are more likely to continue speaking even when they do not receive a response. If the speaker uses C, either females or males (but not participants of inde-terminate gender) are the addressees.

TABLE 10.4. Log-linear model for the use of turn allocational strategies. All estimates significant at $p < 0.05$.

Variable	Estimate
A. The current speaker selects the next speaker	
FS	2.551
MS	0.9594
MS.FA	0.9967
B. The next speaker self-selects	
MS	0.8826
FA	0.4258
MS.FA	1.274
C. The current speaker continues	
MS	1.309
FA	2.087
MA	2.304

TABLE 10.5. Log-linear model for distribution of "no response" by gender. All estimates significant at p < 0.05.

Variable	Estimate
MS	0.5166
FS.FA	−0.3723

TABLE 10.6. Percentage of each turn allocation strategy that gets no response.

Turn allocation strategy	N	Percentage (%)
A. The current speaker selects the next speaker	177	33.5
B. The next speaker self-selects	99	48.3
C. The current speaker continues	2	3.3
Total	278	35.2

We then considered which gender receives more responses to its turn initiations. The average number of responses for the three initiation strategies combined was 0.21 per male message and 0.48 per female message. That is, male participants were less than half as likely to get a response as were female participants. This result is confirmed by the results of the GLMStat analysis shown in table 10.5, in which "no response" was taken as the dependent variable, and gender of speaker, addressee, and speaker–addressee combinations as independent variables.

Table 10.5 shows that male speakers are significantly likely *not* to get a response. In contrast, female speakers are significantly likely to receive responses from females, as shown by the negative value for FS.FA. We also considered which turn allocational strategies are most successful at generating responses. The percentages of "no responses" to each of the three strategies are shown in table 10.6.

About 35% of the initiations receive no response in the sample overall. Strategy A generates a response two-thirds of the time, while B gets a response just over half the time. If a speaker continues after getting no response, however, his or her chances of being responded to increase to 97%. We also used GLMStat to determine which turn allocational strategies were most successful. For this analysis, we considered "no response versus response" as the dependent variable, and strategies A, B, and C as independent variables. The results in table 10.7 are a logistic, rather than a log-linear, model in that the dependent variable is a binomial.

Table 10.7 reveals that strategy B received significantly few responses. In contrast, strategy C received many responses, as shown by the negative value of the estimate. Strategy A also received responses, inasmuch as the value for A was not significant. Because the value for A is close to the mean for the sample overall, it does not show up in the model.

TABLE 10.7. Logistic model for distribution of "no response" by turn allocation strategy. All estimates significant at p < 0.05.

Variable	Estimate
Strategy B	0.05707
Strategy C	−0.2032

TABLE 10.8. Log-linear model for distribution of flirtatious initiations. All estimates significant at p < 0.05.

Variable	Estimate
FA	2.449
MS.FA	3.303

Flirtation

In addition to turn allocation and response patterns, flirtation by both genders was analyzed. We considered the nature of initiations by gender, hypothesizing that male initiations to females would be more flirtatious than other initiations. The results of the GLMStat analyses for all categories of flirtatious behavior combined are shown in table 10.8.

Males initiate more flirtation than do females, and females are the primary recipients of flirtation, especially from males. The overall incidence of flirtation in the corpus was relatively low—only 8.7% of the turn initiations included any flirtatious content, as coded according to the categories described in the methodology section. Table 10.9 shows a breakdown by gender of the frequency of each flirtation strategy.

Females asked for and offered email addesses more than did males, while males asked more directly flirtatious questions ("Do you have a boyfriend?" "Can I date you?") than did females. Moreover, 14 out of the 19 instances (74%) of female initiations regarding email exchange were addressed to other females and were not flirtatious in intent, whereas seven out of seven (100%) of the direct questions asked by males were addressed to participants of the opposite sex and appear to have been intended flirtatiously. Gender-indeterminate participants made the lowest percentage of flirtatious initiations. These individuals also produced the fewest mes-sages (an average of 2.7 messages per person, compared with 15.3 messages per female-identified participant and 12.8 messages per male-identified participant).[17]

TABLE 10.9. Distribution of flirtatious initiations by strategy (raw numbers).

Strategy	Females	Males	Indeterminate	Total
1.1 Email	12	2	0	14
1.2 Phone number	1	1	0	2
1.3 Home/office address	3	2	0	5
2.1 Do you have a bf/gf?	0	4	0	4
2.2 Can I date you?	0	3	0	3
2.3 Sexual prop. or sexual ref.	2	1	0	3
3.1 Chat with me	1	2	0	3
3.2 Email me/I will email you	7	1	0	8
3.3 Phone me/I will phone you	3	0	0	3
3.4 See me	2	2	1	5
Percentage of total initiations	31/382 = 8.1%	18/154 = 11.7%	1/40 = 2.5%	50/576 = 8.7%

DISCUSSION

To interpret these results, we break them into two sets, the first concerning the nature of turn allocation in the chat room, and the second concerning the effects of gender. With regard to the first set, we ask which turn allocation strategies are preferred and which turn allocation strategies are most success-ful. The answer to the first question is that the current speaker selects the next speaker (A), followed by the next speaker self-selects (B), followed by the current speaker continues (C). These results are similar to the observa-tions of Sacks et al. (1974) for face-to-face conversation. They do not support the proposal of Lunsford (1996) that self-selection (B or C) should predomi-nate because everyone in the chat room has an equivalent right to take a turn. Although everyone theoretically has a right to self-select, conversational coherence would be sacrificed if all participants took on the role of speaker all the time. Strategy A promotes coherence by creating linkage between turns, and thus is generally preferred over strategy B, both face to face and in synchronous chat.

At the same time, there are differences in turn taking between the two media. System lag and one-way message transmission not only lead to dis-rupted adjacency (Herring, 1999) but also may affect turn allocation. When a speaker asks a question and does not receive immediate feedback (e.g., because the addressee is in the process of typing a response), other messages may be sent in the meantime, giving rise to apparent speaker self-selection as the speaker waits for the addressee's response. Moreover, because the pantip.com chat rooms have a limited message buffer, allowing a maximum of 150 characters per message, if one wishes to take a long turn, one must first send a message and then continue posting in a second message, creating the appearance of "same speaker continues" (Lunsford, 1996). These properties of the chat medium should logically result in higher incidences of strategies

B and C than in face-to-face conversation. We are unable to evaluate this proposition at present, however, since to our knowledge no one has yet attempted to quantify the use of turn allocation strategies in face-to-face conversation in such a way as to enable a direct comparison.

The answer to which turn allocation strategies are the most successful is strategy A, the current speaker selects the next speaker. Strategy A is responded to 68% of the time. Although strategy C gets a higher rate of response (97%), C is by definition a continuation of an unsuccessful initiation and shows the effects of persistence more than successful initiation. Strategy B—simply speaking up without consideration for ongoing conversations—is the least successful strategy, garnering a response only about half of the time.

The second set of results concerns gender. We found that the use of turn allocational strategies depends in part on participant gender. Females use strategy A more than do males, and males use B and C more than do females. We noted above that A is the strategy that most directly mimics face-to-face conversation. A is also the most interactive strategy, in that it engages the addressee directly, creating social as well as structural cohesion. Our finding is thus consistent with previous research that finds females to be more interactive and other-oriented than are males (Coates, 1993; Edelsky, 1981; Gilligan, 1982; Herring, 1996).

Strategies B and C, in contrast, involve individuals acting independently. Thai males speak out in public CMC forums, regardless of whether they are addressed or responded to (see also Suriyasarn, 1997). This result corresponds to Herring's (1993, 1996, in press) findings on English-language asynchronous discussion groups, in which males tend to adopt an independent, rather than a socially aligned, stance. Further, the fact that male chatters are more likely than female chatters to take a turn without being invited and to persist in posting even when they receive no response is consistent with previous proposals that males experience a greater sense of entitlement to "speak" in public cyberspaces (Herring, 1993, in press).

As for flirtation, although it is not very frequent overall in the Thai chat data, it exhibits familiar gender dynamics. Males are more flirtatious and engage in more direct, explicit flirtation than do females. In contrast, most of the behavior coded as flirtation for females involves requests for email addresses or phone numbers from other females. Flirting is asymmetrical in English-language chat rooms, as well (Bruckman, 1993; Rodino, 1997), with males in the role of pursuer and females in the role of pursued (the "belle of the ball" phenomenon, Herring, 1998). It would be misleading, however, to conclude that because traditional gender roles are evident, males dominate or enjoy greater power in the Thai chat room than do females. On the contrary, females participate more and get more responses in this sample than do males, only a relatively small percentage of which are flirtatious in nature. Furthermore, females interact predominantly with other females and often ignore the males who attempt to get their attention. Males, who are in the minority, must work harder to take the floor, even in their attempted flirtatious interactions.

In part, this may be because males do not use the preferred turn allocation strategy, current speaker selects next, as often as do females. The strategies of self-selection and continuation may be inherently less effective, as suggested above. Alternatively, because females are more numerous than males in the sample (48% female vs. 23% male), as well as in the chat room in general, based on informal observation of other #jaja5 samples in the corpus, they might be empowered by virtue of their majority status, as Herring (1996, in press) found for asynchronous discussion groups.[18] However, this leads to the question of why there are more females than males in this Thai chat room, contrary to the trend in English-language chat rooms. A possible explanation for this is cultural: Thai women may feel comfortable communicating in chat rooms, especially when the topic is casual socializing, because the norms of behavior in Thai contexts are different from those in English-language contexts.

It is interesting to note that the netiquette guidelines posted on the pantip.com website prohibit "messages which contain foul language and sexually explicit content" (as translated by S. Hongladarom, 2000). Given that sexually explicit content in CMC is often used to degrade and objectify women, this guideline may help to ensure a respectful online environment for Thai women. Flirtation in #jaja5 (and the other chat rooms on the site) never approaches crudeness, and we found hardly any instances of sexual references in our corpus. Such behavior would be perceived as rude in Thai culture, and participants could be judged negatively as a result.

In order to determine the relative importance of each of these factors, further empirical research is needed. To explore the effectiveness of different turn allocation strategies, the present findings could be supplemented with qualitative analysis of message content, to determine, for example, whether response rate is influenced by the topic (or by whether the initiation itself is on- or off-topic). Majority gender effects could be assessed by comparing the present findings with chat rooms (or chat samples) on the pantip.com site in which the majority of participants are male. Systematic comparisons of initiation and response patterns by gender could be made across chat rooms frequented by different cultural groups. Ideally, a study incorporating a multivariate design could allow topic, gender, and culture to vary, enabling a more precise determination of their relative contributions to participation patterns. It would also be of interest to compare Thai chat with Thai asynchronous discussion groups and private forms of Thai CMC such as email to assess the stability of gender patterns across CMC modes.

CONCLUSIONS

In this study, we investigated turn allocation and participant gender in a Thai-language chat room, employing methods of analysis adapted from the study of turn taking in face-to-face conversation. We found that turn allocation in the chat room is generally similar to that in face-to-face conversation: Participants preferentially address one another, rather than self-selecting to speak. We also found gender differences, with females making greater use of the preferred strategy to create coherence and orient to their conversational partners, and males initiating more turns independently, as well as initiating more flirtatious exchanges. At the same time, contrary to previous findings on gender in chat rooms, and contrary to culturally based expectations about the subordinate status of Thai women, we found evidence that females appear to be relatively empowered in the Thai chat room sample studied here, participating more often than males and receiving a higher rate of response from both female and male interlocutors. This finding reflects, on the one hand, the numerical predominance of females in the chat room, which enables them to set and enforce interactional norms according to their own preferred practices. On the other hand, it reflects the value placed on politeness and civility in Thai culture, which creates a context in which women can participate comfortably, free from the crude, aggressive behaviors that often characterize public, English-language CMC.

These results stand in a paradoxical relationship to the socialization of Thai females to be submissive and their sexualized reputation in the West. The young Thai women in the #*jaja* chat room sample are generally friendly but not overly accommodating to males; they are objects of flirtatious male attention but less so than are females in English-language chat rooms. This suggests that the relatively higher status of Thai women may be more than just a "refreshing cliché" (van Esterik, 1982) today. More generally, the results indicate that gender interacts with culture online in complex ways, underscoring the need for further comparative research.

Acknowledgment

A previous version of this chapter was published in the *Journal of Computer-Mediated Communication* (volume 9, issue 1, 2003).

Notes

1. Public chat rooms tend to be heterosexual by default, unless otherwise indicated by a modifier such as "gay," "lesbian," or coded terms such as "twinks" (young gay males) in the chat room's name. The chat room in this study is not named in such a way as to suggest that its participants are homosexual.

2. This example is from the IRC EFNET channel #*punjab*. Ssa is an abbreviated form of the Punjabi greeting sat siri akal (literally "God is truth").

3. In research on turn taking in CMC, message posters are often referred to as "speakers," by analogy with face-to-face conversation. Lunsford (1996) follows this practice, as we do also in this study.

4. It is possible that the Thai women who read the newsgroup felt uncomfortable posting in English. Thai men posted to the group, however, so this explanation would require us to posit different linguistic competencies (or different degrees of self-confidence about posting in English) for females and males. It is not clear from Suriyasarn's discussion whether Thai women posted to the newsgroup on other topics.

5. Some Thai women resist such stereotypes by creating websites to identify the problem and to replace myths with facts (e.g., http://www.siamweb.org/ and http://www.busakorn.addr .com/thaiwomen.htm, retrieved September 15, 2005).

6. At the same time, Thai men have traditionally been allowed and even expected to visit prostitutes. This has started to change in recent years due to fears associated with the spread of AIDS in Asia (Simpson, 1997).

7. It is also the fifth largest Thai website (K. Hongladarom & S. Hongladarom, 2005).

8. Chat rooms named #*jaja1*, #*jaja2*, #*jaja3*, and so forth, are also available, with the same theme of social chat.

9. Some Thai–English code switching occurs in the chat room, which displays log-on and log-off messages in English. (The message "I've just logged on" in figure 10.2 was automatically generated by the system.) However, the Thai language is overwhelmingly dominant in the #*jaja* chat rooms. For those who wish to practice their English, pantip.com provides a separate English-language chat room.

10. The first three are male Thai names; the last is a chat-specific nickname that means "seems smart."

11. The first three are female Thai names, the fourth means "seems beautiful," and the last is a foreign name.

12. See note 8.

13. Unlike earlier reports of play with identity in English-language chat rooms (see Bechar-Israeli, 1995), nicknames are relatively stable identifiers on the pantip site. Attempting to pass as the opposite gender online is not common (compare Bruckman, 1993). Todla (1999) interviewed participants in #*jaja* chat rooms at pantip.com; some reported having misrepresented their gender online. However, only one instance of this was observed in our 60-hour corpus. Participants often discuss their gender (and age) explicitly. This evidence, along with nicknames, pronouns, and final particles, allowed us to identify the gender of participants as male or female with a relatively high degree of confidence. "Gender-indeterminate" participants were treated as a separate category for purposes of analysis.

14. Coding categories were developed and refined by both authors; the first author, a native Thai speaker, coded the data.

15. In the spreadsheet for the GLMStat analysis, gender-indeterminate speakers and hearers were coded as "not-female and not-male."

16. This value is computed from the aggregate of the nonsignificant factors in the model.

17. It is partly because these individuals posted so few messages that they were classified as gender indeterminate. Had they posted more messages, they likely would have used gender-specific particles or otherwise indicated their gender.

18. Synchronicity alone cannot lead to female empowerment. If this were the case, we should find similar effects in all chat rooms, regardless of the language used and regardless of the relative percentage of male and female participants (compare Herring, 2003).

References

Bechar-Israeli, H. (1995). From ⟨Bonehead⟩ to ⟨cLoNehEAd⟩: Nicknames, play and identity on Internet Relay Chat. *Journal of Computer-Mediated Communication, 1*(2). Retrieved September 15, 2005, from http:// jcmc.indiana.edu/vol1/issue2/bechar.html.

Bruckman, A. S. (1993). Gender swapping on the Internet. Retrieved September 15, 2005, from http://www.cc.gatech.edu/elc/papers/bruckman/gender-swapping-bruckman.pdf.

Cherny, L. (1994). Gender differences in text-based virtual reality. In M. Bucholtz, A. Liang, L. Sutton, & C. Hines (Eds.), *Cultural performances: Proceedings of the third Berkeley Women and Language Conference* (pp. 102–115). Berkeley, CA: Berkeley Women and Language Group.

Cherny, L. (1999). *Conversation and community: Chat in a virtual world.* Stanford, CA: Center for the Study of Language and Information.

Coates, J. (1993). *Women, men and language* (2nd ed.). London: Longman.

Danet, B. (1998). Text as mask: Gender, play and performance on the Internet. In S. Jones (Ed.), *Cybersociety 2.0* (pp. 129–158). Thousand Oaks, CA: Sage.

Duncan, S. (1972). Some signals and rules for taking speaking turns in conversations. *Journal of Personality and Social Psychology, 23,* 283–292.

Edelsky, C. (1981). Who's got the floor? *Language in Society, 10,* 383–421.

Gay, J. (1985). The "patriotic prostitute." *The Progressive,* February, 34.

Gilligan, C. (1982). *In a different voice.* Cambridge, MA: Harvard University Press.

Glaser, B., & Strauss, A. L. (1967). *The discovery of grounded theory: Strategies for qualitative research.* Hawthorne, NY: Aldine de Gruyter.

Grossman, W. (1997). *net.wars.* New York: New York University Press.

Herring, S. C. (1992). *Gender and participation in computer-mediated linguistic discourse.* Washington, DC: ERIC Clearinghouse on Languages and Linguistics (document ED345552).

Herring, S. C. (1993). Gender and democracy in computer-mediated communication. *Electronic Journal of Communication, 3*(2). Retrieved September 15, 2005, from http://ella.slis .indiana.edu/~herring/ejc.txt.

Herring, S. C. (1996). Two variants of an electronic message schema. In S. Herring (Ed.), *Computer-mediated communication: Linguistic, social and cross-cultural perspectives* (pp. 81–106). Amsterdam: John Benjamins.

Herring, S. C. (1998). *Virtual gender performances.* Talk presented at Texas A&M University, September 25.

Herring, S. C. (1999). Interactional coherence in CMC. *Journal of Computer-Mediated Communication, 4*(4). Retrieved September 15, 2005, from http://jcmc.indiana.edu/vol4/ issue4/.

Herring, S. C. (2003). Gender and power in online communication. In J. Holmes & M. Meyerhoff (Eds.), *The handbook of language and gender* (pp. 202–228). Oxford: Blackwell.

Herring, S. C. (in press). Who's got the floor in computer-mediated conversation? Edelsky's gender patterns revisited. In S. C. Herring (Ed.), *Computer-mediated conversation.* Cresskill, NJ: Hampton Press.

Hongladarom, K., & Hongladarom, S. (2005). Politeness in Thai computer-mediated communication. In R. Lakoff & S. Ide (Eds.), *Broadening the horizon of linguistic politeness* (pp. 145–162). Amsterdam: John Benjamins.

Hongladarom, S. (2000). Negotiating the global and the local: How Thai culture co-opts the Internet. *First Monday, 5*(8). Retrieved September 15, 2005, from http://www.firstmonday .dk/issues/issue5_8/hongladarom/index.html.

Lunsford, W. (1996). *Turn-taking organization in Internet Relay Chat.* Unpublished manuscript, University of Texas at Arlington.

McLaughlin, M. L. (1984). *Conversation: How talk is organized.* Beverly Hills, CA: Sage.

Rodino, M. (1997). Breaking out of binaries: Reconceptualizing gender and its relationship to language in computer-mediated communication. *Journal of Computer-Mediated Communication, 3*(3). Retrieved September 15, 2005, from http://jcmc.indiana.edu/vol3/ issue3/rodino.html.

Sacks, H., Schegloff, E. A., & Jefferson, G. (1974). A simplest systematics for the organization of turn-taking for conversation. *Language, 50*(4), 696–734.

Schegloff, E. A., & Sacks, H. (1973). Opening up closings. *Semiotica, 25,* 289–327.

Simpson, R. C. (1997). *Negotiating identities in Thai conversation: A sociolinguistic discourse analysis of person-referring expressions.* Unpublished Ph.D. dissertation, University of Michigan.

Suriyasarn, B. (1993). *Roles and status of Thai women from past to present.* Retrieved September 15, 2005, from http://www.busakorn.addr.com/women/women-all.htm.

Suriyasarn, B. (1994). *Thai TV career women: Impressions, statistics and reality.* Retrieved September 15, 2005, from http://www.busakorn.addr.com/tvwomen/TVwomen-frame .htm.

Suriyasarn, B. (1997). *Cyberdiscourse on Thai women on soc.culture.thai. A perspective on gender politics on the Internet.* Retrieved September 15, 2005, from http://www.busakorn .addr.com/cyber/cyber-frame.htm.

Todla, S. (1999). *Patterns of communicative behaviour in Internet chatrooms* (in Thai). Unpublished master's thesis, Chulalongkorn University.

UNESCO. (1990). *Status of women: Thailand.* RUSHSAP Series on Monographs and Occasional Papers No. 26. Bangkok: UNESCO Principal Regional Office for Asia and the Pacific.

van Esterik, P. (Ed.). (1982). *Women of Southeast Asia.* Dekalb: Northern Illinois University, Center for South and Southeast Asian Studies.

VanLandingham, M. J., Suprasert, S., Sittitrai, W., Vaddhanaphuti, C., & Grandjean, N. (1993). Sexual activity among never-married men in northern Thailand. *Demography, 30*(3), 297–313.

Werry, C. C. (1996). Linguistic and interactional features of Internet Relay Chat. In S. C. Herring (Ed.), *Computer-mediated communication: Linguistic, social and cross-cultural perspectives* (pp. 47–63). Amsterdam: John Benjamins.

11

SANDI MICHELE DE OLIVEIRA

Breaking Conversational Norms on a Portuguese Users' Network

Men as Adjudicators of Politeness?

Issues of gender in English-language computer-mediated communication (CMC) have been investigated since the late 1980s. While early studies highlighted advantages the new technology offered for greater gender equality (e.g., Graddol & Swann, 1989; Smith & Balka, 1988), by 1992 studies had identified gender differences in communicative style on the Internet. Herring (2003) traces the history of gender research on CMC, concluding that messages posted by men and women reflect "culturally learned" gender styles.

In comparison, research on CMC in Portuguese is scanty and has focused mainly on its use as a tool in foreign language education, especially in the development of writing skills (e.g., Kelm, 1992). With the exception of a few studies (e.g., Cardoso, 1998), little scholarly attention has been devoted to native speakers of Portuguese using the Internet as a means of natural communication.

Previous research on gender in Portuguese has found that media stereotypes resemble those in the English-speaking world (Neto & Pinto, 1998). In Portuguese TV advertisements, men are more often presented as the central figure (66%) and "voices of authority" in voice-overs (91%) and are more than four times as likely as women to have speaking roles, although both genders are more often silent at the end of the ad relative to other nationalities studied. Neto and Pinto concluded that while women account for more than half of the general population and those completing a university degree, they continue to be portrayed in the media in traditionally feminine roles, and women portrayed in the workplace occupy positions of lower rank than do men. Actual gender-based language differences in Portuguese, however, have not been sufficiently investigated.

In contrast to the paucity of research on Portuguese CMC or gendered language use, politeness and especially the sophisticated Portuguese address system have received considerable attention over the past 20 years. For example, Hammermüller (1993) examined social conventions and the acceptability of variable formulations of address. Carreira (1997) considered address as a means of verbal proxemics. Of particular relevance are the studies of Oliveira Medeiros (1985, 1994), which discuss negotiation and renegotiation strategies for developing address form relationships in Portuguese, and Oliveira (2003), a 20-year perspective on actual address form usage.

In this chapter I analyze asynchronous conversational threads posted on a users' network at a Portuguese university over a two-year period (March 2001 to April 2003). The analysis considers linguistic politeness behavior at both sentence and discourse levels. The working hypotheses were that (1) men and women would adhere to the pragmatic norms followed in face-to-face interaction (use of appropriate titles, politeness norms) and (2) gender analyses would reveal women to be the guarantors of standards of politeness, with men the more frequent transgressors, as found in previous research on gender and CMC (e.g., Herring, 1994; Smith, McLaughlin, & Osborne, 1997).

After a presentation of the theoretical foundations for the study and the pragmatic norms of communication at a Portuguese university, the data are examined. The findings indicate that stereotypical patterns of gendered behavior do exist in Portuguese asynchronous CMC. At the same time, contrary to the findings of previous studies, clear evidence exists that men are interested in the overall "decency" and maintenance of communicative "standards" on the users' network.

THEORETICAL FOUNDATIONS

Two related approaches provide the theoretical underpinnings for analyzing politeness (Brown & Levinson, 1987) and impoliteness (Culpeper, 1996), while studies of the Portuguese system of address over a 20-year period (e.g., Oliveira, 2003; Oliveira Medeiros, 1994) provide the cultural focus necessary for a fuller understanding of the data presented.

Brown and Levinson's (B&L) model is based on politeness as a function of a speaker's desire to give or receive respect ("positive face") or to avoid imposition (on oneself or another; "negative face"). The strategies used in conversation are ranked accorded to their ability to "threaten" the face "wants" of the other. The categories are bald on record (direct comments, with no attention paid to the wants or needs of the hearer), positive politeness (statements showing respect for the hearer), negative politeness (statements designed to diminish the imposition on the hearer), off-record (very indirect statements of want), and withholding the face-threatening act (FTA) (silence on the matter, hoping the hearer will understand the speaker's wants without a verbal stimulus).

The B&L model has been criticized on several grounds. First, the strategies are assumed to be universal. Second, the model analyzes text at the sentence rather than the discourse level. Finally, the model ignores the special problems of intentional impoliteness, where a speaker's desire to be impolite would appear to threaten her positive face wants (to be respected).

Culpeper (1996) attempts to fill the latter gap, suggesting that strategic impoliteness exists, with a structure parallel to that of B&L's politeness strategies. He identifies bald on-record impoliteness (deliberate rudeness), positive impoliteness (attacking the positive face wants of the hearer), negative impoliteness (attacking the negative face wants of the hearer), sarcasm or mock politeness (being rude by pretending to be polite), and withholding politeness (avoiding engaging in expected politeness behavior). Unfortunately, Culpeper's categories are not mutually exclusive; positive impoliteness can also be baldly rude, for example. His model also suffers from the first two limitations noted above for the B&L model: assumed universality and focus on the sentence level. These criticisms aside, the two perspectives provide useful terms for consideration, because they integrate the notions of "face" (Goffman, 1956) into a linguistic frame of reference, identifying degrees of politeness and impoliteness along lines of directness.

THE IMPORTANCE OF APPROPRIATE ADDRESS IN PORTUGUESE

Appropriate address is a crucial aspect of smooth communication in Portugal. While everyone has a social title, not everyone possesses an academic degree; fewer still have professional or administrative titles. Unless the speakers have negotiated an address form relationship different from conventionalized norms, they must select the appropriate title for each situation. Oliveira Medeiros (1994) presents strategies speakers use to determine an appropriate address form or to (re)negotiate their address form relationship with others.

Knowing the appropriate rank and educational background of the other person is the responsibility of the speaker, with the relevant information often obtained through third parties. Portuguese speakers commonly "precall" an organization to discover the title of a person to guarantee pragmatic correctness when the "real" phone call is made. Gião (1992) states that when people are introduced, their position and title should be made clear "to avoid embarrassing situations" (p. 171) arising naturally from the social rule that one should not obtain this information through a direct question to the person. Thus, when third parties are not present and people are left to present themselves to others, they do not use their own titles, but furnish supplementary information so their status can be ascertained (e.g., "Hello, I am _____, professor at University X").

Given this preoccupation with correct address, a refusal to acknowledge the other's full status would be highly inappropriate. In instances where the relative status—and thus the appropriate address form—of the parties is (or "should" be) known, Culpeper might consider failure to use it an example of withholding politeness or positive impoliteness (using inappropriate identity markers). In Portuguese society, however, withholding an appropriate address form would be considered an act of bald on-record impoliteness.

INTERACTIONAL NORMS WITHIN THE UNIVERSITY

Appropriate address is no less important in the university environment than in Portuguese society at large. Hierarchy is very important; status is determined by rank and seniority. University faculty and staff are expected to conform to protocol in university council meetings and correspondence. Table 11.1 presents a four-tier hierarchy of forms for address within the university.

TABLE 11.1. Forms of address used to conduct official business at Portuguese universities (all titles used with the third-person singular form of the verb).

Administrative titles	sr.(^{a}) presidente sr.(^{a}) director(a)	
Professional titles	professor(a)	(= rank of assistant, associate, or full professor)

	Variants:
	    title + FN (with men or women)
	    title + LN (with men)
	    Prof.(^{a}) + Doutor(a) or Engenheiro(–a)
	    Senhor(a) Professor(a)	

Academic titles	doutor(a)	(= completion of Ph.D. degree in letters)
	engenheiro(–a)	(= completion of Ph.D. degree in science or engineering)
	dr.(^{a})	(= completion of B.A. degree in letters)
	eng.^{o} or eng.^{a}	(completion of B.A. degree in science or engineering)

	Variants:
	    title + FN
	    title + LN
		(with men or women)
		(with men)

Social titles	(Social titles are used with those who have no academic degree; administrative titles, if possessed, take precedence)	
	sr. + FN or LN dona + FN	(with men) (with women)

In Portuguese, regular feminine nouns are formed either by adding an "a" to a masculine noun ending in a consonant (e.g., director/directora) or by substituting the final "o" with an "a" (e.g., engenheiro/engenheira). By convention, these are indicated by (–a) to signal substitution, or (a) or (^{a}) to signal addition (the superscript form is used with abbreviations). FN, first name; LN, last name.

Obviously, personal relationships exist that transcend the official hierarchy, so one hears *tu* (the second-person pronoun, generally signifying a close relationship), first or last name, or *colega* ("colleague;" used among faculty members or administrative personnel, but not between the two). However, while the tendency to hide close friendships through the use of more formal address forms in the presence of third parties is reduced relative to 20 years ago (see Oliveira Medeiros, 1985; Oliveira, 2003), academic and professional titles are still used in both official correspondence and council meetings.

In correspondence, academic titles are generally omitted in the letter's closing; the administrative title (e.g., President of the Department Council) or rank (Graduate Assistant)[1] appears under the name. It is the reader's responsibility to be able to determine the address from the administrative or professional titles. Use of *tu* in CMC reveals a desire to highlight the personal relationship and/or to take advantage of the closeness implied by that address to achieve conversational goals not otherwise possible (see example 5 below).

In Portuguese CMC, variable use is made of the standardized "signature" (inclusive of information needed for selecting appropriate address). While a standardized signature is not considered offensive, simply presenting one's name and academic title would be considered self-promotion, a pragmatic offense. Absent a signature, respondents frequently use *colega*, considered inoffensive. However, its use is not unambiguous, for while *colega* traditionally emphasizes solidarity, it can also serve to avoid acknowledging the hearer's (superior) status, without fear of reprisal.

Prescriptive gendered behavior at work merits only a single paragraph from Gião (1992). Women are admonished not to expect social niceties (e.g., the opening of a door). As to how women should be addressed, Gião (1992) advises, "True courtesy will be to treat her in accordance with her hierarchical position and not her gender." Women are encouraged to act in a similar fashion (p. 169).

Finally, the computer network users in this study are part of the university community and therefore interact via CMC, face-to-face, telephone, and "regular" written communication. The norms of each channel are potentially relevant in interpreting online behavior.

INTERNET USAGE WITHIN THE UNIVERSITY

For convenience, I have been referring to a "users' network"; in reality, this is the university's IMAP webmail program (asynchronous email). Email addressed to users@university_X, whether from an internal or external address, is sent to everyone holding a university mail account. Internet use at this university is relatively recent. In 1993 the first email accounts were issued, using a UNIX-based system; in 1996 a change was made to a Windows-based program, permitting easier communication. Only in 1998 did the university actively encourage faculty and staff to acquire email accounts.

No official policy exists regarding appropriate use of the network, censorship of messages, or expected language use. When asked, the computer center responds that users should observe the rules of netiquette as found on the Internet. Occasionally they post their "informal" rules (emphasis theirs) to filter out commercial messages, unsolicited junk mail, messages with attachments or images, and messages announcing new viruses (unless validated by the computer center). Nevertheless, unsolicited junk mail from sources outside the university surpasses in number the messages generated internally, a common source of complaint.

User names are not anonymous, so the gender and rank of active participants are verifiable. Most contributors to the conversational threads analyzed are male professors. Thirty-four percent of all professors and 49% of graduate assistants are female.[2]

THE DATA

University faculty and staff posted a total of approximately 2,700 messages between March 2001 and April 2003 (unsolicited junk mail excluded). More than 90% were informational bulletins with no response expected: notices of university events, academic deadlines, university hirings, research opportunities, and so forth. The remaining messages posted by network members were comments or complaints about university services or facilities (directed to all colleagues or as an "open letter" to the university administration) and inappropriate use of the users' network (particularly complaints regarding advertising).

While nearly every message was read (some official bulletins excepted), I chose to analyze the 14 conversational threads (CTs) of five messages or more in the sample, as well as messages containing comments on communicative appropriateness. The sustained CTs, made up of 178 postings, represent approximately 8% of the total, indicating that this network is used primarily for disseminating information and only secondarily to advance discussion.

Women post informational bulletins with roughly the same frequency as do men (see Graddol & Swann, 1989) but demonstrate little participation in extended CTs, rarely initiating general discussion. The ratio of male-to-female participation, greater than 4-to-1 for number of messages and nearly the same ratio for the number of active participants, is disproportionate to the overall university faculty population (2-to-1 male-to-female).[3] An examination of the number of "highly active" participants (those contributing five or more times) shows almost no gender difference (13% of females vs. 15% of males). However, these numbers are not statistically significant, because only two females are "highly active." The list of CTs with a breakdown of participation by gender is given in table 11.2.

TABLE 11.2. Conversational threads analyzed.

Conversation thread	Total postings	Initiated/terminated by male (M) or female (F)	Postings by females		Postings by males	
			Total postings	No. females	Total postings	No. males
1. Complaint: faulty air conditioning	7	M/M	3	3	4	2
2. Debate: university ID card?	11	M/M	1	1	10	8
3. Proposed national law on education	20	M/F (union rep.)	8	6	12	6
4. University newspaper coverage of B.A. course	5	M/M	1	1	4	3
5. Criticism: newspaper article on church as pillar of society	5	M/M	0	0	5	4
6. Responses to publicity placed by female [toys]	5	M/M	1	1	4	4
7. Responses to publicity placed by male [real estate]	13	M/F	1	1	12	10
8. Proposed changes in university statutes	7	M/M	1	1	6	5
9. Complaint: new university procedure	14	M/M	3	3	11	6
10. Responses to action taken by rector	34	M/M	4	3	30	18
11. Complaint: university service	6	M/F	1	1	5	5
12. Possible discontinuation of users	19	M/F	2	2	17	13
13. Responses to mention of religious website placed by female; topic change to users	6 + 13 = 19[a]	M/M	2	2	17	10
14. Apology for posting advertising; topic change to censorship	2 + 4 = 6[a]	F (apology)/M	2	2	4	3
Total	178		33		145	
No. participants			16 (19%)		52 (81%)	
No. "highly active" participants[b]			2 (13%)		8 (15%)	

[a] The number following the + indicates messages with a change in header and shift in content, although the first message clearly continues the CT begun previously.
[b] "Highly active" participants have participated five or more times in the CTs analyzed.

262

ANALYSIS OF CONVERSATIONAL THREADS

The analysis of CTs is separated into three categories: initiation and termination of threads, violation of pragmatic norms (politeness), and inappropriate content of submissions.

Initiation and Termination of Conversational Threads

Only one of the 14 CTs analyzed was initiated by a female (CT-14); it was an apology to users for posting a message containing advertising. CT-2, discussing whether the university should issue identity cards, is particularly interesting in terms of gendered behavior. Table 11.3 summarizes the sequence of messages. Although six males supported the position first espoused by the female respondent, only three credit her with the solution; the others credit their male colleagues (see Herring, Johnson, & DiBenedetto, 1995).

A hypothesis that a man terminated every CT proved incorrect. Four were ended by women, three by the same one (one of the two "highly active" participants). The fourth (CT-3), discussing proposed national education legislation, closed with an official posting by the teachers' union representative, coincidentally female.

Violation of Pragmatic Norms

The next conversational thread CT-4, concerns appropriate address and is notable for the acidic tone of some of the messages. Male 1, a professor,

TABLE 11.3. CT-2 (FN = first name, LN = last name).

Message	Sender	Message content
1	M	Introduces the problem
2	F	Suggests a simple solution
3	M	Agrees with email of "colleague + FN + LN"
4	M	Agrees with Dr.[a] FN + LN
5	M	Agrees with "the colleague" (feminine)
6	M	Agrees with "the colleagues"
7	M	Agrees with "Prof. FN + LN (male colleague, message 4) and other colleagues"
8	M	"I agree with the message of Prof. LN (message 7) and have exactly the same position expressed by Prof. FN + LN (message 4)"
9	M	Long answer to first message, no indication of having read other messages
10	M	Long response to previous message
11	M	Long, general position addressed to "dear colleagues"

questions the coverage given one of the university's B.A.-level programs in a recent issue of the university newspaper. Writing to "dear colleagues," he explains that he is not affiliated with that program or department but feels the university newspaper was unfairly biased. He signs FN + LN, providing no academic title, in accordance with the norms described above.[4]

Example 1. CT-4, Message 1 (Male 1)

Dear Colleagues:
   What is happening with the _____ course? Or rather . . . What is happening with the University Newspaper, so dedicated that it is to speaking poorly about one of our (and its) courses?

   . . .

   Nota Bene: I am not involved in that course, nor do I know any of the article's authors, nor did I gain, in any case, any desire to after reading them. I do not have the least personal stake [in the issue], or belong to a lobby, political party, or religion that leads me to state the following.
   I simply find it inadmissible that the University Newspaper serves to (attempt to) cast such a dark shadow on the image of any of the courses of this university, by people of the university itself, worse, with the knowledge and acceptance—as I cannot imagine that he is not aware of this— of the Rector, who is also the newspaper's Director.
   All of us, at least all those who try to be serious in their work, deserve greater respect. And forgive my letting off steam.
       FN + LN

Caros Colegas:
   Que se passa com [nome do curso]? Ou melhor . . . Que se passa com o Jornal da Universidade, tão dedicado que está em dizer mal de um dos nossos (e seus . . .) cursos?

   . . .

   Nota Bene: não estou envolvido nesse curso, nem conheço nenhum dos articulistas, nem fiquei, aliás, com muito desejo disso depois de os ler. Não possuo o mínimo interesse pessoal, ou de lobby, ou de partido político, ou de religião, para dizer o que vou dizer.
   Acho simplesmente inadmissível que o Jornal da Universidade sirva para (tentar) colocar de rastos a imagem dum curso qualquer da Universidade, por gente da própria Universidade, pior, com a conivência— pois não imagino que esteja desconhecedor da questão— do próprio Reitor que é, também, o Director do Jornal.
   Todos nós, pelo menos todos os que tentam ser sérios no seu trabalho, merecem mais respeito. E desculpem o desabafo.
       FN + LN

Example 2. CT-4, Message 2 (Female 1) (Bold italics indicate inflammatory or aggressive language.)

Sr + FN + LN

I believe we do not live in a ***totalitarian state***, but I am

Sr + FN + LN

Penso que não vivemos num ***estado totalitario***, mas fico muito

very thankful that **Sr. + FN** tells us *all, including the Rector,* when we can or cannot debate **the issues** that are important to our University.	agradecida que o **Sr. + FN** nos diga *a todos, inclusive ao Sr. Reitor,* quando é que podemos *ou não* debater os assuntos que importam a nossa Universidade.
The issue of [the aforementioned] course is, unfortunately, *too serious for light commentaries.* So, *if you wish to be informed, you may contact me.* I am *always* in the Department of _____ [not the department under fire].	O tema do [curso em _____] é, infelizmente, *demasiado sério para comentários ligeiros.* De maneira que, *se quiser ser informado*, pode-me contactar. Estou *sempre* no Departamento de _____ [não o dept.º em questão].
Academic respect is also a victory for democracy.	*O respeito académico é também uma vitória da democracia.*
FN + LN	FN + LN

In example 2, female 1 actively seeks disagreement, insinuating that male 1 is uninformed, undemocratic, and not serious; she engages in sarcasm and mock politeness, inviting him to contact her for further information and suggesting she possesses "the" truth. Ironically, her statement "[a]cademic respect is also a victory for democracy" misfires, as she shows anything but academic respect for her colleague, as evidenced in the tone of her message and inappropriate address.

Use of "Sr. + FN + LN" is inappropriate, first, because the absence of an introductory word (e.g., "Dear") suggests direct address, but this pattern would not occur. Second, and more germane here, is the use of *Sr.* (Mr.) rather than even the academic title *Dr.* to signify completion of a B.A. degree. Male 1 has earned a Ph.D. degree and is a professor. Therefore, he would be addressed as *Professor*, reflecting his rank within the professor category, *Professor Doutor*, reflecting rank plus academic title, or even *Senhor Professor Doutor*, although this last would probably be judged ironic in these circumstances. Either of the first two titles could be followed by first or last name.

Use of *Sr.* is appropriate only if a speaker does not know whether the other has an academic or professional title, knows no one to ask, and has no independent means of discovering that information. If this woman were unfamiliar with her colleague's title, she should have asked a colleague or searched the university's website. By using *Sr.*, rather than even *Dr.*, she strips him of the academic qualifications that would give him the right to use the term "colleagues" in its strictest sense! University janitors, for example, are addressed by *Sr. + FN* (or *LN*). In Portuguese society, this behavior would be viewed as very aggressive, regardless of the speaker's gender.

Jackson (1999) identifies American women as being more often offended than men by the use of inappropriate address. Here we do not have the data to compare the relative frequency of complaint or comparative degree of sentiment by gender, but the online response from male 1 is noticeably sharp:

Example 3. CT-4, Message 3 (Male 1) (Bold italics indicate sarcasm.)

Dear Colleague (***I presume you are for having "responded"*** to my letting-off-steam of the other day addressed to Colleagues):

Without any attempt to diminish you by the address form you chose to address me by, I inform you that what worries me, precisely, is speaking about democracy in the same breath that you insinuate being on the side of one who has more power than ***my poor person***, that is, in ***confounding citizenship with vassalage. I KNOW that THIS Rector does not need defenders.***

. . .

Regards.

FN + LN

Cara Colega (***presumo que o seja ao ter "respondido"*** ao meu desabafo do outro dia dirigido aos Colegas):

Sem qualquer tentativa de a diminuir através da forma de tratamento com a qual optou por se me dirigir, informo-a que o que me preocupa, precisamente, é falar de democracia no mesmo sopro em que se insinua estar do lado de quem tem mais poder do que ***a minha pobre pessoa***, ou seja, ***confundir cidadania com vassalagem. Eu SEI que ESTE Reitor não precisa de defensores.***

. . .

Cumprimentos.

FN + LN

Through the phrasing of "I presume you are [a colleague]" and "without any attempt to diminish you . . .," male 1 employs a standard put-down in Portuguese: He says he will *not* chastise the transgressor, while doing exactly that. It is obvious to all that female 1 has committed a faux pas, despite male 1's not having offered his rank. Still, the same social rules prohibit him, although the injured party, from chastising her directly. Etiquette "demands" that errors committed by those in a subordinate position in the workplace should be handled as follows: "The correct attitude will be to call him aside and explain the error he committed. Never should one expose a subordinate to public humiliation, or even worse, criticize him behind his back without explaining to him his mistake" (Gião, 1992, pp. 166ff.). Thus, had male 1 criticized female 1 more overtly, he could have damaged his public face and appeared pompous, overly concerned with his position. Ironically, he was later accused of that very attitude (by male 3; see description further below).

Male 1's self-reference as "my poor person" is sarcastic and demonstrates mock politeness, but the tone is not biting. He says what worries him is something *other* than the address form used (namely, "confounding citizenship with vassalage"). Still, he apparently feels strongly enough about the inappropriate address to mention it; the alternative would have been to address the message to "Dear colleague" and then talk about the issue of democracy.

There was no response from female 1, and certainly no apology. Consequently, a second male comments further on her transgression. He addresses *colegas* on the importance of proper address, rather than her personally, since a "private" message to her in the public forum would run counter to rules of etiquette.

> *Example 4. CT-4, Message 4 (Male 2) (Words in bold preach etiquette; bold italics indicate sarcasm; and words in bold underline are address forms.)*

Dear **Colleagues,**

Caros **Colegas,**

The tacit meaning of the address form is proof that academic address is done without effort:

O significado tácito da forma de tratamento é uma evidência que o trato académico integra sem esforço:

> Quoting [female informant]:
> I am very grateful that **Sr. + FN** tells us all

> Quoting [informante feminino]:
> fico muito agradecida que o **Sr. FN** nos diga a todos

No. "Senhor FN" is impossible. It won't do. The Academic world is vast, diverse, open, and has its fragility: the respect of *a certain elegance* is not imposed by law. It's just as well, but it imposes greater moral duty.

Não. "Senhor FN", não pode ser. Não dá. O meio Académico é vasto, diverso, aberto, e tem a sua fragilidade: o respeito de *uma certa elegância* não é imposto por lei. Ainda bem, mas mais dever moral impõe.

***

***

P.S. Would it be possible to reread the thesis of <u>***Colleague + FN***</u> ***on "address forms in Portuguese"?***

P.S. Seria possível reler a tese da <u>***Colega + FN***</u> ***sobre "modos de tratamento em Português"?***

Here male 2 has social legitimacy in pointing out female 1's faux pas, arising from the role third parties play as providers of appropriate social information. Accordingly, they are empowered to make social rules explicit. Moreover, and perhaps due to the absence of a public apology from female 1, he felt justified in going bald on record, as evidenced by unequivocal statements that she was wrong and her behavior inexcusable. His suggestion to "colleagues" to read about address form usage in Portuguese is directed essentially to her.

One might speculate on the significance of both male 1 and male 2 holding the rank of professor, while female 1 is a graduate assistant (verifiable on the university's website). However, female 1's manner of address was such a blatant breach of social conduct that its use would have attracted comment irrespective of the transgressor's gender or rank. More interesting, when male 1 "presumes" she is a colleague, he is effectively refusing to acknowledge his awareness of her status or to take the time to seek it out.

Female 1 neither responded to this nor sent any message to users for the following three weeks. Although impossible to prove, a natural conclusion is that she was effectively silenced (Herring, 1999). For that matter, no one (including male 1) acknowledged male 2's comments publicly. However, the exchange provoked a response from a former student of the university (male 3), who wrote to users from an address outside the university system to support the newspaper and further criticize male 1.

As with female 1, male 3 does not notice that male 1 has no tie to the department under fire. He refers to male 1 as "a certain Dr. + FN + LN." By using *Dr.* rather than *Prof.*, he continues the pragmatic offense of diminishing the academic qualifications of male 1. While male 2 does not indicate the address form that is most appropriate, the implication was certainly present that an academic title was missing. Male 3 opted for the lowest academic title (indicative of a B.A. degree), without verifying the true status; this is another instance of going bald on record. Moreover, the addition of "a certain" conveys the impression that the person to whom he refers is nearly an "untouchable," a conversational strategy entirely unacceptable in face-to-face communication that might be overheard by the one being maligned. There was no online reaction to his message.

Herring (1999, p. 156) presents a five-stage progression of online gender harassment:

(1) Initial situation
(2) Initiation of harassment
(3) Resistance to harassment
(4) Escalation of harassment
(5) (a) Targeted participants accommodate to dominant group norms, and/or
     (b) targeted participants fall silent

While the legal definition of harassment refers to repeated abuse (by the same party), analysis of the entire sequence of CT-4 seems to fit the pattern described by Herring, but with an interesting twist: While the original skirmish is between male 1 and female 1, midway through the process the original participants fall silent and the conflict is carried on by others, all male:

(1) Initial situation: male 1's complaint
(2) Initiation of harassment: female 1
(3) Resistance to harassment: male 1; male 2's support of male 1
(4) Continued harassment: male 3 against male 1
(5) All participants (and the entire users' community) fall silent

Not only did the participants fall silent on this, but in the following 18 months no additional messages contained or called attention to inappropriate address. However, one male professor opened discussion of how the users themselves should be addressed. No consensus was reached. The computer center addresses messages to *Caros Utilizadores* ("Dear Users"), a form rejected by the users themselves.

While extreme discord can arise over address (see CT-4), the Portuguese address form system is so complex that it also allows for very subtle snubbing.

In another CT, originated by two males (not the same as in CT-4), the first sends to all a hyperlink to a newspaper article on "Church, moral pillar of society." It provokes a sharp response:

Example 5. CT-5, Message 2 (Male 2) (Words in bold are particularly aggressive; bold italics indicate sarcasm; and words in bold underline are address forms.)

My dear **LN**

    I do not know the reason that led **you** to send to the users the excerpt from the article of _____. I presume that it must be, **with your agreement**, **a certain** desire for anticlerical proselytism, unfortunately still common in **a certain** left[ist group], ***bound by the ghosts of the Enlightenment*** of the 18th century and the positivists of the 19th century. It happens that the Church continues to be the ***great enemy***, which only attests to the permanence of its values, as no one beats on corpses.

    . . .

With the regards of
FN + LN

Meu caro **LN**

    Desconheço a razão que **te** levou a enviar para os users o excerto do artigo do _____. Presumo que será, **com a tua concordância**, um **certo** desejo de proselitismo anticlerical, aliás infelizmente ainda comum numa **certa** esquerda, ***presa dos fantasmas iluministas*** do sec. XVIII e positivistas do sec. XIX. Constata-se que a Igreja continua a ser o ***grande inimigo***, o que só atesta a permanência dos seus valores, já que ninguém bate em mortos.

    . . .

Com os cumprimentos do
FN + LN

Male 2 neither claims to know why the message was posted nor asks, presuming that male 1 intended to spread anticlerical propaganda. He denigrates his colleague using "a certain," accusing him of being leftist as well as anticlerical, and further associating the latter with outdated philosophies.

Commonly, friends choose to use address forms indicative of respect for the other's academic title or rank in online messages, so use of "colleague" or "dear + title" would not have been surprising. Here male 2 deliberately chose "my dear LN" and use of the pronoun *tu* (in the form of the direct object pronoun *te*). Use of *tu* online indicates a relationship sufficiently close to allow an offline response. However, public ridicule seems the intent here: Use of *tu* emphasizes the aggressive tone created by the writer's pompous, sarcastic language; it also "authorizes" the writer to be boldly sarcastic without fear of public redress, for the linguistic behavior of those in a mutual *tu* relationship is negotiated by the speakers, not by social norms (see Oliveira Medeiros, 1985). Even the greeting can be interpreted as ironic;

however, it is within conventionalized norms. Therefore, irony is impossible to prove.

Male 1 responds in example 6 with "dear FN + LN," immediately creating greater distance, as he had been addressed by last name exclusively.

> *Example 6. CT-5, Message 3 (Male 1) (Words in bold underline are address forms.)*

Dear **FN + LN**	Caro **FN + LN**
I take great pleasure in clarifying.	Tenho muito gosto em esclarecer.
I begin by clarifying that I have nothing against religious values. The article itself by _____ also does not appear to me to be against [them]. On the contrary, it says: . . .	Começo por esclarecer que nada tenho contra os valores religiosos. O próprio artigo do _____ também me parece nada ter contra. Pelo contrário, diz: . . .
I only intended to call attention to an interesting article (stimulating), which I happened to see in a newspaper and thought other colleagues might find interesting and might not have seen in the paper. . . .	Pretendi apenas chamar a atenção para um artigo interessante (porque estimulante), que vi por acaso no jornal e que outros colegas poderão achar interessante e poderão, por acaso, não ter visto no jornal . . .
Regards	Cumprimentos
FN + LN	FN + LN

"I take great pleasure in clarifying" and "I begin by clarifying" are formal constructions, deliberately impersonal—both the direct and indirect object pronouns are omitted. Despite use of the first person and the personalized salutation, male 1 appears to be addressing the group, rather than a single individual, and there is no other reference to the colleague to whom he is ostensibly responding. His message is emotionally neutral, and the words selected are clear. He signs his message "regards, FN + LN."

Male 1's response is so neutral and entirely above reproach that it effectively (and sharply) criticizes the tone of the previous message; he takes advantage of his legitimacy as the second party in a *tu* relationship to take redressive action. Absent blatant insinuation, a subtle dig may be found in the comment that some other colleagues may be interested in the article. Unlike the circumstances in CT-4, where the title *Professor* would have been expected, here use of both *FN* and *LN* is appropriate as a response to a personalized greeting using *LN*. If male 1 had used the title *Professor*, the disparity between the two messages might have prompted others to believe he was overreacting. Male 2 did not respond, although two other males contributed comments. Neither made direct reference to the personal exchange, but rather to the content of the article.

Inappropriate Content of Submissions

Despite over 75 postings with advertising content, only four attracted attention resulting in conversational threads of the length studied here; three involved postings by women. In message 1 of CT-14 (example 7), a woman apologizes for having posted a notice containing advertising. A review of the messages revealed no overt objection to which she is responding, so presumably the complaints were sent to her off-list. However, she feels compelled to apologize publicly. She is highly self-deprecatory and adheres to stereotypical norms of "female discourse style" (Herring, 1993). A small number of native speakers of both genders (nonmembers of the users' group) were questioned: They agreed that "only" a woman could have written message 1 and "only" a man could have written message 2. Moreover, in the original Portuguese, it is nearly impossible to enunciate her words and avoid adopting a subservient tone.

Example 7. CT-14, Message 1 (Female Speaker) (In this message, bold indicates self-humbling language.)

Dear Colleagues

It was never my intention to send any publicity **whatsoever** . . . I was "**carried away**" by my **as yet slight** experience in navigating the Internet and Email.

I ask forgiveness.

In the future, **I will be more careful**. I **learned** that I have to pay more attention to the "Subject" line and **I will immediately delete** [messages] when there are words such as "discounts" or others that "**smell**" of publicity.

One more time I present my apologies.

[Have a] good day and good work.

FN

Caros Colegas

Nunca foi minha intenção enviar **qualquer** publicidade . . . Fui "**levada**" pela minha **ainda pouca** experiência nestas andanças da Internet e Email.

Peço desculpas.

De futuro, **vou ter mais cuidado**. **Aprendi** que tenho que passar dar mais atenção à coluna "Assunto" e **vou apagar imediatamente** quando nela figurem palavras como "descontos" ou outras que me "**cheirem**" a publicidade.

Mais uma vez apresento as minhas desculpas.

Bom dia e bom trabalho.

FN

In this short message, the writer formally seeks forgiveness twice. Mentioning her inexperience, she claims to have learned a lesson, promising to behave better in the future. She emphasizes her transgression and proposes a remedy. She addresses everyone; as no single person is responsible for the users' network, it might have received no response. Nevertheless, a male responds in a patronizing and dismissive manner (example 8; in this and subsequent examples, only the English translation is given).

> *Example 8. CT-14, Message 2 (Male Speaker) (In this message, bold italics indicate self-importance.)*

> Dear Colleague:
> You're forgiven, **as far as I am concerned**.
>   Just two weeks ago I sent a notice about an academic event on the Human Genome, promoted by Le Monde Diplomatique, which was not posted nor was I given any explanation for the censure. **That is what is serious**.
>   **As far as you are concerned, be calm.**
> Regards FN + LN

Here a male decides to speak for all in forgiving the female colleague. However, he quickly turns to message censorship. Tangential to the original post, it sparks a new discussion lasting four messages. Thus, although his response is superficially polite (the female colleague is not to worry), it simultaneously conveys to all that her "problem" is uninteresting. This parallels Sandler and Hall's (1982) finding regarding the use of politeness strategies by American male faculty members to demean female students and their work, as well as Herring et al.'s (1995) observation that men "avoided addressing the women's concerns by dismissing them as trivial or by intellectualizing the discussion away from its original focus" (p. 68).

A second complaint against inappropriate use of the users' network was lodged against a woman who sent the hyperlink of a website for prayer or meditation. The issue of censorship again emerged in messages supporting self-regulation. In one, a male states (originally in Portuguese): "It is a question of determining what is reasonable to appear on the internal list of a university. For example, those who wish to visit pornographic sites can do it in the intimacy of their home. It is not necessary for the Users network to display the addresses of the lowest and most 'colorful' sites" (CT-13, message 4).

In the contradictory next message the woman is addressed as *colega* and is informed both that the message was eliminated before it was read and that the person tried to access the site without success! She responds:

> *Example 9. CT-13, Message 6 (Female) (In this message, bold italics indicate irony.)*

> Dear "users,"
> First, I apologize for the **lack of [good] sense** in having sent the message in question to all "users." I thought **only of those for whom it could be of interest, forgetting that there might be others**, as there were, **who would be disturbed**. I had no intention of offending anyone. **Word of honor! My intention was simply to post a notice of the site to those interested. It was not well thought out.**

In the future I will be more careful in using this service. I will use it as if censorship does, in fact, exist. Still, I wonder, if one announces houses and cars for sale, rooms for rent, matters that have little to do with the University . . . why not have a page for interested persons to visit? There are a lot of people who won't care, who will simply delete it, but there are also those who may find it interesting and useful, such as happens with a "For rent" or "For Sale."
Regards FN + LN

Her language is not subservient but ironic; the message can be interpreted as an apology by someone trying to be helpful. A second interpretation is that she is ridiculing as narrow-minded those who reacted negatively to her message. She then justifies her posting as one of many addressing issues outside the direct interests of the university. In essence, she "apologizes" to those who seem to demand it, yet stands her ground by noting that other messages covering nonacademic topics have also been posted. Implied is the notion of unfair treatment, as not all are "required" to justify their actions.

The response, from a male new to the discussion, is not patronizing. Rather, he lends his support by similarly invoking irony, although his message is more gentle and impersonal, with less use of first person and more references to the world at large. No further reference was made to the female's apology; the exchanges continued on the issue of censorship.

Example 10. CT-13, Message 7 (Male) (In this message, bold italics indicate gentle irony.)

Curious times in which we live. *Only gross cultural myopia would allow us to equate the spiritual and religious dimension of humanity (an anthropological universal which not even a basic Jacobinism can eliminate) with political propaganda or pornography.*
As much as I try, I cannot understand (surely the lack is mine) how it is that one can accept the posting of cultural events on the Users' network and be *profoundly disturbed* by the reference to a website of a religious nature, *undisputedly one of the highest forms of culture which the human spirit has ever produced.* Even more so in that the message did not even refer to a specific religion.
FN + LN

A third woman was criticized for announcing the website of a business selling handmade toys for children (CT-6). Three complaints were posted before she responded. She made no apology for having offended users; rather, she justified herself and adopted an aggressive tone: "If the debate initiated could deal with the central issue initiated regarding the type of toy offered a child and the consequences of this same act, taking into account the Christmas season, we will [*sic*] all be certainly more enriched" (CT-6, message 4). Perhaps her lack of contrition was responsible for two additional male postings, the second stating that if the users' network is "open," one day the users will be reading about the sale of "sex-shop products or some such thing," which ended that conversation thread.

Only once did a posting with "inappropriate" content from a male spark a conversational thread large enough for this analysis. He offered five real estate properties for sale (CT-7). The first reaction (from a male) was, "how can such a message be allowed on the users' network?" No personal condemnation was made, however. Moreover, despite 13 postings, no apology was made by the transgressor, nor was there any overt attempt to elicit an apology from him. This may, at least in part, be explained by CT-7, message 5: A male noticed the nonuniversity source of the offending message and complained of usage by outsiders. However, through the university website I verified that the sender was a member of the university community who had opted to respond from an outside address; others could have done the same. Neither he nor any of his colleagues commented publicly on his university affiliation. The next response (CT-7, message 6) was sent 20 minutes later: "In relation to the message originating this crisis in the users' list, I have nothing to say, as there exist no 'official' [their emphasis] rules on the use of this list, it is the responsibility of each one to send what he/she wishes." The remaining messages were either personal condemnations of publicity or statements in support of self-regulation and democracy.

In each of these cases, the discussion eventually revolved around a *systemic* problem—the filtering of messages or censorship. However, some reactions seem gender based. The overall message to female transgressors is that women should not be too self-deprecatory (or they will be patronized), but they should be humble and accept criticism. Moreover, they are criticized differently from males for similar transgressions. In two of the three instances involving females, the possible consequences were extrapolated to be sexual in nature: pornography (from the original matter of a religious site) and sexual toys (from hand-made wooden toys for children). With the male transgressor, however, no such extrapolations were made, and the system was viewed as the only culprit.

CONCLUSIONS

In this chapter I examined asynchronous discussion threads on the users' network of a Portuguese university, focusing on concerns regarding pragmatic and linguistic standards of appropriateness, as well as gendered usage. Concepts borrowed from Brown and Levinson (1987) and Culpeper (1996), as well as the pragmatics of address terms from Oliveira (2003) and Oliveira Medeiros (1985, 1994), were applied in analyzing those violations.

In the absence of official rules and censorship, members themselves set the boundaries for acceptable behavior, and participants of both genders negotiated appropriate interactional norms. Males, however, clearly dominated in initiating (91%) and terminating (71%) sustained conversational threads, as well as in identifying transgressions and meting out interactional "punishment" (resulting in a loss of "face" for the transgressors).

Regarding the first hypothesis, adherence to general communicative norms, the number of messages violating such norms is small, yet of sufficient concern to users to provoke a public response, primarily from males, who used two distinct politeness strategies to respond to messages they considered inappropriate. They addressed the issue directly (e.g., CT-4), using ironic or sarcastic language, or became distant and impersonal, using formal language (e.g., CT-5).

The second hypothesis predicted gender differences in violating politeness norms or serving as guarantors of standards. Both men and women contributed positively, through expressions of support for topics initiated or positions adopted by colleagues. Both, too, were guilty of transgressions, such as inappropriate use of the network through the introduction of topics considered taboo or inappropriate (disrespectful) language. Similarities are found in the way these transgressions were handled, but there are also some notable differences. The first lies in the number of times women, as opposed to men, were chastised for breaking the unofficial rules of the network. A higher percentage of women's than men's transgressions were chastised.

Second, women were expected to apologize. If they did not respond, subsequent messages were more overt in identifying their transgression or extrapolating negative consequences. References were made to possible sexual consequences, highly inappropriate within the university environment. In contrast, even when a man's behavior was criticized, apologies did not seem expected; rather, the conversational thread either shifted focus or died out.

Third, even when the female's position received initial support (from either gender), eventually the original contribution was reattributed to one or more male participants (CT-2). Finally, excepting the union representative, only one female participant had the final word, albeit in three cases.

At the same time, I found evidence that counters the stereotype of men as disinterested in politeness norms. Men not only indicate the transgression but also refer to etiquette standards and even supporting research on address forms. They do not simply complain; they demonstrate concern regarding the behavioral standards of this new medium. While the criticism may be harsh (e.g., CT-4), most of the chastisers are themselves mindful of politeness norms.

The emerging picture is one of traditional gender asymmetry with a culture-specific difference: Portuguese men as adjudicators of politeness. Why do they assume this role? Neto and Pinto's (1998) discussion of male voices of authority suggests a partial explanation. If we consider TV voice-overs, 91% by males, to be somewhat analogous to the messages of chastisement (i.e., they orient the listener to a particular "reality"), then the overwhelmingly male response to perceived inappropriate behavior online seems natural. Portuguese men may simply be demonstrating in a new medium their authority to define and enforce social reality (Spender, 1980).

Several avenues of future research are suggested by this study. One would be the analysis—by gender of transgressors and chastisers—of messages provoking objections, regardless of conversational thread length. Analyses of the "highly active" participants might reveal whether frequency of participation, or some other factor, confers authority. We might also analyze attention to politeness in relation to educational level. Comparative studies of gendered language use in other Portuguese CMC environments are also needed, as is research on language and gender in Portuguese face-to-face communication.

Finally, the Portuguese data show that violations of norms of address provoke vehement reactions, suggesting that the complex communicative norms of address in face-to-face interaction are equally important in asynchronous CMC, at least in the university studied. While men may more likely assume the role of adjudicator, Portuguese men and women agree that a blatantly inappropriate address form, especially when used as a deliberate impoliteness strategy, falls outside the bounds of appropriateness and decency.

Acknowledgment

An earlier version of this chapter appeared in the *Journal of Computer-Mediated Communication* (volume 9, issue 1, 2003).

Notes

1. Graduate Assistants (*Assistentes* and *Assistentes Estagiários[-as]*) are employed as full-time university teachers while preparing their degrees, so their status is higher than their American counterparts.

2. The Instituto Nacional de Estatística (2002) reports that females represent 52.7% of the population and 54% of university graduates, up from 36% of university graduates in 1981 and 47% in 1991.

3. The Minister of the Presidency, of Portugal's Council of Ministers, claims that 27% of females and 34% of males use the Internet (Ministro da Presidência, 2003).

4. All translations from Portuguese to English are by the author. For the Portuguese text of examples 8–10, see the online version at http://jcmc.indiana.edu/vol9/issue1/oliveira.html.

References

Brown, P., & Levinson, S. (1987). *Politeness: Some universals in language usage*. London: Cambridge University Press.

Cardoso, G. (1998). *Para uma sociologia do ciberespaço: Comunidades virtuais em português*. Oeiras: Celta.

Carreira, M. H. A. (1997). *Modalisation linguistique en situation d'interlocution: Proxémique verbale et modalités en portugais*. Paris: Peeters.

Culpeper, J. (1996). Towards an anatomy of impoliteness. *Journal of Pragmatics, 25*, 349–367.

Gião, A. S. (1992). *Etiqueta e boas maneiras. Cortesia e civilidade na vida moderna*. Lisboa: Edições 70.

Goffman, E. (1956). *The presentation of self in everyday life*. Edinburgh: University of Edinburgh Press.

Graddol, D., & Swann, J. (1989). *Gender voices.* London: Basil Blackwell.

Hammermüller, G. (1993). *Die Anrede im Portugiesischen. Eine soziolinguistische Untersuchung zu Andredekonventionen des gegenwärtigen Portugiesisch.* Chemnitz: Nov Neuer Verlag.

Herring, S. C. (1993). Gender and democracy in computer-mediated communication. *Electronic Journal of Communication, 3*(2). Retrieved September 15, 2005, from http://www .internetstudies.pe.kr/txt/Herring.txt.

Herring, S. C. (1994). Politeness in computer culture: Why women thank and men flame. In M. Bucholtz, A. Liang, & L. Sutton (Eds.), *Cultural performances: Proceedings of the Third Berkeley Women and Language Conference* (pp. 278–94). Berkeley, CA: Berkeley Women and Language Group.

Herring, S. C. (1999). The rhetorical dynamics of gender harassment online. *The Information Society, 15*(3), 151–167.

Herring, S. C. (2003). Gender and power in online communication. In J. Holmes & M. Meyerhoff (Eds.), *The handbook of language and gender* (pp. 202–228). Oxford: Blackwell.

Herring, S. C., Johnson, D., & DiBenedetto, T. (1995). "This discussion is going too far!" Male resistance to female participation on the Internet. In M. Bucholtz & K. Hall (Eds.), *Gender articulated: Language and the socially constructed self* (pp. 67–96). New York: Routledge.

Instituto Nacional de Estatística. (2002). Actualidades do INE: Mais de um Milhão de portugueses atingem o Ensino Superior. Retrieved September 15, 2005, from http://alea-estp .ine.pt/html/actual/html/act27.html.

Jackson, C. (1999). *Project on honorifics.* Term paper presented for Linguistics 391, Cal Poly San Luis Obispo. Retrieved September 15, 2005, from http://cla.calpoly.edu/~jbattenb/ Papers/jackson/index.html.

Kelm, O. (1992). The use of synchronous computer networks in second language instruction: A preliminary report. *Foreign Language Annals, 25*(5), 441–454.

Ministro da Presidência. (2003). Gender and information society. Retrieved December 5, 2006, from http://www.mp.gov.pt/mp/pt/GabImprensa/Intervencoes/Ministro/GC15/20030506 .htm.

Neto, F., & Pinto, I. (1998). Gender stereotypes in Portuguese television advertisements. *Sex Roles: A Journal of Research, 39*(1/2), 153–164.

Oliveira, S. M. de (2003, March). *Para além de Poder e Solidariedade: Uma retrospectiva sobre formas de tratamento em Portugal (1982–2002).* Paper presented at Colloque 2p, Paris.

Oliveira Medeiros, S. M. de (1985). *A model of address form negotiation: A sociolinguistic study of continental Portuguese.* Unpublished Ph.D. dissertation, University of Texas at Austin.

Oliveira Medeiros, S. M. de (1994). Winning friends and influencing people abroad: Using native speakers' communicative strategies. *Intercultural Communication Studies, 4*(1), 23–44.

Sandler, B. R., & Hall, R. (1982). *The classroom climate: A chilly one for women?* Washington, DC: Association of American Colleges Project on the Status and Education of Women.

Smith, C. B., McLaughlin, M. L., & Osborne, K. K. (1997). Conduct control on Usenet. *Journal of Computer-Mediated Communication, 2*(4). Retrieved September 15, 2005, from http:// jcmc.indiana.edu/vol2/issue4/smith.html.

Smith, J., & Balka, E. (1988). Chatting on a feminist network. In C. Kramarae (Ed.), *Technology and women's voices* (pp. 82–97). New York: Routledge & Kegan Paul.

Spender, D. (1980). *Man made language.* London: Routledge & Kegan Paul.

12

HIROFUMI KATSUNO AND CHRISTINE YANO

Kaomoji and Expressivity in a
Japanese Housewives' Chat Room

To what extent do online fora such as chat rooms foster feminism and autonomy in Japan, as opposed to reinforcing traditional stereotypes? What characterizes online communication among Japanese women? What role do *kaomoji*—Japanese-style emoticons or "faces" such as (^ ^) or (^_^)—play in the constitution of online community among Japanese housewives? What are the interpersonal dynamics that bind online communities of women in Japan? These are some of the questions that guided the research reported in this chapter, as we lurked in chat rooms for Japanese in their thirties.

In the first few years of the twenty-first century, women have been the primary participants in chat rooms at Yahoo!Japan (http://chat.yahoo.co.jp/). Young *shufu* (housewives)[1] inhabit cyberspace at all hours of the day and night, sharing their lives, thoughts, and interactions with a virtual community of regular users. Japanese female cyber-sociality enacts a kind of virtual intimacy that relies in part on the visual play of *kaomoji* (literally "face mark") to establish a language of familiarity. *Kaomoji* such as (^_^) and (^^;), representations of faces and bodies on the computer screen, are ideographs of emotion, sociality, and playfulness. We analyze text-based chat room interactions including *kaomoji* as critical in forming "communities of imagination and interest" among housewives in Japanese cyberspace (Appadurai, 1996, p. 195). Our analysis looks at the interpersonal dynamics of these communities, addressing ways in which visual play contributes to a sense of "imagination and interest."

In our previous work (Katsuno & Yano, 2002), we described and analyzed the general phenomenon of *kaomoji* in Japanese cyberspace, focusing
on processes of embodiment through emoticons. Drawing upon interviews
with users, we posed theoretical questions concerning subjectivity amid the
"disrupted bodies" of online encounters (Murray & Sixsmith, 1999). Here we
take our ethnographic research to the screen to interpret actual online
encounters through observations and logs.

Among more than 100 chat rooms in Yahoo!Japan, we found interactions
using *kaomoji* extensively, in chat rooms for people in their teens, twenties,
and thirties under the subheading of *deai* (literally, "meet"). In fact, *kaomoji*
at times appeared in nearly every line. Among these age-graded chat rooms,
we found the "thirties chat room" to be especially interesting in terms of the
active participation of housewives.[2] In most cases, we assume the participants
to be physically located in Japan, primarily through their referencing of
places, weather, local events, and Japanese media broadcasts. In order to
sample interactions randomly, our observations took place at different times
of the day, different days of the week, approximately three times a week for
one hour each time from August 2002 through May 2003. We did not participate in the chat rooms, but instead lurked as read-only members and saved
the logs.

We acknowledge that identifying chat room participants as women is an
interpretation of their *performance* as women. Our interpretation is founded
on a combination of their self-identifications, handle names, use of highly
gendered expressions, and descriptions of their life situations. Cyberspace has
frequently been discussed as a realm where one's identity is disembodied from
the physical world (Haraway, 1991; Stone, 1995/1996; Turkle, 1984, 1995).
These studies describe cyberspace identity as fluid, multiple, and free-float-
ing, primarily dominated by play. Susanna Paasonen (2002) criticizes such
postmodernist views of cyberspace as a cyber-fantasy, which masks issues of
power, gender, race, and class. According to Paasonen, pioneering works by
Sherry Turkle, Allucquére Rosanne Stone, and others uncritically appropriate Ervin Goffman's (1959) dramaturgical model equating online perfor-
mativity with playfully free, intentional activity. One problem with these
arguments is their overemphasis on agency unconditioned by external forces.
The supposedly freewheeling Internet filled with anonymous postgendered
cyborgs must be tempered by an everyday groundedness that is part of the
round-the-clock chatter.

In the case of chat room interactions in Japanese cyberspace, users
perform aspects of their real-life identities as young *shufu* through their
choices of topics such as pregnancy, child care, diet, and cooking. They display
their cyber-literacy through use of colors, fonts, and *kaomoji*. Their expressions are littered with age-based slang and language unique to cyber-
communication, for example, *kon kon*, computer slang for *konnichiwa*, "good
day," and *ohatsudosu*, a mixture of computer slang and Kyoto dialect for
hajimemashite, "nice to meet you." Most significant for our interpretation are
the times, frequency, and duration of their participation in these chat rooms.

The last aspect is deeply related to *shufu* "habitus" (Bourdieu, 1990) in the physical world, that is, their relationship to computers in their everyday lives. In those instances in which we have observed the same chat room for an entire day, we noted that different kinds of people participate at predictable times. For instance, *shufu* dominate the room during early morning, late morning, early afternoon, and early evening hours. Company workers tend to log in during their lunch hours and may return in the mid-afternoon. Interactions in the evening show a mix of *shufu* and businessmen logging in from home or work. Thus, participation is not completely free form, but follows closely the schedules and patterns of people's everyday offline lives.

The users studied here interact in Japanese, forming a linguistic boundary that excludes most of the rest of the global audience. As Nanette Gottlieb and Mark McLelland (2003) point out, "Despite the fact that the Internet is often discussed in terms of its 'global' reach and its 'borderless' frontiers, it is important to remember that individuals who log on are real people in actual locations with specific purposes" (p. 2). In a similar fashion, David Crystal (2001) writes, "Most Internet interactions are not global in character; we are not talking to millions when we construct our Web pages, send an email, join a chatgroup, or enter a virtual world" (p. 59). Rather, the typical audiences and recipients of webpages, email messages, and chat room talk—especially in Japan—are limited and local (here, national) or, if geographically dispersed, based on common interest. These Japanese *shufu* speak as straightforward, if often playful, individuals whose cybernetic connectivity has a regular place in their lives.

KAOMOJI AS VISUAL CYBERCULTURE

Since around 1986, computer users in Japan have filled Japanese cyberspace with *kaomoji*. While the American sideways smiley face, :-) or :), first created in 1980,[3] generated hundreds of variants, only a small number are in actual use. Besides the basic smiley face, one occasionally encounters a wink ;-) or a frown :-(. The others remain a form of miniature ASCII art stored in online and print compilations (Godin, 1993; Sanderson, 1993).[4] The Japanese case is quite different: *Kaomoji* rapidly proliferated into thousands of intricate designs, many of them frequently used online, and utilizing a full range of exotic fonts (e.g., λ, ω, ϕ) and other keyboard resources not appearing in Western emoticons.[5] The examples below show *kaomoji* using the symbols Д, λ, and 炎.

オーイッ!!L(ﾟДﾟo)オ---(ﾟ|Д|ﾟ)---イ!!(oﾟДﾟ)」 オーイッ!!

Three *kaomoji* faces looking from left to right, hands gesturing at either side of mouth, calling out "オーイ!!" (Ooi!!) (Hey, is anybody here?). Implies someone looking around for others in the chat room.

仕事落ちっす｜出口｜　λ．．．．．．．．．．ﾄﾎﾞﾄﾎﾞ　　　　"仕事落ちっす"

(*Shigoto ochissu*) (I have to go to work). 出口 (*Deguchi*) (exit). λ *kaomoji* figure walking, head bowed. *Tobotobo*, onomatopoeia for trudging.

/ (@｀＜炎炎炎

Monster-like *kaomoji* in profile—@ depicts the right ear—facing right. 炎, character for flame, three times, suggests flames emitting from monster's mouth.

In the mid-1980s, *kaomoji* flourished as part of primarily male *otaku* (computer aficionado) subculture, only to be appropriated later in the mid-1990s by female teenage pager and cell phone users through text messaging. What enabled this appropriation (and subsequent dismissal by many *otaku*) was the availability of thousands of *kaomoji* in books (e.g., StereoMagic, 2000), downloadable dictionaries (e.g., http://www.kaomoji.com/kao/), and CD-ROMs. They were also preinstalled on Japanese computers and cell phones.[6] With the spread of personal computers from offices into homes, *kaomoji*-based Web interaction became commonplace among *shufu*.[7]

The extraordinary development and ready use of *kaomoji* in Japan may be linked to a number of technological and sociocultural factors. Technically, *kaomoji* use depends on the development of a front-end processor, a conversion system for Japanese word processing that allows a basic phonetic keyboard to be used to produce pictographic ideographs. In this system, the user first enters the romanized syllabary (*kana*) that constitutes a word, after which a choice of homophonic ideographs appears.[8] Users may also customize word processing with designated combinations of characters. They can enter particular *kaomoji* as a macro, or string of keystroke characters for future use when typing in appropriate words. For example, a user may preprogram a computer to produce the *kaomoji* (^_^) automatically when typing in the *kana* for *niko* ("smile").[9] Thus, one need not remember exactly how to produce particular *kaomoji*, but may reproduce them easily with spelled out words. This keystroke conversion greatly facilitated the inclusion of *kaomoji* in computer messages. It is also possible to preinstall multiple smiling *kaomoji* under the word *niko*. In this case, after typing the *kana*, a small window pops up with the proposed pictographs, so that users can easily click on the desired *kaomoji*. Besides these manually installed *kaomoji*, there are a number of websites and CD-ROMs from which users can download thousands of *kaomoji*. Some users create their own or customize existing ones to display their prowess and creativity on the keyboard.

This technological infrastructure would be meaningless, however, without the sociocultural context that has spawned creative *kaomoji*. Development of *kaomoji* owes its greatest debt to another central visual medium in Japan, *manga* (comics). *Manga* visual codes have had a fundamental influence not only on the creation but also the emotional expressivity of *kaomoji*. According to Natsume Fusanosuke and Takekuma Kentarô (1995), a single *manga* frame consists of a complex visual grammar including what they dub *keiyu* (figure symbols) and *on'yu* (sound symbols). Both are expressive means for depicting drama and emotion. *Keiyu* present the physiological and psychological states of individual *manga* characters, as well as provide dramatic nuance to scenes. *On'yu*, the *manga* version of onomatopoeia, make audible the noises that might be difficult to suggest in drawings or explain in words; these symbols add emotional atmosphere to scenes.[10]

Creators of *kaomoji* utilize both *keiyu* and *on'yu* when devising *kaomoji*. For example, the *kaomoji* (^_^;) adds the *keiyu* (;) indicating sweat. In both *kaomoji* and *manga*, this sweat drips because of physical and psychological tension. Therefore, whereas (^_^) indicates simply a smiling face, the *keiyu* (;) gives an added dimension to the smile, suggesting a complex tension between the outer smiling face and inner commentary that informs the smile.[11] Another example is the *kaomoji* (- -#). The *keiyu* (#) depicts a bulging vein at one's temple, indicating anger or rage. In both of these cases, the *manga*-derived symbol somaticizes a particular kind of emotion into a visual code, which is then recast into convenient symbols found on a computer keyboard.

The influence of *on'yu* on *kaomoji* includes use of onomatopoetic expressions embedded within the emoticon as follows:

°。(。o● (エ) ●o。)。°シクシク

Close-up of *kaomoji* with huge dark eyes, crying with tears flying.

(*Shikushiku*) Onomatopoeia for weeping.

ヾ(* ▽ *)Ｂｙｅ ε=ε=ε=ε=ε= タタタ ┌(; ▽)┘…・。. ☆ ドロン♪

First *kaomoji* waving, saying "Bye." ε= depicts movement. タタタタ (*tatatata*) is onomatopoeia for rapid movement. Second *kaomoji* running, arms pumping. ・ ・ ・。. ☆ depicts vanishing, as part of the visual language borrowed from *manga*. ドロン (doron) is *manga*-based onomatopoeia for vanishing. ♪ suggests cheery atmosphere.[12]

In addition to this visual code, *manga* and *kaomoji* are related to processes of reading and meaning developed in the Japanese writing system. Drawing on arguments by Frederik Schodt (1983) and Natsume (1997), Yuko Tanaka (2000) points out that *manga* does not simply consist of images and words, but that images themselves function as a visual language that may be read in its own right. Noting the rapid speed with which Japanese consumers read *manga*, Schodt (1983) suggests that *manga* may be a readily accessible visual language to Japanese readers, in which frames and even pages can be read as rapidly as words. Meanwhile, Natsume (1997) emphasizes that *manga* images have developed as ideographs deeply related to the Japanese reading of *kanji* (Chinese-derived characters of pictorial origin). *Kanji* reading includes both *on'yomi* (Chinese reading) and *kun'yomi* (native Japanese reading), with some *kanji* incorporating multiple readings of even these two. One reads *kanji* both for meaning and for sound. For example, the character 顔 means face and can be read as either *gan* (*on'yomi*) or *kao* (*kun'yomi*).

Confronted with 顔, Japanese readers understand the semantic meaning but must decide based on the context which sound to assign the character.

In the same way that each *kanji* has both *on'yomi* and *kun'yomi* readings, so do *manga* and *kaomoji* require a reader to flip simultaneously between sounds, images, and meanings. Reading becomes a constant, changing experience of multiplicity and flexibility. According to Natsume (1997),

> Japanese language can cross sounds and images, switch time and space easily. Here, it is important to see that they [Japanese] read *kanji* by both *on'yomi* and *kun'yomi*. The way to read the pictograph *kanji* by Japanese *kana* [syllabary; in effect, sound] inseparably connects *kanji* and Japanese *kana* [i.e., sound] so that it usually requires Japanese speakers to translate images into sounds and vice versa. (quoted in Tanaka, 2000, p. 37, our translation)

The dynamic interrelations between image and sound and even among images composed of words or word fragments inform the development of *kaomoji*. In other words, image/ideograph and sound do not exist in a one-to-one relationship, but rather in a one-to-several correspondence, along with the inclusion of both *on'yomi* and *kun'yomi* reading systems. Meaning and sound relationships are multiple.

At the same time, each image/ideograph has a highly marked sound precisely because of that multiplicity. A reader must know, and sometimes even investigate, the intended reading for the *kanji*, making reading a deliberate, conscious process of translation from image to sound and back. This complex relationship between image and sound, embedded in the Japanese language, contributes to the visuality of *manga* and *kaomoji* communication, as part of what Susan Napier (2000, p. 21) has characterized as Japan's "'pictocentric' culture."

What is common among these arguments is that Japanese inscribed communication is not strictly word based. Instead, a nonlinguistic but highly coded visual language not only enriches but perhaps even constitutes communication, particularly with textures of emotion and atmosphere (Kataoka, 1997). *Kaomoji* extend this tendency to computer-mediated communication in Japan, sometimes in conjunction with words, at other times performing the multifaceted work of silence. Although *kaomoji* are related to ASCII art (Danet, 2001), in that they are graphic images realized through typography, they are not ordinarily stand-alone creations, but are "performed" within the context of a string of computer-mediated utterances.

While *kaomoji* often act as straightforward substitutes for communicative cues in the physical world, such as facial expressions and gestures, they may go beyond merely appending emotional comments to written language. They can appear as independent realities integrated within typed messages, functioning as extensions of the bodies of users or as virtual bodies in and of themselves (Katsuno & Yano, 2002). This sort of phantasmic cyberreality emerges as *kaomoji* become more elaborate and highly stylized. For instance, the *kaomoji* below (including a reduplicated face showing movement)[13] all depict surprise, but each has a slightly different nuance.

　ヽ(Д｀ヽ ﾐ ﾉ'Д｀)ﾉ

Panic-stricken, looking from side to side in alarm (reduplicated face), hands raised.

　ヽ(°Д°;)ﾉ!!

Dismayed, cold sweat trickling down side of face, hands raised.

　＼(@o@)／

Sheer fright, eyes wide in astonishment, hands raised.

Such differences are expressed only through the visual language of *kaomoji*. In other words, *kaomoji* users may express subtle shades of emotion and thought through visual rather than strictly linguistic means. In some cases, they can express themselves more compactly with *kaomoji* than with words.

The symbolic resources users draw on to create or manipulate *kaomoji* build on the aesthetic concept of *mitate* (symbolic analogy, allusion), which rests on a sense of play. *Mitate* may be divided into its component parts: *mi* (to see) and *tate* (to stand, to arrange). *Mitate* suggests that one juxtaposes elements in an arrangement meant to be visually apprehended, resulting in meaning that resides in the relationship between the elements. According to Masao Yamaguchi (1991), "*Mitate* is something close to the idea of a simulacrum, . . . always a pseudo-object" (p. 64). Roland Barthes's (1985) notion of an allusive field of writing draws upon similar processes of meaning making: "Allusion, a rhetorical figure, consists in saying one thing with the intention of making another understood" (p. 158). *Mitate* is a special technique widely employed not only in various Japanese art forms such as *kabuki* (theater), *gesaku* (the popular short novel), *waka* (poetry), *ikebana* (flower arranging), *ukiyoe* (woodblock prints), *chadô* (tea ceremony), and *teien* (gardens), but also in everyday life (Yamaguchi & Takashina, 1996).

Mitate depends on referentiality between one realm and another in creating layers of interacting meanings. A creator of a work of art assumes a common pool of intertextual associations in the consumption of the art product. *Mitate* lies in the shared symbolic and semantic resources of creator and viewer.[14] We can recognize *mitate* in everyday food, for instance, in the dish known as *tsukimi* ("moon-viewing")-*soba*, soba noodle soup topped with a raw egg. The moonlike image of the egg floating in the soup suggests a poetic as well as humorous connotation because the lofty sense of the moon, about which many poems have been written, is juxtaposed with the earthly mundanity of an egg.[15] *Mitate*, in other words, overlays a wholly different sense from the original.

Mitate is possible in the speech community because members share a common pool of referents, as well as an expectation of *mitate*. The ever-present possibility of *mitate* frames objects and expressions simultaneously as a source of difference and sameness, as always something upon which one may act. The cultural frame of *mitate* differentiates it from simpler metaphors, which are only used sporadically and secondarily. It is the distance between object and referent, between depiction and the thing depicted, that carves out and preserves the space of play. That distance marks the cleverness of *mitate*. Furthermore, the unexpected juxtapositions of *mitate* deform or "deconstruct" the original (Yamaguchi & Takashina, 1996, p. 16) and thus transform it through a mix of meanings, evocations, and atmospheres.

Thus, *kaomoji* exist in a staging ground of performance, in which users display their competence and creativity and readers display their cyber-literacy in their interpretations and responses (Briggs, 1988; Danet, 2001; Danet, Ruedenberg, & Rosenbaum-Tamari, 1998). According to Richard Bauman (1992), the hallmarks of performance are "an aesthetically marked and heightened mode of communication, framed in a special way and put on display for an audience" (p. 41). The relationship between performer (*kaomoji* users) and audience (readers) is critical. The work of *kaomoji* binds user and reader and their successive exchange of roles in a fluid process of interpretation and meaning. That bond, like the tie between image and sound, is multiple, flexible, and dynamic.

Kaomoji encourage a spirit of competition among users and readers. Competition and, to a certain extent, cooperation create a hierarchy determined by facility at the keyboard, including speed of typing and knowledge and skilled use of *kaomoji* themselves. At the peak of interaction, *kaomoji* may appear in nearly every line of messages generated within a community of expert users.

As our past study shows (Katsuno & Yano, 2002), users derive pleasure in constructing a distinct reality through interchange based largely on *kaomoji*. Beginners are at a disadvantage. One beginner complained, "I just got back from a thirties-chat room without saying anything. I just couldn't get a word in edgewise because of the proliferation of *kaomoji* in that room!" When participating in such chat rooms, many beginners become defensive, immediately and publicly acknowledging their low status by labeling themselves as *shoshinsha* (beginner). They thereby ask for indulgence, as in the example below):

Mimi ←初心者

I am a beginner (初心者) at this. [← indicates pointing to herself, Mimi]

In fact, Yahoo!Japan sets up chat rooms under the category of *shoshinsha* for beginners to learn *kaomoji* at their own pace.

However, this hierarchy does not always alienate beginners. Sometimes experts socialize beginners into the use of *kaomoji*, further promoting their usage. For instance, the log shown in figure 12.1 presents a scene in which *kaomoji* expert Figo teaches Mimi how to incorporate them into her online interactions. Figo inadvertently uses *kaomoji* right after having declared that

8	figo	じゃ　俺も顔文字を使わない ぞ・・・・・ o(ˋ □ ˙*)oエッヘン！	Then, I won't use *kaomoji*, either. [Head thrown back with pursed lips; mock bullish expression; onomatopoeic *ehhen!* depicts slightly defiant attitude of speaker]
9	figo	って、つかってるし	Oops, I inadvertently used *kaomoji*.
10	mimi	誰かおしえてほしい	I wish somebody would teach me how to use *kaomoji*.
11	figo	(*・ε・*)ホイー	[Noncommittal expression; "*hoi*," okay]
12	nana	おぃおぃ＞フィゴ	Hey! [To Figo]
13	figo	あ！また使った・・・・	Oops! I used it again . . .
14	nana	フィゴに、教えてもらえば？＞みみ	Why don't you have Figo teach you? [To Mimi]
15	figo	クセかな？	Using *kaomoji* gets to be a habit, huh?
16	nana	だね。＞フィゴ	I think so. [To Figo]

FIGURE 12.1. Mimi needs to learn to use *kaomoji*.

she won't use them at first. For experts like Figo, using *kaomoji* is so much a part of their computer-based interactions that it is difficult to avoid including them. *Kaomoji* constitute an important part of their performative online personae.

FEMINIZING THE SPACE: CUTE INTERACTION IN JAPANESE CHAT ROOMS

Part of the playfulness of *kaomoji* lies in their link to *kawaii* (cute) culture in Japan. Since the 1970s, the young and female segments of the population in Japan have been enamored of a "cult of cuteness" (Kinsella, 1995; McVeigh, 2000, p. 2). Brian McVeigh (1996, p. 293) calls *kawaii* a "key symbol" in contemporary Japan, encompassing objects, persons, behavior, and attitudes. In 1992, the young women's magazine *CREA* dubbed *kawaii* "the most widely used, widely loved, habitual word in modern living Japanese" (November 1992, p. 58, quoted in Kinsella, 1995, pp. 220–221). As Mark Schilling (1997) writes, "Japan . . . is the Country of Cute" (p. 221).

Consuming and performing *kawaii* has become a way of life, not only for children and young females, as might be expected, but also for the general populace. Banks use cartoon characters in company logos, the Tokyo metropolitan police uses a cartoon figure as a mascot, and Japan Railways uses a doll to promote interpersonal etiquette on trains (McVeigh, 2000). *Kawaii* can be bought in the form of dolls, toys, household goods, and fashion. While it would be misleading to claim that everyone in Japan embraces public displays of cuteness wholeheartedly, cuteness meets with little critique (Yano, 2004).

Japanese sociologist Sôichi Masubuchi (1994) has defined seven elements of *kawaii* as follows: (1) smallness, (2) naiveté and innocence, (3) youth (especially the very young), (4) *amae* (dependency), (5) roundness, (6) pastel colors, and (7) animal-like qualities (p. 208). Masubuchi's list overlaps with John Morreall's (1991) attempt to define the visual dimensions of cuteness: smallness, with distinctively babyish features (e.g., large head in relation to body, round cheeks, plumpness, softness, helplessness) (p. 40). "Cute features,... are the distinctively babyish features which elicit nurturing behaviour in adults" (Morreall, 1993, p. 285). Morreall's cute, like Masubuchi's *kawaii*, takes the human infant as the foundational prototype, both for its physical dimensions and for the emotional response it elicits from adults.

Rather than dwell on visual/physical aspects, although they are relevant for our analysis, we prefer to embed *kawaii* within particular kinds of relations that lie at the core of the concept. In other words, it is not so much "what cuteness looks like" (Morreall, 1991, pp. 39–41), but "what cuteness does" in calling forth particular kinds of responses and practices. Cute thus becomes a performance and a social category, rather than an aesthetic concept. Furthermore, one person's (or culture's) cute may not be quite the same as another's.[16] This holds particularly true when attempting to police the boundaries between the cute and the overly cute, or even kitsch.

Kawaii taps fundamental relationships of helpless and helper, the kept and the keeper, the dependent and the dependable. Lori Merish (1996) comments:

> The cute always in some sense designates a commodity in search of its mother, and is constructed to generate maternal desire; the consumer (or potential consumer) of the cute is expected...to pretend she or he *is* the cute's mother. Valuing cuteness entails the ritualized performance of maternal feeling. (p. 186)

However, the relationship between the cute and the observer becomes more complicated, because the observer may want to become the cute. Merish continues:

> Appreciating the cute ... entails a structure of identification, wanting to be *like* the cute—or more exactly, wanting the cute to be just like the *self*. Appreciating cuteness expresses the double logic of identification, its fundamental inseparability from desire.... The aesthetics of cuteness thus generates an emotional response in accord with what Mary Ann Douane has described as a commercial structure of "feminine" consumer empathy, a structure that blurs identification and commodity desire. Putting a feminine twist on Walter Benjamin's formulations, Douane sees a convergence between the intimate, emotional address of commodities and certain ... empathetic structures of feeling ... that assimilates consumption into the logic of adoption. (pp. 186–187)

Basic *kaomoji* (smile)	Cute *kaomoji* (smile)
(^_^)	(@⌐‿⌐@)
(^^)	(₀ ^ _ ^ ₀)
(^o^)	(● ^ o ^ ●)
>^_^<	(*^ O ^*)

FIGURE 12.2. Basic versus cute *kaomoji*.

What is most important for our research is that *kawaii* is invoked in *kaomoji* performances by women.

Kawaii rests within the bond of *amae* (dependency) between the helpless and the helper, the dependent and person on whom one depends. This bond holds a culturally legitimate place in Japanese society, not only in child–parent relationships but also extending into adult relationships (Doi, 1973). The *amae* bond is not without its abuses. The fact that the epitome of cuteness rests in the young and female (i.e., *shôjo*, young, unmarried female, approximately 7–18 years) positions *kawaii* and its foundational concept of *amae* within larger structures of subordination by older and male members of society.[17]

The cult of cuteness that pervades much of Japanese society in the 2000s creates an umbrella for practices linked through *kawaii*, including the use of *kaomoji* online. *Kaomoji* provide a means to perform oneself as *kawaii* in order to obtain one's own ends, playing upon *amae* (dependency) even with other females. Asserting *kawaii* helps smooth social relations and softens the social hierarchy while not fundamentally changing it (McVeigh, 2000).

Chat rooms, especially those peopled by young women, are one of the most common spaces for performing *kawaii*. The following examples compare basic *kaomoji* developed by (primarily male) *otaku* in the 1980s and those appearing within the feminized *kawaii* space of the 1990s and later as females became widespread users of cell phones and personal computers.

Feminized *kawaii kaomoji* are wider, relatively rounded, and sometimes even pastel-colored compared to their basic counterparts (figure 12.2). Japanese users frequently employ colors in the text of their chat room messages, choosing from an available array of shades and combinations of shades. When a user has selected a shade for her text message, the *kaomoji* have the same color. Color becomes a distinguishing feature of any particular chat room participant's utterances. If one color is already in use, then another person will select a different color to differentiate herself from others present online. The use of color distinguishes Japanese chat room users from their Euro-American counterparts, who tend to stick with the default black text on white background.

Kaomoji frequently appear with onomatopoetic symbols that make sense only within the context of the chat room interaction. For example, *powaan* by itself has little meaning, but when combined with the *kaomoji* (⌒) provides an auditory sense of floating in a relaxed state. Another example is "*po`–*" which combines with (///• •///) or (*ˆoˆ*) to depict embarrassment. This use of sound expressions in combination with pictorial resources is closely linked to that found in *manga*. *Kaomoji* also appear appended to "baby talk" or childish expressions. A number of *kaomoji* websites list similar *kaomoji* under the category of *kawaii kaomoji*. In addition, some users employ these *kawaii kaomoji* as their personal icons in chat rooms, such as ＼ζ6。6ζζ／ (wide-eyed *kaomoji* with curls, hands gesturing on both sides of face) and (ë。ë)／ (*kaomoji* with eye shadow and long lashes, waving with her right hand). In most cases, such *kaomoji* are modeled on stereotypic *shôjo* figures from *manga* and become an essential part of the visual identities of these housewife chat room participants. Housewives thus often use their own signature *kaomoji* repeatedly to perform their individual identities.

In a survey of 100 cell phone users in Tokyo in 2000, Larissa Hjorth (2003) found that men and women used *kawaii* characters roughly to the same extent. However, women "seemed better able to articulate the meanings behind their appropriation of cute characters, . . . using *kawaii* modes for customization in a more reflexive—and thus empowering—way" (pp. 53, 56). Likewise, in our study, *shufu* use *kawaii* in self-conscious ways, performing themselves as *shôjo* through the *kaomoji* they insert in chat room interactions.

The links between *kawaii*, *shôjo*, and *kaomoji* may also be found in *hentai shôjo moji* (cute female writing), a writing style that was wildly popular with young females in Japan from the early 1970s through the mid-1980s. They share exaggeratedly round figures and frequent use of pictorial symbols such as flowers and stars to express emotional states (Kataoka, 1997; Kinsella, 1995; Yamane, 1986). More important than the actual writing style was its use as public display (Miyadai, Ishihara, & Otsuka, 2000; Otsuka, 1989; Yamane, 1986). According to Miyadai et al. (2000), while originally used specifically to write poems romanticizing the writer's inner world in the early 1970s, by the late 1970s *hentai shôjo moji* had become a tool of *shakou* (social relationships) through such popular communication practices as *kôkan nikki* (diary exchanges) and letters. As the faddish writing style became standardized, it became a boundary of inclusion for the community of writers, creating a *kawaii kyôdôtai* (cute community) marked by *hentai shôjo moji* (Miyadai et al., 2000). Cute writing, like the *kaomoji* that followed, became a coded practice of membership, defining a gender and age cohort through the public performance of *kawaii*.

According to Sharon Kinsella (1995), *kawaii* may be seen as a culture of resistance in its escape from reality and abnegation of adult responsibilities. Nevertheless, that escape is temporary, minimal, and superficial. This resistance does little to change overall power structures, even though it manipulates those structures. Furthermore, the resistance maintains a minimum level of compliance (a point to which we return below where we discuss *kaomoji* as an element of cyber-feminism). This straddling of resistance and compliance, rebellion and duty, and the private and the public plunges *kaomoji* (and the *kawaii* culture of which it is a part) into an online language of ambiguity. Within this liminal sphere, *shufu* perform themselves as both responsible mothers/wives and dependent *shôjo*.

SHUFU ADRIFT IN CYBERSPACE

In the chat rooms we observed, the peak periods of interaction are weekday evenings, the down time for most *shufu*, after dinner when young children are likely to be asleep but before husbands have returned home. Our transcripts present *shufu* as idling via cyber-chat in the interstices between periods when others demand their attention. Computers become companions to their daily activities. *Shufu* are also sometimes online during late-night or early-morning hours, and at night, after husbands have returned from work. The fact that significant numbers of *shufu* are online during these other times suggests that these women often engage with their cyber-friends in preference to sleeping or attending to their husbands. In several instances, women commented nervously that their husbands were nearby and might be looking over their shoulders, as in the example in figure 12.3.

Since the late nineteenth century, the primary gender role for women in Japan has been *ryôsai kenbo* ("good wife, wise mother"). This originally urban, upper-middle-class gender role has been extended as an ideological model to all women (Bernstein, 1991; Imamura, 1987; Lebra, 1984). Even working women adopt this model and often justify their work in terms of meeting the demands of "good wife, wise mother" (Roberts, 1994). Marriage and motherhood, then, are foundational to these women's gendered identities both online and offline.

8	masaki19	主婦さんおおいねぇ＾＾	There are a lot of housewives here, huh. [Smiling]
9	masaki19	ダンナさんはいないの？	There are no husbands around?
10	Yuki08	←旦那遊びに行った	[←indicates pointing to herself] My husband went out to play.
11	sons_kei	うち　すぐ	My husband is . . .
12	sons_kei	後ろにいる・・・	Right behind me . . .
13	masaki19	淋しいね＾ ＾＞ユキ	Lonesome, huh. [Smiling face] [To Yuki]

FIGURE 12.3. Housewives chatting online, husband observing.

Within this system of gender roles, women's stereotypical attitude toward their husbands has been immortalized in Japan through common derogatory references to them as *sodai-gomi* (large trash) or *nure-ochiba* (wet leaves, i.e., the leaves that stick to the pavement after a heavy rain). Although these terms are generally used by older women to refer to retired husbands who hang about the house, useless and annoying, even younger couples in their thirties relate to each other in a similar fashion. The chat rooms provide spaces in which *shufu* may roam free of husbands and children, even as obligations of marriage and motherhood intervene in their conversations. Women prefer to discuss romance as a dream of the past, dismissing their husbands as ones for whom they have little feeling in general, much less sexual desire. The picture of marital life represented in these chat rooms is bleak (figure 12.4).

Shufu form their own rules for chat room interaction. If they must leave briefly, for example, to check their laundry or take a bathroom break, they remain in the chat room as "read-only-members" (designated ROM), informing others that they will soon return to engage more actively.[18] If they get called away on a more time-consuming chore such as meal preparation, they let others know why they must leave, and log off, typically in a flurry of *kaomoji* farewells (figure 12.5). They enter and exit, logging on and off chat rooms as time permits between errands and chores and sometimes even in the midst of these duties.

43	koakuma	ん？全く感情ナッシング (ΦωΦ)ふふふ・・・・	Hm? My feelings for my husband are just about nil. [Chuckling to oneself: "*Fu-fu-fu*" (ふふふ), sound of soft laughter.]
44	sons_kei	情もないの？かよ・・・	Not even sympathy?
45	koakuma	いやいや	No, no.
46	masaki19	それは淋しい・・	How lonesome.
47	sons_kei	ん？	Hm?
48	koakuma	家族としてはまだ・・・少しくらいは・・・	I still care a bit for him as a family member.
49	sons_kei	щ(￣□￣)ш ケケケ	[Mockingly evil face; "*Ke ke ke*" (ケケケ), evil laughter.]
50	sons_kei	だよね	That's right.
51	koakuma	子供もいたら でも男としてなんか見れん！	More so if we have children. But, we really can't see them as men!

FIGURE 12.4. Housewives chatting about marital life.

kazu-chan	出勤です、またあそんでね♪	I have to go to work. Let's get together again, OK? [♪ expresses cheerfulness]
pure	p (*^‿^*)q がんばっ♪＞かず	[Smiling *kaomoji* with both fists raised in the air as if cheering] *Ganba* (がんばっ) [abbreviated form of *Ganbatte*, Keep it up!] [♪ expresses cheerfulness] [To Kazu-chan]
hanabi	ﬁ イッテラー(￣‿￣)ノ ロ"フリフリ	*Itterâ* (イッテラー) [abbreviated form of *itterasshai*, Take care] [*Kaomoji* waves a handkerchief in the air as a gesture of farewell] [*Furifuri* (フリフリ) indicates the sound of a fluttering handkerchief]
pure	ロ～～ヾ ^‿^) マタネッ♪＞かず	[ロ～～ emphasizes movement] [*Kaomoji* waves farewell] *Mata ne* (マタネッ), see you later [♪ expresses cheerfulness] [To Kazu-chan]

FIGURE 12.5. A flurry of farewells.

Some of the most extensive *kaomoji* use appears in these entrances and exits as part of cybernetic *aisatsu* (formulaic greetings).[19] Entrances and exits spawn sociality, establishing the tone for what is to follow and affirming what has gone before. This is sometimes done in the most cheerfully rousing manner through *kaomoji*, as in the example above. Instead of a simple verbal expression, using *kaomoji* to greet or bid farewell to other chat room users personalizes the performance of self, even when the *kaomoji* are standardized. In Japanese terms, *kaomoji* "moisten" the chat room space.

Because of the nature of a housewife's life, on call but not always fully engaged in requisite activities, online interaction is a necessarily intermittent activity, secondary to the main work at hand. These women share this common understanding of the place of sociality, both online and offline. Their sociality is thus denigrated as discontinuous and open to interruption, with bouts of selective inattention or split attention, as each keeps an eye on the stove, another on the computer screen, and an ear out for her husband's *kaeru kôru* (returning home phone call), signaling time to sign off and start preparing dinner. Their recognition of shared demands, tasks, and restraints create intimacy in the chat room, including the retreat into *kaomoji* as the coded language of their clubhouse.

PERFORMING SELVES ONLINE

Within this zealously guarded but tenuous space, women stake claim to their own agency through online interactions. The chat rooms are areas that they can control, peopled by women such as themselves. Such shared spaces are characterized by (1) discussing common topics, such as child rearing, cooking, dieting, and romance (or the lack thereof); (2) social relations among themselves; and (3) certain means of expression, especially *kaomoji*.

These three divisions are interrelated, constructing a shared camaraderie often based on self-deprecation. Their conversations are full of complaints about their lives, including misbehaving children, necessary frugality, burdensome housework, boring husbands, and lack of romance. The extract in figure 12.6, for example, illustrates a concern with sleep and weight.

However, it is notable that the mood of these chat rooms is not gloomy, and women are not there to seek help or advice. The mood is playful rather than weighty, informed by a strong sense of parody in which the object of parody is not so much men, children, or chores but themselves. Various social conventions frame these complaints as self-deprecatory jokes mocking *shufu* life. For example, *shufu* sometimes identify themselves specifically as *furyô shufu* ("delinquent housewife") or *hima shufu* ("slacker housewife"), bragging about their negligence of duties:

３６歳不良主婦です

I am a thirty-six-year-old delinquent housewife [*furyô shufu*].

These self-deprecatory remarks express experiences common to many, though sometimes, of course, *shufu* exaggerate. The specifics of each woman's

15	akiwolf	寝てばっかりやんかっ！（滝汗）＜自分	I do nothing but sleep all the time! (Cold sweat pouring down) [To herself]
16	yuiyui	ヾ(*°□°*)ノ あははねることはいいこと＞あき	[Smiling; both arms raised] Yeah, it's good to sleep. [To Akiwolf]
17	akiwolf	良く寝る大人は、横に成長するんだぞ▼・＿・▼（笑）	Adults who sleep a lot will get fat. [This is a parody of the adage, "Children who sleep a lot will grow tall."] [Smiling face] (Laughing)
18	yuiyui	そーなんか＞あき	Is that so? [To Akiwolf]
19	akiwolf	ええもう。立派に成長しました▼・＿・▼（笑）＞ゆいゆい	Oh, yeah. I've really put on weight. [Smiling face] (Laughing) [To Yuiyui]

FIGURE 12.6. Concern with sleep and weight.

life become generalized to encompass the stereotypical image of absent, inattentive, or uncommunicative husbands. If one woman complains, "My husband hardly says a word to me," she is voicing a generalized lament about all husbands' lack of communicativeness. Furthermore, if one woman says, "My husband says little more than ten words to me a day," then another can retort "Yes, but my husband says not more than five words a day," and another can reply, "My husband only grunts." The humor lies in one-upping the others.

This form of humor depends on the meta-message of play. *Kaomoji* provide the winks to their cybertalk. If one were to take these women's words seriously, then the impact of their statements might lead one to think that they were all on the brink of divorce, yet few Japanese marriages end in divorce. Few of these women look forward to any substantive or structural change within the context of their marital/family life. This parody does not effect social change, but simply allows women to voice their complaints with one another as shared sufferers.

That these women are spending countless hours online with each other suggests a certain abnegation of responsibility, however. They go on performing their housewifely duties, but amid cyber-chat activities. It is not that they are neglecting anything at home, but that they are less than ideal *ryôsai kenbo* (good wife, wise mother). They are rebelling by carving out the cybernetic space and taking up real time for their own purposes. The self-mockery conveys the contradictory message: "I am not a proper *shufu*, but I am still a *shufu*." The delinquency of these *shufu* lies in daring to criticize their husbands, presenting themselves as overweight and uncomely, denigrating their children, and spending hours online, although they do little to change their situations. If they were to become truly delinquent as *furyô shufu*, they would violate every goal that had been set for them since they were young girls. The pleasure they feel lies in playing at *furyô shufu*, the housewife who takes the part of a bad girl, while remaining in fact a housewife. These *shufu* find fun in just barely toeing the line; theirs is a performance of rebellion. Delinquency gives them distance from their everyday roles, while the frame of play imparted by *kaomoji* makes that distance instantly retractable. Inasmuch as the humor of mockery includes the coexistence of opposites, within the performance in these chat rooms we find both the delinquent housewife and her opposite, the *ryôsai kenbo*.

The position of a middle-class housewife is the goal to which most females are socialized in Japan because of the rewards it promises of economic security and social standing. If anyone is in a position to critique this role, it is those who have achieved the desired status of housewife—witness the self-mockery found in these chat rooms. These women have the leisure and technology to engage in such play. The anonymity of cyberspace gives these women license to play that much harder and more dangerously. In the end, however, nothing is truly threatened by these playful interactions.

The space they inhabit online straddles the line between anonymity and familiarity. Some women reveal their locations, give details of their daily lives, fill out the electronic personal profiles requested of users, or even arrange to meet their cyber-friends face to face (Holden, Miles, & Tsuruki, 2003). Yet others remain completely anonymous. For many, the distanced intimacy of virtual interaction provides a convenient alternative to the demands and risks of face-to-face friendship. For others, face to face remains a constant draw. This matrix of performed selves gives their online playfulness a mixed and shifting poignancy, providing rebellious commentary on their roles while they continue to perform them. *Kaomoji* and the online language of cuteness form critical components of this poignancy.

CONCLUDING THOUGHTS AND QUESTIONS: WHITHER CYBER-FEMINISM?

Let us return to the questions that we posed at the beginning of this chapter. First, how does the language of visual play contribute to a sense of "imagination and interest" in these communities of *shufu*? Focusing on the visual play of *kaomoji*, we have found that they form a boundary of inclusion and exclusion in these online communities. The inclusiveness of *kaomoji* is based on visual codes developed in Japanese language and *manga* that are also common to these emoticons. The exclusiveness rests on often age-graded familiarity or ability to read the emoticons. For older generations unfamiliar with the visual language of *manga*, some of the more elaborate *kaomoji* can be difficult to decipher. Even those who have grown up with *manga* may have a difficult time understanding how to read certain *kaomoji*. The fact that this is a rapidly shifting subculture makes keeping up with changes difficult. But this rapid change in itself can be a source of "imagination and interest" for devotees. Furthermore, the strong sense of play and creativity that pervades *kaomoji* is crucial for holding the interest and enjoyment of users. *Kaomoji* not only place bodies on the computer screen but invest those bodies with the performed subjectivities of users. Cuteness frames those subjectivities within benign cultural codes of femininity.

Second, what are the interpersonal dynamics that bind these communities? *Shufu* are bound in a virtual community most fundamentally through the commonality of their experiences. It is the very predictability of their lives that makes much of the online conversation readily intimate and comforting. Much of the communication is phatic—low in content, high in emotional expressivity. Little need be said or explained; users enter chat rooms knowing that theirs is a bond of ready-made familiarity. Both competition and cooperation bind these women. They build hierarchies of expertise in technical facility with *kaomoji*, going beyond the resources preinstalled on computers and cell phones by downloading exotic fonts to expand the repertoire of expression, tapping into electronic dictionaries for other *kaomoji*, creating new ones, and personalizing old ones. These housewives share a cyberculture that is rapidly becoming widespread in Japan.

Finally, to return to the question with which we began this chapter, do online fora such as chat rooms foster (cyber)feminism and autonomy in Japan?

Does the Internet provide feminist alternatives in Japanese women's everyday lives? As Paasonen (2002) writes, "gender matters and is made to matter" in online as well as offline communication (p. 25). The question remains, however, in what ways does gender matter and with what kinds of consequences? Susan Herring's (1993, 1996) research on male–female behavior in online communication shows that gender matters in terms of styles, values, and rates of interaction reinforcing male domination. In the examples we observed of primarily female chat rooms in Japanese cyberspace, males are often intimidated by the sense that this is a female space marked by feminine/feminized *kaomoji*.

Does feminized cyberspace spell feminism, empowerment, and autonomy in Japan? Obviously, we cannot answer for all female users of the Internet in Japan or even necessarily for all those who participated or lurked in the chat rooms we observed. However, we venture to speculate that if cyber-feminism implies overt political activism, these *shufu* would vehemently deny any part of it.[20]

These women do not identify themselves as rebels outside of the chat room. They are mothers and wives foremost, as well as friends to each other. On the surface, things remain the same: Men go off to work, children go to school, and women stay at home making meals and folding laundry. No dinners have gone missing, no shirts are left unpressed. Housewifely attention to these duties has been pared down to a minimum, as computer time is squeezed in among the chores. For *shufu*, chat rooms and the *kaomoji* deployed in them allow the publicly powerless a voice that laughs instead of cries, in a virtual space safely marked off from real life.

Notes

1. See Ishii and Jarkey (2002) for the historical development of the concept of *shufu* in modern Japan.

2. Thirties chat rooms are subdivided by maximum number of participants, generally about 30. When we have logged on during peak times, there have been as many as 10 subdivided thirties *deai* chat rooms.

3. Scott Fahlman first invented the sideways smiley in 1980. See http://www-2.cs.cmu.edu/~sef/sefSmiley.htm, retrieved May 16, 2005.

4. See also "The Unofficial Smiley Dictionary," http://paul.merton.ox.ac.uk/ascii/smileys.html, and "Canonical Smiley List," http://www.astro.umd.edu/~marshall/smileys.html, retrieved May 16, 2005.

5. Horizontal icons appear also in Chinese (see Bodomo & Lee 2002; Lee, chapter 8 this volume) and romanized Arabic (Palfreyman & Al Khalil, chapter 2 this volume). Works by Sugimoto and Levin (2000), Matsuda (2002), Yamazaki (2002), and Nishimura (2003, chapter 7 this volume) document use of *kaomoji* in Japanese, although it is not their focus of analysis. In a conference presentation by Ellis (2003), *kaomoji* occurred in primarily English chat (B. Danet, personal email communication). Japanese *kaomoji* also appear sporadically in English chat rooms of fans of Japanese *anime* (cartoons).

6. For more on the development of *kaomoji*, see Katsuno and Yano (2002).

7. When one uses *kaomoji*, they are often slightly personalized, edited, and transformed in the process. Even if *kaomoji* have been preinstalled or downloaded, individual users maintain freedom to modify them to suit their own purposes or tastes.

8. See the explanation in Katsuno and Yano (2002) and Nishimura (2003).

9. Similarly, typing :-) automatically produces ☺ in Microsoft Word.

10. The use of onomatopoeia is extensive in the Japanese language, which places great emphasis on sounds to evoke emotion, atmosphere, and movement.

11. This tension between outer public face and inner private emotions is embedded in Japanese culture, particularly in dichotomous expressions such as *tatemae* (public face) versus *honne* (true feelings) and *omote* (front) versus *ura* (back) (Lebra, 1976).

12. Use of stars, musical notes, and so on, is characteristic of Japanese computer-mediated communication/chat derived primarily from *manga*, as we discuss further below.

13. See also Danet et al. (1998, pp. 60–65) for an example of a reduplicated face in American emoticon usage.

14. A work of art employing *mitate* may be viewed simultaneously in four different ways: (1) literally, as a juxtaposition of particular materials; (2) symbolically, for the elements that the materials represent; (3) historically, with regard to the antiquity of symbols and references; and (4) syncretically, as an admixture of all of the above (e.g., Aoki, 1996).

15. See Palmer (1994) on incongruity and humor.

16. This holds true in spite of ethologist Konrad Lorenz's findings on the distinctive features of infants that garner caregivers' attention and affectionate behavior (cited in Morreall, 1991).

17. That position commingles power and sexuality in highly problematic practices, including the sexualization of young girls/*shôjo* in a phenomenon called *rorikon* (a Lolita complex; sexual attraction of older men to young preadult females, particularly girls in school uniforms), which paves the way for a flourishing market for teenage prostitution and child pornography (Kinsella, 2000; McVeigh, 2000).

18. When users leave and reenter the chat room, they do not change their screen names. This contrasts with the Euro-American practice on Internet Relay Chat, where people sometimes change their nicknames to indicate their absence from their computers (B. Danet, personal communication, August 6, 2003).

19. Although a typology of the uses and functions of *kaomoji* would be extremely useful and would include the examples that we have been discussing, such a comprehensive categorization is beyond the scope of our research and this chapter.

20. See Herring (2003, pp. 219–221) for discussion of feminization and female empowerment through Internet use in the United States.

References

Aoki, T. (1996). *Mitate no bigaku* [Aesthetics of mitate]. *Nihon no Bigaku* [Japanese Aesthetics], *24*, 36–62.

Appadurai, A. (1996). *Modernity at large: Cultural dimensions of globalization.* Minneapolis: University of Minnesota Press.

Barthes, R. (1985). *The responsibility of forms.* Berkeley: University of California Press.

Bauman, R. (1992). Performance. In R. Bauman (Ed.), *Folklore, cultural performances, and popular entertainments* (pp. 41–49). New York: Oxford University Press.

Bernstein, G. L. (1991). Introduction. In G. L. Bernstein (Ed.), *Recreating Japanese women, 1600–1945* (pp. 1–14). Berkeley: University of California Press.

Bodomo, A., & Lee, C. (2002). Changing forms of language and literacy: Technobabble and mobile phone communication in Hong Kong. *Literacy and Numeracy Studies, 12*(1), 23–44.

Bourdieu, P. (1990). *The logic of practice.* Stanford, CA: Stanford University Press.

Briggs, C. (1988). *Competence in performance: The creativity of tradition in Mexicano verbal art.* Philadelphia: University of Pennsylvania Press.

Crystal, D. (2001). *Language and the Internet.* Cambridge: Cambridge University Press.

Danet, B. (2001). *Cyberpl@y: Communicating online.* Oxford: Berg. Companion website: http://pluto.mscc.huji.ac.il/~msdanet/cyberpl@y/, retrieved May 16, 2005.

Danet, B., Ruedenberg, L., & Rosenbaum-Tamari, Y. (1998). Hmmm . . . where's that smoke coming from? Writing, play and performance on Internet Relay Chat. In F. Sudweeks, M. McLaughlin, & S. Rafaeli (Eds.), *Network & netplay. Virtual groups on the Internet* (pp. 41–76). Cambridge, MA: AAAI Press/MIT Press.

Doi, T. (1973). *The anatomy of dependence* (J. Bester, Trans.). Tokyo: Kodansha International.

Ellis, B. (2003, October). *Cardcaptors uncensored: A virtual community.* Paper presented at the annual meeting of the American Folklore Society, Albuquerque, New Mexico.

Godin, S. (1993). *The smiley dictionary: Cool things to do with your keyboard.* Berkeley, CA: Peachpit Press.

Goffman, E. (1959). *The presentation of self in everyday life.* New York: Doubleday.

Gottlieb, N., & McLelland, M. (2003). The Internet in Japan. In N. Gottlieb & M. McLelland (Eds.), *Japanese cybercultures* (pp. 1–16). London: Routledge.

Haraway, D. (1991). *Simians, cyborgs, and women: The reinvention of nature.* New York: Routledge.

Herring, S. C. (1993). Gender and democracy in computer-mediated communication. *Electronic Journal of Communication, 3*(2). Retrieved December 22, 2005, from http://ella.slis .indiana.edu/~herring/ejc.txt.

Herring, S. C. (1996). Posting in a different voice: Gender and ethics in CMC. In C. Ess (Ed.), *Philosophical perspectives on computer-mediated communication* (pp. 115–145). Albany: State University of New York Press.

Herring, S. C. (2003). Gender and power in online communication. In J. Holmes & M. Meyer-hoff (Eds.), *The handbook of language and gender* (pp. 202–228). Oxford: Blackwell.

Hjorth, L. (2003). Cute@keitai.com. In N. Gottlieb & M. McLelland (Eds.), *Japanese cyber-cultures* (pp. 50–59). London: Routledge.

Holden, T., Miles, J., & Tsuruki, T. (2003). Deai-kei: Japan's new culture of encounter. In N. Gottlieb & M. McLelland (Eds.), *Japanese cybercultures* (pp. 35–49). London: Routledge.

Imamura, A. E. (1987). *Urban Japanese housewives: At home and in the community.* Honolulu: University of Hawaii Press.

Ishii, K., & Jarkey, N. (2002). The housewife is born: The establishment of the notion and identity of the *shufu* in modern Japan. *Japanese Studies, 22*(1), 35–47.

Kataoka, K. (1997). Affect and letter-writing: Unconventional conventions in casual writing by young Japanese women. *Language in Society, 26,* 103–136.

Katsuno, H., & Yano, C. R. (2002). Face to face: Online subjectivity in contemporary Japan. *Asian Studies Review, 26*(2), 205–231.

Kinsella, S. (1995). Cuties in Japan. In L. Skov & B. Moeran (Eds.), *Women, media, and con-sumption in Japan* (pp. 220–254). Honolulu: University of Hawaii Press.

Kinsella, S. (2000). *Adult manga: Culture and power in contemporary Japanese society.* Honolulu: University of Hawaii Press.

Lebra, T. (1976). *Japanese patterns of behavior.* Honolulu: University of Hawaii Press.

Lebra, T. S. (1984). *Japanese women: Constraint and fulfillment.* Honolulu: University of Hawaii Press.

Masubuchi, S. (1994). *Kawaii kyôdôtai* [Community of cuteness]. Tokyo: Nihonhôsôkyôkai.

Matsuda, P. K. (2002). Negotiation of identity and power in a Japanese online discourse community. *Computers and Composition, 19,* 39–55.

McVeigh, B. J. (1996). Commodifying affection, authority and gender in the everyday objects of Japan. *Journal of Material Culture, 1*(3), 291–312.

McVeigh, B. J. (2000). *Wearing ideology: State, schooling and self-presentation in Japan.* New York: Berg.

Merish, L. (1996). Cuteness and commodity aesthetics: Tom Thumb and Shirley Temple. In R. G. Thomson (Ed.), *Freakery: Cultural spectacles of the extraordinary body* (pp. 185–203). New York: New York University Press.

Miyadai, S., Ishihara, H., & Otsuka, M. (2000). *Sabukaruchâ shinwa kaitai* [Deconstructing the myth of subcultures]. Tokyo: Parco.

Morreall, J. (1991). Cuteness. *British Journal of Aesthetics, 31*(1), 39–47.

Morreall, J. (1993). The contingency of cuteness: A reply to Sanders. *British Journal of Aesthetics, 33*(3), 283–285.

Murray, C. D., & Sixsmith, J. (1999). The corporeal body in virtual reality. *Ethos, 27*(3), 315–343.

Napier, S. (2000). *Anime from Akira to Mononoke: Experiencing contemporary Japanese animation.* New York: Palgrave.

Natsume, F. (1997). *Manga wa naze omoshiroi no ka: Sono hyôgen to bunpô* [What makes manga enjoyable: Expressions and grammar]. Tokyo: NHK Library.

Natsume, F., & Takekuma, K. (1995). *Manga no yomikata* [How to read manga]. Tokyo: Takarajimasha.

Nishimura, Y. (2003). Linguistic innovations and interactional features of casual online communication in Japanese. *Journal of Computer-Mediated Communication, 9*(1). Retrieved May 15, 2005, from http://jcmc.indiana/edu/vol9/issue1/nishimura.html.

Otsuka, E. (1989). *Shôjo minzokugaku* [The folklore of shôjo]. Tokyo: Kôbunsha.

Paasonen, S. (2002). Gender, identity, and (the limits of) play on the Internet. In M. Consalvo & S. Paasonen (Eds.), *Women and everyday uses of the Internet* (pp. 21–43). New York: Peter Lang.

Palmer, J. (1994). *Taking humour seriously.* New York: Routledge.

Roberts, G. S. (1994). *Staying on the line: Blue-collar women in contemporary Japan.* Honolulu: University of Hawaii Press.

Sanderson, D. (1993). *Smileys.* New York: O'Reilly & Associates.

Schilling, M. (1997). *The encyclopedia of Japanese pop culture.* New York: Weatherhill.

Schodt, F. L. (1983). *Manga! manga! The world of Japanese comics.* New York: Kodansha International.

Sugimoto, T., & Levin, J. A. (2000). Multiple literacies and multimedia: A comparison of Japanese and American uses of the Internet. In G. E. Hawisher & C. L. Selfe (Eds.), *Global literacies and the World-Wide Web* (pp. 133–153). London: Routledge.

StereoMagic. (2000). *Face mark library 2000: Contemporary smileys of Japan.* Tokyo: GOT Co. Ltd.

Stone, A. R. (1995/1996). *The war of desire and technology at the close of the mechanical age.* Cambridge, MA: MIT Press.

Tanaka, Y. (2000). *Kibyôshi to manga* [Kibyôshi and manga]. *Nihon no Bigaku* [Japanese Aesthetics], *30,* 30–41.

Turkle, S. (1984). *The second self: Computers and the human spirit.* New York: Simon & Schuster.

Turkle, S. (1995). *Life on the screen: Identity in the age of the Internet*. New York: Simon & Schuster.

Yamaguchi, M. (1991). The poetics of exhibition in Japanese culture. In I. Karp & S. D. Lavine (Eds.), *Exhibiting cultures: The poetics and politics of museum display* (pp. 57–67). Washington, DC: Smithsonian.

Yamaguchi, M., & Takashina, S. (1996). Dialogue: *Mitate to nihon bunka* [*Mitate* and Japanese culture]. *Nihon no Bigaku* [Japanese Aesthetics], *24*, 4–23.

Yamane, K. (1986). *Hentai shôjo moji no kenkyû* [Study of deviant handwriting of teengage girls]. Tokyo: Kôdansha.

Yamazaki, J. (2002). Global and local in computer-mediated communication: A Japanese newsgroup. In R. T. Donahue (Ed.), *Exploring Japaneseness: On Japanese enactments of culture and consciousness* (pp. 425–442). Westport, CT: Ablex.

Yano, C. R. (2004). Panic attacks: Anti-Pokémon voices in global markets. In J. Tobin (Ed.), *Pikachu's global adventure: The rise and fall of Pokémon* (pp. 108–138). Durham, NC: Duke University Press.

PART IV

LANGUAGE CHOICE AND
CODE SWITCHING

13

MARK WARSCHAUER, GHADA R. EL SAID, AND AYMAN ZOHRY

Language Choice Online

Globalization and Identity in Egypt

As a major new means of global communication, the Internet is having a great impact on language use. Probably the most feared result, voiced most often in the Internet's early years, was that it would encourage global use of English to such a degree that other languages would be crowded out. Indeed, in the mid-1990s, 80% of international websites were reported to be in English (Cyberspeech, 1997). That number remained as high as 72% through 2002 (O'Neill, Lavoie, & Bennett, 2003). English remains even more dominant within certain Internet realms. A study conducted by the Organization for Economic Cooperation and Development (OECD; Default Language, 1999) found that while some 78% of websites in OECD countries were in English, 91% of websites on "secure servers" were in English, and fully 96% of sites on secure servers in the .com domain were in English. This is significant because secure servers (especially those in .com) are used for e-commerce. Presumably, then, while a growing number of noncommercial sites are in local languages, English remains the dominant language of commercial sites.

The strong presence of English online has caused consternation among many. Local opposition to English online has sprung up most notably in France, where a 1994 law mandates that all advertising must be in French (Online, 1998) and where the Finance Minister reportedly banned the use in his ministry of English-derived terms such as "email" or "start-up," in favor of French terms such as *courier électronique* or *jeune pousse*. In other countries, concerns about English online have sparked new efforts to improve English language instruction (Takahashi, 2000).

Of course, the Internet is a boon not only to English but potentially to many other languages, especially minority languages that bridge geographically dispersed speakers or that have insufficient resources to make use of more expensive media. There are numerous examples of technology use for indigenous language revitalization (see Cunliffe & Herring, 2005; Warschauer, 1998). The Internet also fosters written communication in dialects and languages that previously were used principally for oral communication (Warschauer, 2001). In spite of concern about competition between English and other languages online, until recently, very little research had been done on the topic, with the notable exception of two studies on language use in a Usenet group (Paolillo, 1996) and an Internet Relay Chat channel (Paolillo, 2001). These studies highlighted, among other things, the role of code switching between two languages within a particular group of interlocutors.

In this chapter we examine language choice online by a group of Egyptian Internet users, asking in what circumstances, and why, this group uses English and Arabic. We first provide background information on language use and Internet use in Egypt, then introduce and discuss the study, and finally analyze the results in terms of broader global trends of language, identity, and globalization.

LANGUAGE CONTEXT

Language use in Egypt is a classic example of "diglossia," a situation in which one dialect or language is used in formal or written realms and a second dialect or language is used largely in informal or spoken realms (Ferguson, 1972). Diglossia can refer either to the use of two different languages (e.g., English and Tagalog in the Philippines) or to the use of two different varieties or dialects of the same language (e.g., standard German and Swiss German in parts of Switzerland).

In Egypt, the two varieties used are both varieties of Arabic, referred to as Classical Arabic and Egyptian Arabic (Haeri, 1997). Actual usage of Classical or Egyptian Arabic in Egypt falls along a continuum, rather than in complete bipolar opposition (Bentahila & Davies, 1991; Parkinson, 1992), but since most uses tend toward one pole or the other, these two are considered the main Arabic dialects of Egypt. Classical Arabic is the literary dialect that is used in the Qu'ran; in most print publications, including books, magazines, and newspapers; and in formal spoken discourse, including prayer, television news broadcasts, and formal prepared speeches. It is used with relatively little variation throughout the Arab world; Moroccans, Egyptians, Iraqis, and Saudis who know Classical Arabic will be mutually comprehensible in writing or speech.

Egyptian Arabic, also referred to as Egyptian colloquial Arabic (Al-Tonis, 1980), is the spoken dialect of the Egyptian people and is used in conversation, songs, films, and television soap operas. As for written forms, it is used in comic strips and, occasionally, in novels and short stories (similarly to how nonstandard English dialects might be occasionally used either as a literary device or for reporting dialogue and conversation). Both Classical Arabic and Egyptian Arabic use the same Arabic script. Egyptian Arabic is spoken only in Egypt (or by Egyptians elsewhere), but it is understood widely in the Arab world due to the popularity of Egyptian films and songs.

Both Classical Arabic and Egyptian Arabic have their own powerful symbolism for Egyptians. Classical Arabic, as the language of the Qu'ran and the common language of the Arab nation, is central to their identity as members of the nation of Egypt and of the broader Islamic community. Egyptian Arabic, as the language of daily communication, jokes, song, and cinema, is central to their identity as Egyptians. While virtually all Egyptians are competent speakers of Egyptian, only about half of adults in the country can read and write Classical Arabic (Fandy, 2000). The country's low rate of adult literacy—52.7% according to the United Nations Development Programme (2000)—stems in part from the difficulty that Egyptian children have in mastering a written language that is at large variance from their spoken variety.

Beyond this diglossia of Classical and Egyptian Arabic, many other languages are used in Egypt, including the ancient Coptic language sometimes used in Coptic Christian church services (Takla, 2002), African languages used by refugees, and European languages used in business and tourism. The use of European languages has a long history dating back to periods of French and British colonialism. The Egyptian elite often preferred to be educated in French or English (Haeri, 1997). Recently, though, use of English has far surpassed that of French and other foreign languages. According to a study by Schaub (2000), English plays a dual role in Egypt. On the one hand, it is the principal foreign language of the general population. English is the first and only mandatory foreign language taught in schools, with obligatory instruction starting in fourth grade. Hotel workers, shopkeepers, and street salespeople use English to communicate with foreign visitors and residents, especially in major cities and tourist destinations (Schaub, 2000; Stevens, 1994).

Beyond that, English serves as a second language of additional communication for Egypt's elite. The majority of private schools are considered English language schools, which means that English language instruction begins in kindergarten and English is a medium of instruction of other specified subjects (mathematics and science). Recently, the Ministry of Education also launched experimental language schools in the public school system. Seventy-nine of the 80 launched so far are English medium (personal interview with Reda Fadel, former Councilor of English, Egyptian Ministry of Education, April 2000). The elite usually continue their postsecondary education in English, studying either abroad (e.g., in the United States or England), at an English-medium university in Egypt (the most established being the American University in Cairo), or in an English-medium department of an Egyptian public university. Medicine, dentistry, veterinary studies, engineering, the natural sciences, and computer sciences all use English as a main medium of instruction, and other disciplines, such as commerce and law, have English-medium sections that are considered more prestigious and difficult to enter. Graduates from these universities and programs often enter careers in which English continues to be used as a daily medium of communication, such as international business or computer science. Professionals in other elite fields, such as medicine, continue to use English as an additional language through frequent contact with foreigners and through professional activities: For example, the conferences of doctors, dentists, and nurses in Egypt are conducted in English, even without foreigners present, and professional publications of these groups are published in English (see discussion of English as an second language of the Egyptian elite in Haeri [1997] and Schaub 2000).

TECHNOLOGY CONTEXT

The other main contextual factor framing this study is Internet use in Egypt. The Internet was first introduced to Egypt in 1993, when a small university network was established (Information Technology in Egypt, 1998). Commercial Internet use began three years later and has developed with more government support and less censorship than in many other Mideast countries, reaching a total of some 440,000 Internet users by 2000 (Dabbagh Information Technology Group, 2000), representing 0.7% of the population. Although the growth of the Internet in Egypt is constrained by economic (high expense in relation to average income) and infrastructure factors (low teledensity), its impact extends beyond its current limited reach. The Egyptian government is placing great emphasis on information and communication technologies (ICT), and Egypt is said to have one of the fastest growing ICT markets in the world. Initiatives to expand Internet access and use abound in the educational system, the business community, and the nonprofit sector. Those who are already connected disproportionately represent the economic elite, so their influence extends far beyond their somewhat limited numbers, especially in major population centers such as Cairo and Alexandria (Warschauer, 2003).

With this context as background, we conducted an exploratory study of a group of Egyptian Internet users. We sought to find out which languages this group of people used in online communications, and why.

METHODS

Subjects

The study was carried out among 43 young professionals in Cairo known to be Internet users. The category of "young professionals" was chosen because it represents the first generation of Internet users in Egypt. Young professionals are not representative of the overall Egyptian population or even of current Internet users, but they do include many early adopters of the Internet in Egypt. The young professionals in this study were selected through personal contacts of two Cairo researchers who assisted with the study; the subjects may not be representative of all young professionals in Cairo.

"Young professionals" were defined for the purpose of the study as people between the ages of 24 and 36 engaged in introductory or mid-level professional and management positions. All 43 people in the sample had at least a bachelor's degree, and 30 of the group (70%) had a master's or doctoral degree. Areas of study ranged broadly and included engineering, economics, computer science, and medicine. The sample was fairly evenly balanced for gender, with 23 men and 20 women. Twenty-three individuals worked in the information technology industry, including computer engineers, information technology specialists, system engineers, and managers. The remaining 20 worked for business and research industries, including an environmental researcher, librarians, statisticians, and doctors. Almost all had part of their education in English and part in Arabic.

Instruments

Survey

A written survey was developed that inquired about people's language and literacy practices online (see Warschauer et al., 2002, appendix A). The survey included six questions about personal information (e.g., what is your profession?), four general questions about computer and Internet access and use (e.g., how long have you been using the Internet?), eight questions about language use online (e.g., what language[s] do you use in online "real-time" chatting with Egyptians or other Arabic speakers?), and eight questions about print literacy practices (e.g., what kind of things do you write regularly and in what language?) The survey was pilot tested among a small group of people who were not in the final survey, and then finalized and distributed by email to 50 people, who were also asked to include voluntarily examples of any email messages or online chats that illustrated points covered in the survey.

Forty-three of the 50 people returned the survey. Eight of them included examples of email messages or online chats; some of these are included in the analysis. The survey was nonanonymous so that the researchers could conduct follow-up interviews. People were asked their name and email address and whether they agreed to be contacted for a follow-up interview. Thirty-one people volunteered to be interviewed.

Interviews

Four young professionals were selected for interviews who, judging by their survey answers, represented a cross section of language use patterns found in formal and informal Internet communications. Two of the four came in together; the others came in alone. The interviews were conducted by two of the three researchers, using a semistructured approach; that is, a set of interview questions was planned ahead of time related to language and literacy practices online (see Warschauer et al., 2002, appendix B), but the interviews diverged as appropriate to explore interesting points that came up. The interviews lasted from 60 to 90 minutes and were tape recorded with the consent of the subjects.

DATA ANALYSIS

Survey data were tallied to allow the examination of various types of online communication by language, dialect, and script. In addition, after the use of Egyptian Arabic was identified as occurring in online communication, a two-tailed analysis of variance (ANOVA) was performed to investigate which factors were correlated with online use of Egyptian Arabic (with alpha established at 0.05). The interviews were transcribed and the written transcripts were examined by the researchers to identify patterns and illustrative examples of when and why the participants used a particular language, dialect, and script online.

LIMITATIONS

It is important to point out the limitations of this study. The sample is small and nonrandom, having been selected through personal contacts of the researchers. The facts that the subjects were personally known by the researchers and that the survey was nonanonymous (to allow for follow-up contact) may have affected people's responses. The survey was not formally tested for reliability. Only four participants were interviewed, and the interview transcripts were examined for patterns and illustrative examples rather than systematically coded; this examination process was not checked for interrater reliability. In addition, no systematic attempt was made to assess participants' fluency in English, Classical Arabic, or Egyptian Arabic. For all of these reasons, the results of the study cannot be assumed to be generalizable to other populations beyond this group of subjects. Rather, this was an exploratory investigation to identify possible issues and trends for further research.

RESULTS

The most interesting results of the survey concerned language use online. Basically, Classical Arabic in Arabic script, the most common form of writing in Egypt, was seldom used by any of the 43 participants. Rather, online com-

TABLE 13.1. Language and script use (numbers exceed 100% because some people use more than one script).

	Formal email	Informal email	Online chat
English	37 (92.5%)	35 (83.3%)	22 (71.0%)
Classical Arabic (Arabic script)	4 (10.0%)	4 (9.5%)	2 (6.5%)
Classical Arabic (Roman script)	1 (2.5%)	7 (16.7%)	3 (9.7%)
Egyptian Arabic (Arabic script)	0 (0%)	2 (4.8%)	5 (16.1%)
Egyptian Arabic (Roman script)	4 (10.0%)	21 (50.0%)	17 (54.8%)
Total no. of participants using this feature	40	42	31

munications featured a new and unusual diglossia—involving a foreign language, English, and a romanized, predominantly colloquial form of Arabic that had very limited use for these informants prior to the development of the Internet.

Table 13.1 shows the number of people who indicated that they used English, Classical Arabic (in either Arabic script or romanized script), and Egyptian Arabic (in either Arabic script or romanized script in their formal email messages, informal email messages, and online chats).[1] English and romanized Egyptian Arabic are the two main language forms used and will be discussed in turn below.

ENGLISH ONLINE

Table 13.2 indicates the number of people who used English, Classical Arabic (in either Arabic or romanized script), and Egyptian Arabic (in either Arabic or romanized script) in their online communications. Table 13.3 displays a simple comparison between English and any form of Arabic (or English and Arabic combined). Both sets of data indicate that English is the dominant

TABLE 13.2. Language and dialect use.

	Formal email	Informal email	Online chat
English	37 (92.5%)	35 (83.3%)	22 (71.0%)
Classical Arabic	5 (12.5%)	11 (26.2%)	6 (19.4%)
Egyptian Arabic	4 (10.0%)	21 (50.0%)	19 (61.2%)
Total no. of participants using this feature	40	42	31

TABLE 13.3. English versus Arabic.

	Formal email	Informal email	Online chat
English only	33 (82.5%)	13 (31.0%)	6 (20.7%)
Arabic only	5 (12.5%)	7 (16.7%)	6 (20.7%)
English and Arabic	2 (5.0%)	22 (52.4%)	17 (58.7%)
Total no. of participants using this feature	40	42	29

language used in online communication among this group of Egyptian young professionals.

The dominance of English is particularly strong in formal email communication, with 82.5% of the participants using only English in that medium (table 13.3). In informal email communication, the situation is more balanced, with a slight majority of the participants code switching between English and Arabic languages (principally Egyptian Arabic; see tables 13.2 and 13.3). In online chats, the majority also code switch, with smaller and equal numbers using English or Arabic only (table 13.3). An examination of email messages and online chat transcripts submitted indicated that, when English and Arabic were combined in a single message, there tended to be more use of English. In addition, each person interviewed indicated that the majority of their webpage reading was also in English.

The interviews and survey data show that the prominence of English in Internet communication stems from a variety of social, economic, and technological factors that are closely related to the more general role of English in Egyptian society. The following points were stressed by interviewees as to why they use English predominantly in online communication.

Dominance of English in the Professional Milieu

Most formal online communication carried out by the young professionals in this study was done within broader environments that strongly emphasized English. For example, one information technology professional explained that most of his professional contacts are with software or hardware firms that are branches of international companies. Therefore, even if he is contacting a local branch office in Egypt, he is aware that the branch functions in a broader English language milieu, and he therefore writes in English. The study indicated that some 75% of the participants do most of their professional writing in English. It is thus certainly not a surprise that their formal email communication is also in English. Similarly, most types of business and technical information sought by these young professionals are available on the World Wide Web in English, so they naturally search the Web in that language.

Lack of Arabic Software Standards

A second reason for the dominance of English is the lack of a common Arabic software standard. The reasons for this lack are part technical, because computing throughout the world is easier in ASCII code. The larger reason, however, is socioeconomic. Countries such as Japan, Taiwan, and Israel have been able to develop common standards for non-Roman computing and telecommunications due to the prominence of a national bourgeoisie within a single country. Computing leadership within the Arabic world is spread over a number of countries, and the business community in each of these countries—especially in the ICT field—is largely dominated by foreign companies and managers. This is especially true in the oil-rich Gulf countries, which employ huge numbers of foreign managers and technicians.

The lack of a single common standard for Arabic language computing, together with the large presence of foreign nationals in the business community, hinders Arabic language computing. For example, one of the participants in the survey had started an online sales business targeted to consumers in Egypt. Although the majority of his customers were Egyptians, information on his pages was available only in English. He explained that most of his customers accessed the Web at their jobs, and they often worked at foreign companies that had not upgraded to Arabic-language operating systems (due, in part, to the desire to use a single standard throughout their companies, whose headquarters were based outside the Arab world). This budding entrepreneur felt that his best chance of building an audience in Egypt would be to market his product in English.

Computer and Internet Use Learned in English Environments

Most of the participants stressed that they first learned to use computers and the Internet in English environments, either in their English-medium coursework or in English-dominant work environments. Therefore, they were not experienced typists in Arabic, using either Arabic script or Roman script. Several mentioned that they thus wrote principally in English and only used Arabic where there was a special feeling or sentiment that was difficult to express in English.

Early Adopters' Fluency in English

The majority of the people in this survey were educated in English and can write English as well as or better than Arabic. This, together with the other reasons listed above, provides another disincentive to switch to Arabic in online communications, especially for formal interaction.

USE OF EGYPTIAN ARABIC

Another interesting finding of the study was the considerable amount of romanized Egyptian Arabic used by the participants. This is consistent with a more general use of romanized Arabic in computer-mediated communication in the Arab world (Palfreyman & Al Khalil, chapter 2 this volume). In the present study, romanized Egyptian Arabic was found to be widely used in both informal email communications and online chatting, with many people engaging in code switching (between English and Egyptian Arabic) and some writing exclusively in Egyptian Arabic.

The emergence of romanized Egyptian Arabic is especially interesting because it was previously not a widely used language form. As discussed above, Egyptian Arabic is principally a means of oral communication. Although it has been written in certain realms, such as comic books, prior to the Internet it appeared mainly in Arabic script, with several unofficial romanized versions existing principally for the benefit of foreigners (e.g., in language instruction books and dictionaries). Broader written uses of Egyptian Arabic in areas such as business, scholarship, and religion are frowned upon by society and by educational and religious authorities. The use of Egyptian Arabic online thus represents a major expansion of its written use, especially in a romanized form, in a new realm in which informality is considered acceptable and in which no authority discourages its use.

One of the interesting features of this adaptation is the widespread use of the numbers 2, 3, and 7 to represent phonemes that are not easily rendered in the Roman alphabet. The use of these numbers arose among Internet users, spread spontaneously, and is now widely recognized. The use of two of these numbers is seen in the following informal email, which also provides a good example of code switching:

> Hello Dalia, 7amdellah 3ala el-salama ya Gameel. we alf mabrouk 3alal el-shahada el-kebeera. Keep in touch...I really hope to see you all Soooooooooooooooon (Maybe in Ramadan). Kol Sana Wentom Tayyebeen. Waiting to hear from you . . . Laila

> *Translation:* Hello Dalia, Thank God for the safe return, my sweet. Congratulations for the big certificate [sarcastic]. Keep in touch . . . I really hope to see you all Soooooooooooooooon (Maybe in Ramadan). Happy Ramadan. Waiting to hear from you . . . Laila

Participants in the study who engaged in code switching indicated that they most frequently used Egyptian Arabic to express highly personal content that they could not express well in English. Several interviewees explained that they start in English and switch to Egyptian Arabic when they feel the need. Analysis of sample messages indicated that, in bilingual messages, Egyptian Arabic was most often found in greetings, humorous or sarcastic expressions, expressions related to food and holidays, and religious expressions, as in the following:

Greetings:
Salamt [Greetings]
Ezayek [How are you?]
Akhbarek eih [What's new?]

Sarcastic Expressions:
Ya Fandem !! [Sir (sarcastic)]
Rabena yg3al fe weshek el2obol :) [Let God make it easy for us :) (sarcastic)]

Food and Holidays:
Kahek el Eid [Egyptian sweet only, usually to be eaten after Ramadan]
Fanousse Ramadan [Ramadan lantern]
Agazet noss el sanna [Mid-term vacation]

Religious Expressions:
In shaa Allah [God willing]
El hamdoulellah [Thank God]
Besm Allah el Rahman el Raheem [In the name of God the merciful and most compassionate]
As-Salamu alaikum wa rahmatu Allahi wa barakatu [May God give you peace, his mercy and blessing]

Finally, a means test (using a two-tailed ANOVA) was carried out to investigate online use of Egyptian Arabic further. Two factors correlated significantly ($p < 0.05$) with increased use of Egyptian Arabic in online chatting: (1) years of experience using the Internet, and (2) working in an information technology profession. The latter is of interest because information technology professionals in Egypt, in addition to being proficient with computers, are also known for being highly proficient in English (Schaub, 2000), a characteristic that extends to this particular group, as well, based on the researchers' evaluation following extensive personal communication with the subjects. This suggests that there are other explanations for use of Egyptian Arabic than lack of familiarity with English or computers.

One possible, albeit untested, explanation is that the familiarity of information technology professionals with computers and the Internet has led them to want to experiment more, especially in online chatting. At least within this group of young professionals, use of Egyptian Arabic does not appear to be a crutch used by those with less background in computers and English, but rather an additional communicative tool selected by those with expertise and experience with computers and English. Other factors, such as gender or amount of education, did not correlate with use of Egyptian Arabic online.

The use of romanized versions of Arabic online is not unique to Egypt. A detailed discussion of linguistic features of romanized Gulf Arabic chat is found in Palfreyman and Al Khalil (chapter 2 this volume). Finally, while the study reported here focused on email and online chatting, it also should be mentioned that the Arabic language—in any dialect—is woefully underrepresented on the Internet in general.

DISCUSSION

Two interesting findings emerged from this study: first, that English is the dominant language used online among a particular group of early Internet adopters in Egypt, and second, that a previously little-used written form of romanized Egyptian Arabic is also widely used in informal communication by this group. We believe that the meaning of these findings is better understood when examined in a broader context of language, technology, and society in Egypt and internationally.

Sociologists have pointed to the current era as marked by a contradiction between global networks and local identities (Barber, 1995; Castells, 1996, 1997). On the one hand, global flows of capital, finance, markets, and media increasingly impinge on our lives, weakening traditional pillars of authority such as the nation-state, the permanent job, and the family (Castells, 1996). On the other hand, this breakdown of traditional authority has caused a reaction as people attempt to defend their cultures and identity from amorphous, globalized control. Thus, we witness the increased power of transnational corporations, international media, and multilateral institutions such as the World Trade Organization and the International Monetary Fund, and also the rise of religious fundamentalists, anarchist groups, and identity movements. Within this matrix, language is a potential medium of both global networks and local identities (Warschauer, 2000a, 2000b). Economic and social globalization, pushed along by the rapid diffusion of the Internet, creates a strong demand for an international lingua franca, thus furthering English's presence as a global language (Crystal, 2003).

On the other hand, the same dynamics that gave rise to globalization and global English also produced a backlash against both, which gets expressed, in one form, through strengthened attachment to local dialects and languages. This tension—between Internet-led globalization and an increased need for local culture and language—has pushed Singaporeans to cling closely to their highly colloquial dialect (Singlish) even as the government pushes them to adapt standard English in order to market their goods more effectively (Warschauer, 2001). It has also given a push to movements in defense of other languages, such as French (Online, 1998). The Internet can be a convenient medium for both sides of this dynamic. It not only is a medium for global interaction in English but also allows for new forms of communication and interaction in local languages. Eritreans living in Italy or the United States can chat in their native language and read online newspapers. Hawaiians can produce curricular materials in their indigenous language that would have previously been unaffordable (Warschauer & Donaghy, 1997). And, as seen by the use of numbers to represent Arabic phonemes discussed above, new written forms of language can emerge.

In this context, it is not surprising that we witness expanded use of both English and Arabic online among this group of Egyptians—that is, the instrumental use of a global language and the more intimate and personal use of a local one. What is interesting, and worthy of further analysis, is how the main literacy language of Egypt, Classical Arabic, may be getting squeezed from both above and below by this dynamic.

Niloofar Haeri, a sociolinguist who has written broadly on language and power in Egypt (Haeri, 1996), argues that the ties of the Egyptian elite to Classical Arabic are not particularly strong (Haeri, 1997). This stems, in her eyes, from a number of factors, including the elite's immersion in private, foreign language education; elite involvement in occupations demanding use of English (international banking, medicine, and research) or Egyptian Arabic (movie and stage acting) rather than Classical Arabic (government clerk positions); and the elite's distance from Islamic fundamentalist movements (which try to defend Classical Arabic as a religious language). It has also been pointed out that links between the poor and written Classical Arabic as a language of scholarship are weak, since the majority of the poor are illiterate (Fandy, 2000). Thus, the advent of the Internet could be one factor, together with other socioeconomic changes (e.g., globalization), that contributes toward a shift from traditional diglossia in Egypt to increased multilingualism, with both English (from "above") and Egyptian Arabic (from "below") encroaching on the traditional dominance of Classical Arabic in written communication. This might be one expression of a strengthening of global (English-language dominant) networks in Egypt, as well as local (Egyptian) identities, with a corresponding weakening of more "traditional" sources of identity, such as (Arab) nationalism.

The long-term consequences of such a trend, if it continues, are unclear. On the one hand, participants in this study made quite clear that their use of English does not signify an embrace of Western culture or an abandonment of Egyptian identity. In contrast, they tended to describe their use of English in terms of Egypt's long and proud history of being able to absorb the best from a broad array of cultures and make it its own. They also made clear that their own local language, Egyptian Arabic, is a powerful vehicle for expressing their most personal thoughts and feelings. Their use of Egyptian Arabic online thus represents the appropriation of technology toward a people's own communicative purposes.

On the other hand, the continued encroachment of English on the prestigious realms of language use, in business, commerce, and academia—bolstered now by online communications—could be viewed as a threat to the national language and values. While the informants in this particular study, most of whom have been immersed in an English-language environment for years, did not express this concern, press reports indicate that many other Egyptians are worried about the future status of Classical Arabic vis-à-vis English (Fawzy, 1999; Hassan, 1999; Howeidy, 1999). This could portend a class split, suggested by Haeri (1997), with the elite continuing to gravitate toward English as their prestige language, while the lower middle class excels in Classical Arabic.

CONCLUSION

As an important new communication medium, the Internet is bound to have an important long-term effect on language use. It is too early to tell what that impact will be. The trends discussed in this chapter could prove to be temporary, if, for example, the development and diffusion of Arabic language software and operating systems bolster the use of Classical Arabic and stem the tide of online communication in English or in romanized Arabic dialects. However, language use online, in Egypt and elsewhere, will be shaped not just by the capacities that technology enables but also by the social systems that technology encompasses. Moreover, as Castells (1996, 1997) and others (Barber, 1995; Friedman, 1999) have pointed out, the major social dynamic shaping international media and communication in this age of information is the contradiction between global networks and local identities. In that light, it is worthwhile to consider whether the online use of English and Egyptian Arabic by this small group of Egyptian professionals might reflect broader and more enduring social and linguistic shifts.

Acknowledgment

A previous version of this chapter was published in the *Journal of Computer-Mediated Communication* (volume 7, issue 4, 2002).

Note

1. "Formal email messages" are those sent for professional or business purposes. "Informal email messages" are those exchanged between friends and acquaintances for personal reasons. Online chat refers to synchronous communication via, for example, ICQ or Yahoo! Messenger. The numbers in this figure do not add up to 43 because some people indicated they use more than one language, and others indicated no languages used (if, e.g., they never engage in a particular practice, such as online chat).

References

Al-Tonis, A. (1980). *Egyptian colloquial Arabic: A structural review*. Cairo: American University in Cairo.

Barber, B. R. (1995). *Jihad vs. McWorld*. New York: Ballantine.

Bentahila, A., & Davies, E. (1991). Standards for Arabic: One, two, or many. *Indian Journal of Applied Linguistics, 17*, 69–88.

Castells, M. (1996). *The rise of the network society*. Malden, MA: Blackwell.

Castells, M. (1997). *The power of identity*. Malden, MA: Blackwell.

Crystal, D. (2003). English *as a global language* (2nd ed.). Cambridge: Cambridge University Press.

Cunliffe, D., & Herring, S. C. (Eds.). (2005). Minority languages, multimedia and the Web. *New Review of Hypermedia and Multimedia, 11*(2).

Cyberspeech. (1997, June 23). *Time, 149*, 23.

Dabbagh Information Technology Group. (2000). Number of Internet users in Arab countries edges toward 2 million. Retrieved March 2, 2001, from http://www.dit.net/itnews/newsmar2000/newsmar20.html (no longer available).

Default Language, The. (1999, May 15). *Economist*, 67.

Fandy, M. (2000). Information technology, trust, and social change in the Arab world. *Middle East Journal, 54*(3), 378–394.

Fawzy, H. (1999, September 26). Decision banning use of foreign names a step to preserve mother tongue. *Egyptian Gazette*, 7.

Ferguson, C. (1972). Diglossia. In P. Giglioli (Ed.), *Language and social context* (pp. 232–251). Harmondsworth, UK: Penguin.

Friedman, T. (1999). *The Lexus and the olive tree: Understanding globalization*. New York: Farrar, Straus, & Giroux.

Haeri, N. (1996). *The sociolinguistic market of Cairo: Gender, class, and education*. London: Kegan Paul International.

Haeri, N. (1997). The reproduction of symbolic capital: Language, state, and class in Egypt. *Current Anthropology, 38*(1), 795–805.

Hassan, F. (1999, October 21–27). Advocating Arabic. *Al-Ahram Weekly*, 17.

Howeidy, A. (1999, September 23–29). From right to left. *Al Ahram Weekly*, 19.

Information Technology in Egypt. (1998). Cairo: American Chamber of Commerce in Egypt.

O'Neill, E., Lavoie, B. F., & Bennett, R. (2003). Trends in the evolution of the public Web: 1998–2002. *D-Lib Magazine, 9*(4). Retrieved December 5, 2005, from http://www.dlib.org/dlib/april03/lavoie/04lavoie.html.

Online. (1998, July 26). *Chronicle of Higher Education*, A27.

Paolillo, J. C. (1996). Language choice on *soc.culture.punjab*. *Electronic Journal of Communication, 6*(4). Retrieved September 15, 2005, from http://ella.slis.indiana.edu/~paolillo/research/paolillo.publish.txt.

Paolillo, J. C. (2001). Language variation on Internet Relay Chat: A social network approach. *Journal of Sociolinguistics, 5*(2), 180–213.

Parkinson, D. B. (1992). Good Arabic: Ability and ideology in the Egyptian Arabic speech community. *Language Research, 28*, 225–253.

Schaub, M. (2000). English in the Arab Republic of Egypt. *World Englishes, 19*(2), 225–238.

Stevens, P. B. (1994). The pragmatics of street hustlers' English in Egypt. *World Englishes, 13*(1), 61–73.

Takahashi, H. (2000). *Dealing with dealing in English: Language skills for Japan's global markets*. Report 7A. Washington, DC: Japan Economic Institute.

Takla, H. H. (2002). Coptic liturgy: Past, present, and future. Retrieved December 5, 2005, from http://www.stshenouda.com/coptman/colgsurv.pdf.

United Nations Development Programme. (2000). *Human development report 2000*. New York: Oxford University Press.

Warschauer, M. (1998). Technology and indigenous language revitalization: Analyzing the experience of Hawai'i. *Canadian Modern Language Review, 55*(1), 140–161.

Warschauer, M. (2000a). The changing global economy and the future of English teaching. *TESOL Quarterly, 34*, 511–535.

Warschauer, M. (2000b). Language, identity, and the Internet. In B. Kolko, L. Nakamura, & G. Rodman (Eds.), *Race in cyberspace* (pp. 151–170). New York: Routledge.

Warschauer, M. (2001). Singapore's dilemma: Control vs. autonomy in IT-led development. *Information Society, 17*(4), 305–311.

Warschauer, M. (2003). *Technology and social inclusion: Rethinking the digital divide.* Cambridge, MA: MIT Press.

Warschauer, M., & Donaghy, K. (1997). *Leoki*: A powerful voice of Hawaiian language revitalization. *Computer Assisted Language Learning, 10*(4), 349–362.

Warschauer, M., EI Said, G. R., & Zohry, A. (2002). Language choice online: Globalization and identity in Egypt. *Journal of Computer-Mediated Communication 7*(4). Retrieved August 11, 2006, from http://jcmc.indiana.edu/vol7/issue4/warschauer.html.

14

MERCEDES DURHAM

Language Choice on a Swiss Mailing List

In this chapter I examine how the language situation in Switzerland affects, and may be affected by, the choice of languages for Internet use. I focus primarily on language choices on a mailing list for members of a Pan-Swiss medical student organization. English has become the lingua franca, the preferred language of intra-Swiss communication, within this group. The use of English by list members was charted over four calendar years to determine when and how this change occurred. Qualitative analysis of comments by members in the emails themselves and in interviews provides clues as to why English has become so important on the mailing list. I conclude by considering the implications of this case for the linguistic situation in Switzerland and for the global spread of English via the Internet.

THE LANGUAGE SITUATION IN SWITZERLAND

Switzerland has four national languages: German, French, Italian, and Romansh (see figure 14.1). Of these, all but Romansh are considered official languages and are used in government and federal administration. German has the highest proportion of native speakers in Switzerland (64%), followed by French (20%) and Italian (6.5%; Swiss Federal Statistics Office, 2005). Generally, people's main language is the same as that of the canton or region in which they live. Which language they choose to use with Swiss nationals from other linguistic regions in the country is more complicated, however.

Until recently, the school system required that students' first foreign language be another Swiss national language, so German speakers studied French, French speakers German, and Italian speakers studied either French or German. In the past few years, however, English has become more

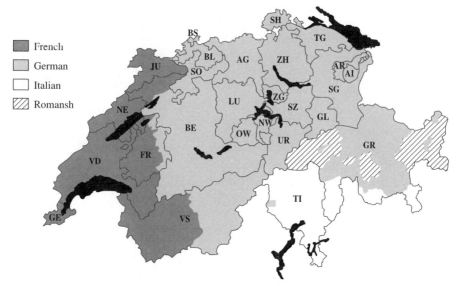

FIGURE 14.1. Regional distribution of the national languages of Switzerland. The canton names are given in the figure by two-letter abbreviations. From left to right: GE: Geneva, VD: Vaud, NE: Neuchatel, JU: Jura, BE, Berne, FR: Fribourg, VS: Valais, BS: Basel-Town, BL: Basel-Country, SO: Solothurn, AG: Aargau, LU: Lucerne, OW: Obwalden, NW: Nidwalden, SH: Schaffhausen, ZH: Zurich, ZG: Zoug, SZ: Schwytz, UR: Uri, TI: Ticino, TG: Thurgau, SG: St. Gall, GL: Glaris, AR: Appenzell-Outer-Rhodes, AI: Appenzell-Inner-Rhodes, GR: Grisons. (Recreated from map by Camillo Kohli, 2003. ©DHS, Dictionnaire Historique de la Suisse, 2003.) *Source*: http://www.snl.ch/dhs/externe/protect/francais.html, retrieved July 7, 2005. Reproduced with permission.

important. The schools of the canton of Zurich, for example, have decided to make English the first foreign language taught in the classrooms. The fact is that a large number of Swiss speakers do not feel at ease speaking in the other national languages and are more comfortable using English.

English Use in Switzerland

Although there are a number of languages spoken in Switzerland, English has gradually gained ground as a lingua franca. This change is relatively new: "Before World War II the presence of English could be felt only where the citizens of the Anglo-American countries—then above all Britain—came into contact with Swiss citizens" (Dürmüller, 2002, p. 115). English was used by Swiss nationals only to communicate with English speakers and never with other Swiss people. This use of English with non-Swiss people obviously still occurs today, and Switzerland places a large emphasis on tourism. However,

> since the end of World War II, particularly since about 1960, the situation regarding the place of English among the languages used in Switzerland has drastically changed. People in Switzerland are now often more familiar with English than

with the languages of their compatriots. English has definitely changed its status, it has moved from the fringes to the centre, from the status of a foreign language to that of an additional language with LINGUA FRANCA function, i.e., a language that can be used for special purposes and for wider communication. (Dürmüller, 2002, p. 116, emphasis original)

In addition to its importance as a lingua franca, the presence of English can also be felt in advertising (Cheshire & Moser, 1994) and to a certain extent on the Internet, in that many Swiss websites provide pages in English, as well as in French, German, and Italian.

In short, while Switzerland is a multilingual country, speakers themselves are not always multilingual, at least not necessarily in the other national languages. Although a sizable portion of the population can speak two or more national languages, apparently there is an even larger percentage of Swiss people who, even though they have studied another Swiss language, do not feel competent enough to use it. Thus, speakers from the various linguistic regions of Switzerland have had to find a different way of communicating with one another. Moreover, as attested in interviews conducted for this study, many do not feel that it would be "fair" for German speakers to use French, if the French speakers cannot use German and vice versa. Using English puts everyone at an equal disadvantage, because it is a foreign language for almost all Swiss people. But how widespread is this practice?

Project on Pan-Swiss English

The study presented here is part of a larger research project investigating whether a focused form of English may be under construction in Switzerland.[1] Focusing is a process through which a language form acquires a series of set norms through intensive contact (Le Page & Tabouret-Keller, 1985). The concept is primarily used when dealing with the formation of pidgins and creoles: languages that are born through the contact of speakers of two or more languages using a language that is no one's native tongue. A pidgin is considered to be a language with no native speakers, and a creole is a pidgin that has acquired native speakers (Todd, 1991). The case for focusing in Switzerland is based primarily on the fact that if English is indeed used as a lingua franca, it is being used by native speakers of a range of languages (French, German, and Italian). Since the three groups are using a language that is not native to any of them, their English may differ from native-speaker English.

While the project's interest lay partly in seeing what might have caused the shift in language use, its primary focus is on the forms that this potentially new pan-Swiss English might take. Having determined that English in Switzerland is indeed a lingua franca and is used by many nonnative speakers, the project attempted to categorize unique features of pan-Swiss English. In this chapter I report on part of the first phase of the research, namely, determining whether the linguistic practices of Swiss speakers involve using English as a lingua franca. In addition to showing to what extent English is used, the emails collected provide insight into the English of Swiss speakers. The language choices and situations found on this mailing list might then help generate predictions about how other groups will deal with similar multilingual situations.

IFMSA-CH

The Association

The association chosen for analysis of language choice on mailing lists in Switzerland is the International Federation of Medical Students' Associations–Switzerland (hereafter IFMSA-CH). As described by one of the members of the association, its "purpose is to enable international cooperation in professional training and the achievement of humanitarian ideals" (01/19/b—Italian speaker).[2] The members of the association help Swiss students find placements in other countries and organize internships (or clerkships, as they are called by the members themselves) for students from abroad. Some of the members also attend general assemblies (GAs) around the world twice a year and meet members of associations from different countries in order to organize new exchanges with them. The worldwide federation, of which IFMSA-CH is a chapter (see http://www.ifmsa.org, http://www.ifmsa-ch.org/), celebrated its 50th anniversary last year and is recognized by the United Nations as a nongovernmental, nonprofit organization. It boasts more than 80 member countries from all parts of the world; the official language of the association is English.

As in most associations, members hold various positions within IFMSA-CH. Unsurprisingly, it is the members holding the main positions, that is, president, secretary, and NEO (National Exchange Officer, who is in charge of supervising all exchanges made), who email most often. Other members either are local exchange officers (LEOs) or in charge of one of the standing committees in Switzerland. At the time of data collection, there were approximately 80 members within the Swiss branch, but only a handful of those were very active, at least on the mailing list. The presidency is quite often shared by two members. From 2000 to 2001 the presidents were an Italian speaker and a German speaker, and in 2002 the presidency was held by two native French speakers.

The universities that the members attend are either German speaking or French speaking, because Ticino, the one Italian-speaking canton, does not have its own medical school at present. Mainly, members go to a medical school in a university in which courses are taught in their native language; French speakers go to the French-speaking universities (Lausanne and Geneva), and German speakers choose the German-speaking ones. There are Italian speakers in both French- and German-speaking universities. (For this reason, in table 14.4, the Italian speakers are assigned two main languages: Italian, which is their mother tongue, and also the language they use for their studies, French or German). This does not mean that there are no medical students whatsoever who choose to go to medical school in a linguistic region other than their own; it merely appears that there were no such members within the association.

The fact that the members of the Swiss association come from three linguistic backgrounds means that they had to decide which language to use as their main language, not only on the mailing list but also at national meetings. Since it was possible to obtain data from the mailing list from the time of its inception until three years later, we can examine how these linguistic choices have taken place.

On a day-to-day basis within their local exchange offices, members are unlikely to use English with one another. Students in Lausanne or Geneva would be expected to use French, and those at the German-speaking universities would be expected to use German or Swiss German. It is only when they are communicating with one another that they would find themselves in a situation where they would need to use a lingua franca.

The Mailing List

In May 1999, IFMSA-CH began using a Yahoo! mailing list to ensure that all interested members received new information as quickly as possible. On the mailing list, members sent messages from their own account to the mailing list address, which were then forwarded to all other registered members. More messages are exchanged at times when events need to be organized (e.g., conferences) than when each local exchange office is working individually; notwithstanding this, emails are very frequent. Swiss German speakers used High German in their emails rather than their native Swiss German, because Swiss German is not generally used in writing. Although the messages are of varying lengths, ranging from a few words to many pages of reports from international meetings, there are enough longer messages that one may form an opinion of how these students use English. It should also be noted that among the most frequent writers, some do not in fact write more than a sentence or two most of the time, whereas some writers do not contribute to the mailing list very often, but when they do, it is always with extensive messages.

DATA AND METHODS

Email Collection

The total number of messages collected for this study is 996. This includes every message sent between May 1999, when the list was started, and June 2002, a total of 38 consecutive months. Thus, counting the number of messages in each language can show us the relative importance of each language.

It was decided to stop further data collection at the end of June 2002, partly because a large number of emails had already been collected, and partly because IFMSA-CH intended to change its mailing list so that, rather than having messages directed to the whole mailing list, it would be possible to send emails only to those most directly concerned. A consequence of this would be to render the need for a lingua franca less important, because the messages would no longer be directed to everyone.

For purposes of simplicity and ease of reference, emails were sorted according to the calendar year in which they were written—1999, 2000, 2001, or 2002—and then numbered one by one, with the numbers starting over each year. All messages in the archives of the Yahoo! mailing list were looked at and numbered, including those that turned out to be international messages, that is, messages sent to all the member countries and not in fact written by Swiss members. The following email is an example of the language production of the Swiss speakers.

> Hi guys, you remember at the past meeting in Bern a red *map* that "b" gave to "c", concerning the activities of SCOPH and the presentation of their activ*ity*? Well, "c" (man! such a stupid NEO!!!) has lost it somewhere. Has *anybody of* the participants of the meeting taken it home? Please, answer quickly! I need that map desperately! A lot of THANKS
> "c", NEO (01/75/c—Italian speaker). [Features deemed nonnative English are italicized ("map" is most likely from the German *Mappe*, meaning folder).]

Although only messages listed in the archives are examined in the quantitative portion of this study reported in "Results," others were added to the corpus for the analysis of linguistic features, described in the section on "Pan-Swiss English?" below. These included messages containing attachments that were not listed in the archive. Furthermore, some messages, which were replies to emails sent off the mailing list, contained the original email as well; the original emails were included in the larger corpus.

The usefulness of the mailing list in investigating language choice derives from the fact that each individual member is relatively free to decide what language to use: "I repeat: if you don't feel writing in english, but you feel like sharing something with us, please write in your language, . . . it is better that not writing anything!" (02/283/b—Italian speaker, all errors in original)

An added advantage in looking at a student association is that the students are unlikely to choose English over their native languages because of a desire to market their company or their products outside the country, as is likely the case for some of the Swiss companies that have decided to use English as their main language because of the global importance of English. The students' use of English is presumably purely determined by the fact that it is the most accessible language for all (Crystal, 1998). It is also the case that English is the language of medical science around the world.

The value of studying emails in relation to language choice is twofold. First, messages can be counted to determine which language is used most often and which ones might have been used at the start but then fell into disuse. Second, quite often members talk about language use on the mailing list, or their language use allows us to infer the reasons for specific uses, providing metalinguistic commentary on their language choices. These two aspects also determine how I present the results in this chapter: Quantitative results for the use of different languages over time are presented first, followed by discussion of individual emails that provide insights into the shift toward English.

Email Classification

In order to calculate the percentages of the use of English versus other languages, the emails were divided into four categories: messages in English, messages in French, messages in German, and a category of miscellaneous messages. The "miscellaneous" category includes messages that do not belong in the research, because they were not written by Swiss speakers (as mentioned above); messages that, for some reason, were sent twice; and messages in languages other than the three mentioned above. A few were in Italian, reflecting the fact that three of the main writers are native Italian speakers. These were primarily short, personal messages. However, the total number of messages in Italian comes to only six, so no separate Italian language category was created. There are few messages in Italian because only a small minority of Swiss people learn Italian as a second (or third) language. In contrast, native French speakers study German at school and German speakers study French.

Some messages cannot readily be classified as in a single language, in that they start off in French or German and then switch to English or vice versa. To ensure that messages containing code switching (Poplack, 1980) were not following different patterns over time from the bulk of the emails, they were considered separately. All messages were sorted into one of three groups: monolingual messages; mixed-dominant messages, where most of the message was in one language with a sentence or two in another language; and mixed-balanced messages, emails in which two (or more) languages were roughly equally represented.

RESULTS

Monolingual versus Mixed-Language Messages

Table 14.1 provides a general introduction to the data and gives the frequency of these three types of messages. In the corpus as a whole, messages containing more than one language are quite rare—only 3.5%: nearly all are

TABLE 14.1. Distribution of monolingual versus mixed-language messages over time.

Type of message	1999	2000	2001	2002	Total
Monolingual messages	97.0%	97.0%	97.0%	95.0%	96.5%
Mixed-balanced messages	—	1.0	0.3	3.0	1.1
Mixed-dominant messages	3.0	2.0	2.7	2.0	2.4
Total	100.0 (64)	100.0 (235)	100.0 (332)	100.0 (251)	100.0 (882)

monolingual, perhaps a surprising result in a multilingual country. This low percentage of mixed-language messages changed only slightly over the four calendar years studied, reaching its peak in 2002 (5%). In the data as a whole, messages in which one language is dominant are slightly more common than those in which the two are balanced, but the incidence of both categories together is extremely low. At the same time, it is worthwhile to examine mixed-language messages more closely, to see what we can learn about the emerging status of English.

"Balanced" versus Mixed-Dominant Messages

A closer analysis of the two mixed types is shown in tables 14.2 and 14.3. Table 14.2 shows that there were only 10 mixed-balanced messages, of which five merely presented the same content translated into one or more languages. In the following German/French/English example, the translation is word for word:

TABLE 14.2. Distribution of mixed-balanced bilingual or multilingual messages by languages.

Mixed-balanced messages	French/ German	English/French/ German	German/ English	English/French/ German/Italian	Total
Translation	4	1	0	0	5
Person specific	0	0	1	0	1
Other	1	1	0	2	4
Total	5	2	1	2	10

Messages classified as "translation" are those in which the additional language(s) did not provide any new information but rather merely translated the accompanying text. "Person-specific" messages are those in which the change to another language appeared to be motivated by a reference to a specific person. "Other" messages are those for which it was not possible to determine the cause of the code switch.

TABLE 14.3. Distribution of messages in two or more languages by dominant language.

Dominant language*	German + French	German + English	French + English	English + French	English + German	English + Italian	English + French + German	Total
Person specific	0	0	0	4	3	2	0	9
Other	3	2	2	4	0	0	1	12
Total	3	2	2	8	3	2	1	21

*The first language given in each column is the dominant one.

> . . . und(et) ich(je) komme(viens) auch(aussi) nach(à) basel(bâle) aber(mais) lcider(malheureusement) nur(seulement) am(au) samstag(samedi). ich(i) hoffe(hope), ihr(you) könnt(cän) mir(to me) verzeihen(forgive). "T".
> (die neue nora, die nun endlich die 84 emails gelesen hat, die sich in der militär—und ferienzeit angehäuft haben!). [02/79/T]
> [Translation: ". . . and I'm coming to Basel as well, but unfortunately only for the Saturday. I hope you can forgive me. 'T'. (the new Nora, who finally read the 84 emails that piled up while he was away in the army and on holiday!)"]

The fact that a number of emails provide the same information in more than one language underlines the extent to which the members place an emphasis on ensuring that messages are easily understood by all.

Mixed-dominant messages (tables 14.1 and 14.3) are also very infrequent in the data ($N = 21$). The code switch in many of these messages appears to have been motivated by an intention to address single comments to specific people, as illustrated in the following English-dominant message containing one French sentence (underlined):

> Dear IFMSA-CH Family, the week-end meeting is approaching, here is the list of people who will hopefully come! (I haven't heard anything from IFMSA-Lausanne, . . . "g" and "q", <u>on veut voir les photos de Malte</u> :-)
> The meeting place : Hôpital des Cadolles, Neuchâtel, it is a hospital on the hills of Neuchâtel, with magnificent view on the lake :-). . . (01/082/b)
> [Translation of French part of the message: "we want to see the pictures from Malta." "g" and "q" are French-speaking members.]

Although these messages are different from monolingual ones, the overall trend is the same: English is the language chosen most often. Of the ten balanced messages (table 14.2), five include English. The case of the dominant language messages (table 14.3) is even clearer: Out of 21 messages, 18 include some English and 14 have English as the primary language.

Because of these similarities with monolingual messages, mixed messages were later coded for the main language used in each (even in mixed-balanced messages, one language was generally used slightly more) and included in the analysis of the spread of English on the mailing list presented below. At the same time, the mixed-language emails show that a certain degree of code switching is present in communication among members and underline their sensitivity to the linguistic needs of a multilingual audience.

Change over Time

Figure 14.2 groups the data by six-month intervals, in order to show the percentage change over time more clearly. Table 14.4 provides specific results for individual speakers, as well as indicating the gender and mother language of each speaker (emailers with fewer than two messages in English were placed in the miscellaneous category).

These data show conclusively that English has superseded the other languages as the main language of email communication for this association. Over a period of about three years, English went from being used a little more than 10% of the time to more than 80% of the time, with the average percentage in English for the entire period 75% (tables 14.4 and 14.5). Whereas French once was the main language (possibly due to the fact that at the time Geneva had the most members), and German came in second, the use of

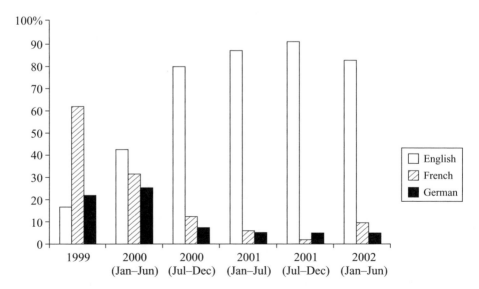

FIGURE 14.2. Spread of English over time: emails by six-month period.

TABLE 14.4. Number of emails in English by individual speaker and gender (emails in French and/or German are given in parentheses).

Speaker	Gender	Native language	No. emails 1999	2000	2001	2002 (through June)	Total	Percentage English use
a	F	Italian/German			27 (5)	39 (1)	66 (6)	92%
b	F	Italian/French	5 (7)	32 (5)	103 (2)	53 (4)	193 (18)	91%
c	M	Italian/German		44 (4)	48 (9)	22 (3)	114 (16)	88%
V	F	Italian/German			1	2 (1)	3 (1)	75%
d	F	German			5		5	100%
h	M	German	(10)	23 (11)	43 (5)	7 (1)	73 (27)	73%
m	F	German			6	7 (2)	13 (2)	87%
n	M	German			5	1	6	100%
o	M	German			7 (1)		7 (1)	88%
p	F	German			10 (1)	6 (3)	16 (4)	80%
r	F	German			5		5	100%
@	F	German	2 (5)	(5)			2 (10)	16%
e	F	French	(10)	23 (21)	5 (5)		28 (36)	44%
f	M	French		(1)	11 (3)	35 (1)	46 (5)	90%
g	F	French			6 (1)		6 (1)	86%
j	M	French			6	4	10	100%
k	M	French			5		5	100%
l	M	French		6	8		14	100%
q	F	French			2		2	100%
s	F	French			2		2	100%
u	M	French	(1)		2	5	2 (6)	25%
w	F	French			1 (1)	6 (1)	7 (2)	78%
&	M	French	3 (4)	10 (2)			13 (6)	68%
*	F	French	(15)	6 (16)			6 (31)	16%
R	F	French				5 (6)	5 (6)	45%
S	M	French				6 (1)	6 (1)	86%
M	F	French/English			2	5	7	100%
Misc.	—	(French/German/Italian)	(2)	3 (23)	1 (3)	10 (8)	14 (36)	28%
Total			10 (54)	146 (89)	296 (36)	208 (43)	660 (222)	75%

TABLE 14.5. Language of emails by native language of writer.

Native language of writer	% in English	% in French	% in German	Total
French	60	37	3	100% (262)
German	65	4	31	100% (209)
Italian	89	7	4	100% (411)
Total	75	15	10	100% (882)

French and German now seem to be similar, and English is the main language used.

The change in percentages from the beginning to the end of 2000 is especially dramatic: English changed from being the main language used to virtually the only language used. Although, as table 14.4 shows, a majority of the emails were written by a small group of people, the rest of the emailers do in fact make the same linguistic choices.

Table 14.4 also shows the extent to which individual members changed their usage. In the earliest messages, most members used their native language (or university language). However, as time went on, they used English more and more, depending on to whom they were writing, until they reached a point when they used English exclusively, answering even messages written in French or German in English. Indeed, almost all of the members who wrote in the first year as well as the second started to use English more than French or German by the second year. For example, "h" wrote 10 messages (out of 10) in German in 1999, but in 2000 wrote 23 in English and 11 in German.

There appear to be two reasons for the use of English even when answering an email in French or German. The first is that often, although the message is directed mainly to one person, it may be useful to all members of the association and should therefore be in a language all can understand. The second reason has to do with the importance of English: These emails are in many ways an ideal place for the students to practice their English language skills; moreover, as mentioned above, international assemblies of the association are conducted in English, and any communication with members from other countries at these meetings is likely to be in English. As one member wrote,

> It is important that you know that you are not "obliged" to write in english if you don't want to, and feel more comfortable in another language. *But as 'M' said it is a matter of practicity* [sic] *and speed. And you can also take it as a training to understand the language used in the international meetings and over the various*

TABLE 14.6. Language of emails by gender and native language of writer.

Gender of writer	No. of speakers	% in English	% in French	% in German	Total
Female		71	20	9	100% (503)
French	12	44	52	4	100% (149)
German	12	51	9	40	100% (86)
Italian	4	90	8	2	100% (288)
Male		81	7	12	100% (359)
French	10	81	17	3	100% (113)
German	9	76	0	24	100% (123)
Italian	2	87	6	7	100% (123)

IFMSA mailinglists (if you don't know what I am talking about, visit www.ifmsa .org) (01/283/b, emphasis original)

The president of the association provided the native languages of the emailing members of the association. Incorporating this information, table 14.5 demonstrates that English is the main language used by all three linguistic groups. At the same time, Italian speakers write in English more often than the others, probably because they do not have the option of writing in their native language. Moreover, although Italian speakers belong to a linguistic minority, they are the most frequent emailers. However, this has more to do with their importance within the association than their minority status (speakers "a", "b," and "c" held the three main positions within the association from 2000 to 2002; see table 14.4).

There are also some differences in gender, as shown in table 14.6. Female emailers are more likely to use their native tongue than are male emailers, if there is an option to do so (Italian speakers cannot do this). However, the high number of emails sent by two female members from the French-speaking part of Switzerland during the first year, one of whom was the president at the time, influenced this result, so the difference should not be considered significant.[3] The greater use of French by the female members overall, when compared to the male members, is also probably not significant, because only one female German speaker emailed in French often (six out of eight emails), and this, too, was during the first year, when many members of the association were in Geneva. Moreover, the main female Italian emailer studied in Geneva and thus would be expected to use French more frequently than German when not using English.

Tables 14.5 and 14.6 also show that when members chose not to use English, they generally used their own language and not the other main Swiss language. Italian speakers, who did not have the option to used their native language on the mailing list when they chose not to use English, generally used their "university" language.

DISCUSSION

Causes of Change

What are the reasons for the shift on the mailing list toward greater use of English over time? One possible explanation is that there was a dominant or core group of emailers who led the shift through their linguistic choices. Tables 14.4 and 14.5 show that Italian speakers contributed the largest number of messages ($N = 411$) and that they were most likely to write their messages in English.

It is not surprising that the Italian speakers used English in such high proportions. Because the Italian speakers have always been in a situation where they needed to use a nonnative language, those members would have understood first-hand the need to ensure that everyone could understand the messages. This is not because the Italian speakers could not cope with other languages. Of the three groups (within IFMSA and Switzerland in general), the Italian speakers appear to be the most multilingual. This is because in order to attend medical school, they have to take courses in one of the other national languages.

Yet English is used by all of the linguistic groups, not just by the Italians. Of all the members who emailed more than once or twice on the mailing list, only one never used English (this member is included under "misc." in table 14.4); every other member used English at some point. It is also noteworthy that most members who only used the mailing list a few times used English (e.g., speakers "d," "j," "k," table 14.4). Given these facts, it does not seem likely that it is solely because of the Italian speakers that English has become the main language used; English is the preferred language for all three language groups.

It may be the case that writing in a foreign language is advantageous in that it forces writers to use simpler language than they normally would (if only because they lack the knowledge to make use of more complicated forms), resulting in a variety of language that is easier to understand. This idea follows from the assumption that it is best for everyone to be at an equal disadvantage, since if the French speakers used French and the German speakers German, their language might be too complex for the others to understand. If both groups use English, presumably neither group will have an advantage.

The general feeling in Switzerland about the position of English vis-à-vis the Swiss national languages must have played a part in language choice, as well. IFMSA-CH's choice to use English as the main language of intranational communication is in no way unusual for the country; many Swiss companies have decided to make English, if not their main language, one of their operating languages. English is seen by many in Switzerland as a necessary tool to further oneself in society, as the decision of the canton of Zurich to make English the second language taught in schools demonstrates. Indeed, the project on pan-Swiss English has revealed many other realms where English is used by Swiss people to communicate with other Swiss nationals. The IFMSA-CH students' language choices are consistent with this trend.

As noted above, English is also the language of the medical sciences worldwide: Many of the important journals and textbooks are written in English, and even within Switzerland many medical research groups use English. In the European Union (of which Switzerland is not a member), it has even been said that "the trend of using English as the teaching medium at continental universities can be seen in almost all scientific areas. It often applies only to single courses, and occasionally to a whole degree" (Phillipson, 2003, p. 77).

Yet despite these facts, medical instruction in Switzerland is not in English. Some students can, and indeed do, manage without speaking English at all. Medical students in Switzerland attend medical school as undergraduates, whereas it is primarily in postgraduate studies that English is used in Swiss universities (Dürmüller, 2001). Even in subjects such as medicine, English is not used at the undergraduate level.

While the reasons discussed above may have influenced language selection on the mailing list, the reasons the members themselves give as to why they chose to use English suggest that in many ways the choice ultimately had more to do with language comprehension and the lingua franca function of English in Switzerland.

Language Comprehension

Evidence for the importance of English is found not only in the numbers of emails written in English, but also in what is said in those emails and how this influences language choice. The emails themselves provide a plausible explanation at the very point when English begins to be used more frequently than the other available languages. As mentioned above, one of the activities of IFMSA members is to attend the general assemblies that take place twice a year. Only eight or nine members from each country are allowed to participate, and it is important for these members to be selected early in order to book flights and make suitable arrangements. Generally, an attempt is made to send one representative from each Swiss university. In 2000, at a point when the members needed to decide who was going to the general assembly, and the president was away in New York and could not give much advice, a misunderstanding occurred because some members had already registered but found they might have to give up their place so that someone from a university with no representative could attend. The president sent the following email:

> Le deadline etait le 1er decembre ... donc je ne sais pas ce que vous voulez faire ... En gros, si Basel a deja fait le transfer on a 9 personnes plutot que 8,

mais si ce n'est pas encore le cas alors on perd notre place en plus . . . Donc si on a 8 place, je pense que soit 'h' soit 'X ' et soit 'u' ou 'e' ne peuvent pas venir . . . et que Lausanne devrait venir, mais je vous laisse decider . . . {. . .} Desolee mais pour l'instant je suis a New York donc ne peut pas beaucoup vous aider. (00/002/*)

[Translation: "The deadline was the first of December . . . so I don't know what you want to do . . . Basically, if Basel has already transferred the money we have nine people rather than eight, but if it isn't the case we lose our extra place . . . So if we have eight places, I think that either 'h' or 'X' and either 'u' or 'e' can't come . . . and that Lausanne should come, but I'll let you decide . . . {. . .} Sorry but for the moment I'm in New York so can't help you much."]

Emails went back and forth among members in French and German in an effort to sort out who was in fact registered and who should give up his or her place. Finally, a member from the university in question wrote: "it's about time that things get clear in this meeting story," and went on to summarize the events as he saw them, in English. The next few emails on this subject were in French and German. Then this member wrote again, summarizing the discussion and ending his message by saying, "Thank you for your answer, so the actual position is." This helped him clarify the position but it benefited other people as well, and other members then thanked him: "vielen dank für die aufklärung!!" (00/013/h—"Thank you for the explanation"). This indicates that the messages in French and German were not immediately understandable by both groups. When the president got back, she then began writing in English, as well: "I'll continue in English as '&' started . . . Sorry for all those strange messages, it would have been simpler if I was in Geneva and I could have phoned you but . . . life is life!" (00/016/*). She then summarized the entire discussion once again. After this episode, the member who had started using English continued to use it for most of his emails, and many of the others who had previously used English only occasionally started using it more often, as well.

Since the main change to English occurred at this time, it seems highly likely that it was in part influenced by these developments. After using both French and German, the IFMSA-CH members had to come to terms with the fact that it was difficult for the French speakers to understand all the German messages, and vice versa. English proved to be a more readily accessible foreign language for both groups. One member wrote, "well i' keep going with english, since my french is even worse." (01/257/h). In Switzerland, English is the most accessible language; speakers are able both to write it and understand it if someone else uses it, to a far greater extent than other non-native languages.

Another email is also very telling. This email followed soon after the switch to English and was sent in response to another member sending out an invitation to a national meeting in French. The subject of the message was

"Switzerland is a multilanguage-speaking country." In this message the member admonishes the others, saying, "please, next time you send a message to IFMSA Switzerland you have to write it *in english*, or to send it *both in french and german*. This thing is even more important when you're sending an official invitation for a national meeting like this one. I think you'll understand why" (00/121/c, emphasis added).

Given that the message sender was one of the very frequent emailers and consistently followed the practice he advocated, it undoubtedly influenced others. This email also raises another point: If English is not used, then both French and German are necessary. The feeling that French or German cannot be used alone is also expressed in much later emails by a member who chose not to use English, if he could avoid it: "Es tut mir leid aber ich kann nicht auf Englisch mit Schweizer kommunizieren . . . Je suis désolé, mais je ne peux correspondre avec des Suisses en Anglais" (02/147 & 148/u—"I'm sorry but I can't communicate with Swiss people in English").

Although this member says that he does not wish to use English, he does recognize that he cannot solely use one of the Swiss languages. To ensure global comprehension he must write in both. He did in fact try to send all his messages in both French and German, but he did not email very frequently, possibly because of the effort involved in producing dual-language messages. He held one of the top posts within the association, however.

Similarly, the member mentioned in example 00/121/c adds as a postscript to a message in German: "Si quelqu'un n'a pas compri mon message, je serai hereux de l'envoyer aussi en français." (01/278/c— "If someone hasn't understood my message, I will be happy to send it in French as well"). The alternative to English is two languages—democratic, but less efficient.

The Situation at Meetings

In addition to collecting emails from the IFMSA mailing list, I attended two of their national meetings and interviewed several of the members about their thoughts on language use in Switzerland.

The first meeting, in May 2002, reflected the conclusions presented in this chapter: A large part of the meeting was conducted in English, and when German was spoken, there were requests to change into another language. There were no requests to change from French when it was used; however, conversations overheard afterward suggest that French was not always readily understood by some of the German speakers.

The second meeting (October 2002) was quite different. First of all, it took place not at a local exchange office but at a high school. Second, fewer members were present, about 20 in all. Furthermore, the ratio of French to German speakers was highly in favor of the French speakers, about three to one. The outcome of this was that this meeting was conducted primarily in

French with the German speakers using German. The main speakers present at the meeting in Basel had either left the association entirely (having graduated from medical school) or simply were not present at this second meeting.

The meetings serve to remind us that the overall distribution of a group determines to a significant extent its language choices, such that in a group with considerably more German speakers than French or Italian speakers, for example, the main language will likely be German. It seems that only in roughly heterogeneous groups is English is spoken, at least within this association. This undoubtedly explains why more French was used on the mailing list at its inception, when the majority of emailers were French speaking.

I learned from language usage at the two meetings and the analysis of emails that English is used when it is important that everyone understand what is said. In smaller groups, or in emails to specific individuals, it is not as important to use English because it is easier for one speaker to ask for further explanation or clarification. These findings support the thesis that English is used as a lingua franca in Switzerland: It is used when the speakers could not otherwise make themselves understood by speaking their own languages.

Pan-Swiss English?

In the emails analyzed in this study, the main concern of the students was to get their point across, not to write perfect English. There was communicative urgency, rather than a desire to create flawless sentences, and members were quite willing to admit that sometimes their English was imperfect. When they did not know the exact word in English, they often replaced it with the corresponding one from their own language. Idiomatic forms were translated literally, sometimes accompanied by the phrase, "as we say in French/German."

Because it was necessary to ask permission from the whole of the association to use their emails in this study, the corpus contains a few emails specifically on the subject of English use, spawned by an email from the president telling them about the project and asking them to give their opinion about it. No one was against the data being used, fortunately. In fact, quite a few members were keen to see what their own special brand of English was like. This suggests that the members were aware that their English was not like the standard English they might hear in the media, but that they did not feel it was bad or incorrect, either. One person commented that he thought it was too bad that they couldn't use one of their own national languages on the mailing list, adding that the English that they used, which incorporated structures from the various Swiss languages, might in fact be a type of Swiss language itself:

> Je comprends le point de vue de "c". Man *muss* aber im fall nicht alles auf english schreiben, but it just so happens that this is what we are (naturally?)

inclined to do in order to get the widest audience and understanding at once (justement pour ne pas avoir à faire ce que tu as gentillement proposé de faire à la fin de ton message "c": traduire pour ceux n'ayant rien capté!). *The study might show that we have our own special swissicized variety of english, at which point you can wonder if it isn't also a type of national language, which combines structures, expressions and mindsets of all the other national languages, une sorte de mélange.* Whatever. Bin auch nicht gegen das projekt und finde es interessant. (01/280/M—emphasis added).
[Translation: "I understand 'c's point of view. But we don't *have* to write everything in English but {text in English} (precisely to avoid having to do what you kindly offered to do at the end of your message 'c': translate for those who didn't get it!) {text in English}, a kind of mix. Whatever. I'm not against the project and I think it's interesting."]

The English used by the IFMSA-CH members might be said, in some ways, to be its own variety, a type of "swissicized" or pan-Swiss English. From emails and other sources, it has been possible to develop a list of features that are common to most of the writers examined in this study and that are present in at least two of the three language groups. A number of features support the hypothesis that the English of the mailing list is relatively homogeneous. The use of "*informations*" or "*infos*" in place of "*information*" or "*info*" (roughly 42% of occurrences in the emails) is present in the three linguistic groups looked at. This is partly because in French, German, and Italian, "*information*" is a count noun. Another feature investigated is the overuse of the infinitive in places where a native speaker of English would use an *-ing* form (e.g., "if you want to stop to smoke," where "if you want to stop smoking" is intended).

Another characteristic is the use of items that on the surface appear to be similar to those of a native English variety (British, American, or other) but that, when examined more closely, do not always appear in the same contexts. For example, although both "will" and "going to" are used to express the future in the Swiss emails, "will" is selected more by the Swiss emailers than by native speakers (~97% of occurrences; Durham, 2003). It may be that these features are characteristic not just of pan-Swiss English but also of international English (or foreign-language English) more generally. The project also investingated to what extent these features are shared by other nonnative users of English, and which, if any, are unique to Swiss English.

CONCLUSION

While results from a single mailing list cannot be generalized to the linguistic situation in all of Switzerland, they provide suggestive clues as to why English has gained in importance as a lingua franca in Switzerland over the past few years. English appears to be the most readily understood and accepted language in mixed language groups, mainly because it is a nonnative language for all. The Italian speakers on the mailing list were at the forefront of this change, since nobody else spoke their native language and they experienced first-hand the need to ensure that people are able to understand one another.

It seems likely that the mode of communication, the mailing list, also influenced the choice of language used. As long as messages (face to face or otherwise) are mainly directed to specific people, there is no need to worry about whether an entire group understands. However, when the aim is to communicate to a broader, multilingual audience, as the Internet makes it easy to do, neither French nor German is able to serve as the main language in the Swiss context, and it becomes necessary to use English. Although it may be possible to use two or more languages for face-to-face interaction (as was demonstrated at the second meeting), it seems that in the case of email, the use of more than one language was impractical and confusing and precipitated the eventual choice of a single language, namely, English.

Undoubtedly, other groups in Switzerland have faced and will continue to face similar problems, as will multilingual groups collaborating online in other cultural contexts. They, too, may choose English as their lingua franca, facilitating cross-language communication and contributing to the increased use of English on a global scale.

Acknowledgment

An earlier version of this chapter was published in the *Journal of Computer-Mediated Communication* (volume 9, issue 1, 2003).

Notes

1. "Language Contact and Focussing: The Linguistics of English in Switzerland," research project funded by the Swiss National Science Foundation. Project Coordinators: Prof. Peter Trudgill, University of Fribourg; Prof. Richard J. Watts, University of Bern; Prof. David Allerton, University of Basel; Research Assistants: Yvonne Dröschel, University of Fribourg; Mercedes Durham, University of Fribourg; Lukas Rosenberger, University of Bern.

2. The messages are coded first for year (e.g., "01") then for message number within that year ("19"), and finally for speaker ("b").

3. Of the 78 emails sent in French by female French speakers, 62 were sent by these two members.

References

Cheshire, J., & Moser, L.-M. (1994). English and symbolic meaning: The case of advertisements in French-speaking Switzerland. *Journal of Multilingual and Multicultural Development, 17,* 451–469.

Crystal, D. (1998). *English as a global language*. Cambridge: Cambridge University Press.

Durham, M. (2003, June). *The future of Pan Swiss English*. Paper presented at the International conference on language variation in Europe 2 (ICLaVE 2), University of Uppsala, Sweden.

Dürmüller, U. (2001). The presence of English at Swiss universities. In U. Ammon (Ed.), *The effects of the dominance of English as a language of science on the non-English language communities* (pp. 389–403). New York: Mouton de Gruyter.

Dürmüller, U. (2002). English in Switzerland: From foreign language to lingua franca. In D. Allerton, P. Skandera, & C. Tschichold (Eds.), *Perspectives on English as a world language* (pp. 114–123). Basel: Schwabe.

Le Page, R. B., & Tabouret-Keller, A. (1985). *Acts of identity*. Cambridge: Cambridge University Press.

Phillipson, R. (2003). *English-only Europe: Challenging language policy*. London: Routledge.

Poplack, S. (1980). Sometimes I'll start a sentence in Spanish y termino en español: Toward a typology of code-switching. *Linguistics, 18*, 581–618.

Swiss Federal Statistics Office. (2005). Les langues en Suisse: Vers la fin du quadrilinguisme. Retrieved September 15, 2005, from http://www.bfs.admin.ch/bfs/portal/fr/index/themen/bevoelkerung/sprachen__religionen/blank/medienmitteilungen.Document.52214.html.

Todd, L. (1991). *Pidgins and creoles*. London: Routledge & Kegan Paul.

15

JANNIS ANDROUTSOPOULOS

Language Choice and Code Switching in German-Based Diasporic Web Forums

Bilingual interaction is still a neglected issue in the study of the multilingual Internet. A review of the literature suggests two main approaches, both of which adapt theories of the pragmatics of code alternation (Auer, 1995) to computer-mediated settings: (1) the study of code switching (CS) or the use of more than one language during a single communicative episode (e.g., Heller, 1988), and (2) the study of language choice, or the distribution of languages used in a bilingual or multilingual community according to factors such as participants, topic, and setting (Auer, 1998; Fishman, 1972; Li, 2000).

Work on CS in computer-mediated communication (CMC) typically draws on interactional sociolinguistics and a conversational approach to bilingual interaction (Auer, 1995; Gumperz, 1982) and investigates CS as a resource for the management of interpersonal relationships and other interactional aims. According to Georgakopoulou (1997), the aim is to examine "how, within frameworks of generic assumptions and expectations, speech communities draw upon their linguistic resources in order to maximize the effectiveness and functionality of their communication" (p. 160). Depending on setting and genre, CS in email, chat, and discussion boards has been found to contextualize shifts in topic, footing, or modality, in order to mitigate potential face threats and to perform social stereotypes (Androutsopoulos & Hinnenkamp, 2001; Georgakopoulou, 1997; Paolillo, in press; Sebba, 2003; Siebenhaar, 2005).

Studies of language choice in CMC, in contrast, operate on a macrolevel, drawing implicitly or explicitly on domain theory and the sociology of language more generally (Fasold, 1984; Li, 2000; Li, Milroy, & Pong, 1992). This work has tended to focus on the dominance of English in multilingual settings. English is found to be favored over indigenous or minority languages in situations of language shift (Paolillo, 1996; Sperlich, 2005); it participates in a new diglossic pattern of CMC among Egyptian professionals, whereby Egyptian Arabic is preferred for informal exchanges and English for formal ones (Warschauer, El Said, & Zohry, 2002, chapter 13 this volume); and it functions as the lingua franca of a multilingual professional network in Switzerland (Durham, 2003, chapter 14 this volume). In contrast to the fine-graded interactional analysis of CS, these studies provide only rough indications of the distribution of languages within individual messages, foregrounding instead their correlation with speakers, genres, or topics.

The assumption of a fixed relationship between language choice and activity type has been criticized as to its theoretical and empirical adequacy (Auer, 1995). While a general tendency of bilingual communities to prefer one language over another with respect to particular situational factors may hold true, this relationship entails ambiguities and complexities, which only a sequential examination of language alternation in interaction can illuminate. Li et al. (1992) have demonstrated that a combined micro/macro approach can be fruitful in the study of language use in bilingual communities. I suggest that this combination can be transferred to computer-mediated settings. Especially as regards the exploration of new arenas of multilingual practice, studies of language choice can provide a window into the linguistic repertoire of an online community, pinpointing contexts in which bilingual "talk" typically occurs. The micro perspective of CS in interaction will then focus on these contexts, examining how CS is creatively employed in ways that cannot be predicted in macrosociolinguistic terms.

In this chapter I examine language choice and CS in the discussion forums of diasporic websites—websites that are produced and consumed by members of diasporic communities. After a brief introduction to German-based diasporic websites and their discussion forums, I outline multilingual practices in the discussion forums in two steps: First, I establish the dominant language, that is, the language most commonly used in the forums. Second, I establish the conditions under which the base language of a forum departs from the dominant language, focusing on aspects of preference-related and discourse-related language choice (Auer, 1995). The remainder of the chapter fleshes out this outline with two case studies. The first isolates the topical organization of discussion forums and examines its influence on language choice. The second case study examines the local significance of CS, based on a conversational approach to bilingual interaction.

DIASPORIC WEBSITES ON THE GERMAN-SPEAKING WEB

The diasporic websites of interest in this chapter address members of ethnic groups that have emerged in Germany as a result of economic migration since the 1960s. Websites currently exist that are dedicated to German-based migrants from Afghanistan, Greece, India, Iran, Morocco, Pakistan, Poland, Romania, Russia, SouthEast Asia, and Turkey. These websites frame their audiences as members of an ethnic community by virtue of their names and slogans, combining an ethnic label with a term such as "portal," "community," or "forum," for example, "Indien-Portal für Deutschland," "Türkische Online-Community," "Die erste asiatische Community im deutschsprachigen Raum" ("The first Asian community in the German-speaking area"), and "Marokko Forum." This chapter focuses on three websites for the Persian, Indian, and Greek ethnic groups, respectively. The Persian website iran-now.net (formerly iran-now.de, figure 15.1) was established in 2000 and launched its discussion forum in 2002. It features a regularly updated news section and is currently the most widely known online resource for Persians in Germany. The same holds true for the Indian website theinder.net, also established in 2000. The Greek website greex. net (figure 15.2) was established in 2003 to compete with an older, larger website; it is less expanded and less popular than the Persian and Indian ones.

There is considerable variance in the audience size of diasporic websites in Germany, as measured by the number of registered users (registration is required to post messages in the forums). The three websites discussed here

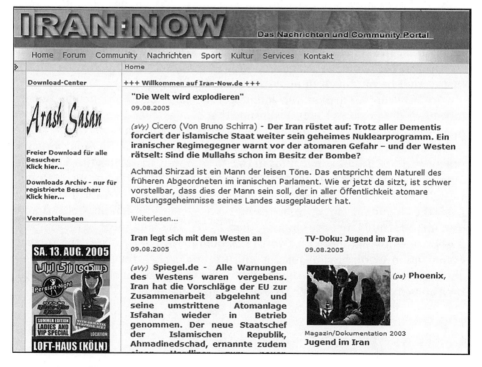

FIGURE 15.1. Iran-Now, portal for Iranian immigrants in Germany. *Source:* http://www.iran-now.de/, retrieved August 9, 2005.

FIGURE 15.2. Greex.net, discussion forum for Greek immigrants in Germany. *Source:* http://www.greex.net/, retrieved August 5, 2005.

are located in the bottom range, comprising 3,000 (Persian), 1,200 (Indian), and 600 (Greek) registered users. A Turkish website, vaybee.de, is in the top range, with approximately 370,000 registered users.[1] These differences reflect the size of the respective ethnic groups in Germany,[2] but they also partly index the popularity of a particular website in an emerging online market. In view of these figures, the cohesiveness suggested by the self-description of the websites should be viewed with caution. Their audience consists mostly of German-based adolescents and young adults from the second and third migrant generations, but it also includes some first-generation migrants and a few nonethnic members; some join from other countries, including the homeland of the diasporic group.

The production of a diasporic website is an instance of media activism, in which members of a diasporic group assume the role and responsibility of creating and maintaining a public space for fellow diasporics (Karim, 2003). German-based diasporic websites are generally commercialized, featuring advertising banners for products and services that are related to the respective ethnic group. Few can be termed a fully professional enterprise, however. The three sites discussed here are produced on a semiprofessional, nonprofit, part-time basis. Their initiators rely on a network of volunteers for content and the maintenance of discussion forums. For example, the Persian website is run by a copy shop owner in his thirties, and the Indian one by three students in their twenties.

Most diasporic websites feature edited content, albeit of varying size, quality, and updating frequency. Depending on available resources, they offer news about the homeland and the diasporic group in Germany, listings of diasporic events, relevant links, and background facts on the home culture. However, their main appeal lies in providing virtual public spaces such as discussion forums and chat channels, where diaspora members "can meet others like themselves, where they can discuss with them and negotiate their we-ness" (Goel, 2004). Participation in these spaces is primarily framed in terms of self-claimed membership in the ethnic group. While the diaspora experience and the negotiation of identity "between the poles of an original home and a newly acquired host culture" (Sinclair & Cunningham, 2000, p. 15) are not the only issues discussed in these spaces, ethnicity is the main frame in which other identity aspects are made relevant and a resource that participants frequently evoke in their various conversational topics.

Previous research on diaspora and new media has focused on what we may call "transnational diasporic networks," users who join a diasporic news-group or chat channel from all over the world, sharing a common ethnic identity but not a common geographical location (Ignacio, 2005; Karim, 2003; Lee & Sau-Ling, 2003; Miller & Slater, 2000; Paolillo, 1996; Sinclair & Cunningham, 2000). In contrast, the websites examined here are "local" with respect to the residence of the majority of their audiences and the reference system of their discourse. In these local diasporic networks, the border between online and offline encounters is fluid. The common location of the audience makes it easier for managers to recruit new volunteers, and to relate to the country's commercial Web industry. It also gives rise to the predomi-nant pattern of bilingualism on these websites, the result of contact between German and the respective migrant (home) language.

INVESTIGATING WEB FORUMS

Web discussion forums—also called bulletin boards, newsboards (Döring, 2003), or cyberforums (Sperlich, 2005)—were selected for analysis because they are the only form of user interaction available on all German-based diasporic websites. A discussion forum is a mode of public, asynchronous CMC and therefore similar to a newsgroup (Döring, 2003; Marcoccia, 2004). While newsgroups are stored on news servers and are part of the newsgroup hierarchy (http://groups.google.com; formerly Usenet), forums are part of a website and closely related to its edited content. Many forums use PHP-based software,[3] which provides a standardized architecture, detailed statistics, and options for the display of member information.

While newsgroups display a single list of all posted messages and visually indicate responding moves in a tree structure (Marcoccia, 2003), Web forums group together topically related threads. The forums examined here are organized in a tripartite scheme. The administrators install a limited number of first-level *sections* that are divided into intermediate *topic groups*, in which the forum members initiate their discussions.[4] The front page of a forum lists all its sections and topic groups, as well as the number of discussion threads and total posts within each group. Figure 15.3 displays three out of five sections in the Persian forum: Kultur (Culture), Wissenschaft (Science), and Community. Figure 15.4 is a more detailed breakdown of discussion threads within Culture, Religion, and Philosophy, one of the topic groups in the Culture section.

Although most forums permit reading by unregistered guests, site registration is required to post messages. Each registered user has a profile page where self-selected information can be displayed and is indexed in a user list that can be sorted by name, location, registration date, and total posts. Participation roles in forum discussions resemble those in newsgroups (and mailing lists), that is, core posters or hosts (Marcoccia, 2003), casual posters, and readers. Web forums are subject to far greater control by administrators than are newsgroups (Paolillo, in press). Forum administrators are entitled to delete contributions that do not conform to the forum's policy and to terminate discussions that have gone off-topic or are otherwise inappropriate.

Kultur			
Kultur, Religion und Philosophie Poesie von Hafez bis Khayyam und alle kulturellen und religiösen Themen Moderatoren Arman, Bibichanoum, minah, Peyman, Sherry, Still Alive	1023	15099	24.07.2005 - 17:19 kimiagar →D
Reise-Forum Informationsplattform für alle Iran-Reisenden Moderatoren Arman, Bibichanoum, minah, Peyman, Sherry, Still Alive	166	1230	22.07.2005 - 16:28 parvana →D
Persische Küche Alles rund um die Iranisch-Persische Küche Moderatoren Arman, Bibichanoum, minah, Peyman, Sherry, Still Alive	123	1525	21.07.2005 - 19:28 naabakhshide →D
Farsi Talk فارسی با پاس واژه Moderatoren Arman, Bibichanoum, minah, Peyman, Sherry, Still Alive	59	669	04.07.2005 - 17:29 fereshteye_darvaeee →D
Wissenschaft			
Wissenschaft und Technik Alles über Wissenschaft, Medizin und Forschung Moderatoren Arman, Bibichanoum, minah, Peyman, Sherry, Still Alive	39	193	24.07.2005 - 16:43 Q. Persi →D
Computer Hardware & Software - Fragen Moderatoren Arman, Bibichanoum, minah, Peyman, Sherry, Still Alive	209	1233	04.07.2005 - 15:21 Agha Pesar →D
Gesundheit Gesundheitstipps und mehr Moderatoren Arman, Bibichanoum, minah, Peyman, Sherry, Still Alive	118	1221	23.07.2005 - 08:04 naabakhshide →D
Schule, Ausbildung und Studium Alles über Schule, Ausbildung und Studium Moderatoren Arman, Bibichanoum, minah, Peyman, Sherry, Still Alive	120	1230	23.07.2005 - 00:09 Q. Persi →D
Psychologie und Gesellschaft Alles über Psychologie, Psychiatrie, Therapie und Gesellschaftslehre Moderatoren Arman, Bibichanoum, minah, Peyman, Sherry, Still Alive	62	1208	24.07.2005 - 14:21 Q. Persi →D
Iran-Now-Community			
Viele Grüsse... Grüße, Geburtstagswünsche und mehr! Moderatoren Arman, Bibichanoum, minah, Peyman, Sherry, Still Alive	71	974	21.07.2005 - 15:38 Ostad JY →D

FIGURE 15.3. Sections and topic groups on Iran-Now's discussion forum.

Kultur, Religion und Philosophie
Foren-Übersicht -> Kultur, Religion und Philosophie

Themen	Antworten	Autor	Aufrufe	Letzter Beitrag
Moderatoren: Arman, Bibichanoum, Sherry, Still Alive, Peyman, minah **Benutzer in diesem Forum:** Keine				
📩 Neues Thema eröffnen ✓ Alle Themen als gelesen markieren				1, 2, 3 ... 32, 33, 34 ➡
ℹ **Ankündigungen: Weisheiten** [Gehe zu Seite: 1 ... 10, 11, 12]	136	Iran-Now	3871	20.07.2005 - 21:48 Shazdeh ➡
ℹ **Ankündigungen: Fragen statt Antworten** [Gehe zu Seite: 1 ... 6, 7, 8]	95	Aran	1380	10.07.2005 - 20:36 Delkesh ➡
ℹ **Ankündigungen: ~*° Antworten °*~** [Gehe zu Seite: 1, 2, 3, 4]	38	golestan	530	16.06.2005 - 15:31 golestan ➡
📁 **FRASH KART**	3	kimiagar	33	24.07.2005 - 17:19 kimiagar ➡
📁 **Hört mal rein... *seufz* :)**	4	Sherry	27	24.07.2005 - 16:09 Sherry ➡
📁 **Informationen über den Islam** [Gehe zu Seite: 1 ... 10, 11, 12]	134	Marianne 6	1909	24.07.2005 - 15:52 minah ➡
📁 **Sadeq Hedayat über Khayyam** [Gehe zu Seite: 1, 2, 3]	33	Hormoz	274	24.07.2005 - 14:29 shekarchia music ➡
📁 **°~*Tagebuch, Gedanken und Erinnerungen*~°** [Gehe zu Seite: 1 ... 29, 30, 31]	366	Sherry	6329	24.07.2005 - 04:57 Sherry ➡

FIGURE 15.4. Threads within Kultur, Religion und Philosophie (Culture, Religion, and Philosophy) on Iran-Now's discussion forum, with number of postings and views.

Forum discussions may range from just a couple to hundreds of posts and may be sustained from several days to several weeks. Some threads remain "idle" for longer periods of time and are "revived" at specific occasions, for example, a national holiday or news on a particular subject. A discussion will often start with a series of replies to the initiating post, which sets the topic for the whole thread, and develop into stretches of interaction, as users start responding to previous posts. These interactions are the site for the management of interpersonal relationships, and their frequency is an indication of the liveliness of a community; however, they tend to get "off-topic" and therefore disrupt the coherence of a thread. As in newsgroups, forum discussions may display conversational fragmentation (Marcoccia, 2003)—simultaneous multiple conversations by several subgroups of users. Forum posts cannot be equated with conversational turns, because one post may convey two or more conversational moves, for example, reply to two or more previous messages (Herring, 1999, 2001).

The findings presented in this chapter are based on data collected from autumn 2004 to spring 2005. Drawing on methods of online ethnography (Döring, 2003, pp. 223–227; Hine, 2000; Miller & Slater, 2000), systematic observation of forum activities on the three websites was conducted. This involved browsing on a regular weekly basis through the forums' sections, locating discussions containing bilingual interaction, and using the statistics and search options of the forums. I examined lists of all posts by member (where available) to determine individual linguistic preferences and used the search function to locate fixed expressions in the home languages or relevant key words such as "language" or "language mixing." The tripartite scheme outlined above was used as a grid for the quantitative analysis of language choice, and a nonrandom sample of approximately 10 discussions from each forum was stored and printed out for sequential analysis. Background information was obtained by offline guided interviews with webmasters.

MULTILINGUAL PRACTICES IN DIASPORIC WEB FORUMS

Systematic observation reveals a broad distinction between home-language–dominant and German-language–dominant forums. In some forums, such as the Russian and the Polish ones, most discussions are carried out in the home language. The Turkish forum features separate language sections for Turkish and German. In the majority of diasporic forums, however, including the ones examined here, German predominates in most discussions.

The predominance of German in the Persian, Indian, and Greek forum seems to depend on different factors. First, it may reflect an ongoing language shift in the respective ethnic groups. Although sociodemographic data are not available, the members of these forums are overwhelmingly young second- and third-generation speakers from ethnic groups of comparatively small size in Germany, which means they have few chances of socializing offline in the home language.[5] This assumption is supported by the metalinguistic discourse of some members who point out their poor competence in the home language or comment on its loss in parts of their ethnic group (similar findings are reported by Paolillo, 1996). To what extent a lack of *written* competence in the home language inhibits its use online is an open question. Moreover, German seems to respond to aspects of ethnolinguistic diversity of the audience. This is particularly salient in the Indian forum, in which German is the common denominator of a community that consists of native speakers of Hindi, Punjabi, Bengali, and other languages of India. German, and to a lesser extent English,[6] helps sustain a national identity, which would possibly collapse with the use of various home languages by member subgroups (Goel, 2004).

Finally, the use of German in the forums mirrors its predominance in the edited sections of these websites. Interviews with site producers confirm that they consciously select German as the main language of their websites. Although there is no evidence of overt pressure by producers on members to use German in the forums, there is evidence of group pressure in favor of German in the discussions themselves. In the Indian forum, for example, users of home languages are occasionally requested to use German or English in order to be understood by everyone. In one case in the Persian forum, a speaker who switches into Persian in the course of a discussion in German is reminded to use German without any further explanation.

In sum, the dominance of German in these three forums appears to be the combined result of several factors that interrelate in specific ways in each forum: ongoing language shift in the ethnic communities, accommodation to the ethnolinguistic diversity of the member population, and producers' language preferences. However, we should be cautious in interpreting German as the "we-code" of these forums (Gumperz, 1982; Sebba & Wootton, 1998) or as a straightforward index of "German" identity. For instance, in the Persian case mentioned above, the user who reminds his fellow discussant to use German declares in the same discussion his disdain of the "hollow" German way of life.

The dominant language of a forum establishes a general frame of expectation for the base language (Auer, 2000) of particular discussions but does not completely constrain members' choices. Native alphabets—Arabic script for Persian, Devanagari (as well as scripts for other languages of India), and Greek—are replaced by romanized transliterations, called "Fenglish" by Persians (see Warschauer et al., 2002, this volume) and "Greeklish" by Greeks (see Koutsogiannis & Mitsikopoulou, chapter 6 this volume; Tseliga, chapter 5 this volume). Whether these transliterations inhibit use of the home language is outside the scope of this chapter. Crucial to our focus is the observation that the home languages are not restricted to a few isolated instances of CS, as in the Hindi and Punjabi newsgroups studied by Paolillo (1996, in press) and the Assyrian ones studied by McClure (2001). In contrast, users sometimes switch to the home language and stick to it for the rest of a discussion, or they conduct a discussion in the home language right from the start, temporarily reversing the default expectation of German and establishing the home language as the base language of interaction.

To explore further such local departures from the forums' dominant language, I draw on the sequential patterns of language choice proposed by Auer (1995, 1998, 1999, 2000). According to Auer's conversational approach, language choice in bilingual interaction is preference related, discourse related, or both. In the first case, "a speaker may simply want to avoid the language in which he or she feels insecure and speak the one in which he or she has greater competence. Yet preference-related switching may also be due to a deliberate decision based on political considerations" (Auer, 1995, p. 125). This pattern also comprises instances of "language negotiation" in which a speaker consistently opposes, or eventually aligns with, the interlocutor's language choice. In discourse-related language choice, on the other hand, switching within a conversational episode "contributes to the organization of discourse in that particular episode" (Auer, 1995, p. 125). This covers a range of well-documented functions of conversational CS such as marking reported speech, change of topic, emphasis, disagreement, specification of addressee, and use as a device for the internal organization of complex turns (Clyne, 2003; Dirim & Auer, 2004; Gumperz, 1982; Li et al., 1992).

With respect to diasporic forums, both patterns of language choice are relevant. My observations suggest that some members indeed prefer the home language throughout their forum activities; if they dominate a particular discussion, they may establish the home language as the base language of interaction. This is not just a matter of language competence. In a discourse environment dominated by German, bilinguals' decision to stick to their home language may be an instance of everyday language politics, a symbol of commitment to the ethnic identity a forum is supposed to represent (McClure, 2001). The case study described below in the section titled "Pragmatics of CS in a Forum Discussion" is illustrative of this.

Analysis of selected discussions from the Persian, Indian, and Greek forums suggests that the discourse functions of CS in diasporic forums comply with established classifications of conversational CS. The direction of the switch is generally (although not exclusively) from German to the home language. Greetings, wishes, and other formulaic uses of the home language are frequent for all diasporic forums. This is congruent with findings on switching between English–Hindi and English–Punjabi (Paolillo, 1996, in press), English–Niuean (Sperlich, 2005), English–Caribbean creole (Sebba, 2003), English–Assyrian (McClure, 2001), English–Egyptian Arabic (Warschauer et al., 2002, chapter 13 this volume), and, German–Turkish and German–Greek (Androutsopoulos & Hinnenkamp, 2001). The home language is also used to enact particular genres such as songs (Paolillo, in press), to mark obvious exaggerations as jocular (Sebba, 2003), and to mitigate face-threatening acts (Georgakopoulou, 1997). CS within a contribution sometimes marks addressee specification, responding to language choices in preceding contributions (Paolillo, in press). This evidence goes against Sperlich's (2005) claim that, in Web forums, "it is virtually impossible to say that any specific member of the . . . audience . . . has any specific influence on the code-switching of a message" (p. 75). CS in the present data is furthermore used to represent direct speech and to emphatically repeat directive or expressive speech acts. The case study further below illustrate some of these discourse functions in context.

TOPIC-RELATED LANGUAGE CHOICE
IN THE PERSIAN FORUM

Since diasporic forums are organized in sections delimited by topic, they lend themselves to a quantitative analysis of the relationship between topic and language choice (Sperlich, 2005). Bilingualism research has established topic as one of the main factors influencing language choice in bilingual communities, alongside participants and setting (Auer, 1998; McClure, 2001; Fasold, 1984; Fishman, 1972). We expect that discussion topics associated with the home country and culture tend to favor the home language, whereas topics associated with the host society favor the majority language, which is also the dominant language of the forums. This is supported by Paolillo (1996) and Sperlich (2005), who suggest that politics and technology disfavor the use of home/minority language in newsgroups and Web forums, while music and traditional poetry favor it. However, it is important to understand this as a broad tendency, not as a fixed relationship. As Gumperz (1982) points out, the association of different codes with different activities is a symbolic one and "does not directly predict actual usage" (p. 66; similarly, see Auer, 1995, p. 118).

Focusing on topic departs from usual practice in the study of bilingualism, which takes participants as the predominant factor in language choice, and examines effects of topic and setting only secondarily. My decision is motivated not only by practical necessities but also reflects the particular organization of discourse in Web forums with thousands of registered users and dozens of new contributions every day. The topical organization of Web forums is relevant to the structure of user activities. Users join the sections and topic groups that happen to be active at the moment, or they regularly join a specific section, perhaps with the expectation that certain fellow users also happen to contribute there. This study does not exclude the possibility that language use in a particular forum section is shaped by specific subgroups of users who regularly join this section; rather, it proceeds on the assumption that if there is a pattern of language choice in these forums, its relationship to topics is the most practicable way to find it out.

The relationship of language choice and topic was examined in a sample from the Persian forum, which is divided into five sections and 21 topic groups (as of March 2005). These are listed on screen in the following order: (1) Section General comprises discussions on Iran, world news, sports, politics, economics and law, and history; (2) Entertainment is devoted to music and events, movies and pictures, jokes, and ethnic radio; (3) Culture (see figure 15.3) offers topic groups on religion and philosophy, travel, Persian cuisine, and "Farsi talk," for discussions in the Persian language; (4) Science is about computers, health, psychology, and education; and (5) Community is for greetings to community members, and also includes a topic on trends and fashion.

A total of 2,084 messages from 49 discussions from all topic groups were coded for language choice, distinguishing between posts that contain *any* items in Persian, regardless of their structure and length, and, as a subset of these, posts that are completely or dominantly in Persian.[7] The difference between the two counts indicates how often Persian is limited to insertional code switches for less than half of a post, or to isolated words and expressions (e.g., proper names of any kind, borrowings, or single-word switches; no further distinction was made in this respect.). Table 15.1 presents an overview of the results. Sections and topic groups are arranged from less to more use of Persian. For instance, the third line from the top indicates that in three discussions on "health" within the Science section, 15 out of 115 posts contain Persian, but only one of these is predominantly in Persian.

TABLE 15.1. Topic-related language choice in the Persian forum (German headings translated into English and partly abridged).

Section	Topic group	No. threads	No. posts	Any Persian		Dominantly Persian	
				N	%	N	%
Science	Computers	2	79	0	0	0	0
	Technology	2	33	2	6.1	2	6.1
	Health	3	115	15	13	1	0.8
	Psychology	2	95	19	20	8	8.4
	Education	2	90	27	30	8	8.9
	Section average	11	412	63	15.3	19	4.6
General	Sports	3	127	13	10.2	1	0.7
	World	3	149	21	14.1	4	2.7
	History	2	96	39	40.6	2	2.1
	Iran	3	159	44	27.7	9	5.7
	Politics	3	143	52	36.3	22	15.4
	Economy	2	72	35	48.6	11	15.3
	Section average	16	746	204	27.3	49	6.6
Community	Trends	2	99	10	10.1	4	4
	Greetings	2	33	22	66.7	8	24.2
	Section average	4	132	32	24.2	12	9.1
Culture	Religion	3	146	41	28.1	22	15.1
	Travel	2	96	67	69.8	7	7.3
	Kitchen	3	135	100	74.1	47	34.9
	Farsi talk	3	95	79	83.1	58	61
	Section average	11	472	287	60.1	134	28.4
Entertainment	Radio	2	89	29	32.6	23	25.9
	Music	2	96	61	63.6	39	40.6
	Pictures	1	42	36	85.7	32	76.1
	Jokes	2	95	87	91.6	85	89.4
	Section average	7	322	213	66.1	179	55.6
Grand total		49	2,084	799	38.3	393	18.9

The overall frequency of posts with any kind of Persian (38.3%) suggests a strong presence of the home language in the forum. However, the frequency of predominantly Persian posts is half that much (18.9%). The average scores by section reveal significant differences across the forum.[8] In both counts, Persian is lower than average in the Science, General, and Community sections and considerably higher than average in the Culture and Entertainment sections. Only within the latter sections do predominantly Persian posts occur.

There are obvious differences by topic group within each section. In the Entertainment section, the groups Jokes and Pictures have the highest frequency of Persian and are unique in their close match between the two counts, suggesting that the activities of joke telling and posting and commenting on photographs (which, as the header of this discussion thread indicates, happen to be erotic pictures) basically take place in the Persian language. Talk about ethnic radio and music is less rich in Persian, although the proportion of predominantly Persian posts is still quite high compared to other sections. In the Culture section, the home language prevails, expectedly, in the area dedicated to Farsi and in talk about Persian cuisine. However, the gaps between the two counts point to a high frequency of Persian words and expressions related to food, religion, and places in Iran.

In the Community section, the striking difference between the two topic groups is consonant with my hypothesis. Greetings, an interpersonal and phatic activity, display a frequency of Persian that is quite close to its use in the culture and entertainment sections, whereas talk about trends and fashion has one of the lowest scores for Persian overall. In the General section, scores for Persian are lowest in discussions on sports and world news, higher in talk on Iran and its history, and highest in politics and finance. At the top end of the table, Persian is completely absent in computer talk (cf. Sperlich, 2005) and slightly present in the remaining topic groups on Science.

Despite considerable variation within sections, these findings provide some support for the hypothesis of a broad association between language and topic. Talk about the homeland and its cultural traditions, and joke telling and greeting score higher for Persian than does talk about sports and world politics, science and technology, or trends and fashion. The differences affect not only the frequency of Persian words and expressions, in part undoubtedly due to referential necessity, but also the occurrence of complete contributions in Persian. However, an examination of variance within topic groups reveals that several groups that are quite low in Persian contain discussions rich in Persian, and vice versa. A selection is given in table 15.2.

TABLE 15.2. Language choice in selected discussions in the Persian forum (German headings translated into English and partly abridged).

Section and topic group	Discussion topic	No. of posts	No. any Persian	No. dominantly Persian
Science > Education	What do you study?	48	26	8
	A question to all students	42	1	0
General > Politics	I flew from Islam	48	9	0
	Does Islam give love?	48	6	0
	Niveau	47	37	22
Culture > Farsi talk	Loftan Faghat Farsi!	70	57	51
	Shahnameye ferdosi!	13	12	7
	The Persian language	12	10	0

The two threads in the education group have a similar subject and an almost equal number of posts, yet Persian is virtually absent from the first and well above group average in the second. Two out of three discussions on politics contain no dominantly Persian posts at all; this is consonant with findings by Paolillo (1996) and Sperlich (2005). Yet in the third one, Niveau ("Level of discussion"), almost half of the posts are in Persian. In the "Farsi talk" area, posts in Persian predominate in two out of three discussions but are completely absent from the third, the subject of which is phrased in German. A detailed examination explains these differences in terms of shifts in topic and footing. In the Farsi talk area, posts *in* Persian are absent in talk *about* Persian. Niveau is a heated argument about the level of discussions in the forum. Significant differences in the distribution of Persian by section and topic group notwithstanding, these data challenge the notion of an unambiguous association between language choice and discussion topic. The distribution of German and Persian is not fully determined by placement of a discussion in a particular topic group but is negotiated by participants, in ways that only a detailed examination of code alternation in its sequential context can reveal.

PRAGMATICS OF CS IN A FORUM DISCUSSION

I now examine a discussion from the Greek forum, to demonstrate how CS into the home language fulfills different discourse and preference-related functions for different speakers, including the negotiation of the language of interaction.

The overall dominance of German in this forum is due both to its being preferred by ethnically Greek members and to the participation of a few non-Greek members who have an interest in Greece or personal relationships with Greeks but are themselves not competent in Greek. The need to accommodate "foreigners" is not met with general acceptance, and some complain that not enough Greek is used in this forum. This tension is part of the group's background knowledge and is indexed by CS in a part of the discussion thread examined here.

This thread was initiated by the webmaster, who has modified some technical features of the forum and now seeks feedback from the community. The excerpt presented here is the first half of the full thread and occurred over nine days. Although Greek does not become the base language of interaction at any time, several posts in Greek occur, as well as some insertional switches within German posts, for example, an addressee specification in (24). Greek is first used in (2), right after the webmaster's initiative move, and again in (10) by the webmaster himself.[9]

    (1)   Webmaster
VOTING NEU GESTARTET!
Da die alte Umfrage nicht besonders repräsentativ ausgefallen ist, starten
wir das Voting erneut! Diesmal gibt es ja auch auf der Startseite einen

*kleinen Hinweis darauf! ;-) Wer will kann zusätzlich zu seiner Stimme auch
gerne einen Kommentar schreiben!*
"VOTING RESTARTED!
We're restarting our voting, because the old voting wasn't quite representative. This time there's a small notice on the homepage! ;-) Feel free to post
a comment besides your vote!"
(2)   Angel
Ftou kai ap'tin arxi! :-)
"Once again the same thing! :-)"
[Posts 3 through 6 omitted.]
(7)   Dennis
und habe ich jetzt was gewonnen? 8-) und was ist es?
"now did I win anything? 8-) and what is it?"
(8)   Fay
eine woche all inclusive mit dem webmaster fidchi-inseln :-) :-) :-)
"a week all inclusive on Fiji islands with the webmaster :-) :-) :-)"
(9)   Dennis
cool :-) also habe ich bald urlaub?
wo ist der webmaster? und die blumen?
"cool :-) that means I'll be on vacation soon?
where's the webmaster? and the flowers?"
(10)   Webmaster
Pame pareoula i protimas na fero kamia Webmeisterin? :-)
"Shall we go together or do you want me to bring along any female
webmaster? :-)"

While the webmaster's initial announcement is in German, Angel uses
Greek to disapprove of the voting. Since she prefers German in other discussions, a preference-related choice of Greek can be ruled out. Because disap-
proval is clearly the dispreferred response here (Levinson, 1983), the switch
seems to mitigate the potential face threat to the webmaster, foregrounding
a reading of the utterance as "playful rejection," enhanced by a laughing
emoticon.

Most subsequent switches are rooted in an off-topic discussion that starts
in posts (7) through (9), when two regulars, Fay (female) and Dennis (male),
playfully reframe the voting as a winning game. Dennis asks whether he has
won anything by voting (7). Fay suggests a fictional prize, a holiday with the
webmaster (8). Dennis accepts the scenario and elaborates it (9). While this
is all done in German, in (10) the webmaster addresses Dennis in Greek,
asking about his preferred company on the holiday trip. Taken at face value,
the webmaster ratifies the holiday plan. However, his choice of Greek is
marked both with respect to the language of the preceding turns and his usual
"voice" as webmaster, which is German. I suggest that the choice of Greek
marks the propositional content of this post as fictional, as part of the holiday
scenario. Greek therefore contextualizes a switch into a fictional, playful
modality.[10]

The community continues to elaborate the holiday scenario in (11) through (20). Greek appears again in the following extract from (21) through (28), in a dialogue between Fay and another regular male, Insatiable, and in two contributions by Mr_Magic:

(21)   Insatiable
ich will auch, bitte bitte . . . darf ich ? tha eimai ganz lieb ["devilish" emoticon]
"I want too, please please . . . may I? I'll be very endearing ["devilish" emoticon]"

(22)   Fay
was willst du? mit dem webmaster auf die fidschi-inseln??
"what do you want? join the webmaster on the Fiji islands?"

[Post 23 omitted]

(24)   Insatiable
fay ich glaube du bist einfach nur neidisch weil du nicht mit kommen kanst . . . . . oso gia sena dennis [refers to #23] deine ideen sind superspitzemegaultrageil . . . . insel ohne frauen ist kaffe ohne koffein oder so . . . .;-)
"fay I think you're just jealous because you can't come along . . .
as for you dennis [refers to #23] your ideas are super-duper . . .
an island without ladies is like coffee without caffeine . . . .;-)"

[Post 25 omitted]

(26)   Fay
*Insatiable, wieso sollte ich neidisch sein? und vor allem worauf? *kopfkratz* *grübel**
"Insatiable, why should I be jealous? and above all, of what? *scratches head* *wonders*"

(27)   Mr_Magic
An kai imaste endelos "off topic"—Thelo kai egooooooooooooooooo! :-)
"Although we're completely "off topic" – I want too! :-)"

(28)   Mr_Magic
   Insatiable wrote:
   (quote of 24)
   E, normal pou tha sou aresoun teteies idees esena!
   Afou ise Mutschi! :-)
"Well, [it's] normal you'd like this sort of idea!
You're a Mutschi! :-)"

Let us first consider the use of Greek in (21) and (27). These posts have the same communicative intent—they convey in an expressive manner the users' wish to join the fictitious holiday trip. In (21), Greek occurs as an insertional switching. The first two clauses of this turn (expression of desire, request for permission) are in German; the third clause (promise of good conduct) switches into Greek for the verb phrase and returns to German for the adjective phrase. In (27), Mr_Magic's turn is entirely in Greek (except for *off-topic*, which can be viewed as a borrowing). A look at other posts by these speakers suggests frequent use of Greek and fondness for switching and mixing. However, their use of Greek here is not entirely preference related, but has a discourse function: to signal their alignment to the webmaster's jocular approval of the holiday scenario in (10). By choosing Greek, in full or in part, speakers contextualize their messages as part of the same fictional frame.

The second post by Mr_Magic (28) is in Greek, interspersed with two German insertions. He quotes Insatiable's post in (24), qualifies his ideas as "normal," and calls him *Mutschi*, a German female nickname, the contextual meaning of which is unclear. I read this as a jocular attack, which signals by code choice that the face-threatening act posed by the evaluation of the addressee's statement and his labeling with a female nickname is to be taken as nonserious. Again, CS joins with an emoticon to signal playfulness.

Up to this point, the use of Greek is discourse related. However, this changes in the remainder of the excerpt, as Greek becomes itself the focus of attention. In (29), Fay shifts to a metalinguistic level by complaining about Mr_Magic's language choice in the previous posts.

(29)   Fay
*hey,Mr_*
du weißt genau,daß ich net so gut griechisch kann
mennooooooooooooooooo
"hey Mr_
you know perfectly well that my Greek is not that good
gosh!"
[30]   Mr_Magic
Aaaaa, na matheis! :-P
"Well, then learn some! :-P"
[31]   Fay
na danke . . . . ["devilish" emoticon]
"thanks indeed . . . ["devilish" emoticon]"
[32]   Insatiable
hei mr. Magic du kennst mich doch ich kann ohne nicht leben (ich heisse nicht um sonst "insatiable":-)
@fay
allh fora tha sou grafo mono ellhnika muahahahaha . . . .
"hey Mr. Magic you know me, I can't live without (that's why my name's "insatiable" :-)
@fay
next time I'll write to you in Greek only hehehe
[33]   Fay
ich sag jetzt nix mehr
"I'm not saying anything more."

Fay frames her post as a protest with an attention-getter, *hey*, that has adversative meaning in German, and rounds it off with an interjection that conveys irritation. She explicitly refers to her poor competence in Greek and to knowledge of this fact by her interlocutor (the adverb *genau*, "precisely," increases the force of this reminder). There follow two adjacency pairs between the two males who address Fay in Greek, while she replies in German. Mr_Magic urges her to learn Greek (30), and Insatiable promises to address her only in Greek in the future (32). This is a remarkable instance of addressee specification, in that Insatiable selects German for his fellow coethnic and Greek for its nonspeaker, Fay. Both Insatiable and Mr_Magic mitigate their aggression with paralinguistic devices, simulating sticking out a tongue via an emoticon in (30) and laughter in (32), thereby demonstrating that they are making fun of Fay, who responds to the first attack with ironic thanks (31) and explicitly quits the conversation in (33).

These are participant-related switches to the extent that they reflect the current speaker's awareness of the linguistic competencies of the recipient (Dirim & Auer, 2004). Both propositionally and by CS, these speakers reject Fay's incompetence in Greek, evoking tension between the predominantly German-speaking reality of this forum and expectations that result from its ethnic alliance. Fay is a native German, a fact that is well known among forum regulars. Her protest occurs precisely at a point where Greek could turn into the base language of interaction, and evokes norms of democratic participation in CMC: Being a regular, she has the right to be addressed in a language she knows well. In contrast, the language choice of Insatiable and Mr_Magic evokes what they presumably perceive as a "natural" link between language and the ethnic character of the forum. Their use of Greek is a symbol of their resistance to the factual dominance of German. In episodes such as this, CS becomes a resource for the negotiation of language norms in a way that no quantitative analysis of language choice can capture.

DISCUSSION AND CONCLUSIONS

Diasporic websites are an increasingly popular mode of CMC in diasporic communities in Germany. They attract second- and third-generation diasporics and integrate online interaction with edited content in ways that go far beyond newsgroups. They must therefore be taken seriously in considering how the Internet is appropriated for the construction of diasporic identities and how it reflects the diversity of societal bilingualism. In this chapter I have presented an exploratory analysis of language use in the discussion forums of three German-based diasporic websites and argued for an integration of quantitative and qualitative methods in the sociolinguistic study of bilingual CMC.

Language use in diasporic online practices is structured in complex ways, the overall predominance of the home language or German depending on the historical depth of migration, the size of an ethnic community, and the audience and policies of each diasporic forum. The predominantly German-speaking forums studied here inevitably raise the question of language maintenance (McClure, 2001; Sperlich, 2005). These forums contribute to the maintenance of home languages to the extent that they provide ample opportunities for use online. Evidence suggests that not only is CS into home languages widespread in these forums, but members also establish niches, as in the Persian case, in which the home language regains dominance. At the same time, the home language undergoes transformations, the most visible aspect of which is its romanized transliteration. The possible effects of this on the literacy skills of young diasporics ultimately depend on their use of the home languages outside the Internet, a consideration outside the scope of this chapter.

The case study of the Persian forum illustrates the usefulness and limitations of a quantitative approach to language choice. Auer (1995) argues that migrant communities in Europe "are too young and culturally unstable to have developed shared norms of language choice" (p. 127). Yet the findings of this chapter suggest a tendency to favor the home language for particular forum activities, while warning against treating this tendency as fixed or restrictive. I see no contradiction in assuming that participants have broad expectations as to where in a given forum the home language is more likely and appropriate yet feel free to depart from this pattern to meet the dynamic requirements of unfolding online interactions.

It was suggested that bilingual "speech" in diasporic forums is comparable to conversational CS in terms of its typical discourse functions. This is not surprising, since forum discussions consist of verbal interactions. What might be surprising is the amount and functional diversity of CS in this asynchronous mode of CMC. Paolillo (in press) predicts that interactional CS will be more frequent in synchronous modes of CMC, because they are more conversationlike than asynchronous ones. Whether this is the case for online diasporic discourse in Germany remains to be investigated. However, unlike the Indian and Punjabi newsgroups studied by Paolillo, diasporic forums in Germany are not restricted to fixed uses of the home language, but contain many instances of interactional CS. Moreover, other cases of rich CS in asynchronous CMC have been documented (Georgakopoulou, 1997; Sebba, 2003). It therefore seems that in addition to interactivity, factors such as the strength of the home language in the repertoire of a user population, the nature of users' relationships, and the discourse genres they engage in are also decisive for the frequency and function of bilingual talk on the Internet.

Classifications of the discourse functions of CS in the forums offer a valuable point of entry into the functions of CS in a community and allow for much-needed comparisons across computer-mediated settings and speech communities. However, the interactional meaning of CS emerges in its sequential context (Auer, 1995). Therefore a sequential analysis is required that takes into account details such as the precise direction of switch, "the place *within* the interactional episode in which languages alternate" (Auer 1998, p. 3), the way switches align to previous code choices by other speakers (Georgakopoulou, 1997), and the way they index participants' background knowledge and language norms.

I examined these issues in a sequence from the Greek forum, in which playfulness is the most conspicuous aspect of home language use. By choosing Greek, participants signal that their utterance should be understood as non-serious, as part of a play frame. In particular, Greek contextualizes contributions as nonthreatening to recipients (jocular attacks, bold disapprovals) and noncommitting to speakers (e.g., the ratification of and subsequent wishes to join the fictitious holiday trip). This parallels the playful use of stylized Jamaican Creole (Sebba, 2003), the use of Egyptian Arabic for humorous or sarcastic expressions within English messages (Warschauer et al., 2002, Chapter 13 this volume), and the use of English and varieties of Greek to signal a shift from a professional to an informal frame of interaction, as well as to mitigate face-threatening acts (Georgakopoulou, 1997). While CS has not previously been discussed in studies of playfulness in CMC (Danet, 2001; Danet, Ruedenberg-Wright, & Rosenbaum-Tamari, 1997), it fits well with what Danet et al. (1997) identified as play with frames of interaction. More specifically, the switches into Greek in this excerpt frame as playful portions of a forum discussion that is not ordinarily intended as such. However, explicitly playful discussions do occur in diasporic forums, and it would be interesting to examine the kinds and functions of CS that occur in them.

In conclusion, this chapter suggests that it is fruitful to combine language choice and CS analysis in the exploration of multilingual practices in CMC. While sequential analysis is essential for understanding the pragmatics of CS, the language choice approach provides the "big picture" and prepares the ground for analysis of particular online interactions. Often studied separately, their combination can contribute to a more coherent picture of the multilingual Internet.

Notes

1. These figures are based on manager information and Web statistics, as of December 2004. The number of registered users does not reliably reflect the effective number of active participants.

2. According to the German Federal Statistical Office, 39,000 Indian, 65,000 Persian, 315,000 Greek, and 1,765,000 Turkish citizens lived in Germany in 2004. These figures do not include naturalized first- or second-generation individuals. From Statistisches Bundesamt, http://www.destatis.de/basis/e/bevoe/bevoetab10.htm, retrieved December 3, 2006.

3. Widely used Web forum software packages include these from phpbb.com and vbulletin.com (retrieved July 25, 2005).

4. "Section" and "topic group" are etic rather than emic labels; participants' naming practices are variable and ambiguous; for example, "forum" is used both for the whole forum and its parts.

5. In contrast, the strong presence of Turkish in the Turkish forum corresponds to a high level of home language maintenance in the German-Turkish community, supported by its size and the resulting density of everyday contacts with coethnics (Dirim & Auer, 2004).

6. Many members of the Indian forum are fluent in English, an official language in India; however, it is much less frequent than German; see Paolillo (1996, in press) on the predominance of English in Indian and Punjabi newsgroups.

7. Although I acknowledge that this is a crude distinction from a conversational analysis perspective, it is inevitable for a quantification of this kind; Sperlich's (2005) Web forum analysis, for instance, distinguishes between "English with Niuean greetings" and "English and Niuean."

8. A chi-square test performed on table 15.1. is highly significant ($\chi^2 = 54.21$, $p < 0.001$, 4 df).

9. In the following excerpts, each post is followed by an English gloss, and Greek is underlined throughout. All screen names have been anonymized; original spelling has been kept throughout; the graphic emoticons used in this forum are replaced by typographic smiley equivalents, unless otherwise indicated.

10. The German word *Webmeisterin* ("female webmaster") is a neologism that perhaps enhances playfulness.

References

Androutsopoulos, J., & Hinnenkamp, V. (2001). Code-Switching in der bilingualen Chat-Kommunikation: Ein explorativer Blick auf #hellas und #turks. In M. Beißwenger (Ed.), *Chat-Kommunikation* (pp. 367–402). Stuttgart: Ibidem.

Auer, P. (1995). The pragmatics of code-switching: A sequential approach. In L. Milroy & P. Muysken (Eds.), *One speaker, two languages* (pp. 115–135). Cambridge: Cambridge University Press.

Auer, P. (1998). Introduction. Bilingual conversation revisited. In P. Auer (Ed.), *Code-switching in conversation* (pp. 1–24). London: Routledge.

Auer, P. (1999). From code-switching via language mixing to fused lects: Toward a dynamic typology of bilingual speech. *International Journal of Bilingualism, 3*(4), 309–332.

Auer, P. (2000) Why should we and how can we determine the "base language" of a bilingual conversation? *Estudios de Sociolingüística, 1*(1), 129–144.

Danet, B. (2001). *Cyberpl@y: Communicating online.* New York: Berg. Companion website: http://pluto.mscc.huji.ac.il~msdanet/cyberpl@y.

Danet, B., Ruedenberg-Wright, L., & Rosenbaum-Tamari, Y. (1997). "Hmmm . . . where's that smoke coming from?" Writing, play and performance on Internet Relay Chat. *Journal of Computer-Mediated Communication, 2*(4). Retrieved September 15, 2005, from http://jcmc.indiana.edu/vol2/issue4/danet.html.

Dirim, I., & Auer, P. (2004). *Türkisch sprechen nicht nur die Türken.* New York: de Gruyter.

Clyne, M. (2003). *Dynamics of language contact.* Cambridge: Cambridge University Press.

Döring, N. (2003). *Sozialpsychologie des Internet.* 2nd ed. Göttingen: Hogrefe.

Durham, M. (2003). Language choice on a Swiss mailing list. *Journal of Computer-Mediated Communication, 9*(1). Retrieved December 15, 2005, from http://jcmc.indiana.edu/vol9/issue1/durham.html.

Fasold, R. (1984). *The sociolinguistics of society.* Oxford: Blackwell.

Fishman, J. (1972). Domains and the relationship between micro- and macro-sociolinguistics. In J. J. Gumperz & D. Hymes (Eds.), *Directions in sociolinguistics* (pp. 435–453). Oxford: Blackwell.

Georgakopoulou, A. (1997). Self-presentation and interactional alignments in email discourse: The style- and code switches of Greek messages. *International Journal of Applied Linguistics, 7*(2), 141–164.

Goel, U. (2004) *The virtual second generation. On the negotiation of ethnicity on the Internet* (research project outline). Retrieved September 15, 2005, from http://www.urmila.de/UDG/Forschung/forschungindex.html.

Gumperz, J. J. (1982). *Discourse strategies.* Cambridge: Cambridge University Press.

Heller, M., Ed. (1988). *Codeswitching.* Berlin: de Gruyter.

Herring, S. C. (1999). Interactional coherence in CMC. *Journal of Computer-Mediated Communication, 4*(4). Retrieved December 15, 2005, from http://jcmc.indiana.edu/vol4/issue4/herring.htm.

Herring, S. C. (2001). Computer-mediated discourse. In D. Schiffrin, D. Tannen, & H. Hamilton (Eds.), *The handbook of discourse analysis* (pp. 612–634). Oxford: Blackwell.

Hine, C. (2000). *Virtual ethnography.* London: Sage.

Ignacio, E. N. (2005). *Building diaspora: Filipino community formation on the Internet.* New Brunswich, NJ: Rutgers University Press.

Karim, K. H. (Ed.). (2003). *The media of diaspora. Mapping the globe.* London: Routledge.

Lee, R. C., & Sau-Ling C. W. (Eds.). (2003). *Asian America.Net: Ethnicity, nationalism, and cyberculture.* New York: Routledge.

Levinson, S. C. (1983). *Pragmatics.* Cambridge: Cambridge University Press.

Li, W. (2000). Dimensions of bilingualism. In W. Li (Ed.), *The bilingualism reader* (pp. 3–25). London: Routledge.

Li, W., Milroy, L., & Pong, S. C. (1992). A two-step sociolinguistic analysis of code-switching and language choice. *International Journal of Applied Linguistics, 2*(1), 63–86.

Marcoccia, M. (2003). On-line polylogue: Conversation structure and participation framework in Internet newsgroups. *Journal of Pragmatics, 36,* 115–145.

McClure, E. (2001). Oral and written Assyrian-English codeswitching. In R. Jacobson (Ed.), *Codeswitching worldwide II* (pp. 157–191). Berlin: Mouton de Gruyter.

Miller, D., & Slater, D. (2000). *The Internet: An ethnographic approach.* Oxford: Berg.

Paolillo, J. C. (1996). Language choice on soc.culture.punjab. *Electronic Journal of Communication, 6*(3). Retrieved December 3, 2006, from http://ella.slis.indiana.edu/~paolillo/research/paolillo.publish.txt.

Paolillo, J. C. (in press). "Conversational" codeswitching on Usenet and Internet Relay Chat. In S. C. Herring (Ed.), *Computer-mediated conversation.* Cresskill, NJ: Hampton Press.

Sebba, M. (2003). "Will the real impersonator please stand up?" Language and identity in the Ali G websites. *Arbeiten aus Anglistik and Amerikanistik, 28*(2), 279–304.

Sebba, M., & Wootton, A. J. (1998). We, they and identity: Sequential vs. identity-related explanation in code-switching. In P. Auer (Ed.), *Code-switching in conversation* (pp. 262–289). London: Routledge.

Siebenhaar, B. (2005). Varietätenwahl und Code Switching in Deutschschweizer Chatkanälen. *Networx, 43.* Retrieved September 15, 2005, from www.mediensprache.net/de/websprache/networx/docs/index.asp?id=43.

Sinclair, J., & Cunningham, S. (2000). Go with the flow: Diasporas and the media. *Television and New Media, 1*(1), 11–31.

Sperlich, W. B. (2005). Will cyberforums save endangered languages? A Niuean case study. *International Journal of the Sociology of Language, 172,* 51–77.

Warschauer, M., El Said, G. R., & Zohry, A. (2002). Language choice online: Globalization and identity in Egypt. *Journal of Computer-Mediated Communication, 7*(4). Retrieved September 15, 2005, from http://jcmc.indiana.edu/vol7/issue4/warschauer.html.

16

ANN-SOFIE AXELSSON, ÅSA ABELIN, AND RALPH SCHROEDER

Anyone Speak Swedish?

Tolerance for Language Shifting in
Graphical Multiuser Virtual Environments

More and more people are spending time in Internet-based multiuser virtual
environments (VEs). English is still the main language in these environments, as on the Internet generally (Crystal, 2001). But as more and more
people gain access to the Internet, nationalities and languages increasingly
meet. The aim of the study described in this chapter was to investigate how
different national languages meet and interact in Active Worlds (AW), a VE
that enables interaction between users in a three-dimensional computer-
generated virtual environment,[1] and to examine the influence of the medium
on language encounters. The most central question we address in this chapter
is whether Internet-based VEs of this kind offer an accepting and tolerant
environment, whether people can use their native language in interaction with
others, or whether they are generally compelled to use English, as is the case
in many international offline contexts. We investigated the circumstances in
which participants use a language other than English and the mechanisms
behind language tolerance in Internet-based VEs.

We begin with an overview of issues concerning language use in various
international offline and online contexts. We then provide details of the
context of our study and present our method and the examples of language
encounters that we analyzed. Finally, we discuss our findings and draw some
general conclusions.

LANGUAGE USE OFFLINE AND ONLINE

There is little doubt that English is the dominant language in the world today.
Even though native Mandarin Chinese speakers outnumber native speakers

of English, English is dominant among those who speak it as a second, third, and fourth language. How English became the world's leading language is a complex story that cannot be discussed here. Suffice it to say that it is the leading language wherever people from all over the world meet, communicate, and exchange ideas: in political debates, at scientific conferences, in the media, as well as more widely in popular culture (Crystal, 1997; Phillipson, 1992). However, as several linguists have pointed out (Fishman, 1998–1999; Graddol, 1997; Schiffman, 1996), the dominance of English in today's world is not absolute. Many national as well as regional languages are becoming strengthened with and without institutional support. Nonetheless, even if some languages are experiencing a revival, there is little doubt that the use of English is becoming more widespread.

There are, of course, a number of advantages to having a global language: speedier communication, easier access to information, and fewer misunderstandings. However, there are also disadvantages: Non-English speakers need to express themselves in a language other than their first language, while native English speakers can express themselves in their mother tongue. From the individual's point of view, the consequences of this situation may seem fairly insignificant. However, as Tsuda (2000) points out, the hegemony of English has more serious implications. Language is not a commodity, a tool of communication, Tsuda argues, but an environment where people live, think, and express themselves. Therefore, when people are deprived of their native language, they are deprived of their informational environment and their human dignity: "They become, in a sense, mute, deaf, and blind. They may be there physically, but are treated as invisible, and are easily ignored" (p. 35). Moreover, Tsuda points out that, on a macrolevel, since language and culture are closely intertwined, the dominance of the English language also means dominance of Anglo-American culture over other cultures.

The early days of the Internet were dominated by English, but as Fishman points out (Fishman, 1998–1999; see also Crystal, 2001), the question is, How long will this dominance last? With an increasing number of non-English Web users[2] and more advanced technology for translation and access to languages other than English,[3] Crystal foresees a multilingual Internet. Yet, as he also points out, English will probably continue to be the most common language online for some time, because it is the most commonly understood language.

Previous Studies of Text-Based Computer-Mediated Communication

Numerous studies in the last 20–25 years have shown that computer-mediated communication (CMC) differs from face-to-face communication. Research on CMC has mainly focused on such issues as the absence of contextual, social, and other nonverbal cues (Hiltz, Johnson, & Turoff, 1986; Johansen, Vallee, & Spangler, 1979; Kiesler, Siegel, & McGuire, 1984), which may foster difficulties in coordination and feedback, problems in reaching group consensus, and so forth. However, the lack of nonverbal cues and the like could also be argued to have positive effects, such as a higher degree of informality and status equalization in CMC compared to face-to-face situations (Hiltz et al., 1986; Kiesler et al., 1984; Misztal, 2000). Synchronous CMC has also been characterized as having traits similar to both spoken and written communication (interactive, and at the same time written) (Du Bartell, 1995; Werry, 1996; Yates, 1996). These features, together with the technical conditions provided by the medium (e.g., keyboard layout, the unlimited number of messages that can be sent at low cost), have given rise in CMC to some unique characteristics, such as the use of iconic signs, smileys, and other means of expressing emotions and nonverbal communication.

Language in Internet-Based Graphical VEs

More recently, several studies of online systems (both text based and graphical) have focused on language as an important component of social interaction (e.g., Allwood & Schroeder, 2000; Cherny, 1999; Herring, 1999; Smith, Farnham, & Drucker, 2002). Allwood and Schroeder (2000), who investigated language in AW, found that much of the communication in AW is taken up by greetings and that English (including English spoken by non-English speakers) is by far the most common language used. The fact that so much communication consists of greetings and questions about where other users come from and what languages they speak is due partly, according to Allwood and Schroeder, to the "cocktail party" nature of the VE conversation (people constantly coming and going) and partly to the medium in which (explicitly verbal) background information about other users has to compensate for the absence of social cues.

Allwood and Schroeder's findings are relevant here, because the language encounters that we describe take place in a VE in which English is dominant, and language introductions in AW are often equivalent to greetings. Since AW began in 1995, many virtual worlds have been created within the system, including some that cater to speakers of non-English languages (the worlds "German," "Wien," and "Russia," to mention a few). In most places, however, non-English languages are mainly spoken where non-English speakers have congregated or "found" each other. AW can therefore best be described as a cosmopolitan cocktail party in English, with pockets of non-English speakers.

Apart from interest in the textual nature of online communication, there have also been more recent studies focusing on graphical aspects of the VE medium (e.g., graphical user representation, limited body language, and the meaning of the spatial metaphor for the interaction) and their influence on interaction and communication behavior (Becker & Mark, 2002; Jeffrey & Mark, 1999; Salem & Earle, 2000). Becker and Mark argue, for example, that the available functionality for representations and communication in a VE (e.g., avatar appearance, possibilities of moving around and communicating) affect the expression of social conventions, which in turn influences the behavior of users. These conclusions are also relevant to our study, since we argue that the functionality of the medium has an effect on language encounters, and on the consequences of those encounters.

The Context of This Study

In recent years social scientists, communication researchers, and computer scientists have become increasingly interested in interaction and communication in Internet-based graphical VEs. This interest is largely because these systems have attracted a large number of people who spend a lot of time in these types of VEs, environments that partly resemble ordinary offline life but also profoundly differ from it in terms of social manners and interactional patterns (see the essays in Schroeder, 2002). AW can be defined as a "social," as opposed to a task-oriented, VE. This is because, although activities take place apart from pure socializing (e.g., education, religious activity, shopping), the main activity in AW is to socialize—to hang out with people, chat, and make new friends.

AW consists of more than 700 interlinked virtual worlds that are typically used by between 100 and 200 users at any time of the day. Communication in AW is mainly text based, but since participants are represented by avatars (three-dimensional representations of themselves via which they can have a first-person perspective on the VE),[4] they can also use a selection of movements and gestures (e.g., jump, wave, happy, angry) to communicate. The VE itself—the graphical environment where users meet and interact—also has a communicative function, since it is a geographical place in which movement is a part of the communicational act (avatars can walk away, come closer, hide, etc.).

This study is an attempt to investigate how participants in AW interact with respect to language use. The main purpose of the study relates to our discussion of offline and online language dominance—to determine whether language minorities are typically accepted or rejected by the language majority, and under what circumstances a minority language is accepted or rejected. Aspects investigated include the type of majority language (English or non-English), the character of the setting (cosmopolitan, language-specific, or themed), and the perceived intention of the language-introducing user (e.g., to establish contact with other users, to initiate language play, or to disturb the ongoing conversation). We also wanted to find out the social consequences of a rejection due to language.

In what follows, we distinguish between "majority language,"[5] which refers to the language of the encounter, and "main language," which refers to the language that is typically used in the world in which the encounter takes place. The "majority language" in each situation may not be English but, rather, the language in which the dominant conversation in each observed language encounter situation is held. We define "main language" as the language in which the world owner or administrator communicates with visitors in the welcoming message, on billboards, in object descriptions, and so forth. In what we call "cosmopolitan settings," the main language is English, but in what we call "language-specific settings" the main language is usually a non-English language (e.g., Spanish, Norwegian, Russian, Italian). The language spoken in each world depends on the character and theme of that world. For example, in the world "Italia," Italian is the main language, while in "Russia," Russian is the main language. Thus, sometimes in our descriptions, the main and majority languages will be different. For example, if a conversation in "Russia" is held mainly in English, the main language is Russian, but the majority language is English. If, in these cases, French, Spanish, or some other language is introduced, that language is called the "introduced language" (see figure 16.1).

Even though a graphical VE is seemingly a richer medium than a text-based system because its multiple functionalities allow users to communicate by means of body language, positioning, and a "physical" appearance, these nontextual elements are little used. Moreover, they are less frequently used among longer term users in the case of a VE similar to AW (Smith, Farnham, & Drucker, 2002). It may be that it is difficult to keep up with text communication in a multithreaded conversation (Herring, 1999), so users may prefer text alone. Much research remains to be done about what combination of text and non-text-based communication is used in graphical-plus-text VE. Here, we focus on text.

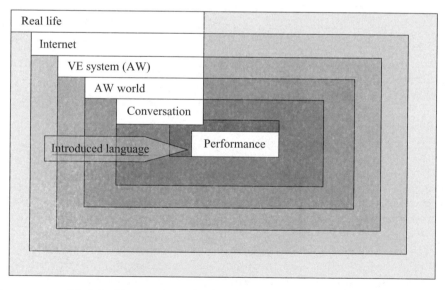

FIGURE 16.1. Model of language use in the context of the VE (adapted from Danet et al., 1997, Figure 1).

Language and Social Interaction in the Context of Graphical VEs: A Model and Preview of Issues

In the "social" setting of AW, a key activity consists of self-presentation, or staging the self and interacting with others who are doing the same. Socializing can thus be analyzed by means of the conventional tools of sociological analysis as applied to microencounters, as they have been developed by Goffman (1959) and his followers. This type of analysis puts the staging of the self into the context of particular frames. In linguistics, the influence of the social context on the communication process has been emphasized in the "activity-based communication analysis" approach (Allwood 1995a, 1995b). The main point for the present study is that the social context must provide the starting point for analyzing communication among participants.

Nevertheless, interaction in a VE does not fit fully into the descriptions given by Goffman, Allwood, and others, since online interactions take place in social settings that are more difficult to analyze because they are in a new medium and participants often do not have clear social roles. However, despite the informal character of the setting, a number of frames influence social interaction and the communication process.

The online conversations analyzed in the present study take place within a partly offline and partly online framework, consisting of a number of frames nested within each other: the real life frame, the Internet frame, the system frame, and the virtual world frame (see figure 16.1, a modification of Danet, Ruedenberg, and Rosenbaum-Tamari's [1997] figure of five nested frames). As Danet et al. (1997, p. 53) have noted, even though only one frame at a time is technically available for action, people operate within several frames simultaneously since the frames are nested within each other. The language encounter that takes place when a minority language is introduced takes place not in an isolated virtual world but also in a VE system, on the Internet, and in a real-world setting—settings where English is the dominant language.

Factors apart from the cultural and linguistic framework also influence the language selection: Since the VE is mainly a text medium and a medium where the main activity is self-presentation, text and language are tools to make oneself seen and known. As already pointed out, even if English is not the native language of the majority offline or online, it is still the language by which one can reach most people. Therefore, if one wants to be seen and known online, one *must* communicate in English. However, in this study we found that AW participants communicate not solely in English but also on many occasions use other languages. The difference between English and other languages seems to be that while English is a "utility language," a lingua franca that is used to make oneself understood and to communicate with others besides native English speakers, non-English languages have more specific uses, such as finding a fellow speaker to chat with, initiating language play, or disturbing an ongoing communication.

To anticipate some of our findings: In public worlds where the main language is English, we found that acceptance of non-English contributions is low, while in themed worlds, people show a far more accepting attitude toward languages that are not understood by everyone. The reason may be that participants in themed worlds are more experienced users who are less eager to communicate and get to know new people online, since they already belong to a core online group. Experienced users are also more familiar with the playful jargon that is characteristic of the Internet, and online text communication generally, which makes them more tolerant of odd-looking words, characters, and signs in the chat window. For a new user, it may be difficult enough to follow a normal conversation in one's own language; a public setting with new users may therefore be less tolerant toward unconventional communication.

Since English is a lingua franca in VEs, as on the Internet and in the world at large, we argue that native English speakers to a large extent dominate text-centered social interactions online, since they have a greater mastery of the language. There are, of course, other skills that can lend one influence in online social interaction, such as fast typing, computer skills, humor, and common social skills. However, if one does not have the language to understand other people and make oneself fully understood, these other skills may be less useful.

METHOD

To study language encounters in AW, we carried out extensive participant observation of ongoing conversations and interaction among users.[6] Approximately 50 hours were spent in observation.[7] In addition to taking notes during the observations, we also logged text conversations.[8] Participant observations were carried out in two main types of settings with respect to language: (1) in central places in the most populated worlds in the AW system, and (2) in language-specific worlds. The reason for studying these two setting types was that in the central places English is the main language, while in the language-specific places other (mostly European) languages are dominant. We also carried out observations in "themed" worlds, worlds that have a specific theme (e.g., role playing, shopping, religious, educational, game playing) that influences social interaction through explicit rules of various kinds (e.g., language rules for "decency;" rules for how to address people; rules for which avatar one may choose). "Themed worlds" can contain any language, but they can be seen as settings distinct from those that we refer to as "cosmopolitan worlds," which do not have any specific theme or rules other than the ordinary and loosely applied rules of the AW system.

After collecting the data, each observer examined his or her material and selected excerpts containing various kinds of language encounter situations.

The encounters were analyzed and classified according to perceived intention of the language introducer, response to the language introduction, and consequence of the language encounter. The text excerpts and the preliminary classifications/interpretations were then distributed to other members of the research team and discussed until we could agree on an interpretation of the language encounters.

LANGUAGE ENCOUNTERS: OVERVIEW

Before presenting examples of text excerpts, we briefly discuss how we interpreted the various elements of the language encounters and display this in tabular format to provide an overview.

Language encounters are common throughout the AW system. In general, language encounters occur most often in the cosmopolitan worlds, which are also predominantly English speaking, compared with the language-specific worlds, which are not visited as often by people trying to speak other languages. There is thus a kind of language inclusion/exclusion evident already at this stage; users choose to go to worlds where they know the language.

Intention/Introduction

The initial phase of a language encounter is the introduction of a new language into a conversation previously held in another language. The reason why a user breaks into an ongoing conversation with a new language is, of course, not easy to determine, since we know nothing about the intentions of the user but see only how the introduction is made and what components (e.g., questions, comments) it contains. Nevertheless, there seem to be three main reasons for users introducing a new language. The most common is to find out if any fellow speakers are present. Lines such as "Anyone speak Swedish?" and "I am Italian" (usually in the introduced language) indicate that the user wants to get in touch with fellow speakers and start a conversation. Another common reason is a desire to initiate language play, that is, to engage the users present in an amusing multilingual conversation. The reason for doing this, apart from the enjoyment of playing together, could be to display one's communication skills and to indicate that one belongs to an international community, or to obtain higher status within the group as an international Internet user. An example is a line such as "Hey The Internationale Community *S* [smiles]."[9] A third common reason for introducing a new language is to disturb the ongoing conversation of others. In this situation, the new language is often accompanied by other disturbing communication elements and behavior that takes up space (e.g., capital letters, graphical figures, text scrolling). The reason for this behavior seems to be to obtain (negative) attention from others.

Response

When a participant introduces a new language, the immediate response, according to our observations, is acceptance, rejection, mixed (both acceptance and rejection), or neutral. When an introduced language is accepted, it is responded to in a friendly way, in the main language, in the introduced language, or in a third language, or it is translated by the language introducer or by a fellow speaker. This response indicates that the introduced language is tolerated in the situation and that its speaker does not have to change to the main language. When it is rejected, a new language introduction is responded to—not always in an unfriendly way—in the main language. The language introducer is told, in different ways, to either change to the main language or to leave. When an introduced language receives a neutral response, it is neither accepted nor rejected but is met by silence.

Consequences

The direct consequences of language introduction are that the introduced language either survives or disappears. Indirect or general consequences of language encounters may also be found, such as how the atmosphere of the situation changes (negatively or positively) and how social interaction is influenced generally, for example, whether the topic of the conversation changes.

Figure 16.2 gives an overview of the types of language encounters and their components: intention/introduction, response, and consequence. Each of these components is divided further into three groups, containing examples from the collected data that describe the components and the language encounter process in more detail. Figures in parentheses refer to the conversation logs that are reproduced below to illustrate these cases.

LANGUAGE ENCOUNTERS: EXAMPLES

Of the many conversation examples logged, we selected a small number for analysis and present an even smaller number here—for reasons of space—in order to illustrate the range of encounters. The number at the beginning of each line indicates where, in relation to the other lines, the line appeared in the original conversation, that is, after the language introduction took place.

Example 1

This example is from a central place in a language-specific world (main language, French) and illustrates a situation where the introduced language receives an accepting response. An informal conversation between two users,

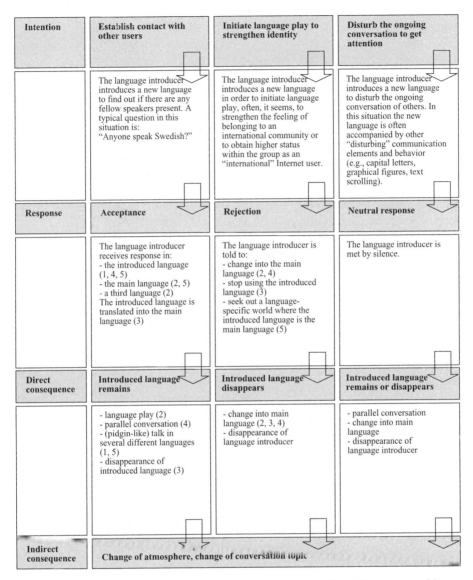

Intention	Establish contact with other users	Initiate language play to strengthen identity	Disturb the ongoing conversation to get attention
	The language introducer introduces a new language to find out if there are any fellow speakers present. A typical question in this situation is: "Anyone speak Swedish?"	The language introducer introduces a new language in order to initiate language play, often, it seems, to strengthen the feeling of belonging to an international community or to obtain higher status within the group as an "international" Internet user.	The language introducer introduces a new language to disturb the ongoing conversation of others. In this situation the new language is often accompanied by other "disturbing" communication elements and behavior (e.g., capital letters, graphical figures, text scrolling).
Response	**Acceptance**	**Rejection**	**Neutral response**
	The language introducer receives response in: - the introduced language (1, 4, 5) - the main language (2, 5) - a third language (2) The introduced language is translated into the main language (3)	The language introducer is told to: - change into the main language (2, 4) - stop using the introduced language (3) - seek out a language-specific world where the introduced language is the main language (5)	The language introducer is met by silence.
Direct consequence	**Introduced language remains**	**Introduced language disappears**	**Introduced language remains or disappears**
	- language play (2) - parallel conversation (4) - (pidgin-like) talk in several different languages (1, 5) - disappearance of introduced language (3)	- change into main language (2, 3, 4) - disappearance of language introducer	- parallel conversation - change into main language - disappearance of language introducer
Indirect consequence	**Change of atmosphere, change of conversation topic**		

FIGURE 16.2. A classification of the language encounter in the AW system and its components: intention/introduction, response, and consequence.

"mimi" and "Rosy," is suddenly interrupted by a third user, "Frederino Toca," who introduces two new languages, English and Portuguese (or Spanish).

  1 Frederino Toca: Hi rose
                        [. . .]
 25 Frederino Toca: ok
 26 Frederino Toca: i understand

38 mimi: *tu hablar portugues ... mi frances y un poco english*
                      ["you speak Portuguese ... me French and a little
                      English"]
                      [...]

40 Frederino Toca: *ablo poco inglês também*
                      ["I speak little English also"]

41 Frederino Toca: *y espanhol* ["and Spanish"]

The communication situation is problematic: The new participant, "Frederino Toca," does not speak French (which is the main language in this case), but only Spanish/Portuguese and English (lines 38, 40–41). The two French speakers, on the other hand, speak French but only very poor Spanish/Portuguese and English (line 38).

Despite the fact that the main language speakers only have poor language skills, it is the main language speakers who adjust to the language introducer and not vice versa. Hence, the conversation turns into a pidgin-language dialogue in several different languages, but mainly in English.

47 mimi: you are a nina or a nino?
                      ["you are a girl or a boy?"]

Finally, the language introducer leaves, probably as a result of the language difficulties.

Example 2

This example is from a central place in a themed world and illustrates a situation where the introduced languages receive a mixed (both accepting and rejecting) response. The conversation, which was characterized by humor and familiarity, involved five users. The first introduced language (Italian, line 1) is accepted by the other users, as it is responded to in both the main language (English, line 2) as well as in a third language (Spanish, line 14).

1 GooDriver: *Molte Bene BellaDaze*
                      ["Very Good BeautifulDaze"]

2 Lady Heartish A: Oh .... what does that mean?
                      [...]

14 daze: *como estas then?*
                      ["how are you then?"]

This acceptance leads to language play where other languages (e.g., German) are introduced and practiced.

16 Albarn Steel LH: *Darf ich hier auch Duetsch reden?*
["May I also speak German (i.e., Deutsch) here?"]

The introduced languages are soon rejected, however, as one user tells the language introducers to change into the main language.

51 Lady Heartish A: Ok . . . english only now please

After this request, the multilingual conversation continues for only a couple of lines. "GooDriver," who has been one of the more active non-English speakers, abandons the introduced languages and returns to English, thereby ending the language encounter situation.

Example 3

In this example, the conversation among approximately five participants has been going on in English for several turns, at a central place in a busy public world. It seems that several participants are nonnative English speakers. They have been carrying on an informal conversation about God and personal beliefs. Abruptly, Benni breaks in with Finnish and is rudely told to "stop talking finnish." GoodCake translates what Benni says, and the conversation during the next few turns comments on whether they have made fun of Benni. Then the conversation continues without further Finnish utterances. (It should also be mentioned that pOpmAn is still on the scene 25 turns after the excerpt below, and that Benni also continues in the conversation for some time.)

1 Benni: *älkääpä pilkatko* ["don't tease"]

2 Stan: brb ["be right back"]

3 pOpmAn: stop talking finnish

4 GoodCake: he don't like us fooling him

5 GoodCake: I mean making fun of him

6 GoodCake.   am I messenger of Benni?

7 Benni: You are better in english cake

8 Twinkle: i'm not making fun of him

9 twister: I was by no means making fun

10 twister: I just had an opinion

11 Benni: I m going to heaven

The reason that the rejection has no further consequences here is that Benni is also able to express himself to some extent in English, as is evident from the surrounding conversation, and he also has a fellow native speaker to help him. In short, this is an example where the introduced language is successfully rejected for a while, but without the disappearance of the introducer. However, 64 lines later Benni is again typing Finnish. This time GoodCake translates for him.

Example 4

Several participants from example 3 are still standing at the central place in the public world some time later, and the conversation has now changed into English, with some German and French mixed in. One person who has been participating for some time, GoodCake, has asked in Swedish if there are any Swedish speakers. Another participant, Mikael, comes onto the scene and says hello six lines later, and when he identifies himself as a fellow Swedish speaker five lines after that (line 1), Mikael and GoodCake start chatting together in Swedish. Kango responds to Swedish in a negative way (line 5, 7, 12) but leaves after a few turns (line 17).

1 Mikael:	*Hej GK . . . Allt väl?* ["Hi GK . . . Everything alright?"]
2 Kango:	and bye Happy . . .)
3 GoodCake:	*allt är bra* ["everything's fine"]
4 GoodCake:	*du?* ["and you?"]
5 Kango:	arrrgh speak englihs
6 GoodCake:	so no-one cares that David Coulthard has been on plane crush!?!!
7 Kango:	or french
8 Mikael:	*Bara bra här också tack . . . *S* . . . Väntar på hockey. . . .* ["Everything's fine here too, thanks . . . [smiles] . . . waiting for the hockey game to start"]
9 Kango:	woops
10 GoodCake:	lol Mikael. . . . we're going to kick your asses!
11 Mikael:	Hi Kango . . . *S* . . . Sorry
12 Kango:	i mean english
13 GoodCake:	hmph . . .
14 Mikael:	Probably GK . . . *S* . . . Our team play like . . . Well
15 GoodCake:	We won Italy 6-0!
16 GoodCake:	but italy was piece of cake!
17 Kango:	ill go bye
18 GoodCake:	bye kang
19 Mikael:	Yes . . . I did see that game
20 Mikael:	Bye Kango . . .

The two Swedish speakers speak in Swedish briefly (about Scandinavian topical affairs, news, and sports) but then change to English with one other, Mikael, apologizing to Kango. This example shows how, in a predominantly English-speaking world, two Swedish speakers switch into English. In spite of this, Kango leaves, possibly because he feels excluded by the topic of the conversation.

The purpose in introducing Swedish in this example is to announce a Swedish speaker to a second Swedish speaker. The rejection results in the disappearance of the introduced language, Swedish, but not of its speakers.

Example 5

In this example from a Spanish-speaking world, eight users are present who are getting to know each other (asking basic age-sex-location questions) and talking about exams in school. Astes, a Portuguese speaker, enters, typing Portugese. His language is accepted by two speakers, who greet him in the main language, Spanish. Astes continues typing in Portugese and he does this throughout the conversation. He is responded to again, after approximately 30 turns, by two other participants. These two type in Portugese, the introduced language, and they ask Astes if he knows Spanish.

66 Mano: *Astes entiendes español?*

["Astes do you understand Spanish?"]

[...]

70 Hans: *falas espanol*

["Do you speak Spanish"]

Astes explicitly states that he likes chatting with the Spanish speakers:

76 Astes: *tambem é muito bueno teclar com voces da Spanha*

["it is also very nice to 'keyboard-button' with you in Spain"]

But Mano suggests that Astes should go to a Portuguese-speaking world:

86 Mano: *Astes en el mundo de BRAZIL hay brasileños que hablan tu idioma ve y podras hablar con ellos*

["Astes in the world BRAZIL there are brazilians who speak your language look and you can talk to them"]

Nonetheless, Astes remains for 126 turns and then takes friendly leave. Overall, the language introducer is treated nicely; he is responded to in Spanish and sometimes in Portugese. The result of the language introduction and the response it receives is that the introduced language survives for a large number of turns. The language is rejected only once, in a polite way, but the language introducer stays. He actively takes part in greetings, has a positive attitude toward the Spanish language, and actively seeks to communicate.

DISCUSSION AND CONCLUSION

As shown in the examples of logged conversations above, language encounters in AW consist of a number of specific components: the way (and the reason why) the new language is introduced, the response to the language introduction, and the consequences of the response. How the encounters develop—the degree of rejection or acceptance of the introduced language—depends, we have argued, mainly on three factors: (1) the main type of language (English or non-English), (2) the character of the setting (cosmopolitan, language specific, or themed), and (3) the perceived intention of the language-introducing user (to establish contact with other users, to initiate language play, or to disturb the ongoing conversation).

In relation to factor 1, English is the main language in AW. English also acts as a shared or backup language in non-English settings. Native English speakers are only rarely bilingual, and therefore they usually ask non-English speakers to speak English when taking part in a predominantly English conversation. Non-English speakers, in contrast, usually have better language skills and are therefore more willing to change into English, even in settings and situations where the majority of users are non-English speaking. As for factor 2, character of the setting (cosmopolitan, language specific, or themed), it seems that English speakers accept non-English languages more in themed settings than in cosmopolitan ones. Factor 3, perceived intention of the language-introducing user (to establish contact with other users, to initiate language play, or to disturb the ongoing conversation), is an important factor, since the manner in which the introduction is made and how other users perceive the intention of the speaker are very important for the response to the language and the outcome of the language encounter. Below we discuss the significance of each of these factors in somewhat greater detail.

When an introduced language is accepted, it is responded to in a friendly way. This response indicates that the introduced language is tolerated within the given situation and that its speaker does not have to change to the main language. Here we can make a comparison with face-to-face settings: It is likely that AW participants are more willing to try out a new language, and respondents are more willing to try out their nonnative language skills, because the absence of social cues means that emotional embarrassment and poor language skills will not have serious consequences. In other words, one could say that the medium facilitates intercultural meetings since "social presence" (Short, Williams, & Christie, 1976) is low (text only, no voice communication) and potential emotional embarrassment is reduced.

In situations where the introduced language is rejected, the language introducer is told either to change to the main language or to leave. Here the absence of social cues, or the narrow bandwidth of the medium, has the opposite effect: In contrast to face-to-face settings, the rejection may be more direct. This is related to the absence of face-to-face embarrassment and because other means of overcoming language problems—gesture and facial expression—are missing.

It is not uncommon for a language introduction to be met with a mixed response, that is to say, with both acceptance and rejection, often by different speakers in the environment (example 2). The introduced language can also, in some cases, be met with neither a positive nor a negative response, but with a neutral one—silence. This response also relates to the character of the medium: In text conversations, it is possible to maintain a silence that would be inappropriate in a face-to-face situation, where a response is always called for. In some cases this silence can be seen as positive, as when two or more language introducers are allowed to maintain a conversation parallel to the one in the main language, but it can also be seen as negative if the language introducer is alone and trying to find someone to talk to.

In addition to being the main language in AW, English acts a shared or default language in non-English settings. Non-English speakers often have good language skills and are therefore willing to change into English, even in settings and situations where the majority of users are non-English speaking. Non-English speakers, we would argue, are thus tolerant toward English because they are used to adjusting to the norm (English). They adjust their behavior toward other language speakers because they are aware of their own and others' minority situation (examples 1 and 2). English speakers are less accommodating of non-English speakers (example 2).

However, English speakers accept non-English languages more in themed settings than in cosmopolitan ones. If they are AW regulars, they probably will have incorporated belonging to an international Internet community into their identity, and they will also have taken on the social conventions of the system, which include such characteristics as openness toward newcomers or a generally friendly attitude.[10] Another factor that may be mentioned in passing is the number of users present. Although we did not study this aspect of the setting in detail, it seems likely that the degree to which an introduced language is accepted or rejected depends on how inhibited or disinhibited the language introducer feels in relation to whether the encounter is with one or a few participants, or if the encounter takes place in a crowd.

Finally, we believe that an important factor influencing whether the introduced language is accepted or rejected is the perceived intention of the language introducer. Of the three main reasons for introducing a new language, the most common is to find out if there are any fellow speakers present. This fits well with what we know about the system generally; participants use greetings and conversation, in the absence of social cues, to find fellow speakers. Another common reason for introducing a new language in a main language setting is to display one's communication skills in a playful way, either to strengthen the feeling of belonging to an international community or to obtain higher status within the group as an international Internet user. We have seen that a third reason for language introduction is to disturb the ongoing conversation of others.

The most tolerant attitude toward users who introduce new languages in order to find fellow-countrymen to chat with can typically be found among English-speaking users, if only because English is the most commonly used language. We also found a tolerant attitude toward users who introduce a new language for playful purposes. But while this behavior is very much appreciated in certain situations, it causes annoyance in others, which in many cases results in rejection of the language. As mentioned above, people in themed settings are often experienced users and more familiar with playful Internet jargon, and therefore more tolerant, while new users perhaps feel unsure in the environment as a whole and are therefore less tolerant toward unconventional behavior. The least accepting attitude toward introduced languages is shown toward introducers whose intention is perceived as being disruptive. This applies to situations where English or a non-English language is the main language.

Relating the characteristics of language encounters to AW as a whole, we can note that English is the most common, default language, except in themed non-English-language worlds. These two settings create different types of language encounters: Unless non-English-speaking participants seek out worlds oriented to their mother tongue, they will need to seek out fellow speakers. Cases where English is rejected are much rarer overall than rejection of non-English languages. Some technical and nontechnical implications can be derived from these findings: It might be helpful to be able to identify speakers of language via information displayed on their avatars, or to provide online translation help to support intercultural communication. As in other cases, new technologies create unanticipated problems, which require both technical and social solutions.

All in all, we have found that the VE medium amplifies certain aspects of language encounters (exclusion, but also embracing language plurality) and diminishes others (embarrassment, nonverbal communication). Here we need to recall how much more important language is in AW than in face-to-face settings, both as a topic of conversation and in structuring encounters. At the same time, the main reason for using AW and the main purpose of conversation is socializing for its own sake. Although it is, of course, important to understand one another in this setting, it is also true that not much hangs on the outcome of the encounter.

Unlike other studies that examine language encounters in intercultural meetings or work situations, in the case of socializing we find a variety of responses when different languages meet. As we have shown, technology plays an important part in shaping these responses, but so, too, do the conventions of real-world conversations. The closest real-world equivalent of AW conversations is informal get-togethers such as cocktail parties. AW conversation is rather loosely structured, taking unexpected turns and involving many options as to how to respond to others. However, unlike real-world settings, much attention is focused on text communication—how the technology shapes the conversation, and what types of social norms are imported into this setting to structure the conversation. This applies particularly to how languages encounter each other, since language encounters are commonplace in this cosmopolitan setting. Put differently, with language encounters so frequent and with so much focus on them, the results of the encounter—how they are shaped—matter more than they do in the real world.

Our main conclusion is that AW is a system in which language encounters result in a variety of outcomes, reproducing but also transforming real-world conversations. Although these occasionally result in non-English speakers being excluded, the most common result of language encounters is quite positive, especially in view of the fact that AW is an exceptionally cosmopolitan place where language encounters are much more commonplace than in the real world.

Acknowledgment

A previous version of this chapter appeared in *New Media & Society* (volume 5, issue 4, 2003).

Notes

1. For a sample of Internet-based multiuser VEs and some images, see http://www.ccon .org.

2. See http://www.internetworldstats.com/, retrieved December 20, 2005.

3. See http://www.google.com/language_tools?hl=en and http://babelfish.altavista.com, retrieved December 20, 2005.

4. The avatar can be humanoid: female, male, child; or nonhumanoid, for example, a bird or a dinosaur.

5. Note that we are using "majority language" in a more context-specific sense than is customary, not merely to refer to a language's status in the physical world.

6. Both user names and names of studied worlds have been anonymized.

7. Apart from time spent specifically observing language, the authors have spent more than 200 hours altogether in AW observing other phenomena.

8. For some of the ethical and methodological issues associated with studying this medium, see Schroeder, Heather, and Lee (1998).

9. This line is taken from our data logs, produced in a language-play situation.

10. AW administrators emphasize the importance of upholding certain communication conventions on the system's webpages. These conventions are displayed next to the window showing the graphical VE. Under the heading "Some chat tips for beginners," users learn that they should be polite to strangers and never type in all-capital letters, harass people who do not want to chat, or be offensive.

References

Allwood, J. (1995a). An activity based approach to pragmatics. In H. Bunt & B. Black (Eds.), *Abduction, belief and context in dialogue: Studies in computational pragmatics* (pp. 47–80). Amsterdam: John Benjamins.

Allwood, J. (1995b). Language communication and social activity. In K. Junefelt (Ed.), *Proceedings of the XIVth Scandinavian Conference of Linguistics and the VIIIth Conference of Nordic and General Linguistics. Gothenburg Papers in Theoretical Linguistics. Vol. 73.* Göteborg, Sweden: University of Göteborg, Department of Linguistics. Retrieved September 15, 2005, from http://www.ling.gu.se/~jens/publications/docs051-075/073.pdf.

Allwood, J., & Schroeder, R. (2000, April). Intercultural communication in virtual environments. *Journal of Intercultural Communication, 4.* Retrieved September 15, 2005, from http://www.immi.se/intercultural/nr4/allwood.htm.

Becker, B., & Mark, G. (2002). Social conventions in computer-mediated communication: A comparison of three online shared virtual environments. In R. Schroeder (Ed.), *The social life of avatars: Presence and interaction in shared virtual environments* (pp. 19–39). London: Springer.

Cherny, L. (1999). *Conversation and community: Chat in a virtual world.* Stanford, CA: CSLI.

Crystal, D. (1997). *English as a global language.* Cambridge: Cambridge University Press.

Crystal, D. (2001). *Language and the Internet.* Cambridge: Cambridge University Press.

Danet, B., Ruedenberg, L., & Rosenbaum-Tamari, Y. (1997). Hmmm . . . where's that smoke coming from? Writing, play and performance on Internet Relay Chat. *Journal of Computer-Mediated Communication, 2*(4). Retrieved September 15, 2005, from http://jcmc.indiana.edu/vol2/issue4/danet.html.

Du Bartell, D. (1995). Discourse features of computer-mediated communication: "Spoken-like" and "written-like." In B. Wårvik, S-K Tanskanen, & R. Hiltunen (Eds.), *Organization in Discourse: Proceedings from the Turku Conference* (Anglicana Turkuensia, vol. 14) (pp. 231–239). Turku, Finland: University of Turku, Department of English.

Fishman, J. (1998–1999). The new linguistic order. *Foreign Policy, 113* (Winter), 26–40.

Goffman, E. (1959). *The presentation of self in everyday life.* New York: Doubleday.

Graddol, D. (1997). *The future of English? A guide to forecasting the popularity of the English language in the 21st century.* London: British Council.

Herring, S. C. (1999). Interactional coherence in CMC. *Journal of Computer-Mediated Communication, 4*(4). Retrieved December 20, 2005, from http://jcmc.indiana.edu/vol4/issue4/herring.html.

Hiltz, R. S., Johnson, K., & Turoff, M. (1986). Experiments in group decision making: Communication process and outcome in face-to-face versus computerized conferences. *Human Communication Research, 13,* 225–252.

Jeffrey, P., & Mark, G. (1999). Navigating the virtual landscape: Co-ordinating the shared use of space. In A. Munro, K. Höök, & D. Benyon (Eds.), *Social navigation of information space* (pp. 112–131). London: Springer Verlag.

Johansen, R., Vallee, J., & Spangler, K. (1979). *Electronic meetings: Technical alternatives and social choices.* Reading, MA: Addison-Wesley.

Kiesler, S., Siegel, J., & McGuire, T. W. (1984). Social-psychological aspects of computer-mediated communication. *American Psychologist, 39*(10), 1123–1134.

Misztal, B. A. (2000). *Informality: Social theory and contemporary practice.* London: Routledge.

Phillipson, R. (1992). *Linguistic imperialism.* Oxford: Oxford University Press.

Salem, B., & Earle, N. (2000). Designing a non-verbal language for expressive avatars. In E. Churchill & M. Reddy (Eds.), *Proceedings of the ACM Conference on Collaborative Virtual Environments* (pp. 93–101). New York: ACM Press.

Schiffman, H. F. (1996). *Linguistic culture and language policy.* London: Routledge.

Schroeder, R. (1997). Networked worlds: Social aspects of networked multi-user virtual reality technology. *Sociological Research Online, 2*(4), Retrieved September 15, 2005, from http://www.socresonline.org.uk/2/4/5.html.

Schroeder, R. (Ed.). (2002). *The social life of avatars: Presence and interaction in shared virtual environments*. London: Springer.

Schroeder, R., Heather, N., & Lee, R. (1998). The sacred and the virtual: Religion in multi-user virtual reality. *Journal of Computer-Mediated Communication, 2*(4). Retrieved September 15, 2005, from http://jcmc.indiana.edu/vol4/issue2/schroeder.html.

Short, J., Williams, E., & Christie, B. (1976). *The social psychology of telecommunications*. London: John Wiley.

Smith, M., Farnham, S., & Drucker, S. (2002). The social life of small graphical chat spaces. In R. Schroeder (Ed.), *The social life of avatars: Presence and interaction in shared virtual environments* (pp. 205–220). London: Springer.

Tsuda, Y. (2000, April). Envisioning a democratic linguistic order. *TESL Reporter 33*(1), 32–38.

Werry, C. C. (1996). Linguistic and interactional features of Internet Relay Chat. In S. C. Herring (Ed.), *Computer-mediated communication: Linguistic, social, and cross-cultural perspectives* (pp. 47–63). Amsterdam: John Benjamins.

Yates, S. (1996). Oral and written linguistic aspects of computer conferencing: A corpus-based study. In S. C. Herring (Ed.), *Computer-mediated communication: Linguistic, social, and cross-cultural perspectives* (pp. 29–46). Amsterdam: John Benjamins.

PART V

BROADER PERSPECTIVES:
LANGUAGE DIVERSITY

17

RUTH WODAK AND SCOTT WRIGHT

The European Union in Cyberspace

Democratic Participation via Online Multilingual Discussion Boards

The European Union has been keen to promote multilingual discussion through the Internet. Such discussion has the potential both to improve decision making and to reduce perception of a democratic deficit by bringing citizens closer together and closer to the institutions themselves. The most important attempt by the European Union (EU) to create such dialogue through information and communication technologies (ICTs) to date is the discussion forum Futurum, hosted on the EU's online portal, "Europa" (http://www.europa.eu.int). The first Futurum debate was inaugurated on March 7, 2001, and continued (sporadically) through the end of 2004.[1] Language policies played an important role in this forum, as they helped mitigate the language barriers that might otherwise have discouraged citizens from participating. In addition, much of Futurum's content reflects European language policies.

The EU's language and communication policies are highly contested, with numerous policy papers covering the subject.[2] Of particular concern in this chapter is their focus on (1) participation of European citizens: Proposals in this area are meant to reduce the so-called democratic deficit of the EU; (2) recognition of the "official national languages" spoken in the member states of the EU: All important documents published by the EU should be translated into all officially recognized EU languages (see also Articles 2 and 3 of the Draft Treaty, European Convention (on the Future of Europe, 2003); (3) minority languages and "diversity": It is important to investigate which languages are spoken when, where, and by whom and which languages are evaluated positively or negatively: autochthonous minority languages, migrant languages, new minority languages, contact languages, and so forth (see Clyne, 2003, for recent definitions[3]); and (4) specific language policies: These have implications for both European integration and citizenship policies for migrants, both major political issues inside the EU (Busch & Krzyzanowski, in press; Delanty, Jones, Krzyzanowski, Wodak, & Ulsamer, 2004; Phillipson, 2003; Wodak & Puntscher-Riekmann, 2003).

In this chapter, we analyze the linguistic/discursive/multimodal aspects of the Futurum discussion forum and how the structures of the discussion forum shape the debates. We also analyze whether the debates achieved their goal of helping to resolve the democratic deficit. From this perspective, two main research questions were developed:

(1) What are the quantitative and qualitative (socio)linguistic characteristics of Internet debate forums as a linguistic genre? Which groups have access, and how does the structure of the forum influence the debate?

(2) In what ways are participation, democratization, communication, and representation related to one another and to language policies? We question this issue on two levels: Are language policies debated in relation to democratization issues? In which languages do the debates take place?

To answer these questions, a quantitative overview of Futurum was combined with qualitative discourse analysis of one thread that focused on EU language politics. We begin by identifying the major theoretical assumptions and concepts underpinning our analysis.

THE COMPLEXITY OF EUROPEAN
LANGUAGE POLITICS/POLICIES

The complex interplay of national, official languages and minority languages forms the core of European language policies. Although the Charter of Fundamental Rights of the European Union (Official Journal, 2000) states that there should be equality of official EU languages, policies for coping with minority/migrant languages are left to each nation state, following the principle of subsidiarity.[4] Research has suggested that English is approaching the status of a lingua franca in EU organizations (Phillipson, 2003). More broadly, 47% of all Europeans speak English in a more or less understandable way, 32% speak German, and 26% French as their second language (de Cillia, 2003). Moreover, native English speakers know very few foreign languages, if any: 66% of British people speak only English.

At the same time, these numbers illustrate that not everyone is prepared for English as the lingua franca and that such a policy could create a further democratic deficit, a linguistic divide to match the digital divide. Some scholars, such as Barbara Seidlhofer (2003), suggest that we should accept "English as lingua franca" (ELF) as a given and teach students and bureaucrats ELF because they need it to communicate and understand other people speaking ELF. Durham's (chapter 14 this volume) analysis of a Swiss mailing list suggests that even relatively narrowcast formats encourage ELF as "the non-native language for all" (although the use of English was not formally imposed or encouraged in the case discussed). Discussion forums such as Futurum where dozens of languages can potentially be used may promote this tendency. This issue is controversial, however, because such suggestions imply that "imperfect" English could become an acceptable means of communication (see also Widdowson, 1994, pp. 377–381). Moreover, the percentages cited above do not include the migrants in European countries who speak many different, non-Indo-European languages. Including migrant languages in EU language policies will necessarily make language policies even more complex.

LINGUISTIC/SEMIOTIC GENRES

Debates about language policies occur in very different settings (Wodak, 2003) and exhibit different characteristic linguistic features. In parliamentary conclusions, for example, policies and proposals are stated in a declarative mode; in the constitution, legal language is used; in speeches, politicians use persuasive rhetoric to convince their audience of certain measures—to justify some and reject others. In spontaneous conversations in semiprivate public domains, rules of dialogue or conversation apply that account for linguistic differences. At the same time, the topical discourses on language policies that take place in such genres overlap; they form a "nexus" of language policies and democratization issues, in the sense of Scollon and Scollon (2004).

Lemke (2001, 2003) labels communication and activities on the Internet as "traversals," as virtual genres, which transcend the traditional norms of time and space in specific, fragmented ways, constructing hybrid patterns of coherence (see also Rusch, 2004; Urry, 2003). Elaborating the notion of "multimodality" (Kress & van Leeuwen, 1996), Lemke introduces the concept of "hypermodality." Through the hypermodality of webpages, every user is able to create her or his new text, by linking different subtexts, images, symbols, icons, and pictures to each other. In this way, people constantly create new semantic hierarchies and an ever newer mixture of "voices." Drawing on Functional Systemic Linguistics, Lemke (1999, 2000) introduces a useful taxonomy that distinguishes between orientational, presentational, and organizational resources and functions, which correspond to the institutional need to present the right image, direct insiders and outsiders through the information flows created by hyperlinks, and provide insight into the organization itself. Below, we briefly point to some relevant features of "Europa" and Futurum, applying those concepts that indicate the intended, meaningful architecture of the discussion forums and the website more generally.

We argue that, in contradiction to Yates (1996), there is a semiotic field in computer-mediated communication (CMC) (Halliday, 1978) generated by the design of the website and, in the case of discussion boards, the body or person hosting and moderating the forum, as well as how the interface is structured.[5] This, following Halliday, influences the genre, which in turn affects linguistic realization of the topic. As Danet (2001) highlights, a number of features distinguish CMC modes both from other genres and from each other. For example, significantly different linguistic features occur in emails, email lists, and discussion forums (Herring, 2002).[6] Of particular interest is Gruber's (2004) study of email lists, such as the Linguist List, for which he provides an interesting model of description. However, topical developments in discussions, the setting of relevance, and argumentation or justification for or against certain stances have been generally neglected so far (see also Abdullah, 2004; Anis, 1999; Neuage, 2003).

Following the proposals for democratization mentioned above, the EU set up a dedicated area on its website to facilitate communication with citizens. Although this was by no means the first discussion forum on "Europa," it marked an attempt to systematize and coordinate online communications between the EU and its citizens. Of particular interest, given the assumed dominance of English as the language of webpages (Stein, 2006), is the fact that people can post in all the official EU languages (although translation software was not made available), and the webpages are themselves available in 10 languages. This means that one person can start a thread in English, another might respond in French, a third in German or Greek, and so forth.

ONLINE DISCUSSION BOARDS AND THE "DEMOCRATIC DEFICIT"

The so-called democratic deficit is a problem that has plagued European leaders to varying degrees since the inception of the European Commission. Recently, the perception of a democratic deficit was noted in a White Paper on European Governance (Commission, 2001), which stated that there is a "widening gulf between the European Union and the people it serves" created by perceptions of an inability of the EU to act even when a clear case exists, that when it does act it does not get credit for it, that when things go wrong "Brussels is too easily blamed by Member States for difficult decisions that they themselves have agreed to or even requested"; that many people simply do not understand the mechanisms of the institutions; and that all these factors lead to a lack of trust and disenchantment (Commission, 2001, pp. 7–8). This analysis suggests that a number of democratic deficits exist, including deficits of knowledge, communication, and perceived closeness, and that they are (1) not entirely of the EU's own making and (2) not always fair.

New technologies are seen as central to resolving these problems. Noting that "[d]emocracy depends on people being able to take part in public debate"

(p. 11), the commission (Commission, 2001) states that the EU must "communicate more actively with the general public on European issues"; that "[t]here needs to be a stronger interaction with regional and local governments and civil society" (p. 4); and that there needs to be a "trans-national space where citizens from different countries can discuss what they perceive as being the important challenges for the Union" (p. 12). This is because "its legitimacy today depends on involvement and participation" (p. 11). Moreover, it is stated that "[i]nformation and communication technologies have an important role" in facilitating such communication and that "Europa" will be redesigned as "an interactive platform for information, feedback and debate" (p. 11).

In response, parallel to the multilevel structure of the European polity itself, a new kind of communication network is emerging (a "nexus"; see above), consisting of multiple communication spheres that mutually refer to each other, initiating topics and engaging with arguments and opinions from other parts of the network.[7] In this communicative process, topics and arguments are not only persistently exchanged but also altered in order to adapt them to new interlocutors/arguments/situations. This discursive process, known in linguistic terms as "recontextualization" (Iedema, 1999; Wodak, 2000), is of central importance when social power is negotiated.

EUROPA

The Europa website was launched in February 1995 to support the then G7 Ministerial Summit on the Information Society and rapidly developed into an overarching communication resource. It is a portal to all the information produced by the institutions of Europe online. The website received a staggering 6,183,955,138 hits in 2003, an average of 16.3 hits per EU citizen.[8] To design a website that simplifies the complexity of the EU into a readily accessible form, while at the same time being representative of the institutions themselves, is obviously a difficult task. Figure 17.1 is a screen capture of the redesigned links page,[9] which appears after the language is selected. The page looks identical in each of the 20 languages. After the redesign, a link was added to the "discussion corner."

There is a permanent set of links on the left-hand side of the page under three titles: Discover the EU, Living in the EU, and Interact with the EU. These hyperlinks relate well to the three functions proposed by Lemke (1999). The titles of these hyperlinks are quasi invitations or proposals, albeit formulated partly as imperatives. "Discover" relates to the presentational function, "living" to the orientational function, and "interact" to one of the organizational functions by which one can ask questions and start a dialogue. Traversals can be created by switching along these links and creating one's own path.

The "Interact with the EU" section provides a number of mechanisms by which people can communicate with the institutions through the Internet.

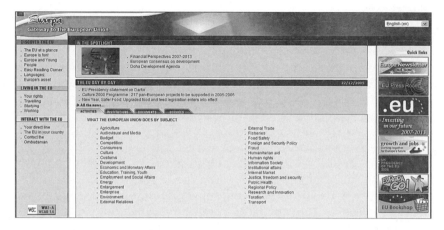

FIGURE 17.1. Europa: Gateway to the European Union. *Source*: http://www.europa
.eu.int/index_en.htm, retrieved December 24, 2005.

First, there is a variety of guidance and question-answering services, including a real-time Internet Relay Chat service with trained staff directing users step by step to the information that they need online. However, the service is only available in English and French. Second, there is a subsection explaining how to contact your local Member of European Parliament. Third, there is a section explaining how citizens can get in touch with local EU information centers and contact points. Fourth, there is the Discussion Corner, and finally a link to contact the European Ombudsman, an official body set up to deal with citizens' complaints about the EU. The central part of the page has a regularly updated news section and a filing cabinet section that gives users access to activities, institutions, documents, and services. In total there are 115 different links on the page. The diversity of topics suggests that the site represents the organizational and functional complexity of the EU itself.

The page has complementary visual and linguistic patterns. The banner features open skies with a picture of workers on scaffolding building an unspecified object superimposed over a flag of the EU, the meanings of which can only be speculated upon: On the one hand, the construction of the EU is symbolized; on the other hand, cooperative practices as well as the diversity of professions are highlighted. This is complemented by the EU's logo, "United in Diversity," with a further EU flag and the Europa slogan, which is "Gateway to the European Union." Thus, many icons and symbols are used to give specific "European" meanings to the website, while alluding to the ongoing debate on European values of justice, democracy, diversity, and equality (Wodak & Weiss, 2004a, 2004b, 2005). There is another photograph, of three black children collecting water from a fountain to promote World Water Day, further highlighting the social values of the EU and "diversity."

THE "FUTURE OF EUROPE" ONLINE DISCUSSION

The discussions on the Future of Europe, revolving around the draft constitution, were undertaken through a variety of offline and online mechanisms. Here we concentrate on the online discussion forum, Futurum,[10] hosted by the "Future of Europe—debate" website on Europa. The discussions are managed by a small team within the Presidency Secretariat and are provided as an addition to the website at no cost. The Futurum forum is intended to "act as a permanent gateway for information on the progress of the debate [on the future of Europe], to provide interactive tools to help fuel the debate (forum), and to gather and publish contributions to the discussion from everyone involved."[11] To this end, it will "address issues crucial to the future of the European Union" and should "help bring the European Union closer to its citizens and reduce the perception of a democratic deficit." However, the online discussions are not analyzed or used at a policy level in any way: They are considered a peripheral part of the broader debate.[12]

Futurum is an asynchronous threaded discussion forum. The structuring of discussion forums is thought to influence the nature of the discussion (Wright, 2005a, 2005b; Wright & Street, in press) and the shape of language interactions. According to Axelsson, Abelin, and Schroeder (2003), "technology plays an important part" because "the medium amplifies certain aspects of language encounters" (p. 495). Thus, it is necessary to devote some discussion to the structures of the Futurum discussion board, such as page layout and moderation policies.

The principal feature of Futurum's interface is its threaded structure, which enables users to see to which post a message responded. The interface also highlights in red the message that is being displayed at the time, making it easier to keep track of where one is within the flow of messages. The date and time of messages are also displayed, as well as when they were edited by the moderator, which helps participants determine how lively the thread is. Finally, personal details are displayed, as provided by the respondent, including username, country of origin, the language used, mother tongue, and the title of the message. Via these latter features, participants can specify whether the language of the text is different from that used in the message header. This is often the case, since when users reply they tend to leave the original message title even if they use a different language.

Futurum is moderated: Messages are read and assessed for content before they are made visible on the forum. There is one moderator who emails participants if their messages are deemed inappropriate, to explain why and how they could be made acceptable.[13] Futurum's moderation policy states that "this discussion corner is designed to give European citizens complete freedom to express their views on, and discuss the future of Europe. This discussion corner is democratic. We do not censure the content or form of contributions IN ANY WAY."[14] However, the editorial policy contradicts this emphatic statement by "merely" having a list of "basic rules of politeness and respect" that, if violated, may lead to a message not being posted. The list is quite comprehensive—although it does not mention respect for linguistic diversity—with nine different areas covered, from the use of foul language to the defense of terrorist activity. Thus, "the moderator reserves the right not to publish certain contributions" because such a restriction is "necessary to ensure a democratic debate, and we are convinced that everyone will support it."[15] According to one senior commission official, only a small percentage of messages were actually subjected to moderation.[16] Nevertheless, the moderation process (or self-censorship due to an awareness of the process) could significantly affect the language of postings as the rules require users to meet certain minimum language standards.[17] In fact, the moderation policy did raise concerns among users. "Josef Langer" complained that "censurship [sic] is an ugly feature of Futurum. It is difficult to understand why an institution which is supposed to be the guardian of European values applies censorship in a political discussion. In any case such behavior raises suspicion about the evil side of EU institutions."[18]

QUANTITATIVE OVERVIEW

To gain an overview of the discussions on Futurum, we conducted a quantitative analysis of the 18,703 posts made to the 19 debates closed as of December 2003. Each debate had an average of 984 posts, with the largest debate having 4,420 posts and the smallest only 73 posts. A "debate" here refers to a discussion topic, as set by the Futurum team. Some debates were closed by moderators because the discussions had run their course, while others, such as the ones in which political leaders participated, appeared to have fixed time limits. We selected a range of sample sizes because each measure required different depths of analysis, and we wanted to analyze the largest feasible sample for each one. This was because the analysis was conducted by tabulating the posts by hand. The measures used analyzed factors such as the language of posts and sex of posters.

WHO IS POSTING?

First, we asked who is posting. This question was answered by analyzing the given country of origin and the sex of participants within the General Debate. Because there is no guarantee that users provided their actual location or name, this analysis can serve only a guide. In fact, a small number of posters repeatedly changed their country of origin. One person gave his location as Holland in 200 messages but made a further 79 posts from 30 different countries. Having noted this problem with the data, we can now analyze the General Discussion. There are too many countries to present the data for each; thus, only the 15 pre-2004 enlargement member states and the two other biggest contributors (the United States and Turkey) are listed.

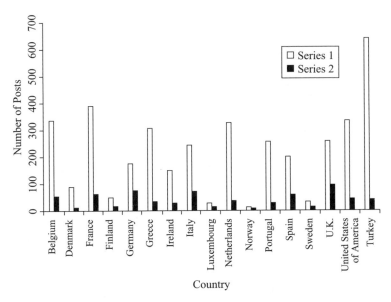

FIGURE 17.2. Posts by country of origin. Series 1, number of posts; series 2, number of posters. From General Discussion, Futurum; $N = 3,721$ of 4,420 total posts.

Series 1 in figure 17.2 refers to the number of posts and shows that there were significant discrepancies from one country to the next. Series 2 refers to the number of posters. This followed a pattern similar to the number of Internet users in each country, although the actual differences were often significantly smaller, suggesting that the digital divide was not prominent.[19] Turkey's strong showing is primarily due to one poster called WolfWolf, who sent 495 posts, the vast majority of which were related to Turkey's proposed EU membership. Nevertheless, there were apparently representatives from each country, and this would suggest that a range of languages might be expected to appear.

The broad range of nationalities participating in the discussion meant that determining the sex of users was not always straightforward. If this was unclear, posts were coded neutrally. The sex of users who started new threads is shown in figure 17.3. By this measure, the General Discussion was not representative of society as a whole but had a considerable bias in favor of male-presenting users. While the uncodable participants (e.g., those using initials, surnames, or a title that did not appear to be a real name) might significantly redress this imbalance if their sex were known and turned out to be mostly female, this seems unlikely. Previous research on public online discussion groups has shown that men tend to participate more, especially in political forums (Herring, 1993, 1996); the Futurum results are consistent with this. Such a significant departure from the societal average suggests serious issues for online discussions in the future because the usefulness of feedback to decision makers may be undermined if it remains dominated by male voices.

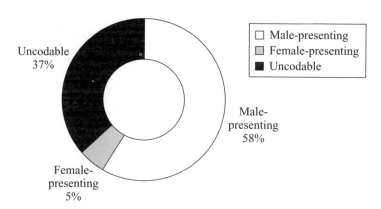

FIGURE 17.3. Sex of participants who started new threads. From General Discussion, Futurum; $N = 472$ participants.

As Herring (1996) has noted, there are "significant gender differences" in online communication styles, which do not necessarily follow stereotypes (p. 104). This may, through both overt and covert censorship, undermine the democratizing potential of the medium (Herring, 1993).

LANGUAGE USAGE

A central focus of this study is determining diversity of language usage and how the different languages interact with one another. Table 17.1 presents as percentages the language(s) used in a representative sample of posts from the General Debate, where the initial seed post was in English. It then presents the same statistic for all the non-English-seeded posts, before finally combining the two together. This division was designed to test our expectation that there would be greater linguistic diversity in non-English-seeded threads. The seed message is important because it effectively frames the debate. Because the base samples were different, we equalized them by multiplying the 10% sample of English-seed posts by 10 so that they were weighted equally.[20]

There were 169 non-English-seeded threads receiving 363 responses for an average of 2.15 replies for each seed post. This is significantly lower than for the general debate, which averaged 5.02 posts per thread while overall the average was 5.84 messages. This suggests that there was less interaction when a language other than English was used for the seed post. This appears to support the conclusion of Axelsson et al. (2003, p. 492; chapter 16 this volume) that "English is clearly a dominant language on the Internet and it is the main language in AW." However, Axelsson et al.'s conclusions are drawn from observations: No statistics were produced on the volume of languages used either on the Internet or the Active Worlds chat environment that they analyzed. The statistics in table 17.1 provide quantitative evidence that both supports and questions their observations.

TABLE 17.1. Language usage (from General Debate, Futurum; N = 442 and 363).

Language	Used in English-seeded threads (% of all posts)	Used in non-English-seeded threads (% of all posts)	Total
English	91.11	14.66	80.15
French	1.89	47.18	8.38
German	0.00	13.15	1.89
Italian	0.27	6.20	1.12
Spanish	2.43	10.34	3.56
Dutch	0.00	1.50	0.22
Portuguese	0.00	3.76	0.54
Swedish	0.00	0.19	0.03
Suomi	0.00	0.19	0.03
English/French	1.89	0.75	1.73
French/English	0.81	0.75	0.80
Dutch/Italian/German/English	0.27	0.19	0.26
English/German	0.27	0.00	0.23
English/German/French	0.00	0.19	0.03
Spanish/Esperanto	0.00	0.19	0.03
Italian/Dutch/German/English	0.00	0.19	0.03
French/English/Spanish	0.00	0.19	0.03
Spanish/French	0.00	0.19	0.03
French/Dutch/English	0.00	0.19	0.03
French/Dutch	0.00	0.19	0.03
Total	100%	100%	100%

Table 17.1 shows that discussions were predominantly in the English language. Although six different languages were used in the sample of English-seeded threads, more than 90% of the posts were solely in English, and only 2.43% of the posts did not feature some use of English. The results for the non-English-seeded threads provide a more even spread, with nine different languages evident. Just under half of the posts were in French, and nearly 15% were in English, although there were nearly as many Spanish and German posts as English ones. In just under three-quarters of the posts that began in a language other than English, users did not go on to use other languages, although as many as five different languages were used in any one thread.

To investigate the language mix within threads further, table 17.2 tabulates the number of languages used in non-English-seeded threads, broken down by the length of each thread. It is thus possible to compare the length of the thread with the number of languages used.

In several threads there were nearly as many languages as posts, for example, four languages used in a thread with five replies, and three languages used in a thread with two replies. Thus a significant minority of threads did feature a range of languages. We observed that some respondents went out of their way to facilitate linguistic intercomprehensibility by providing as many as three different translations of their message. Occasionally, translation

TABLE 17.2. Language diversity within threads (from General Discussion, Futurum; $N = 363$).

No. of replies to seed message	No. of languages used in thread				
	1	2	3	4	5
0	56	0	1	0	0
1	30	5	0	0	0
2	21	4	1	0	0
3	12	7	1	0	0
4	5	4	5	0	0
5	0	1	0	1	0
6	0	4	0	0	0
7	0	0	2	0	0
8	2	1	1	0	0
9	0	1	1	0	0
10–25	0	1	0	1	1
Total	126	28	12	2	1

software was used to achieve this (see quote from Fettes below), although this can be problematic (Climent et al., chapter 9 this volume).

Nonetheless, non-English-seeded posts make up a relatively small part of the whole discussion, and when this is taken into account we can see that English is the predominant language. This shows that even in a public space where discussions can take place across a range of languages—and it is evident that a wide range of languages are spoken by users—English nevertheless became the lingua franca for communication.

These quantitative results have a number of limitations. The results primarily deal with distributional patterns across messages, not the text within messages. Thus, for example, they do not show whether, or how, messages reply, relate, or refer to one another. As noted by Jankowski and van Selm (2000, p. 154), using solely quantitative techniques "to measure the quality of a debate is suspect," especially when the focus is on how people use different languages to *interact*. Quantitative analysis by itself is helpful in giving an overall picture but does not represent the complexity that underlies the numbers. Thus, we conducted a critical discourse analysis of the Futurum discussions to complement and differentiate the empirical findings.

QUALITATIVE CASE STUDY: DISCUSSING MULTILINGUALISM IN MULTIPLE LANGUAGES ONLINE

A single thread was downloaded for analysis. We chose this thread because it discussed EU language policies in relation to enlargement of the EU, and particularly multilingualism and the choice of official and working languages.[21]

Furthermore, the debate took place in several languages and thus illustrates the debate on language policies itself. As we show below, the choice of language appears to be dependent on complex factors, mostly on emotional attitudes toward specific languages rooted in nationalistic and historical ideologies (Clyne, 2003).

"Relevance," in the sense of Sperber and Wilson's (1986) Theory of Relevance, proved to be a useful approach for our analysis. Relevance as regards language choice is primarily constructed by historical connotations and attitudes accompanying languages. In analyzing the sample debate, we distinguish specific frames of reference and cognitive modes of perception when dealing with language issues. Discourse analysis enables us to assess how people use the technologically mediated public spaces provided by the European institutions in their attempt to create a new supranational public sphere.

On June 17, 2003, Marc Fettes[22] from Luxembourg started a thread in the General Discussion of Futurum, focusing primarily on the issue of languages to be spoken in the "new Europe." The subject line is "The next step." His message contains several subtopics on European policies and the future of the EU; the relevance of the elaborated subtopics, however, is not explicitly justified.

Fettes frames his message with an overview of the role of the European convention and discusses the role of power, which—in his view—privileges the big states in the EU, and suggests a concept which is more oriented toward a Europe of regions. In the following, we quote the part of his message that concerns the language issue (spelling and grammatical mistakes are reproduced as in the original):

> This Europe should speedily introduce the European citizenship as well as the single currency. One single working language, the French language, should be taken advantage of in addition to the regional languages. Trough this Europe gets bilingual everywhere. German as European working language would be an additional victory from Hitler and therefore has to be refused. The English language although far more common has only roots in England, Ireland and Scotland This language has been successful only with the American army in Europe. English isn't and never was the language of Europe and English shouldn't becomes the language of Europe.

> Europe should be the over-structure, a Europe of all citizens. No armies of occupation or strange states, no religion states or religions should be allowed to exercise any power here. A state is sovereign only when the political organs must be able to take her decisions freely and give account to only her people.

Fettes does not provide any empirical evidence to support his argument that French should be *the* working language of the EU. His main argument is basically ideological and relates to negative connotations and attitudes associated with German and English. Both arguments are also historically based: German is seen as "the" language of the National Socialist regime, whereas English is the language of the American army in Europe after World War II. Arguing with the *topos of history* (i.e., using relatively stereotypical frames for justifying a certain issue)[23] is a frequent characteristic of persuasive argumentation.

Fettes then moves on to the present and the future—to a discourse of constructing a European Identity, with a single currency, freedom, no occupation, and political accountability: a Europe for all citizens, regardless of language, religion, power, and so on. This macrostrategy of constructing identity (Reisigl, 2004) serves to legitimize Fettes's ideological argumentation. His very emphatic message contains some positively connoted flag words: freedom, sovereignty, accountability, citizens, and so forth. The implication suggested by Fettes, if we analyze the whole text, can be summarized as follows: After the terrible past (Nazi time, occupation), Europe has to be able—very quickly—to decide its future for itself.

The next message, by José M. of Spain, posted on June 25, 2003, with the subject line "Re: The next Step," illustrates the usefulness of the Theory of Relevance approach described above. José M. picks out two points from Marc Fettes's long message and writes in a totally different style: "French as the only working language? 100 regions more important than the national states? Come on! You must be kidding!" José M.'s reply is informal and ironic. There is no formal mode of address in his message; moreover, he explicitly rejects two proposals made by Fettes: the focus on regions and on the French language. He selected these two topics as relevant for reply, ignoring all other subtopics from the first message. Instead of proposing arguments to validate his rejection, José M. makes fun of Fettes in a sarcastic way, moving to a meta-level and thereby rejecting a content-oriented rational discussion.

Marc Fettes replies to José M. on the same day with a short declarative message emphasizing his argumentation and presenting more evidence to support his position. However, this time, only the topic of "regions" is selected: "In my suggestion Europe is the state with 560 million peoples. The 100 regions are the substructures. That is an important state." He also rejects the informal tone and his reply is devoid of sarcastic or aggressive undertones. Gradually, we understand his model: Europe as superstructure, the regions as substructures.

On June 18, Daniel from Germany starts another subdebate with Marc Fettes. Not surprisingly, for Daniel what is most relevant is Fettes's argumentation against the German language, and he refers only to this aspect of Fettes's message:

> Although you have some really interesting ideas, I think that you probably haven't thought through properly what you are writing about the german language. It is an unlegitim offence to the germans and the german-speaking population in Europe, to link our language exclusively to hitler, denying that german is de facto the most spoken native tongue in Europe, the language of some of Europeans best literature, philosophie. Don't get me wrong, I don't think german

is a "better" language than another, but it has not the role in Europe, it fairly should have, just because of unjustified reservations in Europe of the german language of the kind you posted it.

Daniel starts with a polite, face-saving device, giving Marc Fettes the option to change his opinion about the German language. He praises Fettes's ideas ("really interesting") and suggests that Fettes has not had enough time to think about his proposal. After this introduction, he rejects Fettes's evaluation of the German language and redefines it ("our language") as the language of literature and philosophy, as well as the most spoken language in Europe. Thus, he uses a tripartite argument drawing on different kinds of evidence. This statement also marks a broader problem of German postwar identity: the feelings of guilt that many Germans, including the young, still have after the Nazi regime. These ambivalent feelings have made it difficult for postwar generations to reconstruct a positive German identity and positive attitudes toward the German language. Statistics show that in many European countries, the desire to learn German as a foreign language fell significantly after WWII (especially in the Scandinavian countries, Hungary, and France; de Cillia, 2003).

Fettes replies to this posting on June 19, changing his argumentation about the German language as follows:

> Hello
> I don't link our language exclusively to Hitler. I accept that German language is the most spoken native tongue in Europe, but it only part of them. The Europe which I have described has 560 million inhabitants. An acceptable agreement is needed there to bring all the languages and all people under a hat.

Interestingly, Marc Fettes seems to be at least bilingual—as are many people from Luxembourg (German, French); he writes about "our language," meaning "German." The two posters still correspond in English, best described as ELF with the linguistic features accounted for by Seidlhofer (2003; see above). Fettes now moves on, politely, from his first declarative, dogmatic message to a position that allows negotiation with Daniel. This step to compromise is taken up by Daniel on the same day: "I agree with you now, but it sounds very different from what you posted before!" This subdebate is a good illustration of our theoretical approach to relevance: The cognitively and emotionally relevant part of the posting is referred to. A conflict evolves and is resolved through discussion in the European virtual space; specific linguistic and pragmatic devices allow for such negotiations and constructions to take place: politeness features such as mitigation, praise, and forms of address, as well as a shift from a dogmatic mode to an argumentative mode.

On June 18, at the same time, a second subdebate evolves between Shane O'Donnell from Ireland and Marc Fettes, again on issues of language choice and a Europe of regions (we focus on the first topic here). These topics, which slowly evolve to become relevant topoi in this debate, are referred to consistently over the whole thread and are obviously salient for all contributors to this discussion. O'Donnell chooses a different style of writing, an argumentative, persuasive style full of rhetorical questions, comparisons, and irony, refuting Fettes's ideological and historically based arguments and evidence step by step:

> "English is not and never was the language of Europe".
> True
> The same is true of French. It is very arrogant to tacitly suggest that French is the language of Europe.
> "German would be a victory for Hitler" ridiculous and insulting. Hitler did not 'invent' German.
> Incidentally, would a French language Europe be tantamount to a victory for Napoleon?
> Language has divided Europe for too long. Let us enjoy each others languages without politicizing them.

Fettes answers this posting on the same day, apologizing first for his "translation program" and then justifying his argument about the rejection of the German language with new historical evidence (topos of history) and pointing to the fallacy of O'Donnell's argument: "The French language has been used many centuries in Europe. Napoleon was 200 years ago. Hitler was 60 years ago. Hitler forced all occupied peoples to learn and to use German. This will be forgotten in any generations, but not today." This answer implicitly rejects the proposal to "depoliticize" language debates. For Fettes, languages presuppose sociopolitical knowledge and have historical connotations. Language debates are inherently connected with the historical and ideological contexts of nation states and their national identities. This is different for O'Donnell, whose country was not occupied by the Germans, and also for Daniel, who is German. The commonsense knowledge connecting these three discussants and their presuppositions, as well as their background knowledge, differs; however, the choice of the relevant arguments remains constant.

Frederic, from France, posts a different opinion in French on June 19, 2003, and the three final replies follow his linguistic suit, switching to French:

> *Cher Marc,*
>
> *Je ne pense pas qu'on doive imposer aucune langue commune a l'interieur de l'Union Europeenne. Plutôt, il faut ENCOURAGER L'APPRENTISSAGE des langues entrangéres, en augmentant par exemple le poids de la seconde langue vivante lors du passage de l'Abitur, du Matura, ou du Baccalaureat. Il faut que les citoyens europeens puissant parler et comprendre 2 langues en plus de leur langue maternelle, alors*

qu'aujourd'hui, 1 langue etrangére est plus ou moins bien maitrisée par les
eleves.
[Translation: "Dear Marc, I don't think we should impose any common
language inside the European Union. Rather, people should be ENCOUR-
AGED TO LEARN foreign languages, for example by giving greater
weight to the second modern language when they take the Abitur, the
Matura, or the Baccalaureat. European citizens should be able to speak and
understand 2 languages in addition to their mother tongue, whereas these
days, students only more or less manage to master one foreign language."]

Frederic continues his posting, arguing for language diversity, which has been
achieved by learning from historical mistakes. Thus, he also employs the
topos of history in his argumentation. For him, the EU transcends the concept
of the nation-state; he proposes a "humanistic vision" and emphasizes the
equality of all EU member states and citizens. His focus on diversity also
encompasses the "language problem": There is no need for *one* language;
everybody should actually know three. The language policy proposals are
again founded in an ideological vision—the ethical values of "diversity" and
"equality." The use of capital letters emphasizes his views.

On the same day, Marc Fettes replies in French. He presents further evidence and argumentative support for the choice of *one* European language
for general communicative goals. However, he also takes up what he believes
to be Frederic's most relevant point, his emphasis on equality:

> *Le choix d'imposer une langue commune en plus de la langue maternelle sert a*
> *faciliter le dialogue entre tous les citoyens europeens. Aucune richesse des cul-*
> *tures est en danger par ce choix. Si de plus en plus de pays rejoignent l'europe,*
> *quelles langues seront les langues supplementaires? Le but est, de parler n'importe*
> *ou avec n'importe qui dans l'europe et de reussir plus facilement tous dans*
> *l'europe.*
> [Translation: "The choice to impose one common language in addition to the
> mother tongue serves to facilitate dialogue among all European citizens. This
> choice does not threaten any cultural wealth. If more and more countries join
> Europe, which languages will be the supplementary languages? The goal is to
> speak anywhere with anyone in Europe and for all in Europe to succeed in doing
> so more easily."]

Thus, the ideological-political discussion is narrowed down to a pragmatic
problem, namely, how to ensure a maximum amount of communication
among European citizens.

Finally, the last posting considers Fettes's proposal for a "Europe of
regions" as most relevant and does not give an opinion on the language issue
or choice; however, it is in French (June 23, Yannick Bauthiere, subject line
"regions"). This posting changes the focus of relevance, although, as presented above, Marc and José corresponded on the topic of language choice
after June 23.

CONCLUSION

Our quantitative analysis revealed that discussions on Futurum were not dominated by a small range of countries, although they were apparently male-dominated. The analysis of language usage showed that English was the dominant language for discussion, although there was a significant minority that conversed in a range of languages, different from the pattern observed by Durham (chapter 14 this volume). Each of these quantitative findings was supported by the discourse analysis, although it is worth noting that the thread we analyzed belongs to the "significant minority" category in terms of language diversity.

The qualitative discourse analysis of this thread leads to the following observations:

(1) The issue of language policies in Europe is highly political and ideologically loaded. Various arguments are used for supporting one or another language, mostly connected to sociopolitical and historical experiences and events. Moreover, language is clearly connected to (national) identities.

(2) The messages refer to one another, they argue with one another, and, with the exception of one message, they respect politeness conventions, even if they disagree. Thus, negotiations and compromises are achieved. There *is* dialogue.

(3) Reference from one posting to another is achieved by connecting issues seen as relevant and related to the everyday experiences and knowledge of the discussants: issues of language policies and a Europe of regions. All other topics are basically dismissed. A connection is also made through language use: When the messages switched to French, subsequent messages continued in French.

The qualitative analysis illustrated in detail how one discussion evolved and how it succeeded in creating dialogue, while the quantitative analysis shows that these thread-specific findings are part of a discernible trend across the discussions more broadly. Thus, the quantitative analysis and the qualitative discourse analysis mutually enriched and strengthened one another.

This study raises important theoretical and practical questions. First, it brings to mind Habermas's (1989) distinction between the public and the private. Is it the government's role to create a public sphere? If so, how do officials make sense of such debates, and should they listen, given their unrepresentativeness? Although this study has shown that online discussions offer considerable potential for reducing the democratic deficit through discourse, unfortunately, they are not used by policy makers in any way.[24]

Their primary role might be symbolic. The fact that the European Constitution—the principal topic of the Futurum debates—was subsequently rejected in two popular referendums suggests that the final document was indeed out of touch with what the general populace wanted. More controversially, one might suggest that it was not the document itself but the very notion of a European Constitution that was unpopular. Another interpretation is that the genre chosen for the Draft European Constitution did not present a document commonly known as a constitution, but rather another complex treaty (too long, too many issues, too many details, etc.). Unfortunately, people were not allowed to discuss whether it was right or wrong, only what should go in it. Thus, while discussions such as those that took place on Futurum "help fuel the debate" and bring citizens closer to each other, they do not necessarily bring the European Union closer to its citizens and reduce the perception of a democratic deficit.[25] In fact, ignoring such contributions may actually exacerbate the deficit.

Notes

1. We accessed http://europa.eu.int/comm/coreservices/forum/index.cfm?forum=Futurum &fuseaction=debate.home&archive=1, retrieved May 10, 2005. No live discussions were running at the time we last visited the site.

2. Markhardt (2005) and de Cillia (2003) offer critical overviews of the EU's language policy documents. Most important for this chapter are the Charter of Fundamental Rights of the European Union (Official Journal 2000), and the White Paper on European Governance (Commission, 2001).

3. Michael Clyne (2003) distinguishes among pluricentric languages, such as Dutch and Spanish; national languages that are also minority languages in other countries, such as Albanian and Hungarian; languages, such as English and Spanish, that are also employed overseas; and minority languages used by migrants, such as Arabic and Turkish, which are not indigenous to Europe. He suggests four possible models for Europe: polyglot dialogue (or receptive multilingualism, as in Switzerland); multilateral competences in related languages (several Romance, Slavic, or Scandinavian languages used by one person or by communities); unspecified multilingualism (acquiring several non-related languages); and finally, one lingua franca.

4. Subsidiarity, written into the 1992 Treaty on European Union (Official Journal 1992) requires decisions to be taken as close to the affected people as possible (thus nationally).

5. This is supported by analyses of how different groups use discussion forums (Herring, 1993; Kelly-Holmes, 2004). Communicative facilities depend on the design and structure of the discussion board (Wright, 2005a, 2005d; Wright & Street, in press). For example, the style of moderation affects the nature of discussions (Wright, 2005c). For an overview of the Internet as a linguistic domain, see Stein (2006).

6. See Swales (2001), Danet (2001), and Lemke (1999) for detailed descriptions of written and multimodal genres related to professional and everyday language; see Reisigl (2004) and Reisigl and Wodak (2001) for definitions of "genre" as part of "orders of discourse."

7. These communication spheres are related not just to the Internet but have been developed through EU audiovisual policies (e.g., Television without Frontiers) and through 250 European Information Centers located in public libraries. See Schlesinger and Kevin (2000).

8. This is based on Eurostat's estimate for the EU population of 378,988,100.

9. http://www.europa.eu.int/index_en.htm, retrieved September 15, 2005.

10. There are several online discussion forums on Europa—each with different rules, funding, and management. Most are administrative, accessible by password only. Those that were openly accessible did not normally contain any messages (as of October 14, 2004; see http://forum.europa.eu.int/Public/irc/efilwc/board/home). Three further forums were found, but two of these linked to external sites. The third, SIMAP, had 558 visible messages (as of October 14, 2004; see http://simap.eu.int/forumcgi/get.cgi/SIMAP.html).

11. http://europa.eu.int/futurum/about_en.htm, retrieved August 29, 2006.

12. Telephone discussion with senior commission official, May 18, 2004.

13. Telephone discussion with senior commission official, May 18, 2004.

14. http://www.europa.eu.int/futurum/documents/contrib/editorialpolicy_en.htm, retrieved August 29, 2006.

15. Source: http://www.europa.eu.int/futurum/documents/contrib/editorialpolicy_en.htm, retrieved August 29, 2006.

16. Telephone discussion with senior commission official, May 18, 2004.

17. See analyses by Davis (1999) and Wilhelm (2000) of unmoderated discussion boards, where discussions were found to be very limited discursively and with significant "flaming."

18. For instance, one poster wrote, "Censurship [sic] is an uggly [sic] feature of Futurum. It is difficult to understand why an institution which is supposed to be the guardian of European values applies censurship [sic] in a political discussion. In any case such behaviour raises suspicion about the evil side of EU institutions." Source: http://ec.europa.eu/comm/coreservices/forum/index.cfm?forum=Futurum&archive=1&fuseaction=contribution.detail&Debate_ID=-3&Message_ID=2864, retrieved August 29, 2006.

19. See http://www.internetworldstats.com/stats4.htm, retrieved September 15, 2005.

20. This adjustment was made to avoid biasing the results in favor of the non-English posts. The language used was normally obvious. Where the coder had any doubt, it was referred to another coder. Occasionally, others were consulted if coders were still uncertain as to the language being used. In certain circumstances, the use of a different language was not counted. These included cases involving fewer than five words in a language and messages containing only a greeting, a standardized footnote, or a quote or phrase in another language.

21. Source: http://ec.europa.eu/comm/coreservices/forum/index.cfm?forum=Futurum&archive=1&fuseaction=contribution.detail&Debate_ID=-30&Message_ID=-21206, retrieved August 29, 2006.

22. These are posters' usernames, not necessarily their real names.

23. Within argumentation theory, "topoi" or "loci" can be described as parts of argumentation that belong to the obligatory, either explicit or inferable, premises. They are the content-related warrants or "conclusion rules" that connect the argument or arguments with the conclusion, the claim. As such, they justify the transition from the argument or arguments to the conclusion (Kienpointner, 1992).

24. For an analysis of the implications for Futurum as a general or strong public sphere, see Wright (2005c).

25. This quotation comes from http://europa.eu.int/futurum/about_en.htm, retrieved August 29, 2006.

References

Abdullah, N. A. (2004). *Relational communication in organizational email: A Malaysian case study.* Unpublished Ph.D. thesis, University of Malaya, Kuala Lumpur.

Anis, J., Ed. (1999). *Internet, communication et langue française.* Paris: Hermes Science Publications.

Axelsson, A., Abelin, A., & Schroeder, R. (2003). Anyone speak Spanish? Language encounters in multi-user virtual environments and the influence of technology. *New Media & Society, 5*(4), 475–498.

Busch, B., & Krzyzanowski, M. (in press). Outside/inside the EU: Enlargement, migration policies and security issues. In W. Armstrong & J. Anderson (Eds.), *The geopolitics of European Union enlargement.* London: Routledge.

Commission of the European Communities. (2001). *European governance: A White Paper* (COM 2001) 428, Brussels, July 25, 2001. Retrieved August 29, 2006, from http://eur-lex .europa.eu/LexUriserv/site/en/com/2001/com2001_0428en01.pdf.

Clyne, M. (2003). Towards inter-cultural communication in Europe without linguistic homogenization. In R. de Cillia, H. J. Krumm, & R. Wodak (Eds.), *Die Kosten der Mehrsprachigkeit / The Cost of Multilingualism* (pp. 39–48). Vienna: Austrian Academy of Sciences.

Danet, B. (2001). *Cyberpl@y: Communicating online.* Oxford: Berg. Companion website: http://pluto.mscc.huji.ac.il/, retrieved September 15, 2005.

Davis, R. (1999). *The web of politics.* Oxford: Oxford University Press.

de Cillia, R. (2003). Grundlagen und Tendenzen der europäischen Sprachenpolitik. In M. Mokre, G. Weiss, & R. Bauböck (Eds.), *Europas Identitäten. Mythen, Konflikte, Konstruktionen* (pp. 231–256). New York: Campus.

Delanty, G., Jones, P. R., Krzyzanowski, M., Wodak, R., & Ulsamer, F. (2004). *Voices of migrants.* Research Report from the EU-FP5 Research Project "The European Dilemma: Institutional Patterns and Politics of Racial Discrimination." Unpublished manuscript, Liverpool/Vienna.

European Convention (on the Future of Europe). (2003). *Draft treaty establishing a European constitution for Europe,* CONV 850/03, Brussels, July 18, 2003. Retrieved August 30, 2006, from http://european-convention.eu.int/docs/Treaty/cv00850.en03.pdf#search=%2 2draft%20treaty%20establisHING%20A%20EUROPEAN%20CONSTITUTION% 202003%22.

Gruber, H. (2004). Die Globalisierung des wissenschaftlichen Diskurses. *Wiener Slawistischer Almanach, 52,* 91–108.

Habermas, J. (1989). *The structural transformation of the public sphere.* Cambridge: Polity Press.

Halliday, M. A. K. (1978). *Language as a social semiotic: The social interpretation of language and meaning.* London: Edward Arnold.

Herring, S. C. (1993). Gender and democracy in computer-mediated communication. *Electronic Journal of Communication, 3*(2). Retrieved September 15, 2005, from http://ella.slis .indiana.edu/~herring/ejc.txt.

Herring, S. C. (1996). Two variants of an electronic message schema. In S. C. Herring (Ed.), *Computer-mediated communication: Linguistic, social and cross-cultural perspectives* (pp. 81–106). Amsterdam: John Benjamins.

Herring, S. C. (2002). Computer-mediated communication on the Internet. *Annual Review of Information Science, 36,* 109–168.

Iedema, R. (1999). Formalizing organizational meaning. *Discourse & Society, 10*(1), 49–66.

Jankowski, N., & van Selm, M. (2000). The promise and practice of public debate in cyberspace. In K. L. Hacker & J. Van Dijk (Eds.), *Digital democracy: Issues of theory and practice* (pp. 149–165). London: Sage.

Kelly-Holmes, H. (2004). An analysis of the language repertoires of students in higher education and their language choices on the Internet. *International Journal on Multicultural Societies, 6*(1), 29–52.

Kienpointner, M. (1992). *Alltagslogik. Struktur und Funktion von Argumentationsmustern.* Stuttgart: Frommann-Holzboog.

Kress, G., & van Leeuwen, T. (1996). *Reading images.* London: Routledge.

Lemke, J. L. (1999). Discourse and organizational dynamics: Website communication and institutional change. *Discourse and Society, 10*(1), 21–48.

Lemke, J. L. (2000). *Multiplying modalities: Presentational, orientational and organizational meaning.* Unpublished manuscript.

Lemke, J. L. (2001). Discursive technologies and the social organization of meaning. *Folia Linguistica, 35*(1–2), 79–97.

Lemke, J. L. (2003). Texts and discourses in the technologies of social organization. In G. Weiss & R. Wodak (Eds.), *Critical Discourse Analysis. Theory and interdisciplinarity* (pp. 130–149). London: Palgrave/Macmillan.

Markhardt, H. (2005). *Das österreichische Deutsche im Rahmen der EU.* Bern: Peter Lang.

Neuage, T. (2003). *Conversation analysis of chatroom talk.* Unpublished Ph.D. thesis, University of South Australia.

Official Journal of the European Communities. (1992, July). *Treaty on European Union.* Official Journal C 191. Retrieved August 29, 2006, from http://europa.eu/eur-lex/en/treaties/dat/EU_treaty.html.

Official Journal of the European Communities. (2000, December). *The charter of fundamental rights of the European Union,* 2000/C 364/01, Nice. Retrieved August 29, 2006, from http://www.europarl.eu.int/charter/default_en.htm.

Phillipson, R. (2003). *English-only Europe? Challenging language policy.* London: Routledge.

Reisigl, M. (2004). *Wie man eine Nation herbeiredet. Eine diskursanalytische Untersuchung zur sprachlichen Konstruktion der österreichischen Nation und österreichischen Identität in politischen Fest- und Gedenkreden.* Unpublished Ph.D. thesis, University of Vienna.

Reisigl, M., & Wodak, R. (2001). *Discourse and discrimination.* London: Routledge.

Rusch, D. (2004). *Von den Möglichkeiten der Web-Inszenierung zum audio-visuellen Gesamtereignis am Beispiel online-journalistischer Kulturberichterstattung in Österreich und den USA.* Unpublished Ph.D. thesis, University of Vienna.

Schlesinger, P., & Kevin, D. (2000). Can the European Union become a sphere of publics? In E. O. Eriksen & J. E. Fossum (Eds.), *Democracy in the European Union: Integration through deliberation?* (pp. 206–229). London: Routledge.

Scollon, R., & Scollon, S. (2004). *Nexus analysis: Discourse and the emerging Internet.* London: Routledge.

Seidlhofer, B. (2003). Brave new English? Zum bildungs/sprachenpolitischen Desiderat einer Konzeptualisierung von Englisch als Lingua franca. In R. de Cillia, H. J. Krumm, & R. Wodak (Eds.), *The costs of multilingualism* (pp. 243–249). Vienna: Austrian Academy of Sciences.

Sperber, D., & Wilson, D. (1986). *Relevance, communication and cognition.* Oxford: Blackwell.

Stein, D. (2006). Language and Internet: Email, Internet, chatroom talk. In *Elsevier encyclopedia of language and linguistics* (vol. 4, K. Brown, pp. 116–124) (2nd ed.). Oxford: Elsevier.

Swales, J. (2001). *Genre analysis: English in academic and research settings.* Cambridge: Cambridge University Press.

Urry, J. (2003). *Global complexity.* Cambridge: Polity Press.

Widdowson, H. G. (1994). The ownership of English. *TESOL Quarterly, 28*(2), 377–388.

Wilhelm, A. G. (2000). *Democracy in the digital age: Challenges to political life in cyberspace.* London: Routledge.

Wodak, R. (2000). Recontextualization and the transformation of meaning: A Critical Discourse Analysis of decision-making in EU—meetings about employment policies. In S. Sarangi & M. Coulthard (Eds.), *Discourse and social life* (pp. 185–206). Harlow, UK: Pearson Education.

Wodak, R. (2003). Auf der Suche nach einer neuen europaischen Identitat. In R. de Cillia, H. J. Krumm, & R. Wodak (Eds.), *The costs of multilingualism* (pp. 125–143). Vienna: Austrian Academy of Sciences.

Wodak, R., & Puntscher-Riekmann, S. (2003). Europe for all: Diskursive Konstruktionen europäischer Identitäten. In M. Mokre, G. Weiss, & R. Bauböck (Eds.), *Europas Identitäten: Mythen, Konflikte, Konstruktionen* (pp. 283–304). Frankfurt: Campus.

Wodak, R., & Weiss, G. (2004a). Visions, ideologies and utopias in the discursive construction of European identities: Organizing, representing and legitimizing Europe. In M. Pütz, A. van Neff, G. Aertselaer, & T. A. van Dijk (Eds.), *Communicating ideologies: Language, discourse and social practice* (pp. 225–252). Frankfurt: Peter Lang.

Wodak, R., & Weiss, G. (2004b). Möglichkeiten und Grenzen der Diskursanalyse: Konstruktion europäischer Identitäten. In O. Panagl & R. Wodak (Eds.), *Text und Kontext: Theoriemodelle und methodische Verfahren im transdisziplinären Vergleich* (pp. 67–86). Würzburg: Königshausen & Neumann.

Wodak, R., & Weiss, G. (2005). Analyzing European Union discourses: Theories and applications. In P. Chilton & R. Wodak (Eds.), *New agenda in (Critical) Discourse Analysis* (pp. 121–136). Amsterdam: John Benjamins.

Wright, S. (2005a). *A comparative analysis of government-run discussion boards at the local, national and European Union levels.* Unpublished Ph.D. thesis, University of East Anglia.

Wright, S. (2005b). Design matters: The political efficacy of government-run discussion boards. In S. Oates, R. Gibson, & D. Owen (Eds.), *Civil society, democracy and the Internet: A comparative perspective* (pp. 80–99). London: Routledge.

Wright, S. (2005c, April). *A virtual European public sphere? The Futurum discussion forum.* Paper presented to Rethinking European Spaces: Territory, Borders, Governance, Royal Holloway University, London.

Wright, S. (2005d, May). *Moderating censorship? Government-run online discussion forums.* Paper presented to the Second Conference on Online Deliberation, Stanford University.

Wright, S., & Street, J. (in press). *Democracy, deliberation and design: The case of online discussion forums. New Media & Society.*

Yates, S. J. (1996). Oral and written linguistic aspects of computer conferencing. In S. C. Herring (Ed.), *Computer-mediated communication: Linguistic, social and cross-cultural perspectives* (pp. 29–46). Amsterdam: John Benjamins.

18

JOHN C. PAOLILLO

How Much Multilingualism?

Language Diversity on the Internet

In recent years the Internet has had a profound effect on communication around the globe. Qualitatively, it offers a constantly evolving set of communications modes, many of which are unlike those available through other media. Quantitatively, Internet growth has followed an exponential curve, doubling in size approximately every 20 months (Internet Systems Consortium, 2005). Although the Internet is still mostly concentrated in the United States and northern Europe, it has spread to most countries around the globe and now dominates international information policy concerns.

Currently, a major topic of discussion is the extent to which English is prevalent on the Internet, and what effects this might have on the many non-English-speaking people around the world. If English dominates, does this effectively force users to accommodate by learning English, in order to access the services that the Internet makes available? Or does the influx of non-English-speaking users, as claimed by Global Reach (2003), portend the end of English dominance of the technology? Will online global contact lead to greater linguistic homogenization, or will the inherent flexibility of network and multimedia technology lead to a new efflorescence of linguistic diversity (Herring, 2002)? Does the technology and its current social contexts lead to advantages for speakers of particular languages over others?

These questions cannot be definitively answered with our current state of knowledge, because there currently is no comprehensive survey or census of Internet users, or even of materials publicly posted on the Internet. The chief sources of Internet user surveys are marketing companies (Nielsen Net

Ratings, Jupiter Research, Global Reach, etc.) and national government agencies with a vested interest in the outcomes. Consequently, the information we have about languages online may present an exaggerated view of online linguistic diversity. To make matters worse, several aspects of linguistic diversity tend to be overlooked in these studies, most important, the meaning of linguistic diversity itself.

At present, some 6,000–7,000 living languages are catalogued (Gordon, 2005; Nettle & Romaine, 2000), the majority of which have fewer than 100,000 speakers. The best available data for the Internet represent only 11 languages, all of which have speakers numbering in the tens or hundreds of millions, and all of which are national languages of presently or historically powerful nations. The remaining category "others" aggregates all the rest. The discussion of Internet multilingualism is overwhelmingly skewed toward the interests of these language titans. The needs of smaller groups are not even visible. Hence, our appreciation of the issues could be improved by reexamining Internet multilingualism in light of a better understanding of global linguistic diversity. That is my aim in this chapter.

To accomplish this, I examine global linguistic diversity and develop a measure that allows us to compare countries and regions around the world. Subsequently, I consider the distribution of Internet hosts worldwide and apply the linguistic diversity measure to the language population estimates of Global Reach (2003). I then draw inferences about the relation of Internet language diversity to global language diversity. The chapter concludes with a discussion of the sociolinguistic forces operating in the context of Internet multilingualism and recommendations for promoting linguistic diversity on the Internet.

WORLD LANGUAGE POPULATIONS

How many languages are spoken in the world? The most honest answer is that nobody really knows, although the estimates of experts range from a low of about 4,000 to a high of about 7,000 (Crystal, 2000; Dalby, 2002; Nettle & Romaine, 2000). Estimating the number of languages in the world is complicated by a number of factors. First, national boundaries seldom correspond to language boundaries. Often, a language will go by different names on either side of a political border, so counting languages means collating and comparing those names. Naming of languages itself is often fraught with difficulty, because an ethnolinguistic group may have a different name for itself than its neighbors do or may have no name at all. Likewise, the status of a language variety as a "distinct" language may be uncertain. It may be a dialect of another language, or it may be called a dialect for political reasons but be linguistically distinct. These problems cannot be addressed in the same way in all situations.

A reasonably accepted count of distinct languages is found in the *Ethnologue* (Gordon, 2005), a database maintained by SIL International, a linguistic service organization affiliated with Wycliffe Bible Translators. For the *Ethnologue*, "language" is defined primarily in terms of mutual intelligibility of the spoken tongue. Under this definition, the different Chinese "dialects," such as Cantonese, Fuzhou, Mandarin, and Wu, are regarded as different languages, not dialects of one language, even though they share a common written form and are collectively regarded as "Chinese." As of 2003, the *Ethnologue* contained entries for 8,415 language groups by country, with a total of 6,296 recognized distinct, living languages.[1]

In the 2003 edition, meaningful population figures were available for a total of 7,639 *Ethnologue* language group entries; these were obtained from population censuses and field surveys collected between 1919 and 2000.[2] It is possible to display these population estimates as a scatter plot of the raw data points, with population measured on log scale so that the full range of estimates can be compared, as in figure 18.1.

The population estimates for years between 1919 and 1970 tend to be smaller than those between 1970 and 2000. This is an artifact of the way the data are collected and updated. Global population has been growing

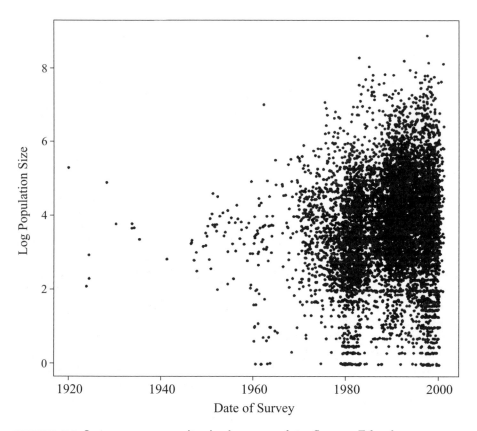

FIGURE 18.1. Language community size by survey date. *Source*: *Ethnologue*, 14th ed.

exponentially throughout the represented period, increasing almost 250% since 1950. Since updated estimates replace earlier estimates, frequently updated entries will tend to reflect this exponential growth, and infrequently updated entries tend to be smaller. Most of the information, especially that about larger language groups, is collected through national censuses and updated regularly. Groups that are missed in later surveys, because of changes in the surveys or other reasons, end up not being replaced with more current, possibly larger estimates.

Furthermore, smaller language groups tend not to be surveyed as often or as reliably as the larger language groups. They are often left out of national censuses entirely or may be aggregated with other groups in an "other" category. Sometimes a survey would require expensive and difficult travel to remote areas or could be politically awkward because of a tendency of nations to limit recognition of subnational groups. Hence, population estimates for some small language groups can be extremely out of date and may appear artificially small.

To compare properly the different language groups by size, it is necessary to adjust the estimates for world population growth. In this chapter, I assume that the proportion of a country's population represented by any particular language group is constant over the years, and project all of the population figures to the year 2001, based on United Nations (UN) population data for each country (United Nations Population Division, 2005). The constant-proportion assumption is in all probability inaccurate for the majority of the sample; other research indicates that smaller languages are disappearing at an alarming rate (Crystal, 2000; Krauss, 1992; Muhlhäusler, 1996; Nettle & Romaine, 2000; Wurm, 1991), and world population growth is not constant in all countries (HarperCollins, 2003). This suggests that the size of smaller groups is shrinking, rather than increasing with world population growth. Unfortunately, the data we would need to estimate this shrinkage of smaller languages are not available.[3] I adopt the constant-proportion assumption as a conservative approach. Twenty-one population estimates in the *Ethnologue* database have dates prior to 1950, predating the UN population data; these were excluded from further analysis.

Grimes (1986), working with an earlier version of the *Ethnologue* database, observed that the sizes of language populations were log-normally distributed, as in figure 18.2, in which the log size of the language groups (adjusted to 2001 levels) is plotted against the number of groups. The mean language group size is approximately 50,000, smaller than the size of a small urban area in the United States, such as Bloomington, Indiana (population ~69,000). Statistically speaking, the world's major languages such as English, Spanish, Arabic, Russian, Chinese, and Malay/Indonesian, with populations exceeding 100 million speakers, are anomalously large.

Nonetheless, languages of more than 10 million speakers represent the norm for most people in the world. This can be seen from a plot of the cumulative proportion of global population, as in figure 18.3. The x-axis in this figure represents language size, sorted from largest to smallest, and measured

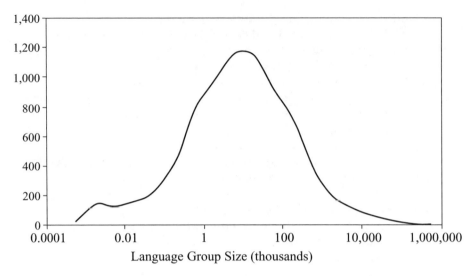

FIGURE 18.2. Sizes of language groups, adjusted to 2001 populations. *Source*: *Ethnologue*, 14th ed.

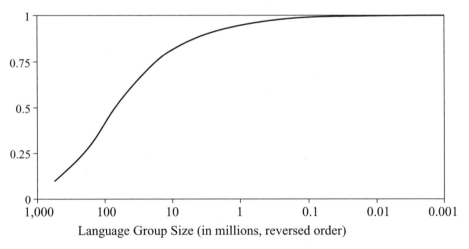

FIGURE 18.3. Cumulative proportions of the world's population by language group size. *Source*: *Ethnologue*, 14th ed.

on log-population scale. The y-axis represents the total proportion of the world's population, and the curve represents the proportion of the world's population having speakers of languages whose population is at least as large as that indicated by the corresponding point on the x-axis. The largest language group in the data set is Mandarin Chinese in China, with 877 million speakers, or approximately 15% of the estimated 5.8 billion global population in 2001; thus, the curve begins with this point. Language groups of 100 million speakers or more (including Mandarin Chinese) account for approximately one-third of the world's population, and those of 10 million or more speakers (including all the previous languages) account for more than three-quarters.

Information technologies such as the Internet do not presently serve very many of the languages having tens of millions of speakers. Among the very largest languages, Chinese, English, Spanish, Japanese, French, and most other European languages, are well served: Standard character encodings, fonts, keyboards, and computer operating systems are available for them, and these standards are well integrated into the communications protocols of the Internet such as the World Wide Web (Unicode Consortium, 2003). Other languages employing a Roman alphabet, such as Indonesian (206 million in Indonesia), Yoruba (18 million in Nigeria), and Guaraní (5 million in Paraguay), piggy-back on these resources, but support varies widely from language to language.[4] In many language communities of substantial size, such as South Azerbaijani (24 million in Iran), even the most basic resources are not available (E. Haghverdi, personal communication, May 2004). Other languages with such resources, such as Hindi with 211 million speakers, lack effective encoding standards, which sometimes hampers the use of Internet technology (Baker, Burnard, McEnery, & Sebba, 1998). Hence, the Internet currently serves the native languages of only a small proportion of the world's population.

GLOBAL LINGUISTIC DIVERSITY

The sizes of language groups worldwide only give a glimpse of the nature of linguistic diversity. Linguistic diversity is a characteristic of locales and regions, and varies from place to place, ranging from highly diverse countries like Tanzania (Fasold, 1984; Mafu, 2004) to relatively homogeneous ones like Norfolk Island (Gordon, 2005). Linguistic diversity may be manifest within the experience of individuals, as well as within countries. Citizens of a country may work or obtain schooling in a language other than the one used at home, may live in a linguistic border area, or may have friends, cohorts, or work contacts with different native languages. Finally, the media contribute to the experience of linguistic diversity: Television, radio, literature, popular film, and digital media may be consumed from foreign sources, either in the original language or in translated, subtitled, or dubbed form (Muhr, 2003).

The great variability in linguistic diversity needs to be quantified in order to be discussed coherently. A quantitative measure of diversity has several requirements. First, it should be able to be used in any situation we might want to investigate, irrespective of its size. It should reflect a reasonable summary of a situation's diversity, an average of sorts. It should have a minimum of zero, meaning no diversity, for completely homogeneous situations. It should have no maximum value, reflecting the idea that the linguistic diversity of any situation, no matter how large, can always be increased a small amount by adding an individual who speaks a language not shared by anyone else. Ideally, it should also have a sound statistical basis, so that it can be used in statistical significance tests.

Unfortunately, quantitative measures of linguistic diversity are rarely employed in linguistic research, and no established measure is widely used. Many approaches quantify diversity somewhat simplistically, using numbers of languages or numbers of language groups, as in Barrera-Bassols and Zinck (2002), Nettle (1998), and E. A. Smith (2001). Greenberg (1956) and Lieberson (1964) proposed various measures of diversity based on the notion of finding the *probability* that a pair of randomly chosen speakers will be unable to communicate in a common language (see Fasold, 1984, for a review). However, these measures do not have the properties described above. They all use a closed-ended scale with a maximum diversity value at 1, which should mean "absolutely diverse," a concept that has no useful meaning. Furthermore, equivalent probabilities can correspond to very different diversities. For example, a community of two people, each of whom speaks a different language, has a diversity value of 1, as does a community of 10 people, each of whom speaks a different language. Both hypothetical situations are maximally diverse for their size, but the latter gives more possible pairs of languages and hence should be treated as more diverse. In recent research on linguistic diversity, these measures appear to have fallen out of use, for unclear reasons. Nettle (1998) employs residuals of a linear regression model as a measure of diversity, an approach related to the one adopted here. This measure does not appear to have been developed beyond its application in a single study, however, nor has its basis been fully articulated. Other attempts to measure diversity (e.g., Nichols, 1992) are based on language family relations, which are not directly relevant to questions of multilingualism.

An appropriate measure for the present purposes can be modeled on the information-theoretic construct *entropy*, first proposed by Shannon and Weaver (1949) as a measure of the information content of messages. Statistically, entropy is a measure of variance, or the degree to which successive observations in a sample vary in value. If we consider our observations to be the languages spoken by individuals in a situation, entropy will measure the extent to which the observed language varies from individual to individual. Entropy is typically calculated as a sum of base two logarithms, because this leads to a natural interpretation in terms of bits, a natural unit of information. That being less important for present purposes, we use instead the natural logarithm (base e), which gives an index that is on the same scale as G^2, a variance measure used for log-linear models (Agresti, 1996).[5] The diversity index may be calculated as in equation 1:

(1) $D = -2\sum p \ln(p)$

In this formula, p is the proportion of the population of each language group. We take the logarithm of this amount and multiply the result by the same proportion, for each group. The diversity index D is -2 times the sum of all these terms. Note that the minimum value of the diversity index is achieved when all individuals are members of a single group, and hence there is only one term where $p = 1$. The logarithm of 1 is zero, so the diversity index itself is zero. There is no maximum value; D reaches infinity for an infinite population in which every individual speaks a different native language. Effectively, D is a weighted average, where the weights are the proportions of the population in each group, giving a per-individual index that is independent of the population size. This means that we can compare the relative diversity of different polities with different population sizes, such as countries or entire regions. The average is expressed as a simple sum, meaning that it can be broken into parts or aggregated with other similar figures by addition, without changing the basic nature of the index.

For example, table 18.1 shows computation of the linguistic diversity index for Albania. The 2003 *Ethnologue* listed seven languages for Albania, the largest two having slightly more than a third of the population each. The 2001 population estimates are given in table 18.1, alongside the proportions of the population they represent, as well as the corresponding terms of the index, $-p\ln(p)$. These figures are summed at the bottom of the corresponding columns, and the sum in the final column is doubled to give the final index value. This value can be compared with values from other situations. For example, if we compute a linguistic diversity index for Croatia (0.352), we can determine that Albania is much more linguistically diverse, as a country, than is Croatia.

We can now consider what the linguistic diversity index can tell us about the distribution of linguistic diversity worldwide. Figure 18.4 displays relative sizes of the index values by United Nations–defined regions, calculated from the language group population data discussed above. Table 18.2 gives the numerical values of the diversity index, alongside the corresponding proportions of the world total. North America's diversity index is divided into a share for the United States and a share for the rest of North America, so that the relative contribution of the United States can be observed. The United States had 170 languages listed in the *Ethnologue* database, but its linguistic

TABLE 18.1. Calculating the linguistic diversity index for Albania.

Language	Population estimate	Proportion (p)	$-p\ln(p)$
Albanian, Gheg	286,969	0.388	0.367
Albanian, Tosk	267,341	0.362	0.368
Greek	55,312	0.075	0.194
Macedonian	27,672	0.037	0.123
Romani, Vlax	54,557	0.074	0.192
Romanian, Macedo	47,077	0.064	0.175
Serbian	500	0.001	0.005
Total	739,428	1.000	1.425
Diversity index			2.849

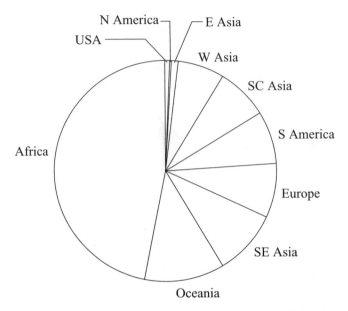

FIGURE 18.4. Worldwide linguistic diversity by region. *Source*: *Ethnologue*, 14th ed.

TABLE 18.2. Linguistic diversity index scores by region.

Region	Language groups	Diversity index
United States	170	0.7809
North America (including United States)	248	3.3843
East Asia	200	4.4514
West Asia	159	26.1539
South Central Asia	661	29.8093
South America	930	30.5007
Europe	364	32.4369
Southeast Asia	1,317	37.6615
Oceania	1,322	46.5653
Africa	2,390	185.6836

diversity index is small because its two largest language populations (English and Spanish) overshadow contributions of the remaining smaller languages.[6]

The largest proportion of the worldwide linguistic diversity index comes from Africa, the smallest from North America. The difference between the two regions is very large, with the value for Africa more than 100 times that for North America. It is instructive to compare this difference with the distribution of Internet hosts (see further below).

Since each region contains a different number of countries, the indices can differ according to the number of countries, as well as the number of languages. If we divide the regional index by the number of countries in the region, we obtain a per-country average diversity for the region. Hence, for the 54 countries of Africa we divide Africa's regional diversity score by 54. Figure 18.5 displays the relative sizes of the regional average diversity indices, and table 18.3 tabulates the same value alongside the number of countries. The discrepancies are not as large as in figure 18.4, but Africa is still the most diverse, and North America among the least. In addition, the per-country Africa index is more than four times the size of the North America index, so North American countries (principally the United States and Canada) are clearly less linguistically diverse than are typical African countries.

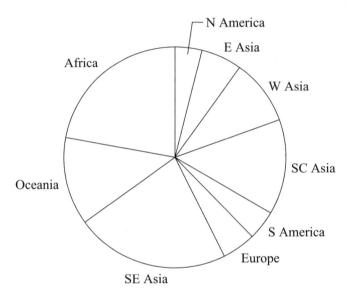

FIGURE 18.5. Per-country linguistic diversity by region. *Source*: *Ethnologue*, 14th ed.

TABLE 18.3. Average per-country diversity index.

Region	Per-country diversity	Number of countries	Lgs/country
United States	0.78092	1	170.00
North America (including United States)	0.67686	5	49.60
East Asia	0.89028	5	40.00
West Asia	1.45299	18	8.83
South Central Asia	2.12923	14	47.21
Latin America and Caribbean	0.66306	46	20.22
Europe	0.75435	43	8.47
Southeast Asia	3.42377	11	119.73
Oceania	2.02458	23	57.48
Africa	3.43219	54	44.26

The probable causes of the differences in linguistic diversity are various. North and South America have histories of European colonialism with long periods of European immigration, and this has led to the replacement of smaller populations of indigenous languages with large populations of speakers of European languages. Europe and East Asia are characterized by nation states founded by powerful ethnolinguistic groups imposing hegemony over smaller groups, resulting in large, linguistically homogeneous populations (Crystal, 2000, 2003; Phillipson, 1992).

In regions with larger diversity per-country indices, such as Africa, Southeast Asia, and to some extent Oceania, South Central Asia, and West Asia, the local histories of colonization did not typically involve large in-migrations. For example, although in-migration radically changed the linguistic makeup of Australia and New Zealand, significant in-migration did not occur in most of Papua New Guinea, which is still today one of the most linguistically diverse countries in the world. Oceania's linguistic diversity index owes much to this one country, while also reflecting the smaller contributions of a few countries with large languages.

GLOBAL LINGUISTIC DIVERSITY AND THE INTERNET

Like linguistic diversity, Internet access is a regional phenomenon. It is widely known that the United States and North America enjoy far more Internet resources than many other countries, but how much more? A revealing look into this can be obtained by taking a random sample of IP addresses and looking up their geographic latitude and longitude using the Unix *whois* networking program. This program consults a set of databases maintained by all the network operators on the Internet, containing essential information about each registered Internet host. Figure 18.6 shows the locations of 1,067 randomly sampled Internet hosts.

The heavy concentration of Internet hosts in North America and Europe is particularly striking, as is the relative absence of hosts in Africa, Asia, and most of Oceania and South America. The greatest concentrations of Internet hosts are in regions with the lowest linguistic diversity, especially North America. Since North America's share of the Internet resources is so large, and since its linguistic diversity is low, it is no wonder that English should be prevalent on the Internet. In addition, Internet access is largely absent for the region with the greatest linguistic diversity, Africa.

Confirmation of these observations can be found in the patterns of Internet host growth in figure 18.7, based on the Internet domain survey conducted by the Internet Systems Consortium (http://www.isc.org/ds), a networking group responsible for a number of basic Internet maintenance tasks. The survey is a semiannual tally of the Internet hosts registered under different domains in the Domain Name System (DNS). Each Internet host normally has a mnemonic address in the DNS consisting of labels separated by periods (e.g., http://www.example.com), the last of which is the top-level domain

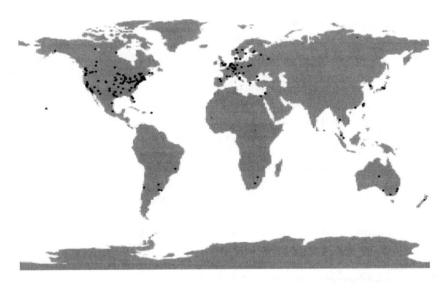

FIGURE 18.6. Global distribution of a random sample of 1,067 Internet hosts. *Source*: Original data, randomly sampled IP numbers from Whois databases worldwide.

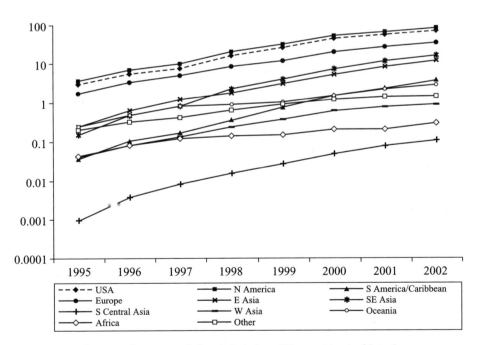

FIGURE 18.7. Internet host growth by region, in millions of hosts (data from www.isc.org/ds), retrieved December 15, 2005. *Source*: Internet Software Consortium (now Internet Systems Consortium), July 2003.

(TLD), representing the authority under which the name is registered. TLDs are either country codes (e.g., .in for India, .pt for Portugal) or "generic." Domains such as .edu, .gov, and .mil are generic TLDs that belong only to hosts registered in the United States. The generic TLDs .net and .com, by far the largest, unlike the other TLDs, are not assigned to a specific country. The domain survey identifies the number of hosts in each top-level domain.

In figure 18.7, country-code top-level domains are aggregated for United Nations–defined geographic regions. For .com and .net, a random sample of hosts in both domains was obtained, and their locations identified from the *whois* database. The totals were then divided among the different country totals according to their proportion in the random sample. Totals for the United States, the vast majority of host counts for North America, are shown separately (the dotted line) for comparison.

While exponential growth is observed in all regions, each region starts with a different level. For the most part, rates of growth are constant across regions, meaning that North America and the United States will continue to lead Internet host growth for the foreseeable future. Notably, Africa is lagging behind other regions in Internet host growth (the slope of its line is flatter). Hence, the most linguistically diverse region in the world is likely to remain relatively unconnected to the Internet, by comparison to other regions.

These observations have consequences for how we should understand the distribution of multilingualism on the Internet. While one can expect to observe Internet communications using French, Dutch, German, Spanish, and other European languages, the sheer concentration of resources in North America will necessarily mean more use of English than any other language on the Internet. Moreover, the majority of language groups—those with small populations existing in linguistically diverse regions—are unlikely to touch the Internet in any great way. Hence, linguistic diversity on the global Internet is rather less than global linguistic diversity. Finally, it is unclear whether Africa, whose contribution to global linguistic diversity is greatest of any region, will ever have a significant impact on Internet linguistic diversity. The rate of Internet host growth in Africa is so low that the proportions of Internet users using African languages are bound to stay very low for the foreseeable future.

LANGUAGES ON THE INTERNET

So far, the inferences drawn about linguistic diversity on the Internet have been indirect. Principally, from the distribution of hosts and languages around the world, we can observe potential opportunities, but not actual uses. What then of the languages people use for Internet communication? Is there any way to observe the diversity of languages as they are actually used? While in principle the answer is yes, the information needed to make these observations is scarce and costly to arrange.

A small number of studies try to quantify the prevalence of English on the World Wide Web (Lavoie & O'Neill, 2000; Nunberg, 1998; O'Niell, Lavoie, & Bennett, 2003); all of them show English to be dominant. Lavoie and O'Neill (2000) and O'Neill et al. (2003) observe the distribution of languages in web pages from comparable samples taken four years apart; these show that linguistic diversity increased slightly in the period between 1998 and 2002 (the dates of the samples), but that English remains the language of more than 70% of the webpages in 2002. According to Lavoie and O'Neill, the resulting linguistic diversity is comparable to that of a U.S. academic library: predominantly English with a scattering of roughly equal levels of one or two dozen foreign languages. A flaw in their method, however, was that the language identifier used (http://www-rali.iro.umontreal.ca/SILC/SILC.en.cgi) could recognize only 29 different languages. Languages not foreseen by the authors of the program could not be revealed with these methods, and the estimate of linguistic diversity may have suffered as a result.

Nunberg (1998) reports on the results of applying a similar program to a large-scale Web crawl. Unlike in the study by Lavoie and O'Neill (2000), adapting the design of the language identifier was an integral part of the methodology. In addition, languages were correlated with the geographic domains of the servers hosting them, and care was taken to validate results by inspecting pages manually. The results are only reported in terms of English and non-English counts, however, and hence cannot address diversity directly. For 1997–1998, the time of Nunberg's data collection, he suggests that a figure of 85% English for the whole of the World Wide Web is probably accurate. At the same time, the proportion of English on websites varies substantially from country to country. Among non-English-speaking countries, the lowest proportions of English were found in Latin America (12–31%), and the largest proportions in countries where Internet penetration was relatively low at the time (e.g., Turkey, 62%; Latvia, 75%; Bulgaria, 86%; Egypt, 95%; Thailand, 95%).

Hence, although previous studies of languages on the Internet provide some revelations about linguistic diversity, they leave many gaps in our current knowledge. We lack sufficient information on systems such as Usenet News and email, which typically precede the Web in their international spread (M. Smith, 1999), and we lack longitudinal data on language growth or spread on the Internet. Moreover, synchronous modes of computer-mediated communication, such as Internet Relay Chat, video chat, and instant messaging, are difficult to collect and analyze on any comprehensive scale, because these communications are not aggregated centrally or archived in the way Usenet and listserv messages are.

The most widely cited figures on Internet multilingualism are those of the Internet marketing firm Global Reach (2003), presented in figure 18.8. Projecting forward from the figures provided by Global Reach, Chinese will overtake English as the dominant language on the Internet by 2015. However, these estimates are based not on actual counts of languages used on the

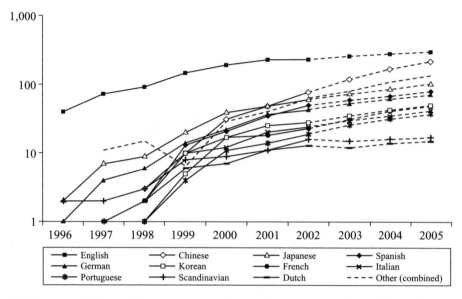

FIGURE 18.8. Estimated language populations of Internet users, in millions. *Source*: Global Reach (July 2003), http://global-reach.biz/globstats/evol.htm, retrieved December 15, 2005.

Internet but on a combination of heterogeneous sources, rendering the results methodologically problematic. Global Reach first acquired a set of user statistics for individual countries from sources such as Nielsen Net Ratings (for the United States), the China Network Information Center, and the International Telecommunications Union (ITU), and then used the *Ethnologue*'s population estimates to estimate proportions of users for each language. The methodologies for estimating user populations vary even within sources such as the ITU, and so methodological comparability among the many sources is not assured. Moreover, these sources are typically governments or marketing companies, both of which have a vested interest in outcomes leading to higher estimates. The estimates are not reliably insulated from this bias. In addition, prorating user populations according to *Ethnologue* populations effectively overestimates the linguistic diversity of the Internet, because access in such countries as China will be differentially available in the linguistically homogeneous urban areas and linguistically diverse rural areas.

A further limitation is that the data beyond 2002 in figure 18.8 (in dotted lines) are based on estimated trends rather than current data, and the trends themselves represent controversial claims. For example, the spread of Internet use among English speakers is thought to be slowing (Lenhart, 2003), but this has been shown recently only for the United States; comparable data do not yet exist for the other English-speaking countries. Likewise, Chinese use is thought to be accelerating, but the survey used to estimate these trends was conducted by telephone among university students (CNNIC, 2003); this is

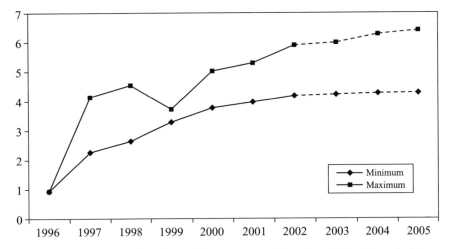

FIGURE 18.9. Estimated diversity of Internet users, based on Global Reach data.

most certainly a biased sample in a country like China where people do not universally have telephones (or receive higher education). Figures of this nature need to be interpreted with due caution.

From the Global Reach (2003) estimates, one can calculate linguistic diversity indices for the global population of Internet users. Since the "other" category represents multiple languages, we cannot do this precisely. We can, however, determine the theoretical maximum diversity by assuming that the "other" category is evenly divided among the world's remaining languages, and the minimum diversity by assuming that a single other language accounts for the remaining diversity and that the remaining languages account for negligible numbers of users. Here, I use 6,000 as the estimate of the remaining number of languages. Both the maximum and minimum diversity figures are unrealistic but place absolute upper and lower bounds on the diversity that could have been observed. Figure 18.9 displays these figures for the Global Reach data.

The wild fluctuation in the maximum index values suggests that there are problems in the estimates of the "other" category, since this is the only component of the index that differs in the two extremes. The actual diversity value is likely to be much closer to the minimum values, because the number of other languages is probably not large (in the dozens at most, rather than hundreds or thousands) and not evenly divided among the different languages represented. In addition, although there were initially large gains in the diversity index from 1996 to 1999, linguistic diversity appears to be leveling off in the projected 2003–2005 values. It is important to consider the reason for this: The projected increase in the number of Chinese-speaking users, because it is so large—Mandarin Chinese accounts for 15% of the global population—actually decreases overall diversity. The entire Internet could shift over to

Chinese as the dominant language and not become any more linguistically diverse in the process. Ironically, the most commonly cited reason for the putative increase in linguistic diversity on the Internet turns out not to cause an increase after all. Finally, the resulting linguistic diversity index is comparable in size to that of a typical African country. At the same time, it is only as large as the least diverse region (North America) and nowhere near as large as that of the world as a whole. The Internet thus looks characteristically North American, not global, in its linguistic diversity.

DISCUSSION AND CONCLUSIONS

The two regions with the greatest concentration of Internet resources, North America and Europe, turn out to be among the least linguistically diverse regions. Moreover, the proportion of linguistic diversity accounted for by these two regions is a very small proportion of global linguistic diversity. Consequently, the Internet in its present form does not provide representative access to the full range of linguistic and cultural groups worldwide. Low linguistic diversity potentially facilitates Internet access, since a small number of standardized technological solutions can serve large language populations. Regions and countries with greater linguistic diversity would need potentially expensive customized solutions for a large number of minority language groups. But even some reasonably large language groups have a disproportionately low online presence. Because some of these languages require special script adaptations, or may not be written in a standard form, significant technical development work may remain before the speakers of these languages can use them on the Internet.

In research conducted as early as 1995, it was observed that the Internet represents a language contact situation of unprecedented scale (Paolillo, 1996; see also Crystal, 2001). The outcomes of such large-scale language contact are uncertain. From one perspective, the Internet represents yet another facet of globalization (Block, 2004). Its technologies originated in the English-speaking United States. Adapting them to many non-European languages is costly, time-consuming, and often not a priority of corporate interests. English speakers and texts predominate, meaning that either people must have a good command of English to use the Internet, or effective control of the resources remains in the hands of a few local English-speaking bilinguals.

A paradigm example of this can be found in the protracted struggle over the internationalization of the DNS, the technical system under which computer systems are assigned mnemonic names. In many ways, the DNS is a technical and social microcosm of the larger Internet. It has been maintained since 1998 by ICANN, a nonprofit corporation based in the United States, under contract with the U.S. Department of Commerce. The technical protocol of the DNS was established in 1983 and permits computers to have names using only a subset of 7-bit ASCII, which excludes distinct capitalization, diacritics, and non-Roman characters. The ICANN board has been dominated by Americans, whose chief policy concern has been the resolution of U.S. commercial trademark disputes over domain-name "squatting." Issues of internationalization of the DNS were until recently relegated to secondary importance, even though ICANN's founding coincided with increased global spread of the World Wide Web and intensified pressure to internationalize the DNS. In 2003, ICANN approved a recommendation for internationalization of domain names, but its implementation suffers from limits on name length imposed by the original DNS, and uptake has been slow. In many other technical domains of the Internet, similar stories can be told. Existing protocols rely on technologies encoding an (often American) English language bias (Yates, 1996). The protocols are maintained by U.S. or international technical organizations whose business is conducted in English and whose agendas are dominated by powerful U.S. corporate interests.

What can we expect from this situation in terms of linguistic diversity? Will speakers of other languages accommodate by learning English in greater numbers, in order to use the Internet? Or will they increasingly use their own languages on the Internet, thereby increasing its linguistic diversity? So far, both trends are evident to some extent. Many of our studies of Internet multilingualism involve individual or national bilingualism with English (e.g., Durham, chapter 14 this volume; Georgakopoulou, 1997; Kelly Holmes, 2004; Koutsogiannis & Mitsikopoulou, chapter 6 this volume; Mafu, 2004; Paolillo, 1996, 2001; Peel, 2004; Warschauer, El Said, & Zohry, 2002). Although bilinguals in some of these situations have reasons extrinsic to the Internet to be using English (e.g., expatriate status), arguably some accommodation is taking place. At the same time, the spread of the Internet is bringing new languages online, and one can find, if one looks hard enough, pockets of bilinguals using even very small languages.

Overwhelmingly, however, the current situation favors large languages, and especially English. The Internet technologies themselves are mostly based on English. Programming and markup languages, communications protocols, operating systems, and network technologies are all developed in international English-speaking fora, under the auspices of the World Wide Web Consortium, the Internet Engineering Task Force, the Unicode Consortium, and other international standards bodies. If one wants to do so much as put up a webpage on a server, one must learn a set of English-based acronymic mnemonics (HTML tags) to properly format the page and a cryptic operating system with English-mnemonic commands in English syntax to host it (e.g., Unix/Linux) and manage a browser with English commands in the menus to view it (e.g., Mozilla).[7] This scenario assumes the lowest cost, most widely available technologies: free software running on inexpensive hardware. Users who want more, such as graphical user interface editors that hide the HTML, will have to pay a premium for software, programmers, or packaged systems. In the past, major products such as Microsoft Word have taken years to become localized for particular language markets.[8] Hence, the environment in which software and Internet content are developed impose high costs on smaller languages. The economics of Internet technology development and use disfavors linguistic diversity.

What, then, of the future of linguistic diversity and multilingualism on the Internet? If current trends are representative, the center of gravity of the Internet will remain in North America and Europe for the foreseeable future. Africa, and most of its linguistic diversity, is likely to remain out of reach of the Internet. Overall linguistic diversity among Internet users may increase slightly, but mainly from speakers of large (national) languages coming online. English, as the international language of the Internet, will continue to enjoy the greatest support. For this picture to change substantially, one or more of several things would need to occur.

First, the primary modes of communication on the Internet (email and the World Wide Web) are textual and asynchronous. A large-scale shift to more synchronous modes would potentially favor greater linguistic diversity since, as observed in Paolillo (in press), bilinguals tend to use their local languages more in synchronous chat than in asynchronous discussion forums. Empirical research is needed to show if this pattern holds for other synchronous modes such as Internet telephony and video chat. If so, adopting official policies favoring synchronous communication modes, such as through eased taxation and subsidy, could promote online linguistic diversity.

A related possibility would be a shift in the uses of the Internet from institutional and official kinds of communication, which favor national languages, toward more personal kinds of communication, where minority vernaculars have an expressive advantage. To some extent, the evolution of weblogs ("blogs") represents a trend in this direction (Herring, Scheidt, Bonus, & Wright, 2004), although the orientation of some weblogs toward (national) politics might mitigate their vernacular effect. A study of language use on the blog-hosting service LiveJournal.com (Herring, Paolillo et al., 2007) found active pockets of vernacular language use in a predominantly English environment. Another possibility would be a large-scale shift in the information production and consumption patterns of different countries. If the markets for internationally produced cultural products or scientific research were to expand suddenly, the result might be a greater spread of languages other than English into these domains.

A final possibility would be increased adoption of automatic translation. If people could use their own languages on either end of a trans lingual communication, with automatic translation mediating the conversation, then they could also use their languages anywhere on the Internet (Climent et al., chapter 9 this volume). However, machine translation, like other Internet technologies, services only a fraction of the world's languages, and the problems of adding more languages to the mix are substantial (Jurafsky & Martin, 2000).

For example, Systran, the provider of the popular Web translation service Babel Fish, uses a direct translation approach from any one language to another. At present, Babel Fish offers 12 languages for a total of 36 source–target pairs (24 of which involve English), out of a possible 132. For 6,000 languages, this approach would require nearly 36 million potential source–target language pairs, a truly forbidding number. Interlingua-based translation systems, which use mediating representations to facilitate translation from language to language, cut down on the number of systems to as little as one per language, but it is unclear whether a single interlingua could work in all translation contexts. Moreover, translation quality in general-purpose systems tends to be poor (Hutchins, 2002), as users of Web translation systems are well aware. Better translations can be obtained by tuning translators to specific domains, but this is a labor-intensive and expensive process (it is where companies such as Systran earn their profits), and one cannot hope to cover all domains to the same degree. Again, multiplied by the number of languages worldwide, the problem is immense.

If a solution to the technical problems were discovered, or if rough translation turns out to be sufficient, we could see increased diversity in the language backgrounds of Internet users. However, we should not take first-language literacy for granted. Text translation is not a guarantee that heretofore unwritten languages, of which there are many, will be able to be used on the Internet. Voice translation is generally a much harder problem to solve. In addition, Muhlhäusler (1996) warns that translation, through importation of foreign concepts, may alter a language's vocabulary and structure and hence promote potentially subversive changes in a minority language that could lead ultimately to its loss. We should not blithely assume that all of machine translation's effects on linguistic diversity will be positive.

As with the dimensions of multilingualism on the Internet today, these possibilities and the issues they raise are not likely to be addressed adequately by marketing surveys or industry estimates of Internet user populations. Future research on Internet multilingualism should seek to go further, through sober, empirical observation of actual language use on the Internet.

Acknowledgments

I wish to acknowledge the generous support of the UNESCO Institute for Statistics in the conduct of this research. Elijah Wright and Hong Zhang served as research assistants on aspects of the research reported here. I am grateful for their assistance.

Notes

1. The fall 2005 estimate on http://www.ethnologue.com is 6,912. The reason for the disparity with the 2003 estimate is unknown but should not be taken as indicating an increase in global linguistic diversity, for reasons described in the text below.

2. The same language is often used in different countries; such languages have multiple entries in the *Ethnologue* database.

3. Oddly, language death and endangerment research does not appear to address this question, but is rather primarily focused on documentation and preservation (linguistic description, archiving, education, etc.).

4. Indonesian has a government-sponsored Linux translation project that appears to be fairly mature (http://www.software-ri.or.id/winbi/). Paraguay is listed on the Linux counter as having 71 Linux users among its 263 total Internet-connected hosts (http://counter.li.org/

bycountry/py.php), but most Internet resources using Guaraní appear to be bilingual or trilingual (using Spanish, English, and/or German with Guaraní), and pages on Linux in Guaraní appear to be entirely in Spanish. Yoruba has a localization project for GNOME, one of the two main Linux desktop environments (http://www.wazobiasoft.org/gnome/yoruba.htm), but it appears to be not as mature as the Indonesian project (all pages are in English). The Nigerian Linux User's Group (http://nglug.org.ng/) posts all of its pages in English, rather than in any other of the 505 living languages of Nigeria; thus, it appears that complete localization of Linux, at least, for Nigeria and Paraguay remains some way off. All pages were retrieved September 15, 2005, except that for Paraguay, which is no longer available.

5. G^2 is chi-square distributed; when calculated this way, the diversity index D can be used in significance tests when the correct degrees of freedom are known. Since this issue is secondary here, I leave it for future discussion.

6. Most of these languages are Native American languages that are either moribund or extinct. Extinct languages have zero population and do not contribute anything to the linguistic diversity index as calculated here.

7. Although popular browsers such as Microsoft Internet Explorer or Mozilla Firefox are localized in 20–30 languages, this is a small number compared to the 6,000+ living human languages, or even the approximately 1,200 standardized languages (Fishman, 1998), that are spoken in the world.

8. Apple introduced WorldScript, its international language support product, in 1992. At that time, because of its fierce competition with Apple, Microsoft refused to support it in its products. By 1994 Microsoft had introduced partly internationalized versions of Word for Windows. Only in 2001 was international language support and WorldScript added to Microsoft Word on the Macintosh.

References

Agresti, A. (1996). *An introduction to categorical data analysis.* New York: Wiley.

Baker, P., Burnard, L., McEnery, A., & Sebba, M. (1998). *Beyond the 8 bit character set: The representation and exchange of Indian and Chinese corpus data.* MILLE working paper 2. Lancaster University, Lancaster, UK.

Barrera-Bassols, N., & Zinck, J. A. (2002). Ethnopedological research: A worldwide review. In *17th World Congress of Soil Science CD-ROM proceedings: Confronting new realities in the 21st century* (pp. 590.1–590.12). Bangkok: Kasetsart University. Retrieved September 15, 2005, from http://www.itc.nl/library/Papers/ arti_conf_pr/barrera.pdf (no longer available).

Block, D. (2004). Globalization, transnational communication and the Internet. *International Journal on Multicultural Societies, 6*(1), 13–28.

CNNIC. (2003). China Network Information Center website. Retrieved September 15, 2005, from http://www.cnnic.net.cn/.

Crystal, D. (2000). *Language death.* Cambridge: Cambridge University Press.

Crystal, D. (2001). *Language and the Internet.* Cambridge: Cambridge University Press.

Crystal, D. (2003). *English as a global language* (2nd ed.). Cambridge: Cambridge University Press.

Dalby, A. (2002). *Language in danger: The loss of linguistic diversity and the threat to our future.* New York: Columbia University Press.

Fasold, R. (1984). *Sociolinguistics of society.* Oxford: Blackwell.

Fishman, J. A. (1998). The new linguistic order. *Foreign Policy, 113,* 26–40.

Georgakopoulou, A. (1997). Self-presentation and interactional alliances in e-mail discourse: The style- and code-switches of Greek messages. *International Journal of Applied Linguistics, 7,* 141–164.

Global Reach. (2003). Evolution of non-English-speaking population. Retrieved August 29, 2006, from http://global-reach.biz/globstats/evol.html.

Gordon, R. G., Jr. (Ed.). (2005). *Ethnologue: Languages of the world* (15th ed.). Dallas, TX: SIL International. Retrieved September 15, 2005, from http://www.ethnologue.com/.

Greenberg, J. (1956). The measurement of linguistic diversity. *Language, 32*(2), 109–115.

Grimes, J. E. (1986). Area norms of language size. In B. F. Elson (Ed.), *Language in global perspective: Papers in honor of the 50th anniversary of the Summer Institute of Linguistics, 1935–1985* (pp. 5–19). Dallas, TX: Summer Institute of Linguistics.

HarperCollins. (2003). *Atlas of the world.* Ann Arbor, MI: Borders Press & HarperCollins.

Herring, S. C. (2002, July). *The language of the Internet: English dominance or heteroglossia?* Keynote speech delivered at the International Conference on Cultural Attitudes Towards Technology and Communication, University of Montreal, Quebec, Canada.

Herring, S. C., Paolillo, J. C., Ramos Vielba, I., Kouper, I., Wright, E., Stoerger, S., Scheidt, L. A., & Clark, B. (2007). Language networks on LiveJournal. *Proceedings of the Fortieth Hawaii International Conference on System Sciences.* Los Alamitos, CA: IEEE Press. http://www.blogninja.com/hicss07.pdf.

Herring, S. C., Scheidt, L. A., Bonus, S., & Wright, E. (2004). Bridging the gap: A genre analysis of weblogs. In *Proceedings of the thirty-seventh Hawaii International Conference on System Sciences (HICSS-37).* Los Alamitos: IEEE Press. Retrieved August 25, 2006, from http://www.blogninja.com/DDGDD04.doc.

Hutchins, J. (2002). Machine translation today and tomorrow. In G. Willée, B. Schröder, & H-C. Schmitz (Eds.), *Computerlinguistik: was geht, was kommt? Computational linguistics: Achievements and perspectives. Festschrift für Winfried Lenders* (pp. 159–162). Sankt Augustin: Gardez! Verlag.

Internet Systems Consortium. (2005). *ISC Internet domain survey.* Retrieved September 15, 2005, from http://www.isc.org/ds.

Jurafsky, D., & Martin, J. H. (2000). *Speech and language processing.* Upper Saddle River, NJ: Prentice Hall.

Kelly Holmes, H. (2004). An analysis of the language repertoires of students in higher education and their language choices on the Internet (Ukraine, Poland, Macedonia, Italy, France, Tanzania, Oman and Indonesia). *International Journal on Multicultural Societies, 6*(1), 29–52.

Krauss, M. (1992). The world's languages in crisis. *Language, 68*(1), 4–10.

Lavoie, B. F., & O'Neill, E. T. (2000). How "world wide" is the Web? In *Annual Review of OCLC Research 1999.* Retrieved November 26, 2005, from http://digitalarchive.oclc.org/da/ViewObject.jsp?fileid=0000002655:000000059202&reqid=9467.

Lenhart, A. (2003). The ever-shifting Internet population: A new look at Internet access and the digital divide. Washington, DC: The Pew Internet and American Life Project. Retrieved September 15, 2005, from http://www.pewinternet.org/reports/toc.asp?Report=88.

Lieberson, S. (1964). An extension of Greenberg's linguistic diversity measures. *Language, 40,* 526–531.

Mafu, S. (2004). From oral tradition to the information era: The case of Tanzania. *International Journal on Multicultural Societies, 6*(1), 53–78. Retrieved September 15, 2005, from http://portal.unesco.org/shs/en/ev.php-URL_ID=3996&URL_DO=DO_TOPIC&URL_SECTION=-465.html.

Muhlhäusler, P. (1996). *Linguistic ecology: Language change and linguistic imperialism in the Pacific Region.* London: Routledge.

Muhr, R. (2003). Language change via satellite: The influence of German television broadcasting on Austrian German. *Journal of Historical Pragmatics, 4*(1), 103–127.

Nettle, D. (1998). *Linguistic diversity.* Oxford: Oxford University Press.

Nettle, D., & Romaine, S. (2000). *Vanishing voices: The extinction of the world's languages.* Oxford: Oxford University Press.

Nichols, J. (1992). *Linguistic diversity in space and time.* Chicago: University of Chicago Press.

Nunberg, G. (1998, October). *Languages in the wired world.* Paper presented at La Politique de la Langue et la Formation des Nations Modernes, Centre d'Etudes et Recherches Internationales de Paris, France.

O'Neill, E. T., Lavoie, B. F., & Bennett, R. (2003). Trends in the evolution of the public Web: 1998–2002. *D-Lib Magazine, 9*(4). Retrieved November 26, 2005, from http://www.dlib.org/dlib/april03/lavoie/04lavoie.html.

Paolillo, J. C. (1996). Language choice on soc.culture.punjab. *Electronic Journal of Communication, 6*(3). Retrieved September 15, 2005, from http://www.cios.org/www/ejc/v6n396.htm (subscription required).

Paolillo, J. C. (2001). Language variation in the virtual speech community: A social network approach. *Journal of Sociolinguistics, 5*(2), 180–213.

Paolillo, J. C. (in press). "Conversational" codeswitching on Usenet and Internet Relay Chat. In S. C. Herring (Ed.), *Computer-mediated conversation.* Cresskill, NJ: Hampton Press.

Peel, R. (2004). The Internet and language use: A case study in the United Arab Emirates. *International Journal on Multicultural Societies, 6*(1), 79–91. Retrieved September 15, 2005, from http://portal.unesco.org/shs/en/ev.php-URL_ID=3996&URL_DO=DO_TOPIC&URL_SECTION=-465.html.

Phillipson, R. (1992). *Linguistic imperialism.* Oxford: Oxford University Press.

Shannon, C., & Weaver, W. (1949). *The mathematical theory of communication.* Urbana: University of Illinois Press.

Smith, E. A. (2001). On the co-evolution of linguistic, cultural and biological diversity. In L. Maffi (Ed.), *On biocultural diversity* (pp. 95–117). Washington, DC: Smithsonian Institution Press.

Smith, M. A. (1999). Invisible crowds in cyberspace: Measuring and mapping the social structure of USENET. In M. Smith & P. Kollock (Eds.), *Communities in cyberspace* (pp. 195–219). London: Routledge.

Unicode Consortium. (2003). *The Unicode standard, version 4.0.* Reading, MA: Addison-Wesley.

United Nations Population Division. (2005). *World population prospects.* Retrieved November 26, 2005, from http://esa.un.org/unpp/.

Warschauer, M., El Said, G. R., & Zohry, A. (2002). Language choice online: Globalization and identity in Egypt. *Journal of Computer-Mediated Communication, 7*(4). Retrieved September 15, 2005, from http://www.ascusc.org/jcmc/vol7/issue4/warschauer.html.

Wurm, S. A. (1991). Language death and disappearance: Causes and circumstances. In R. H. Robbins & E. M. Uhlenbeck (Eds.), *Endangered languages* (pp. 1–18). Oxford: Berg.

Yates, S. J. (1996). English in cyberspace. In S. Goodman & D. Graddol (Eds.), *Redesigning English: New texts, new identities* (pp. 106–140). London: Routledge.

Index